U.S.
CIVIL
AIRCRAFT
VOL. 6

U.S.
CIVIL
AIRCRAFT
VOL. 6

(ATC 501 - ATC 600)

By

JOSEPH P. JUPTNER

ISBN-0-8168-9170-2

AERO PUBLISHERS, INC.

329 Aviation Road Fallbrook, Cal. 92028

ACKNOWLEDGMENTS

Any historian soon learns that in the process of digging for obscure facts and information he must oftentimes rely on the help of numerous people, unselfish and generous people, many of whom were close to, or actually participated in, various incidents or events that make up this segment of history recorded here, and have been willing to give of their time and knowledge in behalf of this work. To these wonderful people I am greatly indebted and I feel a heart-warming gratitude; it is only fitting then that I proclaim their identity in appreciation.

My thanks to Gordon S. Williams of the Boeing Co., to Peter M. Bowers, Harvey Lippincott of Pratt & Whitney Div., Everette J. Payette commercial photographer, Theron K. Rinehart of Fairchild-Hiller, Gerald H. Balzer, Robert Wood of National Air Museum, Walter M. Jefferies, Jr., William Wagner of Ryan Aeronautical Library, John W. Underwood, Ray Brandly of the National Waco Club, William T. Larkins, John Sommerfeld and Bob Von Willer of the Fleet Club, H. Lloyd Child former Curtiss-Wright test pilot, Harry S. Gann of McDonnell-Douglas, Roger F. Besecker, James H. Harvey of the Monocoupe Club, Henri D'Estout, George Townson, Gregory C. Krohn, Edward Peck, Mitch Mayborn of Flying Enterprises, Joe Christy, Ken M. Molson, James W. Borden, Don Hartsig, Boardman C. Reed, J. R. Nielander of Exec-Air, E. L. "Jack" Wright, Earl C. Reed, and Emil Strasser.

FOREWORD

Each year since commercial flying began, there had been steady, or sometimes dramatic improvements in airplanes, but the period of 1934-35 produced greater advancements than in any period since the Wright Brothers first flew in 1903. Here in this volume, as it unfolds, we will find the scientific advancements that nearly doubled the speeds with greater regularity, and provided comfort and security that won the public confidence in traveling by air. Achievement of this phenomenal advancement was a joint effort in refining methods of propulsion, the application of new concepts in aerodynamics, and the introduction of advanced methods in all-metal construction. Oil companies had also developed new fuels that allowed engine manufacturers to design powerplants of fantastic power-to-weight ratios, supercharging had nearly doubled the service ceiling, and the controllable pitch propeller was providing efficient performance from the ground up. Transport airplanes were especially in the limelight, and specifically the "Douglas Commercial" (DC-2) which practically forced all previous airliners into obsolescence. The huge "Clipper Ships" by Sikorsky and Martin blazed new trails in various directions from our shores and opened up the possibility of scheduled trans-oceanic service. Other transport airplanes came out in the new pattern to fit different loads and schedules, and America's air transport system, as the fastest and the finest, became the envy of the world. While it was the airliners that had shown the greater progress, the so-called private airplane was also taking advantage of new advancements to offer more speed, comfort, and reliability at a reasonable price. The sportsman had a prolific array to choose from, the business-man could find exactly what he needed most, and the choice for the private-pilot was only limited by the cash in his pocket. From the tiny "Cub" to the huge "Clipper" there were designs to fire one's enthusiasm and dreams; many of these airplanes became classics that stood the test of time. Surely, advancements continued as the years went by, that is normal, but weren't they mostly refinements of the principles brought out in this memorable 1934-35 period?

Jos. P. Juptner

TERMS

To make for better understanding of the various information contained herein, we should clarify a few points that might be in question. At the heading of each new chapter, the bracketed numerals under the ATC number, denote the first date of certification; any amendments made are noted in the text. Unless otherwise noted, the title photo of each chapter is an example of the model that bears that particular certificate number; any variants from this particular model, such as prototypes and special modifications, are identified. Normally accepted abbreviations and symbols are used in the listing of specifications and performance data. Unless otherwise noted, all maximum speed, cruising speed, and landing speed figures are based on sea level tests; this method of performance testing was largely the custom during this early period. Rate of climb figures are for first minute at sea level, and the altitude ceiling given is the so-called service ceiling. Cruising range in miles or hours duration is based on the engine's cruising r.p.m., but even at that, the range given must be considered as an average because of pilot's various throttle habits.

At the ending of each chapter, we show a listing of registered aircraft of a similar type; most of the listings show the complete production run of a particular type and this information we feel will be valuable to historians, photographers, and collectors in making correct identification of a certain aircraft by its registration number.

In each volume there are separate discussions on 100 certificated airplanes and we refer to these discussions as chapters, though they are not labeled as such; at the end of each chapter there is reference made to see the chapter for an ATC number pertaining to the next development of a certain type. As each volume contains discussions on 100 aircraft, it should be rather easy to pin-point the volume number for a chapter of discussion that would be numbered as A.T.C. #93, or perhaps A.T.C. #176, as an example. The use of such terms as "prop", "prop spinner", "wheel pants", "trim tabs", "chrome-moly", "wash-in", "stub-wing", and "skin", are normally used among aviation people and should present no difficulty in interpretation.

TABLE OF CONTENTS

ATC # 501
(3-16-33)
CURTISS-WRIGHT "CONDOR" T-32

Fig. 1. Prototype "Condor" T-32 shown here on early test flight.

With the unfolding of this volume we come into the fascinating era of the "super airliners" of the 1930's, a period that was to see giant strides in air transportation. Among the first of these new liners, the new Curtiss-Wright "Condor" model T-32 was introduced as the ultimate in transport biplane design, and only slightly inferior to the new monoplane transports also under development at this particular time. Proud of the reputation for passenger comfort and safety acquired with the earlier "Condor" transport (ATC # 193 of USCA/C, Vol. 2) Curtiss-Wright retained the colorful name and concentrated many of the recent aeronautical innovations and aerodynamic concepts into this new design, a design-type which incidently was to become the last of the big biplanes to be used on the American airlanes. Transamerican Air Lines was the first of the lines to place an order for the new 17 place transport, ordering 4 in November of 1932 with an option for 2 more, all to be delivered early in 1933. Before the airplanes were even delivered American Airways had purchased "Transamerican" thereby inheriting the order for the "Condor" liners and adding the Chicago-Detroit-Cleveland-Buffalo route to its expanding system. The "Valley Route" from Chicago to New York, inaugurated in May of 1933, offered a schedule of 5 hours 50 mins. including stops in Detroit and Buffalo. With a one-way fare of $47.50 the new, fast service, soon became very popular. Eastern Air Transport (EAT) had ordered 5 of the new "Condor" also in 1932, with deliveries to commence early in 1933. The very first example of the "Condor" T-32 was delivered to EAT on 3-23-33. After trial runs from Newark to Atlanta and down the eastern seaboard to Miami the new "Condor" transports were soon offering 12 hour (1210 mile) scheduled service between New York and Miami, including a stop in Atlanta. Meanwhile, American Airways (AA) inaugurated service with the T-32 from Cleveland to Fort Worth in Oct. of 1933; the time between terminals was cut to 11 hours. Late in 1933 EAT started an experimental nightly passenger-schedule between Newark and Atlanta; the "Condor" T-32 converted into a sleeper-plane was used. In Oct. of 1933 EAT had fitted one of their 17 place T-32 day-planes with some sleeping berths; Eddie Rickenbacker, adventurous official of the line, was the first to try it out on a trial night-run from Newark to Atlanta. Thus Rickenbacker became the first known passenger to undress in flight and go to bed in an American airplane. Rickenbacker's compliments on the night-time flight prompted conversion of several more T-32 day-planes into "sleepers" with 8 berths and 5 reclining chairs; the night-time service became instantly popular. Very pleased with performance on their new, faster schedules, both AA and EAT ordered additional "Condor" T-32 transports to replace slower and smaller aircraft in their fleets. By mid-1933 each line (AA and EAT) had 9 of the T-32 and American Airways had already placed orders for a number of the newer model AT-32 which promised to be even faster, more luxurious, and with improved

Fig. 2. "Condor" T-32 on delivery flight to Eastern Air Transport.

operating economy.

Development of the new "Condor" model T-32 dates back to a design proposal by Geo. A. Page, Jr. in 1931. Several scale models of this proposed transport had undergone wind-tunnel tests to establish the basic aerodynamic form and arrangement; performance capabilities were calculated around the use of two Wright "Cyclone" 575 h.p. engines. Moving over to the Curtiss-Wright plant in St. Louis, engineer George Page and two assistants started work on the new design in the spring of 1932, already receiving recommendations from several interested airlines. The prototype of the model T-32 airliner was out of final assembly and off on its maiden flight in Jan. of 1933. With only 9 months time from start of construction to first-flight it can be appreciated that every one at Curtiss-Wright (St. Louis) bent towards extra effort to make this possible. Flown on its maiden-flight by Lloyd Child and Geo. A. Page, Jr. the new "Condor" measured up to all expectations and showed promise of a useful future. Tests of the T-32 prototype were performed under the watchful eye of the Army Air Corps; satisfactory performance prompted an order for 2 of the T-32 (as YC-30) with delivery in May of 1933. Certification tests went well and ATC # 501 was issued 3-16-33; a week later the

prototype airplane was delivered to EAT and the first T-32 for AA was delivered early in April. Some 6 months later all 21 of the T-32 type had been delivered and the new AT-32 version was already shaping up on the assembly floor. Amendments to this type certification (# 501) were issued 9-11-33, 9-23-33, and 4-12-34. EAT and AA each had 9 of the model T-32, the Army Air Corps had 2, as the YC-30, and the last of this particular type was used by Adm. Byrd on his Antarctic Expedition to the South Pole. The "Condor" tour of duty on EAT and AA routes lasted into 1935 and slightly beyond, but the longest and most interesting part of its service life came afterward. Practically all of the "Condor" T-32 were eventually exported and every one of them had marked up an interesting and useful career.

The Curtiss-Wright "Condor" model T-32 was a large transport biplane with basic interior arrangement for 15 passengers and a crew of two. Aside from being a large biplane the new T-32 had scarcely anything else in common with the earlier Curtiss "Condor" of 1929. Considerably advanced over transports of previous years this new "Condor" offered a large, quiet cabin in comfortable surroundings; the spacious elegance was accented with individual conveniences and comfort aids to ensure an en-

Fig. 3. "Condor" T-32 offered smooth, pleasant ride for 15 passengers.

joyable trip. Manned by a pilot and co-pilot, the co-pilot served sometime as a "steward" to tend to various simple needs and to chat amiably with nervous first-time passengers. Designed to combat noise and vibration, the big "Condor" offered a smooth, pleasant ride, and had speed enough to maintain 140 m.p.h. schedules. Powered with two Wright "Cyclone" GR-1820-F11 engines rated 650-670 h.p. at sea level the model T-32 delivered a good performance throughout the operating range, and had some power reserve which enabled it to maintain flight to safety at 3000 ft. on any one of its engines. Equipped with several mechanical and aerodynamic assists the big "Condor" was rather easy and enjoyable to fly, and surprisingly manuverable for a ship of this large size. Although the "Condor's" service life on the airlanes of America was rather short the bulk of its exciting history was acquired in foreign countries; it is there they performed a multitude of chores often over forbidding terrain, or in and out of second-rate airfields. Oddly enough, the "Condor" T-32 was more or less a quick, short-term project, designed to fulfill an urgent need and to serve a useful purpose; this it fulfilled with tribute. The "Condor" model T-32 was manufactured by the Curtiss-Wright Airplane Co. at Robertson (St. Louis), Mo. and 21 examples of this particular model had been built. To upgrade this model closely to the standards of the newer AT-32 about 10 of these aircraft were pulled from service at various times and converted by Curtiss-Wright to the model T-32-C under ATC # 547.

Listed below are specifications and performance data for the model T-32 as powered with 2"Cyclone" GR-1820-F11 engines rated 650-670 h.p. each; length overall 48'10"; heighth overall 16'10"; wing span upper 82'0"; wing span lower 74'0"; wing chord upper & lower 106.5"; wing area upper 702 sq. ft.; wing area lower 506 sq. ft.; total wing area 1208 sq. ft.; airfoil NACA-2412; wt. empty 11,235 lbs.; useful load 5565 lbs.; payload with 300 gal. fuel and 2 pilots was 3155 lbs. (15 pass. at 170 lbs. each & 605 lbs. baggage-mail-cargo); gross wt. 16,800 lbs.; max. speed 170; cruising speed 145; landing (stall) speed 59; climb 850 ft. first min. at sea level; ser. ceiling 15,500 ft.; ceiling with one engine out 3000 ft.; gas cap. 300 gal.; oil cap. 30 gal.; cruising range at 70 gal. per hour was 4 hours or 580 miles; price at factory approx. $60,000.; Western Electric radio-telephone and extra navigational equipment added 85 to 200 lbs. to the standard empty weight; the payload was affected accordingly.

The fuselage framework was a spidery web of welded chrome-moly steel tube trusses faired to shape with metal formers and fairing strips, then fabric covered; much of the fuselage forward area was covered with removable dural metal panels. The pilot station, up high and in front, was equipped with adjustable seats, adjustable rudder pedals, and dual control wheels on a Y-type column. All the latest instrumentation and two-way Western Electric radio-telephone were provided for navigation and communication. The floors, walls and roof of the large passenger cabin were insulated with "Seapak" for effective sound-proofing; long tail-pipes also directed engine exhaust noise away from the cabin. Two rows of seats (5 in each row) were on right side of the cabin, and one row of 5 on the left side with a wide aisle between; cabin head-room was 6'6" to enable a comfortable walk in the aisle

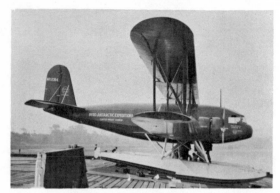

Fig. 4. "Condor" played important role in Byrd's Antarctic Expedition.

even in flight. Passenger seats could be reclined for napping, and hot or cold air adjustment was at each seat; 2 large dome-lights were in cabin roof for general lighting with individual reading lamps at each seat. The cabin was tastefully upholstered in leather and rich fabrics; fabrics were fire-proofed to allow smoking in flight. Luggage racks were mounted in the ceiling for light baggage; the main mail-cargo and baggage compartments were in belly of the fuselage under the cabin floor to avoid disturbing passengers during loading or unloading. The double-bay wing framework was built up of welded chrome-moly steel tube girder-type spar beams with wing ribs of stamped-out dural metal sheet and riveted dural tubing, spaced about 10 inches apart to preserve the airfoil form across the span; the leading edges were covered with dural metal sheet and the completed framework was covered in fabric. Large balanced ailerons were on upper wings only. The center-section panel of upper wing contained 4 gravity-feed fuel tanks of 75 gallon capacity each; electric fuel level gauges were mounted on pilot's panel. Fifteen gallons of oil were provided in each engine nacelle. Engine nacelles were mounted into the truss of lower stub-wing; engines were mounted in rubber bushings to lessen vibration. Each a separate unit, the retractable undercarriage of 20'4" tread was mounted under the engine nacelles; electric motors were used to raise and lower the gear with a hand-lever provided for emergency use. Low-pressure wheels and tires were 15.00x16 with Bendix servo-mechanical brakes; each landing gear unit was fitted with "Aerol" shock absorbing struts. Three baggage-cargo compartments were in underside of the fuselage with capacity for up to 600 lbs. The large fabric-covered tail group was built up of welded steel

tube spars and dural metal ribs; all movable control surfaces were aerodynamically balanced. The elevators and rudder were fitted with "trimming tabs" to trim for direction and attitude. A 7.00x5 swiveling tail wheel, three-bladed adj. metal propellers, 2 engine-driven generators, two 12-volt batteries, 2 large cabin heaters, Western Electric two-way radio, electric inertia-type engine starters, fire extinguishers, Sperry artificial horizon, navigation lights, first-aid kit, and a lavatory were standard equipment. Extra equipment was optional at discretion of operating airline; these options included night-flying equipment and special interior appointments. The next development in the Curtiss-Wright "Condor" series was the improved moded AT-32 as described in the chapter for ATC # 534 of this volume.

Listed below are "Condor" model T-32 entries as gleaned from registration records:

NC-12353;	T-32	(# 21)	GR-1820-Fll;	EAT.
NC-12354;	"	(# 22)	"	AA.
NC-12363;	"	(# 23)	"	AA.
NC-12364;	"	(# 24)	"	AA.
NC-12365;	"	(# 25)	"	AA.
33-320;	"	(# 26)	"	AC.
33-321;	"	(# 27)	"	AC.
NC-12366;	"	(# 28)	"	EAT.
NC-12367;	"	(# 29)	"	EAT.
NC-12368;	"	(# 30)	"	EAT.
NC-12369;	"	(# 31)	"	EAT.
NC-12371;	"	(# 32)	"	AA.
NC-12372;	"	(# 33)	"	AA.
NC-12373;	"	(# 34)	"	EAT.
NC-12374;	"	(# 35)	"	EAT.
NC-12375;	"	(# 36)	"	EAT.
NC-12376;	"	(# 37)	"	EAT.
NC-12377;	"	(# 38)	"	AA.
NC-12378;	"	(# 39)	"	AA.
NC-12383;	"	(# 40)	"	AA.
NR-12384;	T-32-S	(#41)	"	Adm. Byrd.

There were 21 examples of the T-32 type; 9 for EAT, 9 for AA, 2 for Air Corps as YC-30, and 1 as T-32-S (on Edo floats) for Adm. Byrd; 8 were later converted as T-32-C for AA, one converted to T-32-C and 2 converted as T-32-C Spl. for EAT; a few T-32 crashed while in airline service, and several remained as standard T-32 in EAT service until sold; some T-32 also equipped with GR-1820-Fl engines rated 700 h.p. at sea level; YC-30 type had "Cyclone" R-1820-23 engines rated 650 h.p. at sea level—at 18,500 lbs. gross wt. the YC-30 was 19 place with maximum speed of 161 m.p.h.; the Wright GR-1820-F series engines were geared down at a 8:5 or 16:11 ratio, price was $8320, delivered.

ATC # 502
(4-6-33)
WACO "SPORTSMAN", PLA.

Fig. 5. Waco Model PLA with 170 h.p. Jacobs LA-1 engine. Canopy slides forward for entry.

The model PLA as introduced for the 1933 season offered 12 distinct improvements over the previous Waco two-seaters of 1932, and offered all this at no increase in price. Some of these changes were quite noticeable and some were not, but in general, the basic "Model A" design was pretty much the same. Earlier 1932 versions of the A-series were certainly all good airplanes, but even in the best there always seems to be room for some improvement. Striving to make a good airplane better the prime consideration was given now to convenience and more, almost lavish comfort. Fattened up noticeably through its middle, the cockpit of the PLA was now wider for more elbow-room and the new coupe-top canopy, which slid open or closed on rails, was both a convenience and a boon to the appearance. A study of the various other improvements reveals a more generous treatment to streamlining the nooks and crannies, some concessions to better operation, and many other little things that perhaps only added to personal enjoyment. Noticeably longer now with a more rounded appearance, and laced with trappings that also contributed to adding more weight, the model PLA, by comparison with earlier counterparts, was slightly heavier when empty. It was also allowed a little more in useful load, and as a consequence, the gross weight was boosted also. In spite of this the model PLA "Sportsman" for

1933 was even a shade faster, and didn't hardly notice any burden of extra weight. As powered with the 7 cyl. Jacobs LA-1 engine of 170 h.p. the PLA was perhaps one of the most sensible machines for the average sporting pilot of this period. The true sport-plane of this time had to fulfill an almost infinite number of requirements to satisfy the whims and needs of the average amateur sportsman; this was a large order and the "Sportsman" (PLA) demonstrated ability to do it well.

The Waco "Sportsman" model PLA was basically a light sport biplane with side-by-side seating for two. Due to the popularity of the optional "coupe top" on previous models in this A-series, this feature was now more or less a permanent installation specified to be included upon delivery. Besides the added comfort in colder weather the coupe-top did streamline the top side of the fuselage and actually contributed a little toward more speed. The large payload that was available in the PLA permitted up to 275 lbs. for baggage and sporting gear, or an optional 20 gals. of extra fuel for 1.5 hours more cruising range; even with extra fuel there was still weight allowance for up to 150 lbs. of baggage and gear. Weight allowance for all this baggage, or the option to stretch cruising range to 6 hours was greatly appreciated by sportsman-pilots, especially those

Fig. 6. Sporty PLA featured chummy arrangement for two.

that hied away often to places where gasoline was not easily available, or the catering to air travelers was scant and more primitive. Realizing that most sportsmen were more apt to be fitted with bulky clothing in year-around flying the PLA offered a wider cockpit for more shoulder-room and soft contoured cushions for comfort on those longer rides. The companionship of side-by-side seating made pleasant trips even more enjoyable, and dual controls allowed a sharing of piloting experiences. As powered with the 7 cyl. Jacobs LA-1 engine of 170 h.p. the PLA had snappy, effortless performance that allowed practical operation far from the beaten path; a stout frame and rugged character was able to soak up more than normal abuse and held together well even in misuse. Operating expenses of the PLA were not necessarily cheap, but they were quite sensible in proportion to the type of services rendered. Not represented in any large number the PLA "Sportsman" was welcomed anywhere, it was popular for many years, and its good reputation upheld the famous Waco tradition. The type certificate number for the model PLA was issued 4-6-33 and at least 4 examples of this model were manufactured by the Waco Aircraft Co. at Troy, Ohio. This approval was amended 11-2-33 to allow 2300 lb. gross weight.

Listed below are specifications and performance data for the model PLA as powered with 170 h.p. Jacobs LA-1 engine; length overall 23'6"; height overall 8'9"; wing span upper 29'6"; wing span lower 27'5"; wing chord upper & lower 57"; wing area upper 130 sq. ft.; wing area lower 111 sq. ft.; total wing area 241 sq. ft.; airfoil Clark Y; wt. empty 1411 lbs.; useful load 796 (889) lbs.; payload with 40 gal. fuel 363 (457) lbs.; payload with 60 gal. fuel 236 (329) lbs.; gross wt. 2207 (2300) lbs.; figures in parentheses are wts. as later amended; max. speed 122; cruising speed 105; landing speed 41-43; climb 850 ft. first min. at sea level; ser. ceiling 14,500 ft.; gas cap. normal 40 gal.; gas cap. max. 60 gal.; oil cap.3-4 gal.; cruising range at 9.5 gal. per hour 420-600 miles; price $4285. at factory field.

The construction details and general arrangement of the model PLA were basically typical to that of previous models in the A-series except for some improvements and slight changes. Spring-filled form-fitting cushions were provided in the wider cockpit and the sliding canopy for weather protection was an option installed for $195.00 extra; a cabin heater was also offered as an option. A centrally-located throttle control on the wood-grained dash-panel eliminated the previous use of a throttle control on each side; the parking brake handle was placed between the occupants and dual stick-type controls were provided. Baggage compartment doors, both front and rear, were provided with Sesame locks; allowance in front compartment was 150 lbs. and allowance in rear compartment was 36 lbs. The cockpit entry doors, typical of earlier models were now eliminated, but hand-holds in the upper wing and step-pegs on the fuselage still offered easy step-over entry from either wing-

Fig. 7. The PLA two-seater was fun to own and welcomed anywhere.

walk. Two fuel tanks of 20 gal. capacity each were mounted in center-section panel of upper wing, and an extra 20 gal. fuel tank could be mounted in fuselage ahead of the cockpit. The robust landing gear of 71 in. tread was equipped with Waco patented shock absorbing struts and Warner wheels with brakes; 7.50x10 low-pressure tires were fitted on 6.50x10 wheels. A 10x3 tail wheel, speed-ring engine cowling, dual controls, wheel brakes, a parking brake, compass, navigation lights, hot-shot battery, Heywood engine starter, engine cover, tie-down ropes, first-aid kit, tool kit, log books, and a wooden propeller were standard equipment. A metal propeller, coupe-top canopy, extra 20 gal. fuel tank, cabin heater, 8 in. streamlined tail wheel, wing-root fairings, landing lights, parachute-flares, and wheel pants were optional. Ser. # 3714 and #3758 were finished in Loening Yellow fuselage and Nungesser Green wing panels. The next development in the Waco A series was the model ULA as described in the chapter for ATC # 511 of this volume.

Below are PLA entries as gleaned from registration and factory records:

NC-13067; PLA (# 3714) Jacobs 170.
 -13073; PLA (# 3758) Jacobs 170.
 -13401; PLA (# 3759) Jacobs 170.
 -13410; PLA (# 3760) Jacobs 170.

This certificate for ser. # 3714 and up; this approval expired 9-30-39.

ATC # 503
(4-29-33)
FAIRCHILD, MODEL 22-C7D

Fig. 8. Fairchild 22-C7D with 4 cyl. Wright "Gipsy" engine. The "Gipsy" and the "Model 22" were a charming combination.

The development of the new model 22-C7D by Fairchild (Kreider-Reisner) was perhaps dictated by circumstance, and as a consequence it became the cheapest model of the popular series. First-quality construction of Fairchild airplanes surely prevented any invasion of the lowest-price field, but this new "Model 22" for the 1933 season was reasonably low-priced and a very big bargain for the money. By 1933 a continuing production flow of the A. C. E. "Cirrus" engines was becoming doubtful, the Menasco "Pirate" engines were quite expensive and still plagued with overheating problems, as fitted in the "Twenty two", so choice of the popular Wright-Gipsy engine was almost essential in the "air-cooled inline" category. The 4 cyl. Wright-Gipsy developing 90 h.p. at 1950 r.p.m. was certainly a fine little engine, already proven in many interesting installations. Being an upright engine, with cylinders placed above the thrust-line, it changed the face of the new "22" and forced a somewhat higher cowl line at the front cockpit. Although basically similar to previous models of the "Fairchild 22" monoplane, the model 22-C7D somehow showed and enjoyed a subtle difference. Even on the ground it seemed to radiate a feeling of friendliness, and in the air its manner was completely charming. The Rover-

powered, Cirrus-powered, and Menasco-powered "Twenty Two" all shared this attribute to varying extent of course, but these airplanes seemed to put on the air of a "sport plane"; the jolly Gipsy-powered 22-C7D seemed neither a sport-plane nor a trainer either, it was just a pleasant, rather ordinary ship that was adaptable to and quite happy in most any capacity without perceptible change in temperament. It is historical fact that owner-pilots were very happy with the 22-C7D, quickly becoming staunch friends with their ship, and always anxious to share their delight either with joy-rider friends or other pilots. Word of the comparative good nature of the 22-C7D, even in the hands of an embryo-pilot, soon got around so it was inevitable that several of them were forced into pilot-training; "dual" time was usually $10.00 per hour and "solo" time went for about $8.00 an hour. It stands to reason, had the 22-C7D not been introduced at the very bottom of this country's "depression", it would have been seen just about everywhere in far greater number.

The Fairchild model 22-C7D was a light open cockpit parasol-type monoplane with seating arranged in tandem for two. Aimed more or less at the private-pilot, its prime feature was to be its lower cost, but it was not a "cheap" airplane

Fig. 9. The 22-C7D was an excellent trainer.

by any means; the airframe still incorporated all the expensive features of "Fairchild" quality construction. Although delivered price was still rather high for these lean times, the bonus of less frequent maintenance and a longer service life in general tended to make it a better and better bargain as time went by. As powered with the upright 4 cyl. Wright-Gipsy engine of 90 h.p. the model 22-C7D had more than ample performance for the average owner-pilot, and its happy-go-lucky nature was endeared by one and all. Rather spritely in spite of its nominal power, it had absolutely no objectionable handling characteristics and flying it was a pleasant experience. Its rugged structure, fortified against high stresses, also allowed basic acrobatics

without restriction, so this offered peace of mind to pilots who enjoyed doing the various shenanigans called "stunting". Pilots were very enthusiastic about the Gipsy-powered 22-C7D and this was often hard to comprehend by others, that is, until they too had the chance to be properly convinced. The Fairchild model 22-C7D could boast of many friends, and they were not likely to forget an association with this airplane even as the years went by. The type certificate number for the 22-C7D was issued 4-29-33 for ser. # 902 and up; approval was amended 11-9-33. Some 21 examples of this model were manufactured by the Kreider-Reisner Aircraft Co., Inc. at Hagerstown, Md.

Listed below are specifications and perfor-

Fig. 10. Happy-go-lucky nature of the 22-C7D made it ideal for the week-end sportsman.

Fig. 11. Gipsy-powered "Twenty Two" was at home anywhere.

mance data for the Fairchild model 22-C7D as powered with the 90 h.p. Wright-Gipsy engine; length overall 21'8"; height overall 7'10"; wing span 32'10"; wing chord 66"; total wing area 170 sq. ft.; airfoil (NACA) N-22; wt. empty 992 lbs.; useful load 558 lbs.; payload with 21 gal. fuel 244 lbs. (1 pass. at 170 lbs., 34 lb. baggage & 2 parachutes at 20 lb. each); gross wt. 1550 lbs.; max. speed 112; cruising speed 95; landing (stall) speed 45; climb 568 ft. first min. at sea level; ser. ceiling 12,000 ft.; gas cap. 21 gal.; oil cap. 2.4 gal.; cruising range at 6 gal. per hour 320 miles; price $2475. at factory field with standard equip-

ment.

The construction details and general arrangement of the 22-C7D were typical to that of previous models in the "Twenty Two" series. One significant change, in appearance at least, was installation of the 4 cyl. "upright" Wright-Gipsy engine. The aircooled inline engine was mounted on rubber-bushed bearers to lessen vibration in the airframe; a hand-crank starter was provided and the engine swung a "Gardner" wooden propeller. The standard landing gear of 7 ft. 7 in. tread was fitted with 6.50x10 semi-airwheels with brakes; "Fairchild" spring-oil

Fig. 12. Head-on view of 22-C7D shows its slim-waisted figure.

shock absorbing struts had up to 8 in. travel for softer landings. A streamlined sport-type landing gear, with 6.50x10 Warner wheels fitted with streamlined metal wheel pants, was optional at extra cost, or either landing gear (standard or sport-type) could be fitted with 19x9-3 Goodyear low-pressure "airwheels". Normally a tail skid was provided, but an 8x4 tail wheel was optional. Dual stick-type controls were provided, with brake pedals normally in the rear cockpit only; brake pedals in the front cockpit were optional. The 21 gal. fuel tank was mounted high in the fuselage ahead of the front cockpit; baggage allowance was 34 lbs. and 2 seat-pack parachutes at 20 lbs. each were part of the payload allowance. All engine and plane controls operated on ball bearings; full-length narrow chord ailerons and aerodynamically balanced rudder provided sharp control. For trimming, the horizontal stabilizer was adjustable in flight. A compass, air-speed indicator, hand-crank engine starter, and the usual set of engine and flight instruments were standard equipment. Owners of the "Twenty Two", powered with either the "Cirrus" or "Wright-Gipsy" engines, had assurance of replacement parts through Menasco Motors which had bought up all stocks of these 2 engines in 1935. The next development in the "Twenty Two" series was the Warner-powered model 22-C7E as described in the chapter for ATC # 515 of this volume.

Listed below are 22-C7D entries as gleaned from registration records:

NC-13193;	22-C7D	(# 902)	Wright-Gipsy
-2575;	"	(# 903)	"
-2579;	"	(# 904)	"
-2691;	"	(# 905)	"
	"	(# 906)	"
-2722;	"	(# 907)	"
-9478;	"	(# 908)	"
-9479;	"	(909)	"
-9480;	"	(# 910)	"
-9481;	"	(# 911)	"
-9482;	"	(# 912)	"
-14336;	"	(# 913)	"
-14337;	"	(# 914)	"
-14338;	"	(# 915)	"
-14339;	"	(# 916)	"
-14340;	"	(# 917)	"
-14764;	"	(# 918)	"
-14765;	"	(# 919)	"
-14766;	"	(# 920)	"
-14767;	"	(# 921)	"
-14768;	"	(# 922)	"

This approval for ser. # 902 and up; first-flight of ser. # 902-903-904-905-906-907 in 1933; first-flight of ser # 908-909-910-911-912-913-914-915-916-917-918 in 1934; first-flight of ser. # 919-920-921-922 in 1935; this approval expired 9-30-39.

ATC # 504
(5-3-33)
STEARMAN "SPORTSTER", MODEL 80-81.

Fig. 13. Stearman Model 80 with 420 h.p. "Wasp Jr." engine.

The manufacture of Stearman airplanes was at a near stand-still during this particular period (1932-33), but the shop facilities were kept more or less active by offering service, repair, and modification to owners of Stearman, Northrop, and Hamilton aircraft. Any of the previously built "Stearman" models were still available on "45-day delivery" after receipt of order, but orders were just not coming in. Despite the virtual cut-off in manufacturing, the engineering department under Mac Short was still very active and several interesting projects were either "on the board" or in the making. Of necessity, most of the projects and proposals were slanted to military or export requirements; a few commercial designs however were built on speculation or to customer order. One of these custom-built craft was the Model 80, an adaptation of the earlier 4-series design for high-speed special purpose work. As the Stearman "Sportster" the Model 80 was a custom-designed airplane especially built to the order of John L. Vette, Jr. variously of Oak Park, Ill., of Grosse Pointe,

Mich., and of Oakland, Calif. A high-performance utility airplane for the sportsman-pilot the Model 80 was used extensively by Mr. Vette, a 21 year-old master-pilot graduate of the Boeing School of Aeronautics, for nation-wide sales promotion of a new-type rivet, or just for sight-seeing on flights from coast to coast.

As a two-place biplane the Model 80 had a streamlined canopy over the pilot's station and the open passenger cockpit, up front, was covered with a metal panel when not in use. As a single-seater the ship's performance was greatly improved by closing off the front cockpit cavity. With a cruising range of 650 miles or more the "Eighty" was used extensively on long cross-country hops; various pilot aids were installed and instrumentation was unusually complete, including a Sperry directional gyro and artificial horizon. Radio-telephone, a Lear radio receiver, and a full set of night-flying equipment were also provided. As powered with the 9 cyl. supercharged Pratt & Whitney "Wasp Jr." model T3A engine of 420 h.p. the sleek Model 80 was

Fig. 14. Stearman Model 80 was specially built for John L. Vette, Jr. as cross-country commuter.

capable of brilliant performance and rather high cruising speeds. In effect, the performance potential was also greatly enhanced by use of the Hamilton-Standard controllable pitch propeller, an especially new innovation for sport-craft of this type. In all respects, the "Sportster" model 80 was a typical Stearman airplane, and built only in the one example (NC-11720) as shown. The type certificate number for the Model 80 was issued 5-3-33 and amended later on 10-5-33 to include approval of the similar Model 81.

Listed below are specifications and performance data for the Stearman "Sportster" model 80 as powered with the 420 h.p. "Wasp Jr." T3A engine; length overall 25'1"; height overall 9'8"; wing span upper 35'0"; wing span lower 27'0"; wing chord upper 62"; wing chord lower 48"; wing area upper 174 sq.ft.; wing area lower 101 sq.ft.; total wing area 275 sq.ft.; airfoil NACA-4412; wt. empty 2436 (2380) lbs.; useful load 1064 (1120) lbs.; wts. in parentheses for 80 as tested on early flights; payload with 104 gal. fuel 210 lbs.; gross wt. 3500 lbs.; max. speed 175; cruising speed (.88 power) 151; landing (stall) speed 58; climb 1600 ft. first min. at sea level; service ceiling 19,600 ft.; gas cap. 104 gal.; oil

Fig. 15. Stearman Model 81 with 420 h.p. "Wasp Jr." engine.

Fig. 16. Model 81 was secondary trainer for military pilots, built primarily for export.

cap. 8 gal.; cruising range at 23.9 gal. per hour was 4.35 hours or 650 miles; price was not announced.

The fuselage framework was built up of welded chrome-moly steel tubing, lavishly faired with plywood bulkheads and spruce stringers to a well-rounded shape, then fabric covered. The cockpits were provided with dual controls and both cockpits were equipped with instruments for flight and operation. The front cockpit was normally covered with a metal panel when not in use, and the pilot's cockpit was covered by a streamlined canopy with sliding hatch for entry. A large compartment for 100 lbs. of baggage was forward of the front cockpit with a large and convenient door on the left side. A Pyrene fire extinguisher compartment was just ahead of the baggage hold, a safety feature for ground crews when servicing the airplane. The wing framework, consisting of a center-section and 4 panels, was built up of laminated spruce spar beams with spruce girder-type wing ribs; the leading edges were covered with dural metal sheet and the completed framework was covered in fabric. Fuel tanks totaling a 104 gal. capacity were in upper wing. The semi-cantilever landing gear of 87 in. tread was a well-streamlined combination of "Aerol" shock absorbing struts and wire-braced axles; "General" streamlined wheels and tires of 24 in. diameter were equipped with Bendix brakes. A large full-swivel tail wheel was faired with a streamlined metal cover. The fabric covered tail-group was built up of welded steel channels and tubing; the horizontal stabilizer was adjustable in flight and the "balanced" rudder was provided with a fixed metal tab that could be deflected to compensate for engine torque. Rigging was at zero incidence, dihedral of upper wing at 1 deg., and lower wing at 2 deg. Other equipment included Western Electric radio-telephone, a Lear radio receiver, Sperry directional gyro and artificial horizon, fire extinguisher, electric engine starter, battery,

navigation lights, retracting landing lights, 3 parachute flares, and a Hamilton-Standard controllable pitch propeller.

On 10-5-33 this type certificate (ATC # 504) was amended to include approval of the Stearman "Model 81". The Model 81 was a conversion of the basic 80 design that was planned for use as a secondary-trainer of military pilots, or as a fast long-range mailplane. As a prototype, the Model 81 was not built to order, but most likely on speculation in hopes of stimulating some orders for this type of airplane from small foreign countries. The Model 81 was dispatched on a leisurely tour of So. America and demonstrated several times as a high-performance seaplane on twin-float gear. In April of 1935 the "81" was offered for sale to the public in general for $8500.; not yet sold by November it was flown by George Harte to Mexico City for demonstration. By now, the airplane had been modified with installation of a 420 h.p. Wright engine; reportedly, it was finally sold to the Mexican government.

Basically, the Model 81 as shown was quite similar to the custom-built Model 80. As a two-place biplane the "Eighty One" had an extended streamlined canopy that covered both cockpits; normally, the ship was provided with dual stick-type controls. The pilot flew from the front when ship was used as a trainer, and from the rear when used as a mailplane. First powered with a 9 cyl. Pratt & Whitney "Wasp Jr." model SB engine rated 400 h.p., the Model 81 was later equipped with the 420 h.p. "Wasp Jr." T3A engine and a Hamilton-Standard controllable pitch propeller. The proposed Model 82 was to be a military export-version of the 81, but apparently none had been built. The certificate of approval for the Model 81 was combined with ATC # 504 on 10-5-33 and only one example of this model (NC-570Y) was built by the Stearman Aircraft Co. at Wichita, Kan. a div. of the United Aircraft & Transport Corp. J. E.

Fig. 17. Model 81 on Edo floats.

Schaefer was president & general manager; Mac Short was vice-president & chief engineer; Cliff Barron was secretary-treasurer.

Listed below are specifications and performance data for the Stearman Model 81 as powered with the 420 h.p. "Wasp Jr." T3A engine; length overall 25'1"; height overall 9'4"; wing span upper 35'0"; wing span lower 27'0"; wing chord upper 62"; wing chord lower 48"; wing area upper 174 sq. ft.; wing area lower 101 sq.ft.; total wing area 275 sq.ft.; airfoil NACA-4412; wt. empty 2385 (2515) lbs.; useful load 1615 (1385) lbs.; payload with 155 gal. fuel 230 lbs.; gross wt. 4000 (3900) lbs.; wts. in parentheses for trainer-version, other wts. for long-range mailplane; max. speed 170; cruising speed (.87 power) 140; landing (stall) speed 60; climb 1100-1200 ft. first min. at sea level; ser. ceiling 17,000 ft.; gas cap. 155 gal.; oil cap. 10 gal.; cruising range at 23.9 gal. per hour was 6.45 hours or 900 miles; price was not announced.

The construction details and general arrangement of the Model 81 were typical to that of the entry; a complete set of flight, engine, and blind-flying instruments were provided in both cockpits of the trainer version. A metal-lined mail pit was provided in the long-range mailplane. The landing gear was identical to that of the Model 80 and fittings were provided for installation of twin-float seaplane gear. All con-trol surfaces were aerodynamically balanced; the horizontal stabilizer was fixed with adjustable "trimming tabs" on the elevators. The balanced rudder had a fixed metal tab that could be adjusted (on the ground) to trim for engine torque. Streamlined "General" tires were mounted on Bendix wheels with brakes. The airframe was bonded and shielded for radio; a Western Electric radio-telephone and a Lear radio receiver were optional. An electric engine starter, engine-driven generator, Exide battery, navigation lights, landing lights, parachute flares, lighted instrument panels, fire extinguisher, and Hamilton-Standard controllable pitch propeller were standard equipment. As a military fighter-bomber the proposed Model 82 was to be equipped with 2 forward-firing machine guns in center-section of upper wing, 1 flexible machine gun mounted in rear cockpit, and racks for 5 small bombs under each lower wing. Another interesting Stearman development was the Model 75 as described in chapter for ATC # 743.

Listed below are Stearman Model 80 and 81 entries:

NC-11720; Model 80 (# 8001) Wasp Jr. T3A
NC-570Y; Model 81 (# 8101) Wasp Jr. T3A

Model 81 first had Wasp Jr. SB-400 engine and last engine installation was Wright R-975-E2 of 420 h.p.

DOUGLAS "DOLPHIN", MODEL 9.

Fig. 18. Douglas "Dolphin" 9 with two 450 h.p. "Wasp" engines. Navy version was RD-2.

The Douglas "Dolphin" amphibian was presumably designed as a flying-yacht for the wealthy sportsman, but an unmistakable adaptability was engineered into the airplane so that it could be easily modified for use by the government services; at this time, this was the most practical approach. Actually by comparison, there were only a very few "civil" Dolphin because most were either in Coast Guard, U.S. Navy, Marines, and Army Air Corps service. Occasional headlines of the day told the story—"two new Dolphin amphibians recently flown to France Field in Panama Canal Zone by Air Corps pilots"—or, "three Douglas "Dolphin" delivered to Air Corps station in Hawaii",etc. A tally shows that practically all of the "Dolphin" that were in "civil" use were more or less custom-built "Specials" arranged and furbished to the specific instructions of a customer. The flying-yacht, especially built for plane builder Wm. E. Boeing, was a case in point, as was the special "Essowing" built for the Standard Oil Development Co. of N.J.; these and similar specials were manufactured under various Group 2 approvals. As to the Model 9 covered by this type certificate (ATC # 505), records show that 2 were delivered to the U.S. Navy as RD-2 (Bur. no. A9348 and A9349), but no civil versions of this particular model were registered. The Model 9 (Navy RD-2) was

powered with 2 Pratt & Whitney "Wasp" CD-450 engines rated 450 h.p. at sea level; described as 9 place vehicles, it is more than likely they were used as utility transports. An alternate powerplant installation, eligible under an amendment for the "Dolphin 9" (RD-2), were the "Wasp" supercharged S3D1 engines rated 450 h.p. at 5000 ft. The "Dolphin" amphibian series actually came in a large variety of models and it is particularly difficult to distinguish one from the other very readily; this because of the similarity and the scarcity of technical data that separates one model from the other.

Like all other Douglas "Dolphin", the Model 9 was a high-winged cabin monoplane of the flying-boat type with a folding undercarriage to permit operations off land or water. The deep and broad all-metal hull was spaciously arranged for the seating of 9. Designed to take the buffeting of heavy seas, the sturdy hull was divided into 6 water-tight compartments with ample space for movement back and forth in the craft, either at rest or even aloft. The 2 engines were mounted high above the cantilever wing on a system of braces in a tractor fashion; the engine nacelles were cleverly tied together with a small "wing" that added rigidity to the mounting trusses and also provided added wing area for extra lift. The high mounting of the engines provided ample airframe clearance for the whirl-

Fig. 19. View shows unusual "Dolphin" configuration in all its detail.

ing propellers, and kept the blades away from damaging waterspray. The folding long-leg landing gear retracted out of the way for operation on water and could be quickly lowered into position for operation on land, or to come out of the water onto a ramp. Floats mounted out near the wing tips helped to keep the hull on an even keel and prevented wings from heeling into the water when taxiing. Powered with two P&W "Wasp" CD-450 engines rated 450 h.p. each at sea level the performance of this "Dolphin" was quite adequate, especially for a craft of this type. A nominal power reserve at gross load permitted emergency flight with one engine out, at least to a nearby haven of safety. The "Dolphin", by shape and arrangement, was a very good airplane and also a very good boat; it adapted itself quite readily to menial chores or rigorous service. For a multi-engined airplane weighing nearly 5 tons loaded, this craft was surprisingly deft on land or water, and pleasantly maneuverable in the air. It was definitely one of the better amphibian types. The type certificate number for the "Dolphin" Model 9 (U.S. Navy RD-2) was issued 5-8-33 and 2 examples of this model were manufactured by the Douglas Aircraft Co., Inc. on Clover Field in Santa Monica, Calif.

Fig. 20. Versatile "Dolphin" 9 (RD-2) taxis out of water to unload passengers.

Listed below are specifications and performance data for the "Dolphin" model 9 as powered with two 450 h.p. "Wasp" CD-450 engines; length overall 45'3"; height overall 14'7"; wing span 60'0"; wing chord at root 132"; wing chord at tip 86"; total wing area 592 sq.ft.; airfoil at root Clark Y-18; airfoil at tip Clark Y-9; aux. wing airfoil Clark Y; wt. empty 6563 lbs.; useful load 2937 lbs.; payload with 210 gal. fuel 1190 lbs. (7 passengers at 170 lb. each, no baggage); gross wt. 9500 lbs.; max. speed (sea level) 151; cruising speed (.70 power) 130; landing (stall) speed (no flaps) 64; landing speed (with flaps) 58; climb 900 ft. first min. at sea level; ser. ceiling 15,000 ft.; gas cap. max. 252 gal.; oil cap. 20 gal.; cruising range at 48 gal. per hour was 4 hours or 500 miles; price was not announced.

The two-step boat-type hull was an all-metal semi-monocoque structure divided into 6 watertight compartments; 3 external hatches provided emergency exit. The main cabin area was arranged to seat 7 passengers; 3 large windows lined each side and center windows could be jettisoned for emergency escape. A large external hatchway, beyond the wing's trailing edge, provided entry to the main cabin area. Two baggage compartments were provided; one up in front of pilot's station and one to rear of main cabin. A lavatory could be installed in space to rear of main hatchway. The pilot station for two, was high up front ahead of wing's leading edge; a skylight hatchway provided exit or entry from topside of wing. Dual wheel controls were standard equipment for all normal operation. The one-piece cantilever wing was built up of laminated spruce and mahogony plywood box-type spar beams with spruce and mahogany plywood truss-type wing ribs; the completed framework was covered with 3-ply mahogany and spruce plywood sheet. The fuel tanks of 252 gal. capacity were mounted in the wing. The long-leg retractable landing gear used Bendix pnue-draulic shock absorbing struts; 36x8 Bendix wheels with brakes were standard equipment. The landing gear was operated into up or down position by either pilot with a hydraulic hand-pump; position of the landing gear was visible at all times. To operate as a pure "flying boat" removal of the landing gear provided gain of 575 lbs. to the useful load and about 12 m.p.h. to the top speed. The vertical fin and horizontal stabilizer were of riveted metal construction and covered with "Alclad" sheet; the rudder and elevators were metal structures covered with fabric. The elevators were fitted with adjustable "trim tabs" and all movable surfaces had aerodynamic balance. Hydraulically-operated wing flaps were in trailing edge of the wing; deflection of the "flaps" reduced landing speeds by 6 to 8 m.p.h. Metal propellers, electric engine starters, Exide battery, engine-driven generator, fire extinguisher, fuel pumps, anchoring & mooring gear, full-swivel tail wheel, wheel brakes, and dual wheel controls were standard equipment. A radio, night-flying equipment, and controllable pitch propellers were optional. The next "Dolphin" development was the Model 10 as described in chapter for ATC # 506 of this volume.

Ship # A-9348 was delivered to Naval Base in San Diego on 4-13-33 and remained there in varied service until the early part of 1939; from there it went to Quantico and shortly after was at disposal of Naval Attache in Havana, Cuba; it was retired from service in March 1940. Ship # A-9349 was del. to Coco Solo on 6-16-33 and served there continually until 1939; it was retired from service in November 1939.

DOUGLAS "DOLPHIN", MODEL 10.

Fig. 21. Douglas "Dolphin" 10 with two 500 h.p. "Wasp" engines. Navy version was RD-2 Deluxe.

The "Model 10" was one of the more powerful versions of the Douglas "Dolphin" amphibian; the 2 Pratt & Whitney "Wasp" SD-1 engines mounted atop the cantilever wing were rated 500 h.p. each at 7000 ft. This combination points to cross-country use at higher altitudes where faster cruising speeds were easier to maintain. Basically, the "Model 10" was listed as 8 or 9 place, but a 7 place "Executive Model" was also available; one of these plush versions as the RD-2 Deluxe (Bur. no. A-9347) was delivered to the U.S. Navy at Anacostia with special VIP interior. Capable of 162 m.p.h. at 7500 ft. as an amphibian, or 174 m.p.h. as a "flying boat" (minus the landing gear) the "Model 10" substantiated several of the aerodynamic refinements wrought into the new "Dolphin" series; a slight redesign to structure also permitted sizeable gains in useful load. This new series "Dolphin" for 1933-34 was now rightfully described as models primarily developed for military purposes, but also available for commercial or private use. As a military counterpart of the Model 10, one RD-2 Deluxe (Bur. no. A-9347) was delivered to the U.S. Navy, but no civil versions of this model were registered. According to manufacturers tally some 59 "Dolphin" were built in all; 5 for the Wilmington-Catalina Air Line, 47 for the military services, and 7 were delivered to various private owners.

The Douglas "Dolphin" Model 10 was a high-winged amphibious monoplane of the "flying boat" type with seating normally arranged for 8 or 9. An "Executive" model was also available with fancy appointments and plush interior; this version was arranged to seat 7. In general, the Model 10 was typical of other "Dolphin" except for its engines, which in this case were the supercharged "Wasp" of 500 h.p. each. Structural improvements now gave the new series "Dolphin" exceptional seaworthiness even in very rough water, and a care-free life-time in normal service. Lower shape of the hull was redesigned somewhat to control the flow of "wash" and to reduce "spray" for increased visibility during take-off and landing. As powered with 2 Pratt & Whitney "Wasp" SD-1 engines rated 500 h.p. each at 7500 ft., the Model 10 was endowed with extra performance and an ability that comes only with power reserve. As an airplane that was far from compact in its proportion, and weighing nearly 5 tons, the "Dolphin" was surprisingly nimble and practically nothing could upset its pleasant nature. The "Dolphin" was one of the few airplanes that used a true "balanced and slotted" aileron; these control surfaces were designed for Douglas by Stanley H. Evans, formerly of Handley-Page in England. By design the "Dolphin" airframe was flexible enough for various modification; a military version, similar to the Model 10, was delivered to the Army Air Corps as the C-29. It is not known definitely how many "Dolphin" were exported, but one at least, was shipped to a clothing manufacturer (M. Armand Esders) of France in 1934 as a luxuriously appointed personal transport. The type

Fig. 22. RD-2 Deluxe was used to transport VIP personnel. No civil version of "Dolphin" 10 was built.

certificate number for the "Dolphin 10" was issued 5-8-33 for the 7 place Executive Model; an amendment on 5-26-33 included approval for arrangement to 8 or 9 places. As far as can be determined, only one example of the Model 10 was built as the RD-2 Deluxe for the U.S. Navy; manufactured by the Douglas Aircraft Co., Inc. at Santa Monica, Calif. Donald W. Douglas was pres.; Harry H. Wetzel was V.P. and gen. mgr.; Carl Cover was V.P. of sales; and A. E. Raymond was V.P. in charge of engrg. By mid-1933 Douglas was employing an average of 2500 people, of whom 288 were employed in the engineering dept. alone. Sprawled over 11 acres of Clover Field, the plant area was steadily increased and it now stood at 350,000 sq. ft.; big things were shaping up at Douglas Aircraft.

Listed below are specifications and performance data for the "Dolphin" Model 10 as powered with two 500 h.p. "Wasp" SD-1 engines: length overall 45'3"; height overall 14'7"; wing span 60'0"; wing chord at root 132"; wing chord at tip 86"; total wing area 592 sq.ft.; airfoil at root Clark Y-18; airfoil at tip Clark Y-9; aux. wing airfoil Clark Y; wt. empty (7 place Executive) 6750 lbs.; useful load 2450 lbs.; payload with 150 gal. fuel 1055 lbs. (5 passengers at 170 lbs. each & 205 lbs. baggage); gross wt. 9200 lbs.; wt. empty (as 8 or 9 place) 6347 lbs.; useful load 2853 lbs.; payload with 195 gal. fuel 1190 lbs. (7 passengers, no baggage); gross wt. 9200 lbs.; max. speed (at 7500 ft.) 162; cruising speed (7500 ft.) 146; landing (stall) speed (no flaps) 60; landing speed (with flaps) 55; climb 1200 ft. first min. at sea level; ser. ceiling 17,500 ft.; gas cap. max. 250 gal.; oil cap. 20 gal.; cruising range at 55 gal. per hour 395-510 miles; price not announced.

The construction details and general arrangement of the "Dolphin" Model 10 was typical to that of the Model 9 except for powerplant installation and arrangement of the interior. The 7 place "Executive Model" (delivered to U.S. Navy as RD-2 Deluxe) seated 5 passengers in the main cabin with plush comfort; all operations were conducted with 2 pilots on board. Described as a "VIP interior", the main cabin must have been a spacious layout with all manner of creature comforts. A high-performing airplane, even as an amphibian, the Model 10 gained 575 lbs. in useful load and 12 m.p.h. in top speed just by removing the weight and drag of the landing gear components. As a pure "flying boat" the Model 10 was capable of 174 m.p.h. at top speed, and the 155 m.p.h. cruising range could be extended to nearly 700 miles. Because of special treatment in the "Deluxe" version, it is quite likely it was equipped with radio gear and all the latest operational and navigational aids. The 8 to 9 place version of the Model 10 seated 6 or 7 passengers in the main cabin, and interior treatment was no doubt plainer and more serviceable. Hamilton-Standard controllable-pitch propellers, and night-flying equipment were optional. The next Douglas development was the famous DC-2 transport as described in chapter for ATC # 540 of this volume.

The RD-2 Deluxe (Bur. no. A-9347) was delivered to U.S. Navy at Anacostia on 3-24-33; its entire service life was spent working out of the Anacostia or Norfolk air stations and it was transferred to NACA at Langley Field in December 1939; the airplane was retired from service in January 1940.

PITCAIRN "AUTOGIRO", PA-24

Fig. 23. Pitcairn PA-24 with 160 h.p. Kinner R5 engine.

Based on the premise that the average week-end sportsman interested in owning an "autogiro" would probably prefer something more economical to buy and to operate, the model PAA-1 and later the modification called the PA-20, were designed around a 125 h.p. powerplant; this was a preconceived buyer preference and these two designs were calculated to fulfill it. As it later turned out, the performance with this marginal amount of power created no particular enthusiasm among owners and prospects, and the monetary saving in purchase price was not all that important to most of the flying sportsman, anyhow. To salvage this design from downright indifference and possible failure, Pitcairn redesigned several portions of this 'giro and substituted the earlier 125 h.p. engine with one of 160 h.p. The new installation, a 5 cyl. Kinner R5, pumped some 35 h.p. more into the complacent frame and turned its rather timid and reluctant behavior into something a lot more useful and certainly a lot more enjoyable. In the strict sense, the Model

PA-24 was not a new design as such, but rather a set of updated specifications that could be applied to any existing models PAA-1 or PA-20 already in service. Offered and recommended to all owners of the PAA-1 and PA-20, the new PA-24 specifications were eligible for application to about 22 airplanes, airplanes which received the equivalent of a new lease on life and several more years of useful service. In fact, one PA-24 was seen barnstorming through the midwest during 1937, looking very good and still going strong.

The Pitcairn model PA-24 was a sport-type autogiro with open cockpits arranged to seat 2 in tandem. As shown, the PA-24 was actually not a new design, but more of a modification of previously built models PAA-1 and PA-20. The most significant part of the modification was the installation of a more powerful engine and a complete change in the rotor blade system. Other noticeable changes were a new cockpit cowl line, larger windshields of better arrangement, extra stabilizing fins in the tail group, and

Fig. 24. Improvements in PA-24 were suggested by pilots; previous design suffered from low power.

a slightly redesigned engine cowling; in fact, as modified, the PA-24 now very much resembled the earlier PA-18. Standing side by side, the PA-18 and the PA-24 were nearly equals, with the rejuvenated PAA-1 and PA-20 (now designated PA-24) having the edge in many respects. As powered with the 5 cyl. Kinner R5 engine rated 160 h.p. the PA-24 was now a much better airplane and peace of mind was brought about by a little power reserve. The combination of a new rotor system, improved streamlining, more effective controls, and the much-needed boost in horsepower was translated into quicker take-offs, a much better climb-out, some increase in cruising speeds, and certainly much better slow-speed performance. Many of the earlier PAA-1 and even PA-20 would have been eventually abandoned to be sure, had it not been for the PA-24 "modification procedure" that saved them from a dismal fate. With a new strength coursing through its system the PA-24 remained on the active scene for several years afterward. The type certificate number for the Pitcairn model PA-24 was issued 5-19-33 and this modification procedure was eligible at the factory for serial numbers 19, 32 through 41, 52 through 61, and 72. Manufactured by the Pitcairn Autogiro Co. at Willow Grove, Penna.

Listed below are specifications and performance data for the Pitcairn model PA-24 as

Fig. 25. Performance was now greatly improved.

Fig. 26. A group of autogiro buffs pose happily alongside PA-24.

powered with the 160 h.p. Kinner R5 engine; fuselage length 18'7"; height overall 11'10"; rotor dia. 40'0"; rotor blade chord 18.6"; rotor blade area 117 sq.ft.; fixed-wing span 22'9"; fixed-wing chord (constant) 30"; fixed-wing area 51.6 sq.ft.; fixed-wing airfoil Goettingen 429 modified; wt. empty 1257 lbs.; useful load 543 lbs.; payload with 27 gal. fuel 183 lbs. (1 pass. at 170 lbs. & 13 lbs. baggage); gross wt. 1800 lbs.; max. speed 100; cruising speed 87; landing speed 20-25; climb 750 ft. first min. at sea level; ser. ceiling 12,000 ft.; gas cap. 27 gal.; oil cap. 3.5 gal.; cruising range at 9.5 gal. per hour was 2.7 hours or 235 miles; actual price for modification at factory was not announced.

The construction details and general arrangement of the model PA-24 were typical to that of the models PAA-1 and PA-20 as described in the chapter for ATC # 433 of U. S. CIVIL AIRCRAFT, Vol. 5 except for the following modifications. The removal of the 125 h.p. Kinner B5 engine and replacement with a 160 h.p. Kinner R5 engine required a redesign of the engine mount and a modification of the engine cowling panels; 16 lbs. of ballast was clamped into tail-end of fuselage to restore proper

Fig. 27. PA-24 in Canadian service; outfitted here as crop sprayer.

balance. The new rotor system, now with greater diameter and more area, was identical to that used on the model PA-18 (ATC # 478). The landing gear, of slightly different stance and wider tread, used long-travel oleo-spring shock absorbing struts, with 6.50x10 semi-airwheels on Warner wheels with brakes. Auxiliary fins (weighing 4 lbs.) were mounted vertically on the horizontal stabilizer for better directional control at lower speeds. An air-operated Heywood engine starter (weighing 32 lbs.), and a ground-adjustable metal propeller were standard equipment. A safety-wheel in front to prevent nose-over was optional. The next Pitcairn development was the cabin-type model PA-19 as described in chapter for ATC # 509 of this volume.

See chapter for ATC # 433 for registration listing of aircraft eligible for this modification.

Serial numbers 19, 32 thru 41, 52 thru 61, and 72 eligible as PA-24 upon conversion in accordance with approved technical data. Two PA-24 were owned by Earle Eckle of Washington, N. J.; one was all black and one was all blue. One of these was sold to a banner-towing company and finally wrecked in Florida; it is now rebuilt and on display at a transportation museum in Minden, Neb.

Late in 1934 Pitcairn developed the model PA-22, a direct control wingless autogiro, a two-place side-by-side cabin job with a 75 h.p. Pobjoy engine. Rotor diameter was 32 ft., empty wt. 600 lbs., gross wt. of 1140 lbs., max. speed 105, cruising speed 90, and range of 350 miles on 17 gal. of fuel. Take-off speed was 25 m.p.h., with a run of less than 60 ft. This model would have been an ideal sport-type autogiro for the average private-owner, but it was not fully developed.

ATC # 508
(5-22-33)
LOCKHEED "ORION", 9-E.

Fig. 28. Lockheed "Orion" 9-E with 450 h.p. "Wasp" engine.

The Lockheed "Orion" model 9-E had an uncertain beginning and led a somewhat confused existence; even as one of the swiftest airliners of its day, it seemed that it couldn't outrun disaster. The first example of this model was a fuselage on the floor that was started as a parasol-type "Air Express", a cargo-plane with no passenger seating. Some 5 months later the proposed "Air Express" actually became a passenger-cargo "Orion" (ser. # 192) labeled the Model 9-E. This was by the way, the first ATC number awarded the Stearman-Varney group since they had bought out the bankrupted company. This first ship was purchased by Transcontinental and Western Air, Inc. (TWA) in May of 1933 and added to its fleet at Kansas City. Another fuselage frame also started as an "Air Express" was given the same revamping treatment and became another "Orion" model 9-E (ser. # 193) purchased also by TWA in mid-1933. This second example was fitted with the new Goodrich "de-icer boots" that prevented formation of ice on the wing's leading edge. The third example of this model was apparently built from scratch as a 9-E and also purchased by TWA about mid-1933. All 3 examples were painted brightly in red and white marked with TWA fleet numbers of # 256-257-258. After just barely a month's service the first example crashed into the Missouri River; the second 9-E served TWA quite regularly for some 2 years before being sold to an operator in Calif. The third example of the 9-E also served TWA for some 2 years and finally became the ill-fated "Orion-Explorer", a combination of unrelated Lockheed parts, that crashed on take-off in Alaska killing Wiley Post and the famous Will Rogers. Basically, the "Orion" 9-E was very similar to the earlier "Model 9" in dimension and otherwise except for some slight altering of the configuration, the installation of a supercharged "Wasp" SCI engine, and a convertible interior that could be quickly prepared for all-cargo loads; interior was normally arranged to seat 5 or 6 passengers on short hauls, or even a combination of 2 or 3 passengers and balance of the payload in mail and cargo. In the latter part of 1933 the 2 remaining 9-E were converted for TWA into 9-E Specials by installation of the 550 h.p. "Wasp" S1D1 engines; the extra 100 h.p. was initially used for more speed and better performance, and finally used to allow a 5800 lb. gross wt. for the single-place all-cargo version.

The "Orion" model 9-E, a wooden Lockheed, was a low-winged cabin monoplane with variable seating arrangements for passengers, and variable arrangements for hauling cargo loads. The all-passenger version seated

Fig. 29. "Orion" 9-E shivers on wintry ramp in Kansas City.

5 or 6 and a pilot, with provisions for only a small amount of baggage. The 4 place version seated 3 passengers, a pilot, baggage, and some cargo. A single-place version was outfitted to haul all-cargo loads; this late version had a "Wasp" engine of greater power and gross wt. allowance was increased by 400 lbs. As powered with the 9 cyl. "Wasp" SC1 engine of 450 h.p. the model 9-E was the fastest light transport of its day; as powered with the "Wasp" S1D1 engine of 550 h.p. this "Orion" was delivering "air express cargo" on schedules never before thought possible. Transcontinental and Western Air, Inc. (TWA) was the first large airline to buy the "Orion", after the airplane had established its reputation first as a high-speed transport on the smaller lines. The swift "Orion" 9-E put TWA in a better competitive position with its faster mail and cargo schedules on the central transcontinental routes. The 9-E flew the mail for TWA in relays, along with the "Alpha" and "Fleetster", from Newark in the east to Los Angeles in the west. Pilots who flew the mail for TWA liked the "Orion" very much because it was fast, comfortably stable, and rather easy to fly; most pilots were still leary of the retractable landing gear, but finally learned to master its needs. One of the 9-E survived into 1937 and was finally scrapped by Lockheed in 1938. The type certificate number for the "Orion" model 9-E was issued 5-22-33 and only 3 examples of this model were manufactured by the Lockheed Aircraft Corp. at Burbank, Calif. Lloyd Stearman

was pres. & chf. engr.; Carl B. Squier was V.P. & gen. mgr.; Robert Gross was treas.; Cyril Chappallet was sec.; and Richard A. Von Hake was asst. engr. Walter Varney was a large stockholder in the new company; various former Lockheed office and plant personnel were also retained in the new company. The new firm was concentrating on the manufacture of various models of the "Orion" and also planned to develop a ten place single-engined low wing all-metal transport designed by Lloyd Stearman; by May of 1933 development of the twin-engined "Electra" was announced.

Listed below are specifications and performance data for the "Orion" model 9-E as powered with 450 h.p. "Wasp" SC1 engine; length overall 27'6"; height overall 9'8"; wing span 42'9"; wing chord at root 102"; wing chord at tip 63"; total wing area 294 sq.ft.; airfoil at root Clark Y-18; airfoil at tip Clark Y-9.5; wt. empty 3664 lbs.; useful load 1736 lbs.; payload with 105 gal. fuel 850 lbs. (5 pass. at 170 lb. each); gross wt. 5400 lbs.; max. speed 228; cruising speed 205; landing speed 65; climb 1250 ft. first min. at sea level; ser. ceiling 20,000 ft.; gas cap. 116 gal.; oil cap. 10 gal.; cruising range at 25 gal. per hour was 4 hours or 800 miles; price approx. $20,000. at factory field. This certificate was amended 10-20-33 to include approval of the 9-E Special as 1 to 4 place with "Wasp" S1D1-550 engine with wts. of 3890-1510-5400 lbs. for passenger plane and 3831-1769-5600 lbs. as single-place cargo plane; amended 11-16-33 for

Fig. 30. "Orion" 9-E were later converted to "9-E Special" with 550 h.p. "Wasp" engine.

one-place cargoplane with wts. of 3860-1940-5800 lbs.; amended 11-28-33 with wts. of 3859-1541-5400 lbs. as passenger-plane and wts. of 3831-1969-5800 lbs. as one-place cargoplane. The installation of a 550 h.p. engine and the various weight allowances would cause performance figures to vary from those listed above.

The construction details and general arrangement of the "Orion" 9-E were typical to that of the "Model 9" as described in the chapter for ATC # 421 of U. S. CIVIL AIRCRAFT, Vol. 5. The first 9-E was actually started as a high-winged "Air Express", but the transition to the low-winged "Orion" type required only the appropriate fuselage cut-outs for pilot's cockpit and the low mounting of the one-piece wing. The retractable landing gear was fitted to underside of the wing and required "about 18 good pumps" of the hydraulic hand-lever for complete retraction. The early 9-E were powered with the "Wasp" SCl engine of 450 h.p. and gross wt. was held at 5400 lbs. As the 9-E Special, the "Orion" was powered with the 550 h.p. "Wasp" S1D1 engine; gross weight allowance was raised to 5800 lbs. and performance increase was noted, especially in climb-out and service ceiling. TWA outfitted the 9-E with radio gear, all the latest navigational aids, night-flying equipment, and Goodrich de-icer boots. Electric engine starter, a battery, engine-driven generator, ground-adjustable metal propeller, wheel brakes, tail wheel, retractable landing gear, and NACA engine cowl were standard equipment. Options were at discretion of customer. The next development in the "Orion" series was the model 9-F as described in the chapter for ATC # 512 of this volume.

Listed below are 9-E entries as gleaned from various records:

NC-12277; 9-E (# 192) Wasp 450-550.

-12278; 9-E (# 193) Wasp 450-550.

-12283; 9-E (# 195) Wasp 450-550.

Serial numbers 193 and 195 as 9-E Special after 10-2-33.

PITCAIRN "AUTOGIRO", PA-19.

Fig. 31. Cabin-type Pitcairn PA-19 showing off over New York City.

Heretofore, the Pitcairn "autogiro" was built only in sport models or the so-called utility model; their uses ran the gamut of specialized chores that the peculiar ability of the 'giro happened to be best suited for. As a flying machine the autogiro found a limited place in the scheme of things; even by liberals in the air industry it was slow at being fully accepted and every notable flight was still considered not much more than another "stunt". Hoping to change this attitude and to seek a better, more solid future, Harold F. Pitcairn began thinking of the autogiro as a "transport". When Pitcairn finally decided to experiment with a "cabin model" that could carry 4 or 5 people he presented the idea to his engineering staff, but the idea was said to have fallen on skeptical and unreceptive ears; they must have felt that such a dream was beyond any engineering precedent. It was to be a big task and certainly a strong challenge; shopping around for a likely engineer to implement his dream, Harold Pitcairn finally persuaded Robert Noorduyn into accepting the challenge. As executive-engineer of the Pitcairn Autogiro Co., R. B. C. Noorduyn, formerly with Fokker and Bellanca, was assisted by the regular

engineering team and the new PA-19 finally evolved as a mating of many ideas. Beacuse it was the first cabin-type "transport autogiro" the PA-19 stirred up much comment and perhaps some new interest in the capabilities of the novel rotor-plane. Emulating the comfort and the luxury offered in a fine motor-car of this period, the PA-19 represented the last word in both automobile and aeronautical practices. Mechanically and in layout this new cabin 'giro embodied a number of features entirely new to autogiro application; as a result the PA-19 had both good autogiro characteristics and the aerodynamic cleanness, the stability, and the amount of control usually found in well-designed airplanes. The cabin-type model PA-19 was actually luxurious, completely practical from the standpoint of utility, and its comparative reliability was a bonus feature. With such credentials the Pitcairn PA-19 took its place on the market of 1933; based on its ability and its outstanding utility the PA-19 should have found instant favor, but being confronted with the depths of a national depression was more than a craft of this type could bargain for. There was a token interest, of sorts, but financial difficulty at

Fig. 32. Model PA-19 with 420 h.p. Wright engine seated four.

the Pitcairn plant finally halted its production and further development. Actually, the cabin-type PA-19 was an aircraft too far ahead of its time.

The Pitcairn model PA-19 was a cabin-type autogiro with plush and comfortable seating for 4 or 5 people. A cabin-type 'giro was somewhat unusual in itself, but the big PA-19 was doubly unusual because of the unhampered comfort it

offered in tasteful surroundings. The passengers were offered every comfort and convenience, and the pilot was treated with advanced aids and features calculated to make his job much easier. Four large people and 80 lbs. of baggage was a normal load, but 5 people could be squeezed in comfortably on short flights, if no baggage was carried. Flight testing of the PA-19 prototype by veteran James G. Ray was underway in Sept.

Fig. 33. Success of PA-19 caused designers to envision "Giro" transports carrying 20 passengers or more.

Fig. 34. Pitcairn PA-22 was proposed sport model for two.

of 1932 and most of the preliminary testing was completed by November. Another example of the PA-19 was built for approval tests and in Feb. of 1933 one example was sold to the "Year-Round-Club" of Florida. The club's giro was used to ferry club-members on errands or to various points of interest around the area. As powered with the 9 cyl. Wright R-975-E2 engine of 420 h.p. the PA-19 had excellent performance for a ship of this type and handled as well as any good airplane. The type certificate number for the PA-19 was issued 6-23-33 with amendments issued on 6-29-33, 9-1-33, and 9-22-33. Some 4 or perhaps 5 examples of this model were manufactured by the Pitcairn Autogiro Co. at Willow Grove, Penna. Harold F. Pitcairn was pres.; James G. Ray was V.P., gen. mgr., and chief pilot; R. B. C. Noorduyn was executive-engineer on PA-19 project.

During late 1933 Pitcairn concentrated on development of a 3-bladed rotor and the placing of all flight control into the rotor system. This would eliminate the wing and the airplane-type control surfaces as in use up to now. The relative success of Pitcairn's cabin model (PA-19) prompted various engineers to envision "autogiro airliners" up to 50 ft. long with 80 or 90 ft. rotors and carrying 10-15 passengers or more at two miles per minute. The feasability of such a craft was entirely within reason, but development would have been costly and none of the manufacturers had the money to spare. On Jan. of 1934, due to prevailing depressed conditions, Pitcairn announced that it would suspend manufacture of all autogiros until further notice; however, facilities would be available to offer service and repair to autogiros already in use. Meanwhile, with a small crew, development would continue on new designs.

Listed below are specifications and performance data for the Pitcairn model PA-19 as powered with the 420 h.p. Wright R-975-E2 engine; fuselage length 25'9"; height overall 13'0"; rotor dia. 50'8"; rotor blade chord 22"; rotor disc area 2085 sq.ft.; fixed-wing span 38'8"; fixed-wing chord at root 60"; fixed-wing chord at tip 24"; total fixed-wing area 95.5 sq.ft.; airfoil Goettingen modified; wt. empty 2681 lbs.; useful load 1360 lbs.; payload with 90 gal. fuel 590 lbs. (3 pass. at 170 lb. each & 80 lbs. baggage); gross wt. 4041 lbs.; max. speed 120; cruising speed 100; landing speed 0-20; take-off full load (no wind) 260 ft.; climb 850 ft. first min. at sea level; ser. ceiling 12,500 ft.; gas cap. 90 gal.; oil cap. 8 gal.; cruising range at 24 gal. per hour 350 miles; price $14,950. at factory field. Approved wts. as of 6-23-33 were 2681-1360-4041 lbs.; wts. amended later to 4097 lbs. for ser. # H-84 and to 4129 lbs. for all others.

The fuselage framework was built up of welded chrome-moly steel tubing, lightly faired to shape then fabric covered. The cabin walls, ceiling, and floor were insulated and sound-proofed with thick blankets of Dry-Zero; the cabin was upholstered in rich fabrics. A soft bench-type seat of 41.5 inch width was provided in back for 2 or 3 passengers; a baggage compartment with capacity for 80 lbs. was under and behind this seat. Two individual seats were placed in front; the pilot's seat was adjustable for leg-room. All windows were of shatter-proof glass; the rear windows were fixed, but the front windows were raised or lowered with a small crank. Ventilators would circulate fresh air through the cabin, making it unnecessary to lower windows while in flight; cabin heat was also provided for cold weather flying. A large entrance door was on the left side with easy entry from the wing-walk; a steel tube step-ladder, normally concealed in the wing, could be pulled out for access to the walk-way or the ground. The large instrument panel was very complete, including a novel oil-level measuring rod which allowed checking oil even in flight. Dual control was provided by a central column with swing-over control wheel. The tapered fixed-wing was of cantilever design, in 3 sections; the center-section of 10 ft. span was a rigid truss structure of welded chrome-moly steel tubing. The 2 outer panels, tapered in plan-form and section, were of wooden monospar construction; for torsional rigidity the entire wing framework was covered with spruce plywood sheet and then covered with fabric for weather protection. The thick cantilever wing of extreme dihedral used large balanced ailerons of the offset hinge type to provide adequate control down to the lowest speeds. Two fuel tanks of 45 gal. capacity each were mounted under cabin floor; front tank contained a 6 gal. emergency supply. An engine-driven pump provided fuel pressure, with a hand operated wobble-pump provided for emergency use. The landing gear of 12 ft. tread was 2 cantilever tripods fastened to outboard ends of the center-section frame; the splined Bendix oleo shock absorbing struts provided 9 in. travel to soak up an occasional hard landing. The semi-airwheels were 9.50x12; a large locking-type tail wheel was provided and removable cowling at this point allowed inspection and maintenance. The fabric covered tail-group was of cantilever construction; the horizontal stabilizer was built up of wood, and the fins, rudders, and elevators were of welded steel tubing. No cables or control horns were exposed to the windstream. The cantilever rotor pylon was a welded steel tube structure encased in a metal streamlined fairing; angle of incidence of the rotor head was adjustable in flight to maintain the proper "tilt" for maximum performance in level flight, in the climb, or vertical descent. A rotor-starter was used to bring rotor blades to proper r.p.m. for take-off, and a rotor-brake was provided to stop rotor blades after landing. An electric engine starter was engaged by a foot-button, and a parking brake was provided for engine run-up. The 9 cyl. Wright R-975-E2 engine was mounted at negative thrust in rubber blocks to dampen vibration; a modified engine mount would also allow use of the 420 h.p. "Wasp Jr." T3A engine. A metal ground-adjustable propeller was normally used, but a Hamilton-Standard controllable pitch propeller was later optional; the controllable prop allowed maximum climb and still added 7 m.p.h. to the cruising speed. An oil-cooling radiator, cabin heater, panel lighting, a battery, navigation lights, an electric engine starter, engine-driven generator, fuel pump, roll-down windows, fire extinguisher, assist cords, ash trays, map pockets, first-aid kit, engine tools, an engine cover, and dual controls were standard equipment. Landing lights, parachute flares (3), an extra cabin door, extra walk-way, trim-tab on elevators, larger oil cooler, Y-type control column, and controllable propeller were optional.

Listed below are known entries of the Pitcairn PA-19:

NC-13149; PA-19 (# H-84) Wright   420
X-13182; PA-19 (# H-85) Wright 420.
NC-2503; PA-19 (# H-87) Wright 420.
NC-2740; PA-19 (# H-88) Wright 420.

It was occasionally reported that one PA-19 was exported to England, this could have been ser. # H-86; this approval expired 9-30-39.

STINSON "RELIANT", SR & SR-2.

Fig. 35. Stinson SR with 215 h.p. Lycoming engine.

The new Stinson "Reliant" (model SR) was actually a combination of better parts from the previous Model S and Model R with new innovations inserted here and there to make the old and new concepts jell together. Powered with a refined and more reliable Lycoming engine of 215 h.p. the new "Reliant" stressed even more comfort in a harmonious interior, and posed with a rather pleasing exterior that was welcomed to grace anybody's flight line. Much of the operating paraphenalia was also improved, pilot aids were more numerous, and features designed to assure the passenger's comfort and well-being were more practical and efficient. Even though it presented an appearance no one need be ashamed of, the new "Reliant", like all the Stinsons before it, would not shirk from working for its keep and most of them did just that. Announced publicly in May of 1933 for a price of $3995. the new SR was presented as a man-sized airplane for 4 big people and was clearly the biggest bargain that anyone had to offer this season. For the season of 1933, Stinson once again was offering the type of airplane most people were wanting to buy at a price that a majority could still afford to pay. News of this spread fast and by Sept. of 1933 the Model SR was already outselling all the other 2-4-6 place cabin airplanes combined. With some new developments by this time in the Lycoming engine series also, a few variations of the standard SR were introduced as the SR-1, SR-2, and SR-3. The model SR-2,

which mounted a 240 h.p. Lycoming engine and had minor variations to its configuration and specifications, shared this type certificate (# 510) also with the model SR. The model SR-2 would be hard to distinguish from the standard SR because the features that set it apart were not readily noticeable. The differences actually were hardly enough to warrant a new model designation, but aircraft manufacturers did want it to appear they were going all-out to offer selection that would best please the customer.

The Stinson "Reliant" model SR was a high-winged cabin monoplane with seating arranged for four. A relatively large airplane of buxom proportion the SR had a man-sized cabin that offered room and comfort to spare in surroundings comparable to those in aircraft of twice the price. At a rock-bottom price of $3995. one would expect a more or less stripped-down airplane, but the new SR amazed everyone with all that it had to offer. As powered with the Lycoming R-680 engine of 215 h.p. the SR retained all of the famous characteristics attributed to the earlier "Junior" monoplanes plus a slight improvement in utility and overall performance. Rugged, obedient, and predictable, the SR was also rather easy to fly, fairly easy to maintain, and quickly proved quite popular among sportsmen and men of business. The flying-service operator, as always, was also a significant customer. Later in the year the model SR was approved as a seaplane on Edo P-3300 twin-

Fig. 36. Stinson SR seaplane in Canadian service.

float gear. One airplane of this series with added equipment, a more powerful (240 h.p.) version of the Lycoming engine, and at higher allowable gross weight was approved as the model SR-2. The type certificate number for the model SR was issued 6-29-33 with amendments issued on 7-12-33 and 8-5-33; certificate was amended 9-29-33 to include 4-place seaplane on Edo P-3300 floats. Certificate amended 12-18-33 for model SR-2 as seaplane on Edo P-3300 floats with wts. of 2384 lbs. empty, 1085 lb. useful load, and 3469 lb. gross weight. Certificate amended 5-3-34 to include installation of Lycoming R-680-7 engine of 240 h.p. for SR landplane equipped with "Smith" controllable propeller. Some 88 examples of the model SR were manufactured

by the Stinson Aircraft Corp. at Wayne, Mich.; a div. of the Cord Corp.

Listed below are specifications and performance data for the Stinson model SR as powered with 215 h.p. Lycoming R-680 engine; length overall 27'0"; height overall 8'5"; wing span 43'3"; wing chord 75"; total wing area 235 sq.ft.; airfoil Clark Y; wt. empty 2070 lbs.; useful load 1085 lbs.; payload with 50 gal. fuel 575 lbs.; baggage allowance 75 lbs.; gross wt. 3155 lbs.; max. speed (with wheel pants) 130; cruising speed 115; landing speed 55; climb 750 ft. first min. at sea level; ser. ceiling 14,000 ft.; gas cap. 50 gal.; oil cap. 4 gal.; cruising range at 12.5 gal. per hour 460 miles; price $3995. at factory field.

Fig. 37. Many SR owners were part of nationwide "Stinson Air Cab Service".

Fig. 38. Model SR-2, as shown, was slightly modified version.

Model SR as seaplane on Edo model P-3300 twin-float gear. wt. empty 2281 (2384) lbs.; useful load 1085 lbs.; payload with 50 gal. fuel 575 lbs.; gross wt. 3366 (3469) lbs.; wts. in parentheses for SR-2 as seaplane; max. speed 115; cruising speed 100; landing speed 60; climb 600 ft. first min. at sea level; ser. ceiling 12,000 ft.; cruising range at 12.5 gal. per hour 400 miles; performance figures for SR-2 would be slightly higher.

Model SR-2 landplane; wt. empty 2173 lbs.; useful load 1060 lbs.; payload with 50 gal. fuel 550 lbs.; gross wt. 3233 lbs.; max. speed (with wheel pants) 135; cruising speed 120; landing speed 57; climb 850 ft. first min. at sea level; ser. ceiling 14,500 ft.; gas cap. 50 gal.; oil cap. 4 gal.; cruising range at 13 gal. per hour 440 miles; price not announced.

Following data lists allowable variations of model SR and SR-2. Model SR with Lycoming R-680 engine rated 215 h.p.; std. empty wt. of 2070 lbs. includes, engine cowl (22), wheel fenders (13), direct-drive electric engine starter (26), battery (36), cabin heater, metal ground-adjustable propeller, 8.50x10 wheels and tires; 8 in. streamlined tail wheel, 75 lbs. baggage, locking-type baggage door, chromed exhaust collector ring.

Model SR: approved optional equipment (gross wt. increased to 3160 lbs.); 74 gal. fuel cap. (2 tanks in wings at 37 gal. each); 5 gal. oil; (a 21 lb. increase in empty wt. for extra gas-oil tankage); standard engine cowl (22), optional engine cowl (30), wing root and stabilizer fairings (6), radio bonding & shielding (9), radio (25-34), generator (18), fog light (3), 5 parachute flares (16), 25x11-4 Goodyear airwheels with hydraulic brakes (11 lb. increase over 8.50x10 wheels & tires with mech. brakes), leather cabin trim (9), retractable landing lights (26), wheel pants (22), and a Lycoming-Smith controllable propeller (49 lb. increase over standard propeller).

Amendment as of 5-3-34: Model SR also approved to mount R-680-7 engine rated 240 h.p. with Lycoming-Smith controllable prop; max. of 240 h.p. allowed only on take-off and initial climb-out (otherwise engine will be held to max. of 215 h.p.) a placard to this effect to be placed in full view of pilot.

Model SR seaplane on Edo P-3300 floats (9-29-33); empty wt. of 2384 lbs. includes engine cowl (22), battery (36), engine starter (26), cabin heater, anchor & mooring ropes (30), baggage reduced to 45 lbs., fuel cap. 50 gal. (2 tanks in wings at 25 gal. each), oil 4 gal., a metal grd.-adj. propeller on R-680 engine of 215 h.p. or a Lycoming-Smith controllable propeller on R-680-7 engine of 240 h.p.; max. of 240 h.p. allowed only on take-off & initial climb-out; std. gross wt. of 3469 lbs.; gross wt. may be increased to 3500 lbs. with Lycoming-Smith propeller.

Model SR-2 (also approved on ATC # 510): serial # 8910 (NS-13832 registered to State of Penn.) eligible as SR-2 with following specifications; empty wt. 2222 lbs. includes, engine cowl (30), wheel pants (22), wing root & stabilizer fairing (6), battery (36), 5 parachute flares (16), special instruments (10), 8.50x10 wheels & tires, 8 in. streamlined tail wheel, electric engine starter (26), cabin heater, bonding for radio (3), leather cabin trim (9), (figures in parentheses are wts. per item), 50 gal. fuel cap. (2 tanks in wings at 25 gal. each), oil 4 gal., engine on SR-2 was R-680-7 of 240 h.p.; max. of 240 h.p. at 2300 r.p.m. allowed only on take-off & initial climb-out using "Smith" controllable propeller; gross wt. 3233 lbs., baggage 50 lbs.; Model SR-2 basically identical to SR except horizontal tail surfaces and their control system, extra equipment, and increase in allowable gross wt. The next Stinson development was the models SR-1 and SR-3 as described in chapter for ATC # 513 of this volume.

Registration listing for Stinson model SR and SR-2:

NC-12191; SR (# 8700) Lycoming 215
  12198; " (# 8701) "
 -12199; " (# 8702) "
 -13450; " (# 8703) "
 -13451; " (# 8704) "
 -13452; " (# 8705) "

-13453;	"	(# 8706)	"
-13454;	"	(# 8707)	"
-13455;	"	(# 8708)	"
-13456;	"	(# 8709)	"
-13457;	"	(# 8710)	"
-13458;	"	(# 8711)	"
-13459;	"	(# 8712)	"
	"	(# 8713)	"
-13461;	"	(# 8714)	"
-13462;	"	(# 8715)	"
-13463;	"	(# 8716)	"
-13464;	"	(# 8717)	"
-13460;	"	(# 8718)	"
-13465;	"	(# 8719)	"
-13466;	"	(# 8720)	"
-13467;	"	(# 8721)	"
-13468;	"	(# 8722)	"
-13469;	"	(# 8723)	"
-13471;	"	(# 8724)	"
-13472;	"	(# 8725)	"
-13470;	"	(# 8726)	"
-13475;	"	(# 8727)	"
-13474;	"	(# 8728)	"
NS-81Y;	"	(# 8729)	"
-13473;	"	(# 8730)	"
-13476;	"	(# 8731)	"
-13477;	"	(# 8732)	"
-13478;	"	(# 8733)	"
-13482;	"	(# 8734)	"
-13479;	"	(# 8735)	"
-13480;	"	(# 8736)	"
	"	(# 8737)	"
-13483;	"	(# 8738)	"
-13487;	"	(# 8739)	"
-13486;	"	(# 8740)	"
-13481;	"	(# 8741)	"
-13493;	"	(# 8742)	"
-13489;	"	(# 8743)	"
-13488;	"	(# 8744)	"
NC-13490;	SR	(# 8745)	Lycoming 215
-13492;	"	(# 8746)	"
-13491;	"	(# 8747)	"
-13494;	"	(# 8748)	"
-13496;	"	(# 8749)	"
-13495;	"	(# 8750)	"
-13497;	"	(# 8751)	"
-13498;	"	(# 8752)	"
-13800;	"	(# 8753)	"
NC-2612;	"	(# 8754)	"
-13801;	"	(# 8755)	"

-13802;	"	(# 8756)	"
-13803;	"	(# 8757)	"
-13806;	"	(# 8758)	"
-13807;	"	(# 8759)	"
-13809;	"	(# 8760)	"
-13805;	"	(# 8761)	"
-13808;	"	(# 8762)	"
-13804;	"	(# 8763)	"
	"	(# 8764)	"
-13813;	"	(# 8765)	"
-13812;	"	(# 8766)	"
-13815;	"	(# 8767)	"
-13816;	"	(# 8768)	"
-13818;	"	(# 8769)	"
-13819;	"	(# 8770)	"
-13820;	"	(# 8771)	"
PP-IAC;	"	(# 8772)	"
-13821;	"	(# 8773)	"
-13822;	"	(# 8774)	"
	"	(# 8775)	"
NS-6;	"	(# 8776)	"
-13814;	"	(# 8777)	"
-13823;	"	(# 8778)	"
	"	(# 8779)	"
	"	(# 8780)	"
-13825;	"	(# 8781)	"
	"	(# 8782)	"
	"	(# 8783)	"
NC-13826;	SR	(# 8784)	Lycoming 215
-13827;	"	(# 8785)	"
-13829;	"	(# 8786)	"
-13831;	"	(# 8787)	"
NS-13832;SR-2		(# 8910)	R-680-7

This approval for model SR of ser. # 8700 and up, also for model SR-2 of ser. # 8910 and up; ser. # 8700 in Canada as CF-AUS; ser. # 8701 to Alaskan Airways in 1934; ser. # 8708 del. to bandleader Wayne King; ser. # 8713 may not have been used; ser. # 8729 del. to Michigan Department of Aeronautics, registration later changed to NC-13542; ser. # 8739 del. to Stokely Bros. Foods; ser. # 8741 del. to Wien Airways in Alaska, operated on skis in winter; ser. # 8756 also as SR Special; ser. # 8761 and # 8773 del. to Alaska; ser. # 8772 in Brazil as of 3-38; ser. # 8777 del. to Goodyear Tire and Rubber Co.; ser. # 8787 (as SR Special on Group 2 approval # 2-471) del. to Gulf Oil Co. of Penn.; ser. # 8910 (SR-2) del. to State of Penn.; one SR operated in England as G-ACSV.

ATC # 511
(6-30-33)
WACO "SPORTSMAN", ULA.

Fig. 39. Model ULA with 210 h.p. Continental engine was last of the "Waco A" series.

As the last and perhaps the finest of the two-seated Waco "Model A" series, the ULA for 1933-34 was a brave but somehow futile attempt to prolong the life of this interesting design. Waco Aircraft, it was said, was even prepared to lose money on each sale just to help this series endure through the lean depression years, but it became a losing battle. For years now sportsman-pilots had been attracted to the open-cockpit "Waco" biplanes because their wants and needs were well understood and catered to at the factory; the "Model A" sportster was a good example of what the average sportsman wanted and it was offered to him for several years in a prolific array of combinations. Literally loaded with small improvements and many attractive extras the ULA for 1933 was 12 ways better and it posed as one of the better buys in an economical high-performance sport biplane during this period. Most sportsman-pilots of this day had demanded performance above all else, but by now they didn't mind putting up with convenience, utility, and more comfort. As powered with the 7 cyl. Continental R-670 engine of 210 h.p. the ULA was no doubt the ultimate in this

series of sportplanes by Waco, but its introduction in the very bottom of the "depression years" was perhaps a penalty much too difficult to overcome. The urge to buy the model ULA "Sportsman" certainly was not lacking, there actually was plenty of interest, but the money needed to buy and to support this particular type of airplane was something not many had to spare at this time. As a consequence, the ULA was built in only one example. Carefully boxed and loaded on a ship, the ULA was delivered new on 28 June 1933 to Jacques Dupuy of Paris, France. After operating abroad for nearly a year the ULA was returned to Waco Sales of New York on 5 June 1934; it changed hands several times in the next few years and was finally destroyed in a hangar fire late in 1937.

The Waco model ULA was a convertible strictly-for-sport biplane with side-by-side seating for 2 large people, or 2 smaller people bundled in extra heavy clothing. The ULA was a "convertible" to the extent that it could be flown as an open cockpit model or closed in with a coupe-type canopy for comparative comfort in the chill of winter. Being affixed on rails in a more or less permanent installation, the sliding canopy, offered as an option, really became a part of the airplane and would normally be included upon delivery. Blessed with ample weight allowance the ULA had more than enough capacity for heaps of baggage and all sorts of sporting gear; extra fuel capacity allowed better than an hour's increase in cruising range. Thus a pilot bent on a sporting week-end could load up "gear" to his heart's content and head for a playground some 500 miles in the distance without bothering to stop for fuel. Like the previous UBA, the model ULA had practically go-anywhere utility that was nearly without reasonable limit; even the tiniest field was a likely place for the ULA pilot to land in and then take off from again. As powered with the Continental R-670 (Series 2) engine of 210 h.p. the ULA promised performance enough to warm the heart of any true "sport". Inheriting all the features and basic characteristics of the "Waco A" series, the ULA no doubt, was easy to fly well and precise manuverability was one of its better features. Of particularly rugged frame and robust character the ULA was also of handsome proportion and cut quite a figure on the flight line. The type certificate number for the model ULA was issued 6-30-33 and only one example was manufactured by the Waco Aircraft Co. at Troy, Ohio.

Listed below are specifications and performance data for the Waco model ULA as powered with the 210 h.p. Continental R-670 (Series 2) engine; length overall 22'9"; height overall 8'9"; wing span upper 29'6"; wing span lower 27'5"; wing chord upper & lower 57"; wing area upper 130 sq.ft.; wing area lower 111 sq.ft.; total wing area 241 sq.ft.; airfoil Clark Y; wt. empty 1484 lbs.; useful load 796 (816) lbs.; payload with 40 gal. fuel 363 (383) lbs.; payload with 60 gal. fuel 236 (256) lbs.; gross wt. 2280 (2300) lbs.; figures in parentheses are amended wt. allowance; max. speed 134; cruising speed 118; landing speed 43; climb 1500 ft. first min. at sea level; ser. ceiling 15,800 ft.; gas cap. normal 40 gal.; gas cap. max. 60 gal.; oil cap. 3-4 gal.; max. cruising range at 12.5 gal. per hour 535 miles; price $4895. at factory field.

The construction details and general arrangement of the model ULA were basically typical to that of previous models in the A-series except for some improvement and slight changes. The fuselage length was increased by nearly 2 feet and extra width at the cockpit provided more shoulder room. The coupe-type canopy, sliding forward and back on tracks, was more or less a permanent installation that was considerably more serviceable than the flimsier canopies offered on earlier models. The coupe-top was installed for $195.00 extra. The large cockpit doors, used on previous models, were eliminated in the ULA, but hand-holds in the center-section of upper wing and a step-peg on the fuselage still permitted easy step-over entry into the cockpit off the wing-walk. A large baggage compartment, with allowance for 150 lbs., was down low and forward of the cockpit; a smaller compartment of considerable length, with an allowance for 36 lbs., was up high in the turtle-back section behind the seat-back. The bright exterior finish by Berry Bros. was Vermillion fuselage, fin and rudder, trimmed with a "fish-hook" stripe of Black edged in Gold; in pleasant contrast, the wings and horizontal tail surfaces were done in Silver. Two 20 gal. tanks, mounted in center-section of upper wing, were normal fuel capacity; an extra 20 gal. tank mounted high in the fuselage ahead of cockpit provided nearly 5 hours of cruising range. The Continental R-670 (Series 2) engine with 5.4:1 compression ratio using low octane fuel was rated 210 h.p. at 2000 r.p.m. at sea level. The landing gear of 71 in. tread was equipped with Waco patented shock absorbing struts, Warner wheels and wheel brakes; 7.50x10 low-pressure tires were fitted on 6.50x10 wheels. A parking brake, 10x3 tail wheel, speed-ring engine cowl, Hartzell wooden propeller, Heywood engine starter, dual stick-type controls, centrally located throttle control, compass, engine cover, tool kit, tie-down ropes, first-aid kit, log books, and navigation lights were standard equipment. Wing-root fairing, coupe-top canopy, cabin heater, landing lights, battery, parachute flares, metal propeller, extra 20 gal. fuel tank, and wheel pants were optional at extra cost. The next Waco development was the model UKC cabin biplane as described in chapter for ATC # 528 of this volume.

Listed below is the only example of the model ULA:

NC-14300; ULA (# 3761) Cont. 210.

As a recap of the Waco A series we'd like to mention that it was finally built into 9 different models for a total of 21 airplanes. One airplane (X-12435) was used as the prototype for development of 7 different models—this is an example of practical ingenuity.

ATC # 512
(7-19-33)
LOCKHEED "ORION", 9-F.

Fig. 40. Lockheed "Orion" 9-F with 660 h.p. "Cyclone" engine was capable of over 240 m.p.h.

The cigar-shaped Lockheed "Orion" model 9-F was a rather distinctive airplane; being the only one of its kind, it was also the fastest (242 m.p.h.) standard "Orion" that Lockheed had ever built, and for a time it was the fastest privately-owned cabin monoplane in the country. The owner of this particular airplane was equally distinctive, a dapper gentleman named Dr. John R. Brinkley. This Dr. Brinkley was a flamboyant person, to some extent a controversial person, and bent to get all the publicity he could gather for his purpose. No doubt a combination of airplane and powerplant conceived by imaginative Carl Squier, the swift model 9-F with its big Wright "Cyclone" engine was just about as flamboyant an airplane and aptly tailored to the Doctor's liking. The gleaming all-white 9-F, handsomely trimmed in black, was actually registered to Geo. A. MacDonald, pilot for Dr. Brinkley; this it was said, a prudent move fostered to shelter the "Orion" from any lawsuits. As was expected of the good doctor, the "Orion" 9-F was named the "Dr. Brinkley III" and was used to shuttle him speedily from his medical empires in Milford, Kansas to Del Rio, Texas, and often anywhere else in the country the doctor decided to go on urge or business. After some 3 years of intensive flying for Dr. Brinkley, the faithful "Orion" was traded in to Lockheed for one of the new twin-engined

"Electra". The "Orion" 9-F was eventually exported to Spain, via Holland and France in 1937, and subsequently became a casualty of the Spanish Civil War.

The Lockheed "Orion" model 9-F was a low-winged cabin monoplane with seating arranged for 5 to 7 places; listed as "5 to 7 place" the 9-F however was normally operated as a 5 place airplane. Typical of the "Orion" models of 1933, the model 9-F featured a retractable landing gear that folded flush within the bottom-side of the cantilever wing and drag-producing "wing flaps" were introduced to slow down the high landing speed. As powered with the 9 cyl. Wright R-1820-F21 engine rated 645 h.p. at sea level, the hefty "Cyclone" produced a slight nose-heavy condition; lead ballast was carried in the tail to restore a proper balance. With 645 h.p. at its command the 9-F was a terrific performer and could show its tail to just about anything that came along. Compared to other "Orion" models, empty weight of the 9-F was rather high, but this was because of the large engine, extra trappings and custom interior finery; a penalty of no significance when useful load was adjusted accordingly. Although little-known for what it was, the 9-F was a very special "Orion" that was a credit to its developers, and a crowd-gathering sight wherever it landed. The type certificate number for the model 9-F was

Fig. 41. "Orion" 9-F provided speedy travel for Dr. J. R. Brinkley.

issued 7-19-33 and only one example of this model was manufactured by the Lockheed Aircraft Co. at Burbank, Calif.

Listed below are specifications and performance data for the "Orion" model 9-F as powered with the Wright "Cyclone" R-1820-F21 engine rated 645 h.p. at sea level; length overall 27'11"; height overall 9'8"; wing span 42'9"; wing chord at root 102"; wing chord at tip 63"; total wing area 294 sq.ft.; airfoil at root Clark Y-18; airfoil at tip Clark Y-9.5; wt. empty 3708 lbs.; useful load 1692 lbs.; payload with 110 gal. fuel (4 passengers at 170 lbs. each & 104 lbs. baggage) 784 lbs.; gross wt. 5400 lbs.; max. speed 242; cruising speed (.75 power) 220; landing speed (with flaps) 63; climb 1600 ft. first min. at sea level; ser. ceiling 25,000 ft.; gas cap. 116 gal.; oil cap. 10 gal.; cruising range at 42 gal. per hour 450 miles; price was not announced. Approved wts. listed as 3708-1693-5401 lbs.

The construction details and general arrangement of the model 9-F, also a wooden Lockheed, were typical to that of other "Orion" models except for the following. The throbbing heart of the swift 9-F was the big 9 cyl. Wright "Cyclone" engine which coursed some 645 h.p. through its monocoque frame for a rather phenomonal performance. Of course, the extra weight of the big engine up front required ballast clamped in the extreme tail section to restore proper balance; otherwise it was a rather normal installation. The plush interior was normally arranged to seat only four, this to allow plenty of stretch-room in comfort; normally, baggage allowance was 104 lbs. The fuel supply was contained in wing tanks on either side and a gravity-feed header tank up high behind the pilot; a fuel pump transfered fuel from main wing tanks to the header tank, which then fed the engine by gravity flow. A wobble-pump was provided for emergency use. The all-wood tail group was of typical "Orion" construction and configuration except for a 12 in. greater span of the horizontal stabilizer for a higher aspect ratio. A ground-adjustable metal propeller, electric engine starter, a battery, engine-driven generator, fuel pumps, wheel brakes, and tail wheel were standard equipment. The next "Orion" development was the popular model 9-D as described in the chapter for ATC # 514 of this volume.

Listed below is the only example built of the model 9F:

NC-12284; Model 9-F (# 196) Cyclone 645.

Model 9-F mfgd. 7-33; registered in Texas.

Fig. 42. "Reliant" SR-1 was only slightly modified over standard Model SR.

Stinson Aircraft had tried to eliminate the "Junior" label for their four-place cabin monoplanes as far back as 1931, but popular usage among fliers and owners was certainly hard to change. Some 2 years later the 1933 version of the popular 4-place series were officially labeled the model SR "Reliant", but even then the name "Junior" kept creeping in to conversation or printed reference. Introduced earlier in the year of 1933 as the model "SR", several variations were soon prepared as the models SR-1, SR-2, SR-3, and SR-4. The model SR-1 as approved on this certificate (# 513) was basically similar to the standard model SR, but was powered with the Lycoming R-680-2 engine of 240 h.p.; the R-680-2 was originally the R-680-BA transport-type engine of 1932 as used in the earlier models, R-2, R-3, and also the Model U tri-motor. The model SR-3 in turn as a slight variation from the SR-1 described here, also shared this same type certificate at a later date. The models SR-1 and SR-3 were indeed very rare "Reliant" types and were built up especially to customer order. As far as can be determined from record this certificate is concerned possibly with only 3 airplanes. During this period "Stinson Air Cab Service" was offered nation-wide

by "Junior" and "Reliant" owners who belonged to the Stinson Air Cab Operators Assoc.; besides offering charter air-taxi, they also operated flying schools, urging prospects to "learn to fly in the airplane you will eventually buy". Business-men using the convenience of Stinson air-taxi service were often urged to "take the wheel" and were taught some of the basic rudiments of flying during the course of a charter trip; this was to induce them to buy an airplane for their own use—preferably a Stinson, of course. The new "Reliant" was proudly displayed at the "Century of Progress" in Chicago, and the lines of interested viewers were long and continuous.

Technical description states that the model SR-1 version of the 1933 "Reliant" was basically similar to the standard model SR except for the following differences; a 107 lb. increase in empty weight included the installation of several operational aids as standard equipment, equipment that was available on the SR also, but only as optional equipment. Optional equipment for the SR-1 included such other extras as radio, a full complement of night-flying equipment, and extra fuel capacity for a greater cruising range; these optional extras were of course all added to

Fig. 43. "Reliant" delivered to Mexican Army; ship believed to be an SR-3 which also varied from standard Model SR.

the basic empty weight. With gross wt. held to a very unrealistic 3161 lbs. for the SR-1 it was sometimes necessary to leave a passenger behind when carrying extra fuel for extended range. The model SR-3 in turn was a variation of the SR-1 and was described also as being basically identical except for the horizontal tail surfaces and their control system, plus some added equipment, and an increase of the allowable gross wt. to 3323 lbs. Powerplant for both the models SR-1 and SR-3 was the Lycoming R-680-2 (formerly the R-680-BA) of 240 h.p. The non-professional market at this time was about the only field left for any significant expansion in selling, so it was the non-professional pilot-owner that was now having his say. Aircraft manufacturers were now listening closely to what performance he considered satisfactory, how much comfort he really required, what he could afford to pay for an airplane, and what operating-maintenance costs would come within his budget. Once again "Stinson" made careful analysis of the market and designed the "Reliant" series accordingly; slight modifications to the basic SR in power, fuel capacity, and equipment, were slanted to please just about anybody. The type certificate number for the model SR-1 was issued 8-5-33 with amendment added on 9-8-33; certificate was amended 12-18-33 to include the model SR-3. Per available record, one SR-1, one SR-1 Special, and two SR-3 were built by the Stinson Aircraft Corp. at Wayne, Mich.

Listed below are specifications and performance data for the models SR-1 and SR-3 as powered with 240 h.p. Lycoming R-680-2 engine; length overall 27'0"; height overall 8'5";

wing span 43'3"; wing chord 75"; total wing area 235 sq.ft.; airfoil Clark Y; wt. empty 2177 (2330) lbs.; useful load 984 (993) lbs.; payload with 50 gal. fuel 484 (493) lbs.; baggage allowance 50 lbs.; gross wt. 3161 (3323) lbs.; max. speed (with wheel pants) 135; cruising speed 118; landing speed 55 (57); climb 800 (750) ft. first min. at sea level; figures in parentheses for SR-3; ceiling 15,000 ft.; gas cap. 50 gal.; oil cap. 4 gal.; cruising range at 13.5 gal. per hour 440 miles; price variable with amount of equipment added.

Model SR-1 with Lycoming R-680-2 engine rated 240 h.p. for ser. # 8901 and up; empty wt. of 2177 lbs. includes engine cowl (34), wheel pants (22), a battery (37), direct-drive electric engine starter (26), cabin heater, 8.50x10 wheels and tires, 8 in. streamlined tail wheel, metal ground adjustable propeller, assist cords, nickel-plated cabin hardware (5), arm rests, cabin lights, wing root and stabilizer fairing (9), a standard gross wt. of 3161 lbs. Approved optional equipment (all equipment added to empty wt.): Lear radio (25), bonding & shielding (12), Lycoming-Smith controllable propeller (49 lb. increase over standard prop), retractable landing lights (26), leather cabin trim (9), thermocouple system for cyl. head temp. (6), engine-driven generator (18), 5 parachute flares (16), fog light (3), Sperry gyro and artificial horizon (9 lbs. each), fuel cap. to 72 gal. (2 tanks in wings at 36 gal. each), oil cap. 5 gal., gross wt. held to 3161 lbs.—baggage and passenger load to be adjusted accordingly. Note: EM, 9-17-35 for ser. # 8901 (NC-13499): empty wt. of 2270 lbs. included all the above, plus radio (34), special instruments, a pressure-type fire extinguisher, fuel cap. to 72 gal., oil cap. to 5 gal., gross wt. increased to 3180 lbs.

Model SR-3: ser. # 8921 and # 8922 eligible with Lycoming R-680-2 rated 240 h.p. Note: SR-3 is identical to SR-1 except horizontal tail surfaces and their control system, extra equipment, allowable gross wt. increased to 3323 lbs.; fuel cap., oil cap., passenger cap., and baggage allowance same as for SR-1. Model SR-3 (ser. # 8921) with empty wt. of 2330 lbs. includes, engine cowl (30), retractable landing lights (26), 5 para-flares (16), cabin heater, leather cabin trim (9), metal ground-adjustable propeller, wheel pants (22), 8.50x10 wheels & tires, tail wheel, battery (36), direct-drive electric engine starter (26), bonding & shielding (10), radio (25 or 34), assist ropes, nickel-plated cabin hardware (5), figures in parentheses are wt. per unit.

The following construction details and general arrangement were basically applicable to models SR, SR-1, SR-2, SR-3, and SR-4; any variation from this is noted in descriptive analysis of each particular model, as in ATC # 510-513, etc. The semi-cantilever wing framework was built up of solid spruce spar beams with stainless steel wing ribs that were spot-welded into Warren truss form; the leading edges were covered with dural metal sheet and the completed framework was covered in fabric. Two steel-tube lift struts on each side were braced about midway to the wing spars by auxiliary struts, this to stiffen the wing-bracing truss. A 25 gal. fuel tank was mounted in root end of each wing half; two 36 gal. tanks were optional. The unusual landing gear of 120 in. tread consisted simply of 2 one-piece cantilever legs that were connected to Aerol shock absorbing struts; stubs extending from the fuselage provided landing gear attachment as well as attachment for the wing braces. The stubs were heavily faired and filleted into a clean assembly that greatly reduced parasitic resistance. Low-pressure tires were mounted on 8.50x10 wheels with self-energizing mechanical brakes and topped off with wheel fenders to protect propeller from flying debris; streamlined metal wheel pants were optional. A 10.5 in. full-swivel tail wheel provided better ground handling on rough sod or in tall grass. The fabric covered tail group was built up of welded steel tubing; the rudder had aerodynamic balance-horn and horizontal stabilizer was adjustable in flight. Ball-bearings were used liberally throughout the control system to reduce friction and wear, also promoting light control pressures on the ground or in flight. Inspection plates and zippered openings were numerous to provide easy inspection of framework and vital parts. Additional details of "Reliant" construction are noted in chapter for ATC # 519. The next "Reliant" development was the Wright-powered model SR-4 as described in the chapter for ATC # 519 of this volume.

Listed below are SR-1 and SR-3 entries as gleaned from various records:

```
NC-13485; SR-1 (# 8900) Lycoming 240
  -13499;  "   (# 8901)
         : SR-3 (# 8921) Lycoming 240
         :  "   (# 8922)    "
```

Ser. #8900 first registered to Lucius B. Manning as SR-1, later as SR-1 Special with Lycoming 225 on Group 2 approval numbered 2-496; registration numbers for serial # 8921 and # 8922 unknown.

Fig. 44. Lockheed "Orion" 9-D with 550 h.p. "Wasp" engine was used nightly on all-cargo runs.

Introduced in 1931 as the "world's fastest airliner" the Lockheed "Orion" was still the swiftest of them all and was apt to remain so for a while at least. The standard Model 9 of 1931 soon blossomed out into several different versions and one of the most popular of the series was a combination called the model 9-D. The long-nosed 9-D was equipped with a more powerful "Wasp" engine (550 h.p.) and was outfitted quite properly for its role as an airliner. American Airways was the first line to take advantage of using the 9-D on its routes and Northwest Airways soon followed suit. Eventually, after a season or two of top-notch service, the relentless progress of aviation was catching up to the fleet "Orion" and its lustre began fading. By 1935 larger airliners were available that were nearly as fast, so the "Orion" lost its big advantage and found itself being shunted to lesser roles. Some of the 9-D were used on shorter legs of a route where small-capacity airplanes were still feasible, but all of the ones working for American Airways were equipped with night-flying equipment and used nightly on all-cargo runs. In this way the "Orion" still hung onto some of the glamor it had originally created by offering air-express service on a schedule that other airplanes could not meet. Just by comparison, the new "Condor" transports of American Airways were flying the Fort Worth to Cleveland route in 11 hours, and the night-flying "Orion", carrying mail and express shipments only, flew the same route in just 7.5 hours cutting 3.5 hours off the time.

The "Orion" model 9-D, a wooden Lockheed, was a low-winged cabin monoplane with variable arrangements for passengers and cargo. The all-passenger version carried 4 to 6 passengers and a pilot, and the cargo-passenger combination carried 2, 3, or 4 passengers and the balance of payload in cargo. The single-place all-cargo version had special interior for strapping-down freight of all shapes and sizes. Marshall Headle, Lockheed test-pilot, tested

Fig. 45. Trailing edge wing "flaps" were added to slow landing speed.

each one of the 9-D built for American Airways as they came off the line, and delivered them personally to their base in Ft. Worth; deliveries of the 6 airplanes was completed in Oct. of 1933. Northwest Airways had ordered 3 of the model 9-D for their Chicago, Twin-Cities to Seattle route and their ships were the all-passenger type carrying up to 5 or 6 passengers and a pilot; gross weight allowance for the 9-D of NWA was increased by 400 lbs. and they were equipped with "air brake" wing flaps. The "Orion" 9-D of both lines had a very checkered career; some were lost in service, and all were pulled from the line by 1935 to enter other fields of commercial endeavor. One found its way up into Alaska, and 2 found a roundabout way to end their careers in Spain during the Civil War. As powered with the Pratt & Whitney "Wasp" S1D1 engine rated 550 h.p. at 5000 ft. the long-nosed "Orion" 9-D had a tremendous performance and pilots were eager to fly it, especially on the night-runs. Passengers also enjoyed the "Orion" 9-D and bragged to all of their exciting experience. The type certificate number for the "Orion" model 9-D was issued 8-31-33 with amendment on 11-27-33 for increase of gross wt. allowance of cargoplane to 5800 lbs. Amended on 1-9-34 as 1, 5, or 6 place, with wing flaps and gross wt. allowance of 5800 lbs. Nine examples of the "Orion" model 9-D were mfgd. by the Lockheed Aircraft Corp. at Burbank, Calif. Three other

versions of the 9-D (the 9-D1, 9-D2, and 9-D Special) were built as executive transports and one for long-distance flying.

Listed below are specifications and performance data for the "Orion" model 9-D as powered with "Wasp" S1D1 engine rated 550 h.p. at 2000 r.p.m. at 5000 ft.; length overall 28'4"; height overall 9'8"; wing span 42'9"; wing chord at root 102"; wing chord at tip 63"; total wing area (including fuselage portion) 294 sq.ft.; airfoil at root Clark Y-18; airfoil at tip Clark Y-9; wt. empty 3713 lbs.; useful load 1687 lbs.; payload with 116 gal. fuel 742 lbs. (4 pass. at 170 lbs. each & 62 lb. baggage); gross wt. 5400 lbs.; max. speed 226 at 5000 ft.; cruising speed 206 at 8600 ft.; landing speed 63; climb 1650 ft. first min. at sea level; ser. ceiling 22,000 ft.; gas cap. 116-130 gal.; oil cap. 10-11 gal.; cruising range variable; price was not announced. As of 8-31-33 wts. were approved as 3713-1687-5400 lbs. for passenger version and 3676-2105-5800 lbs. for cargoplane; amendment of 1-9-34 as 1, 5, or 6 place (with wing flaps) allowed wts. of 3935-1865-5800 lbs. The various gross wts. affected the performance accordingly.

The construction details and general arrangement of the model 9-D were typical of other "Orion" except for the following. Nose-section of the 9-D was extended 6 in., therefore, they were referred to as "the long-nosed Orion". Other refinements included improved wing root

Fig. 46. Passenger version of 9-D carried 4 or 6, depending on length of route.

fillets, a redesigned tail-group of higher aspect ratio, and landing lights mounted in leading edges of wing; use of a trailing antenna instead of a radio mast also increased the speed by at least 5 m.p.h. Split-type trailing edge wing flaps were used as an "air brake" to lower landing speeds to about 55 m.p.h.; the wing flaps (of dural metal construction) also permitted an increase in gross wt. allowance. The retractable landing gear used "Aerol" shock absorbing struts with 9.50x12 semi-airwheels on Warner wheels with brakes. A sliding hatch for pilot, cabin heat and ventilation, parking brake, a Hamilton-Standard or Smith controllable propeller, Exide battery, Eclipse electric engine starter, Bosch or Eclipse generator, navigation lights, landing lights, 4 parachute flares, Western Electric two-way radio, bonding and shielding, oil-cooling radiator, electrically operated wing flaps, engine mounted in rubber, full-swivel tail wheel, shatter-proof cabin glass, a Pyrene fire extinguishing system, Goodrich

abrasion or de-icer boots on leading edges of wing, rudder, and horizontal stabilizer, and a first-aid kit were standard equipment. An increase of fuel cap. to 130 gal. and oil cap. to 11 gal. was optional. The next Lockheed development was the twin-engined "Electra" model 10-A as described in the chapter for ATC # 551 of this volume.

Listed below are "Orion" model 9-D entries:
NC-12285; 9-D (# 197) Wasp 550.

-12286; "	(# 198)	"
-12287; "	(# 199)	"
NC-229Y; "	(# 200)	"
-23OY; "	(# 201)	"
-231Y; "	(# 202)	"
-13747; "	(# 205)	"
-13748; "	(# 206)	"
-13749; "	(# 207)	"

Serial # 197-198-199-200-201-202 operated by American Airways; ser. # 205-206-207 operated by Northwest Airways; approval expired 9-30-39.

Fig. 47. Line-up of "Orion" 9-D at Northwest Airways home base.

ATC # 515
(9-5-33)
FAIRCHILD, MODEL 22-C7E.

Fig. 48. Fairchild 22-C7E with 125 h.p. Warner "Scarab" was first Model 22 offered with "round" engine.

Up to this point the "Fairchild 22" parasol-type monoplane had been developed into some 5 different models and every one of them had been powered with various aircooled inline engines, both upright and inverted. This dainty-looking airplane, with its raised-up wing and slender fuselage, was indeed a natural for the low frontal area of the inline engine, so the new buxom-looking 22-C7E with its "round engine" and well-padded frame took a little getting used to, at least at first. As cowled in tightly with an NACA-type engine fairing the diameter of the 7 cyl. Warner "Scarab" required extensive fairing down the fuselage length to carry out the flow of natural streamlines; consequently, the new 22-C7E took on a plump, well-rounded look. Actually this was not at all bad because the extra cross-section in form was no detriment to its performance or its personality, but the familiar "Twenty Two" with its slim, girlish figure, now looked like an entirely different airplane. No doubt planning to take advantage of the entrenched popularity of the Warner "Scarab" engine, Fairchild had hopes to make a better showing in the sport-plane market with this new concept, but the skimpy market held few prospects. With what little business there was, manufacturers of sport-planes had to be content

in sharing the sales between them.

The Fairchild model 22-C7E was an open cockpit parasol-type monoplane with seating arranged for two in tandem. All previous models of the "Twenty Two" were slim and lean because they were powered with slender inline engines, so naturally, the new 22-C7E hardly looked like the same airplane, nor a member of the same family. Being powered with a so-called "round" radial-type engine the frame of the new ship had to be altered quite a bit externally to provide a new shape. Fairing of the fuselage was dictated by the circular cross-section of the NACA cowling up front; from the firewall back, the cross-section was carried to the rear on a gradual taper to a completely streamlined shape. This treatment added inches to the girth, but it promoted a better airflow down the fuselage. To compliment the streamlines of the fuselage all strut junctions and landing gear attachments were also faired-in neatly by metal "cuffs" to eliminate as much drag as possible. Because of this treatment the plumpish 22-C7E was a rather fast airplane in spite of its low power. For 1933 the popular Warner "Scarab" engine, previously rated 110 h.p. at 1850 r.p.m., was rerated to 125 h.p. at 2050 r.p.m. As powered with the 7 cyl. Warner "Scarab" engine of 125 h.p. the 22-C7E

Fig. 49. Fairing of "radial" engine provided 22-C7E with plump figure.

had ample performance, but it was also encumbered with an increase in weight which cut down just a little on its inherently frisky nature. Because of the fancy deluxe treatment rendered to this airplane as a whole it would be next to folly to imagine it as a trainer, so it was leveled at the "week ender" and the sportsman; however, of suitable performance and rugged character, the 22-C7E was also eligible for use in acrobatic training during secondary phases of the Civilian Pilot Training Program. What few active sportsmen there were at this time had a wide selection of airplanes to pick from and none of the sport models, by any manufacturer, sold to any extent. The model 22-C7E was a significant milestone in development of the "Fairchild 22" series, but it was represented in

very small number. The type certificate number for the "Scarab" powered 22-C7E was issued 9-5-33 with amendments awarded on 10-16-33, 11-9-33, 12-7-33, and 4-16-34. At least 11 examples of this model were manufactured by the Kreider-Reisner Aircraft Co., Inc. at Hagerstown, Md.

Listed below are specifications and performance data for the Fairchild model 22-C7E as powered with the 125 h.p. Warner "Scarab" engine; length overall 22'0"; height overall 7'11"; wing span 32'10"; wing chord 66"; total wing area 170 sq.ft.; airfoil (NACA) N-22; wt. empty 1102 lbs.; useful load 648 lbs.; payload with 30 gal. fuel 275 lbs. (one passenger at 170 lbs. with baggage allowance of 65 lbs.—2 parachutes at 20 lbs. each as part of the payload); gross wt. 1750 lbs.; max. speed 130;

Fig. 50. Fairchild 22-C7E was designed strictly for the sportsman.

Fig. 51. Sliding canopy provided pilot with protection in colder weather.

cruising speed 110; landing speed 48; climb 650 ft. first min. at sea level; ser. ceiling 17,300 ft.; gas cap. normal 30 gal.; gas cap. optional 50 gal.; oil cap. 3 gal.; cruising range at 7.5 gal. per hour 380 miles; price varied from $2750. at factory field. With 50 gal. fuel payload was reduced by 142 lbs. Also eligible as seaplane on Edo twin-float gear.

The construction details and general arrangement of the 22-C7E were basically typical to that of previous Model 22. The great change to the outward shape was simply accomplished by extensive fairing to the basic fuselage framework. Both cockpits were deep and well protected with entry to the front 'pit through a large door on the left side; the front cockpit was often closed off with a metal panel when not in use. A small baggage compartment, with allowance for 65 lbs., was down low behind the firewall with a door on right side. Normal fuel capacity of 30 gal. was carried in a tank mounted high in the fuselage ahead of the front cockpit; a float-type fuel gauge projected through the cowling. An extra 20 gal. fuel capacity (10 gal. tank in root of each wing half) was optional for a total capacity of 50 gal. The wing framework, mounted on a

maze of struts, was basically the same as previous Model 22; a "spin-strip" was mounted on leading edge to induce buffeting during a "stall" of the wing, and to eliminate "float" on landing. The sport-type landing gear, which was an option on earlier "Twenty Two", was standard equipment on the 22-C7E; 6.50x10 Warner wheels with brakes were encased in metal wheel (pants) fairings. The NACA engine cowl was split vertically in 2 halves to allow removal for inspection or engine maintenance. A metal propeller, sport-type landing gear with wheel pants, wheel brakes, and NACA cowl were standard equipment. A wooden propeller, electric engine starter, and battery were optional. The next development in the "Fairchild 22" series was the model 22-C7F as described in the chapter for ATC # 517 of this volume.

Listed below are 22-C7E entries as gleaned from registration records:

NC-2738: 22-C7E (# 1600) Warner 125.
   -9383:   "   (# 1601)   "
   -9392:   "   (# 1602)   "
   -9393:   "   (# 1603)   "
   -9394:   "   (# 1604)   "
   -9395:   "   (# 1605)   "
   -9396:   "   (# 1606)   "
   -9484:   "   (# 1607)   "
   -9485:   "   (# 1608)   "
   -9486:   "   (# 1609)   "
NC-13286: "   (# 1610)   "

This approval for Ser. # 1600 and up; reports imply that Ser. # 1600-1601 were first powered with Warner 110 h.p.; reports also imply that ser. # 1605 was powered for a time with Warner 90; first-flight date 4 Aug. 33 for ser. # 1600, 12 Jan. 34 for ser. # 1603, 7 Feb. 34 for ser. # 1605, and 21 July 34 for ser. # 1608; a Warner-powered "Twenty Two" (quite possibly a 22-C7E) was reported delivered to Spain early in 1934 as a demonstrator; this approval expired 9-30-39.

ATC # 516
(9-15-33)
KINNER, "SPORTSTER B".

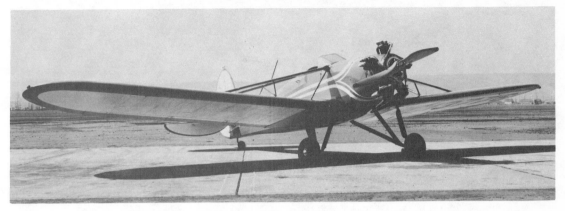

Fig. 52. Kinner "Sportster" B with 125 h.p. Kinner B5 engine.

The earlier 100 h.p. "Sportster K" was still popular and still available, even well into this period, but by now it was becoming industry policy to offer a new and better model for each season. In the "Sportster B" for the 1934-35 season Kinner offered a few added niceties, a more powerful Kinner engine, and of course, the bonus of performance that comes with an increase in horsepower. Because of these extras the Model B became somewhat more attractive as a sport-plane for the sporting amateur and also the week-end flier, but it still remained quite suitable as a pilot-training airplane. One "Sportster B", used primarily as a trainer, operated from the flight-line beginning at early dawn and was still going strong well into dusk; the "board" showed that it had 27 student-pilots

assigned to it for flight instruction. Other examples of the Model B were purchased as personal craft that were used mainly for week-end sport, but being owned by business-men, they also assisted in transacting occasional business. A large grain and milling empire in Montana, in performing its daily business, listed their "Sportster B" as one of its greater assets. Launching the "Sportster B" into the very teeth of a serious national depression was a risky beginning for a new model, but a few customers were rounded up late in 1933 and sales fared just a little better for 1934. As a companion model, also on this type certificate, the model B-1 of 1934 was almost identical to the Model B with hardly enough difference to set one apart from the other. The Kinner model B or B-1, like its

Fig. 53. Lanky "Sportster" B was a pleasant airplane of gentle habits.

Fig. 54. "Sportster" B-1 was a slightly modified version.

earlier sister-ship the Model K, made friends easily and only the lack of money kept admiring pilots from becoming potential customers.

The Kinner "Sportster B" and B-1 was a light open cockpit monoplane with side by side seating for two. Its lanky, sturdy frame, was complimented by simple lines and its reliability was enhanced by its mechanical simplicity. Primarily designed for the owner-pilot the "Sportster B" (or B-1) was a likeable and compatible machine, a vehicle that could assure countless hours of flying pleasure without a lot of attentive fuss or muss into its mechanical innards; some of the flying-service operators were well aware of this trait and enjoyed the advantage of having the "Sportster" on their flight-line. As powered with the 5 cyl. Kinner B5 engine of 125 h.p. the "Sportster B" and B-1, like its earlier sister-ship, was an easy-going airplane that was somewhat reluctant to be in a hurry, but delivered its rather good performance in a gracious and honest manner. Particularly easy to fly and of unusually good manners the "Sportster B" earned itself a reputation of being a very pleasant airplane, and especially tolerant of the student and the amateur; a cooperative nature and a stout airframe did permit a seasoned pilot to coax the "Sportster" out of character occasionally, but this behavior she only tolerated and didn't really enjoy. Because of its willingness to perform any reasonable chore, the "Sportster" was finally relegated to all-purpose service and remained useful and popular for many years after. The type certificate number for the "Sportster B" was issued 9-15-33 and amended on 10-27-33 to include the coupe-top enclosure, modification to the ailerons, and an increase in gross weight allowance. The "Sportster" model B-1, almost identical to the Model B, was first approved (12-1-33) on ATC # 522, but on 5-2-34 the ATC (# 522) was amended for approval of the "Sportwing" B-2 and approval for the model B-1 was then included here with the Model B on ATC # 516. Manufactured

by the Kinner Airplane & Motor Corp., Ltd. at Glendale, Calif.

Listed below are specifications and performance data for the Kinner "Sportster" model B as powered with the 125 h.p. Kinner B5 engine; length overall 24'2"; height overall 7'0"; wing span 39'0"; wing chord 72"; total wing area (including fuselage portion) 227 sq.ft.; airfoil Clark Y; wt. empty 1232 lbs.; useful load 643 lbs.; payload with 35 gal. fuel 244 lbs. (1 passenger at 170 lb. & 74 lb. baggage); gross wt. 1875 lbs.; max. speed 112; cruising speed 98; landing speed 40; climb 900 ft. first min. at sea level; ser. ceiling 15,000 ft.; gas cap. 35 gal. (24 gal. optional); oil cap. 2.5 gal.; cruising range at 7.2 gal. per hour 440 miles; price not announced.

Approved wts. as of 9-15-33 were 1209-616-1825 lbs.; wts. amended on 10-27-33 to 1215-647-1862 lbs. to include cockpit enclosure, balance weights in ailerons, and increase in gross wt.; amended 5-2-34 to include Sportster B and B-1 with wts. of 1215-660-1875 for B and 1197-678-1875 lbs. for B-1; early 1935 wts. changed to 1232-643-1875 lbs.; late 1935 wts. changed to 1272-603-1875 lbs. (this was with 206 lb. payload and 36 lb. baggage); empty wt. for B-1 of 1935 with metal propeller, cabin heater, cockpit canopy, radio gear, and 24 gal. fuel cap. was 1272 lbs.—with useful load of 603 lbs. it carried 1 passenger and 103 lbs. baggage.

The fuselage framework was built up of welded chrome-moly steel tubing, faired out to a nearly oval section with wooden formers and fairing strips, then fabric covered. The short wing stubs which carried the landing gear and points of attachment for the wing panels were also of welded chrome-moly steel tubing and built integral to the fuselage. The deep open cockpit seating two side-by-side was roomy and well protected by a large windshield; a coupe-top enclosure was optional for cold-weather flying. A large door on each side provided easy entry from the wing-walk; the cockpit was upholstered in Fabricoid and dual joy-stick controls were

Fig. 55. "Sportster" B-1 was quite at home on hay-field airports.

provided. A baggage compartment was in each wing-stub with allowance for up to 108 lbs.; parachutes at 20 lbs. each, when carried, were part of the baggage allowance. Model B was allowed 80 lbs. baggage (40 lbs. in each wing compt.) and the B-1 was allowed 54 lbs. in each wing compartment. A 35 gal. fuel tank was mounted high in the fuselage ahead of the cockpit; a 24 gal. fuselage tank was optional to allow increase in payload allowance. The wing panels were built up of solid spruce spar beams with spruce and plywood truss-type wing ribs; the leading edges were covered with dural metal sheet and the completed framework was covered in fabric. The amendment of 10-27-33 required a 3 lb. lead weight in leading edge of each aileron for better mass balance; this added 6 lbs. to empty weight. The landing gear consisted of 2 simple tripod units with oleo-spring shock absorbing struts; 19x9-3 Goodyear airwheels were fitted with brakes. An 8 in. swiveling tail wheel was provided for better ground handling. The fabric covered tail-group was built up of welded chrome-moly steel tubing; the elevators were fitted with adjustable "trim tabs" for longitudinal trim in flight. Various color schemes were available; some were known to be finished two-toned in light green and cream. A Story wooden propeller, Heywood engine

starter, hot-shot battery, dual controls, parking brake, navigation lights, fire extinguisher, and chromed exhaust collector ring were standard equipment. A metal propeller, cabin heater, coupe-top enclosure, 24 gal. fuel tank, bonding, shielding and wiring for radio, a radio, and skis were optional. The next Kinner development was the "Playboy" model R-1 as described in the chapter for ATC # 518 of this volume. Listed below are "Sportster" model B and B-1 entries as gleaned from registration records:

NC-14264; B   (# 46) Kinner B5.
  -13704; "   (# 62)   "
  -13710; "   (# 80)   "
  -13744; B-1 (# 86)   "
  -13654; B   (# 88)   "
  -13776; "   (# 102) "
  -14201; "   (# 122) "
  -14217; "   (# 134) "
  -14235; B-1 (# 138) "
  -14238; B   (# 162) "
  -14288; '   (# 166) "

This certificate for ser. # 46, 62, 80 and up; Kinner airplane serial numbers were all even, as 6-8-10 etc.; ser. # 46 and # 162 first as Model K; NC-234Y (ser. # 28) later modified to Model B; 9 aircraft were mfgd. as Model B and 2 aircraft as Model B-1; approval expired 2-16-39.

ATC # 517
(9-22-33)
FAIRCHILD, 22-C7F.

Fig. 56. Fairchild 22-C7F with 145 h.p. Warner "Super Scarab" engine.

The earlier model 22-C7E launched this series into an entirely new shape, but the power of the Warner "Scarab" (125 h.p.) was just a little short in producing the kind of performance that was expected from a ship of this type. To add a little more punch to the overall performance in general, the new 22-C7F was powered with the recently introduced Warner "Super Scarab" of 145 h.p.; the extra 20 h.p. doesn't seem like much of a boost at first, but it did perk up the performance quite noticeably so that it fell more in line with what the sportsman-pilots were asking for these days, and expecting to get. The whole pity of it was that sportsman-pilots of 1934-35 were becoming a fickle group and could not always be trusted to buy airplanes that were traditionally "designed for the sportsman"; the sportsman's taste was rapidly changing and they were just as apt to buy a small cabin monoplane, an open biplane, or if they could afford it, a custom-designed airplane especially built for them. This development, coupled with the fact that the number of sporting-pilots were extremely small at this time, even on a nationwide basis, caused the manufacturing of "sportplanes" to be a lean and rather risky business. A specially-constructed 22-C7F was ordered by the Navy Dept. as the XR2K-1 for use by the flight-test division of NACA at Langley Field. The airplane was used for the study of experimental

wing sections with various "slot and flap" combinations, a study in actual flight instead of in the wind-tunnel. Fairchild also contracted to build a variety of special wings to NACA specifications; the research conducted with this airplane (XR2K-1) provided much valuable information in the behavior of airplanes with various "slot" and "flap" combinations. Turning to our neighbors in the south, Fairchild exported 6 or 7 of the 22-C7F to Mexico and to So. America. The model 22-C7F was little-known and did not sell very well, but a west-coast distributor of the Fairchild aircraft line reported that business in general was improving, at least in the west; he had just ordered a whole carload of assorted Model 22 and Model 24, most of which had already been ordered and paid for by customers.

In its standard configuration the Fairchild 22-C7F was an open cockpit parasol-type monoplane with seating arranged for two in tandem. Being powered with a so-called "round" radial-type engine the frame fairing of this new series was altered considerably to provide a new shape; the shape was actually dictated by the circular cross-section of the NACA-type engine cowling in front. This fairing treatment added inches to the girth and consequently, the airplane presented a much more bulkier appearance and took on an inevitable gain in

Fig. 57. Wide landing gear on 22-C7F provided stable stance, "parasol" wing provided stable flight.

weight. Streamlined generously to eliminate as much drag as possible the new series "Twenty Two" was fast in spite of its relatively low power, and the performance that was now being expected only came with an increase in the power-to-weight ratio. The earlier 22-C7E with 125 h.p. was just a little shy in get-up-and-go, so the 22-C7F was favored with added power to eliminate this shortcoming. As powered with the new 7 cyl. Warner "Super Scarab" engine of 145 h.p. the 22-C7F responded admirably to the extra horsepower and showed ample gains throughout the whole performance range. Incidently, this was the first certificated installation of the new "Super Scarab" engine and its success in the 22-C7F paved the way to many more interesting installations in the next few years. The special version of the 22-C7F built for NACA (XR2K-1) was modified only to permit easier exchange of various wing configurations for test—otherwise it conformed closely to the standard model. The type certificate number for the model 22-C7F was issued 9-22-33 and amendments were awarded on 11-9-33 and 4-17-34; amendment of 4-26-34 changed wts. to 1102-648-1750 lbs. for more useful load. Records for amount of 22-C7F built are sketchy, but it is

quite probable that at least 9 examples were manufactured by Kreider-Reisner Aircraft Co., Inc. at Hagerstown, Md. Even at this late date the classic "Fairchild 71" transport was still available on order and several had been exported for foreign service. Sherman M. Fairchild was president; W. M. Schwebel was executive V.P.; L. E. Reisner was V.P. and gen. mgr.; H. Eichhammer was sales mgr.; George W. Hardman and A. A. Gassner were project engrs.; R. "Dick" Henson was test-pilot. Eichhammer, formerly with the Aeronca organization, was on extensive tour in the southwest late in 1933 promoting the "Twenty Two" and "Twenty Four".

Listed below are specifications and performance data for the Fairchild model 22-C7F as powered with 145 h.p. Warner "Super Scarab" engine; length overall 22'0"; height overall 7'11"; wing span 32'10"; wing chord 66"; total wing area 170 sq.ft.; airfoil N-22; wt. empty 1133 lbs.; useful load 617 lbs.; payload with 30 gal. fuel 244 lbs. (1 passenger at 170 lb. & 74 lb. baggage); (2 parachutes at 20 lb. each, when carried, were part of the baggage allowance); gross wt. 1750 lbs.; max. speed 138; cruising speed 118; landing speed 48; climb 840 ft. first

Fig. 58. This 22-C7F (XR2K-1) was test-plane at NACA laboratory. Tests were performed on high-lift devices.

min. at sea level; ser. ceiling 19,400 ft.; gas cap. normal 30 gal.; gas cap. max. 50 gal.; oil cap. 3 gal.; cruising range at 9 gal. per hour 377-630 miles; basic price about $3480. at factory.

The fuselage framework was built up of welded chrome-moly steel tubing heavily faired to a rounded shape and fabric covered. Both cockpits were deep and well protected with entry to front cockpit by way of a large door on left side; the front cockpit was often closed off with a metal panel when not in use. A baggage compartment with allowance for up to 65 lbs. was down low behind firewall with a door on the right side. A 30 gal. fuel tank was mounted high in the fuselage ahead of the front cockpit; a float-type fuel gauge projected through the cowling. An extra 20 gal. of fuel (a 10 gal. tank in root end of each wing-half) was optional for a total capacity of 50 gal.—payload was reduced by 142 lbs. The wing framework was built up of I-section spruce spar beams with spruce and plywood truss-type wing ribs; the leading edges were covered with plywood sheet and the completed framework was covered in fabric. The "parasol" wing was mounted high on a system of streamlined steel tube struts. The sport-type outrigger landing gear of 7'1" tread used "Fairchild" oleo and spr-

ing shock absorbing struts; 6.50x10 semi-airwheels were equipped with brakes and encased in streamlined metal wheel pants. The fabric covered tail-group was built up of welded chrome-moly steel tubing; the rudder was fitted with aerodynamic balance horn and horizontal stabilizer was adjustable in flight. A wooden propeller, a tail skid, dual stick-type controls, sport-type landing gear with brakes and wheel pants, a compass, safety belts, and first-aid kit were standard equipment. A metal propeller, 8x4 tail wheel, battery, navigation lights, electric engine starter, front cockpit cover, and 20 gal. extra fuel were optional. The next Fairchild development was the model 24-C8C as described in the chapter for ATC # 535 of this volume. Listed below are the only 22-C7F entries as found in registration records:

NC-9379: 22-C7F (# 1700) Warner 145.
      : 22-C7F (# 1701) Warner 145.
NC-13284: 22-C7F (# 1702) Warner 145.

This approval for ser. # 1700 and up; ser. # 1701, 1703-04-05-06-07 exported to Mexico and So. America in 1934; ser. no. for XR2K-1 was # 1708, sold 17 Sept. 1935; approval expired 9-30-39.

ATC # 518
(10- -33)
KINNER, "PLAYBOY" R-1.

Fig. 59. Rare Kinner "Playboy" R-1 with 160 h.p. Kinner R5 engine.

The "Playboy" model R-1, more or less un-known to all but a few, was to be part of the Kinner Airplanes line-up for 1934. Other new Kinner models in the sport-trainer series, all low-winged monoplanes, were basically of the open cockpit variety, but quickly convertible to closed models by installation of removable "coupe" tops. The "Playboy" model R-1, by comparison, seems to have been designed primarily as a cabin-type airplane for two, but later converted to an open cockpit airplane. Herein lies the mystery. Basically, by its resemblance, the "Playboy" R-1 in prototype was a somewhat smaller version of the earlier Kinner "Sedan P" a 210 h.p. custom-made sportster built (on Group 2-426) especially for Robert Porter. Being primarily a fast sport-type airplane the gleaming all-white model R-1 em-bodied many contemporary racing-airplane features that no doubt contributed heavily to a spirited nature and a swift performance. Such custom features as a fully streamlined landing gear, a rather small wire-braced wing, and the enclosed cabin cockpit were still quite unusual in a small sportplane of this type. As powered with the 5 cyl. Kinner R5 engine of 160 h.p. the "Playboy" model R-1 was certainly an attrac-tive airplane, in either the open or closed con-figuration, and would have been a showy offer-ing in the Kinner Airplanes line-up for the season of 1934. Whatever the reason for curtail-ment of its production it is a pity that it was built only in the one example; it might have well en-joyed an interesting future. Not a total loss, at least it did set a precedent and most likely in-stigated the design of a modified "Playboy", the model R-5 of 1935.

The "Playboy" model R-1 by Kinner Airplanes was a wire-braced low wing cabin or open monoplane with side-by-side seating for

Fig. 60. "Playboy" R-1 as modified to open cockpit.

Fig. 61. Kinner "Playboy" R-1 started out as cabin-type airplane for two.

two. As the model name implies, the pert "Playboy" was designed expecially for the custom pleasures of sport flying. As a handsome airplane of comparatively high performance potential, it can be assumed the R-1 was initially slanted toward the sportsman-pilot of better-than-average means, one who could well afford to enjoy the benefits offered by a machine of this type. As powered with the 5 cyl. Kinner R5 engine rated 160 h.p. this "Playboy" seemed to be of a carefully selected configuration that was almost like a guarantee to playful nature and high performance. Considerable research revealed absolutely no published data on the make-up of the model R-1, so we can only assume by rule-of-thumb that it surely would have been capable of an above-average performance. Judging too by past performance of other "Kinner" designs, notably the popular "Sportster", we can safely assume that this "Playboy" was also of rugged frame and character; it also displayed a beauty of proportion that was enhanced by attention to smaller detail. As is often the case, especially with very rare airplanes, spot stories published at various times often amount to conflicting statements when put together in chronological order; therefore, the "Playboy" model R-1 seemed to be 2 airplanes when in reality it was only one airplane of 2 different configurations. The type certificate number was issued approximately in October of 1933 and only one example of this model was mfgd. by the Kinner Airplane & Motor Corp. at Glendale, Calif. The following data is in CAA Manual as description for model R-1:

Kinner Playboy R-1, 2POLM on ATC # 518.
Kinner R5 engine rated 160 h.p. at 1975 r.p.m.
Fuel cap.: 52 gal. (39 gal. in fuselage & 13 gal. in right stub wing).
Oil cap.: 3.5 gal.
Seating cap.: pilot and one passenger.
Baggage: 71 lbs. (includes 2 parachutes at 20 lbs. each, when carried). Left wing stub compartment 59 lbs., rear of cockpit compartment 12 lbs. (See Note 1).
Standard gross weight: 2200 lbs.
Specification basis: ATC # 518. (for ser. # 84 and up; approval expired 6-30-39.)
Standard equipment: engine nose cowl (10), wheel streamlines (32), radio receiver (13), "B" eliminator (13), 6-volt battery (20), Heywood engine starter (30), tail fairing (5), 8x3 tail wheel, 6.50x10 (Autofan) wheels & brakes with 4-ply tires (66), ground-adjustable metal propeller; figures in parentheses are unit weight.
Note 1: When radio receiver is removed, baggage may be increased to 84 lbs.; the rear of cockpit compartment may then be placarded for 25 lbs.

NC-13703; Playboy R-1 (# 84) Kinner R5

Ser. # 84 registered 1933 in Calif.; photo in Aircraft Year Book for 1934 shows this same airplane (NC-13703) as cabin model; model R-1 had early version of Kinner R5 with front exhaust; the next Kinner development was the "Sportwing B-2" as described in the chapter for ATC # 522 of this volume; for description of the "Playboy" R-5 see chapter for ATC # 554 also of this volume.

ATC # 519
(10-23-33)
STINSON "RELIANT", SR-4.

Fig. 62. Typical of "Reliant" shown, the model SR-4 had 250 h.p. Wright engine.

Except for the years 1931-32, the Stinson plant always had Wright-powered airplanes in their line-up. Since being affiliated with the huge Cord Corp., Stinson more or less standardized on "Lycoming" engines, which were manufactured within the corporation; this a move to keep costs at the lowest possible level. Back in 1929, Stinson Aircraft had contracted for a million dollars worth of "Wright" engines per year, but due to "depression pressures" the contract was unrealistic and finally rescinded. However, in 1933, Stinson once again managed to develop at least one Wright-powered model for the season. Introduced late in the year the Wright-powered "Reliant" for the season of 1933-34 was labeled the model SR-4; the SR-4 was typical of the standard model SR except for the increase in power and a hefty increase to the gross weight allowance, an allowance that permitted the installation of a wide array of extra equipment. As powered with the 7 cyl. Wright R-760-E engine rated 250 h.p. the SR-4 delivered a significant increase in all-round performance, but then, its delivered price was considerably more than the standard "Reliant" with Lycoming engines. By record, it is apparent that only 2 examples of the model SR-4 were built, with one being delivered to Milton Knight of Perrysburg, Ohio. With some of the gloom finally lifting, the outlook for

Stinson Aircraft in 1933 was better than at any time during the past 2 years. More people were now employed, and a large overhauling and rebuilding program was under way; operators and owners of Stinson airplanes were convinced that this work could be done best at the factory at less cost, particularly when considerable modifying was to be done for installation of two-way radio gear, navigational instruments, increased fuel capacity, and other similar features. By year's end, "Reliant" sales were steadily increasing and a considerable export business was also developing.

The Stinson "Reliant" model SR-4 was a high-winged cabin monoplane with seating arranged for four. As the top of the line in the new "Reliant" series for 1933, the model SR-4 was the best equipped, the most expensive, and certainly the best performer. Being more or less a custom-built airplane this "Reliant" (the SR-4) was finished off slowly in finer detail and it was treated to some extra attention in final assembly. As powered with the 7 cyl. Wright R-760-E engine of 250 h.p. the SR-4 responded joyfully to the extra assembly attention and the extra horsepower. Being somewhat costly and therefore somewhat impractical on the flight-line of the average flying-service operator, the SR-4 was naturally slanted toward the sportsman-pilot and men of business. Had times been better for the sportsman-pilot and for the man of business there might have been a somewhat better future for the SR-4; it is known fact too that many owners of Stinson airplanes who would normally be ready to buy a new model about now would instead rebuild to extend the life of their older airplanes for another year or so. The type certificate number for the model SR-4 was issued 10-23-33 and it is quite likely that no more than 2 examples of this model were mfgd. by the Stinson Aircraft Corp. at Wayne, Mich. Bernard D. DeWeese was pres.; Wm. A. Mara was V.P. and gen. mgr.; project engr. for "Reliant" series was C. R. "Jack" Irvine; J. C. "Jack" Kelley, Jr. was demonstration pilot and roving sales mgr. In all, some 100 examples of the SR "Reliant" (including SR-1, SR-2, SR-3, SR-4) were sold and delivered in 1933.

Listed below are specifications and performance data for the model SR-4 as powered with 250 h.p. Wright R-760-E engine; length overall 27'0"; height overall 8'5"; wing span 43'3"; wing chord 75"; total wing area 235 sq.ft.; airfoil Clark Y; wt. empty 2237 lbs.; useful load 1088 lbs.; payload with 50 gal. fuel 588 lbs.; baggage allowance 50 lbs.; gross wt. 3325 lbs.; max. speed (with wheel pants) 138; cruising speed 122; landing (stall) speed 57; climb 900 ft. first min. at sea level; ser. ceiling 15,500 ft.; gas cap. normal 50 gal.; gas cap. optional 72 gal.; oil cap. 4-5 gal.; cruising range at 14 gal. per hour 360 miles; price variable.

CAA data for model SR-4: this approval (ATC # 519) for ser. # 8930-31 and up with Wright R-760-E engine rated 250 h.p. at 2000 r.p.m. at sea level; empty wt. of 2237 lbs. includes engine cowl (36), 12-volt battery (37), cabin heater (3), wheel pants and full fairing (28), electric engine starter (26), assist ropes, cabin fittings & radio bonding (8), 8.50x10 wheels and tires with mechanical brakes, 10.5 in. tail wheel, baggage allowance 50 lbs., gross wt. held to 3325 lbs. Approved optional equipment (weight to be added to std. empty wt.); retractable landing lights (26), 5 parachute flares (16), extra instruments (5), 72 gal. fuel cap. (2 tanks in wings at 36 gal. each), oil 5 gal., Lycoming-Smith controllable propeller (123), with gross wt. held to 3325 lbs. Figures in parentheses are wts. per unit assembly.

The construction details and general arrangement listed here will generally apply to all SR, SR-1, SR-2, SR-3, and SR-4 examples; any variation from this is mentioned specifically in descriptive analysis of each model, as in ATC # 510-513, etc. The fuselage framework was built up of welded chrome-moly steel tubing faired to shape and fabric covered. The auto-like interior had heavily padded seats placed at a restful angle; front seats were adjustable fore and aft as well as up and down. The large cabin doors, one on each side, were fitted with gadget pockets for flashlight, maps, and the like. Heavy soundproofing of the cabin walls, including floor and ceiling, kept noise level to a tolerable minimum; ventilators and a cabin heater of larger capacity provided more comfort during temperature extremes. Dual control wheels were mounted on a Y-type column which was adjustable to suit; "trim control" was accomplished by a small crank overhead. Non-glare safety glass was used in the vee-type windshield and clear shatterproof glass in all other windows. A large baggage compartment, with locking-type door, was down low behind the rear seat and accessible only from the outside; a small hat-shelf in the cabin was behind the rear seat-back. Satin-finish cabin hardware was a compliment to the mohair upholstery of harmonious color that either matched or contrasted the exterior finish. The engine was mounted in big rubber bushings to help deaden sound and reduce vibration in the frame; considerable space was provided in engine compartment for easy access to engine parts and to place a convenient mount for the 12-volt battery used for starting and lighting. Exterior finish was harmonious colors of distinctive Stinson design that were hand-rubbed and polished to a mirror finish. Some of the more popular color combinations were Red & Black, Green & Cream, Blue & Orange, etc. A metal propeller, electric engine starter, 12-volt battery, chromed exhaust collector ring, roll-down windows, wheel brakes, dual controls, cabin heater, and wheel fenders were standard equipment. Retractable landing lights, parachute flares, variable-pitch propeller, and wheel pants were optional. The next Stinson development was the parasol-winged Model O as described in the chapter for ATC # 520 of this volume.

NC-13828; SR-4 (# 8931) Wright 250.

This approval for ser. # 8930, 8931, and up; the registration number for ser. # 8930 is unknown—it may have been exported; ser. # 8931 was registered to Milton Knight of Perrysburg, Ohio and still on register in 1937; approval expired 9-30-39.

STINSON, MODEL O.

Fig. 63. The handsome Stinson "Model O" with 220 h.p. Lycoming engine.

The Stinson "Model O" was a very unusual airplane, unusual primarily in the fact that it was the only open cockpit monoplane that Stinson Aircraft had ever built. Speculation would reveal several good reasons to prompt development of this particular design, but the most logical reason was for Stinson to have a suitable entry into the budding export market. Countries abroad, especially those in our own hemisphere, were looking to the U.S.A. for suitable airplanes with which to form their air forces, and pilot-trainers were especially in demand. Robert L. Hall of "Gee Bee" airplane fame, came to Stinson early in 1933 and joined the design staff; his experience with "Gee Bee" racing airplanes were useful credentials. Soon afterward, one Lowell Yerex arrived at the plant on a mission for the Honduras Air Force; he was shopping for a utility airplane suitable for all phases of pilot-training and for counterinsurgency. Stinson had absolutely nothing to offer off the shelf, so Hall was put to designing a parasol-winged tandem two-seater that would meet the need, on the double. Several weeks later, in May of 1933, a feat pressured by the urgency, the first "Model O" (X-13817) was out of the plant and flying; quite happy with the airplane and with what it could do, Yerex put in an order for three. Eventually, 5 were delivered to the government of Honduras, 3 were delivered to China, and one to Brazil. The prototype airplane, after proving itself for its intended role and winning certification, was used for basic training by a California flight-school until 1946. Freeman Gosden, the Amos of the famous "Amos and Andy" team of radio, learned to fly in the Model O and ordered one like it in his early exhuberance, but later settled for a fancy "Reliant".

The Stinson "Model O" was an open cockpit parasol-winged monoplane with seating arranged for two in tandem. A rather outstanding shape, the Model O was an ingenious adaptation of the basic "SR" configuration, a pilot-trainer that was capable of mounting various pieces of light armament. All necessary fittings were incorporated into the specially designed fuselage for either 2 forward-firing fixed machine guns, a flexible mounted machine gun, and one A-3 bomb rack. The basic SR "Reliant" wing was modified slightly to suit "parasol" mounting, and a severe cut-away in the center section provided excellent visibility from either cockpit. The landing gear was practically identical to that of the SR and the tail-group was only slightly modified. The Model O was not designed primarily as a warplane, but as a training machine to teach pilots the various arts of aerial warfare; it was also adaptable to training pilots in ground support, reconnaiscance, and aerial photography. As powered with the 9 cyl. Lycom-

Fig. 64. Stinson "Model O" dressed for service in Honduras.

ing R-680-4 engine rated 220 h.p. at 2050 r.p.m. the Model O had excellent performance for its varied role and it can be safely assumed that its characteristics and general behavior were typically of "Stinson" nature. Slated for use by smaller foreign countries where facilities tended to be more primitive, the Lycoming R-680-4 engine was specifically selected because of its ability to operate on low (58) octane fuel; as an alternate, using higher octane fuel, the R-680-2 engine of 240 h.p. was also available. The type certificate number for the Model O was issued 11-9-33; an amendment was awarded on 1-8-34. A total of perhaps 10 examples in this model were mfgd. by the Stinson Aircraft Corp. at Wayne, Mich. Robt. L. Hall, formerly associated with "Gee Bee" airplanes, was project engr. on development of the Model O.

Listed below are specifications and performance data for the Model O as powered with 220 h.p. Lycoming R-680-4 engine; length overall 27'8"; height overall 8'0"; wing span 39'11"; wing chord 75"; total wing area 215 sq.ft.; airfoil Clark Y; wt. empty 1907 (1945) lbs.; useful load 710 lbs.; payload with 50 gal. fuel 210 lbs.; gross wt. 2617 (2665) lbs.; max. speed (with engine cowl & wheel pants) 136; cruising speed 122; landing speed 50 (52); climb 1150 (1100) ft. first min. at sea level; ser. ceiling 16,000 ft.; figures in parentheses are for plane with NACA-type engine cowl & wheel fenders; gas cap. 50 gal.; oil cap. 4 gal.; cruising range at 12.5 gal. per hour 450 miles; price variable as plane was custom-built to order; approved wts. of 1907-710-2617 lbs. were for prototype without engine cowl & bare wheels; approved wts. of 1945-710-2665 lbs. included NACA-type engine cowl & wheel fenders; revision in 1934 allowed 2750 lb. gross wt. to 220 h.p. version and 3200 lb. gross wt. to 240 h.p. version; both versions allowed 380 lb. payload to provide for equipment used in gunnery training or aerial photography; stall speed 53 at 2750 lb. gross wt. and 58 at 3200 lb. gross wt.

The fuselage framework was built up of welded chrome-moly steel tubing faired to shape and

Fig. 65. Despite "parasol" configuration, "Model O" retained well-known Stinson characteristics.

Fig. 66. "Model O" borrowed many features from the "Reliant".

fabric covered; forward half was covered with removable metal panels and all necessary fittings were provided for mounting machine guns, aerial camera, and a bomb rack. The pilot's cockpit was in front, but flight controls were provided in both cockpits; wheel brake pedals and parking brake lever were in front cockpit only. Cockpit entry steps were placed in side of the fuselage and hand-holds were provided in the center-section. The wing framework was built up of solid spruce spar beams and truss-type dural metal wing ribs; the center-section and wing roots had severe cut-away for good visibility from front cockpit. One fuel tank of 25 gal. capacity was mounted in root end of each wing-half. The center-section of 7 ft. span was mounted to the fuselage on splayed out struts and wing halves were braced to the lower stub-wing which also formed mounting for the landing gear. The landing gear of 117 in. tread was of 2 cantilever legs equipped with "Aerol" shock absorbing struts and 8.50x10 semi-airwheels with mechanical brakes; 25x11-4 Goodyear airwheels with hydraulic brakes were optional. Wheel fenders were normally provided but streamlined wheel pants were optional. Fittings were also provided in the fuselage for the installation of twin-float seaplane gear. The fabric covered tail-group was built up of welded steel tubing; rudder was provided with aerodynamic "balance horn" and the horizontal stabilizer was adjustable in flight. Both cockpits were equipped with basic flight and engine instruments; front cockpit also fitted with bank and turn indicator and rate of climb indicator. Other optional equipment included a two-way radio, bonding & shielding, parachute flares, navigation lights, landing lights, a 12-volt battery, hand crank inertia-type engine starter, exhaust collector-ring, NACA-type engine cowl, and Lycoming-Smith controllable pitch propeller. The next Stinson development was the "Reliant" model SR-5 as described in chapter for ATC # 530 of this volume.

X-13817: Model O (# 10000) Lycoming 220-240.

Ser. # 10000 registered to Stinson Aircraft in 1933, and later to Lycoming Motors Div.; 5 examples of Model O were delivered to govt. of Honduras, 3 were delivered to China, and one to Brazil which was registered PP-TBG; approval expired 9-30-39.

ATC # 521
(11-15-33)
SECURITY-NATIONAL "AIRSTER", S-1-A.

Fig. 67. Security "Airster" S-1-A with 100 h.p. Kinner K5 engine.

Winfield B. "Bert" Kinner resigned from the Kinner Airplane & Motor Corp. in 1930 and devoted his efforts to designing the basic concept for the popular folding-wing Kinner "Sportster". More or less inactive for several years after, Bert Kinner however couldn't stay away from aircraft and engine development for very long; in early 1933 he organized a new corporation to manufacture his latest design. As the Security National Aircraft Corp. of Downey, Calif. the firm produced 2 examples of the Security "Airster" by mid-1933, a craft strikingly similar but far less expensive than the Kinner "Sportster". The new "Airster" model S-1 was the first full-sized airplane to sell for under $2000. Of the first 3 airplanes built at the former "Emsco" plant in Downey, the first was delivered to a dealer in Santa Monica, the second was delivered to Lee V. Brusse of Downey, and the third was groomed for certification tests to earn an ATC. Formal production of the "Airster" was begun on Dec. 1 of 1933 and tentative schedule was 2 aircraft per week. Among the satisfied owners of the new "Airster" was Edgar Rice Burroughs, author of the popular "Tarzan" stories; the plane was purchased by Mrs. Burroughs and kept at their villa in Palm Springs. Bert Kinner flew an "Airster" demonstrator to Palm Springs several times to show it off in the "film colony" of Hollywood

people. By mid-year of 1934 operations were moved to the Metropolitan Airport in Van Nuys, Calif. where Security-National had 4 large hangars and facilities for production were more suitable. In Nov. of 1934 "Bert" Kinner announced that the Security National Aircraft Corp. had completed and delivered its 15th "Airster" and schedules were being arranged to build 25 more. The company was also beginning manufacture of the new "Security" engine; a 5 cyl. aircooled radial type of 100 h.p., similar to the popular "Kinner K5" engine, the "Security S5" was designed for economy of operation and ease of maintenance. By late 1934 the "Airster" had been approved on Edo model I-1835 floats and the first seaplane was shipped to a flying service in Norway. Because of the lingering depression, aircraft manufacture was still a rocky road during these times; as of July in 1935, W. B. Kinner announced a temporary shut-down of the plant due to financial and legal difficulties. Actually, the temporary shut-down stayed in effect for several years. Subsequent moves were to the Los Angeles Airport in Inglewood and also to Glendale, Calif.; by 1937 the operation had moved to Long Beach, Calif. All listings of the "Airster" after 1935 stated that it was "not in production", but available on order.

The Security "Airster" model S-1-A was a trim low-winged open cockpit monoplane with

Fig. 68. The lean "Airster" was not far removed from its "Kinner" ancestry.

side-by-side seating for two. The roomy 47 in. wide cockpit was well protected by a large windshield designed to offer maximum protection and not interfere with the pleasures of an open-air ride. Pretty much a "Plain Jane" in outward appearance the "Airster" however had many interesting features that appealed to the private-owner pilot. Folding wings were easily operated by one person without tools, and secured to a width of only 9 feet for storage in just 3 minutes; the hinged swing-away motor mount allowed easy access to engine compartment for inspection and service. Designed specifically for the week-end pilot, the "Airster" was rugged of frame, and required a minimum of servicing. As powered with the 5 cyl. Kinner K5 engine of 100 h.p. the model S-1-A offered good performance, broad utility, and its simplicity paid off in dependable service. A rather large ship with long "moment arms" the "Airster" was comfortable to be in and rather pleasant to fly. A student-pilot in Oregon whose first airplane ride was also his first flying lesson, "soloed" in 3½ hours of dual instruction in an "Airster"; it was that easy. Operated mostly in the mountainous country of western U.S.A., the "Airster" accomplished full gross load take-offs quite easily at elevations up to 9000 ft.; at elevations above that something had to stay behind. The first two "Airster" model S-1 were manufactured under a Group 2 approval numbered 2-451 (issued 6-29-33) and the approved type certificate for the S-1-A was issued 11-15-33; some 12 or more of the model S-1-A were mfgd. by the Security National Aircraft Corp. at Downey and Van Nuys, Calif. As of early 1934, W. B. "Bert" Kinner was president; Sam C. Breder was sales mgr.; Lee V. Brusse was in charge of assembly and flight-test; and Benjamin Salmon was chf. engr. As of May 1935, W. B. Kinner was pres.; Max B. Harlow was chf. engr.; and W. B. Kinner, Jr. was the shop foreman. One of the last "Airster", manufactured in 1935, was shipped to Hawaii. For all practical purposes it would be safe to assume that production ceased on 7-1-35 when the approval expired; listings after that time noted "not in production—available on order". In 1937 a new ATC (approval) for the model S-1-B was pending.

Listed below are specifications and performance data for the Security "Airster" model S-

Fig. 69. Coupe-top for "Airster" was optional extra.

Fig. 70. "Airster" with folded wings occupied less space.

1-A as powered with the 100 h.p. Kinner K5 engine; length overall 23'11"; height overall 7'9"; wing span 40'0"; wing chord 84"; total wing area 238 sq.ft.; airfoil Clark Y; wt. empty 1197 lbs.; useful load 555 lbs.; payload with 23.5 gal. fuel 220 lbs. (1 passenger at 170 lbs. & 50 lbs. baggage); gross wt. 1752 lbs.; max. speed 100; cruising speed (.80 power) 88; landing speed 35; climb 800 ft. first min. at sea level; ser. ceiling 14,000 ft.; gas cap. 23.5 gal.; oil cap. 3 gal.; cruising range at 6.9 gal. per hour 300 miles; price $1985. at factory field. Amendment later allowed gross wt. of 1775 lbs. for installation of Heywood engine starter. Seaplane with Edo model I-1835 twin-float gear was allowed gross wt. of 1936 lbs.

The fuselage framework was built up of welded 4130 steel tubing scantily faired and covered with fabric. The large open cockpit had doors on either side for easy entry off the wing-walk; legroom was ample and the adjustable parachute-type seats were padded and placed well enough for hours of comfort. Dual stick controls were provided and wheel brakes were operated by extentions on the rudder pedals. The standard instrument panel was quite bare, but it did offer altimeter and basic engine gauges. A baggage compartment of 6 cu. ft. capacity with allowance for up to 50 lbs. was located in the fuselage behind the seats. The steel-tube engine mount was hinged at the firewall to swing to one side for easy access to accessory section of the engine. The robust wing framework, in 3 panels, was of solid spruce spars routed to I-beam section with spruce and plywood truss-type wing ribs; the leading edges were covered with dural metal sheet and the completed framework was covered in fabric. Outer wing panels were fastened to a 7'6" wide center section and braced to top fuselage longeron by streamlined steel tube

struts. The landing gear of 8'3" tread was of 2 simple tripod assemblys with spring-oil shock struts that were fastened to lower fuselage and outer point of stub-wing. Low-pressure tires on 6.50x10 wheels were fitted with brakes. A 6 in. full-swivel hard rubber tail wheel offered good ground control. As a seaplane the "Airster" was fitted with Edo model I-1835 twin-float gear; gross wt. allowance was 1936 lbs. with 50 lb. baggage allowance plus 23 lb. allowance for anchor and ropes. The fuel tank, of which 3.5 gal. was reserve supply, was mounted in front of the windshield. The fabric covered tail-group was built up of welded 4130 steel tubing into surfaces of high aspect ratio and large area for good low-speed control; the horizontal stabilizer was adjustable in flight. A wooden propeller was standard equipment. Exhaust collector-ring, a coupe-type canopy to fit over open cockpit, Edo floats, metal propeller (seaplane only), Heywood engine starter, and custom colors were optional. The next development of the Security "Airster" was the model S-1-B as described in chapter for ATC # 705.

Listed below are entries for Security "Airster" as gleaned from registration records:

NC-217Y:	S-1	(# 10)	Kinner K5.
NC-13702;	"	(# 11)	"
-13743;	S-1-A	(# 12)	"
-13746;	"	(# 13)	"
-13792;	"	(# 14)	"
-13793;	"	(# 15)	"
-13794;	"	(# 16)	"
-14227;	"	(# 17)	"
-14228;	"	(# 18)	"
-14229;	"	(# 19)	"
-14230;	"	(# 20)	"
-14231;	"	(# 21)	"
-14232;	"	(# 22)	"
-14293;	"	(# 23)	"

Serial # 10 was prototype registered in Calif. on 7-1-33; ser. # 11 reg. in Calif. on 9-1-33; ser. # 10 and # 11 as model S-1 on Group 2 memo # 2-451; ser. # 12 built as Special, modified to S-1-A as first ship on ATC—reg. in Calif. 1933; ser. # 13 reg. Calif. on 11-15-33 to Edgar Rice Burroughs; ser. # 14 reg. Calif. 1933; ser. # 15 reg. 1933 in Long Beach, Calif.; ser. # 16 reg. 1933 in Oregon; ser. # 17 reg. in 1934; ser. # 18 reg. 1934 in New York; ser. # 19 reg. Calif. 1934; ser. # 20 reg. to Cora M. Kinner, wife of Bert Kinner; ser. # 21 reg. 1934 to Security National Aircraft Corp. at Van Nuys, Calif.; ser. # 22 reg. Calif. 1934; ser. # 23 reg. 1935 to Cora M. Kinner, later reg. in Hawaii; seaplane that was delivered to Norway might have been Ser. # 24.

KINNER "SPORTWING", B-2.

Fig. 71. Kinner "Sportwing" B-2 with 125 h.p. Kinner B5 engine.

As a sport-type version of the standard "Sportster" the new "Sportwing" model B-2 was a rather neat and tidy addition to the Kinner aircraft line for the season of 1934. As the illustrations show it was clearly one of the more handsome light sport monoplanes of this period. Standing taut and rather high on streamlined landing gear "boots", with nearly 5 feet trimmed off from the standard wing span, it presented a somewhat cocky and adventurous appearance. There is no doubt, the "Sportwing" in its earliest examples was a very attractive airplane in its glossy coat of gleaming white and it turned heads wherever it went. The large tight-fitting NACA-type engine fairing, adorned with bulging streamlined "blisters" for cylinder head clearance, was another feature that set the "Sportwing" aside from the ordinary. In spite of its small number, only about 8 or 9 were built, the "Sportwing" B-2 became fairly well known by its good reputation and remained popular for years throughout the western states. One George Brent, popular male-lead of the movies, was a proud owner-pilot who enjoyed showing off his "Sportwing" to other Hollywood-ites on jaunts to western resort-towns; another proud owner felt justified to call his ship the "White Beauty". The following was small, but pride of ownership ran high. Largely confined to airports in the west

the Kinner "Sportwing" spent most of its years up and down the Pacific coast, or up among the nearby mountains.

The Kinner "Sportwing" model B-2, an attractive vehicle, was an open cockpit low-winged monoplane with side-by-side seating for two. Basically, it was a sport-type version of the standard "Sportster", but modification was so extensive that it became a distinct shape and a personality of its own. As introduced in the first few examples the "Sportwing" projected a very saucy appearance with its high stance on "wheel boots", and its "blistered" engine cowl; the all-white ensemble presented such a neat appearance it reminded one of a powdered and perfumed lady. Later modifications to the "Sportwing" configuration, with a change in the landing gear and removal of the big engine cowl, changed the face of it by quite a bit—so much so, they looked like different airplanes entirely. Perhaps there was reason enough to do this, we cannot say, but the rather pleasing effect of the earlier shape was lost. The later "Sportwing" type, of more conservative line and of heftier appearance, was eventually mated to a larger Kinner engine and became the B-2-R. Normally the "Sportwing" was operated with an open cockpit, which actually was comfortable enough, but a coupe-top enclosure was available to those

Fig. 72. "Sportwing" with variation in the landing gear.

who flew in colder climes. As powered with the 5 cyl. Kinner B5 engine of 125 h.p. the "Sportwing" delivered a good performance, but in the airplane's enthusiasm for everything it seemed like much more than you were actually getting. The shorter wing-span did improve the roll-rate and added considerably to improvement of overall manuverability. There was some difference in the behavior between earlier and later "Sportwing", however slight, that was instigated by the large engine cowl on the one hand, and also the big difference in landing gear configuration. The type certificate number for the "Sportwing" model B-2 was issued 5-2-34 with amendment issued 6-16-34 for more gross wt. allowance. At least 8 of the "Sportwing" were built by the Kinner Airplane & Motor Corp., Ltd. at Glendale, Calif. This ATC number was first issued to "Sportster" model B-1 on 12-1-33, but on 5-2-34 the ATC was amended for approval of the "Sportwing" model B-2 and the B-1 was then included on ATC # 516 with "Sportster" model B. As the year 1933 was brought to a close, only 26 ATC numbers were issued in that year.

Listed below are specifications and performance data for the "Sportwing" model B-2 as powered with 125 h.p. Kinner B5 engine; length overall 24'2"; height overall 7'2"; wing span 34'5"; wing chord (constant) 72"; total wing area (including fuselage portion) 199 sq.ft.; airfoil Clark Y; wt. empty 1317 (1323) lbs.; useful load 633 (627) lbs.; payload with 35 gal. fuel 235 (229) lbs.; gross wt. 1950 lbs.; max. speed 122; cruising speed (.85 power) 110; landing speed 48;

climb 850 ft. first min. at sea level; ser. ceiling 14,500 ft.; gas cap. 35 gal.; oil cap. 2.5 gal.; cruising range at 7.2 gal. per hour 450 miles; price $4600. at factory with optional equipment at extra cost. Amendment in 1935 changed wts. to 1333-627-269-2000 lbs.; performance was altered accordingly.

The fuselage framework was built up of welded chrome-moly steel tubing, faired liberally to an oval shape, then fabric covered. The open cockpit had side-by-side seating with entry from the wing-walk through door on left side; the large sport-type windshield was of shatter-proof glass. The short stub-wings were built integral to the fuselage for attachment of the cantilever landing gear and mounting of outer wing panels; the wing panels were braced to upper fuselage longeron with inverted-vee struts. A baggage compartment was also provided in each wing stub. The wing panels were built up of solid spruce spars routed to an I-beam section with spruce and plywood truss-type wing ribs; the leading edges were covered with dural metal sheet and the completed framework was covered in fabric. The landing gear was built up of 2 cantilever assemblies covered with streamlined metal boots; shock absorbers (oleo & spring) were Kinner-built and wheels were 6.50x10 with brakes. Landing gear on later model B-2 was nearly identical to that used on Kinner "Playboy", a type of gear quite popular on many racing and sport monoplanes. An 8x3 swiveling tail wheel was used for better ground handling. The fabric covered tail-group was built up of welded steel tubing; elevators were

Fig. 73. Last of the "Sportwing" series did not use NACA-type engine cowl.

equipped with adjustable "trim tabs". A wooden propeller, Eclipse air-operated engine starter, hot-shot battery, navigation lights, a compass, dual stick-type controls, radio shielding & bonding, parking brake, wheel brakes, chrome-plated exhaust collector-ring with tail-pipe, fire extinguisher, two baggage compartments, ad-

Fig. 74. Early Kinner "Sportwing" shows off its cowled engine and "booted" landing gear.

justable seat, first-aid kit, and tool kit were standard equipment. A metal propeller, radio, and coupe-top enclosure were optional. The next Kinner development was the "Envoy" model C-7 as described in chapter for ATC # 532 of this volume. The next "Sportwing" development was the model B-2-R (also as Timm 160) on ATC # 617.

Listed below are "Sportwing" B-2 entries as gleaned from registration records:

NC-13791;	B-2	(# 100)	Kinner B5.
-14200;	"	(# 120)	"
-13797;	"	(# 128)	"
-14214;	"	(# 130)	"
-14212;	"	(# 132)	"
-14224;	"	(# 140)	"
-14234;	"	(# 144)	"
-14927;	"	(# 148)	"

For Ser. # 100 through # 147 with 1950 lb. gross wt.; ser. # 148 and up eligible at 2000 lb. gross wt.; a 3 lb. balance weight (lead) in each aileron raised empty wt. by 6 lbs.; ser. # 144 (with coupe-top canopy) eligible at 1968 lbs. gross wt.; approval expired 6-30-39.

ATC # 523
(12-27-33)
KELLETT "AUTOGIRO", K-4.

Fig. 75. Kellett K-4 with 210 h.p. Continental engine featured improved rotor system.

After a slackening up of the "autogiro boom" in 1931-32 the Kellett firm began laying out a program of design for a new generation of autogiro aircraft. A new design with features promising to overcome most of the problems in low-speed control. This shortcoming of marginal low-speed control near the ground was still the one major thing that kept the "giro" from being a fool-proof airplane. The most promising avenue of development in this respect was the "direct-control" rotor system which would eventually eliminate the use of ineffective airplane-type control surfaces. The fixed wing or lateral stabilizer was the first appendage to be eliminated; the ailerons also then became unnecessary, and the usual tail-group would play only a small part in normal control of the 'giro in its flight range. The direct-control system was a bright new idea for the autogiro and the problems encountered in its perfection promised to take several years of design, test, and study. In the interim, Kellett had introduced the model K-4 as a normal progressive refinement of their standard utility design. Introduced to the flying public in June of 1933 the new model K-4 promised to offer higher cruising speeds, a greater cruising range, more comfort, improved flying qualities, and a better appearance. A few of the new ideas already tested for later use were incorporated into the model K-4, but in general, it was just an overall improvement over the

earlier K-2 and K-3. Several of the earlier (165 h.p.) K-2 had by now been modified into the model K-2-A (On Group 2 approval) which mounted the 210 h.p. Continental engine; the extra 45 h.p. literally forced the K-2 to perform a lot better. During this period (1932-33) the Kellett company was also engaged in further development of its sky-advertising (banner towing) "Sky Ads" business with contracts let to more than 200 advertisers around the country.

The Kellett model K-4 was basically a sport-type open cockpit autogiro with side by side seating for two. A demountable coupe-type canopy, easily installed and removed, was optional to provide cold-weather protection. Improvements to the fixed wing, the landing gear, the pylon, the rotor system, and fuselage, all had purpose to improve performance and efficiency, but in total this added slightly to the empty weight. A higher useful load allowed more fuel for greater range, and the loaded gross weight was slightly higher now (by 100 lbs.) than earlier models. As powered with the 7 cyl. Continental (Series 2) R-670 engine of 210 h.p. the model K-4 showed only small improvement in its total performance range, but overall, it was a much better airplane. As an optional installation, the new 225 h.p. Jacobs L-4 engine was also offered. It is of interest to note that the prototype version of the model K-4 series was actually built up from an early K-2 airframe, one that had already piled up many hours in service and demonstration. In view of the many extensive changes made to the airframe, we can say that it actually did become another airplane. The narrow, tapered semi-cantilever wing reduced the system of braces, and the simpler semi-cantilever landing gear presented far less drag. The redesigned rotor pylon was "cleaned up" considerably and the 4-bladed rotor system also showed some improvement. In the overall, the new model K-4 seemed to be a much better aircraft than either the K-2 or K-3, but its production did not go beyond the prototype example. The type certificate number for the model K-4 was issued 12-27-33 and apparently only one example of this model was built by the Kellett Autogiro Corp. of Philadelphia, Penna. W. Wallace Kellett was pres. and sales mgr.; C. T. Ludington was V.P.; R. G. Kellett was gen. mgr.; Richard H. Prewitt was chf. engr.; testing and promotion was conducted by various area pilots, including Guy Miller. Kellett and Prewitt were in England early 1934 to study recent developments in the autogiro by Juan de la Cierva, its inventor. By now, several Kellett autogiros had also been exported to Europe, Asia, and So. America.

Listed below are specifications and performance data for the Kellett model K-4 as powered with the 210 h.p. Continental R-670 engine; length overall 19'11"; height overall 12'3"; rotor dia. 40'6"; fixed wing span 24'7"; fixed wing chord 45" at root, tapered to tip; rotor disc area 1300 sq.ft.; fixed wing area 63.5 sq.ft.; fixed wing airfoil Clark Y; wt. empty 1707 lbs.; useful load 655 lbs.; payload with 42 gal. fuel 195 lbs. (1 passenger at 170 lbs. & 25 lbs. baggage); gross wt. 2362 lbs.; max. speed 110; cruising speed 95; landing speed 0-15; climb 1000 ft. first min. at sea level; ser. ceiling 5500 ft.; absolute ceiling 13,500 ft.; gas cap. 42 gal.; oil cap. 5 gal.; cruising range at 12.5 gal. per hour 310 miles; price not announced. Gross wt. later increased to 2400 lbs. to allow for coupe-top enclosure and slight increase in payload allowance.

The fuselage framework was built up of welded chrome-moly and 1025 steel tubing, heavily faired to shape with formers and fairing strips, then fabric covered. Dural metal panels covered the whole forward portion of fuselage to edge of cockpit. The wide, open cockpit offered comfortable side-by-seating for two with a large door on each side for exit or entry. An optional coupe-top canopy, installed in just minutes, was offered for coldweather comfort; a baggage compartment with allowance for up to 65 lbs. was in turtleback section behind the seat-back. Seat cushions were thick and resilient for comfort and dual joy-sticks were provided. The tapered semi-cantilever wing (fixed) was built up with solid spruce spar beams and spruce wing ribs, then covered with plywood sheet; the familiar "tip shields" had been eliminated. Angle of incidence was 1.5 deg. and dihedral was 12 deg. The wide-stance semi-cantilever landing gear used long-travel "Kellett" shock absorbers that formed a firm truss with the wing-bracing struts; 8.50x10 semi-airwheels with mechanical (cable operated) Autofan brakes were standard equipment. The streamlined semi-cantilever rotor pylon mounted 4 blades that swung a 40'6" arc; cables kept the blades 90 deg. apart and anti-droop cables kept the blades from sagging to the ground. An engine-driven shaft and clutch arrangement permitted bringing rotor blades up to proper speed for take-off; the rotor "starter" was disengaged for actual flight. The main fuel tank was mounted in lower fuselage under the seat and a small header tank was mounted behind instrument panel; fuel was pumped by the engine from main tank to "header tank" where it then flowed to the engine by gravity feed. A 5 gal. oil tank was mounted in engine compartment. The fabric covered tail group was built up of wooden spar beams and wooden ribs; there was now more fin area and less rudder area, but horizontal surfaces were same as on earlier K-2. A large swiveling tail wheel was provided for better ground handling. A metal propeller, electric engine starter, fuel pump, complete set of normally used engine and flight instruments, a compass, navigation lights, and fire extinguisher were standard equipment. The K-4 was available in custom colors of any combination. A coupe-top enclosure and Jacobs L-4 engine were optional. The next development in the Kellett autogiro was the model KD-1, a direct-control 'giro, as described in chapter for ATC # 712.

Listed below is only known example of model K-4:

NC-11666; Model K-4 (# 23) Continental 210.

Ser. # 23 (NC-11666) was first as model K-2 with ser. # 3.

ATC # 524
(1-3-34)
BOEING, MODEL 247-A.

Fig. 76. Boeing 247-A provided luxurious transport for "United" officials while testing new double-row engines.

The twin-engined Boeing model 247-A was designed as an "executive transport" for the United Aircraft & Transport Corp., differing mainly from the standard Model 247 by its powerplant installation and its cabin interior. The interior was laid out plushly for the comfort of 6 passengers, with a special heating and ventilation system to assure the maximum in creature comforts. Actually, the 247-A was primarily designed as a test-bed for the new twin-row Pratt & Whitney "Twin Wasp Junior" engines, but to give it just a little more purpose it was fitted as a plush transport for officers of the "United" corporation. Engine nacelles were redesigned and the "speed rings" were broadened to shroud the deeper double-row engines. Extra tanks boosted the fuel capacity to 356 gals. for fewer stops on hurried transcontinental flights. The prototype installation was the P & W SGR-1535 engines rated 625 h.p. at 2400 r.p.m. at 7000 ft.; a first-flight on 9-14-33 proved that here Boeing had a promising combination. Rapid development of the twin-row "Twin Wasp Junior" engine prompted installation of the newer S1A1G engines rated 660 h.p. at 2400 r.p.m. at 7000 ft. The 247-A responded admirably to all this extra power and executives were pleased with its comfort and performance; imagine plush "club car" comfort at 7000 ft. at 3 miles a minute. Generally flown by genial "Ben-

ny" Whelan, the 247-A logged some 3000 hours from 1933 to 1942, and as far as Whelan was concerned it was a transport that was a truly good airplane and pretty hard to beat. In its 14 year career the 247-A was always ready for any job, tough or not, and it did them all easily without ceremony; among its normal chores the 247-A carried out 2 mercy flights successfully to save the lives of a girl and a young woman. In its entire career, which radiated out of Hartford, Conn., it never had an accident, not even a little one, and finally was scrapped in 1947.

The Boeing model 247-A monoplane was a low-winged, all-metal, twin-engined airliner especially refurbished as an executive transport. Designed to carry only 2 pilots and 6 passengers, the interior arrangement was strung-out in luxurious fashion to provide the utmost in creature comforts. To provide a little more purpose for the airplane it was also used as a flying test-bed for the recently introduced double-row "Twin Wasp Junior" engines. In prototype, the 247-A was the lightest of the 247 series; it also had the lowest wing loading and the lowest power loading which assured it the lowest landing speeds, the quickest takeoffs, and the best climb-out. It had exceptional ability to operate out of even the smallest airfields and pilots praised it continually for this remarkable ability. As powered with 2 Pratt & Whitney SGR-1535

Fig. 77. 247-A preparing to leave on a night flight; its entire 14-year career was unmarred by accidents.

engines rated 625 h.p. each, the 247-A cruised at 3 miles a minute and top speed was almost 200 m.p.h. As development of the "Twin Wasp Junior" engines continued, the newer S1A1G engines were installed for test; rated 660 h.p. each at 7000 ft. the newer engines perked up the performance, but this performance was soon traded off for (695 lbs.) more gross weight allowance. Then, as the 247-A Special, the transport was equipped with two SA7G engines rated 655 h.p. each and gross weight allowance was jacked up to 13,650 lbs.; even at this stage the 247-A was still one of the best of the Model 247, but it had lost some of its earlier get-up-and-go. The type certificate number for the 247-A was issued 1-3-34 and amended on 5-29-34. Only one example of this model was built by the Boeing Airplane Co. at Seattle, Wash. Claire L. Egtvedt was pres. & gen. mgr.; Erik H. Nelson was V.P. in charge of sales; and C. N. Monteith was V.P. in chg. of engrg.

Listed below are specifications and performance data for the Boeing model 247-A as powered with two 625 h.p. SGR-1535 engines; length overall 51'4"; height overall 16'5"; wing span 74'0"; wing chord at root 180"; wing chord at tip 88"; total wing area 836 sq.ft.; airfoil Boe-ing 106 modified; wt. empty 8975 lbs.; useful load 3430 lbs.; payload with 356 gal. fuel 750 lbs. (3 passengers at 170 lbs. each & 240 lbs. baggage); payload with 290 gal. fuel 1150 lbs. (6 passengers at 170 lbs. each & 130 lbs. baggage); gross wt. 12,405 lbs.; max. speed 198; cruising speed (.60 power) 170 at 12,000 ft.; stall speed 55; landing speed 62; climb 1170 ft. first min. at sea level; ser. ceiling 22,700 ft.; gas cap. normal 290 gal.; gas cap. max. 356 gal.; oil cap. 26 gal.; normal cruising range 1000 miles; price approx. $75,000.

As a ten-place airplane (2 pilots & 8 passengers) the 247-A was allowed 13,100 lb. gross wt.; approved wts. were now 8620-4480-1800-13,100 lbs. with S1A1G engines rated 660 h.p. at 7000 ft., eligible also as 247-A Special with SA7G engines rated 655 h.p. at 7000 ft., allowing 2290 lb. payload and 13,650 lbs. gross wt.; the performance varied considerably from the prototype version; absolute ceiling with one engine out was 6800 ft.

The construction details and general arrangement of the Boeing 247-A were typical to that of the "Model 247" as described in chapter for ATC # 500, that is, except for interior arrangement and installation of more powerful engines.

Fig. 78. Model 247-A shows off its twin-row "Wasp Jr." engines.

The interior of the 247-A executive-transport was specially fitted in "club car" comfort for the enjoyment of "United" executives. Plush seating for 6 was arranged informally about a center aisle that meandered through cabin area; each passenger had access to a reading lamp, gadget pocket, ash-tray, and assist cords. A special "air conditioning" system provided the desired amount of ventilation or heat. All interior decor and appointments were designed for restful and pleasant cross-country travel. Later in its service life the 247-A capacity was extended to 8 passengers and 2 pilots; the interior was then rearranged closer to airline standards. Engine nacelles of the 247-A were designed especially for installation of the new "Twin Wasp Junior" which were encased in deep-chord "speed rings" to cowl the double-row radial engines. Later modifications to the 247-A included newer "Twin Wasp Junior" engines rated 660 h.p., slightly redesigned nacelles and engine cowlings, redesigned radio antennas, and a vertical fin and rudder of the 247-D configuration. One 178 gal.

fuel tank was mounted in each wing stub to provide 356 gal. max. capacity for extended range; normal fuel load was generally less than 300 gals. Baggage compartments were forward and aft, with a complete lavatory in the aft section with convenient access from the cabin area. Three-bladed metal fixed-pitch propellers, electric engine starters, an engine-driven generator, battery, engine-driven fuel pump, emergency wobble-pump, a two-way radio, shielding and bonding, dual control wheels, fire extinguishers, lavatory, and first-aid kit were standard equipment. The next development in the "Model 247" series was the 247-D as described in chapter for ATC # 558 of this volume.

Listed below is the only example of the model 247-A:

NC-13300; Model 247-A (# 1711) 2 Twin Wasp Junior.

This approval for ser. # 1711 only; registered alternately to United Aircraft & Transport Corp. or Pratt & Whitney Div.; approval expired 9-30-39.

ATC # 525
(2-16-34)
TAYLOR "CUB", F-2.

Fig. 79. The "Cub" F-2 had a short romance with the 3 cyl. Aeromarine engine, but the affair didn't last.

C. Gilbert Taylor, innovator and designer of the popular Taylor "Cub", was not entirely happy with the 4 cyl. Continental A-40 engine of 37 h.p., so he was always on the look-out for another suitable engine. As new engines in the 30-40 h.p. range became available, naturally, they had to be considered for use on the "Cub". When the 3 cyl. Aeromarine AR3-40 engine became available in some quantity, it had already been tried out on the two-seated Rearwin "Junior" model 4000, so there was at least some previous operating record to recommend it. The likeable little "Cub", as powered with the 3 cyl. radial-type AR3-40, altered only from the firewall forward, was now labeled the model F-2. Some pilots enjoyed the new engine, saying that it had a healthy bit of thrust, but some remarked it was just a new set of irritations to put up with. Flying extensively behind any light-plane engine of this early day was mostly a matter of cultivating familiarity and a large degree of trust. This can be pictured well by the fact that some owners of the earlier Continental-powered model E-2 hastened to convert their ships into the Aeromarine-powered F-2; then again, some owners of the new F-2

eventually prefered to convert their ships to the (Continental A-40 powered) model E-2. The "Cub" itself, bless her soul, was not as finicky as its pilots and did very well on most any of the small engines, as long as they kept running for a reasonable length of time. Forced landings, due to some slight engine malfunction, were not unusual, but there was always some place to "set her down". The "Cub" was most always the busiest airplane on the airport; many flocked to it for the economy (flying time was cheap), but there were others that came to fly it just for the novelty of it.

Like the Taylor "Cub" model E-2, the model F-2 was an open-sided parasol-type monoplane with seating arranged for two in tandem. A large curved windshield up front transformed the open cockpit into a semi-cabin affair, but this did not lessen the sporty atmosphere of flying out in the open. As an option, the F-2 could be equipped with a rather flimsy detachable enclosure to take some of the bite out of cold weather flying. The demountable cabin sides were often called "storm shelters", even in technical description! Boxy, with square corners all over the place, the F-2 was rather large and generally impressed one of being a real airplane and not just a "flying flivver". The "Cub" was more closely identified with the "flat four" engine, so the F-2 with its 3 cyl. "radial" engine did look a little odd, more like a "Cub" that had been tampered with. However, the "Aeromarine" engine was a fairly good powerplant for its day, and it got along quite well with the eccentricities of the "Cub". As powered with the 3 cyl. Aeromarine AR3-40 engine rated 40 h.p. at 2050 r.p.m. the F-2 was credited with a very substantial increase in performance over the E-2, but it is hard to concede that the difference was actually as much as reported. Some improvement was naturally to be expected, but the amount of difference shouldn't have been all that noticeable. The AR3-40 as used in the F-2 was "de-rated" to 40 h.p. from its normal rating of 50 h.p.; perhaps the pilots knew ways of getting the full 50 h.p.—this would make a good deal of difference. There were enough "Cubs" flying by now, in all parts of the country, to prove that it was an exceptionally rugged airplane, and if it was broken up it was quite easy to fix. Everyone marveled that an airplane with such strength and stamina could fly so well on relatively low power. Some of the things that were possible when a "Cub" and a pretty good pilot got together were amazing. The Taylor "Cub" was not the nicest flying airplane by any means, but it flew good, was quite permissive, and very good-natured; it was perhaps the safest airplane ever built for the amateur pilot, especially in some of its later versions. The type certificate number for the "Cub" model F-2 was issued 2-16-34 with amendment on 4-21-34 and nearly 30 examples of this model were built by the Taylor Aircraft Co. on Emery Airport in Bradford, Penn. C. Gilbert Taylor was pres. & gen. mgr.; Wm. T. Piper was sec-treas.; T. V. Weld was sales mgr.; Walter C. Jamouneau was asst. engr.; and Mary Alice Babb took care of all the office work. To promote some sales in the winter of 1934-35, Bill Piper, Jr. (son of Wm. T. Piper) made a demonstration trip to the west coast; the "Cub" and its pilot were well received.

Listed below are specifications and performance data for the Taylor "Cub" model F-2 as powered with 40 h.p. Aeromarine AR3-40 engine; length overall 22'0"; height overall 6'8"; wing span 35'3"; wing chord 63"; total wing area 184 sq. ft.; airfoil USA-35B; wt. empty 538 (545) lbs.; useful load 412 (405) lbs.; payload with 9 gal. fuel 181 (174) lbs.; gross wt. 950 lbs.; figures in parentheses with winter enclosure; max. speed (with enclosure) 92; cruising speed 82; landing (stall) speed 38; climb 600 ft. first min. at sea level; ser. ceiling 13,000 ft.; gas cap. 9 gal.; oil cap. 4 qts.; cruising range at 2.9 gal. per hour 240 miles; price $1495. at factory field, or $895. without engine and propeller. Approved wts. as of 2-16-34 were 536-407-943 lbs., amended to 538-412-950 lbs.; later changed to (with winter enclosure) wts. of 545-405-950 lbs.; sometime

later gross wt. allowance was boosted to 988 lbs.

The construction details and general arrangement of the "Cub" F-2 were typical to that of the model E-2 (ATC # 455) except for its powerplant installation and any changes necessary for this combination. The Aeromarine AR3 engine normally developed 50 h.p. at 2125 r.p.m. (with twin ignition), but as used in the F-2 the AR3 was operated with a restriction plug in the induction system, smaller fuel jets, and single ignition to hold it down to 40 h.p. at 2050 r.p.m. The AR3-40 engine weighed 140 lbs. and cost $510.00 (crated) with single magneto ($560.00 with dual magnetos). The "Aeromarine" plant was building up one engine per week at this time. The two-place cockpit was well protected by a large Pyralin windshield, but not enough to spoil the enjoyment of an open-air ride; entry and exit was by way of a large let-down door on the right side. The optional cabin enclosure (with weight of 7 lb.) was not noticeably "faster" than the open sides, but it did make a "cleaner" airplane and kept gusts out of the cockpit during certain manuvers. The interior was sparsely furnished in true "Cub" fashion, but for normal short hops it was adequate. A small bin behind the rear seat was allowed 5 lbs. of "baggage", which generally turned out to be a tool kit and tie-down ropes. The fuel tank, of 9 gal. capacity, was mounted high in the fuselage ahead of the windshield, using a float-bobber fuel gauge that bobbed up and down to show the tank's content. The split-axle landing gear of 56 in. tread was sprung by "Rusco" aero-cord shocks using 16x7-3 or 7.00x4 Goodyear airwheels; no brakes were provided. Larger 8.00x4 Goodyear airwheels with brakes were optional. The "Cub" F-2 was also eligible on skis. One example of the F-2 was mounted on floats to operate as a seaplane, but was restricted to pilot only. A wooden Sensenich propeller, and dual stick controls were standard equipment. Standard color schemes were variously as red and silver, blue and silver, black and yellow, or blue and yellow; fuselage was of the darker colors. The next "Cub" development was the rare model H-2 as described in chapter for ATC # 572 of this volume.

Listed below are "Cub" F-2 entries as gleaned from registration records:

NC-12668;	F-2	(# 40)	AR3-40.
-13117;	"	(# 47)	"
-2735;	"	(# 66)	"
X-13272;	"	(# 74)	"
-825M;	"	(# 75)	"
-826M;	"	(# 76)	"
-744N;	"	(# 77)	"
-745N;	"	(# 78)	"
-2142;	"	(# 87)	"
NC-14308;	"	(# 89)	"
-14309;	"	(# 90)	"
-14344;	"	(# 100)	"
-14345;	"	(# 101)	"
-14346;	"	(# 102)	"
-14347;	"	(# 103)	"

-14348;	``	(# 104)	``
-14354;	``	(# 110)	``
PP-TAW;	``	(#)	``
PP-TBH;	``	(# 113)	``
PP-TBK;	``	(# 114)	``
PP-TDH;	``	(# 115)	``
NC-14387;	``	(# 126)	``
-14388;	``	(# 127)	``
-14389;	``	(# 128)	``
-14709;	``	(# 131)	``
-14712;	``	(# 134)	``
-14713;	``	(# 135)	``
-14730;	``	(# 137)	``
-14731;	``	(# 138)	``

-14732;	``	(# 139)	``
-14733;	``	(# 140)	``
-14734;	``	(# 141)	``
-14736;	``	(# 143)	``

This approval for ser. # 40,66,74 and up; PP-TAW (ser. no. unknown), PP-TBH (#113), PP-TBK (#114), PP-TDH (#115) as F-2 in Brazil; PP-TDH as seaplane (F-2S) first reg. in U.S.A. as X-14729; ser. # 40, 47, 66, 75, 76, 77, 78, 110, 131, 143 first as model E-2; ser. # 74, 104, 127, 134, 135, 140 later converted to E-2; approval expired 4-24-37.

ATC # 526
(2-19-34)
FLEET, MODEL 11.

Fig. 80. Fleet Model 11 with 160 h.p. Kinner R5 engine; ship shown exported to Mexico.

The Fleet "Model 11" was primarily developed for military uses, especially slanted to export in smaller foreign countries, but also offered here in the U.S.A. as a high performance sport-plane. Not particularly endowed with smooth flowing lines nor bedecked with some of the finery and niceties offered by other sport-planes of this time the "Fleet 11" would appeal more to the rough-and-tumble type of sportsman. Not a new airplane, it is well apparent that the Model 11 was basically another "Fleet" biplane, quite similar to the Model 10, but there was actually enough variation in its makeup to set it apart from the others. The most significant change was of course the larger Kinner R5 engine that sent 35 more horsepower thumping through the brawny frame, an "extra kick" which translated into increased load limits and a considerable increase in all-round performance. Noted also was a high cowl line for better cockpit protection and an improved tail-group configuration for more positive control in the lower speed ranges. All the other improvements, mostly not noticeable, were of a structural and mechanical nature. There can be no doubt that the "Fleet 11" could have been an admirable sporting-type airplane, well capable to satisfy the needs and the ego of the flying sportsman, but in a comparison with the many beautiful sport-plane offerings of this period, it

failed to excite much interest. It is not known just how many examples of the Model 11 were built, and perhaps no more than 2 were in use in this country; some were actually exported as sport-planes to neighboring countries, but it is quite likely they soon ended up in military service. The "Fleet" trainer was eventually developed into several more models after this, but except for an experimental version or two, all were designed for military uses and none were offered on the civil airplane market.

The "Fleet" Model 11 was an open cockpit biplane with seating arranged for two in tandem; still in the form of lean and brawny lines that made little effort to hide all the muscle that lay underneath. Basically, the "Eleven" was also a pilot-trainer, but it was more concerned with very advanced stages of flight and introduced the fledgling pilot to the intricate art of aerial warfare. Quickly arranged for the various jobs the Model 11 was prepared to teach aerial gunnery to both pilot and observer; various racks were provided for practice in bombing, a camera could be mounted to teach the intricasies of aerial photography, and radio gear was installed for excursions into ground support and reconnaiscance. The versatality of the "Eleven" was such that it could be used first in teaching these various military functions and then could be equipped with military loads and apparatus to

Fig. 81. Fleet Model 10-G with 4 cyl. "Gipsy" engine was designed for European markets.

carry out these various functions, or missions, in actual small-scale warfare. As powered with the 5 cyl. Kinner R5 engine of 160 h.p. the "Fleet 11" was actually a much better trainer than a warplane, but its utility and operating economy were well suited to needs of small foreign countries engaging in self-defense on a small budget. Performance and flight characteristics of the "Eleven" were no doubt typical of the various other "Fleet" types, except that the added power sharpened up manuverability, climb-out was considerably improved, service ceiling was extended, and a little was added to top speed. The type certificate number for the Model 11 (land

or sea) was issued 2-19-34 with amendments attached on 3-16-34 and 4-13-34. The bulk of the "Eleven" were exported, but the amount of examples built is unknown. Manufactured by Fleet Aircraft, Inc. at Buffalo, N.Y. a div. of the Consolidated Aircraft Corp. Rueben Hollis Fleet was pres.; Lawrence D. Bell was V.P. and gen. mgr.; Ray P. Whitman was V.P. and asst. mgr.; I. M. Laddon was chf. engr.

As a military vehicle the "Model 11" was of more complicated nature than most of its (Fleet) sister-ships, and aspired to be much more than just an ordinary pilot-trainer. Touted by its manufacturer as a practical and economical

Fig. 82. Fleet 11-32 was high altitude model with extra wing area.

Fig. 83. Model 11 retains basic lines of the classic "Fleet" design.

fighter-bomber trainer for the smaller foreign countries, the Model 11 was slightly heavier because of provisions for installation of bomb-racks, and both flexible and fixed machine guns; the greater power (160 h.p.) was of course necessary to handle the weight of extra chores. Late in 1933 it was reported that 6 of the new "Model 11" were delivered to the Mexican government for a military pilot-school operating in Mexico City. During 1934 and into 1935, "Fleet" trainers were delivered and operating in Argentina, Brazil, Canada, Northern China, So. China, Colombia, Cuba, Guatemala, also in Hong Kong, Japan, Mexico, Paraguay, Peru, Portugal, Roumania, Russia, Siam, Spain, and Turkey. Later in the year of 1935, Consolidated reported orders for 70 more of the "Fleet" trainers for delivery to various foreign countries; it is not known how many of these were the Model 11. The Fleet model 10-G with an air-cooled inline engine (as shown) was especially developed for the European military markets and the Model 11 with a radial aircooled engine was developed primarily for foreign military markets in our own hemisphere. After a year-long study of suitable factory sites in California, both San Diego and Long Beach were favored, Consolidated finally decided to move their operations to San Diego; work on the new plant-site was started in Nov. of 1933. All tooling and manufacturing rights for the "Fleet" biplane were sold to Brewster Aeronautical Corp. of Long Island City, New York on 4-6-39. Over 500 "Fleet" biplanes were delivered by mid-1935; how many were actually built altogether is not known, but some estimates name a thousand at least.

Listed below are specifications and perfor-mance data for the Fleet model 11 as powered with 160 h.p. Kinner R5 engine; length overall 21'8"; height overall 7'9"; wing span upper & lower 28'0"; wing chord upper & lower 45"; wing area upper 99.7 sq.ft.; wing area lower 94.7 sq.ft.; total wing area 194 sq.ft.; airfoil Clark Y-15; wt. empty 1155 (1175) lbs.; useful load 625 (565) lbs.; payload with 27 gal. fuel 250 (190) lbs.; payload with 52 gal. fuel 100 (40) lbs.; gross wt. 1780 (1740) lbs.; figures in parentheses as amended in 1935; 2 parachutes at 20 lbs. each as part of the payload; max. speed (sea level) 124; cruising speed (.85 power) 109; landing (stall) speed 48; climb 1170-1100 ft. first min. at sea level; ser. ceiling 17,800 ft.; gas cap. normal 27 gal.; gas cap. max. (with belly tank) 52 gal.; oil cap. 3 gal.; normal cruising range at 9.5 gal. per hour 296 miles; max. cruising range (52 gal.) 530 miles; price not announced.

The construction details and general arrange-ment of the Model 11 were typical to that of the models 1-2-7-10, including the following. The beefy wings were of solid (laminated) spruce spar beams with heat-treated and anodized dural metal wing ribs covered in fabric. The fuselage framework was built up of welded chrome-moly steel tubing slightly faired with dural metal strips and fabric covered. Windshields were of Pyralin; normally the front cockpit was the master cockpit. Dual stick-type controls were provided; brake pedals in both cockpits were op-tional. Normal fuel cap. of 27 gal. was in upper wing; a "belly tank" provided 25 gal. extra fuel and a fuselage tank (mounted in front cockpit) provided an additional 35 gal. fuel. A hand operated wobble-pump delivered fuel from belly tank to wing tank; when 35 gal. fuselage tank was installed the airplane was single-seater.

Provisions to mount bomb-racks and various armament was optional. The fabric covered tail-group was built up of welded chrome-moly steel formers and tubing; empennage shape was usually similar to that of the Model 10 and horizontal stabilizer was adjustable in flight. The landing gear of 77 in. tread was equipped with "Consolidated" air-oil shock struts (7 in. travel) and 6.50x10 Autofan wheels with brakes; 6.50x-10 wheels were fitted with 7.50x10 or 8.50x10 low-pressure (2 ply) tires. The "Eleven" was also eligible as seaplane on Edo # 2260 twin-float gear. The Kinner R5 engine (with front exhaust) was rated 160 h.p. at 1975 r.p.m.; the newer (Type 2) R5 engine was also available. A high-altitude wing cellule of 32 ft. span was also available for the Fleet 11; the added area permitted operation with normal gross loads at higher elevations. Rigging of standard (28 ft.) wings was 23 in. positive stagger, angle of incidence upper & lower none, dihedral upper none, dihedral lower was 4 degs. Standard color scheme was yellow wings and horizontal tail surfaces with blue fuselage, vertical tail surfaces, landing gear and interplane struts. As a relatively new process, all aluminum and dural parts of the Fleet 11, except castings and forgings, were "anodized" to combat corrosion. A leaf-spring tail skid, Curtiss-Reed metal propeller, carburetor heat control, fire extinguisher, first-aid kit, and tool kit were standard equipment. A Hamilton-Standard ground-adjustable metal propeller, Heywood engine starter, Exide battery, belly tank, extra fuselage tank, instruments in both cockpits, navigation lights, compass, metal front cockpit cover, and Edo pontoons were optional.

As a military vehicle the "Fleet 11" was used in these various combinations: trainer (dual) landplane, trainer (dual) seaplane, pursuit-observation, cross-country two-seater (seaplane) long range, pursuit (single seater) short & long range, pursuit (single seater) seaplane, and bomber (single seater) short & long range; other missions were optional.

Listed below is only "Fleet 11" entry in the register:

X-14705: Fleet 11 (# 549) Kinner R5

Ser. # 549 also listed as Model 11-32, so it must have been equipped with 32 ft. wing span; only other airplane known to be powered with Kinner R5 engine was a Fleet "Model 2 Modified" (#201) bearing registration NR-625M; in 1932 a Dr. Ross Sutherland was flying a "Fleet" biplane powered with 160 h.p. Kinner R5 engine on visits (as consulting physician) to hospitals in California and Arizona—no other information was available.

ATC # 527
(2-26-34)
GENERAL (CLARK), GA-43A.

Fig. 84. General GA-43A shows its sleek form; a 715 h.p. "Cyclone" engine up front.

As a little-known example in the early development of the so-called modern airliner, the Clark (General) GA-43 fairly bristled with one innovation after another; it must certainly be considered as one of the most advanced single-engined transports to come out of this (1931-34) period. Based on a desire to provide safe, comfortable, and fast transportation at low cost per seat-mile, the design features were calculated to offer the most favorable difference between operating costs and revenue collected. Only the use of advanced design techniques, the use of revolutionary metal structure, the use of highly advanced engines running on high-octane fuels, and newly learned aerodynamic concepts had made this type of airplane possible. As an airliner the GA-43 carried 10 or 11 passengers occupying a spacious cabin in lavish comfort, a cabin ventilated and heated, remarkably free from vibrations, and so quiet that normal conversation was possible nearly from one end to the other. With all of this to offer it is quite ironic that its future was stifled by the corporate and financial problems of two failing aircraft companies that had nurtured its development.

Almost ignored here in the U.S.A. as a contender in the airline market, the second example of the GA-43 was built nearly a year later to the order of "Swissair" (Swiss Air Traffic Co., Ltd.); the craft was in scheduled use for better than 2 years on Alpine routes to Germany and Austria. The third airplane built was retained as a company demonstrator and was the only GA-43 to remain here in this country. A fourth example, actually the only one to be awarded an ATC approval, was used for a time by General Air Lines (formerly Western Air Express) on its mid-continent division serving a run from Cheyenne to Albuquerque; here the GA-43 enjoyed only brief service and it too was delivered to "Swissair" where it was active for at least another year. The prototype airplane, after more test-flights, more redesign and alteration, was delivered to Japan for their study of design and construction techniques. A fifth and final airplane was delivered to an affiliate line of Pan American Airways (SCADTA) as a twin-float seaplane (GA-43J); it operated briefly but successfully on the Magdalena River in Colombia, South America. Despite all that it had to

Fig. 85. Men responsible for prototype which started out as Fairchild (Pilgrim) 150.

offer the big, sleek, GA-43 was built only in the 5 examples and these were wanderers scattered widely to four different continents.

The GA-43 transport had its beginning (in 1931) at the Fairchild plant as the "Model 150". It was inherited from Fairchild into the "Pilgrim" line of airplanes when the American Airplane & Engine corp. took over at Farmingdale. As a design by the well-known Virginius E. Clark the "One Fifty" embodied many of the newest ideas in clean aerodynamic arrangement and in metal semi-monocoque structure. M. Gould "Dan" Beard, former Fairchild test-pilot, took the "150" up on its maiden flight 5-22-32 and commented that it flew beautifully and showed great promise for its intended role of high-speed transport. Tests continued on the fixed-gear version and on 6-17-32 it was tested with a retractable landing gear, accounting for a 16 m.p.h. increase in top speed. All this time a concerted effort was made to promote the airplane, but no orders were in sight. With a termination of practically all production at "American" by Sept. the "150" project was sold to the General Aviation Corp.

(later as General Aviation Mfg. Corp.); with 600 lbs. of Model 150 spare parts on board, Beard delivered it to Dundalk, Md. on 9-12-32. Further development and some redesign by the "General" engineering staff at Dundalk (in the former Curtiss-Caproni plant) had transformed the "One Fifty" into a Model GA-43. Testing and demonstration of this prototype airplane continued for many months, including an evaluation at Wright Field by the Army Air Corps; interest in its capabilities were developing, but still no orders in sight. Perhaps a year later, a second example was built to the order of "Swissair" and shortly after a third airplane was built as a company demonstrator. A merging of General Aviation with Berliner-Joyce late in 1933 had formed North American Aviation, Inc.; a holding company, with Ernest R. Breech as its president. Later that year the capable J. H. "Dutch" Kindelberger was appointed president and perhaps a year later "North American" ceased to be a holding company and became an operating company. In 1935, "North American" won a contract for basic trainers (Army BT-9) which eventually led to its move to

Fig. 86. Seaplane version (GA-43J) was tested for service in So. America.

Fig. 87. GA-43A of "Swissair" was familiar sight on Alpine routes to Germany and Austria.

California and a great prominence in the aircraft manufacturing field.

The General GA-43A was an all-metal low-winged monoplane transport with seating arranged for 11 passengers and a pilot, or 10 passengers and 2 pilots. Borrowing a useful feature from the earlier "Pilgrim 100" the pilots were housed forward and up high where they could maintain a commanding view of any piloting situation. The plush cabin, as shown, was fitted with leather-covered reclining seats that were spaced well for room and comfort. Ventilation and cabin heat assured a comfortable interior and down-filled cabin walls assured a quiet ride. As powered with the 9 cyl. Wright "Cyclone" R-1820-F1 engine rated 715 h.p. the GA-43A had ample performance while sustaining cruising speeds of better than 170 m.p.h. From the pilot's point of view the "General" was well-balanced for nearly effortless control and its flying qualities (behavior) were pleasant and excellent. Operation was generally simple and maintenance was simplified. A seaplane version (GA-43J), built for an affiliate of Pan American Airways, was mounted on Edo 36-9225 floats and performed quite admirably in South American service. The type certificate number for the "General" model GA-43A was issued 2-26-34 with amendments awarded on 3-24-34 and 4-14-34; amendment of 4-28-34 allowed use of the SR-1820-F3 engine rated 710 h.p. at 5000 ft.—empty weight and useful load where then listed as variable. A total of 5 examples in the GA-43 series were manufactures by the General Aviation Mfg. Corp. at Dundalk (Baltimore), Md., a division of North American Aviation, Inc. Ernest R. Breech was pres.; Temple N. Joyce was V.P. and gen. mgr.; F. S. Hubbard was asst. mgr.; Victor E. Bertrandias was sales mgr. and chf. pilot; W. H. Miller was chf. engr.; and M. L. Winter was factory supt. Breech was succeeded as president by J. H. Kindelberger in mid-1933. Victor Bertrandias sailed to the Far East in late 1933 on company promotion; Chas. Froesch then became sales

and service mgr. By Jan. of 1935, General Aviation Mfg. was dissolved and the General Air Lines was dissolved shortly thereafter.

Listed below are specifications and performance data for the General GA-43A as powered with 715 h.p. "Cyclone" R-1820-F1 engine; length overall 43'1"; height overall 12'6"; wing span 53'0"; wing chord at root approx. 11 ft.; wing chord at tip approx. 5.5 ft.; total wing area (including fuselage portion) 464 sq.ft.; airfoil Clark Y; wt. empty 5283 lbs.; useful load 3467 lbs.; payload with 96 gal. fuel (2 pilots) 2476 lbs.; payload with 136 gal. fuel (2 pilots) 2236 lbs.; gross wt. 8750 lbs.; max. speed 195; cruising speed 170 at 5000 ft.; landing speed 65; climb 1100 ft. first min. at sea level; ser. ceiling 18,000 ft.; gas cap. normal 96 gal.; gas cap. max. 136 gal.; gas cap. of 175 gal. optional; oil cap. 10 gal.; cruising range at 38 gal. per hour 425 miles; price approx. $40,000. at factory. Wts. of prototype airplane were 4921-3079-8000 lbs., amended to 5300-3200-8500 lbs.; approved wts. on ATC 527 were 5283-3467-8750 lbs.

Specifications of GA-43J seaplane powered with "Hornet" T1C engine rated 650-700 h.p. were identical to GA-43A landplane, except as follows; height overall 13'9"; wt. empty 6005 lbs.; useful load 2995 lbs.; payload with 175 gal. fuel 1678 lbs.; payload with 136 gal. fuel 1912 lbs. (10 passengers at 170 lb. each & 212 lb. baggage); gross wt. 9000 lbs.; max. speed 165; cruising speed (.75 power) 145; landing speed (with wing flaps) 60; climb 950 ft. first min. at sea level; ser. ceiling 14,500 ft.; gas cap. 176 gal.; oil cap. 12.5 gal.; cruising range at 38 gal. per hour 500-700 miles; all performance figures with Hamilton-Standard controllable propeller.

The semi-monocoque fuselage framework was a riveted duralumin structure of ring-type bulkheads and Z-type stringers covered with smooth riveted "Alclad" sheet. Cabin walls of large oval cross-section were tightly filled with feathers and down (1 in. thick) to provide a sound barrier and all windows were double-paned of shatter-proof glass. Of 352 cu. ft.

Fig. 88. Interior of GA-43A offered room and comfort for ten.

capacity (20'8" long x 63" high x 58" wide) the main cabin was arranged with 10 comfortable reclining chairs, a lavatory in the aft portion, and a 50 cu. ft. baggage compartment was further aft with access from the inside. Cabin entry door was aft on right side with an extra emergency exit up forward on the left. Another baggage compartment of 37 cu. ft. capacity was underneath the pilot's floor with outside door on the right. In addition, a 26 cu. ft. baggage-mail-cargo compartment was in the root end of each wing panel, outboard of the center-section bay. An entry ladder to the main cabin extended to the ground and then folded up against the cabin door. Entrance to pilot's cabin was from the outside via fuselage steps and sliding hatch panels. The all-metal center-section panel was built integral to the fuselage; the retractable landing gear, in 2 units, was fastened to outer ends of this panel and retracted back into 2 streamlined (pod) nacelles. The landing gear of 96 in. tread was extended in 7 sec. or retracted in 18 sec. by a manually operated hydraulic pump; 30x13 Goodyear airwheels were fitted with brakes. The outer wing panels of dural tube-truss spar beams and wing ribs were of all-metal structure covered with smooth rivited "Alclad" sheet skin. Early experiments with built-in "wing slots", to prolong effectiveness of the ailerons, were cancelled in production models. Three fuel tanks of various capacity and housed in the center panel provided for up to 176 gal. of fuel; fuel was delivered to the engine by an engine-driven fuel pump with a hand-operated wobble-pump for emergency use. The cantilever all-metal tail group had metal covered fixed surfaces and fabric covered movable surfaces; the horizontal stabilizer was adjustable thru 9 degs. in flight. The tail wheel swiveled thru 360 degs. and was provided with a fore and and aft lock. The seaplane version was fitted with Edo 36-9225 pontoons which were identical to those used on Chas. Lindbergh's globe-wandering Lockheed "Sirius". The The seaplane version (GA-43J) was also equipped with fabric-covered split-type "wing flaps" to lower its landing speed and this installation was reported as the first of its kind on any seaplane. A relief valve was mounted in the flap system so flaps could fold up if lowered at an excessive speed. A metal propeller, electric engine starter, battery, generator, navigation lights, landing lights, cabin lights, ventilators, cabin heater, radio receiver, Western Electric two-way radio-telephone, fire extinguisher, parachute flares, bonding and shielding, wheel brakes, parking brake, jacking pads, lifting lugs, lavatory, and tail wheel were standard equipment. A Hamilton-Standard controllable propeller, sleeping lounges for night flights, all-cargo interior, Edo pontoons, extra entry door on left side, and pilot station for either 1 or 2 pilots were optional.

Listed below are all of the GA-43 examples:

X-775N: GA-43 (# 7500) Cyclone 650.

X-775N: GA-43 (# 7500) Cyclone 650.

X-82Y: GA-43A (# 2202) Cyclone 710.

X-13901: GA-43A (#2203) Cyclone 715.

NC-13903: GA-43A (#2204) Cyclone 715.

X-13904: GA-43J (#2205) Hornet 660-700.

Serial # 7500 mfgd. by Fairchild and American Airplane & Engine Corp. as Model 150, sold to Japan as GA-43 in 1934; ser. # 2202 del. to Swissair as CH-169 in March 1934; ser. # 2203 as company demonstrator, disposition unknown; ser. # 2204 del. to General Air Lines, later del. to Swissair as HB-ITU in March 1935; ser. # 2205 as seaplane to SCADTA on 11-19-34.

ATC # 528
(3-16-34)
WACO, MODEL UKC.

Fig. 89. Waco UKC warming its 210 h.p. Continental engine on factory airport.

The Waco cabin biplanes for 1934 did not represent any marked structural changes over the concept first introduced by the Model UIC, however, they did offer numerous little aerodynamic refinements and several interior improvements. More attention to detail, both inside and out, added up to a slight increase in performance and a little more to appearance and comfort. Like previous models of the Waco cabin biplane the models for 1934 were basically working airplanes, but now and then a few were spruced up with gay paint and finery to do no more than fly to here and yon on the owner's whim. To create more interest in the new cabin line, and to offer customers the privelege of being choosy, the cabin models of 1934 were offered with 3 different powerplants. The first in the line-up was the model UKC; as powered with the 7 cyl. Continental R-670 engine of 210 h.p. the UKC benefited by the good showing Waco had made the year before, and thus became an early success. Offered also as a seaplane on Edo twin-float gear the UKC also migrated to bush-flying duties in Alaska and Canada. 1934 was a good year for the UKC, but next year in 1935, Waco Aircraft offered still a little more utility to the ship in general and some structural features of dubious importance to owners and operators were eliminated. For 1935 the model UKC

became the UKC-S. Because the "Custom Cabin" models were introduced also in 1935, Waco had to differentiate between the two lines, so the UKC -S (UKC-Standard) became one of the "Standard" cabin biplanes in Waco's line for 1935; its powerplant was an improved version (R-670-A) of the 210 h.p. Continental engine. For the 1936 season the "Standard" cabin biplane, as powered with the 210 h.p. Continental engine, was generally the same without much change and labeled the UKS-6. Delivered price savings and operating economy were stressed as cardinal features of the UKC-S and UKS-6, so they differed greatly from the plush "Custom Cabin" series and were rather plain-looking by comparison. The various seasonal changes wrought into the Continental-powered "Standard" models for 1934-35-36 are shown here in the various illustrations.

The Waco model UKC was a cabin-type biplane with seating arranged for four. Extra dimension inside, over the UIC of the year previous, allowed ample width for 4 big people and more stretch-room for those in the rear. Redesigned appointments offered extra comfort and a more pleasant styling. Ample window area offered good visibility in just about any direction and interior comfort was regulated by ventilation and cabin heat. Pleasant flying was assured

Fig. 90. Model UKC on Edo floats that operated in Alaska.

by heavy insulation of the cabin walls for sound-proofing and inherent stability made the piloting chore a little easier on those long flights. Several practical improvements had been incorporated into the UKC for 1934 and as a workaday airplane its acceptance was certainly justified. To further increase its utility for work or for play the UKC was easily converted into an ambulance-plane, an air-taxi, or mounted on Edo floats to operate off water. Most examples were used for business or sport, but the utility and operating efficiency of the UKC-series was easily adapted to many types of commercial work. As powered with the 7 cyl. Continental R-670-A engine rated 210 h.p. the UKC handled its extra weight allowance very nicely, still giving top-notch performance under most adverse conditions. For 1935 this model was offered as the UKC-S and definitely shows a cost-cutting trend to make possible a considerable drop in delivered price. The most significant change was elimination of the rear upper cabin windows and also the wheel streamlines. As a consequence, the UKC-S was $760.00 cheaper and the 35 lbs. saved in the empty weight was added to the payload; the 5 m.p.h. lost to top and cruising speeds was not worth a quibble in view of the substantial saving in delivered price. This Continental-powered version for 1936 was offered as the UKS-6. Because no factory data was recorded for this model and because none were registered in CAA listings it is quite likely that the UKS-6 was actually offered in the "Standard" line for 1936, but apparently none were built. In 1935 the Continental R-670-B

engine, with a higher compression ratio and using 80 octane fuel, was rated 225 h.p. at 2000 r.p.m.; this was to be an option in the "Standard" line and was labeled the model VKC-S. The following year this 225 h.p. option became the model VKS-6. It could not be determined if any of the VKC-S or VKS-6 were built and sold in the U.S.A., but probably not. The type certificate number for this series was issued 3-16-34 for the UKC with various amendments to include the UKC-S, VKC-S, UKS-6, and VKS-6. These Continental-powered "Waco C" models were built in at least 40 examples and the UKC of 1934 was by far the most popular; manufactured by the Waco Aircraft Co. at Troy, Ohio.

Listed below are specifications and performance data for the model UKC of 1934 as powered with the 210 h.p. Continental R-670-A engine; length overall 25'3"; height overall 8'6"; wing span upper 33'3"; wing span lower 28'3"; wing chord upper & lower 57"; wing area upper 130 sq.ft.; wing area lower 110 sq.ft.; total wing area 240 sq.ft.; airfoil Clark Y; wt. empty 1745 (1755) lbs.; useful load 1105 (1245) lbs.; payload with 50 gal. fuel 605 (745) lbs.; gross wt. 2850 (3000) lbs.; figures in parentheses amended wt. allowance for ser. # 3856 and up; max. speed (with wheel pants) 143; cruising speed at 1900 r.p.m. 128; landing (stall) speed 50 (53); climb 800 (750) ft. first min. at sea level; ser. ceiling 14,000 (13,000) ft.; figures in parentheses for 3000 lb. gross wt.; gas cap. 50 gal.; oil cap. 4 gal.; cruising range at 13 gal. per hour 500 miles; price $6285.00 at factory field. 70 gal. fuel cap.

Fig. 91. A UKC with Dutch registration.

was optional.

All specifications and data for the UKC of 1934 as seaplane on Edo 38-3430 floats were identical to landplane except for the following: length overall 28'10"; height overall 10'7"; wt. empty 2131 lbs.; useful load 1119 lbs.; payload with 50 gal. fuel 619 lbs.; gross wt. 3250 lbs.; max. speed 126 at 2100 r.p.m.; cruising speed 105 at 1900 r.p.m.; landing (stall) speed 56; climb 600 ft. first min. at sea level; service ceiling 11,250 ft.; cruising range at 13 gal. per hour 400 miles; price not announced. Models UKC-S and UKS-6 eligible with Edo 38-3430 floats also; performance would be similar to UKC as listed here.

All specifications and data for UKC-S of 1935 as landplane were identical except for the following: wt. empty 1720 lbs.; useful load 1280 lbs.; payload with 50 gal. fuel 780 lbs.; gross wt. 3000 lbs.; max. speed (no wheel pants) 138; cruising speed 123; landing (stall) speed 53; climb 750 ft. first min. at sea level; ser. ceiling 13,000 ft.; gas cap. normal 50 gal.; gas cap. optional 70 gal.; oil cap. 4-5 gal.; price $5225.00 at factory field. It can be assumed that all specifications and performance data for the model UKS-6 of 1936 would be more or less typical to that of the UKC-S of 1935. The models VKC-S and VKS-6 with the R-670-B engine, had they been built, would have shown a slight improvement in all-

Fig. 92. Model UKC against backdrop of Canadian countryside.

Fig. 93. An experiment with Edo amphibious floats.

round performance.

The fuselage framework was built up of welded 4130 steel tubing faired to shape and fabric covered. The model UKC of 1934 had the upper cabin windows, as introduced in the UIC, for visibility up and to the rear; for 1935-36 this feature was discarded in the interests of simplicity in construction and repair. The wing framework, in 4 panels, was built up of solid spruce spar beams with spruce and plywood truss-type wing ribs; the leading edges were covered with dural metal sheet and the completed framework was covered in fabric. The ailerons, one on each wing panel, were metal-framed and metal covered. The interplane "drag strut", first introduced on the UIC of 1933, was an optional feature, but not particularly popular. The landing gear of 87 in. tread were faired tripods using "Waco" patented shock absorbing struts; Autofan 6.50x10 wheels with brakes were fitted with 7.50x10 low-pressure tires. The UKC was normally fitted with streamlined metal wheel pants, but this feature was an optional extra on 1935-36 models. The fabric covered tailgroup was built up of welded chrome-moly steel tubing; the elevators were aerodynamically "balanced" and the horizontal stabilizer was adjustable in flight. The Continental engine was cowled in tightly with an NACA-type fairing and all upper and lower wing-roots were faired in with metal fillets. A wooden propeller, electric engine starter, battery, tail wheel, navigation lights, throw-over control wheel and dual rudder pedals, a compass, air-speed indicator, fire extinguisher, tie-down ropes, first-aid kit, tool kit, and log books were standard equipment. A metal propeller, night-flying equipment, a Westport radio, and custom colors were optional.

Most of the UKC type seen about the country were a riot of color. One example had fuselage, fin, and interplane struts in Waco Vermillion; wings, rudder, and horizontal tail in Diana Cream. The rudder was scalloped in Vermillion and upper wings were Vermillion on top side; all Vermillion was outlined in Gold. Center stripe on fuselage was Black and outside stripes in Gold; cowl bumps were trimmed with Black and Gold poly-wogs. A more sedate example had fuselage, engine cowl, fin and rudder in Black with wings and horizontal tail in Silver; fishhook stripe on fuselage was Vermillion edged in Silver. The UKC-S was generally seen in solid colors; entire airplane in French Grey with fishhook fuselage stripe in Dark Blue edged in Gold was a popular combination. Custom colors were very popular and varied greatly; combinations of Green and Cream, Blue and Cream, Black and Yellow, or Grey and Red were embellished with varied striping. Fine-line and fish-hook striping were common in 1934-35 models, while funnel-striping or "Lockheed" striping was common in 1936, but the customer's preference prevailed. The next development in the Waco cabin biplane was the model YKC as described in chapter for ATC # 533 of this volume. The next development in the UKS series were the UKS-7 and VKS-7 as approved on ATC # 648.

Listed below are UKC and UKC-S entries as verified by factory records:

NC-13895; UKC   (# 3838) Continental 210.
  -13898; "   (# 3841)   "
  -13897; "   (# 3842)   "
  -13896; "   (# 3843)   "
  -13899; "   (# 3844)   "
  -13891; "   (# 3845)   "
  -13892; "   (# 3846)   "

CF-AUR:	''	(# 3847)	''
-14003:	''	(# 3848)	''
-14004:	''	(# 3849)	''
-14011:	''	(# 3850)	''
-14010:	''	(# 3851)	''
-14016:	''	(# 3852)	''
-14017:	''	(# 3853)	''
-14012:	''	(# 3854)	''
-14007:	''	(# 3855)	''
NS-16:	''	(# 3856)	''
NS-17:	''	(# 3857)	''
NS-18:	''	(# 3858)	''
NS-19:	''	(# 3859)	''
NS-20:	''	(# 3860)	''
-14015:	''	(# 3861)	''
-14022:	''	(# 3862)	''
CF-AVL:	''	(# 3863)	''
-14020:	''	(# 3864)	''
PH-SAN:	''	(# 3865)	''
NC-5003:	''	(# 3866)	''
-14040:	''	(# 3867)	''
-14043:	''	(# 3868)	''
CF-AVN:	''	(# 3869)	''
LN-ABW:	''	(# 3870)	''
CF-AVR:	''	(# 3871)	''
CF-AVS:	''	(# 3872)	''
:	''	(# 3926)	''
-14052:	''	(# 3927)	''
-14088:	''	(# 3928)	''
-14060:	''	(# 3929)	''
-14061:	''	(# 3930)	''
CF-AVV:	''	(# 3931)	''

CF-AWC:	''	(# 3932)	''
CF-AWD:	''	(# 3933)	''
-14047:	''	(# 3966)	''
-14606:	UKC-S	(# 3977)	''
-14611:	''	(# 3978)	''
-14617:	''	(# 3979)	''
NC-3003:	''	(# 3980)	''
-15214:	''	(# 3981)	''
-14086:	UKC	(# 4220)	''
NC-14609:	UKC-S	(# 4235)	''

This approval for ser. # 3838 and up; ser. # 3838 thru # 3855 held to 2850 lb. gross wt.; ser. # 3856 and up allowed 3000 lb. gross wt.; ser. # 3842 del. to Pure Oil Co.; ser. # 3843 on floats in Alaska; ser. # 3844-45-46 del. to Philippine Aerial Taxi Co.; ser. # 3847 del. to Canada; ser. # 3853 del. to Elgin National Watch Co.; ser. # 3856-57-58-59-60 del. to (CAA) Dept. of Commerce; ser. # 3859-60 later registered as NC-1319 and NC-1320; ser. # 3863 del. to Canada; ser. # 3865 del. to Holland; ser. # 3866 del. to Henry B. Dupont; ser. # 3867 del. to Packard Motor Car Co.; ser. # 3869 del. to Canada; ser. # 3870 del. to Norway; ser. # 3871-72 del. to Canada; ser. # 3926 del. to Johannesburg, So. Africa; ser. # 3931-32-33 del. to Canada; ser. # 3966 del. to Shell Oil Co. of Calif.; ser. # 3980 del. to Alice F. Dupont; ser. # 3981 later modified to YKC-S; this approval expired 9-30-39.

ATC # 529
(3-23-34)
MONOCOUPE, D-145.

Fig. 94. Monocoupe D-145 with 145 h.p. Warner "Super Scarab" engine.

During 1933 a brash young airplane evolved to take its place into the "Monocoupe" line of models as the "Model D" or D-145. Its design was greatly influenced by tricks learned in preparing "racing Monocoupes", therefore, for good and for bad, it inherited the assorted benefits and likewise most of the shortcomings. As a consequence, it was hailed on the one hand and condemned on the other; the D-145 tried as best it knew how to please, but it could make no concessions to likes or dislikes—you either liked it and enjoyed it, or you didn't. In defense of the D-145 it stands to reason that a small 160-170 m.p.h. airplane was inbred with all sorts of features that "made it go", so by nature it would be sometimes fidgety and most always demanding of rather close attention. A sportsman-pilot with a sensitive feeling for quirks in behavior and an appreciation for special talents was perhaps the only logical owner for an airplane of this type. The 15 examples of the Monocoupe D-145 operated by the Bureau of Air Commerce were not generally satisfactory for use by inspectors in the field; BAC pilots were plagued with little accidents frequently (ground-loops and that sort of thing) that hampered their schedules in appointed rounds, and this tried their tempers to the edge. The matter here seems plainly a case of an airplane unsuited for a particular kind of work, and of pilots perhaps unwilling to cater to

its particular needs. Many stories remain about the D-145, some in praise and some not, some are true and some are not, but it is fact that association with this airplane was sure to be remembered.

The "Monocoupe" had always been a small, tidy airplane, that was at times rather chummy inside, especially for two larger people. Frederick J. Knack, company engineer, attempted to solve this problem in a new design called the "Model D". Starting with a cockpit a full 6 inches wider, with more head-room gained by using split wing panels, the Model D was cleverly fashioned to be bigger on the inside and yet seem rather small on the outside. The prototype airplane, powered with a 125 h.p. Warner "Scarab" engine, was finished in the winter of 1931-32, but it failed to make any significant impression on those who would be responsible for its development. With nothing much else to do, development of the Model D continued during 1933, now under the direction of Ivan Driggs who for years had displayed aerodynamic know-how and other special talents. A second prototype airplane under construction, at least similar in dimension, featured the 145 h.p. Warner "Super Scarab" engine and a full deep-chord NACA-type engine fairing. This example, upon test, showed better promise but a revision later to the landing gear, strut

Fig. 95. D-145 adhered to normal Monocoupe lines, but was a special breed.

fairings, and tail group, produced even better results and a more pleasant effect. Satisfied that this combination was now worth showing off, Don Luscombe sped off to the east coast on a demonstration tour. Talented maestro that he was, Luscombe demonstrated the new D-145 to best advantage and even brought back a few orders. The future for the new Model D looked especially bright when 10 of the D-145 were ordered by the Bureau of Air Commerce for use by inspectors country-wide; this order was later increased to 15. Development and production of the D-145 was slightly hampered by effects of the stifling depression and bickering of an unsettled household. Fearing a dim future for "Monocoupe", Don Luscombe resigned in Oct. of 1933, taking Ivan Driggs with him. Peter R. Beazley of Detroit then became president bringing Tom Towle with him as chief engineer; it was Towle that completed the ATC program for the D-145 in the first few months of 1934. Reorganization into the Lambert Aircraft Corp. was formed in May of that year. Luther Harris, formerly with the Dept. of Commerce, became general manager and it was more or less he who helped instigate the large order of D-145 by the BAC. John B. Molitor was sales manager. Early in 1935, the entire operation was sold to Clare Bunch.

Like other "Monocoupes" before it the Model D-145 was a strut-braced high wing cabin monoplane with side-by-side seating for two. Extra width in the cabin provided more shoulder-room, and extra height provided more head-room; a little more leg-room was also added. Larger in several dimensions, the D-145 was often called "the big Monocoupe", but it wasn't all that much bigger. Clever design made it bigger on the inside, but still relatively small on the outside. Occasionally the D-145 was called the 'Super Monocoupe" and this it definitely was; compared to previous standards of performance the D-145 was considerably faster, climb-out was very impressive, and by general terms it was a "hot" airplane. As powered with the new 7 cyl. Warner "Super Scarab" (Series 40) engine rated 145 h.p. at 2050 r.p.m. the D-145 was not an airplane to buzz gently around the patch with; it covered ground in a hurry and was much more practical when up high and going somewhere. Cruising easily at 145 m.p.h. the D-145 could pass over 2 miles of ground in less than a minute, and when pushed to the limit it could zip along at speeds up to 170 m.p.h. Such performance was bound to create enthusiasm. George Hard of New York City, who bought the second Model D off the line, took off on a jaunt that covered 45 states, and into Mexico, Yucatan, and Cuba; the trip covered more than 30,000 miles and was stretched over a leisurely period of 6 months. This was the type of vacation that pilots dreamed about. Designed definitely for use by the seasoned sportsman, the Model D-145 got around to most parts of the country and was always surrounded by an amazed gathering, a gathering that was thrilled with its performance and seduced by its saucy good looks. Flight characteristics were generally of "Monocoupe"

Fig. 96. Tunnel-type cowling on D-145 was designed to improve airflow.

nature, so it possessed most of the inherent habits, and added a few feisty ones of its own, but it did make proud pilots. (Of course, she made an ass out of some of them, sometime, but that was when they weren't paying attention). Truthfully, the D-145 was not as well liked as the Model 90 or the 110 for instance, and for obvious reasons, but it did have a tight circle of supporters. Several owners were quite happy with theirs and Chas. "Lindy" Lindbergh, who had one tailored especially to his liking, was fascinated with its special personality. An example rebuilt and flown by "Dick" Austin in the 1960's became well known in many parts of the country and old-time pilots vied with one another just to get a ride in it. The type certificate number for the Model D-145 was issued 3-23-34 and 28 examples of this model were mfgd. by the Monocoupe Corp. on Lambert Field in Robertson (St. Louis), Mo.; a div. of the Lambert Aircraft Corp. Early in 1934, Monocoupe employed at least 125 at the aircraft plant at St. Louis, and 55 at the engine plant in Moline, Ill.

Listed below are specifications and performance data for the Monocoupe D-145 as powered with 145 h.p. Warner "Super Scarab" engine; length overall 20'5"; height overall 6'10"; wing span 32'0"; wing chord 58"; total wing area 129.7 sq.ft.; airfoil NACA-2412; wt. empty 1220 lbs.; useful load 628 lbs.; payload with 34 gal. fuel 224 lbs. (1 passenger at 170 lbs. & 54 lbs. baggage); gross wt. 1848 lbs.; max. speed (with wheel pants) 170; cruising speed at 1925 r.p.m. 145; landing speed 50; climb 1500 ft. first min. at sea level; ser. ceiling 18,000 ft.; gas cap. 34 gal.; oil cap. 4 gal.; cruising range at 8.5 gal. per hour 550 miles; basic price $5600.00 at factory field.

The fuselage framework was built up of welded chrome-moly steel tubing that was faired to the distinctive "Monocoupe" shape then fabric covered. A large door on right side provided entry to the pleasant cabin; larger cabin dimensions provided more room and appointments were comfortable and pleasing. Ample window area and an overhead skylight provided good overall visibility, but the high cowl line in front restricted visibility directly ahead. Side windows opened out for ventilation and a cabin heater warmed things up a little in winter. Baggage (up to 54 lbs.) was stored directly behind the seatback. The wing framework, in 2 panels, was built up of solid spruce spar beams with basswood and spruce "picture frame" wing ribs; the leading edges were covered with dural metal sheet and the completed framework was covered in fabric. A 15 gal. fuel tank was mounted in root end of each wing half and a 4 gal. reserve tank was in fuselage ahead of the instrument panel. The heavily faired landing gear was equipped with oildraulic shock struts mounted in tension; 6.50x10 semi-airwheels with brakes were encased in streamlined metal wheel pants. The fabric covered tail-group was built up of welded chrome-moly steel tubing; horizontal stabilizer was fixed and R.H. elevator was fitted with adjustable "trim tab". A metal propeller, electric engine starter, battery, NACA-type or tunnel-type (Watters) engine cowl, wheel pants, steerable tail wheel, wheel brakes, parking brake, dual stick-type controls, compass, airspeed indicator, fire extinguisher, wiring for navigation lights, clock, cabin heater, bonding for radio, log books, first-aid kit, and tool kit were standard equipment. Radio equipment, engine shielding, and night flying equipment were optional. Custom colors were available on

Fig. 97. D-145 used by Dept. of Commerce inspectors in the field.

order.

Listed below are D-145 entries as gleaned from registration records:

X-12356:	90-X (# D-101-W)	Warner 125.
NC-12370:	D-145 (# D-102)	Warner 145.
-12386:	" (# D-103)	"
-12360:	" (# D-104)	"
-12387:	" (# D-105)	"
NS-39:	" (# D-106)	"
-11725:	" (# D-107)	"
-12389:	" (# D-108)	"
NS-41:	" (# D-109)	"
NS-43:	" (# D-110)	"
NS-45:	" (# D-111)	"
NS-46:	" (# D-112)	"
NS-47:	" (# D-113)	"
NS-48:	" (# D-114)	"
NS-49:	" (# D-115)	"
NS-50:	" (# D-116)	"
NS-51:	" (# D-117)	"
NS-52:	" (# D-118)	"
NS-53:	" (# D-119)	"
NS-54:	" (# D-120)	"
NS-55:	" (# D-121)	"
NS-56:	" (# D-122)	"
NC-11733:	" (# D-123)	"
:	" (# D-124)	"
NR-211:	" (# D-125)	"
:	" (# D-126)	"
:	" (# D-127)	"
NC-17687:	" (# D-128)	"
-11734:	" (# D-129)	"

Ser. # D-106, D-109, D-110, D-111, D-112, D-113, D-114, D-115, D-116, D-117, D-118, D-119, D-120, D-121, D-122 operated by Bureau of Air Commerce; Ser. # D-110 later as NC-13939; ser. # D-114 later as NC-13940; ser. # D-119 later as NC-13941; no listing for ser. # D-124, D-126, D-127.

ATC # 530
(4-5-34)
STINSON "RELIANT", SR-5, SR-5B, SR-5C.

Fig. 98. An SR-5 "Reliant" with 225 h.p. Lycoming engine; 240 h.p. version was SR-5B.

In the "Reliant" for the 1934 season, Stinson engineers made every effort to provide private-owners with technical features borrowed from the modern air-transport and features of comfort and economy from the contemporary automobile. These were the things not easily seen in an overall glance, but greatly appreciated in actual service. Better cabin insulation provided a barrier against heat, cold, and noise, and a larger-capacity heating and ventilating system permitted better regulation of cabin temperatures. The cabin "furniture" was colorful, more luxurious, and design of cabin hardware was derived directly from automobile practice. A rubber-mounted engine lessened vibration through the frame and hydraulic disc-type wheel brakes provided much better ground handling. Although a kinship to the earlier (1933) "Reliant" is unmistakable, most of the exterior improvements wrought into the new SR-5 series are fairly evident. An improved NACA-type engine cowling and a simpler vee-type windshield faired out the front section a little better; by reducing thickness of the wing section at the root end a slight "gull wing" effect had been produced which offered some improvement in visibility and also some aerodynamic benefit. Larger "fillets" at all intersections literally smoothed out the airflow and con-tributed to accumulating gains in speed and performance. A redesigned wing of shorter span and wider chord, reducing the aspect ratio, was optionally equipped with trailing edge flaps; these "flaps" were called speed-arrestors and permitted variable gliding angles (Selectiv-Glide) at lowered speeds to allow landings into smaller 'fields over high-obstructions. This new "Reliant" series in the standard model SR-5 was powered with the 9 cyl. Lycoming R-680-4 engine rated 225 h.p.; also on this approval was the model SR-5B which was powered with the R-680-2 (same as earlier R-680-BA) engine rated 240 h.p. and also the model SR-5C which was powered with the R-680-5 engine rated 260 h.p. The model SR-5C actually did play in the "airliner" role for a while; 4 examples of this model were operated by the Wyoming Air Service on regional routes and 2 were operated by Northwest Airlines. Not having "wing flaps" as did other models in this series, the standard SR-5 was the economy model and surprisingly, only sold in some 8 examples. The proposed SR-5B with a 240 h.p. version of the popular "Lycoming" engine was somehow bypassed, and the SR-5C with a 260 h.p. Lycoming engine was sold in at least 6 examples. This new "Reliant" (SR-5) series promised to have a combination to suit almost everyone, so consequently, it was

Fig. 99. Gulf Oil Co. used colorful SR-5 in promotion of aviation fuels.

eventually offered in 7 different models, plus a few "specials".

The colorful "Reliant" model SR-5 was a high-winged cabin monoplane with seating arranged for four. In general, the new SR-5 series was basically typical of the earlier "SR" type (ATC # 510), but it was actually studded with a large amount of structural and aerodynamic refinements. As the first of the new series for the 1934 season, the SR-5 also became the best bargain in the country for an airplane of this type. As the first of the new series it was also the basis for the popular models SR-5A and SR-5E (approved on another certificate); incidentally, the SR-5A and the SR-5E were the best-selling "Reliants" that Stinson was to have in several years to come. As powered with the Lycoming R-680-4 engine rated 225 h.p. the standard model SR-5 was slanted toward the average private-owner and the average businessman who would want the most airplane for their money. Ironically enough, Stinson almost immediately began offering modified versions of the standard SR-5 with more power, better performance, and one extra or another; this took most of the appeal away from the cheaper (standard) SR-5 and its sales potential soon dwindled away. It probably figures that those who could afford an airplane during these times could certainly afford the little extra money that would buy them more power and extra performance. Every model in the SR-5 series were good-flying airplanes; all were stable, easy to fly, and delivered a caliber of performance that every owner had a right to brag about—and most of them did. Sharing this type certificate number also, along with the SR-5 and the SR-5B, was a 260 h.p. version of the "Reliant" labeled the SR-5C. The model SR-5C as powered with the R-680-5 engine rated 260 h.p. at 2300 r.p.m. leaned more heavily on transport-type features and was perhaps the best per-

former of the series; six of the SR-5C were modified into "small airliners" and were used by Wyoming Air Service on regional routes and by Northwest Airlines on certain schedules in the northwest. There is no evidence of any SR-5B in the record; it is quite likely this version was planned but never built. The type certificate number for the standard model SR-5 was issued 4-5-34 and later amended to include the (240 h.p.) SR-5B and the (260 h.p.) SR-5C; at least 8 examples of the model SR-5 and 6 of the SR-5C were manufactured by the Stinson Aircraft Corp. at Wayne, Mich., a division of the Cord Corp.

Listed below are specifications and performance data for the standard model SR-5 as powered with 225 h.p. Lycoming R-680-4 engine; length overall 27'2"; height overall 8'5"; wing span 41'0"; wing chord 80"; total wing area 230 sq.ft.; airfoil Clark Y; wt. empty 2200 lbs.; useful load 1075 lbs.; payload with 50 gal. fuel 575 lbs. (3 passengers at 170 lbs. each & 65 lbs. baggage); gross wt. 3275 lbs.; max. speed (with wheel pants) 132; cruising speed 120; landing speed (no flaps) 56; climb 775 ft. first min. at sea level; ser. ceiling 14,500 ft.; gas cap. 50 gal.; oil cap. 4 gal.; cruising range at 13 gal. per hour 430 miles; fuel consumption was 13.5 gal. per hour for SR-5B and 14 gal. per hour for SR-5C; price (standard SR-5) was $5775.00 at factory field. Performance of the 240 h.p. version (SR-5B) would be slightly improved over that listed above. Performance of the 260 h.p. version (SR-5C) was much better than both the SR-5 and SR-5B, but it was toned down some by an increase in weight allowance to 3550 lbs. Wts. for standard SR-5 as approved on 4-5-34 were 2200-1075-3275 lbs.; wts. for SR-5B and SR-5C were increased to 3475 lbs. Serial # 9250-A and up were eligible at 3550 lbs. gross wt.

Two large doors, one each side, and a large step offered convenient entry into the cabin. The

Fig. 100. An SR-5C with 260 h.p. Lycoming engine; wing "flaps" slowed landing speed.

two front seats, with padded arm-rests, were adjustable for convenience; the rear couch-type seat was of extra width and all seats were covered in mohair or leather. Roll-down windows were of shatter-proof glass and so was the flat-paned vee-type windshield; adjustable sunvisors and a rear-view mirror were provided for the pilot's convenience. Dual control wheels were adjustable for position and dual rudder pedals were also provided. The instrument panel was lighted, with all flight instruments mounted in rubber. Other interior appointments included a temperature regulator for maintaining proper cabin heat, ash trays, assist ropes, map & gadget pockets, storage bin under rear seat, and thick carpeting on the floor. Normal fuel capacity was 50 gals. (25 gal. in each wing), but the SR-5B and SR-5C were eligible also with cap. of 75, 90, or 100 gals.; wings required reinforcement for 100 gal. (50 gal. in each wing) fuel capacity. The cantilever landing gear of 9'10" tread used "Aerol" shock absorbing struts and 25x11-4 Goodyear "airwheels" with disc-type hydraulic brakes; a parking brake was also provided. The standard "Reliant" was equipped with wheel "fenders", but streamlined "wheel pants" were optional. The model SR-5, SR-5B, SR-5C were eligible with skis at 3300 lb. gross wt.; models SR-5B and SR-5C were also eligible as twin-float seaplanes on Edo 38-3430 pontoons. Vacuum-operated wing flaps (speed-arrestors) with a control system called "Selectiv-Glide" were offered on the SR-5B and SR-5C, but not on the standard SR-5. A lighted baggage compartment, with allowance for 65 lbs., was just behind the rear seat and equipped with a locking-type door. A metal ground-adjustable

propeller, a 12-volt battery, Eclipse electric engine starter, fire extinguisher, compass, standard group of flight and engine instruments, and a tool-kit were standard equipment. The 260 h.p. model SR-5C version was eligible with a Lycoming-Smith controllable-pitch propeller. Each "Reliant" was delivered with a 12-coat high lustre 3-color finish. The next "Reliant" development was the rare model SR-5D as described in chapter for ATC # 531 of this volume.

Listed below are SR-5 and SR-5C entries as gleaned from registration records:

X-13834;	SR-5 Spl.	(# 9200-A)	Lycoming 225.
NC-13836;	"	(# 9201-A)	"
-13837;	SR-5	(# 9202)	
-13838;	SR-5 Spl.	(# 9203)	Lycoming 245.
-13844;	SR-5	(# 9204)	Lycoming 225.
NC-13843;	SR-5	(# 9210)	Lycoming 225.
-13845;	"	(# 9217)	"
-13846;	"	(# 9218)	"
-13849;	"	(# 9220)	"
-13847;	"	(# 9221)	"
-13856;	"	(# 9222)	"
-13872;	SR-5C	(# 9251-A)	Lycoming 260.
-13873;	"	(# 9252-A)	"
-13874;	"	(# 9253-A)	"
-14168;	"	(# 9268-A)	"
-14169;	"	(# 9269-A)	"
-14170;	"	(# 9270-A)	"

This approval for ser. # 9202 and up; ser. # 9200-A and # 9201-A on Group 2 approval number 2-492; ser. nos. ending -A had wing flaps; ser. # 9203 probably on Group 2 approval number 2-494; ser. # 9202 thru # 9211 had small tail surfaces; ser. # 9251-A, # 9252-A, # 9253-A, # 9268-

Fig. 101. An SR-5C on Boeing School of Aeronautics flight-line.

A, and # 9269-A first as SR-5A modified into model SR-5C; ATC # 530 was first issued for models SR-5, SR-5B, SR-5C—sometime later the ATC numbers for SR-5A and SR-5E were cancelled and these two models were added to ATC # 530; approval expired 9-30-39.

ATC # 531
(4-5-34)
STINSON "RELIANT", SR-5D.

Fig. 102. This was the standard "Reliant". Model SR-5D was similar, but stripped of options and 224 lbs. of empty weight.

What the design-engineers had in mind when they were planning the "Reliant" model SR-5D is rather difficult to conceive, but a look at some of the technical details seemed to point out that this could have been a stripped-down, bargain-priced airplane. The main clue is in the "approved weight allowance". With an empty weight some 224 lbs. less than that of the standard (SR-5) "Reliant", it is entirely conceivable that this airplane was planned to operate without the many normal conveniences. Perhaps it would not be too difficult to strip an SR-5 of 224 lbs.; the metal propeller (which is much heavier) could be replaced with a wooden one, the wheel pants weighed at least 30 lbs., a light "Townend" ring could replace the big NACA-type engine cowl, standard seats and the plush interior were also quite heavy, and any number of other things could be whittled at until the amount was met. With the gross wt. held to 3200 lbs., some 75 lbs. less than that of the standard SR-5, the SR-5D here in question was still able to tote a useful load amounting to 1224 lbs.; that was 149 lbs. more than for the SR-5. And, mind you, this SR-5D version was also powered with the old-style Lycoming R-680 engine of 215 h.p.; if Stinson had a good many of these older

engines left over, then their use in the SR-5D would make some sense. So then, what have we here; a stripped-down airplane to haul cargo at lowest possible rates, or perhaps a poor-man's airplane that could be bought very cheaply at the outset, and equipped with normal accessories and finery, one by one, as money became available. This technical fantasy in conjecture is based on approved weights listed as 1976 lbs. empty, with 1224 lbs. of useful load, and a gross weight allowance of 3200 lbs.; if this is the way it was planned, then we have here a very unusual "Reliant".

It is of course safe to assume that the model SR-5D was a high-winged cabin monoplane, typical to that of other models in the (SR-5) "Reliant" series, but it would only be a guess to envision the interior arrangement and what it was destined to hold. As powered with the old-style, low-compression Lycoming R-680 engine rated 215 h.p. at 2000 r.p.m. on low-octane fuel, the SR-5D probably did well enough in performance, perhaps even as well as the more powerful (225 h.p.) SR-5. Until some factual records are uncovered on this particular airplane, anything about its capabilities and behavior would be guess-work. There are some scant records of an SR-5D version that was approved on a Group 2 memo numbered 2-493, but then this airplane was 190 lbs. heavier when empty and tipped the scales at 3241 lbs. gross; it is easy to see that this (SR-5D) airplane must have been normally equipped with accessories and appointments. The type certificate number for the SR-5D as discussed here in the first paragraph, was issued 4-5-34 and there is no evidence of any examples being built.

Specifications and performance data for the SR-5D would be same as for the SR-5 (ATC # 530), except as noted; wt. empty 1976 lbs.; useful load 1224 lbs.; payload with 50 gal. fuel 724 lbs.; gross wt. 3200 lbs.; performance figures would be only slightly less than those of the standard SR-5.

For a better understanding of the different "Lycoming" engines as used in the various "Stinson" airplanes of this period, the chart below lists the engines by designation and characteristics:

R-680	215	2000	5.3	58
R-680-1 (experimental)				
R-680-2	240	2000	6.5	80
R-680-3	200	2000	5.2	58
R-680-4	225	2100	5.5	58
R-680-5	260	2300	6.5	80
R-680-6	245	2300	5.5	58
R-680-7	240	2300	5.3	58

The list, from left to right, shows model designation, max. horsepower rating, max. r.p.m., compression ratio, and minimum octane number of fuel; R-680 same as had been used for previous 3 years; R-680-1 was not produced; R-680-2 same as earlier R-680-BA transport-type engine; R-680-3 developed for Air Corps trainers; R-680-4 was standard powerplant for SR-5; R-680-5 was the new transport-type engine; R-680-5, -6, -7 for use with controllable propellers only.

Except for one example on Group 2 category, there is no listing for any other SR-5D. The next development in the "Reliant" series was the model SR-5A as described in chapter for ATC # 536 of this volume.

ATC # 532
(4-10-34)
KINNER "ENVOY", C-7.

Fig. 103. Kinner "Envoy" C-7 with 7 cyl. Kinner C7 engine of 300 h.p.

The Kinner "Envoy" model C-7 was a four-place low-winged cabin monoplane that seemed to be masquerading as a racing airplane. Of course, it takes more than a "costume" to make a racing airplane, but the "Envoy" C-7 at least managed to look the part. Belonging to a family of airplanes that included such sporty members as the "Sportwing" and the "Playboy", it is perhaps logical that the "Envoy", even tho' a big sister, so to speak, would tend to resemble its kin. However we judge it, it must be conceded that a relatively thin wire-braced wing, a fully streamlined "spatted" landing gear, a full-blown NACA engine cowling, and streamlined fillets at every corner, was something one did not normally see on a fourplace cabin monoplane. All of these were still contemporary tricks of the racing airplane, and not normally considered in the design of a small cabin transport. The "Envoy" - translated all these features into high performance, and all of this high performance most certainly was slanted towards the sportsman-pilot and men of business. By whatever prompting, the U. S. Navy became interested in this unusual airplane and ordered 3 for use as utility transports to convey personnel; no doubt employed in the hauling around of "Navy Brass". Low-winged cabin monoplanes were still quite rare in 1934 and the Kinner "Envoy" was

actually only the second of this type in a small four-place version. The first of this type, by the way, was the revolutionary Alexander "Bullet" of 1929-30. In many ways the low-winged cabin monoplane was a practical configuration better suited to designing tricks employed to reduce parasitic drag. As time went by, the low-winged cabin monoplane took its place on the market with more frequency, but it wasn't to reach a peak of popularity for another 20 years.

The Kinner "Envoy" model C-7 was a roundish, wire-braced, low wing cabin monoplane with seating arranged for four. Stemming from a line of "Kinner" sport monoplanes, and especially from a model called the "Playboy", the "Envoy" was a very unusual airplane in the four-place category. It is to the credit of the designer (Max B. Harlow) for having the daring to apply rather unorthodox techniques to achieve an airplane with uncommon performance. Just from the looks of an airplane of this type one would expect narrow, cramped quarters, and marginal load-carrying capacity, but to the contrary, the "Envoy" was bulging with room and carried a useful load that allowed for all normal requirements, plus extras. As powered with the new 7 cyl. Kinner C7 engine rated 300 h.p. at 1800 r.p.m. the "Envoy" behaved beautifully without straining and its

Fig. 104. Kinner "Envoy" at Santa Monica air station; Naval designation was XRK-1.

above-average performance was quite deceiving. Considering all the performance that was available in this four-seater, its principal features were not just masquerade, but proven tricks gathered together to achieve something not normally available in a 4-place airplane. As it streaked into the flight pattern of any airport, with wing wires whistling, we can well imagine that all heads turned to that direction. Perhaps all sauntered over to see it come in; much about the "Envoy" was still unusual and interesting enough to captivate any audience. Its very uncommon configuration was rather pleasing, but perhaps also a deterent; not many could yet believe that a four-seated private-owner transport ought to look like this. The type certificate number for the "Envoy" model C-7 was issued 4-10-34 and perhaps no more than 7 examples were built by the Kinner Airplane & Motor Corp., Ltd. at Glendale, Calif. Robert Porter was pres. & gen. mgr.; B. L. Graves was V.P.; Lillian Porter was sales mgr.; Max. B. Harlow design-engineer; B. W. James chf. engr.; and Al Lary test-pilot. C. P. Sander was chf. engr. in 1935, and B. T. Salmon was chf. engr. in 1936.

Listed below are specifications and performance data for the Kinner "Envoy" model C-7 as powered with 300 h.p. Kinner C7 engine; length overall 28'7"; height overall 8'8"; wing span 39'9"; wing chord 72"; total wing area 229 sq.ft.; airfoil Clark Y; wt. empty 2530 (2551) lbs.; useful load 1470 (1449) lbs.; payload with 89 gal. fuel 721 (700) lbs. (3 passengers at 170 lb. each, 120 lb. baggage, & 70 lb. allowance for extra equipment); gross wt. 4000 lbs.; figures in parentheses are wts. as allowed in first amendment; max. speed 170; cruising speed (1750 r.p.m.) 150; landing speed (no flaps) 55; landing speed (with flaps) 46; climb 800 ft. first min. at sea level; ser. ceiling 16,000 ft.; gas cap. 89 gal.; oil cap. 6 gal.; cruising range at 18 gal. per hour 700 miles; price not announced.

Early in 1935 amendment allowed wts. of 2723-1527-4250 lbs.; the detrimental factor of the extra weight was somewhat offset by use of the Hamilton-Standard controllable-pitch propeller. Navy version of the "Envoy" with radio gear and a two-position propeller as follows: wt. empty 2723 lbs.; useful load 1527 lbs.; payload with 90 gal. fuel 772 lbs. (3 passengers at 170 lb. each & 182 lbs. for baggage & 4 parachutes); gross wt. 4250 lbs.; max. speed (at sea level) 165; cruising speed (1750 r.p.m.) 150; landing speed (with flaps) 55; climb 850 ft. first min. at sea level; ser. ceiling 17,000 ft.; gas cap. 90 gal.; oil cap. 6 gal.; cruising range 700 miles.

The following were changes in the "Envoy" for 1936; wt. empty 2850 lbs.; useful load 1450 lbs.; payload with 102 gal. fuel 608 lbs. (3 passengers & 98 lb. baggage); gross wt. 4300 lbs.; max. speed 185 at 5000 ft.; max. speed at sea level 170; normal cruising speed 169 at 5000 ft.; cruising speed 155 at sea level; landing speed (no flaps) 62; landing speed (with flaps) 55; climb 1000 ft. first min. at sea level; ser. ceiling 18,000 ft.; gas cap. 102 gal.; oil cap. 8 gal.; cruising range 700 miles; the engine for this version was the supercharged Kinner SC7 rated 370 h.p. at 1900 r.p.m. at 5000 ft.; other changes included a smooth NACA cowl (no blisters), the

Fig. 105. "Envoy" C-7 breaking ground at Seattle airport.

windshield slanted backward instead of forward, oil cooling radiator was required, and engine was mounted in Lord (rubber) mounts. In 1935 the Kinner B5, R5, C5, and C7 were all available with battery ignition as an option.

The fuselage framework was built up of welded chrome-moly steel tubing, heavily faired with wooden formers and fairing strips to a well-rounded shape, then fabric covered; the front portion over cabin area was covered entirely with dural metal panels. Cabin entry, through a novel door on right-rear side, was an easy step from the wing-walk; a suspended foot-step and large hand-hold eased the climb up to the wing-walk for cabin entry or access to baggage in the wing. Individual front seats were adjustable for position behind a (throw-over) control wheel; windshield panes slanted forward to minimize glare. The bench-type rear seat was heavily padded and all seats were upholstered in fine fabrics. Visibility was ample and all windows were of shatter-proof glass; side windows at pilot station slid open for ventilation. Up to 120 lbs. of baggage was allowed in 4 compartments; compartments in wing stub (right and left) were allowed 20 lbs. each, shelf behind rear seat was allowed 10 lbs., and large lower compartment, aft of cabin, was allowed 70 lbs. Twenty lbs. was deducted from this allowance for each parachute carried. The wing framework was built up of solid spruce spars routed to an I-beam section with spruce and plywood truss-type wing ribs; the leading edges were covered with dural sheet and the completed framework was covered in fabric. Outer wing panels were wire-braced with an upper and lower truss; the wing stub, of composite structure, was integral to the fuselage and provided attachment for landing gear and center

Fig. 106. Unusual configuration promoted high performance; racing-plane features quite unorthodox for a personal transport.

wing bracing truss. Fuel was stowed in 2 wing tanks at 30 gal. each, and a fuselage tank of 29 gal. capacity; 47.5 gal. wing tanks and a 21 gal. fuselage tank were standard capacity on ser. #184 and up. The fully streamlined landing gear consisted of 2 fixed vees and horizontal forks with "Kinner" oleo-spring shock struts to take 8.50X10 Autofan wheels fitted with 6-ply low-pressure tires; the entire landing gear was "faired" and wheels were encased in streamlined metal wheel pants. Wheel brakes, a parking brake, and swiveling tail wheel were also provided. Split-type trailing edge wing flaps of partial span were electrically operated; flaps not to be extended above 100 m.p.h. Wing rigging was 0 deg. incidence, and 4.5 degs. of dihedral. The fabric covered tail-group was built up of welded chrome-moly steel tubing; horizontal stabilizer was fixed and elevators were fitted with "trimming tabs". A ground-adjustable metal propeller, Eclipse electric engine starter, Exide battery, wheel brakes, parking brake, throw-over control wheel, navigation lights, chrome-plated exhaust collector-ring, a fire extinguisher, cabin heater, rear-view mirror, wing flaps, wing root and tail-group fairing fillets, 8 in. or 10.5 in.

tail wheel, lighted instrument panel, compass, air-speed indicator, rate of climb, bank & turn, and normal set of flight and engine instruments were standard equipment. Bonding and shielding, Westport radio, generator, oil radiator, landing light (1) in wing, controllable propeller, and 102 gal. fuel capacity were optional. The next Kinner development was the "Playboy" R-5 as described in chapter for ATC # 554 of this volume.

Listed below are "Envoy" entries as gleaned from registration records:

NC-13756; C-7 (# 108) C7-300.
NC-13756; C-7 (# 108) C7-300.
   -14289; C-7 (# 184) C7-300.
   -14929; C-7 (# 192) C7-300.
  X-14930; C-7P (# 194) SC7-370.

Ser. # 192 had wider fuselage and added gross wt.; serial numbers for (3) Navy "Envoy" unknown; ser. # 194 powered with supercharged Kinner SC7 engine; an "Envoy" on twin-float gear was exported to Japan some time in 1936 or 1937; approval expired 6-30-39. The Navy "Envoy" were Bur. no. A-9747-48-49 and designated XRK-1.

Fig. 107. Waco YKC with 225 h.p. Jacobs engine; this was one of the most popular airplanes in the U.S.A.

Hard on the heels of the new UKC, the Waco model YKC was the second offering in the cabin line for 1934. Basically typical of the model UKC, except for its powerplant, the YKC series were powered with the new 7 cyl. Jacobs L-4 engine rated 225 h.p. Offering just a little more in performance, the model YKC was an extremely versatile airplane and became the best seller for Waco Aircraft in 1934. Offered also as a practical good-performing seaplane on Edo twin-float gear, the YKC had soon migrated to areas that abound in water both here in the U. S. and in Canada. For the season of 1935 the basic YKC was modified to some extent as shown; several earlier features of needless expense and questionable import to operators in general were discontinued. As the YKC-S, this model along with the remodeled (1935) UKC-S and the CJC-S became the "Standard Cabin" models for the 1935 season. Because of various modifications, conducive to lower manufacturing costs, a considerable reduction in delivered price was also offered. As compared to the "Custom Cabin" models (UOC-YOC) introduced with pride and flair in 1935, the model YKC-S as shown at the Detroit Air Show was rather plain, but the utility offered at a considerably lower price was a strong point that helped sell this model in good

number. Several of the YKC-S were exported, one as far away as Johannesburg in So. Africa. Offered again for the 1936 season this Jacobs-powered model was altered just a little more to stay in line with operator's changing requirements, and in this configuration it became the popular YKS-6; with a very reasonable price-tag of $4995. This model sold extremely well. Eligible to operate as a seaplane also, several of the YKS-6 migrated to Canada, a few to So. America, and one to Australia. By 1936, "Jacobs" was producing the larger model L-5 engine rated 285 h.p.; this engine was an optional installation in the "Standard Cabin" biplane for 1936 and labeled the ZKS-6. Of these, several went to Canada, and the others operated in the mountainous regions of western U.S.A. It is true that the new "Custom Cabin" biplanes built by Waco Aircraft were hogging the limelight at this time, but the "Standard Cabin" biplane had its advocates too, and in larger number.

The Waco model YKC was also a cabin-type biplane with seating arranged for four; ser. #4419 and up of the later YKS-6 series were eligible to seat 5. Good-looking appointments with good-wearing capabilities offered comfort and pleasant styling that allowed the airplane to

Fig. 108. The YKC-S was slightly improved for 1935, and cheaper.

work steadily without becoming shabby. The visibility was ample and interior comfort was regulated by ventilation and cabin heat. Pleasant flights were assured by heavy insulation against noise and weather, and good solid stability was a boon to the pilots who had to work long hours in dubious weather and capricious air currents. As a versatile airplane readily adaptable for work, business, or play, the YKC-YKS series were certainly among the best of the line and owners were quick to point it out; to further increase its utility the YKC in all its versions was easily converted to a cargo-plane, an air-ambulance, an air-taxi, or mounted on Edo floats to operate off water. Gross weight allowance was progressively increased and allowable fuel capacity was increased also; these weight increases allowed addition of various aids and equipment, or allowed flights of greater cruising range. Physical differences of the various models in the YKC-YKS series are apparent here as shown, and point to a trend of eliminating costly manufacturing processes, or time and material consuming processes, that only increase the delivered price without much practical benefit; as a consequence, the 1935 model was $960. cheaper, the 1936 model was $495. cheaper yet, and each year the airplane was actually as good, or a little better. As powered with the 7 cyl. Jacobs L-4 engine of 225 h.p. the models YKC, YKC-S, YKS-6, were capable of very good all-round performance and suffered only slightly in the progressive increases of gross weight allowance. The model ZKS-6 as powered with the Jacobs L-5 engine of 285 h.p. naturally was capable of much better performance and therefore was picked more often by operators in

the mountainous regions. The models eligible under this approved type certificate were the YKC (1934), the YKC-S (1935), the YKS-6 (1936), and the 285 h.p. ZKS-6 of 1936; of these, 60 examples were the YKC, 22 were the YKC-S, 65 examples were the YKS-6, and 6 were the more powerful ZKS-6. Of note were the 2 examples that were built specially as the DKS-6 (ser. #4463-4464) with 285 h.p. Wright R-760-E1 engines and exported to operate in Lima, Peru. The type certificate number for the YKC-YKS series was issued 4-12-34 with amendments at intervals to include the various models in this series. Manufacture of the series was initiated by the Waco Aircraft Co. of Troy, Ohio in 1934 and continued into early 1937.

Listed below are specifications and performance data for the model YKC of 1934 as powered with 225 h.p. Jacobs L-4 engine; length overall 25'4"; height overall 8'6"; wing span upper 33'3"; wing span lower 28'3"; wing chord upper and lower 57"; wing area upper 130 sq. ft.; wing area lower 110 sq. ft.; total wing area 240 sq. ft; airfoil Clark Y; wt. empty 1800 (1808) lbs.; useful load 1050 (1192) lbs.; payload with 50 gal. fuel 550 (692) lbs.; gross wt. 2850 (3000) lbs.; figures in parentheses are amended wt. allowance; max. speed 149 (148) at 1000 ft.; cruising speed 130 (129) at 1000 ft.; landing (stall) speed 50 (53); climb 850 (800) ft. first min. at sea level; ser. ceiling 15,500 (15,000) ft.; figures in parentheses were at 3000 lb. gross wt.; gas cap. 50 gal.; oil cap. 4 gal.; cruising range at 14 gal. per hour 480 miles; price $6450. at factory field. Just prior to the 3000 lb. gross wt. allowance, the approved wts. were 1837-1013-2850 lbs. Ser. #3878 and up were eligible at 3000

Fig. 109. Rear quarter-windows were eliminated on YKC-S.

lb. gross wt.

All specifications and data for model YKC as seaplane with Edo 38-3430 twin-float gear was identical to YKC landplane except as follows; length overall 28'10"; height overall 10'7"; wt. empty 2186 lbs.; useful load 1064 lbs.; payload with 50 gal. fuel 564 lbs. (3 passengers & 54 lbs. baggage, which includes anchor and mooring rope); gross wt. 3250 lbs.; max. speed 130; cruising speed 109; landing (stall) speed 56; climb 700 ft. first min. at sea level; ser. ceiling 12,000 ft.; gas cap. 50 gal.; oil cap. 4 gal.; cruising range at 14 gal. per hour 400 miles; price not announced.

Specifications and performance data for the YKC-S landplane of 1935 were identical to that of the YKC except as follows; wt. empty 1773 lbs.; useful load 1227 lbs.; payload with 50 gal. fuel 727 lbs.; gross wt. 3000 lbs.; max. speed (without wheel pants) 143; cruising speed 124; landing (stall) speed 53; climb 800 ft. first min. at sea level; ser. ceiling 15,000 ft.; gas cap. 50 gal.; oil cap. 4 gal.; cruising range at 14 gal. per hour 450 miles; price $5490. at factory field; the YKC-S was also eligible as seaplane on Edo 38-3430 twin-float gear - performance would be comparable to that of the YKC seaplane of 1934.

Specifications and performance data for the YKS-6 of 1936 were identical to the YKC and YKC-S except for the following; wt. empty

Fig. 110. Model YKS-6 was "Standard Cabin" version for 1936; note change in landing gear.

Fig. 111. The YKS-6 as seaplane in Canadian service.

1809 lbs.; useful load 1441 lbs.; payload with 50 gal. fuel 941 lbs.; payload with 70 gal. fuel 832 lbs.; gross wt. 3250 lbs.; max. speed 144 at 2100 r.p.m. at 1000 ft.; cruising speed 130 at 1900 r.p.m. at 1000 ft.; landing (stall) speed 54; landing speed (with air-brake) 49; climb 750 ft. first min. at sea level; ser. ceiling 14,000 ft.; gas cap. normal 50 gal.; gas cap. max. 70 gal.; oil cap. 4-5 gal.; cruising range at 14 gal. per hour 480-650 miles; price $4995. at factory field. The model YKS-6 also eligible as seaplane on Edo 38-3430 twin-float gear - performance compared favorably with that of YKC and YKC-S seaplane.

The construction details and general arrangement of the models YKC, YKC-S, YKS-6, and ZKS-6, were basically similar to those of the UKC and UKC-S. The YKC-YKS series were of course powered with the Jacobs L-4 engine of 225 h.p., the ZKS-6 was powered with the Jacobs L-5 engine of 285 h.p., and both offered with either magneto or battery ignition. The YKC-S for 1935 also had discarded the cabin windows beyond the wing's trailing edge, and wheel pants were offered only as an option. In general, this model (YKC-S) was a little plainer than earlier models and a lot cheaper. As the YKS-6 for 1936 this model was changed slightly and delivered price was lowered again. Notable changes in the YKS-6 were a redesigned landing gear and engine cowls on later ones were without the familiar rocker-box humps. The landing gear of 87 in. tread was 2 streamlined legs braced to fuselage in a tripod form; this improved gear was of wider tread and more robust to handle gross weight increases. All models in the YKC-YKS series were eligible as seaplanes on Edo P-3300 or 38-3430 pontoons. A 25 gal. fuel tank in root end of each upper wing-half provided the normal

50 gal. supply. The YKS-6 and ZKS-6 were eligible with 70 gal. fuel; a 35 gal. tank was installed in each upper wing-half. For extra range a 100 gal. fuel capacity was also available; this included a 35 gal. tank in each upper wing-half and a 15 gal. tank in each lower wing-half. Baggage compartment of later models was a 6 cu. ft. capacity with allowance for up to 125 lbs. A Hartzell wooden propeller, patented (Waco) shock struts, 6.50x10 Autofan wheels with 7.50x10 or 8.50x10 low-pressure tires, wheel brakes, parking brake, 8 in. streamlined tail wheel, compass, air-speed indicator, navigation lights, battery, generator, battery ignition, dual rudder pedals and throw-over control wheel, electric engine starter, wing-root fairing, leatherette upholstery, adjustable front seats, ventilators and cabin heater, dome lights, 2 ash trays, assist cords, first-aid kit, tool kit, log books, tie-down ropes, and a basic two-color finish were standard equipment. A Hamilton-Standard ground-adjustable metal propeller, or a Curtiss-Reed (fixed-pitch) metal propeller, Westport radio set, magneto ignition, wheel pants, parachute-type seats, ambulance litter and equipment, Lear or RCA radio, Grimes retractable landing lights, fuel cap. of 70 or 100 gals., increased oil cap. to 6.5 gal., parachute flares, bonding and shielding, misc. instruments, air brake, extra cabin door, Lux fire extinguisher, Y-type control column, Edo P-3300 or 38-3430 twin-float gear, skis, safety belts for 3 passengers on rear seat, and Gunmetal Gray, or French Gray color schemes were optional. Ser. #3873 thru #3877 and #3975 eligible only at 2850 lbs. gross wt. unless equipped with wing spoilers, Ser. #3878 and up eligible at 3000 lbs. gross wt.; these ser. nos. also eligible at 3250 lbs. gross wt. provided late-type landing gear is installed and

spoilers mounted on wings, or if UMF vertical tail surfaces are installed. Seaplanes of ser. #3873 thru #3877 and #3975 must have wing spoilers installed; seaplanes also require larger vertical tail surfaces plus extra fin underneath tail-end of fuselage. Model ZKS-6 requires installation of oil cooler. The next Waco development was the model CJC as described in chapter for ATC # 538 of this volume.

Listed below are YKC, YKC-S, YKS-6, and ZKS-6 entries as verified by factory records:

Registration	Model	Serial	Engine
NC-14008:	YKC	(# 3873)	Jacobs 225
-14009:	"	(# 3874)	"
-14019:	"	(# 3875)	"
-14025:	"	(# 3876)	"
-14023:	"	(# 3877)	"
-14014:	"	(# 3878)	"
-14027:	"	(# 3879)	"
-14000:	"	(# 3880)	"
-14030:	"	(# 3916)	"
-14034:	"	(# 3917)	"
-14042:	"	(# 3918)	"
-14045:	"	(# 3919)	"
-14033:	"	(# 3920)	"
-14049:	"	(# 3921)	"
-14001:	"	(# 3922)	"
-14021:	"	(# 3923)	"
-14032:	"	(# 3924)	"
-14046:	"	(# 3925)	"
-CF-AWJ:	"	(# 3934)	"
-14084:	"	(# 3935)	"
-14006:	"	(# 3967)	"
-14002:	"	(# 3968)	"
-14053:	"	(# 3969)	"
-14039:	"	(# 3970)	"
-14050:	"	(# 3971)	"
-14055:	"	(# 3972)	"
-14057:	"	(# 3973)	"
-14058:	"	(# 3974)	"
-14081:	"	(# 3975)	"
CF-AWI:	"	(# 3976)	"
-14606:	"	(# 3977)	"
-14059:	"	(# 3986)	"
-14062:	"	(# 3987)	"
-14068:	"	(# 3988)	"
-14065:	"	(# 3989)	"
-14073:	"	(# 3990)	"
-14066:	"	(# 3991)	"
-14071:	"	(# 3992)	"
SU-AAN:	"	(# 3993)	"
-14072:	"	(# 3994)	"
-14131:	"	(# 3995)	"
-14078:	"	(# 3996)	"
-14077:	"	(# 3997)	"
-14126:	"	(# 3998)	"
-14064:	"	(# 3999)	"
-14079:	"	(# 4200)	"
CF-AWE:	"	(# 4201)	"
-14083:	"	(# 4202)	"
-14089:	"	(# 4203)	"
-14140:	"	(# 4204)	"
-14135:	"	(# 4205)	"
VP-NAC:	"	(# 4216)	"
-14133:	"	(# 4217)	"
VP-KBJ:	"	(# 4218)	"
-14139:	"	(# 4219)	"
-14086:	"	(# 4220)	"
-14087:	"	(# 4221)	"
NS-14137:	"	(# 4223)	"
-14127:	"	(# 4224)	"
-14600:	YKC-S	(# 4225)	"
-14601:	"	(# 4226)	"
-14605:	"	(# 4227)	"
-14604:	"	(# 4228)	"
:	"	(# 4229)	"
-14608:	"	(# 4230)	"
CF-AWH:"		(# 4231)	"
-14612:	"	(# 4232)	"
-14610:	"	(# 4233)	"
-14620:	"	(# 4234)	"
-14614:	"	(# 4236)	"
-14676:	"	(# 4237)	"
CF-AWL:"		(# 4238)	"
CF-AWK:"		(# 4239)	"
-14689:	"	(# 4260)	"
CF-AWM:"		(# 4261)	"
-15218:	"	(# 4262)	"
-15232:	"	(# 4263)	"
-15236:	"	(# 4264)	"
-15245:	"	(# 4265)	"
-15701:	"	(# 4266)	"
CF-AYS: "		(# 4267)	"
-15708:	YKS-6	(# 4268)	"
CF-BDK:	ZKS-6	(# 4269)	Jacobs 285
-15710:	YKS-6	(# 4408)	Jacobs 225
-15713:	"	(# 4409)	"
CF-CCP: "		(# 4410)	"
CF-CCQ: "		(# 4411)	"
-15720:	"	(# 4412)	"
-15723:	"	(# 4413)	"
CF-AYR:"		(# 4414)	"
-15725:	"	(# 4415)	"
-16211:	"	(# 4416)	"
-16210:	"	(# 4417)	"
-16215:	"	(# 4418)	"
-16216:	"	(# 4419)	"
CF-AYT:"		(# 4450)	"
CF-AYQ:"		(# 4451)	"
-16221:	"	(# 4452)	"
-16225:	"	(# 4453)	"
-16226:	"	(# 4454)	"
-16230:	"	(# 4455)	"
-16237:	"	(# 4456)	"
-16236:	"	(# 4457)	"
CF-AYP: "		(# 4458)	"
-16241:	"	(# 4459)	"
-16245:	"	(# 4460)	"
CF-AZN:"		(# 4461)	"
-16247:	"	(# 4462)	"
-16246:	"	(# 4465)	"
-16249:	"	(# 4466)	"
-16242:	"	(# 4467)	"
-16504:	"	(# 4468)	"
-16505:	"	(# 4469)	"
-16503:	"	(# 4500)	"
-16509:	"	(# 4501)	"
-16507:	"	(# 4502)	"
-16510:	"	(# 4503)	"
-16512:	"	(# 4504)	"
-16513:	"	(# 4505)	"
-16516:	"	(# 4506)	"
-16514:	"	(# 4507)	"
-16517:	"	(# 4508)	"

-16508; ZKS-6 (# 4509) Jacobs 285
-16519; YKS-6 (# 4510) Jacobs 225
-16521;   "   (# 4511)   "
-16523; ZKS-6 (# 4512) Jacobs 285
-16522; YKS-6 (# 4513) Jacobs 225
-16576;   "   (# 4514)   "
-16578;   "   (# 4515)   "
-16581;   "   (# 4516)   "
-16577;   "   (# 4517)   "
-16580;   "   (# 4518)   "
-16582;   "   (# 4519)   "
-16583;   "   (# 4520)   "
-16585;   "   (# 4521)   "
-16598;   "   (# 4522)   "
-16588;   "   (# 4523)   "
CF-BBQ; ZKS-6 (# 4524) Jacobs 285
CF-AZQ; YKS-6 (# 4525) Jacobs 225
-16589;   "   (# 4526)   "
-16593;   "   (# 4527)   "
-16597;   "   (# 4528)   "
-16592;   "   (# 4529)   "
CF-CCS;   "   (# 4530)   "
-16596;   "   (# 4531)   "
-17460; ZKS-6 (# 4532) Jacobs 285
      : YKS-6 (# 4533) Jacobs 225
VH-UYD;"   (# 4534)   "
-17451;   "   (# 4535)   "
      :   "   (# 4536)   "
CF-BDK; "   (# 4537)   "
NC-17456; ZKS-6 (# 4538)   Jacobs 285

This approval for ser. #3873 and up; ser. #3876 on floats in R.I.; ser. #3918 with Italian Embassy in Wash., D.C.; ser. #3934 to Canada; ser. #3971 as YKC to Jacobs Engine Co., modified later with L5-285 engine as ZKC; ser. #3976 to Canada, later modified to ZKS-6; ser. #3977 modified to YKC-S later to UKC-S; ser. # 3988 on floats in Penna.; ser. #3991 modified to YKC-S; ser. #3993 to Egypt; ser. #4201 to Canada; ser. #4216 and #4218 to Kenya, E. Africa; ser. #4220 first as UKC; ser. #4229 to Johannesburg, So. Africa; ser. #4230 to Alaska; ser. #4231 to Canada, later as NC-34215 in U.S.A.; ser. #4237 to Haiti; ser. # 4238-39 to Canada; ser. #4261 to Canada; ser. #4267 to Canada, later modified to ZKS-6; ser. #4269 to Canada; ser. #4410 to Canada; ser. #4411 to Canada, later as NC-34214 in U.S.A.; ser. #4414 to Canada; ser. #4417 to Alaska; ser. #4418-19 were company demonstrators; ser. #4419 and up eligible as 5 place; ser. #4450-51 to Canada; ser. #4458 to Canada; ser. #4461 to Canada on floats; ser. #4463-64 as DKS-6 with Wright 285 h.p. engine, exported to Lima, Peru; ser. #4524-25 to Canada; ser. #4530 to Canada; ser. #4533 to Argentina; ser. #4534 to Australia; ser. #4536 to Argentina; ser. #4537 to Canada; ser. #4269 may be CF-BBK; approval expired 9-30-39.

CURTISS-WRIGHT "CONDOR", AT-32.

Fig. 112. "Condor" AT-32 sleeper-plane with 720 h.p. "Cyclone" engines.

Even while the earlier "Condor" T-32 was busy proving itself daily in scheduled service for American Airlines and Eastern Air Transport, a new and much improved "Condor" airliner was already in the making. While still basically typical of the previous model T-32 the new AT-32 was cleverly redesigned both inside and out. The extra allowance in gross weight, and all the extra performance, was of course attributed to more powerful "supercharged" Wright "Cyclone" engines and the proper harnessing of this power with newly developed "controllable pitch" propellers. A most significant invention, the variable pitch propeller now enabled the pilot to select a "pitch setting" better suited for a certain condition of flight and not have to operate with a compromise setting as in the fixed-pitch propeller. The practical result of selecting " proper pitch settings" was shorter and quicker take-offs, a steeper climb-out, and increased cruising speeds with actually less fuel consumption. Beside having all this extra performance, and being somewhat finer inside and out, the new "Condor" AT-32 was also a convertible "sleeper". The normal day-plane arrangement carried 17 passengers and 2 pilots, while the sleeper-plane was arranged with 12 berths, 2 pilots and a steward or hostess. The "Condor Sleeper" was in scheduled American Airlines service between Los Angeles and Dallas-Fort Worth (first AT-32 delivered to AA on 3-17-34);

the "sleeper" was also on a run from Chicago to New York. A day route from Fort Worth to Cleveland was flown in 11 hours to make connections to New York City. For a time the majestic "Condor" biplane was "queen of the skies", however, its reign was all too short. Still almost new, but fast becoming obsolescent because of advances made in airliner design, the "Condor" was just about finished on major networks in 1935. By end of 1936, both American Airlines and Eastern Air Lines had sold all their remaining "Condor" liners to operators abroad. Hence, it is odd fact that the "Condor" performed far more service outside of this country than here in the U.S.A.

The Curtiss-Wright Airplane Co. took advantage of 70 years of railway sleeper development by the railroads and put it into an airplane. Since October of 1933, Eastern Air Transport had been operating one "Condor" T-32 between Atlanta and Newark with an experimental sleeping section, but the first airplane built from scratch with convertible day-and-night accommodations were the new "Condor" AT-32 ordered by American Airlines. Working in a walled-off corner of the Curtiss-Wright plant, Ralph Damon, Geo. A. Page, Jr., and a few associates, worked on the intricate problem of applying convertible sleeper equipment to an airplane. The crew spent many nights sleeping in the full-scale mockup, or trying out the comfort,

Fig. 113. Big, roomy AT-32 was cradle of comfort for 15 passengers and crew of 3.

and exploring the various possibilities of un-dressing and dressing in the space available. Eventually, the problems were worked out and a Pullman-type atmosphere had been achieved even down to the net hammock for clothes, overhead luggage racks, and sliding curtains for privacy. The spring-mattress berths were 28 in. wide and a good inch longer than railway berths. Each berth was equipped with a reading light, controlled warm or cold air, clothes hangers, and a call button to summon the steward for ser-vice. The mechanical layout had been designed to give maximum comfort and convenience for night flight, and ease of conversion to day-time operation even during flight. Twelve passengers, with a berth for each, were accommodated on night flights, and 15 passengers were carried on day runs. Realizing that passengers would ap-preciate pre-cooled or pre-heated cabins when embarking for a flight, C-W and AA developed a portable air-conditioning unit to prepare each "Condor", while still on the ground, for flight with a comfortable interior. While in flight, nor-mal means provided air circulation and warmth in the cabin as desired. All this had also been railway practice for years, but it was not until 1934 that anything like this had ever been developed for air transport.

The Curtiss-Wright "Condor" model AT-32 was a huge twin-motored transport biplane with seating and accommodations arranged for 15 to 18 places. As an airliner for American Airlines the AT-32 was normally used as a "convertible sleeper" with 12 berths, 2 pilots, and a steward for night flights, or 15 passengers, 2 pilots, and a steward or hostess for day-time flights. Im-proved considerably over the earlier T-32 (ATC # 501), the new AT-32 was equipped with deep-chord NACA-type engine fairings and larger, more streamlined engine nacelles. As powered with newly developed SGR-1820-F2 or -F3 "Cyclone" engines, fitted with Hamilton-Standard controllable propellers, the AT-32 was allowed a handsome increase in gross weight and performance was substantially improved. Higher cruising speeds were now easily achieved at better economy and performance with "one engine gone" was considerably better. In general, the new "Condor" model AT-32 was a much better airplane and just about the ultimate that could be practically achieved in a large multi-motored biplane transport. Several in-teresting variations of this "Condor" were also offered for export; the model BT-32 was arrang-ed as a bomber and the model CT-32 was arranged as an ambulance, a troop-transport, or cargoplane. A model AT-32C, a passenger-version of the CT-32 was a 26 place airliner delivered to "Swissair" for service on a route from Zurich to Berlin. The type certificate number for the "Condor" model AT-32 was issued 4-16-34 (for ser. # 42 and up) and 10 ex-amples of this particular model were built by the Curtiss-Wright Airplane Co. at Robertson (St. Louis), Mo.

Listed below are specifications and perfor-mance data for the "Condor" model AT-32, a convertible sleeper-plane, as powered with 2 Wright "Cyclone" SGR-1820-F3 engines nor-mally rated 720 h.p. at 1950 r.p.m. at 4000 ft.; length overall 49'6"; height overall 16'4"; wing span upper 82'0"; wing span lower 74'0"; wing chord upper & lower 106.5"; wing area upper 702 sq.ft.; wing area lower 506 sq.ft.; total wing area 1208 sq.ft.; airfoil NACA-2412; wt. empty (day-plane) 11,465 lbs.; wt. empty (sleeper) 12,-

Fig. 114. "Condor" CT-32 was all-cargo version; some delivered to Argentine Navy.

235 lbs.; useful load (day-plane) 6035 lbs.; useful load (sleeper) 5265 lbs.; payload with 375 gal. fuel (day-plane) 3050 lbs.; payload with 375 gal. fuel (sleeper) 2280 lbs.; gross wt. (day or night) 17,500 lbs.; max. speed 181 at 4000 ft.; cruising speed (.70 power) 160 at 4000 ft.; landing (stall) speed 62; climb 1200 ft. first min. at sea level; ser. ceiling 19,800 ft.; gas cap. 300-375 gal.; oil cap. 30 gal.; cruising range at 70 gal. per hour 800 miles; basic price $62,500. at factory field. The SGR-1820-F3 engine was also rated 710 h.p. at 7000 ft. (with 87 octane fuel) when used steadily at night in sleeper service. The geared "Cyclone" engines, with 8:5 or 16:11 reduction ratio, cost $8320. each; a hydraulic propeller control mechanism was optional on the -F2 or -F3 engines. All AT-32 also eligible as seaplane on Edo model 16800 floats. Some of the military "Condor" operated with newly developed "Curtiss" electric variable-pitch propellers.

Except for engine nacelles, engine cowling, and some minor detail, construction and general arrangement of the AT-32 was typical to that of the earlier model T-32 as described in chapter for ATC # 501 of this volume. More powerful engines (SGR-1820-F2 or F3) were operating with higher compression ratios and using higher octane fuels. The "geared" engines were also fitted with 3-bladed Hamilton-Standard or Curtiss Electric controllable pitch propellers. As described, the AT-32 was normally a "convertible sleeper" quickly arranged for day-time or night-time flights; all flights carried a steward or hostess in attendance. The all-metal two-bay wing structure was a normal two-spar type with wing ribs spaced at 10 in. intervals to preserve airfoil form across the span; long narrow-chord ailerons were in upper wings only. The redesigned engine nacelles featured NACA-type engine cowlings for better airflow and considerably less drag; nacelles were full and much longer, protruding beyond trailing edge of the wing. Landing gear retraction was operated electrically or with an emergency hand-lever; 15.00x16 Bendix wheels were fitted with 8-ply Goodrich tires. Wheel tread was 20 ft. 4 in.; wheel brakes and a 7.00x5 swiveling tail wheel assisted in ground handling. A toilet and washroom, with running hot and cold water, was in compartment aft of cabin area. Mail and baggage compartments were below the cabin floor; baggage wt. allowance (night) was 200 lbs. front and 271 lbs. rear; wt. allowance (day) was 200 lbs. front and 450 lbs. rear. All fuel was carried in the center-section portion of upper wing; 4 tanks at 75 gal. each and 2 tanks at 37.5 gal. each for max. cap. of 375 gal. Instrumentation was very complete including Sperry artificial horizon and directional gyro, bank & turn indicator, rate of climb indicator, sensitive altimeter, compass, clock, fuel gauges, and radio equipment. Engine starters (hand-electric inertia-type), 2 engine-driven Eclipse generators, 2 Exide batteries, misc. radio equipment (varies from 85 to 200 lbs.), parachute flares, navigation lights, landing lights, 2 cabin heaters, fresh-air ventilators, a Lux (remote control) fire extinguisher system, Pyrene (hand-held) fire extinguishers, dual control wheels, and first-aid kit were also standard equipment. The next Curtiss-Wright development were the T-32-C converted "Condor" as described in the chapter for ATC # 547 of this volume.

Listed below are various "Condor" AT-32 models as gleaned from various records:

```
NC-12390:  AT-32-A  (# 42)  2 Cyclone 710
   -12391:    "      (# 43)        "
   -12392:    "      (# 44)        "
   -12393:  AT-32-B  (# 45)  2 Cyclone 720
   -12394:    "      (# 46)        "
   -12395:    "      (# 47)        "
   -12396:  AT-32-D  (# 48)        "
   -12397:    "      (# 49)        "
   -12398:    "      (# 50)        "
   -12399:    "      (# 51)        "
        :  BT-32    (# 52)        "
 CH-170:  AT-32-C  (# 53)        "
     651:  BT-32    (# 54)        "
     652:    "      (# 55)        "
     653:    "      (# 56)        "
```

```
 A-9584:   R4C-1   (# 57)        "
 A-9585:    "      (# 58)        "
NC-11729: AT-32-C  (# 59)  2 Cyclone 710
   -11730:    "      (# 60)        "
   -11731:    "      (# 61)        "
   -11732:    "      (# 62)        "
   -11756:  CT-32   (# 63)  2 Cyclone 720
 2-GT-11:    "      (# 64)        "
 3-GT-1:    "      (# 65)        "
```

Serial # 42-43-44-45-46-47 as 15 place "sleeper", convertible to 17 place day-plane; ser. # 48-49 as 19 place day-plane convertible to 15 pl. sleeper; ser. # 50-51 as 19 place day-plane only; ser. # 52 del. to China; ser. # 53 as 19 to 26 place day-plane del. to Swissair; ser. # 54-55-56 to Colombian Air Force; ser. # 57-58 del. to U.S. Navy; ser. # 59-60-61-62 del. to Peru; ser. # 63-64-65 del. to Argentina; ser. # 42 through # 51 del. to American Airlines; ser. # 59-60-61-62 were commercial models originally built as military models having certain oversize members in engine nacelles and fuselage.

ATC # 535
(4-28-34)
FAIRCHILD, MODEL 24-C8C.

Fig. 115. Fairchild 24-C8C, a three-seater with 145 h.p. Warner "Super Scarab" engine.

The Fairchild "Twenty Four" model C8C was somewhat of a milestone in small cabin airplane development. Two-place cabin airplanes and four-place cabin airplanes were quite common, but three-place cabin airplanes had more or less been neglected for several years now. A survey of the market by Fairchild revealed that a three-place airplane would certainly be very timely at this point, and no manufacturer was really trying to reach this market, so the new "Twenty Four" for the 1934 season was planned accordingly. Happily, it was found that a slightly larger airplane with just a little more wing and 20 h.p. more would be quite enough to do the job. The larger interior dimension was handily arranged in such a manner that an owner-pilot had choice to take along only one passenger and several hundred pounds of baggage and what-have-you, or two passengers could go along with a smaller amount of baggage. As the fourth model in the 24-series, a series first introduced in 1932, this latest offering (24-C8C) was a sport-utility airplane that would provide comfort for 3, and yield a fairly high performance on relatively low power, with rugged structure requiring a minimum of maintenance. It was a homogenous blend of airframe strength behind a pleasing appearance that was all contained in generous airplane dimension; certainly, these were features that meant so much to the average pilot, be he amateur, week-ender, or otherwise.

Perhaps the 24-C8C is best described by what people had to say of it, and the comment was always favorable. One example that stands out as typical was comment by a prospective customer: "In all my years I have never seen a salesman so steamed-up about a new airplane, and after thoroughly enjoying his sales-demonstration, I honestly felt he was justified for his enthusiasm". Needless to say, the prospective customer bought the airplane and became another proud owner. In aviation circles a good thing gets around fast, so the C8C sold well and was soon popping up all over the country; and, its popularity seemed to increase with each delivery. Even occasional production of 20 airplanes per month was hardly enough to meet the steady demand. With a marvelous production run for 1934 the basic design proved so popular that it was continued almost intact for the 1935 season. In this new version for 1935 a little performance was traded off for an increase in gross weight allowance, and "wing flaps" were added to lower the landing speed. The roster of 24-C8C owners by now was a cross-section of sportsmen, doctors, lawyers, ranchers, businessmen of all caliber, and a few flying-service operators, proving that the 24-C8C had something to please just about anyone. One specially fitted "Twenty Four" was delivered to Alaska for a medical director of Indian Territory, a rancher in Colorado operated out of a field that was 8200 ft. above sea level, one was delivered to Manila in the Phillipine Islands, one to Honolulu in Hawaii, and one to Argentina, so the 24-C8C did get around. All these owners had

Fig. 116. Roll-out of the 24-C8C prototype.

one thing in common, they were enthusiastic about the airplane.

The Fairchild 24 model C8C was a trim high-winged cabin monoplane with seating arranged for 2 or 3. The "rumble seat" in back, normally occupied by a third person, could be folded out of the way to make room for piles of luggage, golf bags, fishing or hunting gear, or just about enough of anything for a week's vacation. On occasion the C8C would even double as a freighter with up to 500 lbs. strapped down in the cabin. Even with 3 husky persons aboard there was still allowance for up to 170 lbs. of baggage and paraphernalia. Standing there fairly tall, there was no need to crouch when walking up to this airplane and a door on either side offered easy entry up into the cabin; spring-filled cushions, cabin upholstery in real leather, and decorative interior trim promoted a desire to fly more often dressed in one's best raiment. Ample window area in front and down the sides, with a sky-light overhead, permitted a broad range of visibility for keeping a close watch on airport traffic. As powered with the 7 cyl. Warner "Super Scarab" engine rated 145 h.p. at 2050 r.p.m. the 24-C8C delivered a very satisfying performance with enough power on tap for that occasional bad situation. A friendly airplane with pleasant manner the model C8C was quite easy to fly well and instilled early confidence in even the most timid; lest we brand it as a fuddy-duddy's airplane, even the experts enjoyed it

because of proper response to proper handling. As one businessman pilot put it: "I am amazed at the excuses I can find to justify my flying somewhere in the "Twenty Four". The rugged innards of the 24-C8C were designed to withstand all sorts of abuse and every assembly was designed to require only a minimum of maintenance. As a bonus feature, all this was wrapped up in a pleasantly feminine appearance that promoted pride and proper care. Several improvements were incorporated into the 1935 model and it was also eligible as a seaplane on Edo twin-float gear. The popularity of the model 24-C8C assured its longevity, so it is not surprising that nearly all those manufactured were still flying actively in 1939. The type certificate number for the model 24-C8C was issued 4-28-34 with amendments awarded on 5-11-34 for 3-seater, and later for a 2400 lb. gross wt. allowance, and an amendment to include the seaplane. One hundred and thirty examples of this model were manufactured by the Kreider-Reisner Aircraft Co., Inc. at Hagerstown, Md.; a div. of the Fairchild Aircraft Corp.

Listed below are specifications and performance data for the Fairchild model 24-C8C as powered with 145 h.p. Warner "Super Scarab" engine; length overall 23'9"; height overall 7'3"; wing span 36'4"; wing chord 66"; total wing area 186 sq.ft.; airfoil N-22; wt. empty 1354 lbs.; useful load 796 lbs.; payload with 40 gal. fuel 363 lbs. (2 passengers at 170 lb. each & 23 lbs.

Fig. 117. The Fairchild 24-C8C had three-place market all to itself.

baggage); gross wt. 2150 lbs.; max. speed 138; cruising speed 120; landing speed 45; climb 750 ft. first min. at sea level; ser. ceiling 18,200 ft.; gas cap. 40 gal.; oil cap. 3 gal.; cruising range at 8.5 gal. per hour 505 miles; price $4000. at factory with basic equipment. Prototype wts. were listed as 1321 lbs. empty, useful load at 773 lbs., payload at 340 lbs., and gross wt. at 2094 lbs. Data for 1935 model of 24-C8c was identical to 1934 model except for following figures; wt. empty 1390 lbs.; useful load 1010 lbs.; payload with 40 gal. fuel 577 lbs. (2 passengers at 170 lb. each, 170 lb. baggage, & 67 lbs. allowed for accessories & extra equipment); gross wt. 2400 lbs.; max. speed 137; cruising speed (1900 r.p.m.) 118; landing speed (no flaps) 49; landing speed (with flaps) 43; climb 700 ft. first min. at sea level; ser. ceiling 15,500 ft.; cruising range at 8.5 gal. per hour 490 miles; price $4990. at factory. Latest versions of the 24-C8C (late 1935) were listed with a 1457 lb. empty weight which cut useful load to 943 lbs.; payload & gross wt. remained same. Seaplanes allowed 2260 lb. gross wt. on Edo L-2260 floats, or 2425 lb. gross wt. on Edo 44-2425 floats. Serial # 2661 and up (landplane) allowed 2400 lb. gross weight.

The fuselage framework was built up of welded chrome-moly steel tubing (round and square section), heavily faired with wooden formers and fairing strips, then fabric covered. The modish interior was arranged to seat 2 or 3; the 2 front seats were side by side and a folding "rumble seat" in back was available for a third person. Baggage was placed on either side of the rear seat, or seat could be folded up and whole area used for baggage; various amounts of baggage were allowed (23 lbs. to 193 lbs.) according to payload available. Cabin walls were lined with

"Seapak" (Kapok) and upholstered in leather or Bedford cord. The large dash-board had ample room for extra instruments and was fitted with a handy glove compartment; all windows were of shatter-proof glass. A large door and assist cords on each side provided easy entry into the cabin; the pilot's seat was adjustable and visibility was quite adequate. The interior was reasonably quiet and all plane-engine controls operated on ball bearings (some 52 in all); sun-shades and dual stick-type controls were also provided. Cabin ventilators and a cabin heater were optional extras. The wing framework, in 2 halves, was of built-up spruce spars in an I-beam section with truss-type wing ribs of spruce members and mahogany plywood gussets; the leading edges were covered with spruce plywood sheet and the completed framework was covered in fabric. 1935 models of the 24-C8C had "slotted ailerons" and "wing flaps". A 20 gal. fuel tank was mounted in root end of each wing-half; a 20 gal. aux. fuel tank could be mounted in the fuselage in place of the rear seat. The streamlined steel-tube wing bracing struts were combined into a rigid truss with the sport-type landing gear. The splayed out landing gear of 9 ft. 3 in. tread used oleo-spring shock struts of 8 in. travel; center vees were "faired" and provided with a cabin entry step. 6.50x10 low-pressure tires on Warner wheels were equipped with brakes and encased in streamlined metal wheel pants. Fittings were provided in the fuselage for Edo L-2260 or 44-2425 twin-float gear; skis were also eligible. Seaplane fuselage required several stronger members to handle extra loads of pontoon gear. The fabric covered tail-group was built up of welded chrome-moly steel tubing; the rudder was fitted with aerodynamic balance-horn and horizontal stabilizer was adjustable in flight. A Hartzell wooden propeller, NACA engine cowl, wheel pants, electric engine starter, Exide battery, wheel brakes, parking brake, wiring for navigation lights, sun-shades, windshield wipers, compass, air-speed indicator, safety belts, first-aid kit, ash trays, assist ropes, and tool kit were standard equipment. A metal propeller, engine or wind-driven generator, navigation lights, landing lights, parachute flares, cabin heater, radio equipment, seaplane gear, skis, and aux. fuel tank were optional extras. The next Fairchild development was the parasol-type model 22-C7G as described in chapter for ATC # 564 of this volume; the next development in the "Twenty Four" was the model 24-C8D with "Ranger" engine as described in chapter for ATC # 576 also in this volume. Listed below are 24-C8C entries as gleaned from registration records:

NC-45V:	24-C8C	(# 2600) Warner 145	
NC-13290:	"	(# 2601)	"
-13291:	"	(# 2602)	"
-13292:	"	(# 2603)	"
-13293:	"	(# 2604)	"
NS-31:	"	(# 2605)	"
NS-33:	"	(# 2606)	"
NS-34:	"	(# 2607)	"
NS-35:	"	(# 2608)	"
NS-36:	"	(# 2609)	"
NS-37:	"	(# 2610)	"
NC-14320:	"	(# 2611)	"
-14321:	"	(# 2612)	"
-14322:	"	(# 2613)	"
-14319:	"	(# 2614)	"
-14318:	"	(# 2615)	"
-14317	"	(# 2616)	"
-14316:	"	(# 2617)	"
-14315:	"	(# 2618)	"
-14314:	"	(# 2619)	"
-14313:	"	(# 2620)	"
-14358:	"	(# 2621)	"
-14359:	"	(# 2622)	"
-14360:	"	(# 2623)	"
-14361:	"	(# 2624)	"
-14362:	"	(# 2625)	"
-14363:	"	(# 2626)	"
-14364:	"	(# 2627)	"
-14365:	"	(# 2628)	"
-14366:	"	(# 2629)	"
-14367:	"	(# 2630)	"
-14390:	"	(# 2631)	"
-14391:	"	(# 2632)	"
-14392:	"	(# 2633)	"
-14393:	"	(# 2634)	"
-14394:	"	(# 2635)	"
-14395:	"	(# 2636)	"
-14396:	"	(# 2637)	"
-14397:	"	(# 2638)	"
-14398:	"	(# 2639)	"
-14399:	"	(# 2640)	"
-14719:	"	(# 2641)	"
-14720:	"	(# 2642)	"
-14721:	"	(# 2643)	"
-14722:	"	(# 2644)	"
-14723:	"	(# 2645)	"
-14724:	"	(# 2646)	"
-14725:	"	(# 2647)	"
-14726:	"	(# 2648)	"
-14727:	"	(# 2649)	"
X-14728:	"	(# 2650)	"
-14745:	"	(# 2651)	"
-14746:	"	(# 2652)	"
-14747:	"	(# 2653)	"
-14748:	"	(# 2654)	"
-14749:	"	(# 2655)	"
-14750:	"	(# 2656)	"
-14751:	"	(# 2657)	"
-14752:	"	(# 2658)	"
-14753:	"	(# 2659)	"
-14754:	"	(# 2660)	"
-14769:	"	(# 2661)	"
-14790:	"	(# 2662)	"
-14791:	"	(# 2663)	"
-14792:	"	(# 2664)	"
-14793:	"	(# 2665)	"
-14794:	"	(# 2666)	"
-14795:	"	(# 2667)	"
-14796:	"	(# 2668)	"
-14797:	"	(# 2669)	"
-14798:	"	(# 2670)	"
-14799:	"	(# 2671)	"
-15035:	"	(# 2672)	"
-15036:	"	(# 2673)	"
-15037:	"	(# 2674)	"
-15038:	"	(# 2675)	"
-15039:	"	(# 2676)	"
-15040:	"	(# 2677)	"
-15041:	"	(# 2678)	"
-15042:	"	(# 2679)	"
-15043:	"	(# 2680)	"
-15084:	"	(# 2681)	"
-15085:	"	(# 2682)	"
-15086:	"	(# 2683)	"
-15087:	"	(# 2684)	"
-15088:	"	(# 2685)	"
:	"	(# 2686)	"
-15344:	"	(# 2687)	"
-15345:	"	(# 2688)	"
-15346:	"	(# 2689)	"
-15347:	"	(# 2690)	"
-15348:	"	(# 2691)	"
-15349:	"	(# 2692)	"
-15350:	"	(# 2693)	"
-15351:	"	(# 2694)	"
-15352:	"	(# 2695)	"
-15353:	"	(# 2696)	"
-15378:	"	(# 2697)	"
-15379:	"	(# 2698)	"
-15380:	"	(# 2699)	"
-15381:	"	(# 2700)	"
-15382:	"	(# 2701)	"
-15600:	"	(# 2702)	"
-15601:	"	(# 2703)	"
-15602:	"	(# 2704)	"
-15603:	"	(# 2705)	"
-15604:	"	(# 2706)	"
-15605:	"	(# 2707)	"
-15606:	"	(# 2708)	"
-15607:	"	(# 2709)	"
-15656:	"	(# 2710)	"
-15657:	"	(# 2711)	"

Fig. 118. Fairchild 24-C8C seaplane at Wall St. ramp in New York City.

-15658:	"	(# 2712)	"
-15659:	"	(# 2713)	"
-15660:	"	(# 2714)	"
-15661:	"	(# 2715)	"
-15662:	"	(# 2716)	"
-15663:	"	(# 2717)	"
-15664:	"	(# 2718)	"
-15665:	"	(# 2719)	"
-15917:	"	(# 2720)	"
-15918:	"	(# 2721)	"
-15919:	"	(# 2722)	"
-15920:	"	(# 2723)	"
-15921:	"	(# 2724)	"
-15922:	"	(# 2725)	"
-15923:	"	(# 2726)	"
-15924:	"	(# 2727)	"
-15925:	"	(# 2728)	"

-15926:	"	(# 2729)	"
NC-15927:	"	(# 2730)	"

NC-45V was prototype airplane—first flight on 2-20-34; serial # 2605-2606-2607-2608-2609-2610 del. to Bureau of Air Commerce; registration nos. for ser. # 2614, 2617, 2673, 2677, 2722, 2730 not verified; ser. # 2627 to Warner Motors Corp.; ser. # 2650 as 24-C8CS on Edo floats—as PP-TAY in Brazil as of 1938; ser. # 2600 thru #2660 were built in 1934; ser. # 2661 and up were mfgd. in 1935; ser. # 2661 and up eligible at 2400 lb. gross wt.; ser. # 2679 and up had wing flaps; ser. # 2728 later as PP-ABA on floats in Brazil as of 1938; ser. # 2729 del. to Grover Loening as 24-C8CS on Edo floats; this approval expired 9-30-39.

ATC # 536
(5-5-34)
STINSON "RELIANT", SR-5A.

Fig. 119. "Reliant" SR-5A against backdrop of California mountains.

The Stinson model SR-5A was the most popular airplane in the (SR-5) "Reliant" series. Most popular because it was a happy medium type of airplane; it attracted more of the bigger business-houses, beckoned to famous people that wanted to enjoy their own airplane, and appealed also to commercial operators that needed extra performance, but were careful to not let performance demands cut too deeply into profit. The 9 cyl. R-680-6 was the heart of this airplane; from the standpoint of dependability and popularity it was the "Lycoming" engine with the most compatible characteristics. The roster of SR-5A owners was an impressive one and it ranged from newspaper syndicates, a number of oil companies, a Hollywood actress, and some were even pressed into airline duty both here in the U.S.A. and in Alaska. Of course, Errett L. Cord (boss of the Cord Corp.) had a new "Stinson" just about every year (he picked an SR-5A for 1934), and the Dept. of Commerce (Aero Branch) had at least 5 of these aircraft. Lovely Ruth Chatterton, famous movie star, was the first actress in the film-colony to own and personally fly her own airplane; as an avid amateur pilot she was very proud of the SR-5A. Miss Chatterton received her new "Reliant" at the factory and flew it all the way home to Hollywood, Calif. In fact, quite a few owners went out to the factory to pick up their new "Reliant" and flew them back home, leaving the little field at Wayne, Mich. in all directions. Because of a more deluxe attitude the SR-5A was generally equipped with all the available options; these included a variable-pitch propeller, radio equipment, night-flying equipment, Irvin air-chute seats, the latest in navigational aids, custom-plush interiors, and fancy color schemes in three-hue combinations. Most owners pampered the SR-5A with the best of care and its behavior reflected the appreciation, but this "Reliant" was no dude, it was also a working

Fig. 120. SR-5A as seaplane on Edo floats.

airplane that seemed to enjoy the most difficult jobs as well as the easy ones.

The Stinson model SR-5A was a high-winged cabin monoplane with seating arranged for four. In general, the model SR-5A was typical of other "Reliant" in this series, but its final assembly was slanted to appeal to a certain clientele; a clientele that had money for the extras and would actually stand to benefit the most with an airplane of this type. As powered with the Lycoming R-680-6 engine rated 245 h.p. the SR-5A performed exceptionally well and brought out all the good qualities credited to the "Reliant" design. All the SR-5A were equipped with trailing-edge "wing flaps" that Stinson called speed-arrestors, coupled with a positioning control called the "Selectiv-Glide" which allowed various nose-down angles to a landing approach; the steepest approach was recommended for smaller fields ringed with high obstructions. To extend its utility the SR-5A was operated on wheels or skis, and it was also eligible as a four-place seaplane on Edo model 38-3430 floats. The SR-5A was also eligible to be equipped with a "Smith" (Lycoming-Smith) variable-pitch propeller, an air-screw which allowed better selection of pitch angles for a considerable improvement in all-round performance. Comfortably stable, with an inherent desire to please, the SR-5A was a compatible airplane that seemed to fit its own response to the operators mood; owner-pilots loved the SR-5A and never failed to heap praise upon it. Its popularity tended to create longevity, so many of the SR-5A were around for quite a while; 2 of the SR-5A served with the U.S.A.A.F. in World War 2 as the L-12

in training and liasion work. The type certificate number for the model SR-5A was issued 5-5-34 and some 73 or more examples of this model were manufactured by the Stinson Aircraft Corp. at Wayne, Mich.

Listed below are specifications and performance data for the model SR-5A as powered with 245 h.p. Lycoming R-680-6 engine; length overall 27'3"; height overall 8'5"; wing span 41'0"; wing chord 80"; total wing area 230 sq.ft.; airfoil Clark Y; wt. empty 2315 (2325) lbs.; useful load 1075 (1150) lbs.; payload with 50 gal. fuel 575 (650) lbs.; payload with 75 gal. fuel 415 (490) lbs.; gross wt. 3390 (3475) lbs.; wts. in parentheses as later amended; max. speed 135; cruising speed 120; landing speed (no flaps) 58; landing speed (with flaps) 50; climb 900 ft. first min. at sea level; ser. ceiling 15,500 ft.; gas cap. 50-75 gal.; oil cap. 4-5 gal.; cruising range at 13.5 gal. per hour 420-645 miles; price not announced. Approved wts. as of 5-5-34 were 2315-1075-3390 lbs.; gross wt. later amended to 3475 lbs. (land) and 3610 lbs. (sea); SR-5A with Lycoming-Smith variable pitch propeller (ser. # 9250-A and up) were eligible as 4 place with 75 gal. fuel and 55 lbs. baggage at 3550 lb. gross wt. Eligible also with 90 or 100 gal. fuel; wings require reinforcing for 100 gal. fuel (50 gal. in each wing); oil increased to 6.75 gal. All SR-5A eligible on Wien or Kammer skis at 3300 lb. gross wt.

The fuselage framework was built up of welded 4130 and 1025 steel tubing, heavily faired to shape with formers and fairing strips, then fabric covered. There was a large door on each side for easy cabin entry, and a convenient baggage door

Fig. 121. Ski-equipped SR-5A in Canadian service.

on the right side. The handsome NACA engine cowl had "blisters" to provide rocker-box clearance and it was formed entirely by hand on a form block. Lower wing-stubs of welded chrome-moly steel tubing protruded from lower fuselage to form a mount for the cantilever landing gear and an anchor for the wing-bracing struts. The landing gear was fitted with 25x11-4 Goodyear airwheels which were encased in streamlined metal wheel pants; "Aerol" shock absorbing struts, mounted inside lower fuselage, were out of the slipstream. SR-5A also eligible as seaplane on Edo model 38-3430 floats at 3610 lb. gross wt. The wing framework, in two halves, was built up of solid spruce spars that were routed to an I-beam section, with wing ribs of riveted dural tubing; the leading edges were covered with dural metal sheet and the completed framework was covered in fabric. Fuel tanks were in the wing, one each side, of either 25 gal. or 37.5 gal. capacity each. The vacuum-operated wing flaps were mounted between the fuselage and the ailerons; a positioning control called "Selectiv-Glide" produced the desired amount of flap deflection for a landing approach. The fabric covered tail group was built up of welded chrome-moly steel tubing; the rudder had aerodynamic balance and the horizontal stabilizer was adjustable in flight. A ground-adjustable metal propeller, Eclipse electric engine starter, a 12-volt battery, hydraulic wheel brakes, 10.5 in. tail wheel, metal wheel pants, parking brake, dual wheel-controls, cabin heat & ventilation, shatter-proof glass throughout, rear-vision mirror, compass, and cloth upholstery were standard equipment. A Lycoming-Smith variable pitch propeller, 75

gal. fuel capacity, radio equipment, navigation lights, night-flying equipment, extra flight instruments, Irvin air-chute seats, leather upholstery, a wind-driven or engine-driven generator, and custom colors were optional. The next "Reliant" development was the model SR-5E as described in the chapter for ATC # 537 of this volume.

Listed below are SR-5A entries as gleaned from registration records:

NC-13841:	SR-5A	(# 9207-A)	R-680-6
NS-9:	"	(# 9212-A)	"
NS-12:	"	(# 9214-A)	"
NS-15:	"	(# 9215-A)	"
NC-13839:	"	(# 9216-A)	"
-13857:	"	(# 9219-A)	"
-13848:	"	(# 9223-A)	"
-13811:	"	(# 9225-A)	"
-13853:	"	(# 9227-A)	"
-13855:	"	(# 9230-A)	"
-13870:	"	(# 9236-A)	"
-13863:	"	(# 9237-A)	"
-13868:	"	(# 9242-A)	"
-13833:	"	(# 9246-A)	"
-14150:	"	(# 9247-A)	"
-14151:	"	(# 9248-A)	"
-13872:	"	(# 9251-A)	"
-13873:	"	(# 9252-A)	"
-13874:	"	(# 9253-A)	"
-14160:	"	(# 9259-A)	"
-14171:	"	(# 9261-A)	"
-14172:	"	(# 9262-A)	"
-14173:	"	(# 9263-A)	"
-14175:	"	(# 9266-A)	"
-14157:	"	(# 9267-A)	"
-14168:	"	(# 9268-A)	"
-14169:	"	(# 9269-A)	"
-14170:	"	(# 9270-A)	"

Fig. 122. Colorful SR-5A was popular in business promotion.

-14176;	"	(# 9271-A)	"
-14180;	"	(# 9273-A)	"
-14182;	"	(# 9274-A)	"
-14183;	"	(# 9275-A)	"
-14163;	"	(# 9276-A)	"
NS-14181;	"	(# 9277-A)	"
-14186;	"	(# 9278-A)	"
-14189;	"	(# 9283-A)	"
-14179;	"	(# 9284-A)	"
-14188;	"	(# 9286-A)	"
-14164;	"	(# 9289-A)	"
-14165;	"	(# 9290-A)	"
-14166;	"	(# 9291-A)	"
-14167;	"	(# 9292-A)	"
-14195;	"	(# 9297-A)	"
-14191;	"	(# 9302-A)	"
-14565;	"	(# 9303-A)	"
-14567;	"	(# 9304-A)	"
-14568;	"	(# 9305-A)	"
-14569;	"	(# 9306-A)	"
-14571;	"	(# 9307-A)	"
-14574;	"	(# 9309-A)	"
-14575;	"	(# 9311-A)	"
-14573;	"	(# 9312-A)	"
-14576;	"	(# 9313-A)	"
NS-14570;	"	(# 9314-A)	"
-14577;	"	(# 9315-A)	"
-14580;	"	(# 9318-A)	"
-14582;	"	(# 9319-A)	"

-14583;	"	(# 9320-A)	"
NC-14586;	"	(# 9323-A)	"
-14587;	"	(# 9324-A)	"
-14588;	"	(# 9325-A)	"
-14590;	"	(# 9328-A)	"
-14595;	"	(# 9330-A)	"
-14589;	"	(# 9332-A)	"
NS-81Y;	"	(# 9336-A)	"
-14596;	"	(# 9337-A)	"
NS-63;	"	(# 9342-A)	"
NS-64;	"	(# 9343-A)	"
-15104;	"	(# 9345-A)	"
-14594;	"	(# 9346-A)	"
-15101;	"	(# 9348-A)	"

NS-9, NS-12, NS-15, NS-63, NS-64 with Bureau of Air Commerce; ser. # 9219-A reg. to Errett L. Cord; gross wt. for ser. # 9250-A and up increased to 3550 lbs.; ser. # 9251-A, 9252-A, 9253-A later modified to SR-5C; ser. # 9268-A, 9269-A, 9270-A later modified to SR-5C; ser. # 9277-A with Penna. Dept. of Revenue; ser. # 9290-A later modified to SR-5E; ser. # 9297-A as seaplane with Maine Dept. of Forestry; ser. # 9302-A to Hans Mirow in Alaska; ser. # 9312-A later modified to SR-5E; ser. # 9314-A with Florida State Road Dept.; ser. # 9330-A to Ruth Chatterton of Hollywood; ser. # 9348-A to Alaska; this approval expired 9-30-39.

ATC # 537
(5-5-34)
STINSON "RELIANT", SR-5E.

Fig. 123. The popular "Reliant" SR-5E with 225 h.p. Lycoming engine.

Stinson Aircraft had two big-selling "Reliant" for the 1934-35 season. One was the 245 h.p. model SR-5A discussed here just previously, and the other was the 225 h.p. model SR-5E. As development of the series progressed, the SR-5E more or less became the standard "Reliant". As powered with the 225 h.p. Lycoming (R-680-4) engine the SR-5E was offered at a lower basic price, but various options were available as the owner would need for his purpose. Equipped with Stinson speed-arrestors (wing flaps) this version was also available with radio gear, wheel pants, extra navigational aids, night-flying equipment, custom color schemes, and the Lycoming-Smith variable pitch propeller. Offering either basic utility or maximum versatility, the handsome SR-5E was attractive to a wide variety of potential customers. The actual roster of SR-5E owners was indeed an impressive one; among these were included several oil companies, some nationally famous people, other aircraft manufacturers, a sportsman or two, and various professional people. For some of these it was their second or third Stinson; loyalty to the breed ran exceptionally high among "Stinson" owners. A surprising number of owners-to-be came directly out to the factory in Wayne, Mich. to take delivery of their new "Reliant", and several brought in an older Stinson to trade. Those that had the time to spare were treated to a tour of the plant, and often some other social entertainment which was "on the house", so to speak. On a casual go-around there was very little difference between the "Reliant" for 1934 and that of 1935, but Stinson practiced a periodic refinement of detail, both inside and out, which occasionally added to the performance and most certainly to the comfort and convenience of the passengers. It is extremely difficult to make a good airplane better, but Stinson was doing it, a little at a time.

The Stinson "Reliant" model SR-5E was a high-winged cabin monoplane with seating arranged for four big people. Basically typical of other "Reliant" in the popular SR-5 series, the model SR-5E was considered more or less as the "standard model" for the 1934-35 season. Had the two been parked together side by side, there was actually very little to distinguish the SR-5A from the SR-5E, except that perhaps the SR-5A was usually embellished with all the optional extras. As the standard model in the series, the SR-5E was also available with all sorts of optional extras at extra cost, but its 225 h.p. engine and its gross weight limit of 3325 lbs. restricted the choice to some extent. All optional equipment installed was naturally deductible from the .

Fig. 124. SR-5E was big seller in 1934-35 season.

useful load, so some swapping was necessary, be this one less passenger, a cut in the baggage allowance, or perhaps a cut in the fuel on board. As powered with the 9 cyl. Lycoming R-680-4 engine rated 225 h.p. the SR-5E was still a lively airplane of good performance and typical of "Reliant" nature and behavior. Dependable and quite economical, the R-680-4 engine as mounted in the SR-5E, provided enough power to get the job done with even a little left over for power reserve; on normal fuel consumption the SR-5E could be flown on 10c a mile, averaging nearly 10 miles per gallon. The nature of the SR-5E was such that it was perfectly at ease in its best bib and tucker to put up a good front for a proud businessman-owner, or work long and hard at all sorts of jobs to earn a commercial operator a fair profit. Hardly anyone ever spoke a harsh word to a "Reliant" and its appreciation was reflected in its behavior. Its popularity and its inherent dependability created longevity, so it is not surprising this "Reliant" was still seen in good number for many years afterward. The type certificate number for the model SR-5E was issued 5-5-34 and at least 52 examples of this model were manufactured by the Stinson Aircraft Corp. at Wayne, Mich. Following resignation of Lucius B. Manning as president, the directors appointed B. D. DeWeese to fill the vacancy; DeWeese had been V.P. and gen. mgr. since 1930. Wm. A. Mara was now V.P. and gen. mgr.; J. C. "Jack" Kelley, Jr. was sales mgr., and C. R. Irvine was chf. engr. for the "Reliant" division.

Listed below are specifications and performance data for the model SR-5E as powered with 225 h.p. Lycoming R-680-4 engine; length overall 27'2"; height overall 8'5"; wing span 41'0"; wing chord 80"; total wing area 230 sq.ft.; airfoil Clark Y; wt. empty 2250 lbs.; useful load 1075 lbs.; payload with 50 gal. fuel 575 lbs. (3 passengers at 170 lbs. each & 65 lbs. baggage); gross wt. 3325 lbs.; max. speed 133 (138); cruising speed (.75 power) 120 (122.8); landing (stall) speed 56; climb 750 (800) ft. first min. at sea level; ser. ceiling 14,000 (14,500) ft.; figures in parentheses with Lycoming-Smith variable pitch propeller; gas cap. 50 gal.; oil cap. 4 gal.; cruising range at 13 gal. per hour 450 miles; price $5775. at factory field with standard equipment. Eligible with skis at 3300 lbs. max. gross wt.; eligible also as seaplane on Edo model 38-3430 floats. A seaplane-type fin was required for increased area in the rear.

The construction details and general arrangement was more or less the same on all models in the SR-5 series (ATC # 530, 531, 536, 537, 550) except as specifically noted in chapter covering the various types. As the "standard model" in the series the SR-5E was also fitted with rich cloth upholstery, map and gadget pockets, sun-visors and rear-view mirror, Kollsman instruments, tilt-down front seat-backs, dual wheel-type controls, shatter-proof glass, roll-down windows, ventilation and cabin heat, two large cabin doors with convenient step on each side, compartment for baggage with allowance for 65 lbs., 50 gals. fuel (25 gal. in each wing), wing flaps with Selectiv-Glide control, 25x11-4 Goodyear airwheels covered with metal fenders, wheel brakes, parking brake, "Aerol" shock absorbers, 10.5 in. swiveling tail wheel, a Hamilton-Standard ground-adjustable metal propeller, Eclipse electric engine starter, Exide

Fig. 125. An SR-5E all dressed up for business promotion.

battery, exhaust collector ring, and 3-hue color schemes as standard equipment. Streamlined metal wheel pants, a generator, navigation lights, night-flying equipment, Lear radio receiver, bonding & shielding, leather up-holstery, Irvin air-chute seats, Edo twin-float gear, skis, a Lycoming-Smith variable pitch propeller, and custom colors were optional. The next Stinson development was the unusual model R-3-S as described in chapter for ATC # 539 of this volume.

Listed below are SR-5E entries as gleaned from registration records:

NS-442M;	SR-5E	(# 9206-A)	R-680-4
NC-13842:	"	(# 9208-A)	"
NS-7:	"	(# 9209-A)	"
NS-9:	"	(# 9212-A)	"
NS-10:	"	(# 9213-A)	"

Fig. 126. SR-5E makes early morning run-up prior to take-off.

NC-13850:	"	(# 9224-A)	"
-13851:	"	(# 9226-A)	"
-13852:	"	(# 9228-A)	"
-13854:	"	(# 9229-A)	"
-13858:	"	(# 9231-A)	"
-14159:	"	(# 9232-A)	"
-13859:	"	(# 9233-A)	"
-13860:	"	(# 9234-A)	"
-13864:	"	(# 9238-A)	"
-13865:	"	(# 9239-A)	"
-13866:	"	(# 9240-A)	"
-13869:	"	(# 9243-A)	"
-13862:	"	(# 9244-A)	"
-14155:	"	(# 9249-A)	"
-14152:	"	(# 9254-A)	"
-14153:	"	(# 9255-A)	"
-14154:	"	(# 9256-A)	"
-14161:	"	(# 9258-A)	"
-14158:	"	(# 9260-A)	"
-14174:	"	(# 9264-A)	"
-14178:	"	(# 9272-A)	"
NS-14181:	"	(# 9277-A)	"
-14187:	"	(# 9279-A)	"
NS-14177:	"	(# 9281-A)	"
NC-14185:	"	(# 9287-A)	"
-14165:	"	(# 9290-A)	"

-14190:	"	(# 9293-A)	"
-14192:	"	(# 9294-A)	"
PP-IAD:	"	(# 9295-A)	"
-14196:	"	(# 9296-A)	"
-14195:	"	(# 9297-A)	"
-14194:	"	(# 9298-A)	"
-14197:	"	(# 9300-A)	"
-14198:	"	(# 9301-A)	"
-14572:	"	(# 9308-A)	"
-14193:	"	(# 9310-A)	"
-14573:	"	(# 9312-A)	"
-14578:	"	(# 9316-A)	"
-14585:	"	(# 9322-A)	"
-14591:	"	(# 9329-A)	"
-14592:	"	(# 9333-A)	"
PP-IAE:	"	(# 9334-A)	"
-14593:	"	(# 9335-A)	"
-15102:	"	(# 9338-A)	"
NS-62:	"	(# 9340-A)	"
NS-64:	"	(# 9343-A)	"
NC-15104:	"	(# 9345-A)	"

Serial # 9206-A, 9212-A, 9277-A, 9297-A, 9343-A, 9345-A modified later to SR-5A; ser. # 9295-A and 9334-A in Brazil as of 3-38; this approval expired as of 9-30-39.

Fig. 127. The Waco CJC with 7 cyl. Wright engine of 250 h.p.

Six brand-new 1934 models of the Waco cabin biplane were ferried from the factory in Troy to the west coast in April for demonstration; the roster of pilots included Paul Schick (Waco factory rep.), Al Jacobs (of Jacobs engines), Lee Brutus (V.P. of Waco), Hugh Perry (Waco sales mgr.), H. C. Lippiatt (west-coast distributor), and genial Tom Colby of Berry Bros. paints. The shiny new airplanes promoted much interest along the way and even instigated several sales. Recognizing early the value of such jaunts for exposure, Waco Aircraft managed to sell and deliver 67 aircraft from Jan. to June of 1934. The model CJC shown here was the third offering in the Waco cabin biplane line for 1934, a trim-looking airplane of slightly altered dimension that performed as well as it looked. The CJC was not particularly a deluxe model, but it did show several alterations over the standard UKC and YKC. Not readily noticeable because of the tight NACA cowl, the CJC was powered with the popular 7 cyl. Wright R-760-E engine of 250 h.p. Another feature significant to its make-up, more readily noticeable, was the different wing cellule which presented a larger upper wing for more lifting area and a slightly more graceful appearance. Otherwise the CJC was fairly typical of the models UKC-YKC, but it had a certain distinction about it that set it slightly apart from the other two models. Like the UKC-YKC cabin models for 1934 it too

(CJC) was offered as a seaplane on Edo twin-float gear; performance of the CJC seaplane was exceptional and at least 2 were soon working in Canada. This Wright-powered model (land or sea) was offered again in 1935 as the CJC-S; a 1935 version with the Wright R-760-El engine of higher output (285 h.p.) was offered as the DJC-S and an example slightly improved as the DJC-6 for 1936. The world-famous Wright engines always did carry a rather high price-tag in comparison with other engines, so the CJC series were noticeably more expensive than the other two "Standard" models. What actually became a sort of detriment to the future of the CJC in this country was the fact it was somewhat above-class in the "Standard" lineup, but it didn't quite fit the "Custom Cabin" category either, so it was left in the middle while customers generally formed to the right and left of it. Considering that the Waco "cabin biplane" design was just barely 3 years old now, it is remarkable the amount of improvement this design had acquired in that length of time. Perhaps the reason for this was the rapid advancements made in all phases of aviation during this time, especially in engine and propeller developments, and some new concepts in aerodynamics.

The Waco model CJC was a cabin-type biplane with seating arranged for four or five people. Ample dimension inside allowed sufficient room for four big people with extra

Fig. 128. CJC was as handsome as it was functional. Most CJC and CJC-S were exported to Brazil.

stretch-room for those in the rear. Fancy appointments offered extra comfort and pleasant styling. A large amount of window area offered good visibility in most any direction, and interior comfort was regulated to a pleasant level by cabin heat and ventilation. Relaxed flying was assured by adequate sound-proofing and insulation, and exceptional inherent stability made the piloting a lot easier on extended flights. Several extra improvements were incorporated into the CJC for 1934 and it was offered as the top of the line in the "Standard Cabin" series. To further increase its utility for work or for play the CJC was easily converted to varied chores as a landplane, or mounted on Edo floats (pontoons) to operate off water. It is interesting to note that the largest portion of the CJC series built were exported to neighboring foreign countries; only 14 examples were registered in the U.S.A. A total of 29 were delivered to the Brazilian government for mail and passenger service, 2 were operated in Canada, 1 was delivered to South Africa, and 1 was delivered to Egypt. The popularity of the CJC series in foreign countries was naturally brought about by the stellar reputation of its "Wright" engine; the Wright aircooled radial engines had an enviable reputation the world over, and especially so in our own hemisphere. As powered with the 7 cyl. Wright R-760-E engine of 250 h.p. the CJC offered bonus performance under the most adverse conditions, with power reserve for that "extra effort" if and when needed. For the season of 1935 this series was offered as the CJC-S and in general remained pretty much the same; the streamlined "wheel pants" were eliminated and the "-S" was tacked onto its

designation (CJC-S) to label it as a "Standard Cabin" model for 1935. A higher-powered model using the 7 cyl. Wright R-760-El engine rated at 285 h.p. was labeled the DJC-S; the extra power increased the utility and improved the performance considerably. The labeling of a model as the DJC-6 (1936) was more or less a cataloging as no aircraft were actually built as such. The type certificate number for the CJC series was issued 5-10-34 with amendments at intervals to include the CJC-S and the DJC-S; 47 aircraft in this series were manufactured by the Waco Aircraft Co. at Troy, Ohio.

Listed below are specifications and performance data for the Waco model CJC as powered with 250 h.p. Wright R-760-E engine: length overall 25'8"; height overall 8'9"; wing span upper 34'10"; wing span lower 28'3"; wing chord upper 66"; wing chord lower 57"; wing area upper 157 sq.ft.; wing area lower 107 sq.ft.; total wing area 264 sq.ft.; airfoil Clark Y; wt. empty 1976 lbs.; useful load 1224 lbs.; payload with 70 gal. fuel 596 lbs.; gross wt. 3200 lbs.; max. speed (with wheel pants) at 1000 ft. 152; cruising speed at 1000 ft. 134; landing (stall) speed 52; climb 850 ft. first min. at sea level; ser. ceiling 16,000 ft.; gas cap. 70 gal.; oil cap. 5 gal.; cruising range at 14 gal. per hour 640 miles; price $8365. at factory field, lowered to $8165. in Sept.

All dimensions and specifications of CJC as seaplane on Edo 38-3430 floats were same except for the following: length overall 28'10"; height overall on water 10'8"; wt. empty 2296 lbs.; useful load 1354 lbs.; payload with 70 gal. fuel 726 lbs.; gross wt. 3650 lbs.; max. speed 132; cruising speed 110; landing speed 56; climb 750

Fig. 129. CJC-S was modified for 1935; 285 h.p. Wright engine was option.

ft. first min. at sea level; ser. ceiling 12,000 ft.; cruising range at 16 gal. per hour 470 miles; price not announced. All dimensions and specifications for CJC-S (land) of 1935 were same as that of CJC for 1934 except for the following: wt. empty 1941 lbs.; useful load 1359 lbs.; payload with 70 gal. fuel 631 lbs.; gross wt. 3200 lbs.; max. speed (without wheel pants) 148; cruising speed 129; landing speed 52; climb 850 ft. first min. at sea level; gas cap. 70 gal.; oil cap. 5 gal.; cruising range at 15 gal. per hour 580 miles; price for CJC-S was $7000. at factory field.

The construction details and general arrangement of the model CJC series were quite typical of the UKC-YKC series except for differences as noted. The larger upper wing was designed to handle the extra weight allowance and its overall construction was similar to other Waco craft in the early C-series. The landing lights on some were mounted in leading edge of lower wing and later mounted to retract in underside of upper wing. The "drag strut" or "air brake" was optional on the CJC also, but apparently not asked for very often. The fuselage of welded 4130 steel tubing, fabric covered, was also typical of the UKC-YKC series, and 1935-36 versions dispensed with the rear-most cabin windows which on occasion transformed the cabin into a literal sun-room. The 70 gal. fuel capacity was divided among a 35 gal. tank in each upper wing; one or two extra 15 gal. tanks in lower wing roots were optional. The baggage allowance was 100 lbs. for landplane; seaplane baggage allowance was 115 lbs. which included tool kit, anchor, and mooring ropes. Landplane was equipped with 6.50x10 wheels fitted with 7.50x10 six-ply tires (wheels must be placarded for these special

tires); the seaplane was mounted on Edo 38-3430 pontoons and larger vertical tail surfaces and a metal propeller were required. The CJC was also eligible to operate on skis. A hot-shot battery, navigation lights, Heywood or electric engine starter, cabin heater, wing-root fairings, a 10.5 in. tail wheel, wheel brakes, parking brake, Hartzell wooden propeller, throw-over control wheel, dual rudder and brake pedals, a compass, air-speed indicator, cabin dome-lights, ash trays, assist cords, tool kit, tie-down ropes, log books, and first-aid kit were standard equipment. A ground-adjustable metal propeller, Exide battery, landing lights, parachute flares, generator, Y-type control column, wheel pants, bonding and shielding, a Lear or Westport radio, fire extinguisher, Irvin air-chute seats, and custom color schemes were optional. Angle of incidence in both wings was 0 deg., and dihedral was 2.5 deg. in each wing. The next Waco development was the open-cockpit model YMF as described in chapter for ATC # 542 of this volume.

Listed below are CJC and CJC-S entires as verified by factory records:

:	CJC	(# 3881)	Wright 250
:	"	(# 3882)	"
:	"	(# 3883)	"
:	"	(# 3884)	"
NC-14013:	"	(# 3885)	"
-14018:	"	(# 3886)	"
:	"	(# 3887)	"
NC-14026:	"	(# 3888)	"
-14028:	"	(# 3889)	"
-14029:	"	(# 3890)	"
-14035:	"	(# 3891)	"
-14036:	"	(# 3892)	"
-14037:	"	(# 3893)	"

Fig. 130. Waco CJC seaplane in Canadian service.

-14038:	"	(# 3894)	"
-14024:	"	(# 3895)	"
:	"	(# 3896)	"
:	"	(# 3897)	"
:	"	(# 3898)	"
-14054:	"	(# 3899)	"
CF-AVW:	"	(# 3900)	"
:	"	(# 3901)	"
:	"	(# 3902)	"
:	"	(# 3903)	"
:	"	(# 3904)	"
:	CJC-S	(# 3905)	"
:	"	(# 3906)	"
:	"	(# 3907)	"
:	"	(# 3908)	"
:	"	(# 3909)	"
:	"	(# 3910)	"
:	"	(# 3911)	"
:	"	(# 3912)	"
CF-AWB:	CJC	(# 3913)	"
-14136:	"	(# 3914)	"
:	"	(# 3915)	"
:	CJC-S	(# 3946)	"
:	"	(# 3947)	"
:	"	(# 3948)	"
:	"	(# 3949)	"

:	"	(# 3950)	"
NC-15231:	DJC-S	(# 3982)	Wright 285
-14129:	CJC	(# 4222)	Wright 250
:	CJC-S	(# 4370)	"
:	"	(# 4371)	"
:	"	(# 4372)	"
:	"	(# 4373)	"

This approval for ser. # 3881 and up; ser. # 3881, 3882, 3883, 3884 del. to Brazil; ser. # 3886 del. to R. Cliff Durant; ser. # 3887 del. to Brazil; ser. # 3888 del. to Toro Mining Co. of Montana; ser. # 3894 del. to Humble Oil Co.; ser. # 3896, 3897, 3898 del. to Brazil; ser. # 3900 del. to Canada, later reg. as CF-AVN; ser. # 3901, 3902, 3903, 3904, 3905, 3906, 3907, 3908, 3909, 3910, 3911, 3912 del. to Brazil; ser. # 3913 del. to Canada; ser. # 3914 del. to Crusader Oil Corp.; ser. # 3915 del. to Johannesburg, So. Africa; ser. # 3946, 3947, 3948, 3949, 3950 del. to Brazil; ser. # 3982 modified to DJC-S, later reg. as DJC-6; ser. # 4370, 4371, 4372, 4373 del. to Brazil; ser. # 3881 thru 3904 and 3913, 3914, 3915, 4222 mfgd. in 1934; ser. # 3905 thru 3912, 3946 thru 3982, 4370 thru 4373 mfgd. in 1935; this approval expired on 9-30-39.

ATC # 539
(5-l7-34)
STINSON, MODEL R-3-S.

Fig. 131. R-3-S conversion was available for all earlier Model R-3.

Actually, the R-3-S was not a new model development; in essence, the new approval was just a set of specified modifications applicable to the earlier Stinson model R-3 already in service. The model R-3, a sister-ship to the Model R and Model R-2, was the unusual high-winged monoplane with retractable undercarriage that was introduced late in l932 (9-1-32) on ATC #493. As an entirely new concept in a high-winged monoplane the Stinson R-3 had more than its share of teething problems and most of these problems seemed to stem from, or because of, the folding landing gear. Most of the grave problems were eliminated eventually, but some not completely. Typical Stinson reliability seemed to be somewhat lacking in the Model R-3; perhaps only because complicated mechanical assemblies were more prone to malfunction and failure, and it seems that proper operating procedure was not always adhered to. All the changes performed to convert an R-3 into tne new R-3-S were not readily obvious because they were just swaps of one item for another. Perhaps the most significant, but less detectable alteration, was a change in powerplants. The original Lycoming R-680-BA transport-type engine of 240 h.p. was replaced with a new R-680-6 engine

rated 245 h.p.; to this engine was fitted the newly approved Lycoming-Smith "controllable" propeller. All the new Lycoming engines now had fuel pump drive, vacuum pump drive, and generator drive, beside many other internal and external improvements which added to performance and also to reliability. This combination of improved engine with a propeller that used more efficient pitch angles on take-off, climb-out, and in level flight too, was to be a considerable shot-in-the-arm to the overall performance of the new R-3-S combination. Factory or published performance figures were not available for the new R-3-S version, but it must be assumed that a noticeable performance increase throughout the entire range was certainly realized.

Like the earlier model R-3 the new R-3-S modification was still a chubby high-winged cabin monoplane with retracting undercarriage and seating was arranged for four. The most significant, and barely detectable, change wrought into the R-3-S version was installation of a new type Lycoming engine that was shrouded tightly with a new "blistered" cowling; because of a smaller diameter cowling the bumped-out "blisters" were necessary to provide

Fig. 132. Specially fitted R-3-S used improved R-680-6 engine; controllable propeller offered better performance.

clearance over the "rocker boxes" of the engine cylinders.

Besides, the blistered cowl was certainly more eye-catching than just a plain smooth one. The "controllable" variable-pitch propeller allowed use of more efficient pitch angles that took the proper "bite" and allowed the more powerful engine to operate at efficient r.p.m.; this obviously translated into shorter take-off, better climb-out, and increased cruising speeds. By virtue of the various items that were included as standard equipment the R-3-S version was fitted quite nicely for standby air-taxi, or long-distance charter work; standard available capacity of 90 gals. fuel extended cruising range to nearly seven hours, and a full complement of night-flying equipment, with radio, allowed operation either day or night. In comparison with the R-3 the R-

Fig. 133. The Model R-3-S with 245 h.p. Lycoming engine; model not very successful, but design led to popular "Reliant" series.

3-S version was 200 lbs. heavier when empty, useful load was 200 lbs. less, but gross weight was the same. With a useful load of 1010 lbs., carrying 90 gal. fuel, 6 gal. oil and a pilot, the payload was only 255 lbs. To carry three passengers and 50 lbs. baggage the fuel load was held to 40 gal. (20 gal. in each wing) or 50 gals. of fuel (25 gal. in each wing) with three passengers and no baggage. As powered with the improved Lycoming R-680-6 engine of 245 h.p. the R-3-S was more than a match against the new Stinson "Reliant" that was coming off the assembly line in 1934-35, but it was a rare breed of airplane, only seldom seen, and its history is confined mostly to the memories of only a few.

Listed below are technical details of the model R-3-S conversion per CAA inspection data: ATC #539 for Stinson model R-3-S of serial #8600 and up as four-place landplane with Lycoming R-680-6 engine rated 245 h.p. An empty wt. of 2490 lbs. include Lycoming-Smith controllable propeller, new engine cowling, landing lights, wheel streamlines, Exide battery, five parachute flares, Eclipse electric engine starter, bonding and shielding for radio, radio receiver, cabin heater, 7.50x10 wheels fitted with heavy duty 6-ply tires (wheels must be placarded for these special tires), 5.00x4 tail wheel, a fuel capacity of 90 gals. in four wing tanks (l tank at 25 gal. and l tank at 20 gals. in each wing), an oil cap. of 6 gal.; Switlik or Irvin air-chute seats were optional. Useful load normally at 1010 lbs., with a 50 lb. baggage allowance, and gross wt.

held to a 3500 lb. maximum.

For construction details and general arrangement of the model R-3-S refer to chapter for ATC #493 of U. S. CIVIL AIRCRAFT, Vol. 5. All details of R-3 will also apply to R-3-S except as previously noted. The Lycoming-Smith variable-pitch propeller was mechanically operated to an almost infinite number of blade settings. The propeller control was operated from the cockpit and blade angle could be changed at any time in flight by the pilot, at his discretion. Lycoming engines were allowed to operate at 2300 r.p.m. with the controllable propeller. The next Stinson development was the "Reliant" model SR-5F as described in chapter for ATC #550 of this volume.

Listed below are R-3 entries that were eligible for R-3-S conversion:

NC-449M; R-3 (# 8600) Lyc. 240
       : R-3 (# 8601) Lyc. 240
NC-12131; R-3 (# 8602) Lyc. 240
       : R-3 (# 8603) Lyc. 240
NC-12187; R-3 (# 8604) Lyc. 240
       : R-3 (# 8605) Lyc. 240

NC-449M; R-3 (# 8600) Lyc. 240
Ser. #8604 (mfgd. 1935) is the only known example to be converted to model R-3-S specifications; registration numbers for ser. #8601, 8603, 8605 unknown; approval for Model R-3 (ATC #493) expired on 9-1-34 so approval as R-3-S on ATC #539 would apply to all examples converted.

ATC # 540
(6-28-34)
DOUGLAS COMMERCIAL, DC-2.

Fig. 134. Douglas DC-2 on inaugural flight out of Grand Central Air Terminal.

The fabulous story of the (DC) "Douglas Commercial" all started with the revolutionary DC-1, and has since been told so many times over. The prototype airplane of this series certainly made a big splash in aeronautical history and shall go down in records as one of the most outstanding airplanes of all time. Yet, even while the DC-1 was out making history, an improved (DC-2) version (bigger and faster) was already on the drawing boards and taking shape on the assembly floor.

As revolutionary as the DC-1 was, the DC-2 was already a decided improvement; this was the fantastic pace of aeronautical development in this period. American Airlines and Eastern Air Lines were happily showing off their new Curtiss-Wright "Condor" liners on prestige routes, and United Air Lines was capturing the public's fancy with their "3 mile a minute" Boeing 247, but the escapades of the Douglas DC-1 operated in test and demonstration by TWA, soon overshadowed everything else that was happening in the airline field. With no one able to offer anything better, it was only a matter of time when the airlines, including "American" and "Eastern", were turning to Douglas and

placing orders for the popular DC-2. In Nov. of 1933, TWA (Transcontinental & Western Air) announced placing orders for over a million dollars worth of the DC-2, and Douglas Aircraft boosted their work force from 800 to well over 900 people to hasten deliveries. The first shiny DC-2 was delivered to TWA in mid-May of 1934 and 9 completed fuselages were already on the assembly floor. By June of that same year there were orders for 75 on the books and 41 of these had been delivered by October. With customers waiting, a shiny DC-2 was rolling out the door every 3 days and by July of 1935 the 100th example was pushed out onto the ramp to fly away and join the American Airlines fleet. Anthony Fokker, aircraft builder of world renown, sensing the great possibilities present, obtained rights for his company in Holland to distribute the DC-2 in Europe; KLM (Dutch) was the first foreign line to place an order, and several more major lines soon followed suit. By 1935, twelve airlines were boasting of "DC-2 Service" serving some 20 nations; the unusual performance and reliability of the DC-2 was indeed making a profound impression on the public both here and abroad. So many nice

Fig. 135. The DC-1 was prototype for "Douglas Commercial" series.

things were being said about the DC-2, and the airplane was proving it so, that airlines without a DC-2 were at a disadvantage. In a sense, the DC-1 "Douglas Airliner" had been a gamble, no one was too sure it could be delivered just as promised, but the job was done to the joy of everyone connected with it, and the events following were a significant turning point in the history of airline development.

Secretly under construction late in 1932 the DC-1 (X223Y) was up on its maiden flight on July 1 of 1933, and from then on was flight-tested and demonstrated continually under all conceivable conditions. To prove its exceptional performance and built-in margin of safety the DC-1 flew on one engine from Winslow, Ariz., up over the Continental Divide, to Albuquerque, N. Mex. Starting at Winslow Field (4256 ft.) the DC-1 climbed out on one engine, climbed well over the (7243 ft.) "Divide" maintaining 120 m.p.h. and landed at Albuquerque. At Albuquerque (4943 ft.) the take-off test and climb-out was repeated. On Feb. 18 of 1934 the DC-1 flew from Los Angeles to Newark in 13 hours 4 mins. averaging over 203 m.p.h. for the 2609 mile trip. This flight bettered the previous transcontinental airline record by 5 hours and its time was only 3 hours slower than the record for pure racing airplanes. For the next 2 years the DC-1 set many other records, it participated in countless new experiments, and it was finally decided in 1936 that its job with TWA was done; it was sold to Howard Hughes. Having no particular plans for the DC-1, Hughes sold it to an Earl in England; changing hands again it went to France, and by

1939 it ended up in Spain as a recco-transport during their Civil War. The illustrious career of the DC-1 "Airliner" finally ended with a crunch in 1940 as it crashed on the end of a runway during take-off; this had been its first and only crack-up!

The Douglas model DC-2 was an all-metal, low-winged, cabin monoplane of a shape and arrangement that made an indelible forecast of things to come. Of generous dimension and scientific aerodynamic proportion the DC-2 had normal seating arranged for 14 passengers and a crew of two; it was the ultimate achievement in air transportation, having more speed, more luxury, more reliability, and geater seat-mile economy than was ever assembled before into any one airplane. It was the DC-2 that made such fantastic schedules possible; New York to Chicago in 4-1/2 hours, New York to Miami in just 8 hours, or overnight from New York to Los Angeles in less than 18 hours. Needless to say, all the big lines were scrambling to place orders for the DC-2; by late 1935 nearly every major airline in the U.S.A. was DC-2 equipped. A rather large airplane, by contemporary standards, the DC-2 was certainly impressive and instilled confidence into the air-traveler; this confidence, making air travel a pleasure, was soon relayed to other air-travelers and the volume of traffic took a healthy jump upward. As powered with 2 Wright "Cyclone" SGR-1820-F3 engines rated 710 h.p. at 1950 r.p.m. at 7000 ft. the DC-2 had terrific performance and reserve power for a substantial margin of safety; for the air-traveler, whether seasoned or a first-timer, it was a "fly-

Fig. 136. Loading cut flowers into DC-2. Shipments flown daily from California to the east.

ing carpet", and for the airlines it was a welcome money-maker. From the pilot's point of view the DC-2 was a "busy airplane", but that was only because there was now much more to do. The DC-2 was fitted with latest two-way radio equipment, the most advanced navigational aids, a retractable landing gear, and (air brake) wing flaps which all required a certain part of the pilot's time, but the mastery of it was not all that difficult and it did make proud, professional pilots. Naturally, all the airlines wanted their DC-2 fitted a little differently, or appointed a little differently, and these were identified by "dash numbers". TWA, GAL, and EAL had the version called the DC2-112; Pan American and Panagra had the DC2-118, and AA had the DC2-120. The type certificate number for the Douglas DC-2 was issued 6-28-34 and amendments were awarded periodically to cover the various modifications. Altogether some 200 of the DC-2 were built in some 20 different models; these included 138 for the civil airlines, 5 for U. S. Navy-Marines, and 57 for the Army Air Corps. All these were manufactured by the Douglas Aircraft Co. on Clover Field in Santa Monica, Calif. Donald W. Douglas was pres.; H. H. Wetzel was V.P. & gen. mgr.; Carl A. Cover was V.P. of sales & chief pilot; A. E. Raymond, asst. engr. since 1928, was appointed chief engr. in mid-1934 after resignation of J. H. "Dutch" Kindelberger; Ed Burton, Fred Her-

man, and Fred Stineman were design-engineers. Edmund T. Allen, a free-lance test-pilot did most of the testing on DC-1 and D. W. "Tommy" Tomlinson was test-pilot for TWA on DC-1 and DC-2 program.

Listed below are specifications and performance data for the Douglas model DC-2 as powered with two Wright SGR-1820-F3 engines; length overall 62'0"; height overall 16'3"; wing span 85'0"; wing chord at root 170"; total wing area 739 sq. ft.; airfoil NACA-2215 at root and 2209 at tip; wt. empty 12,000 (12,010) lbs.; useful load 5880 (6190) lbs.; payload with 510 gal. fuel 2180 (2490) lbs.; payload with 360 gal. fuel 3080 (3390) lbs.; gross wt. 17,880 (18,-200) lbs.; figures in parentheses are wts. as amended; max. speed 205 (213) at 7000 ft.; cruising speed (.75 power) 180 (200) at 14,000 ft.; landing speed (with flaps) 58-60; climb 1120 (1090) ft. first min. at sea level; ser. ceiling 23,200 (23,-600) ft.; figures in parentheses for speed & altitude are with Hamilton-Standard controllable propellers; gas cap. max. 510 gal.; gas cap. normal 360 gal; oil cap. 38 gal.; cruising range (.75 power) at 96 gal. per hour was 700 miles; cruising range at .625 power (with 510 gal. fuel) was 1200 miles; price approx. $65,000. at factory field.

Late 1935 version of DC-2 amended as follows; wt. empty 12,190 lbs.; useful load 6370 lbs.; payload with 510 gal. fuel 2670 lbs.;

Fig. 137. Outstanding performance of DC-2 rendered all other airliners obsolete.

payload with 360 gal. fuel 3570 lbs.; gross wt. 18,560 lbs.; max. speed 210 at 8000 ft.; cruising speed (.75 power) 191 at 8000 ft. & 200 at 14,000 ft.; landing speed (with flaps) 62; climb 1000 ft. first min. at sea level; ser. ceiling 23,000 ft.; ceiling (one engine) 9500 ft.; gas cap. 510 gal; oil cap. 24-38 gal.; cruising range (.625 power) 1225 miles; payloads were variously arranged with passengers, cargo-mail, and baggage; the DC2-112 version carried 14 passengers, with pilot & co-pilot; the DC2-118 version carried 15 pass. with pilot, co-pilot, and steward; the DC2-120 version carried 14 pass. with pilot, co-pilot, and a stewardess. Successive amendments allowed gross wt. to 19,000 lbs. & the following engines: SGR-1820-F2, -F2A, -F3A, -F3B, -F52, and -F53, ranging from 710 h.p. to 875 h.p. for take-off. Airplanes with reinforced landing gear and centersection were eligible at 18,560 lb. or 19,-000 lb. gross wt.; all ser. nos. to # 1322 required modification — ser. nos. # 1323 and up were eligible at factory.

The fuselage framework was a roundish all-metal (17ST, 24ST, 24SO) semi-monocoque structure covered with riveted "Alclad" alloy sheet. Of 26'4" long x 5'6" wide x 6'3" high dimension the cabin was insulated and sound-proofed with "Seapak" (Kapok) and up-holstered in various rich fabrics. Fourteen seats were normally provided in the cabin, 7 on each side, with a fairly wide aisle between; seats were deeply upholstered in leather and mohair, and reclined to various positions. The interior was

kept at comfortable levels by a large-capacity heating and ventilating system. Overhead racks were conveniently placed for hats and coats, and seat-backs were fitted with gadget pockets. Pilot station was up front with a bulkhead door separating them from the main cabin. Main cabin entry was on the left and to the rear; an emergency exit was directly opposite. A large 76 cu. ft. cargo-mail compartment, with allowance for up to 1000 lbs., was just behind the pilot sta-tion; the 112 cu. ft. baggage compartment, with allowance for 420 lbs., was aft of the cabin area. A buffet cabinet for serving light meals in flight, and a complete lavatory were in the rear of cabin section. All windows were of shatter-proof glass. The tapered cantilever wing, in 3 sections, was an all-metal structure of Northrop multi-cellular "stressed skin" design. The 284 in. wide center-section provided mounting for the landing gear and engine nacelles; outer wing panels were bolted to butt ends of center-section panel. A system of split-type, trailing edge (air brake) wing flaps extended across the span from aileron to aileron; flaps were hydraulically operated. The retractable landing gear of 216 in. tread, in 2 separate units, folded upward and forward into engine nacelles, but a small portion of the wheel was left protruding for emergency landings with gear up. Air-oil shock absorbers (2 on each side) soaked up the bumps and 15.00x16 semi-airwheels were fitted with hydraulic brakes; wiveling tail wheel was 17x7. Two main fuel tanks of 180 gal. capacity each and 2 aux. tanks of 75 gal. capacity each were mounted in the center-section; a 19 gal. oil tank was mounted in each nacelle. The cantilever tail-group was an all-metal, multi-cellular, structure typical of the wing; rudder and elevators were covered in fabric. The metal covered fin and horizontal stabilizer were built integral to the fuselage; rudder, elevators, and left aileron were fitted with "trimming tabs". The landing gear and wing flaps could be operated manually (with wobble-pump) in case of failure to the normal system. Three-bladed (Hamilton-Standard) controllable pitch propellers, Eclipse electric engine starters, Exide battery, generator, Lux fire extinguisher, navigation lights, landing lights, dual control wheels, two-way radio, complete set of instruments for day-night flying, landing gear horn & warning light, ice warning gauge, and parachute flares were standard airline equipment. Automatic pilot, and constant-speed propellers were optional. The next development in the DC-2 series was the model DC2-115 as described in chapter for ATC # 555 of this volume.

Listed below are DC-2 entries as verified by various records:

NC-13711;	DC2-112	(# 1237)	2 Cyclone 710
-13712;	"	(# 1238)	"
-13713;	"	(# 1239)	"
-13714;	"	(# 1240)	"
-13715;	"	(# 1241)	"
-13716;	"	(# 1242)	"
-13717;	"	(# 1243)	"
-13718;	"	(# 1244)	"
-13719;	"	(# 1245)	"
-13720;	"	(# 1246)	"
-13721;	"	(# 1247)	"
-13722;	"	(# 1248)	"
-13723;	"	(# 1249)	"
-13724;	"	(# 1250)	"
-13725;	"	(# 1251)	"
-13726;	"	(# 1252)	"
-13727;	"	(# 1253)	"
-13728;	"	(# 1254)	"
-13729;	"	(# 1255)	"
-13730;	"	(# 1256)	"
-13731;	"	(# 1257)	"
-13732;	"	(# 1258)	"
-13733;	"	(# 1259)	"

-13734;	"	(# 1260)	"
-13735;	"	(# 1261)	"
-14268;	DC2-118A	(# 1301)	"
-14269;	DC2-118B	(# 1302)	"
-14270;	DC2-118A	(# 1303)	"
-14271;	DC2-118B	(# 1304)	"
-14272;	DC2-118A	(# 1305)	"
-14273;	DC2-118B	(# 1306)	"
-14290;	DC2-118B	(# 1350)	"
-14291;	DC2-118B	(# 1351)	"
-14292;	DC2-118A	(# 1352)	"
-14295;	DC2-118B	(# 1367)	2 Cyclone 735
-14296;	DC2-118B	(# 1368)	"
-14297;	"	(# 1369)	"
-14298;	DC2-118A	(# 1370)	"
-14950;	"	(# 1371)	"
-14921;	DC2-120	(# 1401)	"
-14922;	"	(# 1402)	"
-14923;	"	(# 1403)	"
-14966;	"	(# 1406)	"
- :	"	(# 1407)	"
-14924;	"	(# 1410)	"
-14925;	"	(# 1411)	"
- :	"	(# 1412)	"

Serial #1237 thru #1256 delivered to TWA; ser. #1257 thru # 1260 del. to General Air Lines & sold to Eastern Air Lines 2 months later; ser. # 1261 also del. to EAL; NC-13736 was ser. # 1286 & numbers ran consecutively to NC-13740 which was ser. # 1290 — all del. to EAL; NC-13781 was ser. # 1291 & numbers ran consecutively thru NC-13790 which was ser. # 1300; ser. # 1291-92 del. to EAL; ser. # 1293 thru # 1300 del. to TWA; ser. # 1237 thru #1300 were all DC2-112 versions; ser. # 1301 thru # 1306 del. to Pan Am & Panagra; NC-14274 was ser. # 1307 & numbers ran consecutively thru NC-14283 which was ser. # 1316 — these were all DC2-120 versions del. to AA; ser. # 1350-51-52 del. to Pan Am; ser. # 1367 thru # 1371 del. to Pan Am in 1935; ser. #1401, 1402, 1403, 1406, 1407, 1410, 1411, 1412 del. to AA in 1935; ser. # 1407 and # 1412 to AA as parts only; all EAL airplanes were leased thru North American Aviation; one DC2-118A (ser. # 1600) del. to Pan Am as parts only; the last civil DC-2 (ser. # 1587) was built in 1937; 59 of the civil DC-2 were still operating actively in U.S.A. during 1939.

ATC # 541
(6-29-34)
RYAN, MODEL ST.

Fig. 138. Prototype Ryan ST tries its wings over San Diego.

The slender and silver-shiny "Ryan ST" was one of the most exciting sport airplanes of all time and one of the biggest surprises in aeronautical history. Its very appearance, whether standing gently on the tarmac or cavorting noisily aloft, was bound to fire one's imagination with all sorts of pleasant dreams. The brilliant part of the concept was not its originality, but the daring of mating the best features from several outstanding designs into a package of harmony and rounded symmetry. The mating of all these select portions is where the unusual surprise came in. It was Claude Ryan's concern for beauty of line and for perfection of each small detail that made the "ST" one of the handsomest airplanes in the sky. Conceived by a master-pilot, the ST must have been designed especially for the light-hearted pilot who was bent on getting the most fun out of flying, and it has never disappointed anyone. By nature the ST (Sport Trainer) was rather spirited and left many interested operators with some apprehension at first as to its adaptability for pilot-training. In due time the ST series surprised everybody by trebling in duty as a mighty good trainer, a versatile sport-plane, and occasionally as a "week-end racer" at air-shows and airport dedications. The "Sport Trainer" gave student-pilots an entirely new feel in flying that overwhelmed many of them at first, but the airplane's nature was contagious and students soon learned to join in on the fun. An airplane with such outstanding performance on only 95 h.p. was bound to create a stir among the flying public and it provoked excited discussion all over the country. Although still recovering from the crippling depression, and hardly able to dig up the money, many inquiries from pilots swamped Ryan's office. Not all queries produced an order, but the wide-spread interest was certainly gratifying. Starting as a very modest operation, the Ryan factory launched slowly into airplane production and picked up momentum as it went along. The prototype airplane was put into use at the Ryan School of Aeronautics to give it a thorough shake-down in daily service; occasionally another "Sport Trainer" or two would be added to the school's growing fleet. The Ryan "ST" as powered with the 4 cyl. Menasco "Pirate" inline engine of 95 h.p. was built in relatively small number, and quite a bargain for $3985., but its companion model (STA) with a 30% boost in horsepower was soon to muscle-in past the ST and dot the skies in far greater proportion.

Virtually born in the shadow of the great depression the ST was a design by T. Claude Ryan that was unique in its harmonious assemblage of advanced ideas. No doubt influenced by racing airplane design in general, and perhaps by some racing airplanes in particular, the ST was a beautiful dream that was to take some figuring. It took Claude Ryan, along with Millard C. Boyd and Will Vandermeer,

Fig. 139. Men responsible for Ryan ST. From left; John Fornasero, T. Claude Ryan, Millard C. Boyd, Will Vandermeer.

almost a year to feather the edges on all these different ideas and put them all together into what turned out as a beautiful and highly advanced airplane. The ST (Sport Trainer) emerged on the scene to strained expectations, but the maiden flight by John Fornasero on 8 June 1934 and its government approval some 3 weeks later, dispelled all doubts and the camp was filled with joy. The good news traveled around fast. With an influx of almost daily inquiries Earl D. Prudden (sales mgr.) announced that the first batch of scheduled production was sold out even before getting started good, and deliveries could not possibly be promised till the end of the year, if then. Claude Ryan personally delivered the first production airplane on 31 March 1935 to a dealer (Leonard R. Peterson) in Seattle. One customer later flew to Calif. and remained close at hand until his ST was completed. The 95 h.p. model ST was a terrific airplane and surely would have kept the factory busy for months to come, but it was such a simple matter to go to a larger (125 h.p.) Menasco engine and offer the unbelievable increases in performance for just a few more dollars.

The Ryan ST was a slender wire-braced low wing monoplane with seating for 2 in tandem. The narrow fuselage of oval cross-section was a little chummy for pilots with big shoulders, but it allowed a good range of visibility around the nose and down past the sides. A canopy enclosure was offered, but most pilots actually preferred the sporty open cockpit atmosphere. To double the cruising range, a 24 gal. fuel tank could be mounted in the front cockpit, which was then covered with a metal panel to produce a one-seater racy appearance. Designed specifically to appeal to the sportsman the ST had beautiful lines and its advanced features marked an owner for constant query and open envy. It was easy to keep it looking new and maintenance and operating costs were very low. As powered with the 4 cyl. aircooled inline Menasco "Pirate" B-4 engine of 95 h.p. the Ryan ST could outstrip anything in its class. Exceptionally maneuverable, the ST could easily satisfy the expert, yet was stable and cooperative enough not to befuddle the novice. Eager and of spirited nature, it was however thoroughly predictable and harbored no hidden tricks. The (95 h.p.) ST was a frisky airplane, but certainly not in the same caliber as its (125 h.p.) STA sister-ship which became an aerobatic champion. The type certificate number for the (95 h.p.) Ryan ST was issued 6-29-34 and only 4 examples of this model were built by the Ryan Aeronautical Co. on Lindbergh Field in San Diego, Calif. T. Claude Ryan was pres. & gen. mgr.; Earl D. Prudden was V.P. & sales mgr.; Millard C. Boyd and Will Vandermeer were proj. engrs.; and John Fornasero was chief pilot.

Listed below are specifications and perfor-

Fig. 140. Ryan ST was a "hot" airplane, but very manageable; pilots adored it.

mance data for the Ryan ST as powered with the 95 h.p. Menasco B-4 engine; length overall 21'6"; height overall 6'11"; wing span 29'11"; wing chord 56"; total wing area 124 sq. ft.; airfoil NACA-2412; wt. empty 1027 lbs.; useful load 543 lbs.; payload with 24 gal. fuel 210 lbs. (1 passenger at 170 lb. & 40 lb. baggage); gross wt. 1570 lbs; max. speed (2000 r.p.m.) 140; cruising speed 120 at 2000 ft.; landing speed (with flaps) 40; landing speed (without flaps) 48; take-off run (fully loaded) 570 ft.; climb 808 ft. first min. at sea level; ser. ceiling 15,500 ft.; gas cap. 24 gal.; oil cap. max. 2.5 gal.; cruising range at 7 gal. per hour 390 miles; price $3985. at factory field. Wts. of prototype were 1022-528-1550 lbs.

The fuselage framework was an oval monocoque structure of 17ST alloy "rings" covered with 17ST "Alclad" metal sheet; except for 2 heavy alloy stringers, all tension and torsional loads were supported by the "metal skin". The 2 open cockpits were small and chummy, but well protected by curved Pyralin windshields; cockpits were equipped with parachute-type bucket seats. The baggage allowance was 40 lbs., but no baggage was allowed when parachutes were carried. The interior was rather plain and bare, but leather trim was optional; dual stick-type controls were provided. A 24 gal. fuel tank was mounted high in the fuselage ahead of front cockpit. The stub-wing was a welded steel tube structure bolted to bottom side of the fuselage; the stub-wing supported the landing gear, the outer wing panels, and all the bracing-wire trusses. The wing framework was built up of solid (laminated) spruce spar beams and stamped-out 17ST alloy wing ribs; the leading edges were covered with dural metal sheet and the completed framework was covered in fabric. Friese-type ailerons were a metal structure covered with fabric; the trail-

Fig. 141. The Ryan ST with 95 h.p. Menasco B-4 engine; racing-plane influence is evident.

Fig. 142. Four cyl. "inline" Menasco provided slender profile and minimum drag.

ing edge "flaps" were also of metal structure and covered with fabric. The (12.54 sq. ft.) flaps were operated by a manual lever with a positive lock in any of the 4 positions. The wing was braced, top and bottom, by heavy-gauge streamlined steel wire. The treadle-type landing gear of 66 in. tread was of 2 streamlined units that employed long-stroke "Aerol" (air-oil) shock absorbing struts; 18x8-3 Goodyear airwheels were fitted with multiple-disc brakes. The landing gear was fully faired and the wheels were encased in streamlined metal wheel pants. An 8 in. full-swivel tail wheel was an aid to ground handling. The fabric covered tail group was built up of 17ST alloy tubular spars with stamped-out 17ST ribs; a "trimming tab" on trailing edge of the elevator eliminated the old-fashioned way of adjusting the whole horizontal stabilizer. The "tab" was adjustable from either seat. The Menasco "Pirate" model B-4 engine of 95 h.p. at 1975 r.p.m. was suspended in rubber and completely encased in metal cowling; the engine cowling was of the NACA-type with a venturi-type slot in the rear for scavenged exit of the hot air. A Hartzell wooden propeller, impulse starter, air-speed indicator, Pyrene fire extinguisher, wiring for navigation lights, parking brake, dual controls, compass, fuel gauge, first-aid kit, tool kit, and log books were standard equipment. A metal propeller, battery, landing lights, leather upholstery in a coice of colors, 24 gal. extra fuel, and front cockpit cover were optional. The next Ryan development was the more powerful model STA as described in the chapter for ATC #571 of this volume.

Listed below are Ryan ST entries as verified by company records:

NC-14223: ST (# 101) Menasco B4-95
  -14909: ST (# 102) Menasco B4-95
  -14911: ST (# 104) Menasco B4-95
  -14985: ST (# 117) Menasco B4-95

This approval for serial # 101 and up; ser. #102 was first production airplane and delivered by Claude Ryan to Seattle; approval expired 9-30-39.

ATC # 542
(6-29-34)
WACO, MODEL YMF.

Fig. 143. The handsome Waco YMF with 225 h.p. Jacobs engine.

By this point in time the three-place open cockpit biplane had all but lost its classic role for all-purpose service and took up the new role of catering almost exclusively to the adventurous business man and the hardy-type of flying sportsman, or sportswoman. Understandably reluctant to drop this classic F-series design, in spite of the greatly reduced market, Waco Aircraft introduced two F-3 models for the 1934 season. The model YMF-3 as powered with the 7 cyl. Jacobs L-4 engine of 225 h.p. did not represent any marked structural changes over corresponding previous models, however, the F-3 certainly did offer numerous aerodynamic refinements and much closer attention to detail; these were changes that added up to a better appearance and some improvement to the performance. A somewhat larger airplane, with more room inside, the F-3 had been lengthened, widened, and softly rounded in places to eliminate that pugnacious look of the earlier F-types. Although the YMF didn't have the aggressive appearance of the F-2, it was still an overall combination of excellent performance and utility. The roster of owners shows that the three-place YMF was either relegated to yeoman duty in various fields of business, or providing the varied utility required of a personal sportplane. Just slightly refined for the

1935 season this model emerged in the prolific "Waco" lineup as the YMF-5. As a bonus of usefulness, for business or sport, the YMF was also eligible as a seaplane on Edo twin-float gear. Generally held in pampered esteem the YMF led a good life and nearly all were still operating actively in 1939. In recent years, several have been completely restored to fly again.

The Waco model YMF was an open cockpit biplane with seating normally arranged for three. Many pleasing and noticeable changes appeared in the F-series for the new season. Both the YMF and its companion model the UMF now had deep-chord NACA-type engine cowlings that contributed measurably to extra speed; the fuselages were faired out more deeply to blend in with the circular cross-section up front. Because of the cross-sectional increases it was easier to provide extra dimension in both cockpits to treat occupants with a little more elbow room. The added fuselage length provided better transition for airflow and the longer moment arm took some of the nervousness out of longitudinal control. Developed for a role that was less demanding than in previous years, this new three-place (YMF) version was usually in fancier dress and seen more often at the better places. This, no doubt, was because the YMF

Fig. 144. YMF shown was operated by Carpenter Paper Co. to drum up sales in the west.

was used mainly for sport, or for the promotion of someone's business. As a consequence, the operating YMF reflected better care and missed the many menial chores that were generally found in all-purpose service. As powered with the 7 cyl. Jacobs L-4 engine rated 225 h.p. at 2000 r.p.m. the model YMF had a relatively broad range of good performance with a substantial bonus of extra speed. Some of the typical "Waco" characteristics, like short short-field take-offs, landings on a veritable postage-stamp, and rat-race maneuverability, were not present in the YMF to the full extent, but nevertheless, a small sacrifice in some of these characteristics was more than offset by the other bonuses offered. A beautiful airplane, especially when bedecked in custom colors, the YMF remained popular through the years and accumulated a very good service record. The type certificate number for the Jacobs-powered model YMF was issued 6-29-34 and 18 examples of this model were manufactured in 1934-35 by the Waco Aircraft Co. at Troy, Ohio.

Listed below are specifications and performance data for the model YMF-3 (YMF-5) as powered with 225 h.p. Jacobs L-4 engine; length overall 23'4"; height overall 8'5"; wing span upper 30'0"; wing span lower 26'10"; wing chord upper & lower 57"; wing area upper 130.8 sq. ft.; wing area lower 102.7 sq. ft.; total wing area 233.5 sq. ft.; airfoil Clark Y; wt. empty 1540 lbs.; useful load 960 lbs.; payload with 50 gal. fuel 460 lbs. (2 passengers at 170 lb. each & 100 lb. baggage); gross wt. 2500 lbs.; max. speed (1000 ft.) 147; cruising speed (1900 r.p.m.) 129; landing (stall) speed 47; climb 1250 ft. first min.

at sea level; ser. ceiling 16,000 ft.; gas cap. normal 50 gal.; gas cap. max. 62.5 gal.; oil cap. 4-5 gal.; cruising range at 14 gal. per hour 420 miles; price $6795. at factory field.

Specifications and performance data for YMF as seaplane on Edo model M-2665 twin-float gear was identical except as follows: length overall 26'8"; height overall (on water) 10'2"; wt. empty 1790 lbs.; useful load 960 lbs.; payload with 50 gal. fuel 460 lbs; gross wt. 2750 lbs.; max. speed (at 1000 ft.) 132; crusing speed (1900 r.p.m.) 116; landing (stall) speed 50; climb 850 ft. first min. at sea level; ser. ceiling 15,000 ft.; cruising range at 14 gal. per hour 375 miles; price not announced.

The fuselage framework was built up of welded chrome-moly steel tubing, lavishly faired with wooden formers and fairing strips, then fabric covered. The front cockpit for two, was now wider and deeper for more stretch-room with easy entry off the wing-walk. The pilot's cockpit was also more spacious and handsomely trimmed in real leather. The brake system was improved and dual stick-type controls were available. A baggage allowance of 100 lbs. was divided among a front compartment (in dash-panel of front cockpit) holding 25 lbs., and a larger compartment in turtleback section (holding 75 lbs.) with a large access door (with Sesame locks) on left side. A large deep-chord NACA engine cowl shrouded the powerplant for better airflow and substantial increases in speed. The Jacobs L-4 engine normally operated with battery ignition using Bosch coils, distributors, and generator; this system provided quick starts, smoother idling, and better acceleration. Dual

Fig. 145. Models YMF and UMF were sportsman's airplane, but used occasionally for pilot training also.

magneto ignition, still the favorite of many, was optional in the L-4M engine. The wing framework of 4 panels and a center-section was built up of solid spruce spar beams with spruce and plywood truss-type wing ribs; the leading edges were covered with dural metal sheet and the completed framework was covered in fabric. The center-section panel, mounted on splayed out N-type struts, held two gravity-feed fuel tanks of 25 gal. each; an extra fuel tank of 12.5 gal. capacity, in root end of right upper wing, was optional. The landing gear of 74 in. tread used patented "Waco" shock struts mounted in faired vees; 6.50x10 wheels mounting 7.50x10 low-pressure tires were equipped with Autofan brakes. Metal wheel streamlines (pants) were optional. An 8 in. streamlined tail wheel was provided, but an old-fashioned tail skid was available as option. The fabric covered tail-group was built up of welded chrome-moly steel tubing; the elevators were aerodynamically balanced and the horizontal stabilizer was ad-

Fig. 146. Fancy scalloped design on this YMF was blue and white.

justable in flight. A Hartzell wooden propeller, electric (or Heywood air) engine starter, battery ignition, generator, battery, NACA engine cowl, wing-root fairings, a compass, parking brake, air-speed indicator, navigation lights, dual controls, tail wheel, tool kit, first-aid kit, fire extinguisher, log books, tie-down ropes, and cockpit covers were standard equipment, magneto (dual) ignition, a metal (Hamilton-Standard or Curtiss) propeller, wheel pants, landing lights, parachute flares, Westport or Lear radio, bonding and shielding, and extra (12.5 gal.) fuel tank were optional. Standard colors were Vermillion, Gunmetal Gray, Insignia Blue, or Silver fuselage with Silver wings; striping at customer's option. Other custom colors were optional. In turn, the next "Waco" development was the fabulous S3HD as described in chapter for ATC #543 of this volume.

Listed below are YMF entries as verified by company records:

NC-14031; YMF-3 (# 3944) Jacobs 225

-14069;	"	(# 3945)	"
-14132;	YMF-5	(# 3957)	"
-15241;	"	(# 3960)	"
-14051;	"	(# 3961)	"
NC-86Y;	"	(# 3962)	"
-14067;	"	(# 3963)	"
-14074;	"	(# 3964)	"
-14063;	"	(# 3965)	"
-14070;	"	(# 4206)	"
-14075;	"	(# 4207)	"
-14138;	"	(# 4208)	"
-14080;	"	(# 4209)	"
-14082;	"	(# 4210)	"
-14134;	"	(# 4211)	"
-14056;	"	(# 4212)	"
-14128;	"	(# 4213)	"
-14607;	"	(# 4214)	"

Serial # 3957 delivered to noted sportsman Henry J. Topping; ser. # 3963 del. to Shell Oil Co. of Calif.; ser. # 3965 del. to Alice F. DuPont; ser. # 4211 del. to Carpenter Paper Co. of Los Angeles; ser. # 4213 del. to Earle Halliburton; this approval expired 9-30-39.

ATC # 543
(6-29-34)
WACO "SUPER SPORT", S3HD.

Fig. 147. The remarkable Waco S3HD with 420 h.p. "Wasp Jr." engine.

The Waco "Super Sport" model S3HD was actually a military-type aircraft, a commercial version of an export model, that was handsomely disguised as a sportplane. Waco Aircraft, like several other manufacturers in the mid-thirties, was anxious to entice a little extra business from foreign military markets, and their "Model D" series was the vehicle prepared specifically for this reason. Of course, it was but a small matter and perhaps a logical step to customize and adapt this high performance design for use by the sportsman. The result of this development was a softly-contoured airplane that belied its brute strength yet held promise for an unusual performance. It is quite easy to imagine that any red-blooded sportsman would want to own this airplane, to bask happily in its glamor, but its limited purpose was rather hard to justify, especially at this time. Not many could afford a special airplane of this type, therefore, in spite of all that it had to offer, it was built only in the one example. As powered with the 9 cyl. Pratt & Whitney "Wasp Junior" TB engine rated 420 h.p. the S3HD was quite an airplane, but performance alone was not its only attraction. Gleaming in glossy Black and shiny Loening Yellow it was an exciting airplane even while standing still, and a circle of admirers gathered quickly wherever it went. The S3HD was the most exciting "Waco" airplane since the celebrated "Taperwing", truly a "Super Waco". Originally delivered (7-27-34) to Waco Aircraft Sales of New York, it was then sold to Miles H. Vernon of Wall Street, New York City. Usually based at the Long Island Aviation Country Club, along with the UMF-3 of Alice DuPont and the YMF-5 of Henry J. Topping, it was used occasionally for business and mainly for sport, frequently participating in various Aviation Country Club tours and activities. Proud of the S3HD, because there was no other like it, Miles Vernon flew and maintained it until 1944. After Vernon finally sold the S3HD, it just sat around in the New York area, gently deteriorating. Too expensive for the average sportsman, the ship was finally disassembled and stored for various periods in Florida, Georgia, and Ohio. In this time, ownership had passed through 7 different people, purchased finally in 1963 by John W. Church. John Church planned immediate restoration of the deteriorated remains, vowing to refurbish the S3HD to its former elegance. Ernest E. Webb, a part-time rebuilder with an excellent feel for fine airplanes, was chosen for the privilege, completing a beautiful restoration in the summer of 1964. Flown to two national aviation conventions that year, it was acclaimed by people and judges alike, receiving two handsome trophies. In June of 1965 it was flown to Troy, Ohio to the great pleasure of Clayton Brukner who was as proud of it then as he had been on its maiden flight some 30 years previous.

Fig. 148. Model S3HD was often called "King of the Waco biplanes".

A year or so later the S3HD was sold to Richard C. Jackson (Air Museum) in New Hampshire where it occasionally flies and reflects the glory of earlier days.

Earlier military-type (armed) models were just conversions of existing Waco designs and were selected for this use because of unusual performance characteristics and the uncanny ability to operate from the most restricted areas. These characteristics were invaluable in the outposts of modern civilization where large well-developed airports were either unknown or terrain did not permit their construction. The success of these various export models prompted Waco Aircraft to design a strictly military airplane embodying requirements for modern military tactics and yet retain most performance characteristics of the typical "Waco" biplane. Development was well along early in 1933 with a Wright-powered model called the WHD, and continued steadily with a resulting "armed model" (WHD-A) ready to offer for export early in 1935. Meanwhile, the S3HD sport model was developed in between the two WHD airplanes. The basic "Model D" airframe, designed to fulfill 12 different functions, was available for varied military purposes with a choice of 6 different engines, ranging from 250 h.p. to 450 h.p. Truly a versatile lineup of low-budget military airplanes. Designation of the "D models" ranged from the 250 h.p. CHD, through the (330 h.p.) JHD, the (320 h.p.) SHD, the (400-450 h.p.) S2HD, the (420 h.p.) WHD, and the S3HD in the armed or unarmed version; the "armed models" carried suffix -A after designation. Group 2 approval, on memo # 2-512 was awarded the models CHD, JHD, and WHD; the S3HD-A, an armed version of the S3HD "Super Sport", was awarded ATC #581 as described later in this volume.

The Waco "Model S3HD" was a custom-built high-performance sport-biplane with seating arranged for two in tandem. The open cockpit configuration was actually available for this model, but the company didn't recommend its use. An integral part of the overall design, the canopy enclosure provided streamlining for the cockpit section while providing a cozy cabin interior for the occupants. Canopy panels could be slid open for take-off and landing, but had to be closed at speeds in excess of 110 m.p.h. As an option, a cockpit heater was available to ward off the bite of frigid temperatures. Complete control and instrumentation was provided in either cockpit; we can easily assume that the experience of flying the S3HD was something one would certainly want to share with another. As powered with the 9 cyl. "Wasp Junior" model TB engine rated 420 h.p. at sea level the S3HD was no ordinary airplane; this airplane had the blood of a "pursuit ship" in its veins. Climbing out from any small field at 1750 ft. per minute the S3HD could level out easily to 166 m.p.h. cruise with a top speed approaching 200 m.p.h. Quick response and excellent maneuverability was backed up by a beefy airframe that was designed to soak up tremendous air-loads and pilot-inflicted punishment. Normal fuel capacity permitted a cruising range up to 500 miles, but stop-offs were generally more frequent because the beautiful S3HD was definitely an airplane worth showing off to people along the way. The company proudly described the S3HD as a typical "Waco", and to some extent it was, but fans will always remember it as the "King of the Waco biplanes". The type certificate number for the model S3HD was issued 6-29-34 and only one example of this model was manufactured by the Waco Aircraft Co. at Troy, Ohio. Clayton H. Brukner was pres. & gen. mgr.; Lee N.

Fig. 149. Model S3HD was sport-plane with fighter-plane performance.

Brutus was V.P.; Hugh R. Perry was sales mgr.; A. Francis Arcier was chf. engr.; Chas. M. Moffitt was service mgr.; and well-known Johnnie Livingston was test-pilot.

Listed below are specifications and performance data for the model S3HD as powered with 420 h.p. "Wasp Jr." TB engine; length overall 25'1"; height overall 8'11"; wing span upper 32'9"; wing span lower 27'0"; wing chord upper 66"; wing chord lower 57"; total wing area 256.3 sq.ft.; airfoil Clark Y; wt. empty 2435 lbs.; useful load 965 lbs.; payload with 87 gal. fuel 212 lbs. (1 passenger at 170 lbs. & 42 lbs. baggage); gross wt. 3400 lbs.; max. speed (2200 r.p.m.) 196; cruising speed (.77 power) 166; landing (stall) speed 60; climb 1750 ft. first min. at sea level; ser. ceiling 21,000 ft.; gas cap. normal 87 gal.; gas cap. max. 103 gal.; oil cap. 8 gal.; cruising range (.87 power) at 28 gal. per hour was 500 miles; basic price $16,100. at factory field. Weight allowance for 1936 version of S3HD listed as 2474 lbs. empty, useful load as 1126 lbs., payload with 90 gal. fuel as 360 lbs., and gross wt. was increased to 3600 lbs.; some performance suffered by the added weight. Model S3HD also eligible as seaplane on Edo model 4000 twin-float gear, with empennage modification.

The extremely robust fuselage framework was build up of welded chrome-moly steel tubing, heavily faired with wooden formers and fairing strips to a well-rounded shape, then fabric covered. The forward fuselage section was fitted with removable metal panels to permit repair and inspection to components in that area. Step-pegs on the fuselage permitted easy step-over into cockpits which were well protected by the sliding canopy enclosure. Both seats, with wells for parachute pack, were adjustable and dual control was provided. The interior was richly trimmed in dark brown leather. A large baggage compartment, with allowance for 100 lbs., was down low behind rear seat; a large access door with Sesame locks was on left side. A 54 gal. fuel tank was mounted high in the fuselage ahead of front cockpit, and a 33 gal. fuel tank mounted under floor in front (referred to as belly-tank) provided an 87 gal. capacity; an 8 gal. fuel tank in root end of each upper wing panel was optional for 103 gal. total capacity. The rugged wing framework, in 4 panels, was built up of solid spruce spar beams with spruce and mahogany plywood wing ribs, spaced only 6 inches apart for strength and to preserve airfoil form across the span; the leading edges were covered with dural metal sheet and the completed framework was covered in fabric. Upper wing panels, tapering in planform and section at the root ends, were mounted on a short two-strut pylon at about eye level; a large cut-out in both upper and lower wing roots, plus excessive stagger in lower wing, provided an excellent range of visibility. The 4 ailerons were cable operated; upper ailerons were connected to lower ailerons by cable housed in a fairing on rear interplane strut. The ailerons were canted for quick roll response. Stall-strips were fitted to upper wings to prevent "float" on landings. Both wings were rigged to 2.5 degs. of dihedral and 2.5 degs. of sweep-back; heavy N-type struts and heavy-gauge streamlined steel wire interplane bracing completed the exceptionally strong wing cellule. The fabric covered tail group was a composite structure of metal and wood; horizontal stabilizer and vertical fin were built up of spruce spars and ribs, while rudder and elevators were built up of steel tube spars and aluminum alloy ribs. The horizontal stabilizer was adjustable in flight and a fixed metal "tab" on the rudder was adjustable on ground only. The semi-cantilever landing gear of 85 in. tread used "Waco" patented shock struts; 6.50x10 wheels mounting 7.50x10 (or 8.50x10) six-ply low-pressure tires were equipped with Autofan brakes. A Hamilton-Standard ground-adjustable metal propeller, electric engine starter, Exide battery, generator, oil cooler, dual stick-type controls, coupe-top canopy, leather cockpit trim, compass, air-speed indicator, fuel pressure gauge, fuel supply gauges, bank & turn indicator, rate of climb, thermocouple for cyl. head temp., voltmeter, clock, adjustable rudder pedals, wing-root fairings, wheel streamlines, streamlined (10.5 in.) tail wheel, fire extinguisher, bonding and shielding for radio, navigation lights, landing lights, parachute flares, tool kit, first-aid kit, tie-down ropes, and log books were standard equipment. A Westport, Lear, or RCA radio, a cockpit heater, controllable-pitch propeller, and extra fuel capacity were optional. The next development in the "Model D" series was the "armed" model S3HD-A as described in chapter for ATC # 581 of this volume.

Listed below is the only S3HD example manufactured:

NC-14048; S3HD (# 3814) TB-420

ATC # 544
(7- -34)
SIKORSKY, MODEL S-42.

Fig. 150. Sikorsky "Clipper" S-42 was at one time the largest airplane in America.

The far-reaching dreams of the Pan American Airways System, America's "Merchant Marine of the Air", envisioned regular transoceanic service by air to the European continent and over to the Orient. In this dream were huge multi-engined flying boats, full of people. The comparative success of the earlier 4-motored Sikorsky S-40, the first of the big "Clipper Ships", prompted design and development of the big S-42, a much better example of an ocean-going flying boat. Difficult requirements proposed by "Pan Am" dictated a large step forward in the refinement of airframe design, so earlier concepts were forsaken and new concepts were selected to fit the future. As it slid into the water for its maiden flight, the first of 3 new "Clipper" ships (822M) was matter for great pride; a huge parasol-monoplane with four 700 h.p. P & W "Hornet" engines suspended above a large sea-going hull. As it sat in the water it was the largest airplane built in the U.S.A. up to this time. Test flights by Boris Sergievsky confirmed predicted performance and the setting of 10 "world records" also confirmed that it was indeed the world's finest com-

mercial flying boat. Delivered to Pan American in Miami in August it soon introduced new schedules from America to the Argentine; at a stop in Rio, on its first voyage to South America, it was christened the "Brazilian Clipper" and many notables were treated to a ride around the bay. This flight to Rio de Janeiro and to Buenos Aires, laden with dignitaries and newsmen, was to be one of the most significant flights in aviation history. Not long after, a second S-42 (NR-823M) was delivered to Pan Am at its base in Miami; equipped with much larger fuel capacity and extensively tested for long-range flights this S-42 was flown to San Francisco early in 1935 as the "Pan American Clipper". Here it poised at anchor with the broad Pacific Ocean before it. In April it took off from Alameda, Calif. and made an easy flight to Hawaii and return, carrying a large crew and several bags of mail, in a round-trip flight in less than 38 hours. This flight can be considered as the beginning of scheduled transoceanic air travel, certainly a new era in air transportation. This flight was followed by the same "Clipper" gradually extending the route

Fig. 151. S-42 leaves the "Golden Gate" on first flight to Hawaii.

further and further across the Pacific. The round-trip to Midway Island was flown in June, the round-trip to Wake Island was flown in August, and a round-trip to Guam was flown in October; round trips to Manila in the Philippines were flown in November and flights to Canton, China were scheduled as soon as facilities were completed. Extensions of the route to Shanghai and Peiping would complete the Pacific Ocean route. Later on, another S-42 inaugurated the longest over-ocean airline in the world from San Francisco to New Zealand. By this time, Pan Am was already considering a scheduled crossing of the Atlantic Ocean. In July of 1937 the S-42 "Clipper" made the first regular airline crossing of the stormy Atlantic; first flights were to England by the northern route and then to Portugal by way of the Bermuda-Azores route. It was the "Sikorsky S-42" that brought about the reality of commercial flights across both oceans to Europe and the Orient.

Designed in 1932 and under construction during most of 1933 the model S-42, after 18 months of closely-guarded development, was ready to fly by December, but the frozen river forestalled testing until March of 1934. Further testing through April determined that the new "Clipper" would carry the contract load easily, and surpassed all performance guarantees by a comfortable margin. In fact, performance potential prompted several record-breaking flights for heavy seaplanes in speed, load, and altitude. In one flight alone the S-42, with Sergievsky at the helm, set 8 world records for

speed with load; a previous flight set world records for greatest load to highest altitude. Much of this performance was possible through the use of powerful new "Hornet" engines and the efficient harnessing of 2800 h.p. with variable-pitch propellers by Hamilton-Standard. It is obvious that certain details of the S-42 carry a marked "Sikorsky" resemblance, but the classic short hull concept and tail booms, with all its bracing, had to be abandoned. The hull was now extended out to carry the tail group, the wing was mounted on a short pylon, and engine nacelles were neatly faired into the wing's leading edge. Wing-mounted tip floats provided stability during maneuvering in the water. Another interesting feature was the large trailing-edge "wing flap", providing increased lift and braking, which slowed the 19-ton "Clipper" considerably for softer landings. It is remarkable to note that as the S-42 was being constructed, great strides were being made also in development of new high-performance engines, new high-octane fuels, the controllable propeller became practical, great strides were made in radio development, the automatic-pilot was perfected, blind-flying instruments were now thoroughly reliable, and accessories performed accurately for long hours in trouble-free service. The Sikorsky S-42 was certainly fortunate to be able to take advantage of all this and thus become the first ocean-going airplane, and the finest airplane of its type.

The Sikorsky "Clipper" model S-42 was a large parasol-type monoplane of the flying boat type with normal seating arranged for 32

Fig. 152. The S-42 was designed to pioneer trans-oceanic flight.

passengers and a crew of 6. The heavy wing-loading cushioned the jolts of wayward air-currents and provided a smoother ride in turbulent air. The plush interior was roomy and heavy sound-proofing provided a cabin environment that was quiet and comfortable. On long flights a steward was in attendance to cater to passenger needs. The large cockpit compartment, like the bridge of a ship, was equipped with several radios, an automatic-pilot, and all the latest navigational devices to ensure unerring flight to various stations which in most cases were just tiny pin-points in the ocean. For long over-water flights, such as from San Francisco to Hawaii, extra fuel had to be carried so passenger load was held to about 8 with allowance for baggage and some mail. On short hops in the Caribbean Sea as many as 40 passengers were often carried. As powered with 4 Pratt & Whitney "Hornet" S5D1G engines rated 700 h.p. each the S-42 was quite lively for a 19-ton airplane. A full-load (8 ton) take-off averaged less than 20 seconds, climb-out to 6000 ft. in just over 7 minutes, and up to 181 m.p.h. in top speed at sea level in ideal conditions. The huge "wing flaps" with all their braking area slowed the big "Clipper" down to soft landings even in rough water. As a margin of safety, normal flight could be maintained with a full load on any 3 engines up to 10,000 ft. The S-42 was a steady airplane with predictable characteristics and rather easy to handle for such a large ship; pilots liked it. The type certificate number for the model S-42 was issued in July of 1934 by Eugene Vidal himself in a small ceremony at the plant. Three examples of this model were manufactured by the Sikorsky Aviation Corp. at Bridgeport, Conn.

Listed below are specifications and performance data for the Sikorsky model S-42 as powered with 4 P & W "Hornet" S5D1G engines rated 700 h.p. at 2150 r.p.m. at sea level; length overall 67'8"; height overall (on water) 17'4"; wing span 114'2"; wing chord (constant section) at 162", tapered to tip; total wing area 1330 sq. ft.; airfoil Sikorsky GSM; wt. empty 21,945 lbs.; useful load 16,055 lbs.; payload 7040 lbs. (32 passengers at 170 lbs. each & 1600 lb. allowance for baggage-mail); gross wt. 38,000 lbs.; max. speed 181 at sea level; cruising speed 160 at sea level; cruising speed 154 at 8000 ft. on .70 power; landing speed (with flaps) 65; climb 1000 ft. first min. at sea level; ser. ceiling 16,000 ft.; normal flight maintained with full load on any 3 engines to 10,000 ft.; normal gas cap. 1240 gal.; normal oil cap. 74 gal.; cruising range at 150 gal. per hour was 8 hours or 1280 miles; price for first airplane was $197,892.34. The S-42 was also eligible to use 4 "Hornet" S1EG engines rated 750 h.p. (800 h.p. for take-off); performance was slightly improved. The Hornet S5D1G engines provided 670 h.p. at 5000 ft. using 87 octane fuel.

The huge hull consisted of a deep keel, transverse frames, and heavy stringers of formed dural sections that were covered with riveted Alclad metal sheet; all seams were sealed with fabric and marine glue. The elongated two-step hull was divided into 9 water-tight compartments. The anchor and mooring compartment was in the bow, next was the pilot's compartment having provisions for up to 5 crew members; the pilot's compartment was equipped with various controls and 71 instruments, plus radios, which even on normal flights was work enough to keep 5 men busy. The third compart-

Fig. 153. Take-off of 19-ton S-42 required less than 20 seconds.

ment was for baggage, mail, and express cargo, with bins on both sides. The next 4 compartments, fitted for 8 passengers each, were amidship and paneled lavishly in walnut veneer; sound-proofing in cabin walls was of rubberized animal hair. Behind the last passenger compartment were 2 complete lavatories and a drinking fountain. The 8th compartment back contained main entrance to the cabin and a small area for steward's quarters; the last compartment was provided with a bin for extra cargo and crew supplies. The huge semi-cantilever wing framework was built up of duralumin girder-type spar beams with duralumin truss-type wing ribs; the framework was covered with smooth "Alclad" metal sheet from rear spar forward and with fabric from rear spar to trailing edge. All metal skin in hull and wing was smooth and flush-riveted to frame to lessen drag; over 400,-000 rivets were used in each airplane. A trailing edge "wing flap" comprised the entire span of the wing's constant-chord section; balanced ailerons were mounted outboard in the tapered portion. Mounted high on a pylon to provide spray clearance for the propellers, the wing was braced to the hull by a system of struts on each side; wing-tip floats were mounted at root end of the tapered section. Engine nacelles were mounted to front spar and faired into wing's leading edge; an 18.5 gal. oil tank was mounted in each nacelle. The 1240 gals. of fuel was contained in 8 tanks that were mounted in the wing adjacent to the engines; there were 4 tanks at 170 gal. each and 4 tanks at 140 gals. each. Aux. fuel of additional 900 gal. was optional; 4 tanks at 170 gal. each and 2 tanks of 110 gal. each were mounted in center compartment of the hull. A 100 gal. aux. oil tank could be mounted in the hull also; the combined weight of aux. fuel and oil eliminated a like amount in passenger-load from the available payload, of course. A heavy

wheeled gear was used for beaching only. The all-metal tail group was riveted together from variously shaped dural sections and covered with fabric; there were twin fins, twin rudders, and all movable surfaces were aerodynamically balanced. Hamilton-Standard controllable propellers, electric engine starters, Exide batteries, navigation lights, parachute flares, landing lights, cockpit & cabin lights, fire extinguishers, anchor & mooring gear, lavatories, ventilation, and cabin heat were standard equipment. Various instruments were by Kollsman, Pioneer, Lewis, General Electric, Sperry, and Eclipse. Radio equipment was specially developed by Pan American technicians. The Sperry automatic-pilot was optional. The next Sikorsky (Clipper) development was the improved models S-42-A and S-42-B as described in chapter for ATC # 592 of this volume.

Listed below are S-42 examples as gleaned from various records:

NC-822M: S-42 (# 4200-X) 4 Hornet 700
NC-823M: S-42 (# 4201) 4 Hornet 700
NC-824M: S-42 (# 4202 4 Hornet 700

This approval expired 9-30-39.

Fig. 154. S-42 was powered with 4 "Hornet" engines of 700 h.p. each. Shown here on its beaching gear.

Fig. 155. Vultee V-1-A soars high above the California mountains.

Most of the single-engined high-speed transports to this point were of small capacity, normally carrying 4 passengers and their baggage. The Vultee V-1-A was designed for larger loads; normally it seated 8 passengers and their baggage. Being slightly related to the Vultee by corporate ties, American Airways was commissioned to put the prototype airplane in test on one of its routes while an order for 10 of the V-1-A was being completed. By November of 1934, 7 of the shiny-new transports were placed on the Fort Worth to Chicago run (via St. Louis) and one example was delivered to Canadian-Colonial Airways for their international run from New York, Albany, to Montreal. American Airways had actually ordered 20 of the V-1-A, to be built in two batches of 10 each, but because of operational changes, limited their delivery to about 10 aircraft and released most of their order to other customers. A plush 8-place executive version of the V-1-A found several customers in the field of business. The earliest owners were Superior Oil and

United Gas, with deliveries following later to Fuller Paints, the San Francisco Examiner, Lang Transportation Co., Crusader Oil, and others. The Bowen Air Lines of Texas ordered 2 transport-versions of the V-1-A in 1935 and placed them on the Fort Worth to Brownsville and Houston runs, offering a 190 m.p.h. schedule to these terminals. Noted for its particularly high cruising speeds the Vultee V-1-A was flown by Jimmy Doolittle to a new transcontinental record. Taking off from Burbank Airport on Jan. 15 of 1935, Doolittle and 2 passengers, including Mrs. Doolittle, flew the west-to-east route to New York City in 11 hours 59 mins., breaking all records for passenger-carrying transport airplanes. On most of the flight he encountered icing conditions and bad weather which forced him to fly at 16,000 ft.; the stretch from Colorado to Virginia was flown entirely on blind-flying instruments. A month later this record was bettered by another V-1-A; Leland Andrews had lopped 26 minutes off the previous record time by Doolittle, but the record

163

Fig. 156. Vultee V-1 prototype was born in E. L. Cord hangar in Glendale.

was broken again in April and so went the year of 1935, a year replete with notable flights. Perhaps the most notable flight by a Vultee V-1-A (an ex-American Airlines ship) was the round-trip flight across the Atlantic and back by "Dick" Merrill, veteran transport pilot, and Harry Richman, veteran entertainer, as part-time co-pilot. In the "Lady Peace" they left New York on Sept. 2 of 1936 for England and returned to New York on Sept. 21, one of the most adventurous flights of the year. Vultee, more or less, discontinued production of transport airplanes in 1936 and concentrated seriously on military aircraft for export, which became the backbone of the company's business ever since.

With hardly enough to keep him busy and somewhat excited with ambitious plans of his own, Gerry Vultee, a former engineer for Lockheed, decided to leave 'Emsco' in Sept. of 1931. With a design proposal for an all-metal high-speed transport monoplane already in his hip-pocket, Vultee had cast about to find a backer for his new project. It was Errett L. Cord who took an interest in the new transport airplane and provided money for its development. A place to work was also provided in Cord's private hangar on United Airport in Burbank. Announcements in April of 1932 stated that Vultee was quietly working on his highly-advanced all-metal monoplane, a high-speed transport of much larger capacity than heretofore offered. By June of 1932 the whole operation was moved to Cord's facility on Grand Central Airport in Glendale, Calif. where the prototype was completed. The Aircraft Development Corp. was formed late in 1932 as a division of the Cord Corp. with "Gerry" Vultee as its general manager and chief engineer. Designated the V-1 and variously called the Cord V-1 or the Cord-Vultee V-1 the prototype airplane was ready to fly early in 1933. Dean

Ferrin flew development and certification tests early in 1934 and Cord announced that American Airlines would soon have a fleet of these fast liners in service. Work on an order for 10 of the improved V-1-A was started in Feb. of 1934; a work force of 125 people promised to have them all flying by late summer. The order was completed by November and an order for another 10 was already in various stages of construction. American Airlines had wanted to use all 20 of the aircraft on various runs, but due to operational changes, they limited their deliveries and released planes to other customers. In Dec. of 1934 a twin-engined version of the Vultee transport had already passed preliminary engineering stages, but its production was cancelled. The production of military aircraft held more promise, so Vultee spent most of his time developing attack-bomber aircraft that were based on the design lines of the V-1-A.

The Vultee model V-1-A was a low-winged transport monoplane with seating arranged for ten. Of monocoque and cantilever structure, the V-1-A offered a bare minimum of parasitic resistance and was one of the fastest transport airplanes in this country. Its colorful airline career with American Airlines was rather brief because of operational changes, so the interesting part of its service history came later. Several of the earliest examples were fitted as executive-transports for oil companies, newspaper firms, etc., while most of the ex-airline airplanes later roamed two hemispheres in private enterprise. The airliner version provided the ultimate in comfort for 8 passengers and the airliner pilot was provided with two-way radio and all the latest in navigational aids. The executive version varied in seating and in layout, to the customer's choice, but most were fitted with reclining lounge, overstuffed chairs, and a very complete lavatory. One was fitted with a

Fig. 157. Powerful "Cyclone" engine provided V-1-A with excellent performance.

typewriter and writing table. As powered with the supercharged Wright "Cyclone" SR-1820-F2 engine rated 735 h.p., the V-1-A was quite lively for its size and capable of fast cruising speeds; it was a cinch to maintain 190 m.p.h. schedules. The V-1-A, in the executive version, was also eligible with later models of the "Cyclone" engine, namely the SR-1820-F52 rated 775 h.p. and the SR-1820-G2 engine rated 850 h.p.; the result was only a slight increase in top speeds, but the boost to allround performance was considerable. Highly advanced for its day the Vultee V-1-A served for a good many years before it became outmoded, and only then because of new "twins" that captured the spotlight. The type certificate number for the model V-1-A was issued in July of 1934 and some 26 examples of this model were manufactured by the Airplane Development Corp. on Grand Central Airport in Glendale, Calif.; a division of the Cord Corp. Don P. Smith was pres.; Gerard F. Vultee was V.P., gen. mgr., and chief engr.; Lee H. Smith was sales mgr. In a reorganization in 1936 this firm became the Vultee Aircraft Div. of the Aviation Mfg. Corp.; T. V. Van Stone, who took over as chief engineer at "Emsco" when Gerry Vultee left in 1931, became engineering test-pilot for Vultee. Early piloting chores at Vultee during 1933-34 were contracted for among local test-pilots.

Listed below are specifications and perfor-mance data for the Vultee V-1-A as powered with Wright "Cyclone" SR-1820-F2 engine rated 735 h.p. at 1900 r.p.m. at 4000 ft.; length overall 37'0"; height overall 10'2"; wing span 50'0"; wing chord at root 11'3"; wing chord at tip 60"; total wing area 384 sq. ft.; wt. empty 5382 lbs.; useful load 3118 lbs.; payload with 206 gal. fuel (one pilot) 1423 lbs. (8 passengers at 170 lb. each & 233 lbs. baggage); gross wt. 8500 lbs.; max. speed 225 at 4000 ft.; cruising speed 205 at 7000 ft.; landing speed (with flaps) 63; climb 1000 ft. first min. at sea level; ser. ceiling 20,000 ft.; gas cap. 206 gal.; oil cap. 15 gal.; cruising range (.70 power) at 32 gal. per hour was 1200 miles; price not announced. With empty wt. of 5457 lbs. (equipped with radio & night-flying equipment) and limited to 160 gal. fuel the payload allowed 8 passengers & 450 lbs. for baggage and cargo; gross wt. at 8500 lbs.

The oval fuselage framework, a true monocoque design, employed smooth "Alclad" metal sheet riveted to numerous aluminum-alloy transverse rings forming a stressed-skin struc-ture; in this type of framework the "skin" sup-ported a big share of the loads. The sound-proofed cabin was lined with 4 seats on a side, separated by a 12 in. aisle, with entry door aft on the right; each seat was provided with a window, ventilator, heater duct, ash tray, reading lamp, assist rope, and a foot-rest. A small lavatory, in-cluding a drinking fountain, was opposite the en-

Fig. 158. Vultee V-1-A in Canadian service.

try door, and 2 baggage-cargo bins with allowance for up to 450 lbs. were further aft. The pilot station up front was separated from cabin area with a bulkhead door; pilot and co-pilot sat side-by-side, but co-pilot's station was often traded for mounting of radio equipment. The plush (58 in. wide x 68 in. high) cabin was upholstered in rich fabrics or leather; hand-baggage and gadget pockets were overhead and in the seat backs. All windows were of shatter-proof glass. The all-metal wing framework was of the "shell" type with all normal loads taken up by the "stressed-skin" covering; the front and rear spars were connected together by corrugated dural sheet, running span-wise, to form a stiff box-type girder, and then covered with smooth Alclad sheet. A detachable leading edge, in 4 sections, was fastened to the front spar. Split-type trailing edge wing flaps were operated electrically, or manually in case of electric malfunction. Narrow-chord ailerons were statically and aerodynamically balanced. The center-section of the cantilever wing was built integral to the fuselage and contained a 103 gal. fuel tank on each side; outer wing panels were bolted to butt-ends of the center-section. The retractable landing gear of 12 ft. tread was 2 separate cantilever units that folded inward into wheel wells in underside of wing; fairing panels provided a smooth underside when gear was retracted. The landing gear was folded or extended electrically with provisions for manual operation if need be. Oleo shock absorbing struts and large roly-poly "airwheels" cushioned the landings; the 30x13-6 Goodyear airwheels were equipped with brakes. The all-metal tail group was also of "shell type" construction with vertical fin and horizontal stabilizer built integral to the fuselage; all movable surfaces were statically and aerodynamically balanced. Rudder and (fabric covered) elevators were provided with adjustable "tabs" for trim; rudder tab was adjusted on ground only. A controllable (Hamilton-Standard) propeller, electric engine starter, Exide battery, generator, cabin heater, lavatory, drinking fountain, cabin lights, navigation lights, landing lights, parachute flares, a two-way radio, pressure-type fire extinguisher, 16x7-3 tail wheel, wheel brakes, parking brake, were standard equipment. Up to 92 gal. extra fuel, 5 gal. extra oil, and special "club interiors" were optional.

Listed below are V-1-A entries as gleaned from various records:

NX-12293; V-1 (# 1) Cyclone 712
NC-13764; V-1-A (# 2) Cyclone 735
-13765; " (# 3) "
-13766; " (# 4) "
-13767; " (# 5) "
-13768; " (# 6) "
-13769; " (# 7) "
-13770; " (# 8) "
-13771; " (# 9) "
-13772; " (# 10) "
-13773; " (# 11) "
-13774; " (# 12) "
-14249; " (# 12-A) "
-14250; " (# 14) "
-14251; " (# 15) "

CF-AWQ;	"	(#16)	"
-14248;	"	(#17)	"
-14252;	"	(#18)	"
-14253;	"	(#19)	"
-14254;	"	(#20)	"
-14255;	"	(#21)	"
-14256;	"	(#22)	"
-16000;	"	(#23)	"
;	"	(#24)	"
-16099;	"	(#25)	"
-17326;	"	(#26)	"

This approval for serial # 2 and up; ser. # 1 (V-1) assigned to American Airlines for test; ser. # 2 thru # 11 delivered to American Airlines; ser. # 8 later became "Lady Peace"; ser. # 12 del. to Superior Oil Co. & later to Phillips Petroleum Co.; ser. # 12-A (# 13 was not used) del. to United Gas Service of Texas; ser. # 14 del. to San Francisco & Los Angeles "Examiner"; ser. # 15 del. to Lang Transportation Co. of Los Angeles; ser. # 16 del. to Canadian-Colonial Airlines; ser. # 17 and # 19 del. to Bowen Air Lines of Texas; ser. # 18 del. to Geo. P. Fuller (Fuller Paints); ser. # 20 not verified; ser. # 21 del. to Crusader Oil Co. of N.Y.; ser. # 22 reg. to Errett L. Cord; ser. # 24 unknown; ser. # 25 del. as V-1-A Special to Hearst "Examiner"; ser. # 26 probably del. to Vimalert Corp.; ser. # 25 mfgd. under Group 2 approval memo # 2-539 — ser. # 18 also eligible; this approval (ATC #545) expired 9-30-39.

ATC # 546
(7-11-34)
WACO, MODEL UMF.

Fig. 159. The Waco UMF with 210 h.p. Continental engine.

Along with its cabin series Waco Aircraft developed two new "Model F" for the 1934-35 season. Offered with the choice of 2 different engines, the Continental-powered version described here was identified as the UMF, or more specifically as the UMF-3 and the UMF-5. Because of higher prices and higher operating costs the UMF was far from being everyman's airplane, so its clientele was limited to a small band of sportsmen and men of business, or a combination of the two. The relatively scant market for the UMF was bolstered somewhat by a few small orders from neighboring foreign governments; foreign sales were expanding to a point of becoming a significant part of the business. Four of the UMF-3 were delivered to the government of Guatemala in 1934, and 3 of the UMF-3 were delivered to the government of Cuba in 1937. Both batches of the UMF-3 were used in the Guatemalan and Cuban pilot-training program. As a utility airplane the UMF was versatile enough for teaching many facets of modern aerial warfare. One UMF-3 was also shipped to Brazil as a factory demonstrator to solicit orders in South America. Neither the YMF nor the UMF had sold in any great number, but it was sufficient to keep the design concept alive and active for several more years. The UPF-6 stemmed from the UMF-5 and the famous UPF-7 was then the culmination of this classic design.

The Waco model UMF was an open cockpit sport-utility biplane with seating arranged for three. As a companion model to the Jacobs-powered YMF the Continental-powered UMF was more or less identical except for its powerplant. The Continental engine for years now had been a compatible combination with the "Model F" series, both working together nicely for mutual benefit. Developed with new lines for the 1934-35 season the 3-seated UMF was basically fashioned around the NACA engine cowl which added considerably to available speeds. Deeper fairing promoted better airflow down length of the fuselage and allowed extra dimension inside for more room. It was a happy coincidence also that while "fillets" and "fairing" were promoting more speed they also contributed to a more beautiful shape. Especially when "dolled up" with a metal prop, wheel pants, and fancy paint, the UMF was a rather handsome airplane. As powered with the 7 cyl. Continental R-670-A engine rated 210 h.p. at 2000 r.p.m. the UMF had much to offer in performance and offered a broad range of utility. Flight characteristics were generally described as typical of previous versions of the "Model F", although some sacrifices had to be made in this heavier, and "cleaner" airplane. Not generally considered as an ordinary training airplane the

Fig. 160. Three Waco UMF for Cuban Navy. Four UMF also exported to Guatemala.

UMF however, was eligible for aerobatics and secondary phases of the CPTP pilot-training program. The type certificate number for the UMF was issued 7-11-34 and some 18 examples of this model were built by the Waco Aircraft Co. at Troy, Ohio.

Listed below are specifications and performance data for the Waco model UMF as powered with 210 h.p. Continental R-670-A engine; length overall 23'2"; height overall 8'5"; wing span upper 30'0"; wing span lower 26'10"; wing chord upper & lower 57"; wing area upper 130.8 sq. ft.; wing area lower 102.7 sq. ft.; total wing area 233.5 sq. ft.; airfoil Clark Y; wt. empty 1485 lbs.; useful load 1015 lbs.; payload with 50 gal. fuel 515 lbs. (2 passengers at 170 lb. each, 100 lbs. baggage, & 75 lb. allowance for radio & extra equipment); gross wt. 2500 lbs.; max. speed (105% power) 143 at 1000 ft.; cruising speed (1900 r.p.m.) 128 at 1000 ft.; landing (stall) speed 47; climb 1100 ft. first min. at sea level; ser. ceiling 14,500 ft.; gas cap. normal 50 gal.; gas cap. max. 62.5 gal.; oil cap. 4 gal.; cruising range at 13 gal. per hour 460 miles; price $6530. at factory field.

Specifications and performance data for UMF as seaplane on Edo M-2665 twin-float gear was identical except as follows; length overall 26'8"; height overall (on water) 10'2"; wt. empty 1735 lbs.; useful load 1015 lbs.; payload with 50 gal. fuel 515 lb.; gross wt. 2750 lbs.; max. speed (1000 ft.) 128; cruising speed (1900 r.p.m.) 112; landing (stall) speed 50; climb 800 ft. first min. at sea level; ser. ceiling 14,000 ft.; cruising range at 13 gal. per hour 390 miles; price not announced.

Construction details and general arrangement for model UMF were typical to that of the YMF as described in chapter for ATC # 542 of this volume. Unless otherwise noted, the following details apply to both UMF and YMF. All steel tube ends were radiused to provide closer fit for stronger welds, the fuselage was faired to a round section in front to match circular cross-section of NACA engine cowl, front cockpit could be closed off with metal panel when not in use, and improved wing-root fairings smoothed out wayward airflow at fuselage junction. It is hard to imagine why, but a tail-skid was available as option to replace the standard tail wheel. The UMF was equipped with the following: removable NACA engine cowl, hot-shot battery, electric (or Heywood air) engine starter, 6.50x10 wheels with 7.50x10 low-pressure tires (wheels must be placarded for these tires), 8 in. streamlined tail wheel, Hartzell wooden propeller, wing-root fairings, front and rear baggage compartments with allowance for 100 lbs; a compass, air-speed indicator, navigation lights, dual stick-type controls, wheel brakes, parking brake, first-aid kit, tool kit, fire extinguisher, log books, tie-down ropes, and cockpit covers. A metal propeller, Lear or Westport radio, bonding & shielding, Exide battery, landing lights, parachute-flares, hand-crank intertia-type engine starter, wheel pants, 12.5 gal. extra fuel in right upper wing, Sperry gyro & horizon, leather upholstery, cockpit heater, 15 gal. extra fuel in fuselage, and Edo twin-float gear were optional. Standard colors were Vermillion, Gunmetal Gray, Silver or Insignia Blue fuselage with Silver wings; striping was customer's option. A beautiful example of custom colors was Stinson Maize fuselage with

Fig. 161. Early UMF-3 belonging to Alice F. DuPont; Duponts were very air-minded family.

Havana Brown wings, accented with fine-line striping. The next Waco development was the "Custom Cabin" model UOC as described in chapter for ATC #568 of this volume.

Listed below are UMF entries as verified by company records:

NC-13071; UMF-3 (# 3689) Continental 210

-13894;	"	(# 3835)	"
-14041;	"	(# 3836)	"
-13571;	"	(# 3936)	"
:	"	(# 3937)	"
:	"	(# 3938)	"
:	"	(# 3939)	"
:	"	(# 3940)	"
-14076;	"	(# 3941)	"
-14044;	"	(# 3942)	"
-14005;	"	(# 3943)	"
-14085;	UMF-5	(# 3956)	"
-14603;	"	(# 3958)	"
-14627;	"	(# 3959)	"
-14687;	"	(# 4215)	"
:	UMF-3	(# 4548)	"
:	"	(# 4663)	"
:	"	(# 4664)	"

This approval for ser. # 3836 and up; ser. # 3835 delivered to Alice F. DuPont; ser. # 3937, 3938, 3939, 3940 del. to Govt. of Guatemala in 1934; ser. # 3941 del. to Tex LaGrone; ser. # 3943 shipped to Brazil in 1934 as factory demonstrator; ser. # 4215 del. to Hope Noyes in 1935; ser. # 4548, 4663, 4664 del. to Govt. of Cuba in 1937; this approval expired 9-30-39.

ATC # 547
(7-16-34)
C-W "CONDOR", T-32-C.

Fig. 162. Modifications to "Condor" T-32-C prolonged its usefulness in airline service.

In 1934 as the newer AT-32 series of the "Condor" transport began taking its place on American Airways routes, the older T-32 models were being pulled from service at various times to be converted to new specifications. After conversion at the Curtiss-Wright factory they were redesignated to model T-32-C and put back into regular service. To upgrade the older T-32 (mfgd. under ATC # 50l) and to extend its service life a little longer, several major modifications were performed; these modifications were calculated to increase operating speeds, improve general performance, and permit a generous boost to the gross weight allowance. The most significant changes made to the basic T-32 design were the installation of redesigned engine nacelles, and the installation of more powerful SGR-1820-F2 "Cyclone" engines rated 720 h.p. at 4000 ft.; these engines were then tightly shrouded in deep-chord NACA-type cowlings for better distribution of airflow and nearly a 20 m.p.h. increase in the top speed. Fitted to the supercharged "geared" engines were huge three-bladed Hamilton-Standard controllable-pitch propellers; these definitely boosted the overall performance to a large degree. The new "controllable props" now allowed the pilot to select the proper "bite" for take-off and better climb-out, a faster, more economical cruising speed, and substantially higher top speeds at altitude. Operation with "one engine out" was also greatly improved. Thus the modifications as performed by Curtiss-

Wright certainly eliminated some of the short-comings as suffered by the earlier T-32 and allowed it to remain a rather respectable carrier for another few years. American Airways (American Airlines) had 8 of their older T-32 converted to the T-32-C specifications; 2 former Eastern Air Transport (EAT) ships were converted also, but without the extensive modification to cowlings and engine nacelles. Sold to a Colombian airline in 1937, these 2 (EAT) air-planes were rebuilt by Curtiss-Wright as T-32-C Specials with installation of the more powerful "Cyclone" engines swinging Hamilton-Standard variable-pitch propellers. The "Condor" was the last of the big biplane transports to be used on the American airlane system; by 1935 it had finally lost out to the speed and efficiency of the new twin-engined monoplanes, especially to the Douglas DC-2. By 1936-37 the stately "Condor" was being shunted to brokerage lots, such as the one operated by Chas. Babb, for export to foreign countries.

As put back into service, the 17-place "Con-dor" model T-32-C (converted) was still basical-ly similar to the earlier T-32 except for modifications performed by C-W to bring it up closely to AT-32 (ATC # 534) specifications. The most significant item in the conversion was the installation of more powerful SGR-1820-F2 supercharged Wright "Cyclone" engines. These new engines rated 720 h.p. at 1950 r.p.m. at an altitude of 4000 ft. were now swinging large 3-bladed "controllable pitch" propellers; these

Fig. 163. "Condor" T-32-C was last of the biplane airliners.

propellers were a shot-in-the-arm to performance of the rejuvenated T-32-C. Replacing the narrow-chord Townsend-type "speed rings" and shrouding the engines closely with deep-chord NACA-type cowls offered a considerable reduction in frontal drag and the longer, more streamlined nacelles promoted better airflow over the lower wing. A better utilization of the added power, brought about by the controllable-pitch propellers, allowed a boost of the gross weight to 17,500 lbs. Conversion to the new specifications added nearly 250 lbs. to the empty weight, but increase to the gross weight allowed for this and still permitted a 75 gal. increase to the fuel capacity. All of the examples converted for American Airlines were permitted the extra gross weight allowance, but the 2 examples converted from former EAT airplanes, not receiving the full conversion, operated as T-32-C Specials and were not allowed the increase in gross weight, unless equipped with variable-pitch propellers. After being retired from airline ser-

vice in this country most of the T-32-C were exported for use in Alaska, Canada, Great Britain, Mexico and several countries in So. America. The approved type certificate for this conversion was issued 7-16-34 and in total, the Curtiss-Wright Airplane Co. produced 10 of these conversions at Robertson (St. Louis), Mo. Ralph S. Damon was pres.; E. K. "Rusty" Campbell was sales mgr.; George A. Page, Jr. was chief of engineering.

Listed below are specifications and performance data for the "Condor" model T-32-C (converted) as powered with 2 Wright "Cyclone" SGR-1820-F2 engines rated 720 h.p. each; length overall 48'10"; height overall 16'10"; wing span upper 82'0"; wing span lower 74'0"; wing chord upper & lower 106.5"; wing area upper 702 sq. ft.; wing area lower 506 sq. ft.; total wing area 1208 sq. ft.; airfoil NACA-2412; wt. empty 11,470 lbs.; useful load 6030 lbs.; payload with 375 gal. fuel & 2 pilots was 3200 lbs. (15 passengers at 170 lb. each & 650

Fig. 164. More powerful engines and controllable propellers provided T-32-C with extra performance.

Fig. 165. One "Condor" of Eastern Air Transport was modified to a T-32-C Special.

lbs. mail-baggage-cargo); payload reduced by 130 lbs. when stewardess was aboard; gross wt. 17,500 lbs.; max. speed 181 at 4000 ft.; normal cruising speed 160 at 4000 ft.; landing (stall) speed 62; climb 1200 ft. first min. at sea level; ser. ceiling 19,800 ft.; ser. ceiling with one engine out 4000 ft.; gas cap. 375 gal.; oil cap. 30 gal.; cruising range at 75 gal. per hour 650 miles; price for conversion not announced.

The construction details and general arrangement of the model T-32-C were typical to that of the T-32 as described in the chapter for ATC # 501 of this volume, except for certain prescribed modifications. Engine nacelle fairings were redesigned to a longer, more streamlined form, and the GR-1820-F11 engines of 650 h.p. were replaced with supercharged SGR-1820-F2 engines of 720 h.p. These engines were then encased in deep-chord NACA-type cowl fairings and were fitted with three-bladed "controllable" propellers. Hydraulically operated, these propellers allowed selection of better pitch angles for the different conditions of flight. Normally, the T-32-C carried 15 passengers, a pilot and co-pilot, but a "stewardess" was often included on some of the longer routes. The "Cyclone" engines were mounted in rubber to dampen vibration, and large-diameter propellers were driven by geared-down engines at slower speeds to lessen propeller tip noise. The appointments, accessories, and equipment on the T-32-C were upgraded to AT-32 standards as replacement became necessary. The next Curtiss-Wright development was the Curtiss-

Courtney amphibian as described in the chapter for ATC #582 of this volume.

Listed below are T-32 that were converted to model T-32-C:

NC-12353:	T-32-C Spl.	(# 21)	Cyclone 720
-12363:	T-32-C	(# 23)	"
-12364:	"	(# 24)	"
-12365:	"	(# 25)	"
-12369:	T-32-C Spl.	(# 31)	"
-12371:	T-32-C	(# 32)	"
-12372	"	(# 33)	"
-12377	"	(# 38)	"
-12378	"	(# 39)	"
-12383	"	(# 40)	"

Serial #21 (former EAT ship) sold to Colombian airline and modified as T-32-C Spl. by C-W in 1937; ser. # 23 converted to T32-C for AA (American Airlines) on 8-6-34, crashed 12-34; ser. # 24 conv. to T-32C for AA on 10-19-34, sold to Chas. H. Babb (broker) in 1937; ser. # 25 conv. to T-32-C for AA on 9-6-34, del. to Mexico in 1936; ser. # 31 (former EAT ship) sold to Colombian airline and modified by C-W to T-32-C Spl. in 1937; ser. # 32 conv. to T-32-C for AA on 10-6-34, sold to Chas. Babb who sold to Alaskan railway company; ser. #33 conv. to T-32-C for AA on 6-20-34, sold in Chile in 1935; ser. # 38 conv. to T-32-C for AA on 9-21-34, sold in Chile in 1935; ser. # 39 conv. to T-32-C for AA on 11-26-34, sold in Chile in 1935; ser. # 40 conv. to T-32-C for AA on 8-24-34, del. to Mexico in 1936; approval for the T-32-C expired 9-30-39.

ATC # 548
(8-8-34)
BEECH, MODEL A-17-F.

Fig. 166. Beech A-17-F lurking behind the big 690 h.p. "Cyclone" engine.

The Beech model A-17-F was actually forced into existence because of a note added to sales brochures on the earlier model 17-R; this note casually read "also available with the Wright "Cyclone" engine". Beech had not yet built an airplane with the big "Cyclone" engine and it is doubtful if they actually had planned one. Calling their bluff, as it were, the Sanford Mills Co. of Sanford, Maine inquired and actually put in an order for a model of this type; it was up to Beech to produce one. In no position to quibble nor to back down Walter Beech promised delivery and manufacture of the unusual craft was started with some apprehension. As it later rolled out from final assembly the A-17-F was long-legged, fat and stubby, and the big-diameter "Cyclone" on its nose certainly looked somewhat out of place. It was definitely a

Fig. 167. The A-17-F in flight was an awesome sight.

Fig. 168. A-17-F was a fiercely beautiful airplane that commanded respect and admiration.

"monster" and the most powerful commercial airplane of this type ever built. Robert S. Fogg, who had been hired by Sanford Mills to be their company pilot, and had been sent to Wichita to accept delivery, had been warned by other pilots he had possibly about one month to live if he planned to fly the fear-inspiring A-17-F regularly! No doubt "Bob" Fogg had some misgivings on his first flight in "the beast", but soon learned that the Cyclone-powered Beech had practically no fault in the air and only became tricky and offensive on take-offs and getting back down. It was exhilerating and a pleasure to fly otherwise; Fogg soon became extremely fond of the thundering airplane. The Sanford Mills Co. operated the A-17-F regularly from Feb. to Oct. of 1934 and had been well pleased with its bonus performance and its inherent utility; a need for a much larger airplane finally provoked sale of the A-17-F to millionaire sportsman Howard Hughes. Except for a brief splash in the headlines of 1937, Hughes kept the A-17-F shrouded in mystery and reports indicate it had been carefully stored; occasional reports hinted it was still in existence as late as 1969.

The Beech model A-17-F was a high-performance cabin biplane quite similar to the earlier Model 17-R; the glaring difference was of course the big 9 cyl. Wright "Cyclone" R-1820-F11 engine of 690 h.p. Seating 4-5 persons in plush and ample comfort the A-17-F was a very unusual personal-type airplane and certainly the most conspicuous. Despite its awe-inspiring appearance and its rather tricky behavior on or near the ground its utility was rather substantial. Sanford Mills used the colorful A-17-F (Stagger-Wing) to transport executives all over the country and on frequent rounds to their various factories which often required operation from small unimproved airfields. Faster even than military fighters of the day the Cyclone-powered Beech was capable of nearly 250 m.p.h. at top speed and normally cruised at around 215 m.p.h.; cruising range could be extended to 1250 miles. On the ground the A-17-F was a nervous tiger that snarled and trembled because of all that horsepower, but in the air the big "Cyclone" settled down smoothly and the unlikely engine-airplane combination seemed quite happy up there in its proper element. Design and manufacture of the A-17-F with its big, powerful Wright "Cyclone" engine certainly must have instigated several abnormal problems, but Walter Beech, design-engineer Ted Wells, and the small staff of able craftsmen proved they were capable to meet the challenge. Beside the lessons learned in harnessing high-horsepower to their "Stagger-Wing" biplane Beech Aircraft also learned that the market for this type of airplane was very scant in the days of mid-depression. The type certificate number for the A-17-F was issued 8-8-34 and only one example was built by the Beech Aircraft Co. at Wichita, Kansas and it was the third airplane they had built since forming in April of 1932. A similar model, the more powerful A-17-FS, was later built under ATC # 577.

Listed below are specifications and performance data for the Beech model A-17-F as powered with 690 h.p. Wright "Cyclone" (R-

Fig. 169. The A-17-F was very unusual, and certainly very conspicuous.

1820-F11) engine; length overall 24'2"; height overall 8'9"; wing span upper & lower 34'6"; wing chord upper & lower 60"; wing area upper 178 sq. ft.; wing area lower (including fuselage portion) 178 sq. ft.; total wing area 356 sq. ft.; airfoil N-9; wt. empty 3285 lbs.; useful load 1915 lbs.; payload with 155 gal. fuel 740 lbs. (3 passengers at 170 lb. each & 230 lbs. for baggage & extra equipment; gross wt. 5200 lbs.; max. speed (2000 r.p.m.) 235; cruising speed (.80 power) 212; landing speed (with flaps) 60; climb 2500 ft. first min. at sea level; ser. ceiling 25,000 ft.; gas cap. 155 gal.; oil cap. 10-12 gal.; cruising range at 40 gal. per hour 780 miles; price $24,-500. at factory.

The stubby fuselage framework was built up of welded chrome-moly steel tubing, heavily faired with wooden formers and fairing strips, then fabric covered. The forward portion was covered with removable metal panels. Two heat-treated trusses below the longerons were placed to carry most of the major loads. The plush interior was arranged with 2 individual seats in front and a wide bench across the back that would seat 3; the cabin walls were sound-proofed and all was upholstered in contrasting shades of Mohair fabric. There was a large entry door on either side and all windows were of (laminated) shatter-proof glass; the windshield was specially bent to fuselage contours. Dual controls were

Fig. 170. A-17-F was faster than military fighters.

provided and all controls were cable operated. Every moving part was equipped with ball bearings. A large baggage compartment, with allowance for 125 lbs., was behind the rear seat with access from outside on the left. The unusual wing framework was built up of welded 4130 steel tube girder-type spar beams and plywood-gusseted spruce wing ribs that were spaced only 6 in. apart; the leading edges were covered with dural metal sheet and the completed framework was covered in fabric. Ailerons were on lower wings only and "decelerator flaps" were fitted to underside of upper wing. The landing gear, in 2 separate units, was encased in large metal fairings; the treadle-type gear was equipped with "Beech" spring-oil shock struts. 9.50x12 low-pressure semi-airwheels were fitted with Autofan brakes; an enormous wing-root fairing was blended into the streamlined wheel "boots". The upper wing was bolted directly to topside of fuselage framework and root fairings blended in with topside of fuselage lines; upper and lower wing panels were connected together with a welded steel I-type interplane strut and braced with streamlined steel wire. The fabric covered tail group was built up of welded chrome-moly steel tubing; the rudder and elevators were aerodynamically balanced and an elevator "tab" was provided for trim. A Hamilton-Standard controllable propeller, electric engine starter, radio, generator, fuel pump, landing lights, Exide battery, navigation lights, parachute-type flares, cabin heater, cabin vents, a compass, wheel brakes, tail wheel, parking brake, airspeed indicator, cyl. head temp. gauge, fuel level gauge, fuel press. gauge, bank & turn indicator, Sperry directional gyro, rate of climb, sensitive altimeter, wing flaps, and dual controls were standard equipment. Extra fuel capacity and Switlik parachute-type seats were optional. The next Beech development was the Jacobs-powered model B-17-L as described in chapter for ATC # 560 of this volume.

Listed below is the only example of the Beech model A-17-F:

NC-12583: A-17-F (# 5) Cyclone 690.

ATC # 549
(8-9-34)
NORTHROP, "GAMMA" 2-D.

Fig. 171. Cargo-carrying Northrop "Gamma" 2-D with 710 h.p. Wright "Cyclone" engine.

More than anything else the Northrop "Gamma" 2-D was a dramatic exercise in highly advanced all-metal construction, in refined aerodynamics, experiments in long-distance cargo-hauling by air, and research into over-weather flying. Basically a stretched out version of the little "Beta" sportplane, the "Gamma" was primarily designed to haul air-cargo at high speeds over long distances, but the concept for cargo-planes had changed drastically since the "Gamma" was ready to fly and perform service, so the airplane was modified and put to other uses. On 13 May 1934 the first "Gamma" for Transcontinental & Western Air (TWA) was flown to a new cross-country record for transport airplanes by Jack Frye, covering the distance from Los Angeles to Newark in 11 hours 31 mins. This flight was the first airmail consignment since the disastrous cancellation of all airmail contracts in Feb. of 1934. Glowing in the publicity, TWA soon after announced it was contracting for 6 of the "Gamma" cargo-haulers, but only 3 were actually acquired and 2 of these were used only for a short time and resold. The need for a cargo-hauler of the "Gamma" type had not materialized. In 1936 TWA was considering the prospect of operating at much higher altitudes, so intensive experiments were undertaken with its remaining "Gamma". The 2-D was specially modified for flights into the sub-stratosphere, and D. W. "Tommy" Tomlinson was soon making research flights at 25,000 feet. This program was designed to study various conditions and forms of icing, the patterns of turbulence, the possibilities of thunderhead penetration, and powerplant efficiency at extreme altitudes; the ceiling for these experiments was finally raised to 35,000 feet. Much useful data was acquired during the course of these tests, and proved highly useful in future operations. Proudly labeled the "Experimental Overweather Laboratory" the aging "Gamma" 2-D was finally disposed of in 1940 because its role had been taken over by newer twin-engine airplanes.

Disillusioned because of consolidation of his company with Stearman Aircraft in Wichita, Jack Northrop resigned and returned to California. In an agreement to work closely with Donald Douglas (Douglas Aircraft), Northrop formed the new Northrop Corp. in Jan. of 1932. Establishing itself in the old Moreland plant, across the street from the Los Angeles Airport, the new firm began construction on several new designs. The "Gamma" was one of the first of the new Northrop designs and incorporated

Fig. 172. Supercharged "Gamma" used in over-weather experiments; flights ranged to 35,000 feet.

many new ideas. The first "Gamma" off the line (a 2-B) went to Lincoln Ellsworth for his Antarctic Expedition, the second (a 2-A) went to Frank Hawks of Texas Oil Co. for research, and a 2-C was being built for the Air Corps. As the Texaco "Sky Chief" the "Gamma" was flown by Frank Hawks to many transcontinental and inter-city speed records, and was known even to the man in the street. A "Gamma" 2-D was delivered to TWA for transport of mail and cargo, and Jack Frye promptly set out to blaze a transcontinental record for transports; the "Gamma" was fast, with "seven league boots", and toted a sizeable load. Because the airplanes built by Northrop were more or less custom-built and tailored to suit a customer's needs, nearly every one that was rolled out was slightly different than the previous one, and every one became a winner in its field. Starting with only a handful of men, in a rather modest facility, business became so good that plant expansion was in order and the handful of craftsmen soon swelled to a thousand employees. The market for commercial airplanes of the type Northrop was building was not very productive, so Northrop turned to export and development of military designs. A "Gamma" 2-C was delivered to the Air Corps and became the YA-13; revised with an 800 h.p. "Twin-Wasp" engine, the YA-13 then became the XA-16. The model A-17 with a Twin-Wasp Jr. engine of 750 h.p. was developed from the XA-16 and became the most famous "attack" airplane of this period.

The Northrop "Gamma" model 2-D was a low-winged all-metal monoplane with seating for a crew of one. The big, round fuselage was fitted with 2 large cargo-holds for up to 1300 lbs. of payload, and the pilot's station was well to the rear. Placing the pilot way behind the load was rather classic and old-fashioned by now, but at least he was afforded the luxury of a heated, canopy-covered cockpit. The rest of the airplane certainly could not be called old-fashioned because it was made up of all the latest ideas in aerodynamics, "stressed skin" metal construction, and in aids to operation. With tankage for over 300 gals. of fuel the "Gamma's" range was up to 1700 miles carrying a mail-cargo load of some 900 lbs.; the Los Angeles to Newark schedule was made in 3 hops. The "Gamma" was ideal for cross-country air-express, but the anticipated tonnage had never developed, so operation of an all-cargo carrier became a losing proposition. As powered with the 9 cyl. Wright "Cyclone" SR-1820-F3 engine rated 710 h.p. the "Gamma" 2-D had performance to spare and operated admirably at high altitudes over rough terrain. Pilots loved to fly the "Gamma" because it was strong and steady. The "Gamma" never really earned the chance to prove itself as a transport of air-freight, but nevertheless, it was a significant development that found its justification in newspaper headlines. The type certificate number for the "Gamma" model 2-D was issued 8-9-34 and only 3 examples of this model were built by the

Fig. 173. When not making headlines the "Gamma" hauled transcontinental air cargo.

Northrop Corp. at Inglewood, Calif. John K. Northrop was pres. & chf. of engrg.; W. K. Jay was V.P. & gen. mgr.; Don R. Berlin was chf. engr.; Art Mankey was asst. engr.; Gage H. Irving was chf. pilot & sales rep. The well-known Vance Breese was contracted for certain phases of test-flying.

Listed below are specifications and performance data for the "Gamma" model 2-D as powered with Wright "Cyclone" SR-1820-F3 engine rated 710 h.p. at 1950 r.p.m. at 7000 ft.; length overall 31'2"; height overall 9'0"; wing span 47'10"; wing chord at root 114"; wing chord at tip 22"; total wing area 363 sq. ft.; airfoil at root NACA-2415; airfoil at tip NACA-2409; wt. empty 4119 lbs.; useful load 3231 lbs.; payload with 334 gal. fuel 892 lbs.; payload with 250 gal. fuel 1396 lbs.; gross wt. 7350 lbs.; max. speed 224 at 7000 ft.; crusing speed (1900 r.p.m.) 215 at 7000 ft.; landing speed (with flaps) 62; climb 1280 ft. first min. at sea level; ser. ceiling 20,000 ft.; gas cap. max. 334 gals.; oil cap. 22 gal.; cruising range at 40 gal. per hour 1700 miles; price not announced. Optional engines for the "Gamma" 2-D were the SR-1820-F52 rated 775 h.p. at 2100 r.p.m. at 5800 ft., or the SR-1820-F53 rated 735 h.p. at 2100 r.p.m. at 9600 ft.; performance varied slightly with these engines.

The round, semi-monocoque fuselage structure was built up of 24ST alloy rings and stringers that were covered with riveted "Alclad" metal sheet; the "stressed-skin" metal covering supported a large share of the stress. The pilot was seated aft in a canopy-covered cockpit, and the large cargo-hold, with 110 sq. ft. capacity, was stretched out in front; the metal-lined compartment was loaded through 2 hatches from the wing-walk and was purposely large for packaged freight. The cantilever wing framework, in 3 sections, was of 24ST alloy in multi-cellular construction and covered with "Alclad" metal skin; the 11 ft. wide center-section was built integral to the fuselage. An extremely large fillet smoothed out the airflow at the fuselage-wing junction. The tapered outer wing panels were bolted to butt ends of the center-section; ailerons were of the "slotted" type and trailing edges of wing were fitted with electrically-operated split-type "air brakes". All fuel was in center-section of the wing; 2 front tanks of 51 gal. each, 2 center tanks of 54 gal. each, and 2 rear tanks of 62 gal. each provided a total capacity of 334 gals. The cantilever landing gear of 9 ft. tread was in 2 separate units that were faired with streamlined metal boots; 2 Aerol shock absorbing struts were employed in each unit and 36x8 Bendix wheels were fitted with mechanical brakes. The cantilever tail group was all-metal in a structure similar to the wing; the rudder was balanced, and both rudder and elevator were fitted with adjustable "tabs" for trim. All engine and plane controls operated on (125) ball bearings for smoothness and a light touch. A Hamilton-Standard controllable propeller, electric engine starter, 12-volt Exide battery, engine-driven generator, fuel pump, oil-cooling radiator, landing lights, navigation lights, parachute flares, cabin heater, tail wheel, radio, fire extinguisher, air-speed indicator, Sperry directional gyro & artificial horizon, rate of climb, ice-warning indicator, fuel gauges, sensitive altimeter, compass, and other normally-installed instruments were standard equipment. The next Northrop development was the "Delta" model 1-D as described in chapter for

Fig. 174. Northrop "Gamma" introduced revolutionary methods in airplane construction.

ATC # 553 of this volume.
Listed below are "Gamma" entries as gleaned from registration records:

NR-12265; 2-A (# 1) Wright 700
NR-12269; 2-B (# 2) Wasp 500
NX-12291; 2-   (# 5) Cyclone 650
NC-13757; 2-D (# 8) Cyclone 710
NC-13758; 2-D (# 9) Cyclone 710
NC-13759; 2-D (# 10) Cyclone 710
NR-13761; 2-G (# 11) Cyclone 800

NR-2111; 2-D2 (# 12) Cyclone 710

This approval for ser. # 8 and up; ser. # 1 as Texaco "Sky Chief"; ser. # 2 on Ellsworth Expedition; ser. # 5 may have been the model 2-C; ser. #3, 4, 6, 7 were probably all "Delta"; ser. # 8, 9, 10 del. to TWA; ser. # 11 a "special" for Jacqueline Cochrane; ser. # 12 del. to Russell Thaw; in 1942 a "Gamma" 2-D served in Air Corps as UC-100; this approval expired 9-30-39.

ATC # 550
(8-10-34)
STINSON "RELIANT", SR-5F.

Fig. 175. Stinson SR-5F with 7 cyl. Wright engine was top of "Reliant" series for 1935.

The last "Reliant" in the popular SR-5 series was the 250-285 h.p. Wright-powered SR-5F. Because of a much more costly engine the SR-5F was the most expensive model of the series, but it also had the best all-round performance, especially in the higher horsepower (285 h.p.) version. Assembled on a more or less custom-built basis, for the discriminating customer, the SR-5F was embellished with all of the available options, and as such, was a plush and comfortable airplane with maximum utility as its paramount feature. Of the 2 examples actually built in the model SR-5F version, the beautiful "Texaco # 19", as operated by the Texas Co. (oil refiners), was used in field-testing various petroleum products and performed various other services to promote goodwill among the oil company's dealers and their customers. Flown frequently by "Duke" Jernigan (and other Texaco pilots), # 19 literally traversed the country in all directions and became a very familiar sight. The other example of the SR-5F was registered in Michigan and it perhaps led a very average existence.

With no other information available we offer the CAA technical description to tell us something about this rare "Reliant".

Model SR-5F on ATC # 550: ser. # 9200-A and up eligible with Wright R-760-E engine of 250 h.p. or R-760-E1 of 285 h.p.; empty wt. of 2285 lbs. includes a ground-adjustable metal propeller, NACA-type engine cowl, streamlined metal wheel pants, wing-root and tail fairing, a battery (aft in fuselage behind baggage compartment), electric engine starter, cabin heater, 25x11-4 Goodyear airwheels with hydraulic brakes, 10.5 inch streamlined tail wheel, 50 gal. fuel (25 gal. tank in each wing), oil 4 gal., 65 lb. baggage, and noted with gross wt. of 3360 lbs. Approved optional equipment: Lear radio (25), bonding & shielding (9 or 12), 3 or 5 parachute flares (16), hammock-type rear seat (15 lbs. less than standard installation), retractable landing lights (26), fixed landing lights (16), wheel fenders (10 lbs. less than wheel pants), engine-driven generator (24), wind-driven generator (12), a Sperry directional gyro (9), artificial horizon (9), thermocouple & cyl. head temp. gauge (6), mis. instruments (add actual weight), 75 gal. fuel (37.5 gal. tank in each wing) for a 15 lb. net increase, 90 gal. fuel (45 gal. tank in each wing) for a 22 lb. net increase, 100 gal. fuel (50 gal. tank in each wing) for a 25 lb. net increase, reinforcement on wings with 50 gal. tanks (7), 5 gal. or 6.75 gal. oil cap. eligible with no increase in net wt. Figures in parentheses are wts. per unit.

Note: All serial numbers with -A suffix were

Fig. 176. Only 2 of the rare SR-5F were built.

SR-5 models with wing flaps. The SR-5F was basically the same as any other SR-5 model except for engine, propeller, engine mounts, oil tank, fuel capacity, wing flaps, engine cowl, and engine installation.

Note: Ser. # 9265-A (NC-14156) is eligible as SR-5F with R-760-E1 engine of 285 h.p. with the following specifications; empty wt. of 2537 lbs. includes all standard equipment (less adj. propeller, 50 gal. fuel, 4 gal. oil), plus bonding &

shielding (12), 5 parachute flares (16), wind-driven generator (12), l00 gal. fuel capacity (50 gal. tank in each wing) for a 25 lb. net increase, reinforced wings for the larger tanks (7), 6.75 gal. oil cap., Sperry directional gyro (9), thermocouples and cyl. head temp. gauge (6), misc. instruments (11), fixed landing lights (16), RCA radio receiver (35), and Lycoming-Smith controllable propeller (106) for a 24 lb. net increase in wt. This was Texaco # 19.

Fig. 177. "Duke" Jernigan and the SR-5F were a familiar sight the country over.

Note: Other planes of this model (SR-5) with ser. # 9250-A and up eligible with R-760-E engine of 250 h.p. after weight & balance; gross wt. 3425 lbs. Planes with ser. no. below # 9250-A also eligible at 3425 lb. gross wt.; standard gross wt. was 3360 lbs. with 65 lbs. baggage.

Note: Model SR-5F with R-760-E1 engine of 285 h.p. and Lycoming-Smith propeller was eligible at 3550 lb. max. gross wt.; model SR-5F with R-760-E engine of 250 h.p. with adj. metal prop, 50 gal. fuel, 4 gal. oil, 65 lb. baggage (in compartment aft of seat) eligible at 3425 lb. max. gross wt.

Under the provisions of this ATC, any model SR-5 was eligible as SR-5F when modified to conform. The next Stinson development was the tri-motored "Model A" as described in chapter for ATC # 556 of this volume.

Listed below are only known SR-5F examples:

NC-14156; SR-5F (# 9265-A) Wright 285
NC-14162; SR-5F (# 9282-A) Wright 250

Fig. 178. "Electra" 10-A with one engine dead. One 400 h.p. "Wasp Jr." could maintain 6300 ft. altitude.

Until the glistening "Electra" soared into the sunlight on its maiden flight, every airplane to leave the Lockheed factory at Burbank had been of the same general type—that is, they were single-engined, all-wood, cantilever monoplanes with the wing placed at either high-wing, low-wing, or "parasol" positions. Of course, the distinguishing "Lockheed" feature had always been the streamlined, cigar-shaped, monocoque fuselage fashioned in a "concrete tub" out of laminates of plywood. As a contrast in shape and structure, to what left the factory in the previous 7 years, the all-metal "Electra" marked Lockheed's entry into the twin-engined transport field. Comparatively small, the 12 place "Electra" was designed to fill a need for an economical airliner of high performance that offered ideal seating capacity and multi-motor reliability to operators of the shorter routes. The design layout and the calculated performance looked so good on the drawing board that Northwest Airways (as Northwest Airlines on 1 June 1934) purchased the first airplane for their

route to Seattle even before construction began. The first "Electra" for NWA was placed in service on 1 June 1934 making 46 round-trips between the Twin Cities and Chicago in the first month. Two more "Electra" liners had joined the airline shortly after on the route from Chicago to the North-west. By June of 1935 the NWA had 13 of the Model 10-A and had "Electra-fied" the whole route from Chicago to Seattle; a schedule of 9 hours was maintained from point to point. The Pan American Airways System ordered 6 of the transports for routes thru Mexico, Central and South America, and 2 were ordered for service in Alaska. Tony Fokker ordered 7 for resale in Europe. In no time at all the Lockheed "Electra" became a sensation; Lockheed's gospel had always been speed and the twin-engined "Electra" continued preaching this gospel far and wide. The first "Electra", a Model 10-A, was powered with 2 Pratt & Whitney "Wasp Junior" SB engines rated 400 h.p. at 5000 ft., but Lockheed engineers assumed that some of the airlines would no doubt prefer

Fig. 179. "Electra" 10-A with British Airways; "Electra" was popular in Europe.

more power, so the robust framework was designed and stressed to take engines up to 550 h.p. The popularity of the Model 10-A on Northwest Airlines routes prompted Braniff to place a sizeable order and several business-houses were ordering the deluxe "Club" version. Of the "Electra" that were shipped to Europe, 4 of the 10-A were delivered to LOT of Poland. Production of the Model 10-A lasted well into 1939 and trickling over into 1940 and 1941. The astounding success of the "Electra" instigated many other famous Lockheed twin-engine designs.

The Lockheed "Electra" model 10-A was an all-metal, low-winged, twin-engined, transport monoplane with seating arranged for 10 passengers and 2 pilots. Basically, the "Electra" was designed as a passenger transport for the shorter routes, but its interior was adaptable to various custom layouts. The "Club" model, for

Fig. 180. Prototype "Electra" put Lockheed on threshold of a new era.

Fig. 181. An "Electra" in war service; ship shown was formerly a Braniff liner.

sportsmen and executives, offered plush comfort with high performance and twin-engine safety. Rather small for a twin-motored airliner the deft "Electra" provided small-airplane handling and economy with large airplane comforts. First used by Northwest Airlines on its route across the top of the U.S.A., the "Electra" revolutionized passenger service on the shorter routes and literally forced other lines to follow suit. Braniff served the sout-west, Eastern Air Lines in the east, and Delta Air Lines in the deep south. Fan-dancer Sally Rand (with a special uniform on and no fans) was honorary "stewardess" for Braniff on inauguration of a new service from Dallas to Corpus Christi. Pan Am was already offering "Electra" service up in Alaska and down thru Mexico, the "Electra" was smashing former schedules in Europe, and making its way into Canada also. Lockheed reputation was well established the world over, even before the "Electra" made its bid, but the "twin" upheld the reputation well and set a few standards of its own. Perhaps its pinnacle of achievement came about in 1937 when an "Electra" rushed first photos of the coronation of King George VI across the Atlantic Ocean from England to America. As powered with 2 Pratt & Whitney "Wasp Jr." R-985-SB engines rated 400 h.p. at 5000 ft. the Model 10-A had terrific performance throughout the entire range of flight, and was the fastest airplane of its kind in the world. Once, with the help of a brisk tailwind, an "Electra" (10-A) flew from Minneapolis to Chicago averaging 267 m.p.h. from point to point; this was a record for several years. With 2 engines totaling some 800 h.p. power reserve was ample enough to fly a full load safely at 6000 ft. on one engine; the "Electra" was a good example of twin-engine safety. Flown on its maiden flight by test-pilot Eddie

Allen in Feb. of 1934 and tested thoroughly for the next 6 months, the "Electra 10-A received its type certificate number on 8-10-34; some 103 or more examples of this model were manufactured by the Lockheed Aircraft Corp. at Burbank, Calif.

Listed below are specifications and performance data for the "Electra" model 10-A as powered with 2 "Wasp Junior" R-985-SB engines rated 400 h.p. at 2200 r.p.m. at 5000 ft. (450 h.p. for take-off); length overall 38'7"; height overall 10'1"; wing span 55'0"; wing chord at root 145"; wing chord at tip 48"; total wing area (incl. fuselage section) 458 sq. ft.; airfoil at root Clark Y-18; airfoil at tip Clark Y-9; wt. empty 6205 (6325) lbs.; useful load 3545 (3775) lbs.; payload with 150 gal. fuel 2200 lbs. (10 pass. & 500 lbs. baggage-cargo); payload with 200 gal. fuel 1900 (2130) lbs.; baggage-cargo allowance up to 670 lbs.; gross wt. 9750 (10,100) lbs.; figures in parentheses as later amended; max. speed 210 at 5000 ft.; cruising speed (.75 power) 195 at 9600 ft.; landing speed with flaps 63-64; climb 1200 (1140) ft. first min. at sea level; ser. ceiling 21,150 (19,400) ft.; gas cap. normal 150 gal.; gas cap. max. 200 gal.; oil cap. 14 gal.; cruising range (.75 power) at 48 gal. per hour 550 miles & 750 miles; absolute ceiling on one engine with full load 6300 (5800) ft.; figures in parentheses for 10,100 lb. gross wt.; Model 10-A later amended for NWA (1936) with two R-985-SB3 engines rated 450 h.p. with gross wt. allowance to 10,500 lbs.; (empty 6450 lbs., useful load 4050 lbs.), performance suffered slightly. Wts. amended to 6450-4050-10,500 lbs. in 1937.

The fuselage framework was a "stressed-skin", semi-monocoque, all-metal (24ST) structure covered with riveted smooth (24ST) "Alclad" metal sheet. The main cabin was 15 ft.

Fig. 182. "Electra" 10-A in Canadian service.

long x 58 ins. wide x 60 ins. high with a volume
of 300 cu. ft.; normally, seating was arranged for
10 passengers. Entry door was on the left side to
the rear and a lavatory was aft of the cabin. The
pilot's cabin up front was arranged to seat two.
A baggage compartment of 40 cu. ft. capacity
was in the nose and a compartment of 14 cu. ft.
capacity was in each side of the wing-stub. The
stressed-skin all-metal cantilever wing was built
around a single spar beam and covered with
riveted "Alclad" (24ST) metal sheet; the center-
section was integral to the fuselage and outer
wing panels were bolted on. The all-metal engine
nacelles were fastened to outer ends of the C/S
and provided support also for the retractable
landing gear. The landing gear of 13 ft. 7 in.
tread used Aerol (air-oil) shock struts; Goodyear
35x15-6 airwheels were fitted with hydraulic
brakes. Electric motors retracted the landing
gear into the engine nacelles. Fuel tanks were in
forward portion of the stub-wing; maximum
capacity for the 10-A was 200 gal. The cantilever
tail group was an all-metal (24ST) structure
covered with riveted Alclad metal sheet; twin
rudders were placed out in the slipstream behind
each engine. Rudders and elevators had trimming tabs. Hamilton-Standard controllable
propellers, electric engine starters, generator,
Exide battery, cabin heat and ventilation,
lavatory, dual wheel-type controls, Western
Electric two-way radio, bonding & shielding,
navigation lights, landing lights, Lux and Pyrene
fire extinguishers, parachute flares, clock, fuel
gauges, and a full set of airline-type instruments
were standard equipment. The custom "Club"
interior with 4 over-stuffed seats, a couch, and a
table was optional. The next "Electra" development was the Model 10-C as described in the
chapter for ATC # 559 of this volume.

Listed below is partial listing of Model 10-A entries as gleaned from various records:

NC-233Y: Model 10-A (# 1001) 2 Wasp Jr. 400.
NC-14243: " (# 1002) "
NC-14244: " (# 1003) "
NC-14263: " (# 1010) "

-14260;	"	(# 1011)	"
NC-3138;	"	(# 1012)	"
-14261;	"	(# 1013)	"
-14262;	"	(# 1014)	"
-14900;	"	(# 1015)	"
-14901;	"	(# 1016)	"
-14905;	"	(# 1018)	"
-14907;	"	(# 1020)	"
-14915;	"	(# 1021)	"
-14934;	"	(# 1023)	"
-14935;	"	(# 1024)	"
-14936;	"	(# 1025)	"
-14937;	"	(# 1026)	"
-14938;	"	(# 1027)	"
-14939;	"	(# 1028)	"
-14940;	"	(# 1029)	"
-14941;	"	(# 1030)	"
-14942;	"	(# 1031)	"
-14945;	"	(# 1032)	"
-14946;	"	(# 1033)	"
-14947;	"	(# 1034)	"
-14948;	"	(# 1035)	"
-14981;	"	(# 1044)	"
SP-AYA;	"	(# 1045)	"
SP-AYB;	"	(# 1046)	"
SP-AYC;	"	(# 1047)	"
SP-AYD;	"	(# 1048)	"
A-0267;	"	(# 1052)	"
-16050;	"	(# 1061)	"
-16051;	"	(# 1062)	"
CF-AZY;	"	(# 1063)	"
CF-BAF;	"	(# 1064)	"
-16078;	"	(# 1068)	"
-16055;	"	(# 1069)	"
-16056;	"	(# 1070)	"
37-65;	"	(# 1071)	"
-16084;	"	(# 1072)	"
37-66;	"	(# 1073)	"
37-67;	"	(# 1074)	"
NC-1700;	"	(# 1075)	"
NC-20Y;	"	(# 1076)	"
YV-ACE;	"	(# 1078)	"
YV-ACI;	"	(# 1079)	"
G-AEPN;	"	(# 1080)	"
G-AEPO;	"	(# 1081)	"
G-AEPP;	"	(# 1082)	"
G-AEPR;	"	(# 1083)	"
NC-16058;	"	(# 1084)	"

This approval for ser. # 1001 and up; ser. # 1001,
1002, 1003, 1010, 1011, 1013, 1014, 1015, 1020,
1021, 1023, 1024, 1025 del. to NWA; ser. # 1012,
1032, 1035, 1062, 1072 del. as "Club" version;
ser. # 1018, 1026, 1027, 1028, 1029, 1030, 1031
del. to Braniff Airways; ser. # 1045-46-47-48 del.
to LOT in Poland; ser. # 1052 del. as XR20-1 to
U. S. Navy; ser. # 1061 del. to Hanford Air
Lines; ser. # 1063-64 del. to Canada; ser. # 1071,
1073, 1074 as YIC-36 in U.S.A.A.F.; ser. #
1078-79 del. to LAV in Venezuela; ser. # 1080-
81-82-83 del. to England; the bulk of the Model
10-A beyond ser. # 1084 were exported to
foreign countries; the last "Electra 10-A" was
built 18 July 1941.

Fig. 183. The Luscombe "Phantom" with 145 h.p. "Super Scarab" engine.

It would not be correct to say, as many have, that the Luscombe "Phantom" was a metal version of the popular "Monocoupe", but we can say that whatever was learned in 8 years of "Monocoupe" development was, more or less, inherited by the "Phantom" design. Don Luscombe, genial fellow who had been the guiding hand at Monocoupe Aircraft all these years, had a pretty good idea of the requirements necessary in a sporty personal-type airplane, so he carefully blended past experience with some brand-new ideas; the sleek and swift "Phantom" was the startling result. Definitely, the "Phantom" had a distinct personality all its own, but familiar hereditary traits came to the surface now and then, and these caused the erroneous comparison. Judging make-up of the "Phantom" we can see that it was certainly revolutionary for an airplane in the private-owner market. The all-metal "stressed-skin" fuselage was an innovation that offered strength, reliability, and practically no maintenance; because it was easier to build it in a streamlined form, speed was an added bonus. The rest of the airplane framework was all-metal also, for strength and to inhibit deterioration. No wood, no nails, no glue. Striving for speed and top ef-

ficiency, Luscombe knew that the "Phantom" with its high performance was not to be for the average owner, so he aimed his promotional efforts at those privileged few who would appreciate and enjoy the "revolution" he had to offer. We must say that people were not used to seeing such a private airplane, and tho' it drew bouquets wherever it went, it suffered some resistance. The Luscombe "Phantom" was nevertheless a remarkable airplane; fashioned in a concept that certainly bordered on the radical, at least for 1934, this airplane introduced certain standards to the light airplane industry that proved to be years ahead.

When Donald A. Luscombe left the Monocoupe Corp. in 1933 he rented a corner of the former Butler Aircraft hangar from Earl Reed in Kansas City, Mo. Luscombe had definite ideas he wanted to incorporate into a new airplane, and he had the able assistance of engineer Ivan H. Driggs. The hammering-out and stretching of metal panels for the new craft attracted the curious and Luscombe had difficulty keeping his project a secret. He meant to surprise the industry, and this he did anyhow. Bart Stevenson, a very able "Monocoupe" pilot, took the "Phantom" up on its maiden flight in early

Fig. 184. Prototype "Phantom" as rolled out of shop in Kansas City.

May of 1934; the tests were highly satisfying, proving a performance beyond the calculations, but the narrow undercarriage made each landing a skitterish project. The "Phantom" was formally introduced at the 1934 National Air Races where it almost panicked the race-goers with its style and innovations. After securing approval for the "Phantom" a batch of 7 were started, but only one or two were completed at Kansas City. Luscombe judged his business would lie more or less in the east, so a move was made in the winter of 1934-35 to the Mercer Airport in West Trenton, N.J. With various parts left over from K.C. they assembled a few more in early 1935 at Trenton. Anticipating a good year, Luscombe made arrangements to build some 25 more of the "Phantom". Oddly enough, most of the metal-work was let out to sub-contractors who specialized in this type of work, and the parts were then prepared and assembled at the Luscombe factory to become a complete airplane. Luscombe was proud of his beautiful airplane, but it wasn't selling; 4 had been delivered in 1935, and probably 6 or 7 in 1936. Limited production continued in 1937-38, but the "Phantom" was finally shunted aside for a new version called the Model 4, and a Model 8 design that was only waiting for introduction of the 50 h.p. Continental engine. Nevertheless, the "Phantom" was a remarkable airplane; it represented a milestone in lightplane manufacturing and it brought the "Luscombe" name to prominence and high regard in America.

The Luscombe "Phantom" model 1 was an all-metal high-winged cabin monoplane with side-by-side seating for two. From any angle the "Phantom" was a combination of soft, round curves that spelled-out speed with a beauty of line that had many green-eyed with envy. Because of its speed and its desire to be unfettered, this "Luscombe" was strictly a let's-go-somewhere airplane; it covered a lot of ground in an hour. The all-metal framework was unusually tough, strong enough if need be, to withstand the stresses of amateur aerobatics, and it certainly eliminated frequent airframe maintenance. Airplanes like this came rather high, so the "Phantom" had to be leveled at a certain clientele, those few that would enjoy this airplane and be willing to pay for it. As powered with the 7 cyl. Warner "Super Scarab" (Series 50) engine of 145 h.p. the "Phantom" drained every ounce of power from the engine and put it to good use; a testimony of this airplane's aerodynamic cleanness. Not burdened with a heavy, clumsy framework, the "Phantom" was quick and very deft in its maneuvers. A thorough pleasure to fly, the narrow-geared airplane was however, often skitterish on landing and required complete attention; some pilots did not like this. The "Phantom" was not really a difficult airplane, once you got wise to its habits, but it was feisty enough to quickly discourage sloppy flying. It was a high-performance airplane and really showed-off for high-performance pilots. The type certificate number for the "Phantom" model 1 was issued 8-18-34 and perhaps up to 25 or so examples of this model were manufactured by the Luscombe Airplane Development Corp. on Mercer Airport in West Trenton, N.J. Don A. Luscombe was pres. & gen. mgr.

Fig. 185. A "Phantom" on Edo floats.

Listed below are specifications and performance data for the Luscombe "Phantom" model 1 as powered with 145 h.p. Warner "Super Scarab" engine; length overall 21'6"; height overall 6'9"; wing span 31'0"; wing chord 62"; total wing area (incl. fuselage section) 143 sq. ft.; airfoil NACA-2412; wt. empty 1320 lbs.; useful load 630 lbs.; payload with 33 gal. fuel 236 lbs. (1 pass. & 66 lbs. baggage); gross wt. 1950 lbs.; max. speed 168 at sea level; cruising speed (1950 r.p.m.) 143 at sea level; landing speed 55; landing speed (with drag flaps) 45; climb 1400 ft. first min. at sea level; ser. ceiling 19,000 ft.; gas cap. 33 gal.; oil cap. 3.5 gal.; cruising range (1950 r.p.m.) at 9.5 gal. per hour 485 miles; price approx. $6000. at factory field.

The all-metal fuselage framework was a "stressed-skin" monocoque structure of 17ST dural bulkheads covered in .065 in. "Alclad" metal sheet. The 42 in. wide cabin seated 2 side-by-side on thick, spring-filled cushions covered in leather; an 8 cu. ft. baggage compartment behind the seat-back had allowance for 66 lbs. An unusually large door on each side provided easy step-up into the cabin; a large curved windshield and Pyralin side windows, plus rear quarter windows and a skylight, offered good visibility in all directions. The instrument panel was tidy with ample room for extra equipment, and dual stick-type controls were provided. The sound-proofed cabin was upholstered in imitation leather and equipped with heat and ventilation. The all-metal wing framework was built up of extruded dural I-section spar beams with stamped-out dural wing ribs; the leading edge was covered with dural metal sheet and the completed framework was covered in fabric. "Drag flaps" of stainless steel were fastened on under-

side of the wing ahead of the aileron hinge line; operation was electrical or manual. A 16.5 gal. fuel tank was in the root end of each wing-half; fuel gauges were visible in the cabin. The stout wing was braced to the fuselage by streamlined vee-struts and faired into the fuselage junction with a large metal fillet. The semi-cantilever landing gear of rather narrow tread was of 2 oleo-legs braced with streamlined steel wire; the landing gear was completely faired with metal cuffs and fillets. Twenty-one inch streamlined wheels and tires were fitted with brakes; the spring-leaf tail skid was fitted with a hard-rubber wheel. The tail group was a composite structure; fixed surfaces were a riveted dural structure covered in Alclad sheet, and movable surfaces were a welded steel framework covered in fabric. Movable surfaces were aerodynamically balanced and the horizontal stabilizer was adjustable in flight. A metal propeller, electric engine starter, battery, generator, fire extinguisher, dual controls, navigation lights, wheel brakes and a complete instrument panel were generally ordered as standard equipment. A radio set, bonding & shielding, landing lights, parachute flares, 6.50x-10 low-pressure wheels and tires, and Edo 44-2425 twin-float gear were optional. The next Luscombe development was the 90 h.p. Model 4 as described in the chapter for ATC # 687.

Listed below are "Phantom" entries as gleaned from registration records:

NC-272Y:	Phantom 1	(# 1)	Warner 145
-275Y:	"	(# 101)	"
-276Y:	"	(# 102)	"
-277Y:	"	(# 103)	"
-278Y:	"	(# 104)	"
;	"	(# 105)	"
-1286;	"	(# 106)	"

Fig. 186. Rear view of "Phantom" shows trim figure.

Fig. 187. Young couple pose happily with new "Phantom".

-1007:	"	(# 107)	"
-1008:	"	(# 108)	"
:	"	(# 109)	"
:	"	(# 110)	"
-1010:	"	(# 111)	"
-1025:	"	(# 112)	"
-1028:	"	(# 113)	"
-1043:	"	(# 114)	"
-1235:	"	(# 115)	"
-1048:	"	(# 116)	"
-1278:	"	(# 117)	"
:	"	(# 118)	"
-30449:	"	(# 119)	"

-1249:	"	(# 120)	"
:	"	(# 121)	"
-1265:	"	(# 122)	"
-1323:	"	(# 123)	"
:	"	(# 124)	"
:	"	(# 125)	"
-25234:	"	(# 126)	"
-28779:	"	(# 131)	"

This approval for ser. # 101 and up; ser. # 131 assembled from parts in 1941; ser. # 105 probably registered as HB-EXE; approval expired 7-7-41.

ATC # 553
(8-23-34)
NORTHROP "DELTA", 1-D.

Fig. 188. "Delta" poses majestically as flying yacht for sportsman Powell Crosley.

Overshadowed by exploits of the more dramatic "Gamma" the lesser-known Northrop "Delta" was a highly advanced single-engined airliner, a speedy conveyance designed primarily for medium loads on the trunk airline routes. In general, the "Delta" airliner was typical of the "Gamma" cargo-carrier, using the same wing and landing gear, but the semi-monocoque fuselage was enlarged considerably in cross-section to carry 8 people. Finally discarding the long-established tradition of having the pilot sit out in the open behind his load, the "Delta" pilot was up front in an enclosed cabin slightly above the passenger level; the main cabin behind the pilot station was suitable for various passenger and cargo arrangements. Best of all the "Delta" had racing-plane performance that was applied to the transport of air-travelers. Of all-metal, multi-cellular, "stressed-skin" construction similar to the earlier "Alpha" transport, the prototype "Delta" (Model 1-A) was the first of an order for 15 to be delivered to TWA (Transcontinental & Western Air) for test late in 1933, but its promising career as an airliner was stifled by circumstance and the order was cancelled. The second "Delta" was especially built as an airliner for Aerovias Centrales, a Pan American Airways subsidiary, to operate from Los Angeles into Mexico, but was lost in service on a flight to Mexico City. Two of the "Delta" liners were shipped to Sweden and operated by A. B. Aerotransport. Much like the General GA-43 and the Vultee V-1-A the Northrop "Delta" 1-D was denied the chance to prove itself, in this country, by a government directive; this directive, hastily employed because of a few accidents, prohibited the use of large single-engined airliners on the trunk-line routes. But, they could be exported to other countries. However, the plush "executive model" of the "Delta", with custom arrangements for 5 to 7 people, was not affected by the directive and were sold to several sportsmen and business houses.

The husky-looking Northrop "Delta" model 1-D was an all-metal, low-winged, cabin monoplane with seating arranged to suit various functions. The "Delta", a cabin version of the illustrious "Gamma", was originally designed as a high speed passenger-transport, but the future of the large single-engined airliner was stifled in this country, so the "Delta" was then offered as

Fig. 189. The heart of "Delta" performance was 735 h.p. Wright "Cyclone" engine.

an executive-transport in the field of big business. The roster of plush "Delta Executive" owners included such famous names as Richfield Oil, Powell Crosley, Jr., Earl P. Haliburton, Wilbur May, Hal Roach, Stewart Pulitzer, and other big names in the business world. Two of the "Delta" airliners were exported to Sweden, but other than confirmation of the order, no reports on their service there were available. By this time Northrop had already turned to various experiments in military aircraft, so the loss of commercial business was not all that important. In fact, it had been a nuisance that interfered with the planning, and all the secret projects that were shaping up on the assembly floor. As powered with the big 9 cyl. Wright "Cyclone" engine rated 710-735 h.p. the shiny "Delta" could prove that its forte was high speed with comfort and efficiency. Business-men found it ideal for those long hops around the country. Pilots marveled in its strength and passengers were comforted in its safety. The type certificate number for the "Delta" model 1-D was issued 8-23-34 and perhaps 6 or more examples of this model were manufactured by the Northrop Corp. at Inglewood, Calif. A few of the early "Delta" versions, differing slightly from the 1-D, were built and approved on Group 2 certificates before the ATC was awarded.

Listed below are specifications and performance data for the "Delta" model 1-D as powered with Wright "Cyclone" SR-1820-F2 engine rated 735 h.p. at 2100 r.p.m. at 4000 ft.; length overall 33'1"; height overall 10'1"; wing span 47'9"; wing chord at root 114"; wing chord at tip 22"; total wing area 363 sq.ft.; airfoil at root NACA-2415; airfoil at tip NACA-2409; wt. empty 4540 (4600) lbs.; useful load 2810 (2750) lbs.; payload with 328 gal. fuel & 1 pilot 515 (455) lbs. (2 pass. & 175 lbs. baggage); payload with 250 gal. fuel & 2 pilots 813 lbs. (4 pass. & 133 lbs. baggage); gross wt. 7350 lbs.; max. speed 219 at 6300 ft.; cruising speed (.75 power) 200 at 8000 ft.; landing speed (with flaps) 62; climb 1200 ft. first min. at sea level; ser. ceiling 20,000 ft.; gas cap. max. 328 gal.; oil cap. 21 gal.; cruising range (.75 power) at 42 gal. per hour 1500-1100 miles; price $37,500. at factory with standard equipment. The "Delta" was also available with Wright SR-1820-F52 engine rated 775 h.p. at 2100 r.p.m. at 5800 ft.

The fuselage framework was a semi-monocoque structure of transverse dural rings covered with longitudinally stiffened "Alclad" metal sheet. The main cabin of 58 in. width was heavily sound-proofed and arranged to seat up to 8 passengers; an entry door was on the left side. The custom-built "Club" or "Executive" version was generally arranged to seat 4 or 5 people and accommodations were very plush. The normal layout was overstuffed chairs, a divan, and complete lavatory. A 25 cu. ft. baggage compartment was behind the cabin and 35 lbs. was allowed under the divan; some were upholstered in red and tan leather. The cantilever wing panels of multi-cellular construction were a series of vertical webs, bulkheads with flanged lightening holes, and covered with Alclad metal sheet. The riveted metal "stressed skin" on the fuselage and on the wing was designed to carry a large share of the load. The 11 ft. wide center-section (C/S) was built in-

Fig. 190. Cantilever construction of "Delta" provided strength and minimum drag.

tegral to the fuselage; outer wing panels were bolted to the stub end. The fuel capacity of 328 gal. was divided among 6 tanks that were mounted in the C/S; 2 front tanks at 47 gal. each, 2 center tanks at 55 gal. each, and 2 rear tanks at 62 gal. each. Electrically operated wing flaps were outboard of the C/S and occupied trailing edge up to the ailerons. The spatted landing gear of 9 ft. tread was 2 cantilever assemblies fitted with "Aerol" shock struts and 36x8 Bendix wheels with hydraulic brakes; tires were heavy duty 6 ply. The all-metal tail group was also of multi-cellular construction; rudder and elevator were fitted with adjustable trim tab. A Hamilton-Standard controllable propeller, electric engine starter, generator, Exide battery, oil-cooling radiator, navigation lights, landing lights, parachute flares, fire extinguisher, bonding & shielding, Western Electric radio, window curtains, and a full set of airline-type instruments were standard equipment. A special "Club" interior, complete lavatory, Sperry auto-pilot, and extra instruments were optional. Listed below are "Delta" entries as gleaned from various records:

NC-12292: 1-A (# 3) Cyclone 710.
X-236Y: 1-B (#   ) Hornet 650.
NC-13777: 1-D (# 28) Cyclone 710.
   -14241: 1-D (# 38) Cyclone 735.
   -14242: 1-D (# 39) Cyclone 735.
   -14265: 1-D (# 40) Hornet 650.
   -14266: 1-D (# 41) Cyclone 710.
   -14267: 1-D (# 42) Cyclone 735.
   -14220: 1-D (# 73) Cyclone 710.

This approval for ser. # 38 and up; first 4 "Delta" had sliding canopy; ser. no. for 2 to Sweden unknown; Swedish examples had Hornet 660 and controllable props; Aerovias Centrales ship as XA-BED (formerly X-236Y) had Hornet 650; first model 1-D on Group 2 memo # 2-484; Model 1-A on Group 2 memo # 2-456; one "Delta" reported as shipped to Canada in parts - a few built there by Vickers under license; approval expired 9-30-39.

Fig. 191. A Vickers-Northrop "Delta" assembled in Canada.

ATC # 554
(8-28-34)
KINNER "PLAYBOY", R-5.

Fig. 192. Kinner "Playboy" R-5 with 160 h.p. Kinner engine.

Patterned after the earlier "Playboy", which couldn't decide half the time whether it should be an open cockpit airplane, or a cabin airplane, and after the Kinner "Envoy" to some extent, the new "Playboy" model R-5 evolved into an interesting sport-utility airplane. As a fully enclosed coupe-type airplane, slightly on the heavier side, the Model R-5 was now fitted with more wing area to carry 2 large people, with a respectable pile of baggage, and weight allowance left over to stuff in all sorts of little comforts and pilot aids. With a 5 cyl. Kinner R-5 (Series 2) engine up front putting out 160 h.p. the "Playboy" R-5 responded eagerly and delivered a rather good performance. Left to fend for itself in the sport-plane market of 1934 the "Playboy" was up against some serious competition, but fortunately the Bureau of Air Commerce (BAC) took interest in the model R-5 and gave it ample exposure among the flying public. Assigned to government inspectors who roamed in the field in pursuit of BAC duties the Bureau of Air Commerce purchased 5 examples of the new "Playboy" and ran up an impressive operating record. A few sportsmen were also attracted to the new R-5, one trading his Kinner "Sportwing" in on the "Playboy"; one sportsman, recently a licensed pilot, claimed he

bought the "Playboy" as a Xmas present for his wife, but she couldn't even fly. No doubt he planned to be the pilot of her airplane. Interest in the "Playboy" was very big, it should have done well, but the total production of this model was rather small.

The Kinner "Playboy" model R-5 was a wire-braced, low-winged cabin monoplane with side-by-side seating for two. As a comfortable sportplane for 2 people, with a certain amount of utility that would be attractive to an aggressive man of business, the "Playboy" had much to offer, but it was up against some terrific competition in its particular field. It was a distinctive airplane that stood out well in a crowd and its manner was impressive, but it couldn't grasp the assurance of a bright future. Its duties with the Bureau of Air Commerce were perhaps its only claim to fame. As powered with the 5 cyl. Kinner R-5 (Series 2) engine rated 160 h.p. at 1850 r.p.m. the "Playboy" R-5 (a Max Harlow design) was blessed with plenty of muscle and it performed its duties with a certain amount of dash. In a walk-around the "Playboy" looked rather dainty, but it was actually tough and asked no favors. Pilots liked it. The type certificate number for the "Playboy" model R-5 was issued 8-28-34 and 8 examples of this model were

Fig. 193. "Playboy" as fitted for use by Dept. of Commerce inspectors.

manufactured by the Kinner Airplane & Motor Corp., Ltd. at Glendale, Calif. Robert Porter was pres. and gen. mgr.; B. L. Graves was V.P.; Lillian Porter was sales mgr.; and B. W. James was chf. engr.

Listed below are specifications and performance data for the Kinner "Playboy" model R-5 as powered with 160 h.p. Kinner R-5 (Series 2) engine; length overall 24'3"; height overall 7'9"; wing span 32'9"; wing chord 72"; total wing area 189 sq. ft.; airfoil Clark Y; wt. empty 1461 lbs.; useful load 809 lbs.; payload with 48 gal. fuel 325 lbs. (1 pass. & 155 lbs. baggage); gross wt. 2270 lbs.; max. speed 138 at sea level; cruising speed (1800 r.p.m.) 125; landing speed 55; climb 800 ft. first min. at sea level; ser. ceiling 14,000 ft.; gas cap. 48 gal.; oil cap. 3.5 gal.; cruising range (1800 r.p.m.) at 9 gal. per hour 600 miles; later versions amended to empty wt. 1481 lbs.;

useful load 789 lbs.; payload with 44.5 gal. fuel 325 lbs.; gross wt. 2270 lbs.; max. gas cap. 44.5 gal.; range 550 miles; price not announced.

The fuselage framework was built up of welded C/M steel tubing, heavily faired with wooden formers and fairing strips, then fabric covered. Metal panels surrounded the cabin area. A large door on the right side provided entry into the cabin right off the wing-walk. The side-by-side arrangement was more than ample for 2 on a well-padded adjustable seat; dual stick-type controls were provided. The cabin walls were soundproofed, all windows were of shatter-proof glass, the cabin was ventilated and cabin heat was available. Normally, the cabin interior was upholstered in DuPont Fabricoid, but other materials were optional. A baggage compartment behind the seat was allowed up to 40 lbs., and 60 lbs. was allowed in the right wing-stub.

Fig. 194. Racing-plane influence is readily apparent in "Playboy" design.

Fig. 195. Eight "Playboy" were built and this was the last one.

The wing-stub of welded C/M steel tubing was built integral to the fuselage. The framework of the outer wing panels was built up of solid spruce spar beams with spruce and plywood truss-type wing ribs; the leading edges were covered with dural sheet and the completed framework was covered in fabric. The streamlined "spatted" landing gear, typical to that as used on many racing airplanes, was fastened to each side of the wing-stub and braced as part of the wing bracing truss; wings were braced from top and bottom with heavy-gauge streamlined steel wire. The landing gear was "sprung" independently on "Kinner" oleo-spring shock struts; wheels were 6.50x10 Autofan fitted with 4-ply low-pressure tires and brakes. A parking brake was also provided. The main 35 gal. fuel tank was in the fuselage and a 13 gal. aux. tank was in the left wing-stub. The fabric covered tail group was built up of welded C/M steel tubing; the elevators were fitted with adjustable "tabs" for trim. A metal propeller, Heywood or Eclipse air-operated engine starter, 6-volt Exide battery, navigation lights, chromed exhaust collector ring, dual controls, bonding & shielding, wing-root and empennage fairing, Pyrene fire extinguisher, 8 in. steerable tail wheel, clock, car-buretor heater, compass, fuel gauge, and first-aid kit were standard equipment. Landing lights, parachute flares, generator, radio, extra instruments, cabin heater, "Lord" engine mount bushings, Thermos bottle (1 qt.) for drinking water, and a "speed-ring" engine cowl were optional equipment. A 44.5 gal. fuselage fuel tank was available to replace the 35 gal. main tank and 13 gal. wing-stub tank. The next Kinner development was the B-2-R project that was taken over by Timm on ATC # 617 and called the Model 160.

Listed below are "Playboy" R-5 entries as gleaned from registration records:

NC-13778; R-5 (# 106) Kinner R5.
NS-21; R-5 (# 112) Kinner R5.
NS-22; R-5 (# 113) Kinner R5.
NS-23; R-5 (# 114) Kinner R5.
NS-24; R-5 (# 115) Kinner R5.
NS-25; R-5 (# 116) Kinner R5.
NC-14920; R-5 (# 227) Kinner R5.
NC-14963; R-5 (# 228) Kinner R5.

This approval for ser. # 106, 112 and up; ser. # 112-113-114-115-116 operated by Bureau of Air Commerce; ser. # 227-228 mfgd. in 1935; this approval expired 6-30-39.

ATC # 555
(8-28-34)
DOUGLAS COMMERCIAL, DC2-115.

Fig. 196. Douglas DC2-115 series were designed for export.

Anthony H. G. Fokker, aircraft designer and builder of world renown, sensing the great possibilities of an airplane such as the "Douglas Commercial", and realizing the competition it would give his own production, obtained rights for his company in Holland to assemble and distribute the DC-2 in Europe. KLM (Royal Dutch Air Lines) was the first foreign line to place an order and several more major lines began to follow suit. Especially, since the KLM "Stork" (PH-AJU) had won second place in the international MacRobertson Race from London, England to Melbourne, Australia in 1934. This was a great tribute to the Douglas DC-2 since it was bested only by a custom-built racing DeHaviland built especially for the long race. All of the Douglas DC-2 type were basically the same, but there were numerous variations; these variations, mostly in interior arrangements and other things unseen, were awarded design specification numbers such as the DC2-112, DC2-115, etc. The DC2-115 series under discussion here, were all assigned to Tony Fokker and as the European distributor he delivered them to various airlines and governments on the continent. The bulk of these went to KLM, some 20 or more, but other examples went to such airlines as Swissair, Lufthansa, KNILM, LOT of Poland, LAPE and Iberia of Spain, to a line in

Italy, Czechoslovakia, and a few for private use in Austria, France, and Holland. The DC-2 revolutionized airline service in Europe just as it had here in the U.S.A., and many of them were serving continuously into 1940. When Adolph Hitler's marauders were over-running Europe, many of the KLM liners were destroyed on the ground and several were captured for use by the Germans. The 3 operated by KNILM in the Netherlands East Indies escaped to Australia where they were safe for several more years. After the war in 1945 the remaining DC-2 in Europe were put back into service and most were still active in the 1950's; one old veteran survived all the tribulations until 1961.

The Douglas model DC-2-115 was an all-metal, twin-engined cabin monoplane with seating arranged for up to 18 places. Typical of the examples flying here in the U.S.A., the DC2-115 introduced airline supremacy on the continent and European travelers loved it. Now they could save hours on trips such as Zurich, Switzerland to Vienna, Austria, and cut days from long jaunts such as from Amsterdam to Batavia in the Orient. Pleased with the speed, and the safety, the European air traveler also reveled in the comfort and the convenience. All over the continent the DC2-115 was now rubbing elbows with aircraft that had been Europe's

Fig. 197. DC2-115 of Swissair line loads at Zurich.

finest, and in its fetching way was proving that aeronautical progress in America had just about over-shadowed everything else in the transport field; this was having some effect, of course, and it spurred the European industry into an effort to catch up. By 1935 some 100 of the DC-2 transports were in service under the flags of 12 nations. So many nice things were being said about the "Douglas Commercial", and it was reflected in the increasing traffic, so that airlines without a DC-2 were at a noticeable disadvantage. Tony Fokker was a good airplane salesman, as he had proven in the previous 10 years, but he found that the DC-2 was practically selling itself and 40 of the all-metal liners were criss-crossing European skies in less than 2 years' time. As powered with 2 Wright "Cyclone" SGR-1820-F2 engines rated 720 h.p. each the DC2-115 was typical of the versions used here on American airlines, turning in the same unbeatable performance and twin-engined safety that was converting many to airway travel. The type certificate number for the Douglas model DC2-115 was issued 8-28-34 and some 40 examples of this model were handled through the Fokker shops in Holland.

Listed below are specifications and performance data for the Douglas model DC2-115 as powered with 2 Wright "Cyclone" SGR-1820-F2 engines rated 720 h.p. each; length overall 62'0"; height overall 16'3"; wing span 85'0"; wing chord at root 170"; total wing area 939 sq.

Fig. 198. The world-famous "Uiver" of KLM line.

ft.; airfoil at root NACA-2215; airfoil at tip NACA-2209; wt. empty 12,010 lbs.; useful load 6190 lbs.; payload with 360 gal. fuel 3405 lbs. (16 pass. & 685 lbs. baggage-cargo); gross wt. 18,-200 lbs.; max. speed 213 at 7000 ft.; cruising speed (.75 power) 200 at 14,000 ft.; landing speed (with flaps) 60; climb 1090 ft. first min. at sea level; ser. ceiling 23,600 ft.; gas cap. normal 360 gal.; gas cap. max. 510 gal.; oil cap. 38 gal.; cruising range (.75 power) at 96 gal. per hour 700 miles; range (.625 power) 850 miles; price approx. $65,000, plus erection and delivery. The DC2-115 was also eligible with SGR-1820-F52 engines rated 750 h.p. at 1950 r.p.m. at 7000 ft.; the extra horsepower produced a slight performance gain. This version same as above except as follows: wt. empty 12,185 lbs.; useful load 6375 lbs.; payload 3485 lbs.; gross wt. 18,560 lbs.; landing speed 62; climb 1000 ft. first min.; ser. ceiling 22,400 ft.

The construction details and general arrangement of the DC2-115 were typical to that of the model DC2-112 as described here in the chapter for ATC # 540. Variations in one model or another were categorized by a design specification number, such as DC2-112, DC2-115, DC2-120, etc. The specification numbers, if modified, were categorized further by a suffix letter such as A, B, C, etc. As a case in point, the DC2-115 series were also subdivided into DC2-115A, DC2-115B, and so on. The first airplane delivered to KLM, the famous "Stork", was a DC2-115A, but the next 14 airplanes were DC2-115E. One airplane delivered to KLM was the DC2-115H, 3 were delivered as the DC2-115L, and 3 were delivered to KNILM as the DC2-115G. Other versions were the DC2-115B for Swissair, the DC2-115D to Spain, France and Germany, and the DC2-115K to Czechoslovakia. One each were also delivered of the DC2-115J, DC2-115M, and DC2-115U. It would be interesting to know how these versions differed from one another, but information such as this is buried rather deep. The next "Douglas Commercial" development was the model DC-2H as described in the chapter for ATC # 570 of this volume.

Listed below are DC2-115 entries as gleaned from the Journal of the American Aviation Historical Society:

PH-AJU:	DC2-115A	(# 1317)	2 Cyclone
D-ABEQ:	-115D	(# 1318)	"
I-EROS:	-115B	(# 1319)	"
HB-ISA:	-115B	(# 1320)	"
HB-ITI:	-115B	(# 1321)	"
HB-ITE:	-115B	(# 1322)	"
HB-ITA:	-115B	(# 1329)	"
EC-AAA:	-115D	(# 1330)	"
EC-AAB:	-115D	(# 1331)	"
HB-ITO:	-115B	(# 1332)	"
F-AKHD:	-115D	(# 1333)	"
EC-AAC:	-115D	(# 1334)	"
PH-AKF:	-115E	(# 1335)	"
PH-AKG:	-115E	(# 1353)	"
PH-AKH:	-115E	(# 1354)	"
PH-AKI:	-115E	(# 1355)	"
PH-AKJ:	-115E	(# 1356)	"
PH-AKK:	-115E	(# 1357)	"
PH-AKL:	-115E	(# 1358)	"
PH-AKM:	-115E	(# 1359)	"
PH-AKN:	-115E	(# 1360)	"
PH-AKO:	-115E	(# 1361)	"
PH-AKP:	-115E	(# 1362)	"
PH-AKQ:	-115E	(# 1363)	"
PH-AKR:	-115E	(# 1364)	"
PH-AKS:	-115E	(# 1365)	"
PH-AKT:	-115H	(# 1366)	"
PK-AFJ:	-115G	(# 1374)	"
PK-AFK:	-115G	(# 1375)	"
PK-AFL:	-115G	(# 1376)	"
SP-ASK:	-115F	(# 1377)	"
SP-ASL:	-115F	(# 1378)	"
EC-EBB:	-115U	(# 1417)	"
EC-BFF:	-115J	(# 1521)	"
:	-115M	(# 1527)	"
OK-AIA:	-115K	(# 1581)	"
OK-AIB:	-115K	(# 1582)	"
PH-ALD:	-115L	(# 1583)	"
PH-ALE:	-115L	(# 1584)	"
PH-ALF:	-115L	(# 1585)	"

Fig. 199. Stinson "Model A" with 3 Lycoming 260 h.p. engines.

The tri-motored Stinson "Model A" of 1934, as "America's fastest and most economical Tri-Motor", had the three-engined transport field all to itself, but found itself competing also with the Boeing 247 and the Douglas DC-2. At about only half the cost the "Model A" was a cheap airliner that could just about match the speed and comfort of the 247 and the DC-2, and yet beat the pants off them in short-field operation. For the "Stinson A" it was a simple chore to drop in at the smaller airfields every few hundred miles, or even less, to drop off or pick up a passenger or two. The new low-winged Stinson "Tri-Motor" was master of the short high-speed runs at low altitude where less capacity was more suitable. Announced in Nov. of 1933 the rather unusual "Model A" was rolled out and flown on its maiden flight by Ralph DeVore of American Airlines on April 27 of 1934; by August of that year the "A" was being readied for production. The "Stinson A" was proudly displayed at the Detroit Air Show for 1935 and the plant was already working on a batch of 15 airplanes ordered by American Airlines, but delivery was delayed for several months by requested changes. In the meantime, the first production "Model A" was delivered to Delta Air Lines which inaugurated service from Dallas to Tyler, Shreveport, Monroe, Jackson, Meridian, Birmingham, and Atlanta in July of

1935; this a route with 8 stops across 5 southern states. The second batch of 5 airplanes went to Central Airlines which offered Stinson "Tri-Motor" service between Detroit and Washington, D.C. with stops at Cleveland, Akron, and Pittsburgh. Late in 1935 the American Airlines was operating a route from Detroit to Chicago which included 5 stops across the breadth of Michigan; the "Model A" was good at this type of service. When their Wash., D.C. to Chicago run lost some traffic American Airlines replaced the Douglas DC-2 on this route with a more practical "Stinson A". In April of 1936 the first of 4 "Model A" were delivered to the Airlines of Australia, Ltd. for a route from Sydney to Brisbane; the "A" was ideal for the primitive airstrips of Australia. Two of the Australian "Model A" had crashed because of cyclone and fog, and the remaining 2 were converted into a twin-engined configuration in 1943 using two 450 h.p. "Wasp" engines. A few examples of the "Model A" were sold to China; Walter J. Carr, noted flier and aircraft designer, delivered an example to a Chinese transport company in 1936 and remained to train native personnel to operate and maintain the airplane. Four of the "Model A" were delivered as plush executive-transports in the field of business. The tri-motored "A", made obsolete by new-generation "twins" was phased

Fig. 200. "Stinson A" was America's fastest and most economical "tri-motor".

out of production by 1937 and most were retired from airline service by 1938. Surviving examples slipped off into Mexico and the far north where they served well for at least another decade.

The Stinson tri-motored "Model A" was a low-winged transport monoplane with seating arranged for 1 or 2 pilots, 8 passengers, and a stewardess. Fat and contoured to rounded lines the "Model A" was short-coupled and wide-bodied with an interior that placed passengers in a friendly cluster, attended by a comely stewardess, instead of stringing them out into long rows. The executive model had plush over-stuffed chairs, a sofa, a table, and numerous other provisions for creature comforts. The Model A managed to look like a Stinson, but its wing of double taper in planform and in thickness, and its monospar construction was

rather unique. Robert W. Ayer designed it this way and his preliminary performance calculations were substantiated in the wind-tunnel by Prof. Peter Altman. Ayer was given some mighty tough requirements to meet in his design, but the Model A fulfilled his promises and then some. As powered with three 9 cyl. Lycoming R-680-5 engines rated 260 h.p. each at 2300 r.p.m. the Model A was a deft air-plane for its size and it scooted along at a pretty fast clip. Fully-loaded take-offs required less than 800 ft., climb was nearly 1000 f.p.m., and landing runs averaged 600 ft.; it was this kind of performance that made it so popular in the boondocks of the U.S.A. The story goes that designer Bob Ayer would take the "A" off from the factory's 1200 ft. strip, clear an imaginary obstacle in less than 800 ft., chop the throttles to

Fig. 201. The unique "Model A" was the best and the last "tri-motor" by Stinson.

Fig. 202. Tri-motored "Model A" prototype high over Detroit.

land, and then brake to a stop in the remaining 400 ft. This was even before its maiden flight! In every-day service the Model A was dependable, very stable, quiet, and comfortable; pilots enjoyed flying it. Power reserve allowed it to climb out after take-off on 2 engines, and to maintain at least 8000 ft. altitude on any 2 engines. Stinson had built some wonderful tri-motored airplanes, the Model A was no doubt the best, and it was also the last. The type certificate number for the Model A was issued 9-25-34 and some 35 examples of this model were manufactured by the Stinson Aircraft Corp. at Wayne, Mich. Robert W. Ayer was chief engineer of the transport division.

Listed below are specifications and performance data for the Stinson "Model A" as powered with 3 Lycoming R-680-5 engines rated 260 h.p. each; length overall 36'10"; height overall 11'6"; wing span 60'0"; max. wing chord 134"; wing chord at tip 67"; total wing area (incl. fuselage section) 500 sq. ft.; airfoil "2R-18/10"; wt. empty 7200 lbs.; useful load 3000 lbs.; payload with 140 gal. fuel, 1 pilot, & stewardess 1780 lbs. (8 pass. & 420 lbs. baggage); payload with 160 gal. fuel, & 2 pilots 1610 lbs. (8 pass. & 250 lbs. baggage); gross wt. 10,200 lbs.; max. speed 180 at sea level; cruising speed (.75 power) 163 at 5000 ft.; cruising speed (1950 r.p.m.) 170 at 7000 ft.; landing (stall) speed (with flaps) 63; climb 980 ft. first min. at sea level; ser. ceiling 17,000 ft.; gas cap. normal 160 gal.; gas cap. max. 220 gal.; oil cap. 12-15 gal.; cruising range (.75 power) at 42 gal. per hour 490 miles; ser. ceiling on 2 engines 8400 ft.;

price $37,500. at factory field.

The fuselage framework was built up of welded C/M steel tubing, contoured to a rounded shape with formers and fairing strips, then fabric covered; the forward section was covered in dural metal panels. The cabin was soundproofed, ventilated, and equipped with cabin heaters; all windows were of shatter-proof glass. Passengers were seated 3 across, with large entry door to the rear on right side. A large baggage bin of 41 cu. ft. capacity with allowance for 500 lbs. was located behind the passenger section, and so was the lavatory; a 15 cu. ft. baggage or mail bin with allowance for 150 lbs. was available in each engine nacelle, or each of these compartments could be used for 30 gal. extra fuel. The unusual tapered wing was a sesqui-spar design built up of welded C/M steel tubing with a girder-type spar beam and truss-type wing ribs; the metal-covered center-section (C/S) was integral to lower fuselage and braced to top of fuselage with parallel struts. The fabric covered outer wing panels were fastened to stub-end of the C/S. Outboard engine nacelles were mounted to the C/S and the landing gear of 17 ft. tread retracted up and forward into underside of these nacelles. Goodyear 35x15-6 airwheels were fitted with vacuum-boosted hydraulic brakes; the swiveling tail wheel was 12x5-3 with heavy duty tire. An 80 gal. fuel tank was mounted in the C/S, each side of the fuselage; an extra 30 gal. tank could be mounted in each wing-mounted engine nacelle. Trailing edge wing flaps were mounted across span of the C/S; both landing gear and wing flaps were electrically operated with provision for hand operation in emergency. The fabric covered tail group was built up of welded C/M steel tubing; rudder and elevators were fitted with trimming tabs. All movable controls were aerodynamically balanced. Lycoming-Smith or Hamilton-Standard controllable propellers, 3 electric engine starters, battery, generator, cabin heater, drinking water Thermos, fire extinguisher, toilet compartment, landing lights, navigation lights, parachute flares, bonding & shielding, two-way radio, wheel fenders, and first-aid kit were standard equipment. Extra fuel cap., custom "Club" interior, custom colors, and wing de-icers optional. The next Stinson development was the "Reliant" model SR-6 as described in the chapter for ATC # 580 of this volume.

Listed below is a partial listing of Model A entries as compiled from various sources:

NC-14141:	Model A	(# 9100)	3 Lycoming 260.
-14597:	"	(# 9101)	3 Lycoming 245.
-14598:	"	(# 9102)	3 Lycoming 260.
:	"	(# 9103)	"
-14566:	"	(# 9104)	3 Lycoming 245.
:	"	(# 9105)	"
-15106:	"	(# 9106)	3 Lycoming 260.
-15107:	"	(# 9107)	"
-15108:	"	(# 9108)	"
-15109:	"	(# 9109)	"
-15110:	"	(# 9110)	"
:	"	(# 9111)	"
:	"	(# 9112)	"
-15153:	"	(# 9113)	3 Lycoming 260.
-15154:	"	(# 9114)	"
-15155:	"	(# 9115)	"
-15156:	"	(# 9116)	"
-15157:	"	(# 9117)	"
-15158:	"	(# 9118)	"
-15159:	"	(# 9119)	"
-15160:	"	(# 9120)	"
-15161:	"	(# 9121)	"
-15162:	"	(# 9122)	"
-15163:	"	(# 9123)	"
-15164:	"	(# 9124)	"
-15165:	"	(# 9125)	"
VH-UHH:	"	(# 9126)	"
:	"	(# 9127)	"
VH-UKK:	"	(# 9128)	"
-16110:	"	(# 9129)	"
VH-UYY:	"	(# 9130)	"

This approval for ser. # 9102 and up; ser. # 9101, 9104 were "Club" models; no listing for ser. # 9103, 9105, 9111, 9112, nor any beyond ser. # 9130; approval expired 9-30-39.

Fig. 203. The Lockheed "Orion" 9-F1 with 650 h.p. Wright "Cyclone" engine.

Among its many fine attributes the model 9-F1 had the distinction of being the very last "Orion" cabin monoplane that was built by Lockheed Aircraft. Sold and delivered to the Phillips Petroleum Co. of Bartlesville, Okla. in late 1934, it was regularly flown by Will D. Parker, their aviation department manager, until 1936. Quite similar to the earlier "Orion" model 9-F built for Dr. Brinkley in 1933, the model 9-F1 of 1934 was also powered with the big, supercharged Wright "Cyclone" engine and its performance was more or less comparable; in some instances better and in some just slightly inferior. Fitted as a rather plush executive transport the 9-F1 roamed the countryside in all directions to promote the use of "Phillips 77" aviation fuel and some of their other petroleum products. In 1936 the 9-F1 was sold and exported to Mexico. Its operational record in Mexico is unknown, but in 1937 it was exported to Spain where it was involved in the Civil War, serving the Spanish Republican Air Force. What became of it we cannot say, there is no record of

its disposition. The swift "Orion" had a world-wide reputation and were especially in demand in foreign countries; in 1937 the "Orion" was bringing a fairly good price and 12 of them, retired from American service, had found their way into Spain through various dealers and brokers. Thirty-six "Orion" were built from 1931 into 1934 and the model 9-F1 was the very last; some say it was also the very best.

The Lockheed "Orion" model 9-F1 was an all-wood, low-winged cabin monoplane with seating arranged for five. Outfitted as a rather plush executive transport, with special interior, the custom-built 9-F1 was heavy with all its trappings and operated normally at a 5800 lb. gross weight. It was one of the heaviest of the various "Orion", but she handled the poundage with verve and grace. Of course, the big, supercharged "Cyclone" engine, swinging a Hamilton-Standard controllable-pitch propeller, was the combination that made it all possible. As powered with the 9 cyl. Wright "Cyclone" SR-1820-F33 engine rated 650 h.p. at sea level, the

Fig. 204. Wiley Post and "Billy" Parker perhaps discussing the 9-F1.

9-F1 had more than enough horsepower and its abundance of power was reflected in the airplane's high performance. The 9-F1 was fast, very fast, but she was also smooth, quiet and steady, and a distinct pleasure to fly. Manufacture of the "wooden Lockheed" had come to a close in 1934, but they left an indelible mark in the records of aviation history, and will never be forgotten. The type certificate number for the "Orion" model 9-F1 was issued l0-8-34 and only one example of this model was manufactured by the Lockheed Aircraft Corp. in Burbank, Calif.

Listed below are specifications and performance data for the "Orion" model 9-F1 as powered with 650 h.p. Wright "Cyclone" SR-1820-F33 engine; length overall 28'2"; height overall 9'5"; wing span 42'9"; wing chord at root 102"; wing chord at tip 63"; total wing area 294 sq. ft.; airfoil Clark Y-18 at root and Clark Y-9.5 at tip; wt. empty 4100 lbs.; useful load 1700 lbs.; payload with 110 gal. fuel 795 lbs. (4 pass. & 115 lbs. baggage); gross wt. 5800 lbs.; max. speed 235; cruising speed (.75 power) 212; landing speed (with flaps) 65; climb 1480 ft. first min. at sea level; ser. ceiling 24,000 ft.; gas cap. 116 gal.; oil cap. 10 gal.; cruising range (.75 power) at 42 gal. per hour 500 miles; price approx. $25,000. at factory. Special interior was $200. extra.

The construction details and general arrangement of the model 9-F1 were typical of all other "Orion" except for the powerplant installation and special treatment of the interior. Mounting of the big, supercharged "Cyclone" engine required a little strengthening in the forward fuselage, but otherwise it was a normal installation. The engine swung a Hamilton-Standard "controllable" propeller and was "shielded" to eliminate ignition static in the radio reception. An oil-cooling radiator was installed to keep oil temperature from becoming too high. The special cabin interior, upholstered in leather, was described as very plush; special attention was paid to elimination of noise and vibration. The 9-F1 was equipped with split-type trailing edge wing flaps to lower the landing speed, and long-travel "oleo" shock struts softened the landing jolts. Wing flaps could not be lowered above 125 m.p.h. An Eclipse electric engine starter, Eclipse generator, Exide battery, fuel pump, radio equipment, cabin heater, navigation lights, landing lights, parachute flares, wheel brakes, ll.00x12 wheels and tires, cabin lights, and 10.5 in. swiveling tail wheel were standard equipment. Many other options were available on customer order. The next Lockheed develop-

Fig. 205. The sleek 9-F1 was the last "Orion" built.

ment was the twin-engined "Electra" model 10-C as described in the chapter for ATC # 559 of this volume.

Listed below is the only "Orion" 9-F1 entry:

NC-14246; 9-F1 (# 212) Cyclone 650.

This approval for ser. # 212 only; ser. #212 operated in Mexico as XA-BDO in 1936-37, then exported to Spain.

Fig. 206. Boeing 247-D was improved version of world's first modern airliner.

In 1933 the Boeing "Model 247" startled the industry and forecast of things to come when it appeared as the world's first "modern airliner"; almost quite suddenly all other transports became obsolete, and the "247" set a snow-balling trend for the immediate future. So now, in less than 2 years' time found itself in the peculiar situation of being made almost obsolete by transport designs brought out by other manufacturers, manufacturers who were stirred into imitative action by the success of the "Two Forty Seven" itself. This was possible, of course, because of the rapid, almost daily, advances being made in aeronautical development right at this time. From the time the "Model 247" was designed, built, and put into service, the state of the art had moved forward fast enough to make last year's airplanes nearly obsolete by comparison. Luckily, the basic "247" design could still be altered enough to bring it up to date, so to speak, and thus salvage the whole project from a pitiful fate. As the "Model 247-D" this new version used newly-developed supercharged and geared engines that were mounted in larger, more streamlined nacelles, and encased tightly in deep-chord NACA engine cowls for less drag and a gain in speed. This new power was now harnessed more efficiently by using the newly-developed Hamilton-Standard "controllable pitch" propellers for better utilization of engine thrust. These changes alone were enough to add over 20 m.p.h. to the cruising speed with better economy, allowing safety margins for operating better out of smaller airfields, and allowing a half-ton increase to the gross weight; this extra weight allowance permitted more payload, and some extra fuel. Now the 247-D was at least on a par with the best. Altho' only 13 examples of the new "Model 247-D" were built it was fortunate that the "247" already in service were easily updated to the new specifications, and thus could hold their own in transcontinental competition for several more years. By 1937, its accomplishments already eclipsed by the very competition it had fostered, many of the 247-D (modified) were leased or sold to the smaller airlines who were tickled pink to get them, and in 1942 some 27 of these were pressed into military service as the C-73. Most of these were pulled from USAAF service by 1944 and returned to former owners, or found their ways into foreign countries by various routes, many to eventually return back to the U.S.A. The pinnacle of international achievement for the "Model 247-D" was perhaps in the famous MacRobertson Race of 1934, a race from London to Melbourne that

Fig. 207. 247-D shows off its new supercharged engines and controllable propellers.

traced a torturous course of 11,300 miles across the face of 3 continents. Turner and Pangborn placed the 247-D in 3rd position behind a special British raceplane, and a powerful Douglas DC-2. After a varied career, known as "Adaptable Annie" for awhile, this same airplane was retired to the National Air Museum (Smithsonian Institution) in 1953. Other examples of the 247-D, tired but still willing, were in service as late as 1964.

The all-metal Boeing "Model 247-D" was a low-winged twin-engined transport monoplane with seating arranged for 10 passengers, a crew of 3 that included a stewardess, and stowage capacity for 750 lbs. of baggage and cargo. Most of the changes in the 247-D were for the sake of increased performance, but several improvements were added to passenger convenience and comfort, and additional aids were installed to make piloting a little easier. Whereas the earlier "247" was a three-mile-per-minute transport at its maximum speed, the new "247-D" could set the same pace at three-quarter power. Whereas the 247 was limited to a ceiling of 4500 ft. with one engine out, the 247D was able to maintain a ceiling of 11,500 ft. with gross load and one engine out; this was a substantial margin of safety in emergency. Thirteen examples of the "Model 247-D" were built as such at the Boeing factory in Seattle, but the ex-

isting 247 that were modified into 247-D were pulled from service at varying periods and the transformation was performed at the United Air Lines overhaul base in Cheyenne, Wyo. As powered with 2 Pratt & Whitney "Wasp" S1H1-G engines rated 550 h.p. at 8000 ft. the 247-D showed very little improvement in take-off or climb-out because of the half-ton added to its gross weight, but the increase in speed was an advantage that allowed more attractive schedules from point to point, and a saving of hours on a transcontinental flight. When UAL retired all the 247-D for larger and faster equipment the Boeing transports were sold or leased to smaller airlines where they enjoyed several more useful years. Altho' outmoded by newer airplanes in less than a decade, we should remember that the "Boeing 247" was the world's first modern airliner and it did set the pace in air transportation. The type certificate number for the Model 247-D was issued 10-11-34 and amended later to include the one-only 247-E which was used in test as the prototype of the new series. Thirteen of the 247-D were manufactured by the Boeing Airplane Co. in Seattle, Wash. and 33 of the earlier 247 were converted to conform.

Listed below are specifications and performance data for the Boeing "Model 247-D" as powered with 2 P & W "Wasp" S1H1-G engines

Fig. 208. Boeing 247-D was now three-mile-a-minute airliner.

rated 550 h.p. at 2200 r.p.m. at 8000 ft.; length overall 51'7"; height overall 12'2"; wing span 74'0"; wing chord at root 180"; wing chord at tip 88"; total wing area (incl. fuselage section) 836 sq. ft.; airfoil Boeing 106 modified; wt. empty 8940 lbs.; useful load 4710 lbs.; payload with 273 gal. fuel, 2 pilots & stewardess 2447 lbs. (10 pass. & 747 lbs. baggage-cargo); gross wt. 13,-650 lbs.; max. speed 202 at 8000 ft.; cruising speed (.75 power) 184 at 8000 ft.; cruising speed (.80 power) 189 at 12,000 ft.; landing speed (with flaps) 62; take-off run (sea level) 925 ft.; climb 1150 ft. first min. at sea level; climb to 11,000 ft. in 10 mins.; ser. ceiling 25,400 ft.; absolute ceiling on one engine 11,500 ft.; gas cap. 273 gal.; oil cap. 20 gal.; cruising range (.75 power) at 66 gal. per hour 800 miles; cruising range at .625 power 890 miles at 8000 ft.; price $69,000. for factory-built 247-D.

The construction details and general arrangement of the 247-D were the same as for the Model 247 as described in the chapter for ATC # 500 of USCA/C, Vol. 5, and as noted. The most significant change was replacement of the direct-drive "Wasp" S1D1 engines with geared (3:2) S1H1-G engines that were supercharged at higher (12:1) "blower" speeds. Developing 550 h.p. at 2200 r.p.m. at 8000 ft. these engines were mounted in larger, more streamlined nacelles, and cowled much better with deep NACA fairings. The two-bladed propellers were also replaced with 3-bladed "controllable pitch" props to provide more blade area and to reduce tip speeds; tip speed was the culprit that produced annoying "propeller noise". The 247-D also

had a new windshield design that sloped backward, instead of forward as on the earlier 247, but not all of the modified 247-D were fitted with the new windshield. There were some interior improvements in the 20 ft. long x 6 ft. high cabin, including a more efficient heating and ventilating system, a more practical lavatory, and reclining seats were fitted with more comfortable head-rests. A 60 cu. ft. baggage-cargo compartment was in the fuselage nose, and a 65 cu. ft. compartment was in the rear fuselage; total wt. allowance was up to 882 lbs. Fuel tanks were mounted in the wing; 136 gal. in the left wing and 137 gal. in the right wing, of which 70 gal. was reserve. Sheet metal on leading edges of wing and horizontal stabilizer was installed with "flush rivets" to provide smoother entry for the airfoil and better attachment of "de-icer boots". The new tail group was constructed entirely of dural, but elevators and rudder were now covered with fabric instead of dural sheet. A large double tab (or flap) on the rudder acted as an aerodynamic balance and as trim for direction; elevators and the left aileron were also fitted with "trimming tabs". The instrument panel and sub-panel contained more than 35 devices, including two-way radio and automatic pilot. Standard equipment on the 247-D was comparable to that of the Model 247 except where replaced with accessories of more recent design and manufacture. The Sperry autopilot and Goodrich de-icer boots were optional. The next Boeing development was the Model 314 flying boat as described in the chapter for ATC # 704.

Listed below are Model 247-D entries as gleaned from registration records:

NC-12272;	247-D	(# 1946)	Wasp S1H1-G.
-13361;	"	(# 1947)	"
-13362;	"	(# 1948)	"
-13363;	"	(# 1949)	"
-13364;	"	(# 1950)	"
-13360;	"	(# 1951)	"
-13366;	"	(# 1952)	"
-13369;	"	(# 1953)	"
-13367;	"	(# 1954)	"
:	"	(# 1955)	"
-13368;	"	(# 1956)	"
-13370;	"	(# 1957)	"
-13365;	"	(# 1958)	"

Ser. # 1946 thru # 1958 were built originally as Model 247-D; of the previously built Model 247, ser. # 1682, 1686, thru 1691, 1693 thru 1700, 1702, 1704, 1706, thru 1710, 1712, 1714, thru 1726, 1728 thru 1737, 1740, and 1741 were eligible as Model 247-D when modified to conform, but only 33 of these were recorded as being modified; 3 of the Model 247-D and 24 of the 247-D (modified) were in USAAF service as C-73 in 1942; ser. # 1682 with "Wasp" S1D1-G engines designated as 247-E during tests and modifications made to it while serving as prototype of development of Model 247-D; ser.

Fig. 209. Nose compartment of 247-D offered ample space for air express.

1944-45 started as 247-D, but shipped to Germany as Model 247; ser. # 1946 was 11 place "Club" model; ser. # 1952 and 1955 shipped to China; as NR-257Y used by Turner & Pangborn, ser. # 1953 was returned to airline service as NC-13369.

ATC # 559
(10-29-34)
LOCKHEED "ELECTRA", 10-C.

Fig. 210. "Electra" 10-C warming its 450 h.p. "Wasp" engines.

The "Electra" airliners ordered by the Pan American Airways System for Aerovias Centrales and Pacific-Alaska Airways, as the Model 10-C, were powered with the big (9 cyl.) service-proven Pratt & Whitney "Wasp" SC1 engines of 450 h.p., and for a special reason. Most of the routes served by these 2 carriers were over primitive and very difficult territory, so the big "Wasp" was chosen for its muscle, stamina, and reliability. The "Wasp" SC1 was of much larger displacement than the smaller "Wasp Junior" and delivered its rated horsepower very easily; the over-sized "innards" were at far less strain and therefore, the engine did not get all out of breath, so to speak, to deliver full power if need be for an extended period. The established reliability was something you could trust, and this was peace of mind to pilots and air-travelers alike. The big, round "Wasp" had a beautiful drone and the comforting hum made the jagged peaks below look less forbidding. As compared with the "Electra" 10-A, the 10-C with its bigger engines was several hundred pounds heavier when empty, and this had some effect on the useful load, but in view of the purpose, it was a fair exchange. Aerovias Centrales, an affiliate of the Pan Am System, was the first to get the Model 10-C and inaugurated the first multi-motor service on 1 Nov. 1934 from Los Angeles

to Mexico City on a 10.5 hour schedule. For the first few months full loads of passengers were not carried because some of the weight allowance and space was needed to transport supplies for stock-rooms at the various air-stations. Pacific-Alaska Airways, also a Pan Am affiliate, received the first of their Model 10-C at Fairbanks in Jan. of 1935, spanning a route in 3 hours that normally required 3 weeks by dog-team; another 10-C was acquired later in 1935. The expanded route of Fairbanks-Nome-Juneau was 2000 miles of airway over the snow-clad peaks of Alaska, a true test of men and machines.

The Lockheed "Electra" model 10-C was an all-metal, low-winged, twin-engined, transport monoplane with seating normally arranged for 10 passengers and 2 pilots. Basically, the Model 10-C was designed as a passenger transport that offered high performance and twin-engine safety on the shorter routes. Rather small for a twin-motored airliner the deft "Electra" provided small-airplane handling and economy with large airplane comforts. The interior was adaptable to various custom layouts, such as the plush "Club" model, or an all-cargo version to haul freight. Quite often Aerovias Centrales used a combination passenger-cargo layout on portions of their route thru Mexico. Right from the start

Fig. 211. An "Electra" 10-C on airline duty in Cuba.

the "Electra" 10-C was smashing all schedules in Mexico and in Alaska, upholding a reputation established years earlier by the wooden "Vega". As powered with 2 "Wasp" SC1 engines rated 450 h.p. each the Model 10-C was a rather spritely airplane for a 12-passenger transport and proved its mettle beyond question over the difficult terrain of Mexico and Alaska. There was also power reserve enough to maintain an altitude of 6000 ft. on one engine with full gross load under normal conditions. Pilots and passengers alike enjoyed the twin-engine safety and over the years the "Electra" amassed an enviable record. The type certificate number for the Model 10-C was issued 10-29-34 and some 8 or more examples of this model were manufactured by the Lockheed Aircraft Corp. at Burbank, Calif. Lloyd C. Stearman was pres. & chf.

engr.; Carl B. Squier was V.P. & gen. mgr.; Robert E. Gross was treas.; Cyril Chappallet was sec.; Hall L. Hibbard as proj. engr. was in charge of "Electra" development with a crew of 25 engineers and draftsmen. About 300 were on Lockheed's payroll Nov. 1933, this increased to 400 by early 1934, and 600 were employed by the end of that year. When Lloyd Stearman decided to vacate the presidency, Robert E. Gross was elected to fill the position, and Hall Hibbard then became V.P. and chf. engr. By now, Richard Von Hake was factory superintendent and Morton Bach, formerly builder of the Bach "Tri-Motor", was head of final assembly on the "Electra" line. Production schedule was 4 aircraft per month, increasing steadily as the orders kept coming in.

Listed below are specifications and perfor-

Fig. 212. Aerovias Centrales used 10-C on route to Mexico City.

Fig. 213. An "Electra" 10-C on airline duty in Alaska.

mance data for the "Electra" model 10-C as powered with 2 "Wasp" SC1 engines rated 450 h.p. at 2100 r.p.m.; length overall 38'7"; height overall 10'1"; wing span 55'0"; wing chord at root 145"; wing chord at tip 48"; total wing area (incl. fuselage section) 458 sq. ft.; airfoil at root Clark Y-18; airfoil at tip Clark Y-9; wt. empty 6710 lbs.; useful load 3590 (3790) lbs.; payload with 250 gal. fuel & 2 pilots 1625 (1825) lbs. (8 pass. & 265 (465) lbs. baggage-cargo); payload with 190 gal. fuel & 2 pilots 1985 (2185) lbs. (10 pass. & 285 (485) lbs. baggage-cargo); gross wt. 10,300 (10,500) lbs.; figures in parentheses as later amended; max. speed 205; cruising speed (.75 power) 192; landing speed (with flaps) 65; climb 1050 ft. first min. at sea level; ser. ceiling 22,750 ft.; ser. ceiling 6000 ft. on one engine with gross load under normal conditions; gas cap. max. 250 gal.; oil cap. 17 gal.; cruising range (.75 power) at 56 gal. per hour 620-805 miles; price not announced.

The construction details and general arrangement of the "Electra" 10-C was typical to that of the Model 10-A as described here in the chapter for ATC # 551, except as follows. Engines mounted in the 10-C were the big 9 cyl. "Wasp" SC1 of 450 h.p. with mounts and nacelles modified to the extra weight and larger diameter. The fuel cap. (250 gal.) was contained in 6 tanks, all mounted in the stub-wing. Baggage-cargo compartment in the nose was allowed 300 lbs.; and 250 lbs. was allowed in each wing compartment. Because of operation in Mexico, where facilities were more primitive, the 10-C was outfitted with extras not normally provided. A 1 gal. container of drinking water was mounted near the lavatory, a flashlight was mounted in either end of the cabin, a pressure-type fire extinguisher system was installed, 6-ply tires were fitted with cactus-proof liners, and leading edges of horizontal stabilizer and both fins were fitted with "abrasion strips". Typical

of all the "Electra" the landing gear was retracted by electric motor, but manual retraction was possible in emergency; 35x15-6 Goodyear airwheels were fitted with metal fenders to ward off debris. The split-type trailing edge wing flaps were electrically operated, with manual operation in emergency. A 16x7-3 tail wheel was fitted with 4-ply tire; tail wheel centering lock was available. A few of the early "Electra" had windshields that slanted forward to reduce glare, but all subsequent aircraft had windshields that slanted back in the normal manner. Cabin walls were sound-proofed and the interior was kept comfortable by a heating and ventilating system. Ash trays, assist ropes, reading lamps, and a hat net were provided for passenger convenience. Controllable propellers, electric engine starters, Exide battery, generator, two-way radio, fire extinguisher system, bonding & shielding, navigation lights, landing lights, lavatory, parachute flares, oil-cooling radiators, dual wheel-type controls, wheel brakes, parking brake, a full set of airliner type instruments, and first-aid kit were standard equipment. A custom "Club" interior, or cargo interior was optional. The next "Electra" development was the Model 10-B as described in the chapter for ATC # 584 of this volume.

Listed below are "Electra" 10-C entries as gleaned from various records:

XA-BEM; 10-C (# 1004) 2 Wasp 450.
NC-14258; " (# 1005) "
  -14259; " (# 1006) "
XA-BEO; " (# 1007) "
PP-PAS; " (# 1008) "
NC-13762; " (# 1009) "
  -14906; " (# 1019) "
XA-BEQ; " (# 1022) "

This approval for ser. # 1004 and up; the Model 10-D was a design proposal for a twin-engined military bomber, but an example of this model was never built.

ATC # 560
(12-4-34)
BEECH, MODEL B-17-L.

Fig. 214. Walter Beech stands proudly in front of B-17-L.

Walter Beech amazed the world of aviation with his unusual 17-R, and startled them all again with his thundering A-17-F, but he soon realized that these airplanes were particularly hard to sell. The bulk of the business in the U.S.A. was being shared by Waco and Stinson with their four-place airplanes in the 200 h.p. range, so Beech and his staff conceded it would be more practical to enter this field for whatever they could get out of it. A huddle with his men produced some exciting ideas and a successor to the 17-R began taking shape. It was agreed that the negative-staffer configuration would remain the same, but the airplane had to be simpler, cheaper, and a lot easier to build; a 225 h.p. Jacobs engine would drive it, so Beech asked for the most he could possibly get with that much power. With the jutted-out lower wing being practically an integral part of the undercarriage, it was decided to have the gear fold up into it, and that was the stroke of genius that cinched the new airplane's future. The new wings were thicker to allow better methods of manufacture with cheaper materials, provide room to tuck in the landing gear, and the use of a different airfoil promoted better behavior at lower speeds. "Clean as a whistle" the new B-17-L was a surprisingly fast airplane, and its performance was

exceptional for the amount of power it was allowed. It was hard to believe, but this airplane showed a 4 to 1 ratio between its top speed of 175 and its landing speed of 45; performance like this was hard to achieve. Making its maiden flight in late Feb. of 1934, in relative secrecy, the modest B-17-L found early favor and quite a few were built and sold in that year; 1935 was a good year for the B-17-L also, since it had been exhibited at the Detroit Air Show where it became an instant hit. The first few Beech were built in one corner of an idle factory, but the success of the B-17-L required larger quarters and instigated a move back home to the old "Travel Air" plant in April of 1934 where Walter Beech was more at ease. As if equipped with "seven league boots" the Jacobs-powered B-17-L quickly made great strides in the world of aviation. One was loaded on the ocean-liner "Europa" and made an extensive tour of Europe for "Mobiloil". Another made an extensive tour into Central and South America making over 600 landings and take-offs, some at altitudes nearing 10,000 ft., and 17,000 ft. was reached in a flight over the Andes mountains. The three-month trip covered some 12,000 miles without the least mishap. In Oct. of 1935 the B-17-L was approved as a seaplane on Edo floats and its

Fig. 215. A B-17-L lashed to deck of "Europa" for visit to European continent.

mettle as an outstanding utility airplane was firmly established. For the first time since its forming back in 1932, Beech Aircraft was showing a little profit, and the future sure looked exciting.

Technically the Beech model B-17-L was a cabin biplane with seating arranged for four, but physically this airplane was a rather unusual machine. The inverse (negative) stagger was a feature that still had people scratching their heads, and the retractable landing gear, tucked neatly into the lower wing, was a source of wonder at all the airports. There's no denying that the Beech was still quite a novelty, but the B-17-L didn't cost all that much and sportsmen and business-houses were taking a chance on the

investment. In less than a year's time the B-17-L proved what an outstanding bargain it really was, and it became quite competitive in its field. It had more to offer than any airplane in its class, whether it be range, speed, or all-round performance, but it wasn't "a regular airplane" and this was still a slight deterent. As powered with the Jacobs L-4 engine rated 225 h.p. at 2000 r.p.m. the B-17-L was remarkable in what it could do; it was the fastest airplane of its class in the whole world, it stretched more mileage out of every gal. of fuel, carried just about as much as any airplane in its class, and was not particularly fussy where it operated from. Its flight characteristics were pleasant, altho' it required a certain amount of finesse, and it would do a

Fig. 216. A B-17-L presents its unusual profile.

Fig. 217. A B-17-L on Edo floats.

"loop the loop" with a full load—now that is something! When Jacobs introduced the L-5 engine, which was rated 285 h.p. at 2000 r.p.m., this airplane was approved for this installation also as the model B-17-B. Later on, when the L-4 engines approached overhaul time, some of the B-17-L were converted into the B-17-B by a change of engines. For extra utility or for special purpose, both the B-17-L and the B-17-B were approved as seaplanes (SB-17-L and SB-17-B) on Edo twin-float gear in Oct. of 1935. The type certificate number for the model B-17-L was issued 12-4-34 with amendment later included for approval of the model B-17-B and the seaplanes. Some 40 examples of this model were manufactured by the Beech Aircraft Co. at Wichita, Kansas.

Listed below are specifications and performance data for the Beech model B-17-L as powered with 225 h.p. Jacobs L-4 engine; length overall 24'6"; height overall 8'6"; wing span upper & lower 32'0"; wing chord upper & lower 60"; total wing area 273 sq. ft.; airfoil Clark CYH; wt. empty 1800 lbs.; useful load 1350 lbs.; payload with 50 gal. fuel 843 lbs. (4 pass. & 163 lbs. baggage); gross wt. 3150 lbs.; max. speed 175 at sea level; cruising speed (.75 power) 162 at 5000 ft.; cruising speed 152 at sea level; landing speed (with flaps) 45; climb 850 ft. first min. at sea level; ser. ceiling 15,500 ft.; gas cap. 50 gal.; oil cap. 5 gal.; cruising range (.75 power) at 13.2 gal. per hour 560 miles; price $8000. at factory field in 1934, raised to $8550. in late 1935.

SB-17-L seaplane on Edo 38-3430 twin-float gear, same as above except for the following; wt. empty 2173 lbs.; useful load 1337 lbs.; payload with 50 gal. fuel 830 lbs. (4 pass. & 150 lbs. baggage); gross wt. 3510 lbs.; max. speed 145; cruising speed (.75 power) 133 at 5000 ft.; landing speed (with flaps) 55; climb 700 ft. first min. at sea level; take-off (full load) under 30 seconds.

Model B-17-B as powered with 285 h.p. Jacobs L-5 engine same as B-17-L landplane except as follows: wt. empty 1850 lbs.; useful load 1300 lbs.; payload with 50 gal. fuel 793 lbs. (4 pass. & 113 lbs. baggage); gross wt. 3150 lbs.; max. speed 185 at sea level; cruising speed (.75 power) 173 at 5000 ft.; cruising speed 165 at sea level; landing speed (with flaps) 45; climb 1100 ft. first min. at sea level; ser. ceiling 18,000 ft.; gas cap. 50 gal.; oil cap. 5 gal.; cruising range (.75 power) at 17.5 gal. per hour 500 miles; price $9000. at factory.

The fuselage framework was built up of welded 4130 steel tubing, heavily faired to shape with plywood formers and spruce fairing strips, then fabric covered. The cabin walls were sound-proofed and windows were of shatter-proof glass. Front seats were individual and the rear bench-type seat was wide enough to seat three. A large door on the left side provided entry off the wing-walk. The wing framework was built up of solid spruce spar beams with spruce and plywood truss-type wing ribs spaced approx. 8 inches apart; the leading edges were covered with dural metal sheet and the completed framework was covered in fabric. Differential ailerons were on the lower wing and trailing edge wing flaps were on underside of upper wings. The upper wing, in one piece, was fastened directly to top of the fuselage; a steel built-up I-strut connected the wings together and interplane bracing was of streamlined steel wire. A 25 gal. fuel tank flanked either side of the fuselage in the upper wing; an extra 20 gal. fuel tank could be mounted in the root end of either lower wing. Thus, a fuel capacity of 50-70-90 gallons was available. Two welded steel tube trusses were fitted to underside of the fuselage

Fig. 218. B-17-L had 225 h.p. Jacobs engine; 285 h.p. Jacobs version was the B-17-B.

for fastening of the lower wings and mounting of the landing gear; landing gear folded inward to retract into fuselage belly. Retraction of the landing gear was manual, but an electric motor drive was available. 7.50x10 Autofan wheels with (4 or 6 ply) low-pressure tires were fitted with brakes. The fabric covered tail group was a composite structure of welded steel tubes, steel channel, and spruce; the elevators were fitted with trimming tabs. A Hartzell wooden propeller, Heywood or Eclipse engine starter, Exide battery, generator, navigation lights, 10x3 tail wheel, throw-over control wheel, cabin heater, compass, fuel gauges, normal set of engine and flight instruments, assist ropes, and first-aid kit were standard equipment. A metal propeller, landing lights, parachute flares, radio, bonding & shielding, extra fuel capacity, engine-driven fuel pump, and 24 in. General streamlined wheels and tires were optional. A Hamilton-Standard controllable prop was eligible upon modification as required. The next Beech development was the model B-17-E as described in the chapter for ATC # 566 of this volume. Listed below are B-17-L and B-17-B entries as gleaned from registration records:

NC-270Y;	B-17-L	(# 3)	Jacobs 225.
NC-12584;	"	(# 4)	"
-12570;	"	(# 6)	"
-12589;	"	(# 7)	"
-12590;	"	(# 8)	"
-12591;	"	(# 9)	"
NR-12569;	"	(# 10)	"
-12592;	"	(# 12)	"
-12594;	"	(# 13)	"
-12597;	"	(# 14)	"
-12598;	"	(# 15)	"
-14403;	"	(# 16)	"
-14404;	"	(# 17)	"
ZS-BBC;	"	(# 18)	"
-14406;	"	(# 19)	"

-14408;	B-17-B	(# 20)	Jacobs 285.
-14409;	B-17-L	(# 21)	Jacobs 225.
G-ADDH;	"	(# 23)	"
-14405;	"	(# 24)	"
-14412;	"	(# 25)	"
NS-66;	"	(# 26)	"
-14414;	"	(# 27)	"
-14415;	"	(# 28)	"
-14416;	"	(# 29)	"
-14417;	"	(# 30)	"
-14418;	"	(# 31)	"
-14453;	"	(# 32)	"
-14454;	"	(# 33)	"
-14455;	"	(# 34)	"
-14456;	"	(# 35)	"
-14457;	"	(# 36)	"
-15400;	"	(# 37)	"
-15401;	"	(# 39)	"
-15402;	"	(# 40)	"
-15403;	"	(# 41)	"
-15404;	"	(# 42)	"
-15405;	"	(# 43)	"
-15406;	"	(# 44)	"
-15407;	"	(# 45)	"
-15408;	"	(# 46)	"
-15409;	"	(# 47)	"
CZ-116;	B-17-B	(# 48)	Jacobs 285.
-15484;	B-17-L	(# 57)	Jacobs 225.
-15485;	"	(# 58)	"
-15486;	"	(# 59)	"
NC-278V;	"	(# 60)	"
NC-15488;	"	(# 61)	"

This approval for ser. # 3 and up; ser. # 10 later registered as XB-AIZ in Mexico; ser. # 18 del. to Johannesburg, So. Africa; ser. # 20 was first as B-17-L; ser. # 23 del. to Amy Mollison in England; ser. # 24 later del. to King of Ethiopia; ser. # 26 operated by Bureau of Air Commerce; ser. # 33 later del. to Spain; ser. # 40 and 43 as SB-17-L seaplane on Edo floats; ser. # 48 del. to Isthmian Airways in Panama Canal Zone; ser. # 58-59-60-61 mfgd. in 1936; this approval expired 9-30-39.

ATC # 561
(1-15-35)
WILEY POST, MODEL A.

Fig. 219. The Straughan "Model A" with 40 h.p. Ford auto engine.

Looking very much like an oversized model airplane, the "Wiley Post" biplane was a very interesting lightplane design and its appearance in various parts of the midwest created all sorts of comment among amateur pilots. Being the cheapest approved, factory-built airplane one could buy at this time, it was often hailed by scribes as the likely airplane to put the average man in the sky. This was hardly the case, of course, because the "Wiley Post" was an airplane of basically standard design, requiring handling with certain finesse and technique, and not hardly "fool-proof" enough for the average man off the street. However, such as it was, the "Wiley Post" did make a hit with the "grass roots" flying fraternity, especially in the midwest, and for awhile its future looked rather rosy. It certainly promised to be a sky-full of fun for a rather small investment. As powered with a converted Ford "Model A" automobile engine the little biplane was relatively simple and comparatively cheap to operate; low-cost maintenance and parts replacement by the average owner-pilot himself was to be one of its biggest features. Partly by scheme and partly by chance the "Wiley Post" biplane was an airplane one would see staked out in some flying-farmer's pasture lot, or tied down on the edge of some little-known grassy airstrip; this was not a very

sophisticated airplane and rarely ever seen in the big city. With really no need for dash-board trinkets the "Wiley Post" was equipped with little more than 2 basic engine instruments and sometimes an altimeter; this elfish little biplane had not much else to offer than the joy of flight itself. An enterprising pilot on the west-coast, realizing that scarcity of money kept people from learning to fly, offered instruction in his "Wiley Post" for $1.00 per lesson; 40 lessons or $40.00 later, the student was usually ready to solo. They say the "school" operated more on dedication than profit.

Frank Straughan was a "Ford" motor-car dealer in Marshall, Okla. who financed the building of airplanes designed and built by Ross Holmes. The first airplane designed and built by Holmes was a "parasol" monoplane powered with a Ford "Model A" engine; at least 2 more parasol monoplanes were later built by Holmes in a corner of the former Cessna plant before he decided to try his hand at a small biplane. As the "Straughan-Holmes" the first biplane was engineered by Glenn Stearman and built in Wichita during 1932; lanky Ted Anderson was pilot on the maiden flight and he liked it just fine. By Nov. of 1933 announcement was made that plans had been formed for manufacture of the "Straughan A" in Wichita; it was to sell for

Fig. 220. The "Wiley Post" boasts of being built in Oklahoma.

less than $1000. A group 2 approval (# 2-478) was issued 6-26-34 and dealers were clamoring for airplanes, but production was slow in getting started. As the Straughan Aircraft Corp. the firm took over the entire plant of the former Yellow Aircab Co. in June of 1934, the largest single-unit factory in the southwest. The plant was so large that someone suggested the little biplane could be test-flown indoors when the weather was bad! Four airplanes were built by July and the schedule was set for one airplane per week; plans were shaping for one aircraft per day. Before things got going, financial difficulties forced a sale to Mark Kleedon, an Oklahoma oil-man, who acquired assets of the company for $50,000. which included 10 airplanes and all the machinery. All was moved to Oklahoma City under direction of Burrell Tibbs and plans were soon laid for volume production. The name of the little biplane was changed to "Wiley Post" and an ATC was acquired on 1-15-35; the plant was going into a batch of 15 airplanes in June of 1935. The price was raised to $1438. and the volume production predicted failed to happen. "Wiley Post" engineers had a new model on paper by Nov. of 1935, but all the excitement had cooled by now and all production was halted. Whatever the hang-up was, perhaps the untimely death of Wiley Post the famous pilot, or trouble with finances, it certainly wasn't the fault of the airplane.

The Wiley Post A was a light open-cockpit biplane with side-by-side seating for two. The whole aviation fraternity was excited about this little airplane when it was introduced in national tradepapers, because it promised the average man a chance to own a cheap airplane and to fly cheaply. Almost immediately, the company was flooded with inquiries, but all the people could get was promises. Basically, this was an airplane strictly for local sport flying; much in its favor was the fact that it was the first airplane to receive an ATC approval with a converted automobile engine, and as planned, it was to be the first approved airplane to sell for less than $1000. In all sincerity, this airplane had not much more to offer than the simple joy of flight itself, but for thousands of people in this country, especially in the rural areas, this would have been enough. As powered with the 4 cyl. water-cooled Straughan AL-1000 (a converted Ford "Model A") engine the Wiley Post A had adequate performance to satisfy the week-end flier and enough inherent ability to satisfy even the expert. Simple of airframe with a simple powerplant, this airplane would also satisfy those with tinkeritis who gauged this as part of the fun of owning an airplane. The Wiley Post had all the makings for a terrific success, but it was finally manipulated into bankruptcy, and into another "might have been". The type certificate number for the Wiley Post A was issued 1-15-35 and apparently no more than 13 examples of this model were completed. Wiley Post Aircraft Corp. at Oklahoma City, Okla. Wiley Post was pres.; Mark Kleedon was V.P.; J. H. Burke was gen. mgr.; Thomas J. Ruddy was sec.-treas. and sales mgr.; Evert E. Stong was chf. engr.; R. T. Dutcher was chf. pilot.

Listed below are specifications and performance data for the "Wiley Post A" as powered with Straughan AL-1000 (conv. Ford "Model A") engine rated 40 h.p. at 1900 r.p.m.; length overall 19'9"; height overall 7'9"; wing span upper 28'6"; wing span lower 24'6"; wing chord upper 56"; wing chord lower 42"; wing area up-

Fig. 221. The "Wiley Post" was a sky-full of fun.

per 126.7 sq. ft.; wing area lower 79.3 sq. ft.; total wing area 200 sq. ft.; airfoil USA-27; wt. empty 581 (605) lbs.; useful load 417 (393) lbs.; payload with 7 gal. fuel 197 (173) lbs.; gross wt. 998 lbs.; max. speed 82 at 1400 ft.; cruising speed 70 at 1400 ft.; landing (stall) speed 28; climb 450 ft. first min. at sea level; take-off time 6 secs.; ser. ceiling 10,000 ft.; gas cap. 7 gal.; oil cap. 5 qts.; cruising range at 4 gal. per hour 110 miles; price $990. as "Straughan A" in Wichita;

price $1438. as "Wiley Post" at factory in Oklahoma City during early 1935 and later raised to $1692.

The fuselage framework was built up of welded 4130 and 1025 steel tubing, faired to shape with spruce fairing strips, then fabric covered. The open cockpit seated 2 side-by-side with right seat staggered back 4 in. to provide shoulder room. The cockpit was well protected by a large Pyralin windshield; dual stick-type controls were

Fig. 222. "Wiley Post" lined up at the Oklahoma factory.

provided. The wing framework, in 3 panels, was built up of solid (routed) spruce spar beams with spruce and mahogany plywood truss-type wing ribs; the leading edges were covered with plywood sheet and the completed framework was covered in fabric. The upper wing was a continuous piece and supported above the fuselage on a cabane of steel tube struts; the lower wing halves were fastened to the lower longeron. Steel tube (N-type) interplane struts and steel wire bracing completed the wing cellule. The upper wing had a large cut-out for visibility upward; ailerons were on upper wing only. The converted "Model A" engine was neatly cowled and a water-cooling radiator was slung under forward edge of upper wing, similar to many installations used during the "OX-5 era". Engine oil was to be changed every 15 hours of flying time. A 7 gal. fuel tank was mounted high in the fuselage ahead of the cockpit; a "bobber" type float served as a fuel-level gauge. The landing gear was a simple steel tube tripod on each side; early models were stiff-legged and later models were snubbed with a spool of rubber shock cord. Goodyear 16x7-3 "airwheels" were not equipped with brakes. A spring-leaf tail skid was mounted on the stern. The fabric covered tail group was built up of welded steel tubing; there was no adjustment for trim during flight. A wooden (Stone or Supreme) propeller, Eiseman magneto, tachometer, oil temp. gauge, altimeter, dual controls, Pyrene fire extinguisher, firstaid kit, and log books were standard equipment. The Wiley Post Aircraft Corp. had a new model on paper by Nov. of 1935, but it was not developed. Listed below are Holmes, Straughan, and Wiley Post entries as gleaned from various records:

-11919;	Holmes Parasol	(# 1)	Ford A-40.
X-493N;	Straughan B	(# 101)	Ford B-60.
-12561;	Straughan-Holmes	(# 2)	Ford A-40.
NC-12582;	Straughan A	(# 2)	"
NC-12571;	Wiley Post A	(# 3)	"
-12595;	"	(# 4)	"
-12596;	"	(# 5)	"
-13951;	"	(# 6)	"
-13952;	"	(# 7)	"
-13955;	"	(# 8)	"
-13956;	"	(# 9)	"
-13957;	"	(# 10)	"
-13958;	"	(# 11)	"
-13961;	"	(# 12)	"
-13964	"	(# 13)	"

ATC # 562
(3-4-35)
SIKORSKY "CLIPPER", S-40-A.

Fig. 223. Sikorsky S-40-A was updated with new equipment and supercharged "Hornet" engines.

The Sikorsky model "S-40" was the first of the big "Clipper" ships, a grand and majestic flying monster that was 17 tons of miscellaneous steel and duralumin framework. A revolutionary vehicle for over-water travel between North and South America when it was introduced in 1931, but aeronautics in general had advanced tremendously in the next 3 years, making the unusual S-40 look rather archaic by comparison with the latest. Having already put in thousands of hours in service, all of the S-40 were coming due for complete overhaul, so the down-time was convenient to perform a conversion, bringing the airplanes up to a more modern level. The "S-40-A conversion" consisted mainly of removing the old "Hornet B" engines of 575 h.p. each and replacing them with 4 of the new supercharged "Hornet" T2D1 engines that were rated 660 h.p. at 2000 r.p.m. using 80 octane fuel. Having avoided use of the wheeled landing gear as much as possible, it was also decided to eliminate the undercarriage entirely and operate the S-40-A as pure flying boats; most Pan Am bases were adapted to seaplane service anyhow. The saving in weight, by discarding the undercarriage, was substantial and performance took a noticeable

jump also. Operating as a grand shuttle-bus by Pan American Airways in the Caribbean Sea the converted S-40-A amassed several more years of useful service. One of them, the "Caribbean Clipper", was still operated by Pan Am at the Dinner Key Seaplane Base in 1942; stripped of its former interior finery, the cabin was converted into a 23-place classroom for training British (R.A.F.) navigation students during the early part of World War 2.

The Sikorsky model S-40-A was a big airplane, a large four-engined "parasol" monoplane of the flying boat type with seating arranged for 40 passengers and a crew of four. Basically similar to the familiar "Sikorsky" concept, used since 1926, except that it was about 3 times as large, the model S-40 was the largest airplane in the world at one time, and its 114 foot wing span towered nearly 18 feet above the water. Its plush cabin interior was actually wider than a Pullman car, and appointments were fancier and even more comfortable. The large, stubby vee-bottom hull contained all accommodations for the passengers, the crew of 4, and all the baggage-cargo. Even the tip-floats, suspended to the wing's rigging were almost as

Fig. 224. S-40-A "Clipper" leaving its base in Miami.

big as the hull of the average small flying boat. It is questionable that Sikorsky should stick to the spidery boom-and-strut arrangement for an airplane so large, but it did prove that this maze of framework was actually much more durable than it looked. The large wheeled undercarriage as used earlier, was discarded in favor of more useful load (a half-ton or more), and elimination of its parasitic drag was a boost to the all-round performance. As powered with 4 big 9 cyl. "Hornet" engines the S-40-A was a thundering spectacle, and even years later, people would travel for miles just to see it arrive or depart. With the 4 big "Hornets" hung under the large "parasol wing" in a line abreast there was a never-ending maze of struts and wires that were required for their mounting; colorful to be sure, but it must have been an engineering challenge. Water characteristics were very good and the stout hull was classed as an ocean-going vessel, but it is doubtful if all that superstructure above the hull could weather much of a storm. The S-40-A could hardly be described as dainty and nimble, but it was light and deft for a ship so large; pilots liked it, the passengers liked it, and everyone enjoyed a confortable ride. The type certificate number for the S-40-A conversion was issued 3-4-35 and all previously-built model S-40 were eligible. Engineering was prepared by the Sikorsky Aviation Corp. at Bridgeport, Conn. and the actual conversion took place at

Pan Am's overhaul center.

Listed below are specifications and performance data for the Sikorsky model S-40-A as powered with 4 Pratt & Whitney "Hornet" T2D1 engines rated 660 h.p. each; length overall 76'8"; height overall (on water) 17'10"; wing span 114'0"; wing chord 16'0"; total wing area (incl. lift struts) 1875 sq. ft.; airfoil Sikorsky GS-1; wt. empty (as flying boat) 23,787 lbs.; useful load 10,813 lbs.; payload with 400 gal. fuel, 60 gal. oil, & crew of four was 7283 lbs. (40 pass. & 483 lbs. baggage-cargo); payload with 1060 gal. fuel, 80 gal. oil, & crew of 4 was 3173 lbs.; gross wt. 34,600 lbs.; max. speed 140; cruising speed 120; landing (stall) speed 65; climb 750 ft. first min. at sea level; ser. ceiling 12,500 ft.; gas cap. max. 1060 gal; oil cap. 60-80 gal.; cruising range at 125 gal. per hour 350-950 miles; price for conversion not announced. Performance on any 3 engines; max. speed 120; cruising speed 105; climb 400 ft. at sea level; ser. ceiling (estimated) 6000 ft.

The construction details and general arrangement of the S-40-A conversion was typical of the standard S-40 as described in the chapter for ATC # 454 of USCA/C, Vol. 5, except as noted. The most significant change in the "conversion" was replacement of the "Hornet B" engines with the newly-developed "Hornet" T2D1 engines of greater power. The new T2D1 engines were greatly improved over the older B-series engines,

Fig. 225. All 3 of the S-40 "Clipper" were eligible for S-40-A conversion.

delivering more power with even greater reliability. The big 9 cyl. engines were cowled tightly with deep-chord fairings and fitted with improved three-bladed adjustable metal propellers by Hamilton-Standard. Fuel capacity was increased to 1066 gals., divided among 4 wing tanks of 143 gal. each and 2 outboard tip-float tanks of 247 gal. each; fuel transfer was by engine-driven fuel pumps, or a hand operated wobble-pump in emergency. Front baggage compartments (2) were allowed up to 900 lbs. each and the rear compartment was allowed 350 lbs. for a total allowance of 2150 lbs. On long flights with maximum fuel and a full load of cargo on board only 6 passengers were allowed on the trip. The variable payload was adjustable according to trip needs. The next Sikorsky development was the model S-42-A "Clipper" as described in the chapter for ATC # 592 of this volume. Over 1600 aircraft for commercial use were built during 1934 for domestic sales, and altho' this was only some 15 per cent of the grand total of aircraft produced, the outlook was much brighter for the years ahead.

Listed below are S-40-A entries eligible for conversion:

NC-80V: S-40-A (# 2000-X) 4 Hornet T2D1.
NC-81V: S-40-A (# 2001) 4 Hornet T2D1.
NC-752V: S-40-A (# 2002) 4 Hornet T2D1.

This approval for ser. # 2000-X, 2001, 2002 only; approval for this conversion expired 9-30-39.

ATC # 563
(3-16-35)
BELLANCA "AIRCRUISER", 66-70.

Fig. 226. Bellanca "Aircruiser" 66-70 with 710 h.p. Wright "Cyclone" engine.

The stately and quietly impressive "Aircruiser" sesqui-plane was actually a refinement and enlargement of the earlier Bellanca "Airbus"; improvements to the design, with subsequent power increases, were developed through the experience gained in building the Air Corps C-27 utility-transports. In effect, the new "Aircruiser" was just an old "Airbus" (see ATC # 360 and 391 of USCA/C, Vol. 4) with a little more guts and a lot more muscle. Long noted for its unbeatable efficiency, this Bellanca design was however, handed a mortal blow here in the U.S.A. by regulations that practically prohibited the use of large single-engined transports in airline service. Thus hampered, with no other recourse, the "Aircruiser" became a back-woods airplane that made a name for itself in a neighboring country. Most single-engined transports of this particular day, with comparable horsepower, were fast enough to run away and hide from the unhurried "Aircruiser", but when it came to load-carrying ability, or operation from a primitive area, this airplane just had no equal; it was perhaps the most efficient single-engined airplane ever built. As powered with the supercharged Wright

"Cyclone" SGR-1820-F3 engine rated 715 h.p. the "Aircruiser" (66-70) carried a useful load that was greater than its empty weight; there was some penalty in speed because of the tremendous lifting-area that was employed, but delivering a two-ton payload at 145-155 m.p.h. was not all that bad. Ironically enough, all examples of the "Aircruiser" were eventually delivered to Canada where they became a familiar and joyful sight to miners and trappers for years to come; happy in its element the "Cruiser" (nickname) hauled just about anything that could be put into it or lashed to its sides. For the type of work it was doing the "Aircruiser" was an ageless design, so it is not surprising that it was available from the factory into 1940. Some examples were still in service on the lakes of Canada into 1964.

The Bellanca "Aircruiser" model 66-70 (66-75) was a large high-winged monoplane that approached the sesqui-plane configuration. The long and spacious cabin had room enough to seat 15 people, or with seating removed, there was floor space enough to stack over 2 tons of cargo. The most significant features on the "Aircruiser" were the large lower stub-wings and the large airfoiled wing bracing struts, a practical

Fig. 227. The "Aircruiser" as a seaplane in Canada.

combination that contributed heavily to the air-frame strength and to overall lifting area. Typical of "Bellanca" design, most everything within reason had to double in duty, so we find bracing struts that contributed to lift, stub-wings that were stuffed with baggage and cargo, and a wheeled landing gear that could be replaced with floats without hardly any penalty to drag. With nearly every square foot of airframe devoted to some useful purpose, the "Aircruiser" was the pinnacle of achievement in airplane efficiency; there has never been anything to match it. As powered with the geared and supercharged Wright "Cyclone" SGR-1820-F3 engine rated 715 h.p. at 6900 ft. the model 66-70 had an un-usual performance; short-field performance out of difficult territory was outstanding and made-to-order for operating in the depths of rugged "bush country". Whether on wheels, skis, or floats, the stately "Aircruiser" with its serene behavior and majestic splendor became a way of life to miners and trappers who depended on its periodic arrival, meeting it with expressions of joy and a feeling of confidence. An ageless design, for the type of work it was doing, the "Aircruiser" was updated as the years went by with most of the current developments. Available first with a "Cyclone" engine at 670 h.p. (as the 66-67) the "Aircruiser" was later available with "Cyclone" engines of 715-735-760 h.p. and finally with the SGR-1820-G3 engine of 850 h.p. Of course, performance was improved with each power increase and modification; the "Aircruiser" had limits, but it also had capability to go well beyond the bounds of its intended capacity on occasion. Pilots spoke highly of the "Aircruiser" and jumped at the chance to fly it; it must have been an un-forgettable experience. The type certificate

number for the "Aircruiser" model 66-70 was issued 3-16-35 with amendments awarded at various intervals for models 66-75, 66-76, and 66-85. At least 5 examples of the "Aircruiser" were manufactured by the Bellanca Aircraft Corp. at New Castle, Dela.

Listed below are specifications and performance data for the "Aircruiser" model 66-70 (passenger version) as powered with 715 h.p. "Cyclone" SGR-1820-F3 engine; length overall 43'4"; height overall 11'9"; wing span 65'0"; wing chord 94"; main wing area 465.7 sq. ft.; area of lift-struts & stub-wings 198.5 sq. ft.; total lifting area 664.2 sq. ft.; airfoil "Bellanca B"; wt. empty 5983 lbs.; useful load 4870 lbs.; payload with 200 gal. fuel & pilot 3380 lbs. (14 pass. & 1000 lbs. baggage-cargo); payload with 200 gal. fuel & 2 pilots 3210 lbs.; gross wt. 10,853.; max. speed 165 at 6900 ft.; cruising speed (.85 power) 155 at 12,000 ft.; landing speed (with flaps) 58; climb 750 ft. first min. at sea level; ser. ceiling 16,000 ft.; gas cap. 200 gal.; oil cap. 16 gal.; cruising range (.85 power) at 42 gal. per hour 700 miles; price $31,600 at factory. Data for model 66-75 with SGR-1820-F53 engine rated 730 h.p. at 2100 r.p.m. at 11,000 ft. (using 3-bladed Hamilton-Standard controllable prop) same as above except as follows: wt. emp-ty 6115 lbs.; useful load 5285 lbs.; payload with 200 gal. fuel & 2 pilots 3625 lbs.; gross wt. 11,-400 lbs.; landing speed (with flaps) 64; climb 700 ft. first min. at sea level; gas cap. max. 300 gal.; oil cap 16 or 19 gal.; also available with Wright SGR-1820-G3 engine rated 850 h.p. at 7500 ft. Price raised to $35,800.

Specifications and performance data for 1 or 2 place cargo-plane with SGR-1820-F3 engine same as above except for following; wt. empty 5731 lbs.; useful load 6100 lbs.; payload with 150

Fig. 228. Army C-27A cargo-carrier was kin to "Aircruiser".

gal. fuel & 1 pilot 4920 lbs.; payload with 150 gal. fuel & 2 pilots 4750 lbs.; gross wt. 11,831 lbs.; max. speed 165; cruising speed (.85 power) 155; landing speed 65; climb 700' ft. first min. at sea level; ser. ceiling 15,000 ft.; gas cap. normal 150 gal.; oil cap. 14 gal.; cruising range 540 miles.

Specifications for model 66-76 cargoplane with SGR-1820-F53 engine rated 760 h.p. at 5800 ft. same as above except as follows: wt. empty 6348 lbs.; useful load 5042 lbs.; payload with 125 gal. fuel & 1 pilot 4000 lbs.; gross wt. 11,400 lbs.; max. speed 172 at 5800 ft.; cruising speed (.85 power) 162; landing speed 60; climb 850 ft. first min. at sea level; (using 860 h.p. for take-off & initial climb-out); ser. ceiling 20,000 ft.; Model 66-85 cargoplane was available with Wright SGR-1820-G3 engine rated 850 h.p. at 7500 ft. using Hamilton-Standard controllable propeller.

Specifications of model 66-70 as 15 place

seaplane on Edo model 12700 floats same as landplane except as follows: wt. empty 6908 lbs.; useful load 4261 lbs.; payload with 185 gal. fuel & 2 pilots 2706 lbs. (13 pass. & 496 lbs. baggage-cargo); gross wt. 11,169 lbs.; max. speed 160; cruising speed (.85 power) 150; landing speed 63; climb 700 ft. first min. at sea level; ser. ceiling 15,000 ft.; gas cap. normal 185 gal.; oil cap. 16 gal.; cruising range (.85 power) at 42 gal. per hour 650 miles. As model 66-76 seaplane available with SGR-1820-F53 engine rated 760 h.p. at 5800 ft.; 860 h.p. available for take-off. As model 66-85 seaplane was available with SGR-1820-G3 engine rated 850 h.p. at 7500 ft. A Pratt & Whitney "Hornet" S1EG engine rated 750 h.p. at 7000 ft. also available for the model 66-75.

The fuselage framework was built up of welded 4130 steel tubing of rather large diameter at points of greater stress, trussed rigidly with steel tubing in the forward section and braced with

Fig. 229. The "Aircruiser" shows its unusual silhouette.

heavy steel tie-rods in the aft section. The framework was faired to outline and shape with spruce formers and fairing strips, then fabric covered. Two rows of steel-framed seats were arranged on a dias some 12 in. high which provided convenient space for personal baggage; outlets for cabin heat and ventilation were provided at each seat. The cabin was arranged with 13 seats and a small lavatory in the rear; entry was provided thru a large door on each side with a convenient fold-in step. A center aisle ran full length of the cabin providing access to pilot compartment also. With all seating removed, floor space was available for up to 2 tons of cargo. An extra large cargo door on the right side, and a large hatch in the roof, were also available for loading machinery and bulky freight. A small door on each side up front provided separate entry for either pilot. The cabin walls were sound-proofed and insulated against extremes in noise and temperature, and all windows were of shatter-proof glass. The large main wing was built up of solid (routed) spruce spar beams with spot-welded stainless steel wing ribs; the leading edges were covered with dural sheet and the completed framework was covered in fabric. Electrically operated trailing edge wing flaps were attached to the inboard sections. The lower stub-wings, of modified "Clark Y" section, had depth to provide a metal-lined cargo compartment of 30 cu. ft. cap. on each side; additional baggage space (18 cu. ft.) was provided in top-side of the long nose-section just ahead of pilot's station, with allowance for 450 lbs. Stub-wings were built up of welded steel tube spar beams and steel tube truss-type ribs covered in fabric. The airfoiled wing bracing struts were built up of heavy steel tube spar beams with steel tube ribs, then fabric covered; being of a special "Bellanca" airfoil section these struts contributed heavily to lateral stability and overall lifting area. The stub-wings slanted down into anhedral and the bracing struts slanted upward into extreme dihedral. The inverted apex of these 2 units, where they joined together, provided fork-type attachment for the wheels. The landing gear of 18 ft. tread was fitted with double "Aerol" shock struts and 36x-16 Goodyear airwheels were fitted with hydraulic brakes. Fuel tanks of 100 or 150 gal. cap. each were mounted inboard in each upper wing-half; oil tank was mounted in engine nacelle. The fabric covered fin, rudder, & elevator were built up of welded steel tubing; horizontal stabilizer was of spruce spar beams and spot-welded stainless steel ribs. Rudder and elevators were fitted with trimming tabs. A 3-bladed metal propeller, combination hand-electric engine starter, generator, battery, throwover control wheel, navigation lights, cabin lights, cockpit lights, landing lights, fire extinguisher, Fabricoid upholstery, lavatory, 16x7 tail wheel, clock, compass, tool kit, first-aid kit, and complete set of engine and flight instruments were standard equipment. Cargo interior, Pyralin port-holes, bonding & shielding, radio, controllable propeller, skis, and Edo model 12500 or 12700 floats were optional. The next Bellanca development was the "Skyrocket" model 31-50 as described in the chapter for ATC # 565 of this volume.

Listed below are "Aircruiser" entries as gleaned from various records:

CF-AWR: 66-70 (# 719) SGR-1820-F3.
CF-BKV: 66-67 (# 720) SGR-1820-F32.
CF-BTW: 66-75 (# 721) SGR-1820-F53.
CF-BBJ: 66-75 (# 722) SGR-1820-F53.
CF-BLT: 66-75 (# 723) SGR-1820-F53.

This approval for ser. # 719 and up; CF-BTW previously registered as NPC-41 in the Philippines; all examples listed above operated in Canada.

ATC # 564
(4-26-35)
FAIRCHILD, MODEL 22-C7G.

Fig. 230. Fairchild 22-C7G with 145 h.p. "Super Scarab" engine.

Owner-pilots of sport-planes were always dropping hints on what they would like in their airplane. By now they usually wanted engine starters to eliminate "propping" by hand, a battery and a generator then became almost necessary, night-flying equipment was becoming increasingly popular to extend the day into night if necessary, and a radio set was also among the most-wanted options. Bearing this in mind, Fairchild designed the husky 22-C7G "parasol" to handle all these options and more, so as to give the sportsman-pilot an airplane replete with all the options and still retain the classic characteristics of the sport-plane. The disappointment came to Fairchild, however, in the realization that sportsman-pilots could no longer be grouped into a category that fitted everyone. There were those yet that enjoyed a wind-in-the-face encounter with the elements, but an increasing number chose to go "indoors" and enjoy the more comfortable way of owning an airplane. Of course, Fairchild captured some of these new sportsman-pilots with their enclosed "Model 24", but the market originally anticipated for the redesigned "Twenty Two" all but disappeared. The 22C7G was the end of the line for the "Model 22", but the series had a very good reputation, had blossomed into many interesting versions, and shall forever remain as a credit to Fairchild history.

The model C-7, the first of the "Fairchild 22", proved that the open "parasol" monoplane with inline engine was an ideal combination for the private-owner pilot, and it sold well. The C7A offered the boost in power that many were asking for, but that particular engine supply began to run out. The C7B with its still higher power was offered to the sportsman-pilot, but the newly-developed Menasco inline engine was still plagued with development problems. The rare C7C was powered with a D.H. "Gipsy" III engine to operate in Canada, but only one example was built. The C7D with the Wright-Gipsy engine was perhaps the darling of the whole "Twenty Two" series; cheap to buy and cheap to operate, it offered exceptional utility and carefree flying. The C7E was the first model to be powered with a radial engine, but the 125 h.p. Warner "Scarab" failed to deliver the punch that was expected from a sport ship of this type. Powered with the 145 h.p. Warner "Super Scarab" engine the C7F offered a considerable increase in performance, but pilots were now asking for engine starter, radio, and other pilot aids. These were all incorporated into the new C7G which enjoyed only a limited acceptance and was the last model in the "Twenty Two" lineup. Even the so-called sportsman was taking to the "Model 24", which was by now into its fifth modification, and it was offering just about

Fig. 231. 22-C7G glistens against backdrop of wintry skies.

all the "Model 22" could offer, and in a lot more comfort besides.

The Fairchild model 22-C7G was an open-cockpit parasol monoplane with seating arranged for 2 in tandem. In general, the C7G was typical of the earlier C7F, but it had been redesigned to incorporate most of the called-for options that led to a higher gross weight. The brand new wing was a sturdy structure that enhanced the maneuverability, was capable of standing up to unrestricted aerobatics, and yet stable enough to lend itself to pilot training. The rugged fuselage framework was pretty much the same, except for a slightly altered contour that was pleasant and more mindful to the harsh demands of airflow. As "strutted" together into several rigid trusses, the whole C7G combination was extremely tough; tough enough to withstand 11G positive and 9G negative. This was probably the strongest light commercial airplane ever built in the U.S.A. As powered with the 145 h.p. Warner "Super Scarab" (Series 50) engine the 22-C7G performed everything with much gusto, and led one to believe that this would really be some airplane with a little more power. In later years, a 22-C7G was restored using an engine of some 200 h.p. and the result was a fantastic experience. The type certificate

Fig. 232. Parasol-winged 22-C7G was designed for the hardy sportsman.

Fig. 233. Special streamlined version of the 22-C7G.

number for the model 22-C7G was issued 4-26-35 and 6 examples of this model were manufactured by the Fairchild Aircraft Corp. at Hagerstown, Md.

Listed below are specifications and performance data for the Fairchild model 22-C7G as powered with 145 h.p. Warner "Super Scarab" engine; length overall 22'3"; height overall 7'11"; wing span 33'0"; wing chord 66"; total wing area 173 sq. ft.; airfoil (Navy) N-22; wt. empty 1240 (1284) lbs.; useful load 860 (816) lbs.; payload with 40 gal. fuel & 2 parachutes 382 (338) lbs.; figures in parentheses as equipped with battery & engine starter; gross wt. 2100 lbs.; max. speed 135; cruising speed (.80 power) 120 at sea level; landing speed 50; climb 750 ft. first min. at sea level; ser. ceiling 16,500 ft.; gas cap. normal 40 gal.; gas cap. max. 60 gal.; oil cap. 3.75 gal.; cruising range (.80 power) at 9 gal. per hour 480 miles; price $3400. to $3900. at factory.

The construction details and general arrangement of the 22-C7G were typical to that of the model 22-C7F as described here in the chapter for ATC # 517, including the following. Turtle-back fairing was made up of spruce T-strips over wooden bulkheads; bottom and side fairing was of rectangular aluminum alloy tubing attached to the frame by metal clips. Except for metal cockpit cowling the fuselage was covered in fabric. A large door on the left side offered easy entry into the front cockpit; step-holes in the fuselage were placed at either cockpit and in front for servicing. Bucket-type metal seats were designed to fit a parachute pack; 2 'chutes (40 lbs.) were normally part of the useful load. A

baggage compartment was behind the firewall with allowance for up to 133 lbs. The engine was equipped with a hot-air box for the carburetor; an oil-cooling radiator was optional. The stout wing, in 2 halves, was patterned after that of the Model 24 and equipped with balanced and slotted ailerons; trailing edge wing flaps were optional. A 20 gal. fuel tank was mounted in root end of each wing-half; an extra 20 gal. fuel tank mounted in the fuselage was optional. The vertical fin was built up of spruce members and mahogany plywood; other tail surfaces were built up of welded steel tubing and all was covered in fabric. A Hartzell wooden propeller, electric engine starter, Exide battery, navigation lights, dual stick-type controls, compass, wheel brakes, tail wheel, fuel gauges, Pyrene fire extinguisher, and first-aid kit were standard equipment. A metal propeller, landing lights, parachute flares, bonding & shielding, radio set, generator, brake pedals in front cockpit, 19x9-3 Goodyear airwheels, 20 gal. extra fuel, and wing flaps were optional. The next Fairchild development was the Ranger-powered model 24-C8D as described in the chapter for ATC # 576 of this volume.

Listed below are 22-C7G entries as verified by factory records:

NC-14306: 22-C7G (# 1800) Warner 145.
PP-TBD: 22-C7G (# 1801) Warner 145.
NC-14786: 22-C7G (# 1802) Warner 145.
  -14787: 22-C7G (# 1803) Warner 145.
  -14788: 22-C7G (# 1804) Warner 145.
  -14789: 22-C7G (# 1805) Warner 145.
This approval for ser. # 1800 and up; ser. # 1801 del. to Brazil; this approval expired 9-30-39.

ATC # 565
(4-26-35)
BELLANCA "SR. SKYROCKET", 31-50.

Fig. 234. Bellanca "Senior Skyrocket" with 550 h.p. "Wasp" engine displays aggressive beauty.

With an airplane such as the "Skyrocket" there is little else one could do to improve it, but in this new series 31-50 the original basic design had moved right up to the very peak of quality and performance. Developed for a small band of operators who wanted an airplane of the "Pacemaker" type, but with more power and a definite sporting nature, the "Senior Skyrocket" was a combination of abilities that were quite surprising. Judging from the "bouquets" tossed about in its favor, it must have been just what the owners had in mind. To offer an elegant and more spacious interior the fuselage was now widened, the familiar joy-stick was replaced by a throw-over control wheel, custom features were practically unlimited, and substantial gains in performance were instigated by a husky boost in horsepower and several aerodynamic refinements. Because of Bellanca policy in manufacture the model 31-50 was not developed in one big leap; the "Skyrocket" had been improved steadily since the CH-400 of 1930, and as was G. M. Bellanca's wish, each airplane off the assembly line was a little bit better than the one before it. So, the airplanes built in this 31-50 series differed from one another also, and usually reflected the owners special wish or personal needs. Offered in a "Standard" and "Deluxe"

version, the roster of "Senior Skyrocket" owners were generally representatives of big-business who used their airplanes for transportation or sales promotion.

The Bellanca "Senior Skyrocket" model 31-50 (31-55) was more or less a custom-built high winged cabin monoplane with seating normally arranged for six. Despite its comparatively compact-looking proportion the 31-50 (31-55) was enlarged considerably over earlier "Skyrocket" models to offer a lot more room in the spacious cradle of plush comfort. While it was visibly fattened and widened to offer the stretch-room only possible through added dimension, with some wing added to handle the sizeable increase in useful load, the 31-50 (31-55) could not very well forget that it was a "Skyrocket" and behaved much more like a sport-type airplane instead of a transport for six. The "Senior Skyrocket" had unusual abilities and this, of course, was possible because of the big supercharged "Wasp" engine that was tightly shrouded with a deep-chord NACA-type cowling, and driving an efficient Hamilton-Standard controllable propeller. The model 31-50 was hitched to the 9 cyl. "Wasp" S1D1 engine rated 525 h.p. at 2100 r.p.m. at 7000 ft., and the model 31-55 was mated to the "Wasp"

Fig. 235. "Sr. Skyrocket" seaplane in Canadian service.

S3H1 engine rated 550 h.p. at 2200 r.p.m. at 5000 ft. As powered with the S3H1 engine the "Sr. Skyrocket" could romp along at 190 m.p.h., or cruise for hours at 180 m.p.h. at 12,-000 ft.; offhand, this hardly seems likely for such a fat, boxy-looking airplane, but the wizardry of "Bellanca" design has time and again proven that "the old maestro" knew what it was all about in aerodynamics. There was a saying that once bitten by the "Skyrocket" bug, one was addicted forever more; in many cases this was true. Wallace Beery, likeable movie-actor and avid sportsman-pilot, traded his 1931 "Skyrocket" for one of the 1935 models. A "Senior Skyrocket Deluxe" with "Wasp" S3H1 engine, his new airplane was finished in hand-rubbed Rubicon Red and had soft brown genuine leather upholstery; naturally, Beery beamed with pride every time he flew it somewhere. A custom-built airplane, no reasonable expense was spared to make the 31-50 (31-55) the finest airplane of this type, so it was liberally fitted with special comforts, many operating accessories, and the latest in flying aids. Most "Skyrocket" owners could afford to pay for the best, and in the 31-50 or 31-55 that's just what they received. The type certificate number for the "Senior Skyrocket" model 31-50 was issued

Fig. 236. Odd combination of wheels and skis fitted to "Skyrocket" in Canada.

Fig. 237. The new "Skyrocket" 31-55 was fast despite its buxom and boxy proportions.

4-26-35 and amended to include the 31-55; perhaps 10 or more of the 31-50 (31-55) were mfgd. by the Bellanca Aircraft Corp. at New Castle, Dela. Guiseppe Mario Bellanca was pres. & gen. mgr.; Frank Bellanca was V.P.; N. F. Vanderlipp was chf. of engrg.; L. W. Ashton was sales mgr.; and Andrew Bellanca was sec.

Listed below are specifications and performance data for the "Senior Skyrocket" model 31-50 (Standard) as powered with 525 h.p. Pratt & Whitney "Wasp" S1D1 engine; length overall 27'11"; height overall 8'6"; wing span 56'0"; wing chord 81"; total wing area (incl. struts) 359 sq. ft.; airfoil "Bellanca" B; wt. empty 3150 lbs.; useful load 2450 lbs.; payload with 185 gal. fuel 1065 lbs. (5 pass. & 215 lbs. baggage); gross wt. 5600 lbs.; max. speed 183 at 7000 ft.; cruising speed (.70 power) 159; landing speed 60; climb 1240 ft. first min. at sea level; ser. ceiling 23,000 ft.; gas cap. normal 185 gal.; gas cap. max. 200 gal.; oil cap. 12.5 gal.; cruising range (.70 power) at 30 gal. per hour 920 miles; price $21,950. at factory in 1935; price (with wing flaps) was $22,700. at factory in 1936.

Specifications and data for model 31-55 (Deluxe) as powered with "Wasp" S3H1 engine rated 550 h.p. same as above except as follows; wt. empty 3300 lbs.; useful load 2300 lbs.; payload with 160 gal. fuel 1070 lbs. (5 pass. & 220 lbs. baggage); gross wt. 5600 lbs.; max. speed 187 at 5000 ft.; cruising speed (.85 power) 172; landing speed (with flaps) 56; climb 1250 ft. first min. at sea level; ser. ceiling 25,000 ft.; gas cap. normal 160 gal.; gas cap. max. 200 gal.; oil cap. 14 gal.; cruising range (.85 power) at 36 gal. per hour 750 miles; price variable. "Senior Skyrocket" 31-55 (Deluxe) with "Wasp" S3H1 engine, Hamilton-Standard controllable propeller, and extra equipment, as follows; wt. empty 3440 lbs.; useful load 2160 lbs.; payload with 150 gal. fuel 994 lbs. (5 pass. & 144 lbs. baggage); gross wt. 5600 lbs.; max. speed 190 at 5000 ft.; cruising speed (.85 power) 180 at 12,000 ft.; landing (stall) speed (with flaps) 56; cruising range 700 miles; price variable.

Specifications and data for model 31-55 (Deluxe) as seaplane on Edo twin-float gear same as above except as follows: wt. empty 3690 lbs.; useful load 2190 lbs.; payload with 155 gal. fuel 994 lbs.; gross wt. 5880 lbs.; max. speed 172 at 5000 ft.; cruising speed (.75 power) 158 at 12,000 ft.; landing speed (with flaps) 62; climb 1100 ft. first min. at sea level; ser. ceiling 23,000 ft.; gas cap. max. 200 gal.; oil cap. 14 gal.; cruising range at 32 gal. per hour 700 miles; price not announced.

The fuselage framework was built up of welded 4130 steel tubing with gussets and plates at all points of extreme stress, faired to shape with plywood formers and spruce fairing strips, then fabric covered. Cabin walls were lined with "Dry Zero" for sound-proofing and all windows were of shatter-proof glass. The pilot's seat was adjustable and a throw-over wheel provided dual control. All seats with arm-rests, were padded heavily with foam rubber and upholstered in leather or fine fabrics. Heat and ventilating outlets were at several points for cabin comfort. With all seating removed the 124" long x 58" high x 46" wide cabin interior offered ample floor space for cargo. The "Deluxe" version was available with a fold-out seat-couch and various

Fig. 238. A post-war version of the "Senior Skyrocket".

other interior arrangements with custom decor. A cabin entry door and convenient step were to the rear on each side; a 15 cu. ft. baggage compartment was behind the rear seat and accessible from inside or out. The wing framework, in 2 halves, was built up of solid (routed) spruce spar beams reinforced with plywood gussets and birch blocks at all fittings, and spruce and mahogany plywood truss-type wing ribs; the leading edges were covered with plywood sheet and the completed framework was covered in fabric. The distinctive wing-bracing "lift struts" were heavy steel tubes with dural ribs forming the airfoil and covered in fabric; an aux. truss near outer end of struts prevented twisting loads produced by the ailerons. Narrow-chord ailerons were of the slotted-hinge type and quite effective even beyond the "stall". A 100 gal. fuel tank was mounted in root end of each wing-half providing gravity flow; wings reinforced in the tank area. The new-type landing gear of 96 in. tread consisted of single-strut cantilever legs with "Aerol" shock struts mounted in the belly; 31 in. streamlined General tires, or 9.50x12 semi-airwheels, were fitted with Bendix brakes. Wheel fenders were standard, but streamlined metal wheel pants were optional. A 4x5 tail wheel (full swivel) was an aid in ground handling. The fin, rudder, and elevators were of welded steel tubing and covered with fabric; rudder was of balanced type. The horizontal stabilizer was built up of spruce spar beams with spruce and plywood ribs covered with fabric; elevators were fitted with adjustable trim tabs. A metal propeller, Eclipse hand-electric inertia-type engine starter, 12-volt Exide battery, oil-cooling radiator, cabin heater, ventilators, adj. windows, wheel brakes, compass, fire extinguisher, clock, throw-over control

wheel, wheel fenders, full set of engine and flight instruments, first-aid kit, tool kit, and engine cover were standard equipment. Deluxe equipment included all the above plus generator, navigation lights, landing lights, parachute flares, bonding & shielding, radio, Sperry gyrohorizon, air-speed indicator, rate of climb, turn & bank, cyl. head temp. gauge, fuel gauges, and hand-rubbed custom colors. A Hamilton-Standard controllable propeller, Edo twin-float gear, skis, wing flaps, and "Wasp" S2H1 engine were optional. The next Bellanca development was the "Senior Pacemaker" model 31-40 as described in chapter for ATC # 578 of this volume.

Listed below are "Senior Skyrocket" entries as gleaned from registration records:

NC-14700; 31-55 (# 806) Wasp S3H1.
   -14701; 31-55 (# 807) Wasp S3H1.
   -14761; 31-55 (# 808) Wasp S3H1.
   -15015; 31-55 (# 809) Wasp S3H1.
   -15016; 31-55 (# 810) Wasp S3H1.
   -15300; 31-55 (# 811) Wasp S3H1.
   -15953; 31-55 (# 812) Wasp S3H1.

Ser. # 806 first built as "Skyrocket F" on Group 2 approval # 2-475 delivered to Frank W. Fuller, Jr. and later modified to 31-50 and 31-55; ser. # 807 first built for Wallace Beery as "Skyrocket F" and later modified to 31-55 Deluxe; ser. # 809 first registered as NC-10528; ser. # 810 del. to Gilmore Oil Co.; ser. # 812 del. to Des Moines Register & Tribune; an XB-AAZ operated in Mexico, ser. no. unknown; no listing for ser. # 813-814-815; one "Skyrocket" 31-55 del. to U. S. Navy as JE-1 in 1937; CF-DCH operating in Canada appears to be final example of the 31-55 series.

ATC # 566
(5-9-35)
BEECH, MODEL B-17-E.

Fig. 239. The Beech model B-17-E with 285 h.p. Wright engine.

Some of the inquiring customers had a natural preference for the famed "Wright" engines, and especially the 7 cyl. R-760-E1 engine rated 285 h.p., so Beech developed a new model designated the B-17-E especially for these customers. Basically, the model B-17-E was quite typical of the (Jacobs-powered) B-17-B except for the installation of the Wright engine and a slight customizing to various other details. It has been often said that of the 15 or so important characteristics of an airplane, including price, Walter Beech put performance and quality at the top of the list; this was especially evident in the Wright-powered B-17-E. The 4-5 place B-17-E turned out to be a combination of rather uncommon beauty, a practical luxury in relative economy, and the fastest transportation available in this type of airplane. The B-17-E quickly appealed to sportsmen and many men of business, but Beech was also promoting new models coming up with higher horsepower, so oddly enough, many potential B-17-E customers took on an attitude of let's-wait-and-see. Louise Thaden, famous aviatrix, was by now a Beech factory representative and had just made a demonstration tour out to the west-coast; she was well known out there and helped to sell a few airplanes.

The Beech model B-17-E was a cabin biplane with seating arranged for 4 or 5; altho' a cabin biplane, it certainly was no ordinary cabin biplane, as we can see. Inverse (negative) stagger was the worldwide trade-mark of the Beech by

now, and with its landing gear tucked up into the belly, it was still the most novel commercial airplane of this time. More speed per horsepower was its paramount feature, but quality, luxury, and premium performance were also built in to make it one of the best buys of the decade. Ironically enough, the search for more speed and better performance was still tied-in directly to horsepower available, so despite the speed and performance the "Beech" was already delivering with 225 h.p. (B-17-L) there were always those that wanted just a little more. As if to satisfy this need in easy stages, Beech was going up on the horsepower in moderate amounts. As powered with the 7 cyl. Wright R-760-E1 engine rated 285 h.p. at 2100 r.p.m. the model B-17-E delivered substantial amounts of performance increase in proportion to the amount of power added. The extra 60 h.p. added 10 m.p.h. to the top speed, and all else (take-off, climb-out, etc.) was improved accordingly. The Wright engine was relatively expensive, so those that were willing to pay the difference, more or less expected the best of everything to go with it. In the B-17-E this is just what they got, the best of everything. The type certificate number for the model B-17-E was issued 5-9-35 and 4 examples of this model were manufactured by the Beech Aircraft Co. at Wichita, Kan. Walter H. Beech was pres.; R. K. Beech was V.P.; Wm. A. Ong was sales mgr.; Ted A. Wells was chf. engr. George Harte, local test-pilot, did testing for both Beech and Cessna during this period. Beech started out with 8 men in 1932, by mid-1934 the staff had swelled to 150 and former "Travel Air" employees were hired as fast as they came in.

Listed below are specifications and performance data for the Beech model B-17-E as powered with 285 h.p. Wright R-760-E1 engine; length overall 24'5"; height overall 8'2"; wing span upper & lower 32'0"; wing chord upper & lower 60"; total wing area 267 sq. ft.; airfoil Clark CYH; wt. empty 2000 lbs.; useful load 1263 lbs.; payload with 70 gal. fuel 617 lbs. (3 pass. & 107 lbs. baggage); gross wt. 3263 lbs.; max. speed 185 at sea level; cruising speed 165 at sea level; cruising speed (.75 power) 173 at 5000 ft.; landing speed (with flaps) 50; climb 1200 ft. first min. at sea level; ser. ceiling 18,000 ft.; gas cap. normal 70 gal.; oil cap. 7.5 gal.; cruising range (.75 power) at 17.5 gal. per hour 680 miles; price $12,980. at factory field. Approved gross wt. later increased to 3600 lbs., allowing 1600 lb. useful load and 954 lb. payload with 70 gal. fuel.

The construction details and general arrangement of the model B-17-E were typical to that of the B-17-L as described here in the chapter for ATC # 560. The following pertains to the Beech 17 series in general and the B-17-E in particular. The large safety-glass windshield was curved and sloped to fit the streamlines of the fuselage. The lower fuselage was encased in a large metal wing fillet and the forward portion of the fuselage was covered in metal panels. Entry door was on the left side and an extra door was available for the right side. The front seats were adjustable and Switlik or Irvin parachute-type seats were available. Baggage compartment for 125 lbs. was down low behind the rear seat with access door on left side of fuselage; the baggage compartment was limited to 75 lbs. when 3 persons occupied the rear seat. The landing gear of 86 in.

tread used "Beech" oleo-spring shock struts and was shortened to improve landing flare-out; landing gear retraction was normally by electric motor and manual in emergency. Tail wheel retracted also. All controls were cable-operated using ball bearings on every moving part. Differential ailerons were on the lower wing panels, and decelerator (drag) flaps were on underside of the upper wing. Two fuselage tanks, one of 28 gal. and one of 42 gal. were under the cabin floor; an engine-driven fuel pump or a hand wobble-pump provided fuel flow to the engine. Two extra 25 gal. fuel tanks could be mounted in the upper wing. A Curtiss-Reed metal propeller, electric engine starter, generator, Exide battery, navigation lights, oil-cooling radiator, cabin heater, 24 in. streamlined wheels with heavy-duty tires, wheel brakes, 10x3 full-swivel tail wheel, engine-driven fuel pump, fuel gauges, compass, clock, normal set of engine & flight instruments, fire extinguisher, assist ropes, and first-aid kit were standard equipment. A radio set, bonding & shielding, landing lights, parachute flares, extra fuel tanks, custom colors, and Hamilton-Standard controllable propeller were optional. The next Beech development was the monstrous A-17-FS as described in the chapter for ATC # 577 of this volume.

Listed below are B-17-E entries as gleaned from registration records:

NC-12593; B-17-E (# 22) Wright 285.
   -14413; B-17-E (# 38) Wright 285.
   -14458; B-17-E (# 49) Wright 285.
   -15412; B-17-E (# 51) Wright 285.

This approval for ser. # 22 and up; ser. # 38 later converted into B-17-R with 420 h.p. Wright engine; this approval expired 9-30-39.

ATC # 567
(5-9-35)
PORTERFIELD "FLYABOUT", 35-70.

Fig. 240. The Porterfield 35-70 with 70 h.p. LeBlond engine.

The Porterfield "Flyabout" was a brand-new airplane, but it had enough "American Eagle" ancestry in it to endorse its debut into the lightplane market. For many the re-entry of "Ed" Porterfield into the lightplane market-place was a joyous occasion and they backed their enthusiasm by pouring in orders, sight unseen. Announcement of the "Model 35" (Flyabout) in 1934 invited early inquiries that became the nucleus of a nation-wide dealer organization. First batches of production were nearly all fly-away deliveries. In the rush to get back home, shakedown tests on cross-country deliveries confirmed Porterfield's claims for performance and general ability; the general impression was that the "Flyabout" was a helluva lot of airplane for $1695. On a delivery from Kansas City west to California one dealer was so enthused with the airplane that he boasted about it at every gas stop, all the way home. The 2485 mile flight, averaging 100 m.p.h., cost only $34.00 for gas and oil. Delivery flights to the east were generally quicker and cheaper. The Flyabout 35-70 was formally introduced at the Detroit Air Show for 1935 where it was greeted with enthusiasm; prospects were enticed with free flying lessons and pay-as-you-fly contracts. Other showings were at New York and Los Angeles where interest was also high. A good

thing gets around and soon there were agencies in Mexico, the Canal Zone, and in South America. Private operators that usually started out with one airplane were making money training student-pilots, and usually had to get a second or third "Flyabout" to handle all their business; cheap to buy, cheap to operate, and sturdy enough to take punishment without breakage, the 35-70 was putting money in the till. Of course, the "Flyabout" was progressively refined as each new year approached, making it a continually better airplane, but manufacturing costs were now rising too and each year it cost a little more to buy one. In spite of this the "35-70" was still one of the biggest bargains in the country. By 1937 the "Flyabout" was already available with several different engines, thus dividing up the business among several different models, and popularity of the new "Flat four" engines was causing Porterfield to revise their future. The LeBlond-powered 35-70 finally came to the end of the line, but for more than 3 years it was a mighty popular airplane.

During the winter of 1931-32, in the manual training shop of the Wyandotte High School in Kansas City, Kan., students built an airplane under the supervision of Noel R. Hockaday. This design by Hockaday became known as the Wyandotte "Pup" and the features of this design

Fig. 241. Porterfield 35-70 was a lot of airplane for $1695.

were later incorporated into 2 other airplanes that became very popular in this country during the "thirties". The little "Pup" was powered with a 3 cyl. Aeromarine AR3-40 engine of 40 h.p., and tho' somewhat underpowered it flew and performed rather well. When Ed Porterfield made an offer to purchase the "Pup" design for a percentage of stock in his new aircraft company, Noel Hockaday accepted and became designer, factory manager, and test pilot for the budding enterprise. Thus, with a little redesigning and the installation of a 60 h.p. LeBlond engine, the new "Porterfield" airplane was born. The two-seated airplane was an early success forcing moves to succeedingly larger quarters and soon the ships were rolling out the door at 10 per week. The various components were transported to Richards Field and there they

were assembled for fly-away deliveries. A few of the early examples (Model 35) were powered with the old-style "LeBlond 60", but bulk of the production was of the model 35-70. Noel Hockaday, who started the ball a-rolling, left Porterfield in 1937 for California where he planned to build a new design called the Hockaday "Comet".

The slender Porterfield "Flyabout" model 35-70 was a light cabin monoplane with seating arranged for 2 in tandem. Favored by economic circumstance, the model 35-70 was able to fill the role of pilot-trainer, a useful tool in business, or dressed-up a little as a sportplane for the less affluent sportsman-pilot, those who found pleasure enough in flight itself and not in the possession of a custom, high-powered airplane. Fortunately, the "Flyabout" found itself a com-

Fig. 242. 35-70 offered big-airplane performance with small-airplane economy.

Fig. 243. Wyandotte "Pup" instigated "Porterfield" design.

fortable niche in the market place, just a row above the low-priced flivver-planes, where it attracted considerable attention and sold in rather good number. A fair number of the 35-70 were exported and they were flying in at least 35 states here in the U.S.A. As the Model 35 the early "Flyabout" was powered with the old-style 5 cyl. LeBlond 5D engine of 60 h.p., and as the Model 35-70 with the improved LeBlond 5DE engine of 70 h.p.; some of the latest examples were powered with the "Ken Royce" engines. The "Ken Royce" engine was actually the LeBlond engine as later manufactured by Rearwin. As powered with the 5 cyl. LeBlond 5DE engine rated 70 h.p. at 1950 r.p.m. the model 35-70 mustered up a decent range of good performance and it operated from just about anywhere. Pilot-owners were lavish in their praise ("I like it better every time I fly it") and thousands of students were trained to be good pilots. It was easy to own a "Flyabout" on the pay-as-you-fly plan, and lessons to fly the airplane were free if you were not a pilot. Because of its popularity and hardy nature the "35-70" was around for a long time and several are flying yet. The type certificate number for the Model 35-70 was issued 5-9-35 and some 200 or so examples of this model were manufactured by the Porterfield Aircraft Corp. at Kansas City, Mo. E. E. Porterfield, Jr. was pres., gen. mgr., and sales mgr.; Hugh L. Thompson was chf. engr.; Noel R. Hockaday was designer, test pilot, and plant superintendent; L. A. Bichelmaier was assy. foreman; and M. S. Porterfield was V.P. In 1936 Edgar F. Smith was sales mgr. and H. W. Barlow was chf. engr. In 1937 D. H. Hollowell was V.P. and sales mgr., and Wayne Archer was chf. engr.

Listed below are specifications and performance data for the Porterfield "Flyabout" model 35-70 as powered with 70 h.p. LeBlond 5DE engine; length overall 20'3"; height overall 6'7"; wing span 32'0"; wing chord 56"; total wing area (incl. fuselage section) 147 sq. ft.; airfoil Munk M-6; wt. empty 750 (806) lbs.; useful load 485 (504) lbs.; payload with 17 gal. fuel 195 (214) lbs.; gross wt. 1235 (1310) lbs.; figures in parentheses as later amended; max. speed 115; cruising speed (1850 r.p.m.) 100 at 700 ft.; landing speed 38-40; climb 810 (790) ft. first min. at sea level; ser. ceiling 15,500 (15,000) ft.; figures in parentheses at 1310 lbs. gross; gas cap. 17 gal.; oil cap. 2.5 gal.; cruising range (1850 r.p.m.) at 4.7 gal. per hour 360 miles; price at factory field was $1695. in early 1935, $1795. in late 1935, $1895. in 1936, and $2095. in 1937, showing the periodic price raises necessary to offset increases in manufacturing costs.

The fuselage framework was built up of welded C/M steel tubing, faired to shape with wooden formers and fairing strips, then fabric covered. Seats were placed in tandem and a large rectangular door on the right side provided entry. The baggage compartment with allowance for up to 30 lbs. was behind the rear seat. The curved windshield and all side windows were of Pyralin, including a sky-light in the cabin roof. The dash-panel was fitted with basic engine-flight instruments, and dual stick-type controls were provided. The 17 gal. fuel tank was mounted high in the fuselage just behind the firewall; the firewall was of terne-plate. The wing panels were built up of solid spruce spar beams with spruce and plywood truss-type wing ribs; the leading edges were covered with dural sheet and the completed framework was covered in fabric. Wing panels were fastened to upper longerons and strut-braced by parallel streamlined steel tubes on each side. The landing gear of 66 in. or 69 in. tread was a simple vee-type arrangement fitted with 7.00x4 semi-airwheels and Rusco shock absorbing rings; wheel brakes and metal wheel pants were optional. Goodyear 18x8-3 airwheels with brakes were also optional. The fabric covered tail group was built up of welded C/M steel tubing; horizontal stabilizer was adjustable in flight. The completed airplane was finished with 6 coats of Berryloid nitrate dope and several coats of hand-rubbed Berryloid lacquer; Black and Orange were standard colors, but other color combinations were available from time to time. A Fahlin or Sensenich wooden propeller, dual controls, wiring for navigation lights, fuel gauge, Pyrene fire extinguisher, spring-leaf tail skid, and first-aid kit were standard equipment. Wheel brakes, tail wheel, metal wheel pants, battery, navigation lights, air-speed indicator were optional. The next Porterfield development was the Velie-powered Model 35-V as described in the chapter for ATC # 606.

Listed below is partial listing of "Flyabout" entries as gleaned from registration records:

NC-14400;	Model 35	(# 101)	LeBlond 60
-14421;	"	(# 102)	"
-14424;	35-70	(# 103)	LeBlond 70
-14427;	"	(# 104)	"
-14431;	"	(# 105)	"
-14434;	"	(# 106)	"
-14435;	"	(# 107)	"
-14437;	"	(# 108)	"
-14438;	"	(# 109)	"
-14439;	"	(# 110)	"
-14440;	"	(# 111)	"
PP-TBE;	"	(# 112)	"
:	"	(# 113)	"
-14444;	"	(# 114)	"
-14445;	"	(# 115)	"
-14446;	"	(# 116)	"
-14447;	"	(# 117)	"
-14448;	"	(# 118)	"
-14449;	"	(# 119)	"
-14450;	"	(# 120)	"
:	"	(# 121)	"
-14462;	"	(# 122)	"
-14463;	"	(# 123)	"
-14464;	"	(# 124)	"
-14465;	"	(# 125)	"
-14466;	"	(# 126)	"
-14467;	"	(# 127)	"
-14468;	"	(# 128)	"
-14469;	"	(# 129)	"
-14470;	"	(# 130)	"
-14471;	"	(# 131)	"
-14475;	"	(# 132)	"
-14476;	"	(# 133)	"
-14477;	"	(# 134)	"
-14478;	"	(# 135)	"
-14479;	"	(# 136)	"
-14480;	"	(# 137)	"
-14481;	"	(# 138)	"
-14482;	"	(# 139)	"
-14483;	"	(# 140)	"
:	"	(# 141)	"
-15442;	"	(# 142)	"
-15443;	"	(# 143)	"
-15444;	"	(# 144)	"
-15445;	"	(# 145)	"
-15446;	"	(# 146)	"
-15447;	"	(# 147)	"
-15448;	"	(# 148)	"
-15449;	"	(# 149)	"
NS-15450;	"	(# 150)	"

This approval for ser. # 132, 135 thru 138, 140 and up; ser. # 101 thru 131, 133, 134, and 139 were mfgd. under Group 2 approval #2-498 (issued 2-21-35) but were also eligible on ATC # 567 at 1235 lb. gross wt.; ser. # 113, 121, 141, 162 thru 166 not listed, may have been exported; this approval expired 1-25-41.

Fig. 244. The rare Waco UOC with 210 h.p. Continental engine.

The "Waco" lineup for the season of 1935 was handsomely garnished with the introduction of the new "Custom Cabin" models. One of the first of these, the model UOC, was part of the company's display at the Detroit Air Show for 1935, and interested viewers, lingering by the hundreds, was a good indication that the "Custom Cabin" was certainly heading for a pretty good future. As we can see, the new "line" was considerably different from the standard "Cabin Waco" not only in configuration and aerodynamic proportion, but also in room available and in interior decor; actually, they were rather beautiful airplanes both inside and out. In comparison to the "Standard Cabin" biplane the "Custom" models were plush airplanes of the "sedan" type with rich decor and enough gadgetry to please just about anybody. As powered with the 7 cyl. Continental R-670-A of 210 h.p., or the R-670-B engine of 225 h.p., the Model UOC itself was not destined to enjoy much of a future; for some reason the "Continental" engine was side-lined for this particular series of airplanes. The "Custom" models one would see most often over the countryside were either powered with "Jacobs" or the "Wright" engines. Being thus quite rare, the Model UOC deserves credit no less for being a part of this early development of the "Custom" series and actually it was built in some 3 examples. The

first was delivered to Henry B. DuPont, an avid aviation enthusiast, and the other 2 were exported. The surprising thing about the "Custom Cabin" series was the fact they sold quickly and in good number in spite of the much higher price tag. We must consider then, even in these depressed times, that to some people at least, the plain lower-priced airplane was not necessarily the best bargain. Waco Aircraft was, of course, happy because the "Custom Cabin" became a very big part of their business.

The Waco model UOC was a cabin biplane with seating arranged for 4 or 5. The "Custom" series contained no radical departure from normal design practice, but the differences, as compared to the "Standard" series, were considerable. The most noticeable difference was, of course, the configuration and its aerodynamic proportion. The shortened lower wing and the eliptical shaping of the wing-tips gave the new "Custom" a look of speed and dash in spite of its increased dimension and bulk. The roomy interior which offered adjustable front seats a full 17 inches wide and a bench-type seat in back that was wide enough for 3, was bound to become bulkier on its outside, but this had no detrimental effect whatever. In fact, the "Custom" was 7 m.p.h. faster than the smaller "Standard" using the same horsepower. A typical "Waco" in every sense, the "Custom

Fig. 245. Waco UOC operating in New Zealand.

Cabin" in a choice of 3 different engines was a well-blended combination of speed, comfort, safety, and reliability. As powered with the 210 h.p. Continental R-670-A engine the model UOC offered excellent performance with pinch-penny economy, while still inheriting all the commendable "Waco" flight characteristics. The first production version of the UOC was delivered to Henry B. DuPont, industrialist who for the past decade had been an avid airplane enthusiast. When he traded the UOC for a newer "Waco" the ship was then registered to Fred Foote of Chicago. Two more examples of the UOC were built and these were exported; one went to Argentina and the other to New Zealand. The prototype airplane (X-14613) was used for development of all 3 "Custom" models for 1935. The type certificate number for the Model UOC was issued 5-17-35 and 3 examples of this model were manufactured by the Waco Aircraft Co. at Troy, Ohio.

Listed below are specifications and performance data for the Waco model UOC as powered with 210 h.p. Continental R-670-A engine; length overall 25'4"; height overall 8'3"; wing span upper 35'0"; wing span lower 24'6"; wing chord upper 72"; wing chord lower 48"; wing area upper 165.6 sq. ft.; wing area lower 73.2 sq. ft.; total wing area 238.8 sq. ft.; airfoil Clark Y; wt. empty 1895 lbs.; useful load 1205 lbs.; payload with 50 gal. fuel 705 lbs. (3 pass. & 195 lbs. baggage, or 4 pass. & 25 lbs. baggage); gross wt. 3100 lbs.; max. speed 150 at 1000 ft.; cruising speed (1900 r.p.m.) 133 at 1000 ft.; landing speed 53; climb 710 ft. first min. at sea level; ser. ceiling 14,500 ft.; gas cap. normal 50 gal.; gas cap. optional 70-95 gal.; oil cap. 4-6 gal.; cruising range (1900 r.p.m.) at 13 gal. per hour 465 miles; price $6850. to $7375. at factory field. Eligible at 3100 lb. gross wt. on 7.50x10 tires, and 3200 lb. gross wt. on 8.50x10 tires. Eligible at 3200 lb. gross wt. max. with wooden or adj. metal propeller, and 3350 lb. gross wt. with controllable propeller.

The fuselage framework was built up of welded C/M (chrome-moly) steel tubing, faired to shape with wooden formers and fairing strips, then fabric covered. The cabin walls were sound-proofed and upholstered in mohair and other fine fabrics; the windshield and side windows were of shatter-proof glass while rear quarter windows and skylight were of Pyralin. Front seats were individual and bench-type seat in rear was wide enough to seat 3 across. The front seats were adjustable and a throw-over control wheel was provided. A large door on the left side offered easy entry off the wing-walk. A large baggage compartment was behind the rear seat with access from inside or out. The wing framework, in 4 panels, was built up of solid spruce spar beams with spruce and plywood truss-type wing ribs; the leading edges were covered with dural sheet and the completed framework was covered in fabric. The wing cellule was braced together with N-type struts and a heavy tension-compression strut that eliminated the usual criss-cross interplane wires. A 25 gal. fuel tank was in the root end of each upper wing-half. The oleo-spring landing gear of 86 in. tread was of 2 streamlined legs braced to the fuselage; 7.50x10 or 8.50x10 wheels and tires were fitted with brakes. The fabric covered tail group was a composite structure; fixed surfaces were of wooden spars with sheet metal ribs and movable surfaces were of welded steel tubing. The rudder was balanced and the horizontal stabilizer was adjustable in flight. A Curtiss-Reed metal propeller, electric engine starter, Exide battery, generator, navigation lights, dual control wheel, wheel brakes, tail wheel, cabin heat and ventilation, fuel gauges, dome light, fire extinguisher, assist cords, ash trays, first-aid kit, tool kit, and log books were standard equipment. A radio set, bonding & shielding, landing lights, parachute flares, extra fuel tanks, extra instruments, drag flaps, and Edo twin-float gear were optional. A Hamilton-Standard con-trollable propeller was also optional. The next Waco development was the model YOC as described in the chapter for ATC # 569 of this volume.

Listed below are UOC entries as verified by factory records:

X-14613: UOC (# 3952) Continental 210.

NC-500: UOC (# 4295) Continental 210.

    : UOC (# 4333) Continental 210.

ZK-AEL: UOC (# 4336) Continental 210.

Ser. # 3952 used as prototype for models UOC-YOC-CUC; registration for ser. # 4295 was changed to NC-303E when NC-500 was transferred to an EQC-6; ser. # 4333 del. to Buenos Aires, Argentina; ser. # 4336 del. to Wellington, New Zealand — also reg. as ZK-ALA and NZ-575; approval expired 9-30-39.

ATC # 569
(5-17-35)
WACO, MODEL YOC.

Fig. 246. The YOC displays its handsome figure.

Somewhat like a healthy and curvy matron lady, the model YOC was a gently beautiful airplane, perhaps the most beautiful cabin biplane that Waco Aircraft had ever built. Curving and bulging in all the right places, the Jacobs-powered YOC "Custom Cabin" was a pleasant arrangement that was easy on the eyes and its "figure" played along nicely with the harsh demands of high-speed airflow. In the Waco "Custom Cabin" series the emphasis was more upon things attractive, comfortable, and stylish; therefore, it was a more or less pampered airplane and generally owned by a sportsman or an executive of some business-house. Of course, like any Waco, the YOC had no particular aversion to working, but it was treated more like a limousine rather than a station-wagon. About 4 of the YOC were exported, and the rest were scattered rather evenly around the U.S.A. Equipment varied in the YOC, according to customer's needs, but generally the airplanes were quite plush and embellished with numerous extras. Up to this point in early 1935, Waco airplanes, both open and cabin, were operating in Alaska, Argentina, Austria, Brazil, British E. Africa, Canada, Chile, China, Cuba, Egypt, England, France, Germany, Guatemala, Holland, Honduras, Mexico, Nicaragua, New Zealand, Norway, Paraguay, Philippine Islands, Salvador, and So. Africa; various 1933 and 1934 models had already been delivered to 14 of these countries.

The Waco model YOC was a cabin biplane with seating arranged for 4 or 5. The model YOC series contained no radical departure from normal Waco design practice, but the apparent differences, as compared to the "Standard" series, were considerable. The first noticeable difference was, of course, the configuration and the way it was proportioned. The shortened lower wing and the elliptical shaping of the wing-tips gave the new "Custom" series a look of speed and dash, in spite of its increased dimension and the taking on of some bulk. The roomier interior which offered extra space in front, and a rear seat wide enough for 3, was bound to become bulkier on the outside, but this had no detrimental effect whatever. In fact, the larger and bulkier "Custom" was some 7 m.p.h. faster than the smaller "Standard", using the same horsepower. A typical "Waco" airplane in every sense, the "Custom Cabin" series in a choice of 3 different engines for 1935, was a well-balanced combination of speed, comfort, safety, and reliability. The "Waco" airplane had come a long ways in ten years! As powered with the 7

Fig. 247. The Waco YOC with 225 h.p. Jacobs engine.

cyl. Jacobs L-4 engine rated 225 h.p. the model YOC offered excellent performance with pinch-penny economy, while still inheriting all the commendable "Waco" features. When the 285 h.p. Jacobs L-5 engine became available, several of the 225 h.p. model YOC versions were modified to take this new engine and became the YOC-1. The extra 60 h.p. made a noticeable difference in the entire performance range. The type certificate number for the model YOC was issued 5-17-35 and later amended to include the (285 h.p.) YOC-1. At least 50 examples of the model YOC were manufactured by the Waco Aircraft Co. at Troy, Ohio. The YOC was the

Fig. 248. Like other "Waco" biplanes, YOC was a go-anywhere airplane.

Fig. 249. YOC rides gently on Edo floats.

most popular of the 1935 "Custom" series.

Listed below are specifications and performance data for the Waco model YOC as powered with 225 h.p. Jacobs L-MB engine; length overall 25'6"; height overall 8'3"; wing span upper 35'0"; wing span lower 24'6"; wing chord upper 72"; wing chord lower 48"; wing area upper 165.6 sq. ft.; wing area lower 73.2 sq. ft.; total wing area 238.8 sq. ft.; airfoil Clark Y; wt. empty 1908 lbs.; useful load 1192 lbs.; payload with 50 gal. fuel 692 lbs. (3 pass. & 182 lbs. baggage, or 4 pass. & 12 lbs. baggage); gross wt. 3100 lbs.; max. speed 155 at 1000 ft.; cruising speed (1900 r.p.m.) 137 at 1000 ft.; landing speed 53; climb 760 ft. first min. at sea level; ser. ceiling 16,000 ft.; gas cap. 50 gal.; oil cap. 4 gal.; cruising range (1900 r.p.m.) at 14 gal. per hour 450 miles; price $6895. to $7295. at factory field. Note: 3100 lb. max. gross wt. allowed on 7.50x-10 tires, and 3200 lb. max. gross wt. allowed on 8.50x10 tires; 3200 lb. max. gross wt. with wooden or adj. metal propeller and 3350 lb. max. gross wt. with controllable propeller.

The model YOC-1 with Jacobs L-5MB engine rated 285 h.p. was identical to specifications above, except as follows: length overall 25'4"; wt. empty 2260 lbs.; useful load 1090 lbs.; payload with 50 gal. fuel 590 lbs. (3 pass. & 80 lbs. baggage); gross wt. 3350 lbs. with Hamilton-Standard controllable propeller; max. speed 162 at 1000 ft.; cruising speed 132 at 1000 ft.; landing speed 57; climb 920 ft. first min. sea level; ser. ceiling 16,500 ft.; gas cap. 50-70 gal.; oil cap. 4-5 gal.; price approx. $7995. at factory field.

The construction details and general arrangement of the YOC were typical to that of the model UOC as described here in the chapter for ATC # 568. Unless otherwise noted, the following will apply to either UOC-YOC-CUC. Three persons were allowed on the rear seat when adjustment was made to baggage allowance to compensate for the added weight. Front seats were 17 inches wide, rear seat was 3 inches wider than on the "Standard" series, and 6 inches was added to floor space between seats. Curved panels in the windshield were shatter-proof glass; quarter windows and skylight were of Pyralin. The baggage compartment (with allowance for 100 lbs.) was enlarged for bulkier bags, with access from the inside or a large door on left side of the fuselage. Metal-framed ailerons were covered with dural sheet and mounted on the upper wings only; adjustable "tab" was provided on one aileron for lateral trim. Electrically operated "drag flaps", on underside of upper wing, were optional; not to be extended above 112 m.p.h. A 25 gal. fuel tank was mounted in root end of each upper wing-half; 35 gal. or 47.5 gal. tanks were optional. A Hartzell wooden propeller, electric engine starter, generator, battery, and throw-over control wheel were standard equipment. Landing lights, parachute flares, bonding & shielding, radio set, metal wheel pants, Curtiss-Reed metal propeller, leather upholstery, Y-type control column, extra door and wing-walk on right side, skis, Edo pontoons, and custom colors were optional. The YOC-1 was eligible with a Hamilton-Standard controllable-pitch propeller. The next development in the "Custom Cabin" series was the Wright-powered model CUC as described in the chapter for ATC # 575 of this volume.

Listed below are YOC and YOC-1 entries as verified by company records:

NC-14613; YOC (# 3952)   Jacobs L-4
   -14615;   "   (# 4240)   "

Fig. 250. YOC in service for State of Indiana.

-14616:	"	(#4241)	"
-14619:	"	(#4243)	"
:	"	(#4244)	"
-14621:	"	(#4245)	"
-14624:	"	(#4246)	"
-14626:	"	(#4248)	"
-14622:	"	(#4270)	"
-14628:	"	(#4271)	"
-14629:	"	(#4272)	"
-14678:	"	(#4273)	"
-14677:	"	(#4274)	"
-14681:	"	(#4275)	"
-14680:	"	(#4276)	"
:	"	(#4278)	"
NS-40Y:	"	(#4279)	"
-14686:	"	(#4280)	"
-14682:	"	(#4281)	"
-14683:	"	(#4282)	"
-14684:	"	(#4283)	"
-15200:	"	(#4287)	"
-14690:	"	(#4288)	"
-15201:	"	(#4289)	"
-15204:	"	(#4291)	"
-15208:	"	(#4292)	"

-15202:	"	(#4293)	"
-15206:	"	(#4294)	"
-15207:	"	(#4296)	"
-15209:	YOC-1	(#4297)	Jacobs L-5
-15210:	YOC	(#4298)	Jacobs L-4
-15212:	"	(#4299)	"
-15216:	YOC-1	(#4300)	Jacobs L-5
-15211:	"	(#4301)	"
-15215:	YOC	(#4305)	Jacobs L-4
-15217:	"	(#4306)	"
-15219:	"	(#4307)	"
-15225:	"	(#4308)	"
-15221:	"	(#4310)	"
-15226:	"	(#4315)	"
-15229:	"	(#4317)	"
-15235:	"	(#4320)	"
-15234:	"	(#4321)	"
-15239:	"	(#4325)	"
:	"	(#4326)	"
-15244:	YOC-1	(#4327)	Jacobs L-5
-15242:	YOC	(#4328)	Jacobs L-4
-15243:	"	(#4329)	"
-15248:	YOC-1	(#4330)	Jacobs L-5
-15247:	YOC	(#4331)	Jacobs L-4
-15246:	"	(#4332)	"
-15704:	"	(#4337)	"
PP-EAA:	"	(#4338)	"

This approval for ser. # 3952 and up; ser. # 4244 and 4278 del. to Johannesburg, So. Africa; ser. # 4279 del. to State of Indiana, later registered as NC-17740; ser. # 4282 and 4289 later modified to YOC-1; ser. # 4288 static tested to destruction at Wright Field 3-1-37; ser. # 4292 del. to Hanford Air Lines; ser. # 4294 del. to Ball Bros. (Mason Jars); ser. # 4297 first as YOC; ser. # 4300, 4301, 4327, 4330 first reg. as CUC-1; ser. # 4320 del. to Alaska; ser. # 4326 del. to Buenos Aires, Argentina; ser. # 4338 del. to Brazil—later reg. as PP-TBI; this approval expired 9-30-39.

Fig. 251. Douglas DC2-115H with 720 h.p. "Hornet" engines poses in Holland.

Of the seventy-five to one hundred DC-2 airliners that were already flying it would be imposible to tell at a glance that a few of these were powered with Pratt & Whitney engines. The big 9 cyl. radial Wright "Cyclone" engine was the normal installation in the various versions of the DC-2, whether used here or abroad, but as is often the case, a few customers would want powerplants that differed from the standard installation. When the Standard Oil Co. of Calif. ordered a DC-2 (as # 8 in their fleet) they specified a plush "Club" version for transport of executives, with a custom interior; the powerplants in this airplane were Pratt & Whitney "Hornet" SDG engines of 700 h.p. each. It would be interesting to know what dictated the preference. World-famous KLM, the far-flung Royal Dutch airline, already had several of the standard DC-2 with Wright "Cyclone" engines, but for some reason one ex-

ample, a DC2-115H, was powered with 2 "Hornet" S8EG engines rated 720 h.p. each. Perhaps this was done to run a comparison between the two installations. The Standard Oil Co. version, also referred to as the DC-2A, was used regularly for nearly a year and then it came to grief. For some unknown reason the craft made a forced landing into the Great Salt Lake of Utah; the crew aboard survived the crash, but perished when trying to swim to safety. The DC2-115H version, called the "Toekan" in Dutch, was delivered to KLM in May of 1935 and served almost without incident until May of 1940. As war clouds were gathering in Europe, it was captured by the German Air Force as a war prize.

The Douglas DC2-115H was an all-metal, low-winged, transport monoplane with seating arranged for 16 to 17 passengers, 2 pilots, and a steward or stewardess. The (Standard Oil Co.)

Fig. 252. DC-2H in service for Standard Oil Co. of Calif.

DC-2A-127 was an executive-type transport with max. seating for 16 people. Both of these airplanes were similar to other craft in the DC-2 series except for the engine installation; the modification was, of course, dictated by personal preference in either case. The engines are the very heart of an airplane, and if a customer felt more at ease with having one "brand" of engine over another, it behooved Douglas Aircraft to comply and the customer was liable for the extra expense. Because of similar power output, no matter what engines were used, be they "Wright" or "Pratt & Whitney", the airplanes performed more or less the same; the only difference noted, to a trained ear, would be the sound because engines do sound different if you listen to their distinctive "tune". There may have been more DC-2 powered with Pratt & Whitney engines, but available listings failed to confirm it. The type certificate number for the DC2-115H was issued 5-20-35 and perhaps no more than one example of this model was built. It is believed, at this point, that the DC-2A for Standard Oil Co. was manufactured under a Group 2 approval. The Douglas Aircraft Co. was at Santa Monica, Calif. Donald W. Douglas was pres.; Harry H. Wetzel was gen. mgr.; Arthur E. Raymond had replaced "Dutch" Kindelberger as chf. engr.; and Carl A. Cover was demo-pilot and sales mgr. By 1936, in a veritable criss-cross of the nation, DC-2 equipped airlines could fly you anywhere overnight; wherever you are you can be anywhere else by tomorrow morning, they promised.

Listed below are specifications and performance data for the Douglas DC2-115H as powered with 2 "Hornet" S8EG engines rated 720 h.p. each; length overall 62'0"; height overall 16'3"; wing span 85'0"; wing chord at root 170" tapered to tip; total wing area 939 sq. ft.; airfoil at root NACA-2215; airfoil at tip NACA-2209; wt. empty 12,010 (12,185) lbs.; useful load 6190 (6375) lbs.; payload with 360 gal. fuel 3405 (3590) lbs. (16 pass. & 685 or 870 lbs. of baggage-cargo); gross wt. 18,200 (18,560) lbs.; figures in parentheses as later amended; max. speed 212 at 7500 ft.; cruising speed (.75 power) 195 at 14,000 ft.; cruising speed (.63 power) 186 at 10,000 ft.; landing speed (with flaps) 62; climb 1000 ft. first min. at sea level; ser. ceiling 22,400 ft.; gas cap. normal 360 gal.; gas cap. max. 510 gal.; oil cap. 38 gal.; cruising range (.75 power) at 96 gal. per hour 650 miles; price approx. $65,000.

The Douglas DC2-115H and the DC-2A-127 were both identical to other aircraft in the DC-2 series except for the engine installation and the changes necessary for this modification. The DC-2A for the Standard Oil Co. of Calif. was an "executive transport" and the DC2-115H for KLM (Royal Dutch Airlines) was a regular airliner with seating arranged for up to 20 people. The DC-2A was listed with "Hornet" SDG engines rated 700 h.p. at 2100 r.p.m. at 6500 ft., and the DC2-115H was listed with "Hornet" S8EG engines rated 720 h.p. at 2100 r.p.m. at 7000 ft. Both engines were swinging 3-bladed Hamilton-Standard controllable propellers. Electric engine starters, battery, generator, fuel pumps, dual controls, Lux and Pyrene fire ex-

Fig. 253. DC2-115H of KLM line awaits loading for night flight.

tinguishers, navigation lights, landing lights, parachute flares, lavatory, pantry, heating & ventilation, cabin dome lights, reading lamps, luggage rack, hat net, complete set of engine & flight instruments, and first-aid kit were standard equipment. Two-way radio, auto-pilot, and custom interior were optional. The next Douglas development was the model DST "Sleeper" as described in the chapter for ATC # 607.

Listed below are only known DC-2 as powered with Pratt & Whitney engines:

NC-14285; DC-2A-127 (# 1328) 2 Hornet 700.
PH-AKT; DC2-115H (# 1366) 2 Hornet 720.
Ser. # 1328 (Standard Oil Co.) del. Nov. 1934, crashed Oct. 1935; ser. # 1366 del. to KLM in May 1935, captured May 1940.

Fig. 254. Legend on side of DC2-115H translates loosely into Royal Dutch Air Lines.

Fig. 255. Ryan STA with 125 h.p. Menasco engine; Peter Dana aboard.

One of the biggest surprises in airplane development has been the history of the Ryan ST. The first reaction upon its introduction in 1934 was more or less—"It's cute, but who is gonna buy it"? A dour industry grown edgy and vitriolic after several disappointing years, predicted very little success for the noisy upstart. True, nothing much happened to the model ST that first year or so, but then this little airplane began selling faster than it could be produced. Claude Ryan was smart enough to know where aviation's money was spent, and he went after the business. Before the first surprise was barely over, another surprise was brewing on the assembly floor. The Ryan STA "Super Sport" was the new surprise; it was practically identical to the 95 h.p. ST, but the 125 h.p. Menasco C-4 engine coursed extra vigor through the frame of the new STA and it clamored for attention. To make people notice, the model STA went after various records and it wasn't very long before everyone in aviation knew just what the Ryan STA was, and what it could do when it took the notion. Twenty-year old Peter Dana, a great grandson of Henry Wadsworth Longfellow, and at one time the youngest "transport pilot" in the U.S.A., started things off by flying from Calif. to the east coast in 22 hours 6 mins. for a lightplane record. Jovial "Tex" Rankin had set an altitude record for lightplanes by climbing to 19,800 ft. over Florida. Rankin loved this airplane and became one of its loudest boosters; as a factory representative in 1936 he demonstrated the airplane nationwide. As it turned out, he really showed the STA off by some very fancy flying, but did very little selling because he couldn't stay out of the cockpit long enough to talk business. In May of 1937 at St. Louis,

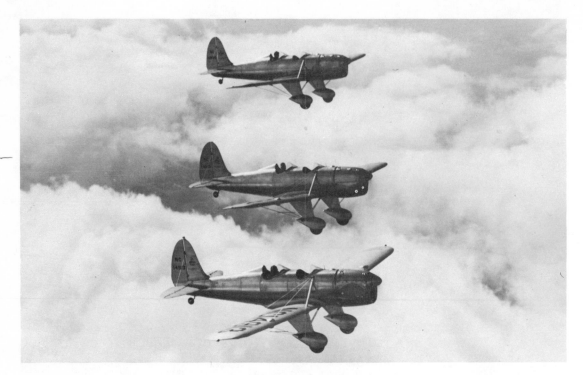

Fig. 256. Trio of STA over clouds above San Diego.

"Tex" Rankin won the International Aerobatic Championship in a Ryan STA against a field of special "stunt planes". The STA he used was strictly stock, in fact it had been training students for 7 months prior to the contest at St. Louis. A gathering of slender shapes melted into a form that was pleasant from any angle, people were first attracted to the Ryan STA by its silvery beauty, and then thrilled by its remarkable performance. The STA was selling in good number and it held a promise of a great future; some were delivered fly-away and some were delivered in box-car loads. Because of its advanced basic design the model STA remained "new" for at least the next decade; as a true sportplane it will never be outmoded. Even what few are left today will draw a crowd of admirers at least 4 deep, and some will wonder why they don't build airplanes like that any more.

The Ryan model STA was a metal-framed, wire-braced, low-winged, open cockpit monoplane with seating arranged for 2 in tandem. Patterned like a racing airplane the STA was actually a sportplane at heart, but it could be bridled into training student pilots. The Ryan School of Aeronautics had several model STA in its lineup and it was used from the first timid maneuvers of a fledgling pilot to the advanced maneuvers of expert aerobatics. The flying school that had an STA in its lineup was assured of extra business. Because of its nature the Ryan STA was attracted to the sportsman and the roster of owners was studded with many famous names. In aviation circles the good news travels fast and the good word about the "STA"

soon brought inquiries from all over the world; the silvery little monoplane was the subject of excited hangar-talk in many far-flung countries. As powered with the 4 cyl. inverted inline air-cooled Menasco C-4 engine rated 125 h.p. at 2175 r.p.m. the slender STA was a lively piece of machinery that was definitely a tom-boy in nature and pretty much of a show-off. For just flying around in gentle patterns it was a perfect lady with good manners, but if you were so inclined, the STA could do just about anything you were willing to try; it was not the least bit awkward in any maneuver. Trim of figure, with curves in the right places, the STA had a definitely feminine personality; it was lovely, vivacious, and didn't like to be ignored. A few of the Ryan STA are still flying and despite their age, have lost none of their feminine charms. The type certificate number for the Ryan model STA was issued 5-23-35 and at least 71 examples of this model were manufactured by the Ryan Aeronautical Co. on Lindbergh Field in San Diego, Calif.

Listed below are specifications and performance data for the model STA as powered with the 125 h.p. Menasco C-4 engine; length overall 21'6"; height overall 6'11"; wing span 29'11"; wing chord 56"; total wing area 124 sq. ft.; airfoil NACA-2412; wt. empty 1027 (1035) lbs.; useful load 543 (565) lbs.; payload with 24 gal. fuel 214 (236) lbs.; gross wt. 1570 (1600) lbs.; baggage 40 lbs.; figures in parentheses as later amended; max. speed 150 at sea level; cruising speed (.75 power) 127 at 2000 ft.; landing speed (no flaps) 50; landing speed (with flaps) 42; take-

Fig. 257. Lineup at factory of STA awaiting delivery.

Fig. 258. Ryan STA shows its slender figure.

Fig. 259. Early morning lineup of STA trainers.

off run 525 ft.; climb 1200 ft. first min. at sea level; ser. ceiling 17,500 ft.; cruising range (2000 r.p.m.) at 8.4 gal. per hour 350 miles; price $4685. at factory field.

The construction details and general arrangement of the model STA were typical to that of the Ryan ST as described in the chapter for ATC # 541 of this volume. It is only natural that some changes and improvements were made as production continued. For the trainer, dual stick controls and instruments in the front cockpit were optional. As a single-place sportplane, extra fuel (16.5 or 24 gal.) and extra baggage were optional in front cockpit; in this case the front cockpit was covered with a removable metal panel. Normal baggage allowance was 40 lbs. in a compartment between the cockpits. The flap operating mechanism was changed to the lever type, replacing the worm-gear type. When flown solo, pilot must occupy the rear cockpit; parachutes, when carried, were deducted from the baggage allowance. The swiveling tail-wheel was provided with a fore-and-aft lock. On later models, the Menasco D-4 engine with down-draft carburetor was optional; a wooden propeller was standard, but a metal propeller was optional. Seat cushions, safety belts, 18x8-3 Goodyear airwheels, wheel streamlines, 8 in. tail wheel, wheel brakes, wiring for navigation lights, wing flaps, elevator trim tab, Pyralin windshields, and first-aid kit were standard equipment. Electric engine starter, battery,

navigation lights, dual sticktype controls, and radio equipment were optional. The next Ryan development was the 150 h.p. STA Special as described in the chapter for ATC # 681.

Listed below are Ryan STA entries as verified by company records:

NC-14910:	STA	(# 103)	Menasco C-4.
-14912:	"	(# 105)	"
-14913:	"	(# 106)	"
-14914:	"	(# 107)	"
-14952:	"	(# 108)	"
-14953:	"	(# 109)	"
-14954:	"	(# 110)	"
-14955:	"	(# 111)	"
-14956:	"	(# 112)	"
-14957:	"	(# 113)	"
-14982:	"	(# 114)	"
-14983:	"	(# 115)	"
-14984:	"	(# 116)	"
-14986:	"	(# 118)	"
-14987:	"	(# 119)	"
-16031:	"	(# 120)	"
-16033:	"	(# 122)	"
-16034:	"	(# 123)	"
-16035:	"	(# 124)	"
-16036:	"	(# 125)	"
-16037:	"	(# 126)	"
-16038:	"	(# 127)	"
-16039:	"	(# 128)	"
-16040:	"	(# 129)	"
-16041:	"	(# 130)	"

-16042:	"	(# 131)	"
-16043:	"	(# 132)	"
-16044:	"	(# 133)	"
-17300:	"	(# 134)	"
-17301:	"	(# 135)	"
-17302:	"	(# 136)	"
-17303:	"	(# 137)	"
-17304:	"	(# 138)	"
-17305:	"	(# 139)	"
-17306:	"	(# 140)	"
:	"	(# 142)	"
-17343:	"	(# 143)	"
-17344:	"	(# 144)	"
:	"	(# 145)	"
:	"	(# 146)	"
:	"	(# 147)	"
-17345:	"	(# 148)	"
-17346:	"	(# 149)	"
-17347:	"	(# 150)	"
-17348:	"	(# 151)	"
-17349:	"	(# 152)	"
-17350:	"	(# 153)	"
-17351:	"	(# 154)	"
-17352:	"	(# 156)	"
-17353:	"	(# 157)	"
ZS-AKZ:	"	(# 158)	"
-17354:	"	(# 159)	"
-17355:	"	(# 160)	"

-17356:	"	(# 161)	"
-17357:	"	(# 162)	"
-17358:	"	(# 163)	"
-17360:	"	(# 165)	"
-17361:	"	(# 166)	"
-17362:	"	(# 167)	"
:	"	(# 168)	"
:	"	(# 169)	"
-17365:	"	(# 170)	"
-17366:	"	(# 171)	"
-17367:	"	(# 172)	"
-17370:	"	(# 175)	"
-17371:	"	(# 176)	"
-17364:	"	(# 177)	"
-16037:	"	(# 178)	"
-18901:	"	(# 179)	"
-18902:	"	(# 198)	"
NC-9:	"	(# 355)	"

This approval for ser. #103 and up; ser. #103 delivered to Peter Dana; ser. # 108, and 114 del. to Hawaii; ser. # 126-127 del. to Brazil; ser. # 130 del. to Betty Lund; ser. # 132 and 147 del. to Australia; ser. # 142, 145, 146, 158, 168, 169 del. to So. Africa; ser. # 165 del. to Venezuela; ser. # 179 to Laura Ingalls; ser. # 355 (mfgd. 1940) del. to C.A.A.; this approval expired 7-24-41.

ATC # 572
(5-28-35)
TAYLOR "CUB", H-2.

Fig. 260. Taylor "Cub" H-2 had 3 cyl. Szekely engine; the H-2 was extremely rare.

According to (airplane designer) C. Gilbert Taylor's own words he was not entirely satisfied with putting the 4 cyl. Continental A-40 engine in the two-seated "Cub". He did favor the little (French) 9 cyl. radial Salmson AD-9 because it intrigued him, but it was impossible to expect continuous large shipments of these engines from France, so he cast about for other engines made in the U.S.A. The "Cub" did well with the 3 cyl. Aeromarine AR3-40 as the model F-2, but various little problems ruled this out as a choice also. Of considerable mechanical aptitude, Taylor went so far as to design his own engine which he installed in a "Cub" model G-2, and while he was working out various details in and about the new engine he decided to try the 3 cyl. Szekely SR-3-35 engine as a powerplant for the "Cub" also. The Szekely-powered "Cub" as the model H-2, was more or less an experiment too and nothing ever happened with this combination either. Only a few of the model H-2 were built and some of these were shipped off to foreign countries, apparently where operators were less apt to be dissatisfied and less likely to complain. Much about the "Cub" H-2 is a mystery due to scarcity of data and the unreliability of memory. It raises a question why this combination was ever certificated in the first place. The Szekely engine and its manufacturer

were both having problems of one sort or another at this time and the Bureau of Air Commerce was actually considering to disqualify certain Szekely engines for installation in approved airplanes. However, the model H-2 like the E-2, F-2 and G-2 models before it, was a milestone in "Cub" development and should be given its due credit in this family of airplanes. Meanwhile, the Continental A-40 engine was steadily being improved and was installed in the model J-2, a version that skyrocketed the "Cub" to unbelievable popularity.

The rarely-seen Taylor "Cub" model H-2 was a light high-winged monoplane with seating arranged for 2 in tandem. Normally, the cabin area was left with open sides, but a bolt-on enclosure was available for cold-weather flying. Except for one example, which was a test-bed for other engines also, most of the Szekely-powered H-2 were modified into this new version from existing model F-2. Why the Aeromarine engines were pulled from the F-2 and replaced with the Szekely SR-3-35 engines we cannot say; it seemed to be an unlikely swap. The "Cub" was not one to complain no matter what engine was up front, within reason of course, and tried to do her best even under handicap. A remarkable thing like this can get to you in time, and that is probably one reason why the "Cub" became so popular around the country. The model H-2, like all "Cubs", was flown solo from the rear seat only. As powered with the 3 cyl. Szekely SR-3-35 engine rated 35 h.p. at 1700 r.p.m. we can assume that the model H-2 was perhaps capable of a performance quite similar to that of the E-2. In fact, a low-revving engine such as the Szekely, swinging a larger propeller, would generally have the advantage over a fast-turning engine swinging a smaller prop, if the horsepower ratings were nearly equal. It would be interesting to hear from pilots that flew the H-2, but the odds against that are of needle-in-the-haystack proportion. Every one knows of the "Cub", but not many know about the model H-2. A small claim to fame happened to the H-2 on 19 June 1937 when Miss Beverly Dodge, carrying a woman passenger, flew the Szekely-powered "Cub" to an altitude of 16,800 ft. over Honolulu for a new record for women pilots. This was some indication that the model H-2 was not a complete dud. The type certificate number for the "Cub" model H-2 was issued 5-28-35 and at least 4, or perhaps more, were modified under this type certificate. Modification was engineered by the Taylor Aircraft Co. at Bradford, Penn.

Listed below are specifications and performance data for the "Cub" model H-2 as powered with 35 h.p. Szekely SR-3-35 engine; length overall 22'1"; height overall 6'6"; wing span 35'3"; wing chord 63"; total wing area 184 sq. ft.; airfoil USA-35B; wt. empty 582 lbs.; useful load 406 lbs.; payload with 9 gal. fuel 175 lbs.; gross wt. 988 lbs.; max. speed 80; cruising speed 70; landing speed 30; climb 435 ft. first min. at sea level; ser. ceiling 12,000 ft.; gas cap. 9 gal.; oil cap. 4 qts.; cruising range at 2.5 gal. per hour 220 miles; price for modification not announced.

The construction details and general arrangement of the "Cub" model H-2 were practically identical to that of the models E-2 and F-2 except for the engine mount, engine cowling, and whatever modifications were necessary for this combination. Two seats were arranged in tandem and occupants were protected by a large Pyralin windshield in front; the cabin sides were open, but a Pyralin enclosure was available. A large let-down door on the right side provided step-over entry; a baggage shelf with allowance for 5 lbs. was behind the rear seat. A 9 gal. fuel tank was mounted high in the fuselage ahead of the windshield; a bobber-type float was used as a fuel-level gauge. The fabric-covered wing framework, in 2 halves, was braced to fuselage longeron with streamlined steel tube struts. The landing gear of 56 in. tread, with faired in vees, was a simple tripod affair and snubbed with rubber shock-cord rings; the Goodyear 7.00x4 airwheels were not equipped with brakes. The welded steel tube tail group was fabric covered; horizontal stabilizer was adjustable in flight. A wooden Sensenich propeller, and dual stick-type controls were standard equipment. Wheel brakes, and winter enclosure were optional. The next "Cub" development was the famous model J-2 as described in the chapter for ATC # 595 of this volume.

Listed below are "Cub" H-2 entries as gleaned from registration records:

NC-12668; H-2 (# 40) SR-3-35.
NC-2735; H-2 (# 66) SR-3-35.
NC-13272; H-2 (# 74) SR-3-35.
NC-14756; H-2 (# 149) SR-3-35.

This approval for ser. # 40, 66, 74 and up; ser. # 40, 66, and 74 were first as model F-2 with Aeromarine AR3-40 engine; PP-TCX was an H-2 in Brazil, ser. no. unknown; X-14756 (ser. # 149) first as model G-2 with Taylor 40-50 h.p. engine; this approval expired 3-24-37.

ATC # 573
(6-8-35)
CESSNA, MODEL C-34.

Fig. 261. The remarkable C-34 with 145 h.p. "Super Scarab" engine.

There was suppressed excitement during mid-year of 1934 in the reopened Cessna plant at Wichita. Largely because a new "Cessna Cantilever Monoplane" was shaping up on the assembly floor. From some angles it looked rather familiar, but anyone could soon tell it promised to be a better "Cessna" airplane in every way. Finally rolled out in June of 1935 the orange and blue prototype was flown by George Harte on its maiden flight, and even the most optimistic calculations made had been justified. Tutored by Clyde V. Cessna, the old master, nephew Dwane L. Wallace had learned his lessons well and they fit in perfectly with what he had in mind. Using the basic design of previous "Cessna" monoplanes and applying aeronautical techniques developed since, Wallace and Tom Salter managed to improve on past performance and introduced a bright new personality. Labeled simply as the Model C-34 the new "Cessna" monoplane was entered in the 1000 mile All-Kansas Air Tour to show it off to local operators; a highlight of the air tour was a 25 mile free-for-all race which Geo. Harte and the new C-34 had won easily. Cessna Aircraft was not one to say "we told you so", but they did say emphatically and often that the new Cessna C-34, using only 145 h.p., was perhaps the most efficient airplane of its time. To justify what they had been saying all along, Cessna entered the fourth C-34 off the production line in the

National Air Races held at Cleveland in Aug.-Sept. of 1935. With Geo. Harte again doing the flying, the yellow and blue C-34 proved itself beyond doubt to be a most efficient airplane by winning 7 trophies, including the coveted 4-event "Detroit News Air Transport Trophy" awarded for highest efficiency. In this event the formula was based on speed, economy, minumum takeoff and minimum landing capabilities with full load; extra points were also earned for comfort and safety. The "Cessna" C-34 won this trophy at the N.A.R. held in Los Angeles the next year also with Dwane Wallace flying and was finally acclaimed the "World's Most Efficient Airplane" by having won this event 3 times; Eldon Cessna flying a "Cessna AW" had won this event for Cessna Aircraft the first time in the air races of 1931. Everyone at the Cessna plant was happy, of course, but Clyde V. Cessna was not surprised—he had been preaching the efficiency of "Cessna Cantilever Monoplanes" since 1927. Clyde V. Cessna sold his interest in the company to his 2 nephews, Dwane and Dwight Wallace, in 1935. He still puttered around the factory and finally retired in Oct. of 1936; he was happy with the way things were going.

The "Cessna" model C-34 was a high-winged cabin monoplane with seating arranged for four. Typical of previous Cessna designs the C-34 was a cantilever (internally braced) monoplane that

Fig. 262. A C-34 delivered to Mexico; others went to Argentina, Portugal, So. Africa, and England.

eliminated all of the drag-producing struts and braces normally seen on other airplanes. As far back as 1927 the "Cessna Cantilever Monoplane" was known for its speed and its uncanny performance with engines of low horsepower. The models A and AW were lean and sassy machines, but the new C-34 was padded and fattened to a rather nice figure, and conducted itself with a nice even temper. The remarkable thing about the C-34 was the way it wrung out all that performance from 145 h.p. without seeming strain or very much fuss. Unencumbered by braces and struts the airframe was fashioned in simple grace and blessed with plenty of strength; the C-34 was nice to have around and most of them led a long and useful life. The roster of owners contained no famous names, nor names in big business, but ownership was scattered all over the country and owners were quick to show-off and to praise their airplane. Two of the C-34 were exported to England, one to Canada, and one to Mexico. As powered with the 7 cyl. Warner "Super Scarab" engine rated 145 h.p. at 2050 r.p.m. one must admit the C-34 had remarkable capabilities with this amount of power. Carrying 4 average people, and baggage, the C-34 operated well from the high country and all the little airports; with range enough for 550 miles the C-34 covered better than 35 miles every 15 minutes. The C-34 was a pleasant airplane with no bad habits and no worrisome tendencies; certainly not as capricious as the older "Cessna AW", but she tippy-toed on a rather narrow landing gear and had to be led around firmly like a partner on the dance-floor. The type certificate number for the Model C-34

was issued 6-8-35 and some 41 or more examples of this model were manufactured by Cessna Aircraft Co., Inc. at Wichita, Kan. Clyde V. Cessna was pres.; A. K. Longren was V.P.; Dwane L. Wallace was gen. mgr. & chf. engr.; Tom Salter asst. engr.; and George Harte was contracted for test and promotion. After retirement of Clyde V. Cessna in 1936, Dwane Wallace became president. In 1942, 2 of the C-34 were pressed into war-time service with the USAAF as the UC-77B.

Listed below are specifications and performance data for the Cessna model C-34 as powered with 145 h.p. Warner "Super Scarab" engine: length overall 24'7"; height overall 7'3"; wing span 33'10"; wing chord at root 84"; wing chord at tip 58.6"; total wing area 180.5 sq. ft.; airfoil NACA-2412; wt. empty 1220 (1300) lbs.; useful load 980 (920) lbs.; payload with 35 gal. fuel 574 (514) lbs. (3 pass. & up to 64 lbs. baggage); gross wt. 2200 (2220) lbs.; figures in parentheses as later amended; max. speed 162 at sea level; cruising speed (1925 r.p.m.) 143; landing speed (with flaps) 47; landing speed (no flaps) 54; climb 800 ft. first min. at sea level; ser. ceiling 18,900 ft.; gas cap. 35 gal.; oil cap. 3.5 gal.; cruising range (1925 r.p.m.) at 9 gal. per hour 550 miles; normal baggage allowance 48 lbs.; price $4985. at factory. Landplane gross wt. later increased to 2250 lbs. The C-34 was also eligible as a seaplane on Edo pontoons; with Edo 44-2425 twin-float gear & Curtiss-Reed metal propeller the C-34 was 1476 lbs. empty, useful load was 1024 lbs., and gross wt. was at 2500 lbs. Performance suffered accordingly from extra drag and weight.

Fig. 263. The C-34 shows profile of speed and strength.

The fuselage framework was built up of welded chrome-moly steel tubing, faired to shape with wooden formers and fairing strips, then fabric covered. The engine was mounted in rubber, encased in an NACA cowl, and fitted with cooling-air pressure baffles; front of the fuselage was covered with dural panels back to the doors. A large entry door and convenient step was provided on each side; front seats were individual with a bench-type seat in back. Tastefully upholstered, the sound-proofed interior was fitted with fresh air vents and cabin heat; a baggage compartment was behind the rear seat with allowance for up to 64 lbs. The cantilever wing framework was built up of solid (laminated) spruce spar beams of one continuous piece, with spruce and plywood truss-type wing ribs; the leading edges were covered with plywood sheet and the completed framework was covered in fabric. Split-type trailing edge wing flaps of wooden framework (later of metal) were worm-gear actuated by hand crank or electric motor; not to be lowered above 108 m.p.h. Two fuel tanks of 17.5 gal. each were mounted in the wing. The cantilever landing gear, with a single leg on each side, used oil-spring shock struts of 6 inch travel; 21 in. streamlined wheels with brakes were fitted with "General" streamlined tires. Goodyear 22x10-4 airwheels or 6.50x10 Warner wheels with brakes and low-pressure tires were optional. The C-34 was planned with a retractable landing gear, but mechanical complexity voided its use. The C-34

was also eligible as a seaplane on Edo 44-2425 twin-float gear. The vertical fin and horizontal stabilizer were of wooden cantilever framework with formed plywood leading edges; rudder and elevators were of welded steel tubing. All control surfaces were covered with fabric. The 8 in. tail wheel was full-swivel with a fore-and-aft lock. A Hartzell wooden propeller, electric engine starter, Exide battery, wheel brakes, combination parking brake and rudder lock, dual controls, safety belts, tail wheel, NACA engine cowl, trim tab on left elevator, compass, fuel gauges, cabin heater, and first-aid kit were standard equipment. A metal propeller, engine-driven or wind-driven generator, navigation lights, landing lights, parachute flares, fire extinguisher, radio, bonding & shielding, extra fuel tank, skis, and Edo pontoons were optional. The next "Cessna" development was the model C-37 as described in the chapter for ATC # 622. Listed below are Cessna C-34 entries as gleaned from registration records.

NC-12599: C-34 (# 254) Warner 145.
   -14425;   "   (# 255)   "
   -14460;   "   (# 300)   "
   -15462;   "   (# 301)   "
   -15463;   "   (# 302)   "
   -15464;   "   (# 303)   "
   -15465;   "   (# 304)   "
   -15466;   "   (# 305)   "
   -15467;   "   (# 306)   "
   -15468;   "   (# 307)   "
   -15469;   "   (# 308)   "

Fig. 264. C-34 that was a big winner at 1936 National Air Races.

-15470;	"	(# 309)	"
-15471;	"	(# 310)	"
-15819;	"	(# 311)	"
:	"	(# 312)	"
:	"	(# 313)	"
G-AEAI;	"	(# 314)	"
-15821;	"	(# 315)	"
-15820;	"	(# 316)	"
-15850;	"	(# 317)	"
-15851;	"	(# 318)	"
-16409;	"	(# 319)	"
-15852;	"	(# 320)	"
-16402;	"	(# 321)	"
-16403;	"	(# 322)	"
-16404;	"	(# 323)	"
-16405;	"	(# 324)	"
-16406;	"	(# 325)	"
-16407;	"	(# 326)	"
-16408;	"	(# 327)	"
-16453;	"	(# 328)	"
-16452;	"	(# 329)	"
X-17070;	"	(# 330)	"

-16454;	"	(# 331)	"
-16455;	"	(# 332)	"
-17050;	"	(# 333)	"
-17051;	"	(# 334)	"
-17052;	"	(# 335)	"
:	"	(# 336)	"
-17054;	"	(# 337)	"
-17055;	"	(# 338)	"
VH-KWM;	"	(# 339)	"
:	"	(# 340)	"

This approval for ser. # 254, 255, 300 and up; ser. # 255 later as XB-AJO in Mexico; ser. # 301 was flown to victory at 1935 National Air Races; ser. #312 to Portugal; ser. # 313 to Argentina; ser. # 336, 340 to So. Africa; ser. # 339 to Australia; ser. # 314 del. to England; ser. # 319 later as G-AFBY in England; ser. # 320 was flown to victory at 1936 National Air Races—later as CF-BDI in Canada; ser. # 330 later used as prototype for C-37 series; this approval expired 9-30-39.

ATC # 574
(6-12-35)
REARWIN "SPORTSTER", 7000.

Fig. 265. Rearwin "Sportster" 7000 with 70 h.p. LeBlond engine.

At first glance it would appear that the new "Sportster" by Rearwin Airplanes and the previously-introduced "Flyabout" by Porterfield were cut out with the same cookie-cutter. Perhaps Rearwin did borrow the cookie-cutter from Porterfield and bent the edges around for a slightly different shape; both airplanes were no doubt influenced into development by Noel Hockaday's "Wyandotte Pup" and the similarity of one with the other was frequently disconcerting. By comparison with the "Porterfield" the Rearwin "Sportster" was a little longer, a bit taller, slightly heavier, had more wing area, had vee-shaped struts to hold the wing on, the windshield was rounder, and the fuselage was faired out a little deeper; otherwise, they were pretty much the same and this was no discredit to either airplane. In some ways, the Rearwin had more to offer and was a better airplane. As a tandem-seated monoplane the Rearwin "Sportster" was an ideal trainer, but it was presented more often as a sport-plane to pilots of moderate means. Rearwin Airplanes suspended all production in 1932 and spent the following two years developing several new airplanes, notably the famous "Speedster" and the "Sportster". Based on previous developments, the "Sportster", more or less, was a refinement of the earlier "Junior" design; the new design

and its engineering was largely the work of Wm. Henry Weeks. As powered with the 5 cyl. LeBlond 5DE engine of 70 h.p. the prototype "Model 7000" was lifted off on its maiden flight by Jack LeClaire on the 30th of April in 1935; everyone was enthused with the new airplane. In July the "Sportster" 7000 was shown at the Detroit Air Show for 1935 in the new Exposition Hangar at Detroit City Airport. Later in the year, Kenneth Rearwin, accompanied by his wife, embarked with a new "7000" on a six-week demonstration tour largely through Okla., Texas, and Calif.; Ken Rearwin sold 6 airplanes on this trip, finally selling the demonstrator in California and they hopped a train back to Kansas City. Orders for the "Sportster" came in at a brisk rate and several were exported to So. Africa, Manila, Alaska, So. America, Puerto Rico, and Australia. Of the 18 privately-owned airplanes in Brazil at one time during 1936, 5 of them were Rearwins.

The Rearwin "Sportster" model 7000 was a light high-winged cabin monoplane with seating arranged for 2 in tandem. As a utility-type airplane the "Sportster" was on the one hand a vehicle far better than the popular puddle-jumper for student training., and also as a modestly-endowed sportplane for the enthusiastic sportsman who loved to fly, but had

Fig. 266. Rearwin 7000 lines up for landing.

to do it on less investment. It also appealed to the business-man who neither had need for "club comfort", nor the ability to quickly span the nation. The "Sportster" was no raving beauty, but it was a trim, handsome airplane with strength far beyond the average need, and it was equipped or could be equipped with the many things that make for a pilot's happier life. The "Sportster" was rather slim-waisted, but it had an abundance of leg-room, and plenty of head-room. With a larger than average fuel capacity the "Sportster" could stretch a flight to nearly 500 miles, getting 20 miles to the gallon at about one cent per mile; even for back in the thirties this was cheap and efficient transportation. As powered with the 5 cyl. LeBlond 5DE or 5E engine rated at 70 h.p. at 1950 r.p.m. the "Model 7000" was certainly out of the flivver class and performed in a fashion quite surprising to those who flew it for the first time. The "Sportster" was agile, yet handled like a heavier airplane and its inherent strength offered peace of mind. Pilots liked it. The type certificate number for the "Sportster" model 7000 was issued 6-12-35 and at least 75 examples of this model were mfgd. by Rearwin Airplanes, Inc. on Fairfax Field in Kansas City, Kan. Rae A. Rearwin was pres.; A. R. Jones was V.P.; Royce Rearwin was sec.; Geo. M. Prescott was sales mgr.; Wm. H. Weeks was chf. engr.; J. B. LeClaire was purch. agent & occasional test-pilot; and B. Ralph Hall was chief pilot. Rearwin Airplanes, Inc. was later a partnership between Rae, Royce, and Kenneth Rearwin, that is, father and two sons.

Listed below are specifications and performance data for the Rearwin "Sportster" model 7000 as powered with the 70 h.p. LeBlond 5DE engine; length overall 22'3"; height overall 6'9"; wing span 35'0"; wing chord 62.5"; total wing area 166 sq. ft.; airfoil NACA (Munk) M-6; wt. empty 835 (853) lbs.; useful load 515 (557) lbs.; payload with 24 gal. fuel 186 (228) lbs.; gross wt. 1350 (1410) lbs.; figures in parentheses as later amended; max. speed 110; cruising speed (1850 r.p.m.) 100; landing speed 38-40; climb 700-625 ft. first min. at sea level; ser. ceiling 14,000 ft.; gas cap. 24 gal.; oil cap. 2 gal.; max. baggage 50 lbs.; cruising range (1850 r.p.m.) at 4.75 gal. per hour 480 miles; price $2095. at factory field in 1935, raised to $2468. in 1937. Wts. were amended in 1937 to 853 lbs. empty, 607 lbs. for useful load, and 1460 lbs. allowed for gross wt.; landing speed, take-off, climb, and ser. ceiling were affected. Serial # 401 thru 413 eligible only at 1365 lbs. max. gross wt.

The fuselage framework was built up of welded chrome-moly steel tubing, faired to shape with wooden fairing strips, then fabric covered. High-backed seats were upholstered and arranged in tandem; one baggage compartment with allowance for 20 lbs. was behind the rear seat with an optional compartment underneath the hinged rear seat. Max. baggage allowance was 50 lbs. A large rectangular door on the right side offered access to either seat; the windshield and cabin sides were of Pyralin. The wing framework was built up of reinforced solid spruce spar beams with spruce and plywood girder-type wing ribs; the leading edges were covered with dural

Fig. 267. The 7000 graced the flight-line of several flying-schools.

sheet and the completed framework was covered in fabric. A 12 gal. fuel tank was mounted in root end of each wing half with fuel gauges visible in the cabin; the wing was braced to lower longerons by vee-struts of streamlined steel tubing. The landing gear of 70 in. tread was a tripod assembly of faired vees incorporating an oleo-spring leg on each side; 7.00x4 wheels (no brakes) were fitted with 4-ply tires. Goodyear 18x8-3 airwheels with brakes were optional. A spring-leaf tail skid was standard equipment, but a tail wheel was optional. The fabric covered tail group was built up of welded steel channels and tubes; the horizontal stabilizer was adjustable in flight. A Flottorp or Fahlin wooden propeller, dual stick-type controls, exhaust collector ring, fuel gauges, and tail skid were standard equipment. Navigation lights, a battery, wind-driven generator, landing lights, cabin heater, speed-ring engine cowl, wheel brakes, parking brake, Eclipse engine starter, Pyrene fire extinguisher, and radio equipment were optional. The next Rearwin development was the "Model 8500" as described in the chapter for ATC # 591 of this volume.

Listed below are "Model 7000" entries as gleaned from registration records:

NC-14443: 7000 (# 401) LeBlond 70.
   -14474:   "   (# 402)   "
   -14485:   "   (# 403)   "
   -14487:   "   (# 404)   "
   -14488:   "   (# 405)   "
   -14486:   "   (# 406)   "
   -14489:   "   (# 407)   "

   -14490:   "   (# 408)   "
   -14491:   "   (# 409)   "
   -14492:   "   (# 410)   "
   -14493:   "   (# 411)   "
   -14494:   "   (# 412)   "
   -15415:   "   (# 413)   "
   -15416:   "   (# 414)   "
   -15417:   "   (# 415)   "
   -15418:   "   (# 416)   "
   -15419:   "   (# 417)   "
   -15420:   "   (# 418)   "
   -15421:   "   (# 419)   "
   -15422:   "   (# 420)   "
   -15474:   "   (# 423)   "
   -15475:   "   (# 424)   "
   -15476:   "   (# 425)   "
   -15478:   "   (# 426)   "
   -15480:   "   (# 428)   "
   -15481:   "   (# 429)   "
   -15482:   "   (# 430)   "
   -15491:   "   (# 431)   "
   -15492:   "   (# 432)   "
   -15493:   "   (# 433)   "
   -15494:   "   (# 434)   "
   -15495:   "   (# 435)   "
   -15800:   "   (# 436)   "
   -15801:   "   (# 437)   "
   -15802:   "   (# 438)   "
   -15804:   "   (# 440)   "
PP-TBL: "   (# 441)   "
   -15823:   "   (# 442)   "
   -15807:   "   (# 443)   "
   -15809:   "   (# 445)   "
   -15825:   "   (# 449)   "
   -15828:   "   (# 451)   "
   -15829:   "   (# 452)   "

Fig. 268. A pair of 7000 practice formation take-off.

-15854:	"	(# 454)	"
-15806:	"	(# 456)	"
-15856:	"	(# 457)	"
-15857:	"	(# 458)	"
-15827:	"	(# 459)	"
-15861:	"	(# 460)	"
-15863:	"	(# 462)	"
-15889:	"	(# 465)	"
-15890:	"	(# 466)	"
-15891:	"	(# 467)	"
-15866:	"	(# 472)	"
-15897:	"	(# 477)	"
-16456:	"	(# 481)	"
-16458:	"	(# 483)	"
-16460:	"	(# 485)	"
-16457:	"	(# 486)	"
-17002:	"	(# 488)	"
-16464:	"	(# 489)	"

-16463:	"	(# 493)	"
-16465:	"	(# 494)	"
-16461:	"	(# 496)	"
-16469:	"	(# 499)	"
-16476:	"	(# 503)	"
-16478:	"	(# 506)	"
-18024:	"	(# 539)	"
-17044:	"	(# 556)	"
-18768:	"	(# 590)	"

This approval for ser. # 401 and up; ser. # 401 thru 413 eligible only at 1365 lbs. max. gross wt.; ser. # 441 delivered to Brazil; no listing for ser. # 446, 447, 473, 475, 476, 482, 484, 487, 490, 491, 497, 498; ser. # 469 to Alaska on floats; ser. # 471 also as seaplane on Edo floats; ser. # 485-486 del. to Puerto Rico; ser. # 539, 556, 590 mfgd. 1937.

ATC # 575
(6-25-35)
WACO, MODEL CUC.

Fig. 269. The Waco CUC with 250 h.p. Wright engine.

A full-figured and rather curvacious machine, the Waco model CUC was perhaps the "grand dame" of the "Custom Cabin" lineup for the 1935 season. Spurred on by the relentless obligation of leadership, Waco Aircraft offered the Model CUC as part of a line of custom airplanes that perhaps excelled all previous attainment in an airplane of this type. The CUC was a custom-built airplane manufactured to the tastes and dictates of each individual customer; each airplane was written up thoroughly beforehand to specify any custom interior treatment, the exterior finish, or addition of mechanical equipment, and no work was even started until a substantial deposit was received to make the order binding. The purpose for this was two-fold; the customer was assured the airplane would be built absolutely to his liking, and Waco Aircraft was in turn assured that all the time and effort spent on a job was destined to be appreciated by a proud and well-pleased owner. As a consequence, the roster of CUC owners were generally wealthy and a cross-section of the biggest names in business; those not used directly in the pursuit of business matters were private airplanes used in an occasional escape from the pressures of business. Afforded the best of care and usually pampered, the various CUC were certainly worth more than a casual glance and were usually surrounded by a ring of admirers wherever they went. Most of the CUC were kept by owners for years of service, and those that were not kept were most always traded in for a newer "Waco".

The Waco model CUC was a custom-built cabin biplane with seating arranged for 4 or 5. Of the 3 "Custom Cabin" models (UOC-YOC CUC) for 1935 the CUC was naturally the more elegant. Customers that specified installation of the more expensive "Wright" engine in their "Custom" airplane would hardly be expected to economize on interior trappings or gadgetry, therefore, the CUC was always more plush and more completely equipped. The CUC that were "involved in business" were most always equipped with radio sets, night-flying equipment, and fancy custom colors; the "controllable propeller" which converted engine horsepower into more efficient performance was another extra that was quite popular. The CUC owned by sportsmen were naturally "show-off" airplanes, so most were brilliantly colored and stuffed to the doors with elegance. As powered with the 7 cyl. Wright R-760-E engine rated 250 h.p. the CUC gave good account of itself with a performance that was rather outstanding and often led to owner-boasting. With introduction of the improved R-760-E1 engine, which was

Fig. 270. CUC series were top of "Custom" line for 1935.

rated 285 h.p., several CUC owners swapped engines for a performance that was even that much better. The designation used for the 285 h.p. version was CUC-1. Flight characteristics of the CUC were pleasant, reliability was a taken-for-granted feature, and pride of ownership was just something that developed by association. The type certificate number for the Model CUC was issued 6-25-35 and some 30 or more examples of this model were manufactured by the Waco Aircraft Co. at Troy, Ohio.

Listed below are specifications and performance data for the Waco model CUC as powered with 250 h.p. Wright R-760-E engine; length overall 25'3"; height overall 8'3"; wing span upper 35'0"; wing span lower 24'6"; wing chord upper 72"; wing chord lower 48"; wing area upper 165.6 sq. ft.; wing area lower 73.2 sq. ft.; total wing area 238.8 sq. ft.; airfoil Clark Y; wt. empty 2017 lbs.; useful load 1183 lbs.; payload with 70 gal. fuel 556 lbs. (3 pass. & 46 lbs. baggage); gross wt. 3200 lbs.; max. speed 162 at 1000 ft.; cruising speed (.80 power) 145 at 1000 ft.; landing speed (no flaps) 55; climb 850 ft. first min. at sea level; ser. ceiling 16,500 ft.; gas cap. normal 70 gal.; gas cap. max. 95 gal.; oil cap. 5-7 gal.; cruising range (.80 power) at 16 gal. per hour 570 miles; price $8400. at factory field.

The model CUC-1 with R-760-E1 engine rated 285 h.p. using Hamilton-Standard controllable propeller was identical to that above, except as follows; wt. empty 2076 lbs.; useful load 1274 lbs.; payload with 70 gal. fuel 647 lbs. (3 pass. & 137 lbs. baggage); gross wt. 3350 lbs.; max. speed 168 at 1000 ft.; cruising speed (.80 power) 160 at 6000 ft.; cruising speed 150 at 1000 ft.; landing speed (no flaps) 58; climb 900 ft. first min. at sea level; service ceiling 17,000 ft.; gas cap. normal 70 gal.; gas cap. max. 95 gal.; oil cap. 5-7 gal.; cruising range (.80 power) at 18 gal. per hour 540 miles; price $8975. at factory field. A few examples were converted to models CUC-2 with Wright R-760-E2 engine rated 320 h.p.; the performance was improved accordingly.

The construction details and general arrangement of the model CUC was typical to that of the models UOC and YOC as described here in this volume. The fuselage front of the CUC, being otherwise similar, was modified to mount the 7 cyl. Wright engine, and because of extra weight, the nose was shortened by several inches. The interior was normally upholstered in rich Broadcloth fabrics, but real leather was optional. The unusually large baggage compartment was loaded from the outside, but luggage was accessible even in flight; baggage allowance was governed only by permissible weight rather than by available space—it was that big. The landing gear of 87 in. tread was fitted with 8.50x-10 wheels and tires; wheels were usually encased in metal wheel pants. The wing roots were faired gently into the fuselage junction by metal wing fillets; the landing gear and wing strut junctions were faired with metal cuffs. Metal-framed ailerons were covered with corrugated dural sheet; one aileron had adjustable tab for lateral trim. Drag flaps, in underside of upper wing, were inset from the trailing edge and spanned the space from aileron to fuselage; numerous hand-holes were provided in the wings for adjustment or inspection. A throw-over control wheel provided dual controls, but a Y-type column with 2 wheels was optional. Front seats were adjustable to fit stature of various pilots. A

Fig. 271. Waco CUC-1 with 285 h.p. Wright engine.

Curtiss-Reed metal propeller, electric engine starter, generator, battery, wheel brakes, tail wheel, navigation lights, unusually complete instrument panel, fuel gauges, fire extinguisher, assist ropes, ash trays, cabin heat & ventilation, first-aid kit, tool kit, and log books were standard equipment. Generally speaking, hardly any model CUC left the factory with just standard equipment, being variously equipped with a radio set, bonding & shielding, landing lights, parachute flares, latest navigational aids, extra engine instruments, extra fuel capacity, wheel pants, and custom color schemes. Installation of the Hamilton-Standard controllable propeller permitted gross weight increase to 3350 lbs. The next Waco development was the "armed" Model D as described in the chapter for ATC # 581 of this volume.

Listed below are CUC and CUC-1 entries as verified by company records:

NC-14618:	CUC-1	(# 4242)	Wright 285.
-14623:	"	(# 4247)	"
-14626:	"	(# 4248)	"
-14625:	CUC	(# 4249)	Wright 250.
-14679:	CUC-1	(# 4277)	Wright 285.
-14688:	"	(# 4284)	"
-14685:	"	(# 4285)	"
-15203:	"	(# 4286)	"
-15205:	"	(# 4290)	"
-15210:	"	(# 4298)	"
-15216:	"	(# 4300)	"
-15211:	"	(# 4301)	"
-15213:	"	(# 4302)	"
:	CUC	(# 4303)	Wright 250.
PH-VDL:	"	(# 4304)	"

-15220:	CUC-1	(# 4309)	Wright 285.
-15222:	CUC	(# 4311)	Wright 250.
-15223:	CUC-1	(# 4312)	Wright 285.
-15227:	"	(# 4313)	"
-15224:	"	(# 4314)	"
-15228:	"	(# 4316)	"
-15233:	"	(# 4318)	"
-15230:	"	(# 4319)	"
-15240:	"	(# 4322)	"
-15238:	"	(# 4323)	"
-15237:	"	(# 4324)	"
-15244:	"	(# 4327)	"
-15248:	"	(# 4330)	"
-15703:	"	(# 4334)	"
-15702:	"	(# 4335)	"

Serial # 4242 later modified to model CUC-2 with 320 h.p. Wright R-760-E2 engine; ser. # 4247 del. to Standard Oil Co. of Ohio (SOHIO); ser. # 4248 del. to Packard Motor Car Co.—was first as model YOC; ser. # 4284 del. to Henry King of Hollywood; ser. # 4298 first as model YOC; ser. # 4300 del. to Leland Hayward of Hollywood; ser. # 4300 later as model YOC-1; ser. # 4301 later modified to model YOC-1 with 285 h.p. Jacobs L-5 engine; ser. # 4302 as X-15213 was test-bed for 320 h.p. Wright R-760-E2 engine; ser. # 4303 del. to Johannesburg, So. Africa; ser. # 4304 del. to Holland; ser. # 4312 del. to Gar Wood, famous speed-boat king; ser. # 4313 was model YOC at one time; ser. # 4322 del. to Victor Fleming of Hollywood; ser. # 4327 and 4330 later modified to model YOC-1; ser. # 4335 del. to Howard Hawks of Hollywood; one CUC impressed into USAAF service as UC-72F during 1942; this approval expired 9-30-39.

Fig. 272. Fairchild 24-C8D with 145 h.p. "Ranger" engine.

Fairchild had been toying with the "6-390", a 6 cyl. inverted inline aircooled engine, off and on since 1929. There had been several obstacles to overcome in an engine of this type, but eventually it was developed and approved into several satisfactory installations. As mounted in the KR-125 and KR-135 sport biplanes the engine was literally trouble-free and showed particular promise in a utility airplane. It seems logical that Fairchild would want to install the inverted inline engine in one of its "Model 22" parasol monoplanes, which seemed to be an ideal design for the "inline" installation, but apparently the project was not even considered. By 1935 the Fairchild 6-390 had since become the "Ranger" engine and was finally installed into a Fairchild 24. Becoming recently quite popular with a (Warner) "radial engine" installation (24-C8C) the new "Twenty Four" looked just a little odd with the long, slender nose that shrouded the 6 cyl. "Ranger" engine, but the lines were indeed quite pleasant and quickly accepted. Inherently smooth, the "Ranger Six" provided a ride that was practically free of vibration, exceptionally quiet, and it offered very good visibility over and around the nose. As the first production batch of the "Ranger 6-390" engine, Fairchild received

15 of the crated powerplants from Farmingdale and these were installed into the new model 24-C8D. The new model created considerable interest and provoked some much-deserved praise; acceptance on the east coast was fairly quick, but orders eventually trickled in from Penn., Ohio, and Calif. Invited to the First International Aircraft Exhibit a Ranger-powered 24-C8D was shipped to Milan, Italy for the two-week showing in Oct. of 1935, and Fairchild was proud to show off their engine-airplane combination. Reports in service had been favorable and published reports had been complimentary, but apparently the buying public had assumed a wait-and-see attitude.

When Fairchild abandoned development of the 4 cyl. "Caminez" engine (see ATC # 37 of USCA/C, Vol. 1) in early 1929 they had already begun experiments on a new engine designed by Walter P. Davis. This new engine, a 6 cyl. inverted inline aircooled powerplant, had many aerodynamic advantages and promised unusual reliability. In 5 months the new engine, a 6-370 (6 cyls. of 370 cu. in. displacement), was built and mounted on a test-stand; a 50 hour run-up showed it delivering 110 h.p. at 1900 r.p.m. This first engine was then flown in a Fairchild KR-31

Fig. 273. 24-C8D shows a handsome profile; this was prototype airplane.

biplane in Jan. of 1930 with satisfactory results. Engine # 2 was also flown in a KR-31 for several hundred hours. Engine # 3 was installed in a modified KR-21 biplane, redesignated the KR-125 (see ATC # 368 of USCA/C, Vol. 4), and it was still flying in 1945. Engine # 4 was converted from a 6-370 to a 6-390 by boring out the cyls. to greater displacement, and block-tested for several hundred hours; each engine after this was a 6-390. Engine # 5 was used by Huntington Aircraft Co. in the mock-up of a new cabin airplane; the engine was later disassembled and parts were returned to stock. Engine # 6 was installed (1930) in a flying boat designed by Chas. Ward Hall and used by him as a personal airplane until 1936. Engine # 7 was installed in another version of the KR-21 biplane, redesignated the KR-135 (see ATC # 415 of USCA/C, Vol. 5). Engine # 8 was installed in a Gee Bee "Sportster" flown by Lowell Bayles; after 100 hours of racing and exhibition the engine was pulled for study and Engine # 9 was installed. The "Sportster" was then wrecked by a pilot unfamiliar with the airplane's characteristics and the engine was returned for salvage. Engine # 10 was sold to "Matty" Laird in 1931 and installed in one of his racing biplanes. Engine # 11 was installed in another KR-135 biplane and sold to a sportsman. Quantity production of the "Ranger" engine finally began in 1935, starting with Engine # 12, and a batch of 15 engines was shipped to Fairchild in Hagerstown for installation in the new "Twenty Four".

The Fairchild model 24-C8D was a rather neat high-winged cabin monoplane with seating arranged for 2 or 3. The "rumble seat" in back, normally occupied by a third person, could be folded back out of the way to make room for piles of luggage, sporting gear, or just about enough of anything for a week's vacation. If need be, the 24-C8D could even double as a freighter with about 500 lbs. strapped down in the cabin. Standing there quite tall, it was easy to walk up to this airplane, and a large door on each side offered simple step-up into the cabin area; soft cushions, handsome upholstery, and decorative interior trim promoted a desire to fly more often dressed in one's finest. Ample window area, with a skylight overhead, permitted a broad range of visibility to better enjoy the scenery and to keep a watchful eye on airport traffic. As powered with the 6 cyl. inverted "Ranger" 6-390B engine, which developed 145 h.p. at 2250 r.p.m., the 24-C8D surprised everyone with its seemingly effortless performance and there was plenty of reserve power to pluck one from a bad situation. The "Ranger" engine had some beautiful characteristics and the "Twenty Four" seemed quite happy with its new-found power. The long, slender nose produced a gracefully streamlined appearance that was pleasant to look at and it added an apparent steadiness to the flying that was quite pleasant in itself. This was the first Fairchild 24 with "Ranger" power and it was now to be offered in progressive versions for the next decade. The type certificate number for the model 24-C8D was issued 6-26-35 and at least 14 examples of this model were manufactured by the Kreider-Reisner Aircraft Co., Inc.; during 1935 the K-R division was renamed as the

Fig. 274. 24-C8D also available as seaplane on Edo floats.

Fairchild Aircraft Corp. of Hagerstown, Md. George Hardman was project engineer on development of the Model 24 series, and A. A. Gassner was busy developing the world's fastest single-engined amphibian. R. "Dick" Henson was flying tests on the 24-C8D with Edo twin-float gear and it was approved as a seaplane (24-C8DS) on 3-30-36.

Listed below are specifications and performance data for the Fairchild model 24-C8D as powered with 145 h.p. Ranger 6-390B engine; length overall 24'6"; height overall 7'3"; wing span 36'4"; wing chord 66"; total wing area 186 sq. ft.; airfoil Navy (NACA) N-22; wt. empty 1440 lbs.; useful load 960 lbs.; payload with 40 gal. fuel 527 lbs. (2 pass. & up to 187 lbs. baggage); gross wt. 2400 lbs.; max. speed 135; cruising speed (2000 r.p.m.) 120; landing speed (no flaps) 49; landing speed (with flaps) 43; climb 700 ft. first min. at sea level; ser. ceiling 15,500 ft.; gas cap. 40 gal.; oil cap. 3 gal.; cruising range (.75 power) at 8.5 gal. per hour 500 miles; price $4990. at factory field. The 24-C8DS seaplane on Edo 44-2425 pontoons operated at 2550 lbs. gross weight; the tail wheel was replaced with an aux. fin and baggage was held to 70 lbs. Approved wts. were 1707-843-2550 lbs.; performance figures would be slightly lower than that of landplane. Price was approx. $1000. extra for seaplane.

The construction details and general arrangement of the 24-C8D was typical to that of the model 24-C8C as described here in the chapter for ATC # 535. From the firewall back these 2 models were nearly identical. The modish in-terior was arranged to seat 2 or 3; the 2 front seats were side-by-side and a folding "rumble seat" in back was erected for a third person. Baggage was placed on either side of the rear seat, or the seat could be folded up and the whole area used to strap down baggage; baggage amounts varied with payload available. Cabin walls were lined with "Seapak" (Kapok) and up-holstered in real leather or Bedford cord; all windows were of shatter-proof glass. A large door and handy assist cords on each side provided an easy step-up into the cabin. The pilot's seat was adjustable and visibility out was quite adequate. The interior was reasonably quiet and all plane-engine controls operated on ball bearings; sun-shades and dual stick-type controls were also provided. Cabin vents and a cabin heater were optional extras. The engine was completely cowled in with removable metal panels and baffled for even cooling. The fabric covered wooden wing, typical to that of the 24-C8C, had "slotted" ailerons and wing flaps were optional. A 20 gal. fuel tank was mounted in the root end of each wing-half; for longer range a 20 gal. aux. tank could be mounted in the fuselage in place of the rear seat. The sport-type landing gear was typical to that of the 24-C8C with 6.50x10 low-pressure tires on Warner wheels with brakes; the wheels were encased in streamlined metal wheel pants. Fittings and extra members in the fuselage were provided (later) for installation of Edo 44-2425 twin-float seaplane gear; tail wheel was replaced with an aux. fin. The seaplane and some of the landplanes were fitted with trailing edge wing flaps; flaps not to be extended above

Fig. 275. The 24-C8D was quite happy with its "inline" power.

94 m.p.h. The fabric covered tail group was identical to that of the 24-C8C; rudder was fitted with balance horn and the horizontal stabilizer was adj. in flight. A Hartzell wooden propeller, electric engine starter, Exide battery, wiring for navigation lights, wheel brakes, parking brake, 8 in. tail wheel, windshield wipers, a compass, sunshades, safety belts, assist ropes, ash trays, first-aid kit, and tool kit were standard equipment. A metal propeller, generator (engine-driven or wind-driven), navigation lights, landing lights, parachute flares, cabin heater, bonding & shielding, radio, skis, seaplane gear, and a 20 gal. aux. fuel tank were optional. The next Fairchild development was the Model 91 "Baby Clipper" as described in the chapter for ATC # 587 of this volume.

Listed below are 24-C8D entries as gleaned from registration records:

NC-45V: 24-C8D (# 3000) Ranger 6-390B.

NC-15044: 24-C8D (# 3001) Ranger 6-390B.
　-15090: 24-C8D (# 3002) Ranger 6-390B.
　-15091: 24-C8D (# 3003) Ranger 6-390B.
　-15092: 24-C8D (# 3004) Ranger 6-390B.
　-15093: 24-C8D (# 3005) Ranger 6-390B.
NC-5050: 24-C8D (# 3006) Ranger 6-390B.
　-15384: 24-C8D (# 3007) Ranger 6-390B.
　-15385: 24-C8D (# 3008) Ranger 6-390B.
　-15386: 24-C8D (# 3009) Ranger 6-390B.
　-15387: 24-C8D (# 3010) Ranger 6-390B.
　-15608: 24-C8D (# 3011) Ranger 6-390B.
　-15609: 24-C8D (# 3012) Ranger 6-390B.
　-15961: 24-C8D (# 3013) Ranger 6-390B.

Serial # 3000 (NC-45V) was used as prototype airplane for both models 24-C8C and 24-C8D; this approval for ser. # 3001 and up; ser. # 3006 first registered as NC-15383 by Fairchild, later changed to NC-5050 by Henry B. DuPont; ser. # 3013 as seaplane (24-C8DS) on Edo pontoons; this approval expired 9-30-39.

ATC # 577
(7-6-35)
BEECH, MODEL A-17-FS.

Fig. 276. Beech A-17-FS with 700 h.p. Wright "Cyclone" engine.

Achieving surprising success with the first "Cyclone-powered" model A-17-F, prexy Walter Beech dreamed of prestige and prize money, so he decided to build another of the high-powered monsters. This second example, the model A-17-FS, was built on the speculation that Robert Fogg and famous aviatrix Louise Thaden could perhaps each fly one of the Cyclone-powered airplanes in the upcoming London to Melbourne race for the lucrative MacRobertson Trophy. This international event promised worldwide prestige and considerable prize money; Walter Beech actually felt confident that either one of his two airplanes could win. However, this being a race of great distance the smaller, faster airplanes requiring frequent stops for fuel would eventually lose out to larger, slower airplanes of greater range, so both the Beech A-17-F and A-17-FS were withdrawn. Construction on the A-17-FS was started 15 June 1934 and finally completed on 15 July 1935. For some time the new A-17-FS could not be sold, no one seemed to want it, and Beech saw it turn into a very expensive hangar-queen. Eventually it was sold to the Bureau of Air Commerce and flown by them occasionally until some time in 1937. Being an airplane of limited usefulness to the Department it was evidently dismantled and used up for its various parts. Despite the excitement generated by both the A-

17-F and the A-17-FS a chance for lasting greatness eluded both of the Cyclone-powered Beech airplanes and they are almost universally remembered as the Stagger-Wing "monsters".

The Beech model A-17-FS was a 4 place high-performance cabin biplane and quite similar to the earlier inverse-stagger A-17-F except for its particular engine installation. The A-17-FS mounted the big 9 cyl. supercharged Wright "Cyclone" SR-1820-F3 engine rated 710 h.p. at 1900 r.p.m. at 5000 ft. and was actually capable of a better performance than the 690 h.p. model A-17-F. By 1935 the flying public was becoming increasingly sophisticated, but the use of 710 h.p. for a personal airplane still seemed highly extravagant and a 235-250 m.p.h. top speed, as quoted for the A-17-FS, was really quite startling. The A-17-FS was a fiercely beautiful airplane, none would deny that, and wherever it went it graced the flight-line with an air of beligerent dignity. Like any unorthodox airplane the Beech A-17-FS appeared strange at first, perhaps even dangerous and out of proportion, but gradually it developed a character that was tolerated and acceptable to those who were familiar with it. Operational record of the A-17-FS while it was used by the Bureau of Air Commerce (BAC) has been sketchy and very elusive, but its use was apparently relegated to various special missions. Every flight must have

Fig. 277. The A-17-FS was a mechanical monster that commanded awe and respect.

been quite an experience, so it is hard to see anyone nonchalantly climbing into the A-17-FS just to make a routine flight. Walter Beech had by now realized that monstrous high-powered engines in his "Stagger-Wing" biplane created great publicity and stimulated exciting hangar-talk all over the country, but they were bad business — who would buy them? The type certificate number for the Beech model A-17-FS was issued 7-6-35 and only one example of this model was built by the Beech Aircraft Co. at Wichita, Kansas.

Listed below are specifications and performance data for the Beech model A-17-FS as powered with Wright "Cyclone" SR-1820-F3 engine rated 710 h.p. at 1900 r.p.m. at 5000 ft.; length overall 24'3"; height overall 8'7"; wing span upper & lower 34'6"; wing chord upper & lower 60"; wing area upper 178 sq. ft.; wing area lower 160 sq. ft.; total wing area (incl. 1/2 of the fuselage section) 338 sq. ft.; airfoil Navy (NACA) N-9; wt. empty 3285 lbs.; useful load 1915 lbs.; payload with 155 gal. fuel 725 lbs. (3 pass. & 215 lbs. baggage); gross wt. 5200 lbs.; max. speed 235; cruising speed (.75 power) 215 at 5000 ft.; landing speed (with flaps) 65; climb 2000 ft. first min. at sea level; ser. ceiling 20,000 ft.; gas cap. 155 gal.; oil cap. 12 gal.; cruising range (.75 power) at 40 gal. per hour 750 miles; price approx. $30,000. The SR-1820-F3 engine alone cost $7320.!

The construction details and general arrangement of the Beech A-17-FS were typical to that of the model A-17-F as described here in the chapter for ATC # 548, except for minor differences as mentioned. The only significant difference in the A-17-FS was use of the supercharged "Cyclone" SR-1820-F3 engine which was a so-called "altitude engine" allowing greater horsepower output at cruising altitude; the -F3 engine developed its max. h.p. at 5000 ft. Wing flaps were on trailing edge of the upper wing, and ailerons were on the lower wing. A throw-over wheel provided control from either front seat. Some sources quote that the "Smith" variable-pitch propeller was used on the A-17-FS, but generally it was shown with the Hamilton-Standard controllable propeller. The instrument panel was literally loaded with instruments and every navigational aid that was available at that time. Finished in a colorful pattern of Cherry Red, Silver, and Blue, colors that were hand-rubbed to a mirror-finish, the A-17-FS was left as is and not repainted (in their standard drab colors) when it was procured by the BAC. More often, the A-17-FS was listed as a 3 place airplane and this suggests that the weight of a passenger or two was traded off for more fuel capacity. Switlik parachute-type seats were optional equipment. The next Beech development was the model B-17-R as described in the chapter for ATC # 579 of this volume. Listed below is the only entry for the model A-17-FS:

NS-68: A-17-FS (# 11) Cyclone 710.

The A-17-FS was briefly registered by Beech as NR-12569, the number was reused when the aircraft was sold to BAC.

ATC # 578
(7-20-35)
BELLANCA, "SR. PACEMAKER", 31-42.

Fig. 278. Bellanca "Sr. Pacemaker" with 420 h.p. Wright engine.

The Bellanca "Pacemaker" was still being manufactured, but its demand in the U.S.A. was falling off, and it was taking a back seat to other developments at the factory. Bellanca had just finished an order for 14 of the C-27 "Aircruiser" type that were delivered to the Army Air Corps, 4 of the 77-140 twin-engined bombers (patterned after the Aircruiser) were developed, built, and delivered to the government of Colombia, and the famous "Bellanca Flash" (or Irish Swoop) was being readied for the famous MacRobertson Race. Twelve of the "Pacemaker" were built on order and delivered to Brazil, a few were sold here in this country, and a few exported to other countries. Meanwhile, development of the 28-90 mailplane, a design stemming from the unusual "Flash", kept the factory quite busy; 42 of the mailplanes were slated for France, but somehow wound up in Mexico and then off to China. By 1938 the demand for the Pacemaker, Skyrocket, and Aircruiser had fallen off to nothing, but Guiseppe Bellanca and his design team had not been idle; the Model 14-9 "Junior" (later the "Cruisair") was completed in Dec. of 1937 and it was a sensation that put Bellanca back in volume business. The Bellanca "Pacemaker", even tho' it was still basically similar to the WB-1 of 1925, was continually refined and the model 31-42 of 1934-35-36 was perhaps the zenith of

achievement for this type of airplane. By now the "Pacemaker" had gotten much fatter, and bigger, but it surely was not lazier; it could still out-do any airplane of its type. As powered with either the 9 cyl. Wright R-975-E2 or -E3 engine rated 420-450 h.p. the Model 31-42 had remarkable performance and an unlimited utility; it was available on wheels, skis, or floats, as a personal airplane, an executive-transport in business, or as a freighter in the "bush". The versatile "Pacemaker" was a yeararound airplane that asked no favors and it never failed to make a profit. The Bellanca "Pacemaker" was a blue-ribbon airplane, it had more to its credit than many popular airplanes of this type, and tho' its mechanical make-up seemed outdated by 1940, its ability never will be.

The Bellanca "Pacemaker" model 31-42 was a medium-sized cabin monoplane transport with a large, convertible interior. Numerous arrangements were possible from a 5 or 6 place "executive" transport with plush surroundings, to a more austere setting that accommodated up to 8 people. The "Freighter" generally seated a pilot only, and the lined interior could just about carry anything that would go through the door. Being an all-season airplane, designed to work for its keep, the 31-42 performed equally well on wheels, on skis, or on floats. It is unbelievable

Fig. 279. A "Sr. Pacemaker" (31-42) in Norwegian service.

that this airplane, with 3 hours of fuel on board, could still carry nearly a ton of paying load. This fat, boxy-looking machine was no beauty, an airplane that only a pilot could love, but it proved G. M. Bellanca's wizardry with aerodynamics and design; every square foot of airframe was contributing to more than one useful purpose. Bellanca pilots were adventurous people and the "Pacemaker" seemed to revel in adventure, so it is understandable why it was always found in primitive parts of the world. As powered with the 9 cyl. Wright R-975-E2 or -E3 engine rated 420 h.p. at 2200 r.p.m. (450 h.p. available for take-off) the "Pacemaker" model 31-42 was capable of speed and performance that belied its bulk and its plain, slab-sided figure. Whether loaded with miners, machinery, precious metals, or animal pelts, the 31-42 asked no favors and operated in and out of places that were nearly impossible. Pilots put an uncommon trust in the abilities of the "Pacemaker" and their plaudits formed an aura of story and fame that shall live forever. The type certificate number for the "Senior Pacemaker" model 31-42 was issued 7-20-35 and it is likely that no more than 6 examples of this model were manufactured by the Bellanca Aircraft Corp. at New Castle, Dela.

Listed below are specifications and performance data for the "Senior Pacemaker" model 31-40 (6 pl. landplane) as powered with 420 h.p.

Fig. 280. The 31-42 was rather frisky for its size.

Fig. 281. A 31-42 on Edo floats operated as freighter in Canada.

Wright R-975-E2 or -E3 engine; length overall 27'11"; height overall 8'6"; wing span 50'6"; wing chord 81"; total wing area (incl. lift struts) 359 sq. ft.; airfoil "Bellanca"; wt. empty 3000 (3250) lbs.; useful load 2350 lbs.; payload with 175 gal. fuel 1040 lbs. (5 pass. & 190 lbs. baggage); gross wt. 5350 (5600) lbs.; figures in parentheses are for model 31-42 with R-975-E3 engine; max. speed 165 at sea level; cruising speed (.75 power) 145; cruising speed (.85 power) 155; landing (stall) speed (with flaps) 54-58; climb 900-750 ft. first min. at sea level; ser. ceiling 18,000 and 14,000 ft.; gas cap. 175-200 gal.; oil cap. 12 gal.; cruising range (.75 power) at 25 gal. per hour 900 miles; price $16,800. at factory early in 1935 — price was $19,975. at factory in 1936. A deluxe version with everything in it would cost about $24,000.

Specs and performance data for 31-42 (1 pl. freighter or 8 pl. coach) as powered with 420 h.p. Wright R-975-E3 engine same as above except as follows: wt. empty 2950 lbs.; useful load 2650 lbs.; payload with 150 gal. fuel 1500 lbs.; payload with 100 gal. fuel 1800 lbs.; gross wt. 5600 lbs.; max. speed 160 at sea level; cruising speed (.80 power) 145; landing speed (with flaps) 58; climb 750 ft. first min. at sea level; ser. ceiling 14,000 ft.; gas cap. max. 200 gal.; oil cap. 12 gal.; cruising range 840 miles; price $19,700. at factory in 1936. Also available on skis or Edo pontoons.

Specs and performance data for 31-42 (seaplane) as powered with 420 h.p. R-975-E3 engine same as either table above except as follows; wt. empty 3470 lbs.; useful load 2430 lbs.; payload with 150 gal. fuel 1270 lbs. (cargo, or mixed load of passengers-cargo) gross wt. 5900 lbs.; max. speed 150 at sea level; cruising

speed (.75 power) 140; climb 700 ft. first min. at sea level; landing speed (with flaps) 62; ser. ceiling 12,000 ft.; cruising range 800 miles; price not announced. Available as 5 or 6 pl. transport, 1 pl. cargo-plane, or an 8 pl. coach with high-density seating.

The construction details and general arrangement of the "Senior Pacemaker" are similar to "Senior Skyrocket" models 31-50 (31-55) as described here in the chapter for ATC # 565, or as noted. The 9 cyl. Wright R-975-E2 engine was fully cowled with an NACA-type fairing of unusually deep chord; the engine cowl was split and hinged to allow easy inspection and quick maintenance. The improved Wright R-975-E3 engine, also rated 420 h.p., was an optional installation. A variety of interiors were available including the modestly plush 6 pl. transport, the 1 or 2 pl. freighter with payload for up to one ton of cargo, or the 8 pl. coach with folding bench-type seats. A baggage compartment for up to 148 lbs. was behind the rear-most seat, or some baggage could be stowed in a belly compartment with allowance for up to 100 lbs. A throw-over control wheel was standard, but a Y-type column with 2 wheels was available for operations requiring 2 pilots. Extra large cabin entry doors were optional to ease loading of bulky cargo into the 124" long x 58" high x 46" wide interior. A 100 gal. fuel tank was mounted in root end of each wing-half; the right tank had a built-in "reserve" of 12 gal. for about 30 mins. of extended flight after both tanks were emptied. Fuel load and cargo payload were variable according to requirements. The single-strut cantilever landing gear of 96 in. tread was equipped with 31 in. General streamlined tires on Bendix wheels with brakes; 9.50x12 low-pressure 6-ply

Fig. 282. A "Sr. Pacemaker" in Alaskan service.

tires were optional. Metal wheel fenders were available to protect the propeller from slung-up debris. The "Senior Pacemaker" was also available on skis, or on Edo twin-float gear; the seaplane was popular in Canada and other foreign countries. A Hamilton-Standard controllable propeller, combination hand-electric engine starter, Exide battery (under floor), engine-driven generator, cabin ventilators, navigation lights, cabin lights, fire extinguisher, compass, full set of engine-airplane instruments, clock, oil-cooling radiator, 5x4 full-swivel tail wheel, fuel gauges, cabin assist ropes, first-aid kit, tool kit, and engine cover were standard equipment. Landing lights, parachute flares, wing flaps, radio, bonding & shielding, cabin heater, lavatory, skis, Edo pontoons, and custom colors were optional. There was enough latitude in the "Senior Pacemaker" design to provide an owner-operator with just about any combination that suited his purpose best; for this reason the models 31-40 and 31-42 were just

about the best airplanes of this type. The same basic design was still manufactured many years later, but only on order. The next Bellanca development was the tiny "Junior" (Cruisair) model 14-9 as described in the chapter for ATC # 716.

Listed below are "Sr. Pacemaker" entries as gleaned from various records:

CF-ANX; 31-42 (# 251) Wright 420.
NC-20Y; 31-42 (# 252) Wright 420.
LN-ABO; 31-42 (# 253) Wright 420.
NC-16707; 31-42 (# 254) Wright 420.

This approval for ser. # 251 and up; CF-ANX del. to Canada on floats; NC-20Y later registered as NC-11642 when reg. no. (NC-20Y) was awarded to a Lockheed "Electra"; ser. # 253 del. to Norway in Feb. of 1936 — LN-ABO was used year-around for tourist service out of Norway; ser. # 254 del. to Alaska; each airplane manufactured after 18 July 1941 must be inspected individually for compliance to pass certification.

ATC # 579
(7-22-35)
BEECH, MODEL B-17-R.

Fig. 283. Beech B-17-R with 420 h.p. Wright engine.

The Beech model B-17-R was kin to the earlier 17-R, but nearly 3 years of development had greatly improved the breed. Just by comparison, the new B-17-R was a little bit longer, not quite as tall, the thicker wing (with a more docile airfoil) was of less span and less area, the weight empty was at least 500 lbs. less, the gross weight was 900 lbs. less, and the airplane was about $4000. cheaper. This sounds like a lot less airplane, but the B-17-R was actually a better airplane by far. As the top of the Beech line for 1935 the (420 h.p.) B-17-R was definitely aimed at the limousine trade and at discriminating men of big business; the roster of owners was studded with many famous names. Mrs. Margaret Dorst of California took delivery of a B-17-R and was said to be the first woman in America to own and fly her own 200 m.p.h. airplane. Jimmy Haizlip, famous racing pilot, owned one also. Most of the B-17-R were kept very busy flying around the country on errand or whim, and several became more or less famous, at least by the frequency of their appearances, but the most famous by far was G-ADLE. Flown by Capt. Harold L. Farquhar, a British sportsman and a friend, the B-17-R (G-ADLE) made a leisurely globegirdling trip from New York to London, but by flying to the west instead of east across the Atlantic. Leaving New York as a seaplane (on Edo 39-4000 floats) without removing the landing gear (it remained folded up in the belly) the B-17-R flew out across the expanse of Canada to Alaska, then across the Bering Straits to Siberia and into Manchuria. At Manchuria the float gear was disconnected, the wheels folded out as needed and the airplane continued on as a landplane. The next leg was across China, into India, and then along the Persian Gulf to Egypt. From there they struck out across No. Africa, past the island of Corsica, and into France, from where it was just a short hop to London, England. This was a sight-seeing flight just for the fun of it, but it was sprinkled with its miserable moments, and it emphasized just how primitive aviation facilities could be in other countries of the world. The 21,332 mile journey was accomplished in 153 hours of flying time, the engine never missed a beat, and the B-17-R flew like a charm all the way around.

The Beech model B-17-R was a cabin biplane with a retracting landing gear and seating arranged for 4 people. Development of the model B-17-R was instigated by the query of a customer. The Loffland Bros., an oil-drilling company, with Eddie Ross as its pilot, previously owned a 420 h.p. Beech (the 17-R) and more recently had ordered one of the Wright-powered

Fig. 284. The amazing G-ADLE prior to its globe-girdling jaunt; Capt. Farquhar seated on lower wing.

(285 h.p.) model B-17-E. Not entirely satisfied with performance of the B-17-E, as compared to their earlier 17-R, Ross inquired if it would be possible to install a 420 h.p. engine in the B-17-E to get the performance he was more familiar with. Ted Wells (chief engineer) calculated it would be possible, with limitations, so the B-17-R was approved accordingly. The new combination was approved with the 420 h.p. Wright engine, but with the stipulation that no more than 285 h.p. (.68 power) be used for cruising speed, with the max. of 450 h.p. used only on take-off. Even with the limitation imposed the B-17-R was quite an airplane and Eddie Ross was more than pleased. As powered with the 9 cyl. Wright R-975-E3 engine rated 420 h.p. at 2200 r.p.m. at 1400 ft. the model B-17-R was just slightly heavier than the B-17-E and its performance potential increased as it went up; it was quite content at 10,000 ft. while cruising easily at 200 m.p.h. The B-17-R had ability beyond belief and from a pilot's point of view it generated nothing but sincere admiration; those who had the good fortune to fly it were lavish with their praises. The type certificate number for the model B-17-R was issued 7-22-35 with amendment shortly after to include the seaplane version. Some 16 examples of this model were manufactured by the Beech Aircraft Co. at Wichita, Kansas. Farquhar's ship G-ADLE was first shown at the Detroit Air Show for 1935 (July 19-28) and then flown to the Edo factory for the fitting of floats.

Listed below are specifications and perfor-mance data for the Beech model B-17-R as powered with 420 h.p. Wright R-975-E3 engine; length overall 24'5"; height overall 8'2"; wing span upper & lower 32'0"; wing chord upper & lower 60"; total wing area 267 sq. ft.; airfoil Clark CYH; wt. empty 2238 lbs.; useful load 1362 lbs.; payload with 93 gal. fuel 589 lbs. (3 pass. & 79 lbs. baggage); gross wt. 3600 lbs.; max. speed 211; cruising speed (.68 power) 195 at 5000 ft. and 202 at 9000 ft.; cruising speed (sea level) 185; landing speed (with flaps) 55; climb 1600 ft. first min. at sea level; ser. ceiling 22,000 ft.; gas cap. 93 gal.; oil cap. 6 gal.; cruis-ing range (.68 power) at 23.5 gal. per hour 760 miles; price $14,500. at factory field.

The B-17-R as seaplane on Edo 39-4000 twin-float gear same as above except for following: wt. empty 2610 lbs.; useful load 1362 lbs.; payload with 70 gal. fuel 635 lbs.; gross wt. 3972 lbs.; max. speed 175 at sea level; cruising speed 130 at sea level; cruising speed (.68 power) 150 at 9000 ft.; landing speed (with flaps) 60; climb 1200 ft. first min. at sea level; ser. ceiling 18,000 ft.

The construction details and general arrange-ment of the model B-17-R were typical to that of the B-17-E as described here in the chapter for ATC # 566. The only significant difference in the B-17-R was mounting of the Wright R-975-E3 engine and any slight modifications necessary for this installation. A 28 gal. fuselage tank and a 42-gal. fuselage tank (under cabin floor), and a 23 gal. tank mounted in the right upper wing provided normal fuel cap. of 93 gal. An extra 23

Fig. 285. This B-17-R was formerly a B-17-E.

gal. tank in the left upper wing and one in each wing root of the lower wing were available for a 116 gal., 139 gal., or 162 gal. capacity; payload was adjusted accordingly. When a Hamilton-Standard controllable propeller was fitted to the B-17-R, a 25 lb. tool kit (or ballast) was fastened in the tail cone to balance the extra weight. The B-17-R had differential ailerons on the lower wing and wing flaps on underside of the upper wing. A reshaping of the elliptical wing-tips on the B-17-E and B-17-R caused a loss of 5 sq. ft. in wing area, but the higher wing-loading was barely noticed. There was some difficulty in getting the tail down to a 3-point attitude in landing, so the landing gear was shortened by 4 in. to reduce the 3-point angle. A Curtiss-Reed metal propeller, electric engine starter, an Exide battery, Eclipse generator, fuel pump, dual controls, cabin heater, wheel brakes, tail wheel, navigation lights, complete set of engine-flight instruments, compass, clock, fuel gauges, fire extinguisher, assist ropes, safety belts, and first-aid kit were standard equipment. A Hamilton-Standard controllable propeller, radio, bonding & shielding, landing lights, parachute flares, and all the latest navigational aids were optional. The next Beech development was the model C-17-L as described in the chapter for ATC # 602.

Listed below are B-17-R entries as gleaned from registration records:

NC-14413;	B-17-R	(# 38)	Wright 420.
G-ADLE;	"	(# 50)	"
-15413;	"	(# 52)	"
-15414;	"	(# 53)	"
-15411;	"	(# 54)	"
-15410;	"	(# 55)	"
-15483;	"	(# 56)	"
NPC-28;	"	(# 63)	"
-15490;	"	(# 64)	"
-15489;	"	(# 65)	"
-15811;	"	(# 66)	"
NC-281Y;	"	(# 68)	"
-15814;	"	(# 69)	"
-15815;	"	(# 70)	"
-15816;	"	(# 71)	"
-15817;	"	(# 72)	"

This approval for ser. # 38, 50 and up; ser. # 38 converted to a B-17-R from a B-17-E; ser. # 50 flew New York to London via westerly route around the world; ser. # 63 operated in the Philippine Islands; ser. # 66 del. to France where it operated as F-APFD; ser. # 69 operated by Prest-O-Lite Battery Co.; ser. # 71 operated by Jimmy Haizlip; B-17-R served as UC-43H in USAAF during W.W.2; this approval expired 9-30-39.

Fig. 286. The Stinson SR-6 with 245 h.p. Lycoming engine.

Exciting things were brewing at the Stinson plant in 1935; both day and night shifts were working to fill accumulated orders. A brand-new, rather revolutionary "Reliant" was shaping up too, but it wasn't quite ready for release, so the "Reliant" for the model year beginning in mid-1935 was basically just a refinement of the previous year's model. This model was the SR-6 which was for the most part a refinement of the previous SR-5, but many Stinson customers traded for newer models every year, so there was a fairly good demand for the SR-6 series. These trade-ins flown to the plant in Wayne, Mich. had formed a sizeable "used plane lot" at the factory, but they didn't stand around long because they were all bargain-priced, and older models of the "Stinson" were still very much in demand. The SR-6 "Reliant" for 1935 was offered with 4 different Lycoming engines and most of the improvements were aimed at more comfort. Two shiny-new SR-6 (an SR-6A and an SR-6B) were flown to Detroit right off the production floor where they were displayed at the All-American Aircraft Show for 1935, an annual industry reunion which had suffered a 3-year lapse. The "Tri-Motor" Stinson (Model A) was also shown and spectator interest was running high. A glistening array of new Lycoming engines were also displayed in the Stinson booth. The week-long show (July 20-28) was a big hit and a pageant of the progress made in aviation since the past 3 years. Chas. J. Correll, the Andy of the famous "Amos and Andy" show on radio was the proud owner of an SR-6B, and many other national luminaries were also on the roster. The new airplane was also popular with big business firms that for years had put their trust in Stinson for reliable transportation. Despite the fact that the SR-6 was regarded as just an improvement over the previous year's model, it was quite an airplane and now generally remembered as the last of the straight-wing "Reliant".

The Stinson model SR-6 was a high-winged cabin monoplane with seating arranged for 4 or 5 people. Because of higher horsepower and greater gross weight allowances the SR-6 and SR-6B were eligible to carry 5; the SR-6A and SR6C were limited to 4. Likewise, the SR-6 and the SR-6B were eligible for greater fuel capacity which extended range to nearly 700 miles. Much of the improvement lie in the interior which was more spacious and arranged for better moving about; window area was increased and entry doors were much wider. Contours of the fuselage were more rounded for a slight gain in speed and wing tips were "washed up" to improve control at low speeds and in the "stall". Vacuum-operated wing flaps made any little strip a useable airport. Everything in and about the air-

Fig. 287. "Reliant" SR-6 was popular in the field of business.

plane was pretty much the same as in earlier "Reliant", but everything seemed to be a little better. As powered with the 9 cyl. Lycoming R-680-6 engine rated 245 h.p. at 2300 r.p.m. with a Lycoming-Smith controllable propeller the SR-6 was rather lively and quite a capable airplane. The SR-6B was powered with the Lycoming R-680-5 engine rated 260 h.p. at 2300 r.p.m. also with a Lycoming-Smith controllable prop did not register that much increase in performance statistics, but it was clearly a much better airplane for those long trips. The SR-6A as powered with the Lycoming R-680-4 engine rated 225 h.p. at 2100 r.p.m. with a fixed-pitch metal propeller was the economy model of the series and the overall best bargain. The SR-6C as powered with the Lycoming R-680-2 engine rated 240 h.p. was a modification available for the SR-6A which improved performance for a little extra cost. All models in the series were very stable, delightfully active when spurred, and exceptionally reliable. The SR-6 series was the lesser-known of the "Reliant", but it surely contributed its share to a commendable reputation. The type certificate number for the SR-6 series was issued 7-23-35 and some 50 examples in this series were manufactured by the Stinson Aircraft Corp. at Wayne, Mich. Lucius B. Manning was pres.; Wm. A. Mara was V.P.; B. D. DeWeese was V.P. & gen. mgr.; J. C. "Jack" Kelley was sales mgr.; C. R. Irvine was chf. engr. of the Reliant div., with Robert L. Hall on the design staff.

Listed below are specifications and performance data for the "Reliant" model SR-6 as powered with 245 h.p. Lycoming R-680-6 engine using a Lycoming-Smith controllable propeller; length overall 27'0"; height overall 8'5"; wing span 43'3"; wing chord 80"; total wing area 235 sq. ft.; airfoil Clark Y; wt. empty 2315 lbs.; useful load 1235 lbs.; payload with 50 gal. fuel 735 lbs. (4 pass. & 55 lbs. baggage); payload with 75 gal. fuel 578 lbs. (3 pass. & 68 lbs. baggage); max. baggage allowance 150 lbs.; gross wt. 3550 lbs.; max. speed 140; cruising speed 128; landing speed (with flaps) 52; climb 770 ft. first min. at sea level; ser. ceiling 14,500 ft.; gas cap. normal 50 gal.; gas cap. max. 75 gal.; oil cap. 4-5 gal.; cruising range at 13.5 gal. per hour 470-695 miles; basic price $5995. at factory field. Price was nearly $9000. with all optional equipment.

Specifications and data for model SR-6A with 225 h.p. Lycoming R-680-4 engine using a fixed-pitch metal propeller same as above except as follows: wt. empty 2310 lbs.; useful load 1015 lbs.; payload with 50 gal. fuel 515 lbs. (3 pass. & 5 lbs. baggage); gross wt. 3325 lbs.; max. speed 137; cruising speed 125; landing speed (with flaps) 50; climb 725 ft. first min. at sea level; ser. ceiling 14,000 ft.; gas cap. 50 gal.; oil cap. 4 gal.; cruising range at 13 gal. per hour 470 miles; price not announced.

Specifications and data for model SR-6B with 260 h.p. Lycoming R-680-5 engine using Lycoming-Smith controllable propeller same as basic SR-6 except as follows: wt. empty 2347 lbs.; useful load 1203 lbs.; payload with 50 gal. fuel 703 lbs. (4 pass. & 23 lbs. baggage); payload with 75 gal. fuel 546 lbs. (3 pass. & 36 lbs. baggage); gross wt. 3550 lbs.; max. speed 142; cruising speed 130; landing speed (with flaps) 52; climb 800 ft. first min. at sea level; ser. ceiling 15,200 ft.; gas cap. normal 50 gal.; gas cap. max. 75 gal.; oil cap. 4-5 gal.; cruising range at 14 gal. per hour 455-660 miles; price $6995. at factory

Fig. 288. An SR-6B with 260 h.p. Lycoming engine; ship shown was cargoplane in Alaska.

field. The SR-6C was a model available with the 240 h.p. Lycoming R-680-2 engine, but no examples of the model SR-6C appear in any registration listings.

The fuselage framework was built up of welded chrome-moly steel tubing, faired to shape with wooden formers and fairing strips, then fabric covered. Entry doors were much larger and front seat-backs folded down to provide better moving about. Both front seats were adjustable up, down, forward, and aft. The Y-type control column was replaced with separate wheels that protruded from the dash-board; rudder pedals were also adjustable. The sofa-type rear seat was wide enough for 3 across; a baggage bin with allowance for 50 lbs. was under this seat. The main baggage compartment with allowance for up to 100 lbs. was behind the rear seat with access thru a door on right side of the fuselage. The cabin was heated, ventilated, sound-proofed, and all windows were of shatter-proof glass. The wing framework, in 2 halves and of more area, was built up of solid spruce spars that were routed to an I-beam section, and spot-welded stainless steel wing ribs; the leading edges were covered with dural sheet and the completed framework was covered in fabric. The metal-framed ailerons were of the balanced and slotted type and trailing edge wing flaps were vacuum-operated. Fuel tanks were mounted in the root end of each wing half; 25 gal. or 37.5 gal. tanks were standard and 50 gal. tanks were

optional. The landing gear was identical using 7.50x10 wheels fitted with 8.50x10 tires; wheels were fitted with multiple-disc brakes. Tail wheel was fitted with a 10.5 in. streamlined tire, and parking brakes were also provided. The fabric covered tail group was built up of welded C/M steel tubing; all movable controls were balanced and the horizontal stabilizer was adjustable in flight. Rudder was fitted with adjustable trim tab. A metal propeller, electric engine starter, battery, wheel pants, cabin heater, rear-view mirror, cabin lights, roll-down windows, navigation lights, assist cords, ash trays, and a 3-color exterior finish was standard equipment. Landing lights, parachute flares, generator, Pyrene or Lux fire extinguishers, radio, bonding & shielding, extra fuel capacity, a cargo interior, and Edo twin-float gear were optional. The next "Reliant" development was the revolutionary SR-7 as described in the chapter for ATC # 594 of this volume.

Listed below are SR-6 entries as gleaned from registration records:

NC-15103; SR-6   (# 9601) Lycoming 245.
  -15111;   "   (# 9602)   "

  -15112;   "   (# 9603)   "
  -15113;   "   (# 9604)   "
  -15114; SR-6B (# 9605) Lycoming 260.
  -15115; SR-6 (# 9606) Lycoming 245.
  -15116;   "   (# 9607)   "
  -15117; SR-6B (# 9608) Lycoming 260.

Fig. 289. Stinson management pose with experimental SR-6X.

-15118;	SR-6	(# 9609)	Lycoming 245.
-15119;	SR-6B	(# 9610)	Lycoming 260.
-15120;	SR-6	(# 9611)	Lycoming 245.
-15121;	"	(# 9612)	"
-15122;	"	(# 9614)	"
-15123;	"	(# 9615)	"
-15124;	"	(# 9616)	"
-15125;	"	(# 9617)	"
-15126;	"	(# 9618)	"
-15127;	SR-6A	(# 9619)	Lycoming 225.
-15128;	SR-6	(# 9620)	Lycoming 245.
-15129;	SR-6A	(# 9622)	Lycoming 225.
-15130;	SR-6	(# 9623)	Lycoming 245.
-15131;	"	(# 9624)	"
-15133;	"	(# 9625)	"
-15132;	"	(# 9626)	"
-15140;	"	(# 9627)	"
-15141;	"	(# 9628)	"
-15142;	"	(# 9629)	"
-15143;	"	(# 9630)	"
-15144;	"	(# 9631)	"
-15145;	"	(# 9632)	"
-15146;	"	(# 9633)	"
-15147;	"	(# 9634)	"
-15148;	"	(# 9635)	"
NS-15150;	"	(# 9636)	"
-15135;	"	(# 9637)	"
-15149;	"	(# 9639)	"
-15136;	"	(# 9640)	"
-15139;	SR-6X	(# 9641)	"
-15137;	SR-6	(# 9642)	"
-15167;	SR-6A	(# 9643)	Lycoming 225.
-15138;	SR-6	(# 9644)	Lycoming 245.
-15168;	"	(# 9645)	"
-15169;	"	(# 9646)	"
-15170;	"	(# 9647)	"
-15171;	"	(# 9648)	"

This approval for serial # 9601 and up; ser. # 9601 delivered to Auburn Automobile Co. of Ind.; ser. # 9607 del. to Morrell Packing Co.; ser. # 9608 del. to Chas. J. Correll of "Amos and Andy"; ser. # 9613 apparently not used; ser. # 9615 not verified; ser. # 9621, 9638, 9649 probably exported; G-ADJK was SR-6A in England, ser. no. unknown; ser. # 9629 del. to Lycoming Mfg. Co.; ser. # 9631 del. to Ruth Chatterton, famous movie actress and a great "Stinson" fan; ser. # 9636 del. to Penn. Aero. Dept.; ser. # 9643 del. to (Texaco) Texas Oil Co.; ser. # 9644 del. to Merrimac Finishes; this approval expired 9-30-39.

Fig. 290. Waco S3HD-A with 420 h.p. "Wasp Jr." engine as fitted for service in Cuba.

The military aspirations of Latin-American countries was beginning to build up because of world events, but being held to a modest budget they generally had to be satisfied with commercial airplanes that were modified to serve as military machines. Several of the earlier Waco "Straight-Wing" and the "Taper-Wing" were already serving in various countries as military machines, but in the "Model D" Waco Aircraft now had a high-performance biplane that would require no modification to become a top-notch military airplane. In fact, the S3HD "Super Sport" (ATC # 543) was no less than a stripped military machine in disguise as a custom-built airplane for the sportsman. As an armed military machine the S3HD-A was designed for a rather wide variety of equipment to perform diverse duties; in addition to the standard two-place "pursuit" version, the basic airplane could easily be converted to delivering bombs, as an aerial ambulance, or to haul mail and cargo. As an "armed" airplane, ready to participate in war, the S3HD-A mounted one fixed (.30 caliber) machine gun in each lower wing, one flexible mounted (.30 caliber) machine gun in the observer-gunner cockpit, and provisions for one or two bomb racks. The bomb-racks under the fuselage belly were able to mount five 25 lb. bombs or two 125 lb. bombs for troop harrassment or demolition. As a weapon to repel insurgence the "Model D" promised to be quite effective. As if calculated to appeal to the romanticism of Latin-American people the S3HD-A was contoured with a flair and its jaunty behavior went hand-in-hand with show-of-strength and military pomp.

Earlier military-type (armed) models were just conversions of existing Waco designs and were selected for this use because of unusual performance characteristics, and the uncanny ability to operate from the most restricted areas. These characteristics were invaluable in the outposts of modern civilization where large well-developed airports were either unheard of or terrain did not permit their construction. The success of these various "export models" prompted Waco Aircraft to design a strictly military airplane embodying the requirements for modern military tactics, and yet retain most performance characteristics of the typical "Waco" biplane. Development was well along early in 1933 with a Wright-powered model called the WHD, and continued steadily with a resulting "armed" model (WHD-A) ready to offer for export early in 1935. Meanwhile, the S3HD sport model was developed in between the two WHD airplanes. The basic "Model D" airframe, designed to fulfill 12 different functions, was available for varied military purposes with a choice of 6 different engines, ranging from 250 h.p. to 450 h.p. Truly a versatile lineup of low-budget military airplanes.

The Waco model S3HD-A was a military-type biplane with seating arranged for a crew of

Fig. 291. The S3HD-A as holstered with military armament.

two. As an attraction to smaller nations that had less money to spend for military aircraft, the S3HD-A offered utility and unusual versatility. Wrapped up here in one machine was the capability to do "pursuit" work, attack the enemy as a two-place "fighter", engage in troop "strafing", or the "bombing" of critical targets. For duties of less aggressive nature the S3HD-A was also adaptable to "observation" with radio communication, photo-reconnaissance, or the evacuation of litter patients, if need be. In less than an hour's time the "Model D" could be converted from one duty to another. For a high-performance airplane that cost less than $30,-000. this was indeed a bargain in jack-of-all-trades. The pilot's cockpit was in front, but the rear cockpit also had controls and instrumentation for emergency; the back seat was adjustable to rearward-facing or forward-facing positions. Both occupants were protected by a canopy enclosure with sliding panels; the gunner was partially enclosed even in normal use of the flexible gun. Considerable wing stagger, wing root cut-outs, and the position of occupants relative to the upper wing provided exceptional visibility. As powered with the 9 cyl. "Wasp Junior" TB engine rated 420 h.p. at sea level the S3HD-A had the spirit of a sport-plane with the performance necessary for a war-machine that shared no apology. Quick response and excellent maneuverability was backed up by a beefy airframe that was designed to soak up tremendous air-loads or pilot-inflicted punishment. In comparison, the S3HD-A "Fighter" was pretty much like the S3HD "Super Sport" except that it was holstered down with firearms, so it was hampered just a little by the extra weight. The S3HD-A in its dress of gleaming white was never called upon to serve in actual combat, so it was not proven in the heat of battle, but the

capability was there, had it been needed. The type certificate number for the model S3HD-A was issued 7-26-35 and only one example of this model was manufactured by the Waco Aircraft Co. at Troy, Ohio.

Listed below are specifications and performance data for the Waco model S3HD-A as powered with 420 h.p. "Wasp Junior" TB engine; length overall 25'6"; height overall 8'11"; wing span upper 32'9"; wing span lower 27'0"; wing chord upper 66"; wing chord lower 57"; wing area upper 156.2 sq. ft.; wing area lower 100.1 sq. ft.; total wing area 256.3 sq. ft.; airfoil Clark Y; wt. empty 2442 (2598) lbs.; useful load 1458 (1378) lbs.; payload was variable; gross wt. 3900 (3976) lbs.; figures in parentheses with extra armament; max. speed 188 at 1000 ft.; cruising speed (.70 power) 163 up to 6000 ft.; landing speed 65; climb 1600 ft. first min. at sea level; ser. ceiling 20,000 ft.; gas cap. max. 109 gal.; oil cap. 8 gal.; cruising range (.70 power) at 26 gal. per hour 640 miles; price $19,-750. to $23,775. according to options installed, plus crating and delivery to P.O.E. Reasonable loads in excess of gross weight allowance could be carried with safety, but with some loss of performance. As fitted with a Hamilton-Standard controllable propeller an overload to 4200 lbs. was acceptable.

The construction details and general arrangement of the model S3HD-A were typical to that of the S3HD as described here in the chapter for ATC # 543, including the following. As a two-place pursuit, the airplane had 2 lower wing-mounted fixed machine guns (Colt or Browning) of .30 caliber; remote controls and gun sight was in the front cockpit. Magazines provided for up to 1000 rounds of ammo; electric counters showed rounds fired. A flexible-mounted gun in observer's cockpit (.30 caliber Colt or Browning)

Fig. 292. WHD-A was Wright-powered sistership to S3HD-A.

was provided with up to 500 rounds of ammunition (5 boxes of 100 rounds each). Two Air Corps type A-3 bomb racks were mounted under fuselage belly in tandem; bombs totaling to 250 lbs. could be released by either occupant. By reducing fuel or armament, a two-way radio and Fairchild aerial camera could be installed. A ground-adjustable metal propeller, electric engine starter, generator, battery, bonding & shielding, navigation lights, dual controls, wheel brakes, wheel pants, tail wheel, sliding cockpit enclosure, fuel gauges, clock, complete set of engine & flight instruments, adjustable seats, fire extinguisher, first-aid kit, tool kit, tie-down ropes, and log books were standard equipment.

A Hamilton-Standard controllable propeller, Fairchild camera, two-way radio, landing lights, parachute flares, extra instruments, 20 gal. extra fuel, and Edo twin-float gear were optional. The next Waco development was the model CPF as described in the chapter for ATC # 583 of this volume.

Number 23: S3HD-A (# 3954) Wasp Jr. TB.

This approval for ser. # 3954 and up; the one-only S3HD-A was sold and delivered (7-30-35) to Govt. of Cuba through Len J. Povey who was director of aeronautics in that country; this airplane also available with 320 h.p. "Wasp Junior" T1B as model SHD-A or with 450 h.p. "Wasp Junior" SB as model S2HD-A.

Fig. 293. Lineup of "Model D" slated for Uruguay.

CURTISS-WRIGHT "COMMUTER", CA-1.

Fig. 294. Curtiss-Wright "Commuter" poses on its unusual tricycle landing gear.

All discussions readily concede that the "amphibious airplane" is the most useful airplane ever designed. In terms of utility, pleasure value, and convenience, it is hard to beat an airplane that can operate as easily off land as it can off water. However, the price one must pay for all this utility and convenience reflects in penalties of excessive weight, a lot more parasitic drag, and added maintenance problems. Poor performance was also a prime penalty unless excessive power was used to offset the losses. Some "amphibians" were better than others, but they all suffered the same penalties, simply because of traditional design. Having had experience with airplanes of this type, Capt. Frank T. Courtney, famous flier and engineer, analyzed their shortcomings and felt confident there were ways to overcome some of these penalties and produce an amphibian that would perform almost as efficiently as the average landplane. The configuration that was finally developed was an ingenious combination that eliminated many of the normal difficulties and allowed performance far above normal for this type of craft. Many features of the "Courtney Amphibian" may seem unconventional, but all

have been tried previously in one form or another. Under supervision of Courtney the hull of the revolutionary craft was built by the Edo Corp., a firm famous for their pontoons, while wings and engine drive were put together at the former Curtiss-Caproni plant. The Courtney amphibian was first registered as a "Curtiss-Caproni", but development was later taken over by Curtiss-Wright in St. Louis. Courtney ran certification tests on the 2nd example, which was built at St. Louis, and approval was awarded in Sept. of 1935. Here the ship was called "Curtiss-Courtney" and then changed to Curtiss-Wright "Commuter" model CA-1. A third ship was built, and finally sold to a customer from Japan. Three years of development and a whole lot of money produced one of the most efficient "amphibians" ever built, but it failed to get the chance to prove that this was so.

The Curtiss-Wright "Commuter" model CA-1 was an amphibious biplane of the flying-boat type with seating arranged for five. The airplane was a harmonious blend of many novel features that specifically contributed to its efficiency and high performance. After extensive study each feature was selected for its particular contribu-

Fig. 295. The Curtiss-Courtney with 365 h.p. Wright "pusher" engine.

tion and how it could benefit in several ways. The result was efficiency and performance unparalleled by any similar craft. The "Courtney" amphibian was formally introduced on an invitational round-trip seaplane cruise from New York City to the Thousand Islands in the St. Lawrence River. Fourteen assorted seaplanes and amphibians were included in the aerial armada; the "Courtney" looked very good by comparison and was easily the star of the show. Occupants of the "Commuter", treated to the utmost in comfort, sat well forward in the hull and extreme stagger of the lower wing offered no detriment to their visibility. The engine was placed well for mass balance and cowled-in extremely well for reduction of drag; the high "pusher" installation was of course best suited for a "flying boat". The tricycle landing gear was a novel feature providing excellent ground control, eliminating problems that top-heavy amphibians suffered on normal gear. As powered with the 9 cyl. Wright R-975-E1 engine rated 365 h.p. at 2100 r.p.m. the C-W "Courtney" delivered performance not normally possible in an airplane of this type, with passenger enjoyment and operational convenience never before offered in an "amphibian". Flight characteristics were amiable and the rugged structure was capable of continuous hard service. For the sportsman that wished to fly conveniently off land or water, the Curtiss-Wright (Courtney) "Commuter" was perhaps the best amphibious airplane ever built. The type certificate number for the "Commuter" model CA-1 was issued 9-3-35 and it is likely that no more than 3 examples of this model were built. The first example was ap-

proved on a Group 2 memo # 2-497 (issued 1-9-35) and subsequent examples were manufactured at the Curtiss-Wright Airplane Co. plant in Robertson (St. Louis), Mo. Capt. Frank T. Courtney was assisted by Edo engineers on the prototype, and by Curtiss-Wright engineers on subsequent versions.

Listed below are specifications and performance data for the Curtiss-Wright "Commuter" model CA-1 as powered with 365 h.p. Wright R-975-E1 engine; length overall 31'0"; height overall (on wheels) 12'2"; wing span upper 40'0"; wing span lower 35'0"; wing chord upper & lower 60"; total wing area 335 sq. ft.; airfoil NACA-2412; wt. empty 3100 lbs.; useful load 1600 lbs.; payload with 80 gal. fuel 900 lbs. (4 pass. & 220 lbs. of baggage & marine gear); gross wt. 4700 lbs.; max. speed (2150 r.p.m.) 153; cruising speed (.75 power) 126; landing (stall) speed 60; climb 835 ft. first min. at sea level; ser. ceiling 13,000 ft.; gas cap. 80 gal.; oil cap. 6.75 gal.; cruising range (.75 power) at 21 gal. per hour 470 miles; price not announced.

The all-metal hull framework of 51 in. width was built up of riveted dural members that were anodized and painted, then covered with smooth "Alclad" metal sheet. Right side half of the windshield frame opened out to provide hatchway for entry into cabin; steps on the hull were provided for climbing top-side. The bench-type seat in back seated 3 across and front seats were individual; right seat-back folded down to form step into cabin. The engine was mounted "pusher" fashion above the hull on a system of struts and fitted with a 31 in. extension shaft to bring propeller well beyond wing's trailing edge; the novel streamlined nacelle also formed the

Fig. 296. The Courtney amphibian was at ease on land or water.

center-section to which upper wings were attached. Leading edge of engine cowl also formed a reservoir for oil supply. The lower wings were mounted to the hull with extreme stagger to provide clear visibility and eliminate wing structure in the cabin area; the wing cellule was braced together by N-type interplane struts and a tension-compression strut was used instead of criss-cross wires. The wing framework, in 4 panels, was built up of solid spruce spar beams with spruce and plywood truss-type wing ribs; the leading edges were covered with dural sheet and the completed framework was covered in fabric. Metal-framed ailerons were on lower wings only. All-metal tip floats were mounted to underside of lower wings. The 80 gal. fuel tank formed the rear seat and was actually part of the cabin structure; a Romec fuel pump provided fuel flow to the engine. The tricycle landing gear of 66 in. tread retracted into the hull; the main wheels retracted into wells on either side and the nose-wheel folded up into the bow. Autofan wheels were fitted with "General" streamlined tires and mechanical brakes; tricycle configuration permitted hard braking without fear of nose-over. The all-metal vertical fin was built integral to

the hull; the all-metal horizontal stabilizer was fastened high on the fin and braced to the hull frame. For trim, the horizontal stabilizer was adjustable in flight. Metal-framed rudder and elevators were covered in fabric; a dual water rudder was provided for better maneuvering in water. A fixed-pitch metal propeller, an electric engine starter, Exide battery, Romec fuel pump, fuel gauge, compass, navigation lights, anchor & mooring gear, fire extinguisher, and first-aid kit were standard equipment. Night-flying equipment, dual controls, and custom interior were optional. The next Curtiss-Wright development was the "Coupe" model 19-L as described in the chapter for ATC # 589 of this volume.

Listed below are "Courtney" entries as gleaned from registration records:

X-13298; Curtiss-Courtney (# 101) Wright 365.
NC-11780; Curtiss-Wright   (# 102) Wright 365.
    ; Curtiss-Wright   (# 103) Wright 365.

Serial # 101 approved on Group 2 certificate # 2-497; ser. # 102 and up on ATC # 582; ser. # 101 believed sold to John Lapham; ser. # 103 sold to customer in Japan, registration no. unknown.

Fig. 297. Waco CPF with 250 h.p. Wright engine; landplanes were delivered to Brazilian Army.

In the telling of the story, the unusual part about the Waco model CPF is the fact that out of the 41 aircraft of this type that were actually built in all, only one example operated here in this country. That single airplane, a model CPF-1 with 285 h.p. Wright R-760-E1 engine, was delivered to Col. R. L. Montgomery of Philadelphia, Penn. in Dec. of 1935 as a personal sport-plane. All the rest of the CPF, powered with 250 h.p. Wright R-760-E engines, were boxed and shipped to the government of Brazil. Thirty of the CPF were assigned to the Brazilian Army and 10 were assigned to the Brazilian Navy; the naval versions occasionally operated off water on Edo twin-float gear. The model CPF was not basically a primary trainer, but as an airplane with remarkable utility they were well suited for the job, and especially in the more intricate secondary phases. In their own training program the Brazilian Navy equipped some of the CPF with blind-flying hoods to teach pilots how to fly on instruments. Casa Meyrink Veiga in Rio de Janeiro were purchasing agents for the Brazilian forces and the airplanes had been ordered to bolster up the nation's air forces. Fourteen of the CPF were rolled off the assembly floor in Sept. of 1935, 16 were rolled off in Oct., and 10 were rolled off in Nov.; they were all boxed, shipped, and delivered shortly after. Typical of "Waco" reliability the Brazilian CPF were still going strong by March of 1943. Waco Aircraft always did have a little export business since 1928, and each year the foreign business was improving, but by 1935 its export business was taking on sizeable proportions. And, as mentioned, the CPF was a rare airplane in this country; about the only time one was ever seen it was getting ready to leave the country.

The Waco model CPF was an open cockpit biplane with seating arranged for 2 or 3. Normally, the bigger front cockpit seated 2, but for training purposes, as in the case of the Brazilian Army models, the front seat was fitted with a "bucket" to seat one. Outside of one airplane, all of the CPF were fitted as trainers and sent off to Brazil. The extent of the training program used in Brazil by their Army and Navy is not known, but it is obvious the CPF was able to handle whatever the program required. Seven-cylinder R-760-E (250 h.p.) engines were chosen for the Brazilian order because "Wright" engines had a good reputation in South America, and incidentally, the CPF was the first model in the "Series F" to be powered with Wright engines. One sport-model, a CPF-1, was

Fig. 298. Waco CPF riding gently on Edo floats.

delivered to Col. Montgomery with the R-760-E1 engine which was rated 285 h.p., and for 1936 a model DPF-6 was offered with this same engine, but apparently none were built. As powered with the 7 cyl. Wright R-760-E engine rated 250 h.p. at 2000 r.p.m. the model CPF was able to deliver a creditable performance from the word go. With the 285 h.p. Wright engine, as in the CPF-1, the performance gain was enough to raise a few eye-brows in disbelief. Waco Aircraft bragged on the flight characteristics, naturally, so we can assume they were typical of the new-generation F-series (such as UMF-YMF) or better, and that's not bad. The CPF was a beautiful airplane softly rounded and of full figure, but it was not a frail beauty; those in Brazil were still flying actively in 1943 and it would be interesting to know the actual extent of their service. The type certificate number for the model CPF was issued 9-14-35 and amended to include the CPF-1, CPF-6, and DPF-6. Forty-one examples were manufactured by the Waco Aircraft Co. at Troy, Ohio.

Listed below are specifications and performance data for the Waco model CPF as powered with 250 h.p. Wright R-760-E engine; length overall 23'2"; height overall 8'5"; wing span upper 30'0"; wing span lower 26'10"; wing chord upper & lower 57"; wing area upper 135.8 sq. ft.; wing area lower 107.8 sq. ft.; total wing area 243.6 sq. ft.; airfoil Clark Y; wt. empty 1725 lbs.; useful load 925 lbs.; payload with 50 gal. fuel 425 lbs. (2 pass. & 85 lbs. baggage); gross wt. 2650 lbs.; max. speed (105% power) 150; cruising speed (.75 power) 135; landing

(stall) speed 48; climb 1150 ft. first min. at sea level; ser. ceiling 18,000 ft.; gas cap. normal 50 gal.; gas cap. max. 73.5 gal.; oil cap. 16-19 qts.; cruising range (.75 power) at 15 gal. per hour 405 miles; price approx. $8000. at factory. Model CPF as seaplane on Edo 45-2880 twin-float gear eligible at 2880 lbs. gross weight.

Specifications and data for model CPF-1 or DPF-6 with 285 h.p. Wright R-760-E1 engine as offered in 1935-36, same as above except as follows: wt. empty 1741 lbs.; useful load 909 lbs.; payload with 50 gal. fuel 409 lbs.; gross wt. 2650 lbs.; max. speed (105% power) 156; cruising speed (.75 power) 142; landing speed 48; climb 1250 ft. first min. at sea level; ser. ceiling 20,000 ft.; gas cap. 73.5 gal.; oil cap. 19 qts.; cruising range (.75 power) at 17 gal. per hour 400 miles; price $8775. at factory field.

The fuselage framework was built up of welded chrome-moly steel tubing, heavily faired to a rounded shape with wooden formers and fairing strips, then fabric covered. A bench-type seat for 2 was in the front cockpit, but a bucket-type seat for one was optional. Rear cockpit had bucket seat for one; both seats were adjustable. A baggage compartment with allowance for up to 100 lbs. was in the turtle-back behind the rear cockpit. A large door provided entry to front cockpit and fuselage steps provided step-over entry to the rear seat. The Wright engine was encased in a deep-chord NACA cowl with humps on its surface to provide clearance for the rocker boxes. The wing framework, in 4 panels, was built up of spruce spar beams with spruce truss-type wing ribs reinforced with mahogany

Fig. 299. The CPF seaplanes were delivered to Brazilian Navy.

plywood gussets; the leading edges were covered with dural sheet and the completed framework was covered in fabric. Ailerons, one on each wing, were connected together in pairs with a push-pull strut. The center-section panel was mounted above the fuselage on N-type struts; 2 fuel tanks of 25 gal. each were mounted in the center-section panel. A 12.5 gal. fuel tank in the root end of each upper wing-half was optional. The Brazilian Navy models (seaplanes) were fitted with stainless steel interplane bracing wires and stainless steel control cables. The seaplanes were mounted on Edo 45-2880 twin-float gear with water rudders. The landing gear of 77 in. tread was of 2 faired vees fitted with "Waco" oleo-spring shock struts; struts were splined to hold alignment. Autofan 6.50x10 wheels were fitted with 4-ply 7.50x10 low-pressure tires and wheel brakes. The fabric covered tail group was a composite structure of wood and welded steel; rudder and elevators were aerodynamically balanced. The horizontal

Fig. 300. Of 41 CPF built only one was in civilian service.

stabilizer was adjustable for trim in flight. A Curtiss-Reed metal propeller, electric engine starter, battery, generator, dual controls, compass, air-speed ind., navigation lights, tail wheel, wheel brakes, parking brake, fire extinguisher, cockpit covers, engine cover, tool kit, and first-aid kit were standard equipment. A metal controllable propeller, oil cooler, brake pedals in front cockpit, landing lights, parachute flares, wheel pants, and extra fuel capacity were optional. The next Waco development was the Jacobs-powered model YPF as described in the chapter for ATC # 586 of this volume.

Listed below are CPF entries as verified by company records:

CPF (# 4250) Wright 250.

" (# 4251) "
" (# 4252) "
" (# 4253) "
" (# 4254) "
" (# 4255) "
" (# 4256) "
" (# 4257) "
" (# 4258) "
" (# 4259) "
" (# 4340) "
" (# 4341) "
" (# 4342) "
" (# 4343) "
" (# 4344) "
" (# 4345) "
" (# 4346) "
" (# 4347) "
" (3 4348) "
" (# 4349) "
" (# 4350) "
" (# 4351) "
" (# 4352) "
" (# 4353) "
" (# 4354) "
" (# 4355) "
" (# 4356) "
" (# 4357) "
" (# 4358) "
" (# 4359) "
" (# 4360) "
" (# 4361) "
" (# 4362) "
" (# 4363) "
" (# 4364) "
" (# 4365) "
" (# 4366) "
" (# 4367) '"
" (# 4368) "
" (# 4369) "
NC-15249; CPF-1 (# 4376) Wright 285.

This approval for ser. # 4250 and up; ser. # 4250 thru 4259, 4340 thru 4359 were Brazilian Army models; ser. # 4360 thru 4369 were Brazilian Navy models; all Brazilian aircraft del. in 1935; NC-15249 (ser. # 4376) a CPF-1 was mfgd. 12-4-35; ser. # 4376 was only CPF model sold in U.S.A.; this approval exired 2-28-41.

Note: Brazilian Army models powered by 250 h.p. Wright engines, swinging Hamilton-Standard fixed-pitch metal propellers, had full NACA-type engine cowl. Equipped with U. S. Army type toe brakes, Sperry gyro horizon, detachable engine mount, and 75 gal. fuel capacity. These airplanes were still in use by Brazilian Army in March of 1943; disposition unknown.

Note: Brazilian Navy models equipped same as Brazilian Army models except they were standard 3 place models, had blind-flying hood, Edo 45-2880 twin-float gear, Breeze shielding on engine ignition system, stainless steel interplane wires, stainless steel control cables, were painted Insignia Blue with Silver stripe edged in Gold. Circle insignia on upper surface of upper wings was Green outer, then Yellow with Blue center. These airplanes were still in use by Brazilian Navy in March of 1943; disposition unknown.

Fig. 301. The "Electra" 10-B with 420 h.p. Wright engines.

As part of its "Great Silver Fleet" on the eastern seaboard of the U.S.A., Eastern Air Lines ordered 5 of the Lockheed "Electra" transports, but specified they be powered with "Wright" engines; by corporate ties and by preference EAL was particularly partial to Wright engines. As the Model 10-B the twelve-place twin-engined "Electra" was powered with 2 Wright R-975-E3 engines rated 440 h.p. each and placed by EAL on schedules between New York to New Orleans, via Atlanta, and the Chicago to Miami route via Indianapolis; the "Electra" 10-B, like a local bus, also handled the intermediate stops on the way along each route. Some of these were only flag-stops. The fleet of 5 "Electra" were all operating for EAL by Dec. of 1935. Delta Air Lines, practically a neighbor of EAL, was also impressed with the Wright-powered "Electra" and ordered 3 of the Model 10-B for their route from Atlanta to Dallas; a route across 6 of the so-called cotton states, the "Electra" served 12 of the leading cities in the south. This route stretched into North Carolina by 1936. In 1937, Delta acquired another new 10-B and also one from EAL; for EAL (Eastern Air Lines) routes the 10-B had become too

small. Over in the mid-west, the Chicago and Southern Air Line ordered a fleet (5) of the Model 10-B for their route from Chicago to New Orleans via St. Louis and Memphis; inaugurating service May 1, with 7 stops on the "Valley Route" to the south, C and S cut 3 hours off former schedules and traffic had soon more than doubled. J. R. Brinkley, the famed "gland doctor", traded in his fast Cyclone-powered "Orion" for a "Club" model of the 10-B, stating he outgrew the capacity of the smaller Lockheed "Orion". With a diversified fleet already in its service the U. S. Coast Guard ordered a 10-B for its rescue system and labeled it the XR30-1; the interior was quickly converted to an ambulance, cargo-hauler, or personnel transport. By 1937, Lockheed was experiencing a lucrative export business, with all versions of the "Electra". Three of the 10-B were delivered to Ansett Airways in Australia, and soon the "Electra" was flying in 10 other countries. At the onset of World War 2 several of the Model 10-B were pressed into USAAF service as the UC-36C; generally, they were used as utility-transports. Two of the 10-B found their way to the RCAF in Canada where they joined 8

Fig. 302. Delta had 5 of the 10-B on routes across the south.

other "Electra" that were shipped there also. At the end of hostilities, those 10-B that were left were scattered in all directions for service on small feeder-lines; the longevity and continuing usefulness of the stalwart "Electra" was certainly commendable.

The Lockheed "Electra" model 10-B was a twin-tailed, all-metal, low-winged, twin-engined, transport monoplane with seating normally arranged for 10 passengers and a crew of 2. The Model 10-B, like its sisterships, was also designed as an airliner that offered high performance and twin-engined safety on routes that required shorter hops and frequent stops. Comparatively small for a twin-motored airliner the nimble "Electra" provided small-airplane handling and small-airplane economy with large-airplane comforts. The interior was adaptable to various layouts depending on the need. The airline versions were equipped with 5 seats on each side of a center aisle, and the "Club" version, like the one for Dr. Brinkley, was fitted with a divan and over-stuffed chairs. The example built for the U. S. Coast Guard was easily convertible for the many functions that lie within its duty as a utility transport. As powered with two 9 cyl. Wright R-975-E3 engines rated 440 h.p. each the "Electra" 10-B had an outstanding performance record in the low-lands of eastern U.S.A. and maintained 3-mile-a-minute schedules with ease and safety. It would be hard to judge one "Electra" version against another because pilots swear by one type of engine, and swear at another type, so this is no practical basis for comparison. The Wright-powered "Electra" 10-B had a large circle of admirers and it performed its job well, even in far-off Australia. The type certificate number for

the Model 10-B was issued 9-18-35 and some 18 examples of this model were manufactured by the Lockheed Aircraft Corp. at Burbank, Calif.

Listed below are specifications and performance data for the "Electra" model 10-B as powered with 2 Wright R-975-E3 engines rated 440 h.p. at 2200 r.p.m. at 1400 ft.; length overall 38'7"; height overall 10'1"; wing span 55'0"; wing chord at root 145"; wing chord at tip 48"; total wing area (incl. fuselage section) 458 sq. ft.; airfoil at root Clark Y-18; airfoil at tip Clark Y-9; wt. empty 6300 (6520) lbs.; useful load 3700 (3980) lbs.; payload with 194 gal. fuel & 2 pilots 2091 (2371) lbs.; payload with 150 gal. fuel & 2 pilots 2355 (2635) lbs.; max. baggage 655 lbs.; gross wt. 10,000 (10,500) lbs.; wts. in parentheses as amended with controllable propeller; max. speed 205 at 1400 ft.; cruising speed (.75 power) 186 at 7500 ft.; landing speed (with flaps) 64-65; climb 1230 (1080) ft. first min. at sea level; ser. ceiling 18,200 (17,000) ft.; figures in parentheses at 10,500 lbs. gross wt.; gas cap. 150-200 gal.; oil cap. 14 gal.; cruising range (.75 power) at 52 gal. per hour 500-650 miles; absolute ceiling (full load) on one engine 4000 ft.; price approx. $50,000. at factory.

The construction details and general arrangement of the Model 10-B were typical to that of all other "Electra" models described here in this volume, including the following: the only difference between the Model 10-B and any other model in the "Electra" series was the installation of Wright R-975-E3 engines. It was a relatively simple task to modify the nacelles for mounting of the 9 cyl. Wright engines and the cowling was modified to suit also. Four fuel tanks in the wing's center-section provided a

Fig. 303. Several 10-B were delivered to Australia, some served as C-36C in USAAF.

capacity of 194 gal.; a 7.5 gal. oil tank was mounted in each engine nacelle. A 230 gal. fuel capacity was optional. The main baggage compartment in the nose was allowed 300 lbs. and 250 lbs. was allowed in each wing compartment. Cabin appointments included ash trays, hat nets, curtains, a dome light, and reading lamps. A lavatory, drinking water, and a buffet with icebox was also provided in the airliner interior. Fixed-pitch metal propellers, electric engine starters, battery, generator, oil-coolers, dual controls, navigation lights, landing lights, parachute flares, wheel brakes, parking brake, 35x15-6 Goodyear airwheels, a 16x7-3 tail wheel, 2 flash lights in brackets, wing flaps, trimming tabs on rudder and elevator, two-way radio, bonding & shielding, antenna, cabin heat and ventilation, and a complete set of airline-type instruments were standard equipment. Hamilton-Standard controllable props, de-icing equipment, abrasion strips on fixed control surfaces, wheel fenders, extra fuel capacity, extra fire extinguishers, cargo interior, a custom "Club" interior, leather upholstery, automatic pilot, ski gear, and custom color schemes were optional at extra cost. The next "Electra" development was the Model 10-E as described in the chapter for ATC # 590 of this volume.

Listed below are Model 10-B entries as gleaned from various records:

NC-14958:	10-B	(# 1036)	Wright 440.
-14959:	"	(# 1037)	"
-14960:	"	(# 1038)	"
-14961:	"	(# 1039)	"
-14962:	"	(# 1040)	"
-14990:	"	(# 1049)	"
-14991:	"	(# 1050)	"
-14992:	"	(# 1051)	"
V-151:	"	(# 1053)	"
-16021:	"	(# 1056)	"
-16022:	"	(# 1057)	"
-16023:	"	(# 1058)	"
-16024:	"	(# 1059)	"
-16054:	"	(# 1066)	"
-16052:	"	(# 1067)	"
-16053:	"	(# 1077)	"
VH-UZN:	"	(# 1106)	"
VH-UZO:	"	(# 1107)	"
VH-UZP:	"	(# 1109)	"

This approval for ser. # 1036 and up; ser. # 1036, 1037, 1038, 1039, 1040 delivered to Eastern Air Lines; ser. # 1049, 1050, 1051, 1077 del. to Delta Air Lines; ser. # 1053 to Coast Guard as XR30-1; ser. # 1056, 1057, 1058, 1059, 1067 del. to Chicago & Southern Air Lines; ser. # 1066 del. to Dr. J. R. Brinkley; ser. # 1106, 1107, 1109 del. to Ansett Airways of Australia; ser. # 1021 (NC-14915) a model 10-A with Northwest Airlines, later del. to Alaska as a 10-B; this approval expired 10-7-41.

Fig. 304. As the "China Clipper" the Martin M-130 was an imposing sight.

The huge Martin M-130 flying boat will probably always be remembered as the "China Clipper", the grandiose airplane that inaugurated scheduled service for Pan American Airways across the Pacific to the Orient. Three of these majestic "Clipper" ships were built by Martin (Hawaii Clipper, Philippine Clipper, and China Clipper) and immediately caught the fancy of the entire U. S. public. Flying to the Orient was a romantic dream and it has been reported that tickets were being sold in Nov. of 1935 for a flight that was to actually leave nearly a year later. The first flight of the Martin M-130 "Clipper" across the vast Pacific Ocean was inauguration of "Trans-Pacific Mail" on 11-22-35; cheered by a crowd of 25,000 well-wishers, the "Clipper" took off with nearly 100,000 letters in its hold and headed for Honolulu; most of the crewmen on board were veterans that had made 9 Pacific crossings already in the trail-blazing Sikorsky S-42 "Clipper", so the Martin "Clipper" was in capable hands. The over-water hops to Hawaii, Midway Island, Wake Island,

Guam, and the Philippines were a "cruise" for the crew and the 8200 mile crossing was made 2 minutes under schedule. The schedule was 60 hours. The return flight to San Francisco was uneventful, except for some anxious moments in the edge of a typhoon just out of Guam, and an instrument landing in San Francisco Bay. The historic round-trip flight had set 19 world records and there had been no delay due to weather or to maintenance. While the "China Clipper" was making history, the other two Martin M-130 flying boats were being readied and both joined the "China Clipper" in Dec. of 1935; the other 2 were the "Hawaii Clipper" and the "Philippine Clipper". By early 1936 all 3 of the M-130 were in active service over the Pacific on shuttle service with airmail and non-revenue passengers between California and the Orient. Regular passenger service was inaugurated 10-21-36 when a load of dignitaries boarded the "Hawaii Clipper" for a five-day trip to Manila; the trip to Manila and the return to San Francisco were described as uneventful, but to some

Fig. 305. The "Hawaiian Clipper" in an enchanting setting.

of the people aboard it was the highlight of a lifetime. What the Sikorsky "Clipper" (S-42) had proven earlier could be done, was now routine for the Martin "Clipper". The Martin "flying boats" continued in the headlines because they were newsworthy, having gained fame and public acclaim for their accomplishments. Tragic headlines of 7-28-38 reported the "Hawaii Clipper" was lost somewhere between Guam and Manila; 16 vessels and 10 aircraft searched for it, but no trace was ever found. As the remaining two "Clipper" continued on what had become routine flights by now, they were occasionally updated with the latest equipment; improved propellers, more powerful engines, and navigational aids were added as they became available. In 1938 large American flags were painted on the bows and wings to prevent attack from Chinese or Japanese war-planes in the Orient where war-clouds were gathering. Early in 1942 the "Philippine Clipper" and the "China Clipper" were turned over to the U. S. Navy; they were overhauled, given a coat of drab war-paint and operated by Pan Am crews. The "Philippine Clipper" was lost in a storm on 1-21-42, but the "China Clipper" served until 10-13-43 and was then returned to Pan Am. Checked and repainted to original Pan Am colors, the "China Clipper" was removed from the Pacific and started tests on a run over the

Atlantic from Miami to Africa. While making a routine landing at Trinidad on 1-8-45 the "China Clipper" hit an object in the water which ripped her hull open; she sank rapidly in 30 feet of water just barely after her 10th birthday. Thus ended the saga of the Martin "Clipper". Their contribution to the development of aviation cannot be over-stressed; they probably did more to stimulate the public's interest in aviation during the 1935-40 period than anything else since Lindbergh landed in Paris in May of 1927.

The all-metal Martin M-130 was a huge 4-motored monoplane of the flying boat type with various seating arrangements up to 52 places. For stability in the water the M-130 had novel "sea wings" (sponsons) fastened to the lower hull, such as that used on the (German) "Dornier" flying boats for many years earlier. The keel of the first M-130 was laid in May of 1933 and as the first ship slid down the slip into the water on 10-30-34 it was the largest and the heaviest flying boat in the world. Chas. Lindbergh was supposed to test-hop the big "Clipper", but he was not available, so the chore went to Wm. K. Ebel. All of the early flights were ceremonial affairs with dignitaries aboard and newspapers were lavish in their coverage. All 3 of the M-130 were delivered to Pan Am by Nov. of 1935 and regular Trans-Pacific passenger schedules were inaugurated in 1936. Because of the more or less uneventful crossings

Fig. 306. The Martin 'Clipper" heads out to sea.

of the broad Pacific, the service soon became rather routine and Martin had proven that large multi-engined flying boats were quite capable of practical trans-ocean service. The huge interior of the Martin "Clipper" was plush and quite adaptable to various layouts, but the most popular set-up was 14 passengers in either day-lounge or sleeping berths, 2000 lbs. of mail and cargo, 30 lbs. of baggage per passenger, and fuel for a range of 3000 miles. Actually, any combination of passenger-cargo loads were possible according to cruising range desired; with a max. of 4000 gal. of fuel on board, in 6 tanks, a cruising range of 4000 miles was normally possible. As powered with four 14 cyl. Pratt & Whitney "Twin Wasp" (double-row) S1A2-G (supercharged & geared) engines rated 830 h.p. at 2400 r.p.m. at 6000 ft. the Martin M-130 was an impressive mass of machinery that brought people out from miles around just to watch it come in or leave. The "Twin Wasp" engines thundered and roared, and it was quite a spectacle to watch the huge "Clipper" leave its wake and spray as it lifted off. When loaded to its 26-ton gross the big boat was not exactly spritely, but it could operate normally even with only 3 of its engines. Engines of 950 h.p. each were later installed, with improved "Hydromatic" propellers, and it was a great help. The type certificate number for the Martin M-130 was issued 10-9-35 and 3 examples of this model were

manufactured by the Glenn L. Martin Co. at Baltimore, Md. Glenn L. Martin was pres. & gen. mgr.; Lessiter C. Milburn was V.P. & chf. engr.; B. C. Boulton and L. D. McCarthy were project engrs. on the M-130 development; Andre' Preister was Pan Am's chief engineer and had considerable influence in development of this airplane, especially the interior.

Listed below are specifications and performance data for the Martin M-130 as powered with 4 "Twin Wasp" S1A2-G engines of 830 h.p. each; length overall 90'7"; height overall 24'7"; wing span 130'0"; wing chord at root 246"; wing chord at tip 123"; total wing area (incl. sea wings) 2315 sq. ft.; airfoil Goettingen 398 mod.; wt. empty 24,611 lbs.; useful load 26,389 lbs.; payload with 3200 gal. fuel & 5 crew 4380 lbs. (14 pass., 420 lbs. pass.-baggage, 2000 lbs. mail-cargo); payload was actually variable with the cruising range desired; gross wt. 51,000 lbs.; max. speed 180 at 6000 ft.; cruising speed (.75 power) 163 at 7000 ft.; cruising speed (.60 power) 130 at sea level; landing speed 70; take-off run 45 secs.; climb 557 ft. first min. at sea level; ser. ceiling 17,000 ft.; ser. ceiling with any 3 engines 8400 ft.; gas cap. normal 3500 gal.; gas cap. max. 4077 gal.; oil cap. 216 gal.; cruising range (.60 power) at 130 gal. per hour 3200 miles; price approx. $430,000. at factory. Weights were amended to 25,350-26,650-52,000 lbs. in late 1936. Landings not permissible over

Fig. 307. An interior view of the Martin M-130.

48,000 lbs. gross wt.; excess weight had to be jettisoned.

The large two-step hull was an all-metal (24-ST) semi-monocoque structure covered in a combination of corrugated and smooth "Alclad" metal sheet. The 45 foot long cabin interior was divided into 5 water-tight compartments; there were 3 sound-proofed sleeping compartments for 6 people in each and the berths converted into comfortable settees for day flights. A 16 foot informal day-lounge was also used as a dressing-room for night-time flights; hot and cold water was available. Two complete lavatories were also provided at rear of cabin area. The bow of the hull had anchor compartment and place for all the sea gear; the so-called "bridge" had seating for pilot, co-pilot, navigator, and radio operator. Behind the bridge, in the pylon structure, was the engineers room with all controls for the engines, propellers, fuel, and other mechanical auxiliaries. Behind and below the bridge were compartments for luggage, mail and cargo, and a small galley. Sleeping quarters for crew (2 bunks) were aft of the cabin with emergency exit hatch in the ceiling; a storage compartment for crew belongings was just aft. Main entrance to the cabin area was a large split-type door on the left side just behind the bridge area; this was convenient to the luggage and cargo areas. Large windows on each side were of shatter-proof glass; the interior was very plush and arrangements were mixed and informal. The huge all-metal wing was perched atop a streamlined pylon and braced to the hull with heavy struts; the sea-wings stabilized the large boat in the water and also provided extra lifting area. 970 gal. of fuel was in each sea-wing. The 2 main fuel tanks were under the cabin floor and 2 aux. tanks were mounted up in the wing. The four engine nacelles were built into leading edge of the wing; fold-out portions of the wing's leading edge provided a work-stand on each side for servicing and maintenance of the engines. The huge tail group was an all-metal (24-ST) structure; the vertical fin and horizontal stabilizer were covered in Alclad sheet, while rudder and elevators were covered in fabric. The ailerons, rudder, and elevators were fitted with adjustable "tabs" for trimming in flight. Three-bladed metal Hamilton-Standard controllable propellers, hand-electric engine starters, generators, Exide batteries, fuel pumps, fuel gauges, fire extinguishers, dual controls, navigation lights, landing lights, parachute flares, bonding & shielding, first-aid equipment, complete set of airline-type engine and flight instruments, including radios and automatic-pilot as standard equipment. The next Martin development was the Model 156-C flying boat as described in the chapter for ATC # 697.

Listed below are Martin M-130 entries:

NC-14714; M-130 (# 556) 4 Twin-Wasp 830.
NC-14715; M-130 (# 557) 4 Twin-Wasp 830.
NC-14716; M-130 (# 558) 4 Twin-Wasp 830.

This approval for ser. # 556 and up; ser. # 556 was "Hawaii Clipper"; ser. # 557 was the "Philippine Clipper"; ser. # 558 was the "China Clipper"; this approval expired 9-30-39.

Fig. 308. Martin M-130 "on the step" and heading for the Orient.

Fig. 309. Capt. Sullivan at the controls.

ATC # 586
(11-19-35)
WACO, MODEL YPF-6.

Fig. 310. The Waco YPF-1 with 225 h.p. Jacobs engine.

A steady transition since 1933 was progressively lifting the "Model F" series right out of the traditional all-purpose class (when an airplane could earn a few dollars now and then) and into the special-purpose or sport-type category. These new "Model F" were now beautiful airplanes, and true, any of them were still able and even willing to work at something, if need be, but the "Series F" was getting pretty fancy and pilots were finding it almost distasteful to subject them to menial affairs not befitting their station. Two very fine examples of this new trend were the Waco models YPF and ZPF. The model YPF was normally a 3-seater and powered with the 225 h.p. Jacobs L-4 engine; for 1936 it was known as the YPF-6 and for 1937 it was known as the YPF-7. The model ZPF was similar, but powered with the 285 h.p. Jacobs L-5 engine; for 1936 it was known as the ZPF-6 and for 1937 it was known as the ZPF-7. Both were primarily designed for special chores in business and for the more affluent sportsman or sportswoman. Certainly not trading off any of their utility for the sake of a handsome figure, both of these F-type were also eligible to operate on Edo pontoons off water. Considering that either of these airplanes would more often be flying without passengers, Waco provided a metal cover to close off the front cockpit and in-

troduced a sliding-hatch canopy over the pilot's cockpit. By closing off the gaping hole in front and streamlining the pilot's station the turbulence and drag was reduced considerably to realize smoother handling and a bit more speed. Oddly enough, these 2 airplanes (YPF-ZPF) were the fastest of the "Model F" and could outrun any of the F-type built years later. The models YPF-ZPF were small in number, but had an exciting part in Waco history. A ZPF-6 was reported (1946) to be at the bottom of the Niagara River, and a YPF-6 was recently being restored in Colorado.

The Waco models YPF-ZPF were sport-type open cockpit biplanes with seating normally arranged for 3. The front cockpit was fitted either with a bench-type seat for 2, a bucket-type seat for one, or the cockpit could be closed off with a metal cover when not in use. The pilot's cockpit in the rear was fitted with a sliding-hatch canopy that faired right into the turtle-back and provided the pilot a cozy station in the cold of winter. Having an open cockpit for the passengers in front and a cozy, enclosed cockpit for the pilot in back was a rather odd combination; it must have drawn chiding remarks from the passengers occasionally. On the other hand, the removable metal cover over the front cockpit transformed it into a handy, oversized luggage

Fig. 311. The Waco ZPF-6 with 285 h.p. Jacobs engine.

compartment and faired over the large gaping hole. These F-6 models were offered with either the Jacobs L-4 or L-5 engine, and numerous options were available; for 1937 they were even more deluxe and of course, cost a bit more. As powered with the 7 cyl. Jacobs L-4 engine rated 225 h.p. at 2000 r.p.m. the YPF-6 and YPF-7 were airplanes of remarkable performance, and as powered with the 7 cyl. Jacobs L-5 engine rated 285 h.p. at 2000 r.p.m. the ZPF-6 and ZPF-7 were even better. Responsive and maneuverable, both were eligible for use in secondary phases of the CPTP pilot-training program. At this point it would be timely to say that design of the UMF-YMF, the CPF, and the YPF-ZPF led directly into development of the famous PT-14 and the UPF-7. The type certificate number for the YPF and ZPF series was issued 11-19-35 and perhaps no more than 8 examples were manufactured by the Waco Aircraft Co. at Troy, Ohio.

Listed below are specifications and performance data for the Waco model YPF-6 as powered with 225 h.p. Jacobs L-4 engine; length overall 23'4"; height overall 8'5"; wing span upper 30'0"; wing span lower 26'10"; wing chord upper & lower 57"; wing area upper 135.8 sq. ft.; wing area lower 107.8 sq. ft.; total wing area 243.6 sq. ft.; airfoil Clark Y; wt. empty 1675 (1694) lbs.; useful load 975 (956) lbs.; payload with 48.5 gal. fuel 484 (465) lbs. (2 pass. & 144 or 125 lbs. baggage); gross wt. 2650 lbs.; max. speed (105% power with wheel pants & cockpit canopy) 150 at 1000 ft.; cruising speed (.75 power) 135 at 1000 ft.; max. cruising speed (2000 r.p.m.) 143 at 6000 ft.; landing speed 50; climb 1100 ft. first min. at sea level; ser. ceiling 17,500 ft.; gas cap. normal 48.5 gal.; gas cap. max. 73.5

gal.; oil cap. 16-19 qts.; cruising range (.75 power) at 14.5 gal. per hour 405 miles; price $7295. at factory, lowered to $7095. later in the year. YPF-7 same as above except more deluxe, heavier empty, and cost $8395. at factory.

Specifications for model ZPF-6 with 285 h.p. Jacobs L-5 engine, same as above except as follows; length overall 23'2"; wt. empty 1698 (1725) lbs.; useful load 952 (925) lbs.; payload with 50 gal. fuel 452 (425) lbs. (2 pass. & 112 or 85 lbs. baggage); gross wt. 2650 lbs.; max. speed (105% power, with wheel pants & cockpit canopy) 156; cruising speed (.75 power) 142 at 1000 ft.; max. cruising speed (2000 r.p.m.) 149 at 6000 ft.; landing speed 52; climb 1250 ft. first min. at sea level; ser. ceiling 19,500 ft.; gas cap. normal 61 gal.; gas cap. max. 73.5 gal.; oil cap. 19 qts.; cruising range (.75 power) at 17 gal. per hour (with 50 gal.) 420 miles; price $7835. at factory. ZPF-7 same as above except, more deluxe, heavier empty, and price was $8935. at factory.

The construction details and general arrangement of the models YPF-ZPF were typical to that of the model CPF as described here in the chapter for ATC # 583, including the following. The most significant difference in the YPF-ZPF was the enclosed canopy over the pilot's cockpit. This coupe-top provided shelter from the slipstream, and the cockpit was fitted with heat and ventilation. A baggage compartment with allowance for up to 100 lbs. was behind the rear cockpit and 25 lbs. was allowed in the dash-panel of the front cockpit, but extra luggage was also allowed on the front seat (strapped) when passengers were not carried. Early examples had "humps" or "blisters" on the engine cowl, but later examples all had the smooth cowl. Two fuel tanks of 25 gal. each were mounted in the center-

Fig. 312. A Waco ZPF-7 on Edo floats.

section panel; a 12.5 gal. tank in the root end of each upper wing was optional. The landing gear of 77 in. tread was a simple tripod affair fitted with "Waco" oleo-spring shock struts; 6.50x10 wheels with 7.50x10 low-pressure tires were fitted with wheel brakes. Autofan 7.50x10 wheels with 8.50x10 tires were optional. The ZPF series were eligible as seaplanes at 2880 lb.

gross weight on Edo 45-2880 twin-float gear. With twin-float gear the empty weight was increased by 230 lbs. A Curtiss-Reed metal propeller, Eclipse electric engine starter, generator, battery, wheel brakes, 10.5 in. tail wheel, dual controls, compass, navigation lights, fuel gauges, fire extinguisher, first-aid kit, tool kit, and log books were standard equipment. A

Fig. 313. Traditionally the F-series of 1936-37 were rugged airplanes.

Fig. 314. Pilot of YPF is wearing a felt Fedora hat and a business suit.

controllable-pitch propeller, landing lights, parachute flares, bonding & shielding, radio, wheel pants, metal cockpit cover, adj. seats, brake pedals in front cockpit, leather upholstery, Edo pontoons, and custom color schemes were optional. The next Waco development was the Wright-powered "Custom Cabin" model DQC-6 and EQC-6 as described in the chapter for ATC # 597 of this volume.

Listed below are models YPF-ZPF as verified by company records:

NC-15711; YPF-6 (# 4374) Jacobs 225.
NC-15700; YPF-6 (# 4375) Jacobs 225.
NC-15707; ZPF-6 (# 4377) Jacobs 285.
NC-16579; ZPF-6 (# 4378) Jacobs 285.
NC-17470; ZPF-6 (# 4383) Jacobs 285.
NC-17710; ZPF-7 (# 4650) Jacobs 285.

; YPF-7 (# 4657) Jacobs 225.
NC-17715; ZPF-7 (# 4658) Jacobs 285.

Serial # 4374 delivered to Burr Bush of Chicago, Ill. with 1 pl. adj. front seat, replaced with standard 2 pl. seat 11-9-36; ser. # 4375 del. to Connie Johnson of Ambler, Pa. with special color scheme in Bronze Plum with Nassau Blue wings; ser. # 4377 del. to Williams Gold Rfg. Co. of Buffalo, N.Y. on Edo floats — this ship reported at bottom of Niagara River; ser. # 4383 del. to Texas Company; records have been lost for ser. # 4379, 4380, 4381, 4382; ser. # 4650 del. to customer in Oklahoma City; ser. # 4657 del. to Japan; ser. # 4658 del. to rancher of Palo Duro, Texas; ser. # 4650, 4658 had 99 in. Curtiss-Reed props and 73.5 gal. fuel cap.; this approval expired 2-28-41.

Fig. 315. Fairchild A-942-A being readied for delivery to Pan Am. Wing-top nacelle contained 750 h.p. "Hornet" engine.

In all accounts the Fairchild "Jungle Clipper" was always portrayed as high adventure along the steamy Amazon River, and it played in this romantic role for nearly 10 years. This unusual high-speed amphibian was developed by Fairchild, in cooperation with Pan American Airways engineers, for use in coastal and sheltered waters of South America. Enthused about the airplane and the service it would perform, Pan Am ordered 6 for early delivery. In 1933 the Pan American Airways System started a weekly service from Para to Manaos, a 932 mile run up the Amazon River into the interior of Brazil; a twin-motored Sikorsky S-38 was used at first, but this route was actually meant for the "Jungle Clipper". The first "Jungle Clipper", known as the Fairchild A-942-A in particular and as the "Model 91" in general, was off on its maiden flight on 5 April 1935 and all went well. It was delivered to the Pan Am base in Miami on 1-21-36 and outfitted there for service in Brazil. Another similar aircraft was

delivered shortly after. Realizing soon that the "Jungle Clipper" was operating off water more often than from the land, the landing gear assemblies were stripped from the hull, and the ships were used as a pure "flying boat"; shedding of the weight allowed increases to the payload. Operating under Panair do Brazil the route did not justify the 6 examples that were originally ordered, so orders for 4 were cancelled and only 2 were used on the river line. The 4 aircraft cancelled by Pan Am, already on the factory floor in various stages of assembly, were finally sold; one to Gar Wood the speed-boat king, one to Richard Archbold for an expedition into the New Guinea interior, and the other 2 were delivered to Japan. Meanwhile, the "Jungle Clipper" had been flying up and down the Amazon River route and kept at it until 1945. The development of airports along the river during days of World War 2 brought in multi-engined landplanes that rendered the "Jungle Clipper" almost unnecessary. Late in 1945, in a

Fig. 316. Known as the "Jungle Clipper" the A-942-A flew a route along the Amazon River.

chore filled with sadness, the "Jungle Clipper" (A-942-A) were stripped of useable items, chopped up into small pieces, and then scrapped along with some aging Consolidated "Commodore" and a few worn-out Sikorsky S-38. To the foreman who supervised the scrapping, it was long a vivid memory.

The Fairchild model A-942-A (of the Model 91 series) was a single-engined cantilever high-wing monoplane of the flying boat type with seating arranged for 8 passengers and a crew of 2. The unusual monoplane was carefully designed to eliminate the drag-producing factors usually associated with an airplane of this type, and thus at one time, it happened to be the fastest single-engined "amphibian" in the world. Most amphibians paid dearly in loss of performance to achieve the ability to operate off land or water, but outside of a little extra weight the "Ninety One" suffered very little loss. Graceful and roundish to its very tail-post, the "Model 91" bristled with advanced ideas and fell heir to the formula for utility and efficiency suggested by Pan American engineers. Tailor-made for the river route in Brazil, operated by Panair do Brazil, the "Jungle Clipper" also proved its robust nature by plying up and down the Amazon for nearly a decade. Pan Am had originally ordered 6 of the Fairchild amphibians for proposed river routes throughout the interior of So. America and China, but a change in plans caused cancellation of the original order and only 2 airplanes were procured. The 4 aircraft cancelled were finally built into another "Model 91" version and sold. As powered with the 9 cyl. Pratt & Whitney "Hornet" S2EG geared engine rated 750 h.p. at 2250 r.p.m. at 2500 ft. (800 h.p. for take-off) the model A-942-A turned in a

respectable performance and was considerably faster than the average airplane of this type. It had good characteristics in the water and pleasant habits in the air. Due to control arrangements and all the things it was necessary to perform, it actually took 2 pilots to fly this airplane, but this was later remedied and 1 pilot could do the job. The type certificate number for the model A-942-A was issued 11-22-35 and only 3 examples of this model were manufactured by the Fairchild Aircraft Corp. at Hagerstown, Md. A. A. Gassner, who earlier had worked for Anthony Fokker and had developed the Fokker F-11 "Amphibian", was largely responsible for design of the Model 91 series.

Listed below are specifications and performance data for the Fairchild "Model 91" (A-942-A) as powered with 750 h.p. "Hornet" S2EG engine; length overall 46'8"; height overall (on wheels) 16'3"; wing span 56'0"; wing chord at root 130"; wing chord at tip 65"; total wing area 483 sq. ft.; airfoil at root Clark Y-18; airfoil at tip Clark Y-11; wt. empty 6500 lbs.; useful load 3200 lbs.; payload with 180 gal. fuel & 2 pilots 1668 lbs. (8 pass. & 308 lbs. baggage); gross wt. 9700 lbs.; max. speed 173 at 2500 ft.; cruising speed (.75 power) 155 at sea level; cruising speed (.66 power) 151 at 8000 ft.; landing speed (with flaps) 63; take-off from water 22 secs.; climb 950 ft. first min. at sea level; climb to 10,000 ft. in 13 mins.; ser. ceiling 17,900 ft.; gas cap. normal 180 gal.; gas cap. max. 350 gal.; oil cap. 15-25 gal.; cruising range (.75 power) at 42 gal. per hour 620 miles; cruising range (.66 power) at 36 gal. per hour 730 miles; price $42,-060. at factory. Gross wt. allowance later increased to 10,500 lbs. for amphibian and to 10,-700 lbs. when operated as flying boat without

Fig. 317. Alfred A. Gassner, designer, poses with prototype Model 91.

landing gear.

The graceful two-step hull was a semi-monocoque dural framework covered with smooth Alclad sheet; the metal skin was riveted to the framework with flush-type rivets. The 75 in. wide hull was divided into 5 water-tight compartments; stowage for mooring gear was in the nose compartment, then came a freight hold of 50 cu. ft. capacity for up to 650 lbs., and aft of that was the cockpit compartment that seated 2 pilots. The main cabin was divided into two compartments with seating for 4 in each; seats in the front compartment were easily removed to haul extra cargo. A lavatory and a baggage compartment with allowance for 350 lbs. were aft of the cabin area; the entrance hatch was top-side behind the wing. Cabin walls were sound-proofed and interior comfort was regulated by heat and ventilation. The thick center-section was built integral to the fuselage and outer wings were bolted to stub ends; outer wings were water-tight and wing tips were detachable. Walk-ways were provided on center-section for servicing of engine and the fuel tanks; two fuel tanks of 90 gal. each were mounted in the C/S. The tripod engine mount was a steel tube unit housed in a streamlined nacelle and fastened to the front and rear spars of the center-section; rear portion of nacelle had space for storage of tools and a life raft. The cantilever wing framework was built up of dural girder-type spar beams and dural truss-type wing ribs; the wing was covered with smooth Alclad "stressed-skin" metal sheet. Wing-tip floats were fastened to a point to prevent "heeling" into the water. Metal-framed ailerons were covered with fabric and split-type wing flaps were of all-metal dural structure. The vertical fin and horizontal stabilizer were all-metal assemblies built integral to the hull; metal-framed rudder and elevators were covered in fabric. Elevators and rudder were fitted with adjustable trimming tabs. The retractable undercarriage, fitted with 30x13-6 Goodyear (8 ply) airwheels with hydraulic brakes, folded up into wheel wells in underside of the wing. The retractable full-swivel tail wheel was fitted with a 16x7-3 heavy duty tire. When operating as a pure "flying boat", removal of landing gear and tail wheel assemblies added extra allowance to the payload. A Hamilton-Standard controllable propeller, hand-electric engine starter, generator, battery, oil-cooling radiator, navigation lights, landing lights, parachute flares, pressure-type Lux fire extinguisher, anchor & mooring gear, life raft, fog horn and bell, bilge pump, Very pistol, tool kit, and first-aid kit were standard equipment. Radio equipment, bonding & shielding, and extra fuel capacity to 354 gal. were optional. The next "Model 91" development was the Cyclone-powered A-942-B as described in the chapter for ATC # 605.

Fig. 318. The Fairchild 91 was once the fastest amphibian airplane in the world.

Listed below are A-942-A entries as verified by factory records:

NC-14743; A-942-A (# 9401) Hornet 750.
NC-14744; A-942-A (# 9402) Hornet 750.
NC-15952; A-942-A (# 9403) Hornet 750.

This approval for ser. # 9401 and up; only ser. # 9401-02-03 were A-942-A, but also eligible as A-942-B when modified to conform; ser. # 9402 as PP-PAP and ser. # 9403 as PP-PAT with Panair do Brazil; ser. # 9401 retained by Fairchild as demonstrator.

Fig. 319. The Fairchild "Model 45" with 225 h.p. Jacobs engine.

The "Model 45" as "Sedan of the Air" was designed specifically as a small high-speed transport having the capacity, comfort, and convenience generally associated with an expensive automobile. Outstanding features included a large, roomy cabin that was entered effortlessly through 2 large doors, a luxurious interior that invited one to settle down in comfort, and an above-average performance with miserly economy. Designed under the supervision of Geo. W. Hardman, chief engineer of Fairchild's commercial aircraft division, the "Forty Five" was flown on its maiden flight (31 May 1935) by Richard A. Henson, Fairchild's test pilot, and pronounced a complete success. It is logically assumed that "Dick" Henson must have been enamored by the airplane because the first flight lasted 3 hours 20 minutes, and a flight a few days later lasted 2 hours 21 minutes; it is doubtful if a pilot would have stayed up that long in a new airplane that didn't please him. In appearance the new "45" was an appealing airplane; the aerodynamic features were truly impressive and they all had definite performance functions. Built with traditional Fairchild quality the structure as used in the Model 45 was somewhat complex and costly, yet to have varied from this design would have resulted in just another airplane. The first airplane in the Model 45 series was delivered to the Superior Oil Co. of

Houston, Texas for speedy transportation of company executives. As is quite often the case, before a second airplane is built, there was pondering about "what a terrific airplane this would be if it had more power"! As a consequence, only one example, the prototype, was built with the 225 h.p. Jacobs engine. Subsequent airplanes in this series were powered with 320 h.p., actually more to the liking of the wealthy people that were buying these airplanes. Perhaps man's progress is driven by his faculty of never being satisfied.

The graceful Fairchild "Model 45" was a cantilever low-winged cabin monoplane with seating arranged for five. The primary objective in creating the "Forty Five" was to give the private-owner an economical five-place airplane which combined speed, luxury, and strength with flight characteristics and handling features that would permit operation from the smaller fields by non-professional pilots. In uncrowded seating to tolerate the longer flights, there was ample visibility and room for plenty of baggage. To obtain the combination of high speed, range, and payload with reasonable horsepower it was necessary to take advantage of the useful aerodynamic features of the low-wing design. Most aircraft of this type were designed for professionals and flown by expert pilots. The "45", however, was a gentle airplane that could

Fig. 320. Model 45 over checker-board of Maryland landscape.

be flown by any average pilot without difficulty. And too, it was loaded with thoughtful details that produced convenience for the pilot and luxurious comfort for his passengers; Fairchild wanted this to be the best in an airplane for personal transportation. As powered with the 7 cyl. Jacobs L-4 engine rated 225 h.p. at 2000 r.p.m. the Model 45 made every ounce of power count and delivered a performance well above the average. Inherently kind to non-professional pilots the "Forty Five" was gentle to its very bones and everyone loved it. It was planned to have the "45" also available with Lycoming 225, Continental 210, and other engines to 285 h.p., but these plans were cancelled in favor of the 320 h.p. Wright engine. The type certificate number for the Model 45 was issued 12-3-35 and only one example of this model was manufactured by the Fairchild Aircraft Corp. at Hagerstown, Md.

Listed below are specifications and performance data for the Fairchild "Model 45" as powered with 225 h.p. Jacobs L-4 engine; length overall 28'11"; height overall 8'0"; wing span 39'6"; wing chord at root 90"; wing chord at tip 47"; total wing area 248 sq. ft.; airfoil at root NACA-2218 tapering to NACA-2209 at tip; wt. empty 2277 lbs.; useful load 1323 lbs.; payload with 60 gal. fuel 755 lbs. (4 pass. & 79 lbs. baggage); gross wt. 3600 lbs.; max. speed 160; cruising speed (.75 power) 147; landing speed (with flaps) 48; stall speed (no flaps) 60; climb 640 ft. first min. at sea level; ceiling 16,000 ft.; gas cap. 60 gal.; oil cap. 5 gal.; cruising range (.75 power) at 13.2 gal. per hour 620 miles; price

$8000. at factory field.

The fuselage framework was built up of welded chrome-moly steel tubing, heavily faired to shape with plywood formers and spruce fairing strips, then fabric covered. The sound-proofed cabin was 51 in. wide x 110 in. long and all windows were of shatter-proof glass. The bench-type front seat (16 in. deep x 47 in. wide) was ample for 2 and a throw-over control wheel was provided; the large instrument panel included a glove compartment for flash-light, maps, and misc. gadgets. The ultra-soft rear seat (18 in. deep x 51 in. wide) was wide enough for 3 with shoulder and leg room for all; a trap-door in the floor opened on a baggage compartment for items that needed to be handy, but not clutter up the cabin. Front seat-backs were fitted with magazine pockets and a shelf behind the rear seat was handy for jackets and hats. A door on the left in front provided entry to the front seats, and a door on the right side opened directly into the rear section. Interior comfort was regulated by heat and ventilation. The all-metal center-section (C/S) of aluminum alloy beams and ribs was covered with dural sheet and fastened to underside of the fuselage frame; outer wings were bolted to stub ends. The tapered wing panels were built up of spruce box-type spar beams with spruce and plywood truss-type wing ribs; the leading edges were covered with plywood sheet and the completed framework was covered in fabric. Slotted and balanced ailerons were metal framed and covered in fabric. The metal-framed wing flaps, in 3 sections, were covered with fabric and hand-operated to 3 positions; 60 degs.

Fig. 321. Fairchild 45 was designed as "Sedan of the air".

was full deflection. The thick C/S housed two 30 gal. fuel tanks and provided attachment for the retractable landing gear. The landing gear of 8 ft. 10 in. tread was 2 separate assemblies that folded up into wheel wells; the wheels extended 11 in. below the wing when retracted to protect the "belly" in wheels-up landings. Oleo-spring shock struts of 7 in. travel were fitted with 8.50x-10 semi-airwheels with hydraulic brakes. The full-swivel tail wheel was fitted with an oil-spring shock strut. The cantilever tail group was an all-metal structure covered with fabric; rudder and elevators were of the balanced-hinge type. Elevator was fitted with an adjustable "trim tab". The "Jacobs" engine was mounted in rubber and encased in an NACA-type cowling. A wooden propeller, electric engine starter, battery, compass, fuel gauges, parking brake, air-speed indicator, and first-aid kit were standard equipment. A metal propeller, navigation lights, landing lights, parachute flares, bonding & shielding, and radio equipment were optional. The next development in the Model 45 series was the Wright-powered 45-A as described in the chapter for ATC # 603.

Listed below is the only example of Model 45 as mfgd. with Jacobs engine:

NC-15060; Model 45 (# 4000) Jacobs 225.

Fig. 322. The "Forty Five" was a gentle airplane with high performance.

Fig. 323. The distinctive Model 19-L with 90 h.p. Lambert engine.

The unusual "Coupe" was a venture sponsored by the Bureau of Air Commerce to design and build an all-metal personal airplane for private-owners who were not necessarily veteran pilots. This was, by the way, another project added to the list of new-type airplanes which the BAC was purchasing in its private-owner aircraft development program. Eugene L. Vidal, director of Air Commerce, awarded a contract to Curtiss-Wright for one airplane early in 1935. As specified, the new "Coupe" was to utilize the same techniques used in building large, all-metal

Fig. 324. The 19-L was used by BAC to evaluate all-metal construction for private planes.

Fig. 325. In prototype the 19-L was tested with "wing slats"—these were later discarded.

transports, adapting these techniques to the fabrication of small airplanes. Carl W. Scott of the Curtiss-Wright engineering staff was the project engineer directly responsible for design and construction of the "Coupe", while George A. Page, the chief engineer, participated in the early planning and followed the progress through various stages. As specified in the contract the "Coupe" rolled out as a very unusual all-metal airplane, certainly taking advantage of all latest techniques, both in structure and in aerodynamics. As a result, the performance of this little airplane was outstanding, and it proved to be almost too much for the average amateur pilot to cope with. As flown in the prototype, the "Coupe" model 19-L was powered with the 90 h.p. Lambert R-266 engine and even in this combination it was considered "a hot little airplane". When modified into the model 19-W, which was powered with the 145 h.p. Warner "Super Scarab" engine, the "Coupe" literally surprised everyone with its unusually high performance and its vivacious nature. It is doubtful this was the airplane that Eugene Vidal originally had in mind for the non-professional pilot, but for Curtiss-Wright it was a good exercize, a rewarding experience, and the basic concept of configuration and construction fostered the design of several outstanding C-W airplanes. From this airplane Curtiss-Wright developed the 19-R basic trainer, and compare if you will, similar lines of the CW-21, CW-22, and the CW-23.

The Curtiss-Wright "Coupe" model 19-L was a cantilever low-winged cabin monoplane with side-by-side seating for two. The lovely little monoplane was the result of a BAC-sponsored project to develop an all-metal personal-type airplane for the amateur pilot that would embody strength, performance, and safety. Its aerodynamic arrangement was planned for stability, but the quest for speed and high performance introduced characteristics requiring a watchful eye. Hailed as an ideal airplane for the private pilot, it is reasonable to agree, but it was not necessarily for just any ham-fisted amateur. An airplane of this type quickly discourages inept or sloppy flying. Mindful of the all-metal construction and the methods used in fabrication, it can be assumed the price would be rather prohibitive for the average pilot, so it would have to be offered to the sportsman-pilot who could afford it. Then too, a flier of this type was generally a pretty good pilot. As powered with the 5 cyl. Lambert R-266 engine rated 90 h.p. at 2375 r.p.m. the "Coupe" 19-L utilized every ounce of power for its purpose and turned in a rather outstanding performance. In the hands of a pretty good pilot, it was maneuverable and practically stall-proof or spin-proof. In the model 19-W version, which was powered with the 145 h.p. Warner "Super Scarab" engine, the performance was almost phenomenal and Curtiss-Wright quickly realized the vast potential of this basic design. Whether the "Coupe" fulfilled Eugene Vidal's purpose is not known, but it was a rewarding experience for Curtiss-Wright. The type certificate number for the "Coupe" model 19-L was issued 12-2-35 and only one example of this model was built by the Curtiss-Wright Airplane Co. at Robertson (St. Louis), Mo.

Fig. 326. Also a Curtiss-Wright "Coupe" this was the Gipsy-powered CR-1 of 1930.

Listed below are specifications and performance data for the Curtiss-Wright "Coupe" model 19-L as powered with 90 h.p. Lambert R-266 engine; length overall 25'7"; height overall 7'2"; wing span 35'0"; wing chord at root 84"; wing chord at tip 40"; total wing area 174 sq. ft.; airfoil CW-19-Spl.; wt. empty 1154 lbs.; useful load 646 lbs.; payload with 30 gal. fuel 261 lbs. (1 pass. & 91 lbs. baggage); gross wt. 1800 lbs.; max. speed 130 at sea level; cruising speed (2100 r.p.m.) 115 at 5000 ft.; landing (stall) speed 44; climb 525 ft. first min. at sea level; ser. ceiling 15,500 ft.; gas cap. normal 30 gal.; gas cap. max. 50 gal.; oil cap. 4-5 gal.; cruising range (2100 r.p.m.) at 5.8 gal. per hour (30 gal.) 500 miles; price was not announced.

Specifications and data for "Coupe" model 19-W as powered with 145 h.p. Warner "Super Scarab" engine were identical except as follows; length overall 25'2"; wt. empty 1360 lbs.; useful load 940 lbs.; payload with 50 gal. fuel 435 lbs. (2 pass. & 95 lbs. baggage); gross wt. 2300 lbs.; max. speed 162 at sea level; cruising speed (1850 r.p.m.) 142 at 5000 ft.; landing speed (with flaps) 48; climb 850 ft. first min. at sea level; ser. ceiling 17,600 ft.; gas cap. 50 gal.; oil cap. 5 gal.; cruising range (1850 r.p.m.) at 9 gal. per hour 700 miles; price not announced.

The fuselage framework was an all-metal semi-monocoque structure of heavy gauge 24-ST "Alclad" ring-type bulkheads, stringers, and riveted-on smooth metal skin. The stressed-skin 24-ST metal covering supported much of the major loads. Two seats were arranged side-by-side in the cabin and either was adjustable; dual wheel-type controls were provided. A large baggage compartment was behind the seats, or this area could be used for a third seat. A large door on either side provided entry from the wing-walk, and judicious use of Pyralin panels offered excellent visibility. The engine, fastened to a steel tube frame and mounted in rubber, was encased in a deep-chord NACA cowl that blended well into fuselage lines; for maintenance and inspection the engine cowl was opened and raised like an automobile hood. The 30 or 50 gal. fuel supply was carried in 2 tanks located one each side of the fuselage in the wing; oil tank was attached to the firewall. The multi-cellular wing framework was built up around 5 alloy (24-ST)

Fig. 327. Cowl sides opened for access to engine.

spar beams that were covered with heavy gauge 24-ST Alclad metal skin; right and left panels were bolted together on centerline and then fastened to the fuselage. All-metal split-type wing flaps extended nearly 70% across the span and were operated by a hand crank.

All-metal ailerons had up-movement only to eliminate adverse drag in the outside wing during a turn. Fixed "slats" were fastened to the leading edge of each wing to prolong effectiveness of aileron control at high angles of attack. The landing gear of 7 ft. tread was of 2 cantilever oleo-legs encased in large streamlined metal "boots"; the oleo-legs of 10 in. travel were fitted with Goodyear 16x7-3 airwheels and hydraulic brakes. The cantilever tail group was of 24-ST all-metal structure similar to the wing; elevator was fitted with adjustable trim tab. A fixed ground-adjustable tab was fitted to rudder and the left aileron. A Curtiss-Reed metal propeller, Eclipse electric engine starter, battery, fuel gauges, 6 gal. reserve fuel in left wing tank, tail wheel, navigation lights, cabin ventilators, rear-view mirror, parking brake, fire extinguisher, and first-aid kit were standard equipment. A Hamilton-Standard metal propeller, Warner "Super Scarab" engine, and radio equipment were optional. The next Curtiss-Wright development was the model A-19-R as described in the chapter for ATC # 629.

Listed below is the only example of the Model 19-L:

NS-69; 19-L (# 1) Lambert 90.

This airplane also eligible as Model 19-W with 145 h.p. Warner "Super Scarab" engine.

ATC # 590
(12-5-35)
LOCKHEED "ELECTRA", 10E.

Fig. 328. The high-performance "Electra" 10-E with two 550 h.p. "Wasp" engines.

Preaching the gospel of speed since 1927, Lockheed strived for swifter and better airplanes as each design came off the drawing-board. Committed to progressive demands and constant improvement, Lockheed groomed the new, powerful Model 10-E "Electra" as the fastest version of the popular twin-engined transport. Because of difficult routes in Mexico, So. America, and Alaska, the Pan American Airways System was largely responsible for development of the high-performance 10-E and eventually had 6 examples placed on critical portions of their far-flung system. The 10-E was blessed with power enough to spare and it was comforting to be able to top a lofty mountain range with altitude left over, or lift a gross load out of some high-altitude field without overrunning the runway. That is why more than half of the 10-E were seen in such places as Alaska, Mexico, Brazil, Argentina, Colombia, and even Yugoslavia. Here in the U.S.A. a few examples were operated by big business and 2 were groomed for trans-oceanic flight. Amelia Earhart, world-famed aviatrix, made a record-setting trip in her 10-E from Oakland to Honolulu, and then announced plans to circle the globe. Unfortunately, her "Flying Laboratory" (purchased for her by a Purdue University grant) became lost over the So. Pacific Ocean and no trace of Amelia Earhart or Noonan, her navigator, was

ever found. Perhaps the pinnacle of achievement for the twin-engined transport came about in May of 1937 when Merrill and Lambie flew an "Electra" 10-E on a round-trip crossing of the Atlantic Ocean; on the way home they rushed first photos picturing the coronation of King George VI from England to America. Because of the large number of "Electra" exported to Europe, Lockheed sent Marshall Headle, their test-pilot, to teach pilots in Britain, Poland, and elsewhere the art of flying a twin-engined "Electra". Moye Stephens, another Lockheed pilot, accompanied 3 "Electra" to New Zealand to help launch a new airline. The last Model 10-E was built in 1940 on an order from Yugoslavia, and at the onset of World War 2, four business-houses released their 10-E to serve in the USAAF as UC-36B utility-cargo transports.

The Lockheed "Electra" model 10-E was an all-metal, low-winged, twin-engined transport monoplane with seating normally arranged for 10 passengers and a crew of two. Fortified with more than 200 extra horsepower, as compared with other "Electra" versions, the Model 10-E was able to grab for the sky a lot quicker, vault over the highest mountains, and cover more ground in an hour's time. Five of the (1100 h.p.) model 10-E were working for the Pan American Airways System, five were "in business", the Argentine Army and Navy each had one, and

Fig. 329. An "Electra" 10-E on airline duty in Colombia.

one was exported to Yugoslavia. The Army Air Corps tested a high-altitude version of the "Electra" 10-E (the XC-35) and during early years of W.W.2 four of the 10-E were pressed into service as the UC-36B. Two of the 10-E made international headlines, one on a happy note and one on a sad note. As powered with two 9 cyl. Pratt & Whitney "Wasp" S3H1 engines rated 550 h.p. each the Model 10-E had spirit, grit, and muscle to spare, and was usually asked to work among natural hazards that tore at the heart of an ordinary airplane. The 10-E was popular among pilots for its ability, and it piled up a good operating record. The type certificate number for the "Electra" model 10-E was issued 12-5-35 and 15 examples of this model were built by the Lockheed Aircraft Corp. at Burbank, Calif. Lloyd C. Stearman, who was at the helm of

Lockheed since 1932, resigned in 1935 because he wasn't enjoying being an executive; he yearned to rid himself of administrative pressures and get back to the drawing-board where he could dream and design airplanes.

Listed below are specifications and performance data for the "Electra" model 10-E as powered with 2 "Wasp" S3H1 engines rated 550 h.p. at 2200 r.p.m. at 5000 ft.; length overall 38'7": height overall 10'1"; wing span 55'0"; wing chord at root 145"; wing chord at tip 48"; total wing area (incl. fuselage section) 458 sq. ft.; airfoil at root Clark Y-18; airfoil at tip Clark Y-9; wt. empty 7100 lbs.; useful load 3400 lbs.; payload with 250 gal. fuel & 2 pilots 1455 lbs.; payload with 200 gal. fuel & 2 pilots 1755 lbs.; gross wt. 10,500 lbs.; max. baggage 422 lbs.; max. speed 215 at 10,500 ft.; cruising speed (.75

Fig. 330. The 10-E for Amelia Earhart being readied for her round-the-world attempt.

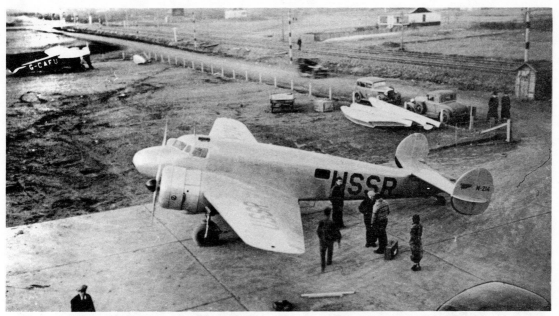

Fig. 331. The famous 10-E that flew a round-trip across the Atlantic.

power) 205 at 9600 ft.; landing speed (with flaps) 65; climb 1200 ft. first min. at sea level; ser. ceiling 25,800 ft.; gas cap. 200-250 gal.; oil cap. 17 gal.; cruising range (.75 power) at 70 gal. per hour 600-700 miles; absolute ceiling (full load) on one engine 9500 ft.; price not announced.

The construction details and general arrangement of the Model 10-E were typical to that of all other "Electra", including the following. You could tell the 10-E was a rather special "Electra" by the large engine nacelles which housed the big 550 h.p. "Wasp" engines that usually swung Hamilton-Standard controllable-pitch propellers. The big radial engines were equipped with oil-cooling radiators and the ignition system was shielded for radio. With 8 passengers on board the baggage-cargo allowance was over 400 lbs. A fuel capacity of 250 gal., in 6 wing tanks, provided range for at least 700 miles, but normally only 200 gal. of fuel was carried. A plush "Club" version of the "Electra" 10-E was usually arranged for 6 passengers in a custom interior that featured over-stuffed chairs, a divan, table, and lavatory. Any other appointments or special arrangements were available on demand. In shiny metal skin, studded with row after row of rivets, the twin-tailed airframe was a rather distinctive Lockheed trademark, but not for long, because the configuration was copied by several other small "twins". Metal propellers, electric engine starters, battery, generator, dual controls, Goodyear 35x15-6 airwheels, wheel brakes, parking brake, 16x7-3 tail wheel, cabin ventilation and cabin heat, navigation lights, landing lights, parachute flares, fire extinguishers, assist ropes, hat net, ash trays, reading lamps, dome lights, and first-aid kit were standard equipment. Hamilton-Standard

controllable props, custom "Club" interior, a two-way radio set, bonding & shielding, lavatory, leather upholstery, and de-icing equipment was optional. The next Lockheed development was the twin-enginge Model 12-A "Zephyr" as described in the chapter for ATC # 616.

Listed below are "Electra" 10-E entries as gleaned from various records:

PP-PAS: 10-E (# 1008) 2 Wasp 550.

XA-BAU:	"	(# 1041)	"
NC-14972:	"	(# 1042)	"
XA-BAS:	"	(# 1043)	"
NC-14994:	"	(# 1054)	"
NR-16020:	"	(# 1055)	"
NR-16059:	"	(# 1065)	"
:	"	(# 1115)	"
NC-18139:	"	(# 1117)	"
-19982:	"	(# 1118)	"
:	"	(# 1125)	"
NC-18987:	"	(# 1129)	"
-30077:	"	(# 1133)	"
-30078:	"	(# 1134)	"
YU-SDA:	"	(# 1139)	"
NC-1621:	"	(# 1140)	"

This approval for ser. # 1008, 1041 and up; ser. # 1008 first as Model 10-C; ser. # 1042 later as PP-PAX with Panair do Brazil; ser. # 1055 del. to Amelia Earhart, lost at sea 7-2-37; ser. # 1065 used by Merrill and Lambie on round-trip Atlantic flight 5-37; ser. # 1115 del. to Argentine Navy; Ser. # 1125 del. to Argentine Army; ser. # 1139 del. to Yugoslavia, was last "Electra" built; ser. # 1060 (no listing) may have been XC-35 high-altitude 10-E del. to Army Air Corps; ser. # 1054, 1117, 1129, 1140 as UC-36B with USAAF in 1942.

ATC # 591
(12-7-35)
REARWIN "SPORTSTER", 8500

Fig. 332. Rearwin "Sportster" 8500 with 85 h.p. LeBlond engine.

The sportsman pilots that were forced to fly on a low budget were taking an interest in airplanes like the "Sportster", so Rearwin developed the "Model 8500" which offered a little more power and the extra benefits that more power would introduce. With the 5 cyl. LeBlond 5DF engine rated 85 h.p. the "Sportster" (Model 8500) was able to take off much quicker, climb out at a better rate, cruise just a little faster, and handle a lot better in mountainous regions of the west. All these extras were available for just a little more money, so the "8500" was a rather good bargain. Then too, there were always a number of customers that were willing to go a little deeper in their pockets for better performance. When the 5 cyl. LeBlond engine was rerated to 90 h.p. as the 5F, the "Sportster" was designated the Model 9000-L with this new engine, and later as the Model 9000-KR when powered with the new 90 h.p. Ken-Royce engine. Rearwin had acquired the LeBlond engine works sometime in 1938 and renamed the engines to "Ken-Royce"; the engines were basically the same, but continually improved. The model 8500 and the 9000-L were very similar to each other except for the engine,

but the 9000-KR was modified considerably, especially around the front end. The deep NACA cowling changed its looks, and also added a bit to the available speeds. By 1937 the "Sportster" was available also on skis and "Edo" pontoons, thus further enhancing its broad utility. For a little extra money the 8500, 9000-L, and 9000-KR were available as a "Deluxe" version; the pilot aids and other popular extras were well worth the extra investment. Oddly enough, the "Deluxe" model was outselling the "Standard" version, and the seaplane was popular for export. Seaplanes were shipped to Sweden, Norway, and Brazil; in the winter they were flown on skis. One seaplane was delivered to Juan Trippe, prexy of the Pan American Airways System. With the records available it has been estimated that about 260 examples of the "Sportster" were built in all, and the last rolled out of the factory in 1941. In 1942 the USAAF acquired 2 of the 90000-KR as the UC-102 for shuttle duty as a light utility transport. Perhaps about a dozen of the Rearwin "Sportster" are still flying.

The Rearwin "Sportster" model 8500 and subsequent versions of this model were light,

Fig. 333. Several "8500" were exported to Siam for training of military pilots.

high-winged cabin monoplanes with seating arranged for 2 in tandem. The earlier "Sportster" was basically a utility airplane, but the 8500 and its companion models (9000-L and 9000-KR) were leveled more often at the sportsman. Having sufficient weight allowance for extra equipment any version could be dressed-up with an engine speed-ring, wheel pants, an engine starter, night-flying equipment, and radio gear if so desired. The "Deluxe" version with all the goodies on it and in it was listing for several hundred dollars more, but in spite of this, the "Deluxe" was actually outselling the bare "Standard" version. The Rearwin "Sportster" was a rather handsome airplane, and tough enough to overcome occasional ham-handed abuse. With "the slimness of an arrow" the "Sportster" was a little slender-waisted, but it had more than enough leg-room, and plenty of head-room. As powered with the 5 cyl. LeBlond 5DF engine rated 85 h.p. at 2125 r.p.m. the Model 8500 was at the top of its class in performance and handled quite well at the higher altitudes. As powered with the 5 cyl. LeBlond 5F engine or the Ken-Royce 5F engine (both rated 90 h.p. at 2250 r.p.m.) the models 9000-L and 9000-KR were slightly better airplanes and there

Fig. 334. "Sportster" 8500 on Edo floats, destined for Alaska.

Fig. 335. A "Sportster" 9000-L over Kansas City.

was extra performance to prove it. Rearwin airplanes had always been popular, and the "Sportster" (in any of the versions) was especially so; they were seen often from one end of the country to the other and most were around for a long time. The type certificate number for the "Sportster" model 8500 was issued 12-7-35 and amended at intervals to include the models 9000-L and 9000-KR. At least 50 or more of these models were manufactured by Rearwin Airplanes, Inc. on Fairfax Airport in Kansas City, Kansas. R. W. Rummel had replaced Wm. H. Weeks as chief engineer in 1937 and was responsible for design of the 9000-KR and subsequent Rearwin models.

Listed below are specifications and performance data for the "Sportster" model 8500 as powered with 85 h.p. LeBlond 5DF engine; length overall 22'3"; height overall 6'9"; wing span 35'0"; wing chord 62.5"; total wing area 166 sq. ft.; airfoil NACA (Munk) M-6; wt. empty 830 lbs.; useful load 580 lbs.; payload with 24 gal. fuel 251 lbs.; gross wt. 1410 lbs.; max. baggage 50 lbs.; max. speed 116; cruising speed (1900 r.p.m.) 103; landing speed 40; climb 700 ft. first min. at sea level; ser. ceiling 15,200 ft.; gas cap. 24 gal.; oil cap. 2 gal.; cruising range (1900 r.p.m.) at 5 gal. per hour 480 miles; price $2370. at factory field. Model 8500 eligible as seaplane on Edo floats at 1615 lbs. gross weight.

Specifications for model 9000-L with 90 h.p. LeBlond 5F engine same as above except as follows: wt. empty 830 lbs.; useful load 630 lbs.; payload with 24 gal. fuel 300 lbs.; gross wt. 1460 lbs.; max. baggage 50 lbs. and 70 lbs. allowable for equipment extras; max. speed 118; cruising speed (1950 r.p.m.) 108; landing speed 42; climb

720 ft. first min. at sea level; ser. ceiling 15,000 ft.; cruising range 490 miles; price $2760. at factory field, raised to $2895. in late 1937. Model 9000-L eligible also as seaplane on Edo floats at 1615 lbs. gross weight.

Specifications for model 9000-KR as powered with 90 h.p. Ken-Royce engine same as above except as follows: wt. empty 870 lbs.; useful load 610 lbs.; payload with 24 gal. fuel 281 lbs.; max. baggage 50 lbs. & 61 lbs. allowable for extra equipment; gross wt. 1480 lbs.; max. speed 123; cruising speed (1950 r.p.m.) 113; landing speed 45; climb 700 ft. first min. at sea level; ser. ceiling 14,800 ft.; cruising range (1950 r.p.m.) at 5.2 gal. per hour 510 miles; price not announced.

The "Sportster" model 8500 was quite similar to the earlier Model 7000 except for installation of the 5DF engine and the introduction of a few more custom features. With a max. baggage allowance of 50 lbs. the "Deluxe" version was allowed 31 lbs. for extra features such as battery, engine starter, or navigation lights, control system on ball bearings, and a hinged rear seat over the optional baggage compartment. The model 9000-L was also similar except for installation of the improved 5F engine of 90 h.p. and a 50 lb. allowable increase in the gross weight. The "Deluxe" version of the 9000-L was allowed 50 lbs. max. baggage, and 70 lbs. for extra equipment which included all the abovementioned extras, plus wheel pants. The model 9000-KR with the new Ken-Royce 5F engine was basically the same except the engine was shrouded with a deep-chord NACA cowl, the fuselage shape in front was altered to fair into new lines, and the windshield was a one-piece assembly of smoother contour. The "Deluxe"

Fig. 336. The handsome 9000-KR had 90 h.p. Ken-Royce engine.

version of the 9000-KR was also eligible with extra equipment. All models were also eligible on skis, or as seaplanes on Edo H-1525 or 46-1620 twin-float gear. A Flottorp or Fahlin wooden prop, exhaust collector ring, 7.00x4 wheels & tires without brakes, dual controls, tail skid, and first-aid kit were standard equipment. An engine cowl (Townend ring on 8500, 9000-L and NACA-type on 9000-KR), battery, navigation lights, 18x8-3 Goodyear airwheels with brakes, tail wheel, engine starter, wind-driven generator, cabin heater, landing lights, parking brake, brake pedals in rear cockpit, fire extinguisher, skis, and Edo pontoons were optional "Deluxe" equipment. The next Rearwin development was the Warner-powered Model 9000 as described in the chapter for ATC # 624.
Listed below are available entries for models 8500, 9000-L, 9000-KR:

NC-15472:	8500	(# 421)	LeBlond 85.
-15473;	"	(# 422)	"
-15479;	"	(# 427)	"
-15800;	"	(# 436)	"
-15803;	"	(# 439)	"
-15808;	"	(# 444)	"
-15824;	"	(# 448)	"
-15826;	"	(# 450)	"
-15830;	"	(# 453)	"
-15855;	"	(# 455)	"
-15862;	"	(# 461)	"
-15864;	"	(# 463)	"
-15892;	"	(# 468)	"
-15831;	"	(# 469)	"
-15832;	"	(# 470)	"
-15858;	"	(# 471)	"
-15896;	"	(# 474)	"
-15898;	"	(# 478)	"
-15899;	"	(# 479)	"
-15894;	"	(# 480)	"
-16459;	"	(# 492)	"
-16466;	"	(# 495)	"
PP-TBW;	"	(# 500)	"
-16473;	"	(# 502)	"
-16474;	"	(# 504)	"
-16477;	"	(# 507)	"
-16479;	"	(# 508)	"
-16486;	"	(# 512)	"
-17016;	"	(# 518-D)	"
-17046;	9000-L	(# 524-S)	LeBlond 90.
-17015;	8500	(# 529-D)	LeBlond 85.
-17041;	"	(# 531-D)	"
PP-TCO;	"	(# 534-D)	"
-18007;	9000-L	(# 540-D)	LeBlond 90.
-18751;	"	(# 545-S)	"
-17048;	8500	(# 542-D)	LeBlond 85.
-18021;	9000-L	(# 551-D)	LeBlond 90.
-18022;	"	(# 552-D)	"
-18544;	"	(# 553-S)	"
-18071;	"	(# 557-D)	"
PP-TCZ;	"	(# 584-D)	"
PP-TDV;	"	(# 599-D)	"
PP-TEE;	"	(# 606-D)	"

This approval for ser. # 427, 436 and up; ser. # 436 first as Model 7000; no listings available for ser. # 446-447-464-473-475-476-482-484-487-490-491-497-498-501-505-509-510-511 and beyond — several of these could have been Model 8500 and exported to foreign countries; ser. # 518-D modified to 9000-L; ser. no. suffix D denotes "Deluxe", ser. no. suffix S denotes "Standard"; ser. # 500, 534-D, 584-D, 599-D, 606-D del. to Brazil; no accurate listing could be compiled beyond 1936; ser. # 524 and up mfgd. 1937.

Fig. 337. The Sikorsky S-42-A had taken on several improvements.

While 3 of the earlier S-42 "Clipper" ships were blazing new trails for Pan Am (Pan American Airways System) in the Pacific and establishing new frontiers in the Caribbean Sea, Sikorsky was preparing 2 new versions of the big 4-engined flying boat. As the model S-42-A the new ocean-going liners were powered with 4 of the newer "Hornet" S1EG engines that were rated 750 h.p. each at 7000 ft., and consequently, the gross weight allowance was increased by one ton to 40,000 lbs. Among the several other changes the new day-time interior was easily convertible to a 14-berth "sleeper" at night. After three of the S-42-A were built the keels were laid for 4 of the model S-42-B. The new S-42-B, using the same "Hornet" S1EG or the improved S2EG engines, was equipped with the newly-developed Hamilton-Standard "constant speed" propellers. The "constant speed" props were a great improvement over the earlier "controllable" type which operated only in 2 positions. There were some changes in the engine nacelles and the NACA-type engine cowlings were modified for better airflow. The several aerodynamic improvements, coupled with use of the new "constant speed props", permitted a gross weight allowance increase by another ton which brought the fully-loaded weight to 42,000 lbs. A 21-ton flying boat with

nearly 120 feet of wing was a pretty large airplane for these times. To complete Pan Am's trans-Pacific route, which was served by 3 of the huge Martin M-130, an S-42-A was kept at Manila for the shuttle run to Hong Kong and back. In March of 1937, Capt. Edwin Musick commanded an S-42-B "Clipper" on a 7000 mile survey flight from the Hawaiian Islands to New Zealand and Austrailia; the 5 month survey established a route in the South Pacific. In July of 1937, another S-42-B was dispatched across the Atlantic Ocean on a survey flight to the British Isles; this was a route that spanned the Atlantic over-night. On one flight in Aug. of 1937 the S-42-B left New York on a southern route via Bermuda, the Azores, and Lisbon; the return trip from England was by way of the northern route across the expanse of the lonely North Atlantic. The sky over the Atlantic Ocean was full of airplanes at this time; the British, the French, and the Germans, were also trail-blazing flights across the Atlantic to various ports in America. The giant Sikorsky "Clipper" had pioneered both Pacific and Atlantic routes and then settled down to various Pan Am routes scattered all over the hemisphere.

The Sikorsky S-42-A and S-42-B were 4-motored ocean-going monoplanes designed and developed specifically for the Pan American

Fig. 338. The Sikorsky S-42-B was a further refinement.

Airways System; blessed with generous dimensions of a flying boat, normal seating was arranged for 26 to 32 passengers and a crew of 5. On early trail-blazing flights across the Atlantic Ocean the cabin was stuffed with several fuel tanks for the extra range that was necessary, but otherwise the spacious cabin was comfortable and quite plush. On over-night flights the day-time interior was quickly convertible to a "sleeper" with 14 large berths and nearly all the comforts of home; sound-proofing of the cabin walls with rubberized animal hair reduced the terrible engine roar to a pleasant hum. The heavy wing-loading, some 31 lbs. to the square foot, cushioned the uncomfortable jolts of wayward air currents and provided a creamy-

smooth ride in even the roughest air. On long flights a steward was in attendance to cater to passenger needs. The large cockpit compartment up front, quite like the bridge of a ship, was equipped with several radios, an automatic-pilot, and all the latest navigational devices to ensure unerring flight to the various stations; many of these stations were just tiny pin-points in the vast ocean. As powered with 4 of the new Pratt & Whitney "Hornet" supercharged and geared S1EG engines rated 750 h.p. at 2250 r.p.m. at 7000 ft. the S-42-A and the S-42-B got around very well for a 20-ton and a 21-ton air-plane; both airplanes were surprisingly lively and handled well in the water. A full load take-off averaged less than 20 secs. and the huge "wing

Fig. 339. An S-42-A docked at the home base in Florida.

Fig. 340. The "Alaskan Clipper", an S-42-B, an instant before becoming airborne.

flaps" lowered the big "Clipper" down to soft landings even in the roughest water. The S-42 type "Clipper Ship" was a steady airplane with predictable habits and rather easy to handle for such a large airplane; pilots liked it. The type certificate number for the model S-42-A was issued 12-19-35 and amended later to include the S-42-B. Seven airplanes of this type were manufactured by the Sikorsky Aircraft Div. at Bridgeport, Conn.

Listed below are specifications and performance data for the Sikorsky model S-42-A as powered with 4 "Hornet" S1EG engines rated 750 h.p. (800 h.p. for take-off) each; length overall 68'0"; height overall (on water) 17'4"; height overall (out of water) 21'5"; wing span 118'2"; max. wing chord 13'6"; mean aerodynamic chord 12'4"; total wing area 1340 sq. ft.; airfoil Sikorsky GSM-3; wt. empty 23,-200 lbs.; useful load 16,800 lbs.; payload with 1240 gal. fuel & 5 crew 7960 lbs.; gross wt. 40,-000 lbs.; max. speed 188 at 7000 ft.; cruising speed (2000 r.p.m.) 165 at 7000 ft.; landing speed (with flaps) 65; climb 850 ft. first min. at sea level; ser. ceiling 16,000 ft.; gas cap. 1240 gal.; oil cap. 74 gal.; cruising range (.75 power) at 170 gal. per hour 1150 miles; price not announced. 32 place as day-plane or 14-berth sleeper.

Specifications and data for model S-42-B were identical as above except as follows: wt. empty 24,000 lbs.; useful load 18,000 lbs.; payload with 1240 gal. fuel & 5 crew 9160 lbs.; gross wt. 42,000 lbs.; max. speed 177 at sea level; max. speed 188 at 7000 ft.; cruising speed (.70 power) 163 at 7000 ft.; landing speed (with flaps) 67; climb 800 ft. first min. at sea level; ser. ceiling 15,500 ft.; cruising range (.70 power) at 168

gal. per hour 1200 miles; normally operated as 37 place day-plane or 14-berth sleeper. Absolute ceiling with any one engine not operating was approx. 6000 ft.

The construction details and general arrangement of the models S-42-A and S-42-B were typical to that of the earlier S-42 except for the following changes. In a very significant change, 24-ST aluminum alloy was used in the structure instead of 17-ST alloy for greater strength and a saving in weight. The new wing, with a Sikorsky-developed "GSM-3" airfoil, had greater span and more lifting area; the wing flaps were also revised and improved. The tail group was revised and improved. There were minor changes in lines and structure of the hull and cabin interior was modified to a looser seating arrangement providing more comfort for fewer passengers; the 32 passenger day-plane was quickly convertible to a 14-berth sleeper, and vice versa. The interior was arranged to provide 138 cu. ft. of cargo space, and a 64 cu. ft. compartment for passenger baggage. Powerplant nacelles for the geared "Hornet" S1EG or S2EG engines were improved and the NACA-type engine cowls were modified slightly on the S-42-B. The engines were fitted with more efficient oil-coolers, and the S-42-B were fitted with the new "constant speed" propellers. Later, the S-42-A were also fitted with the new propellers. Normal tankage of fuel (in 8 tanks) provided a 1200 mile range, but extra tankage in the cabin section and bilge boosted cruising range beyond 3000 miles. In this case, some payload was swapped in favor of extra fuel. Electric engine starters, generators, Exide batteries, fuel pumps, navigation lights, landing lights, parachute flares, Pyrene and

Kidde fire extinguishers, bonding & shielding, two-way radio equipment, a galley, lavatory, crew quarters, mooring gear, and a first-aid station were standard equipment. Each airplane was equipped with an automatic-pilot by Sperry, and the most extensive array of engine and flight instruments that man had devised to now. The next Sikorsky development was the twin-engined model S-43 amphibian as described in the chapter for ATC # 593 of this volume.

Listed below are Sikorsky S-42-A and S-42-B entries as gleaned from registration records:

NC-15373: S-42-A (# 4203) 4 Hornet 750.
   -15374: S-42-A (# 4204) 4 Hornet 750.
   -15375: S-42-A (# 4205) 4 Hornet 750.
   -15376: S-42-B (# 4206) 4 Hornet 750.
      : S-42-B (# 4207) 4 Hornet 750.
   -16735: S-42-B (# 4208) 4 Hornet 750.
   -16736: S-42-B (# 4209) 4 Hornet 750.

This approval for ser. # 4203 and up; reg. no. for ser. # 4207 unknown; this approval expired 9-30-39.

ATC # 593
(12-24-35)
SIKORSKY "AMPHIBION", S-43.

Fig. 341. The graceful Sikorsky S-43 on an early test flight.

Posing in the bay as a "Clipper" ship in miniature the twin-motored Sikorsky S-43 brought modernized, rapid inter-island air service to the Hawaiian Islands. Coincidentally, while the big 4-motored S-42 "Clipper" was being feted in Honolulu for its flight from San Francisco, a steamer was pulling into the harbor with a disassembled S-43 lashed to the deck; this was the first of 2 of the high-speed "Amphibions" for Inter-Island Airways. The cross-channel service was to offer daily trips from Honolulu to all of the other islands in the group; the longest hop, a 2-hour flight, was to Hilo. Assembly of the S-43 in the Inter-Island hangar on John Rogers Airport, gathered daily throngs to watch it go together. Chas. Elliott, as chief pilot for Inter-Island Airways, had been with the ship constantly since it left the factory and was anxious to get it ready for service. Turnout for the acceptance flight was quite a festive occasion. Earlier in the year, this same S-43 was flown on its maiden hop by Boris Sergievsky over Long Island Sound, and the pilot was flabbergasted to find he had taken off on only one engine! Needless to say, with both engines running, performance of the new airplane was even beyond expectations. Enthused with the air-

plane, Sergievsky later invited Igor Sikorsky aboard and together they set many world records for speed, load, and altitude in the category for large amphibian aircraft. A second S-43 was delivered to Inter-Island Airways shortly after the first one was operational, and the Pan American Airways System ordered a whole fleet. As the largest and fastest twin-engined amphibian in the world the S-43 made quite a name for itself and attracted buyers from all corners of the world; quite a few were exported to Europe. Twelve were delivered to the Pan Am System and affiliates for Pacific and Latin American routes, 4 to Air France for its service to Africa, 2 were delivered to Russia, and others to China, Norway, and Chile. In 1937 the Army Air Corps procured 5 of the S-43 as the OA-8, eleven U. S. Navy versions were the JRS-l, and as late as 1942 the Air Corps procured one as the OA-11. The Sikorsky S-43 served well through the years, but their disposition is unknown; the only known airworthy example left at this time is one owned by multi-millionaire Howard Hughes.

Patterned largely after the big Sikorsky (S-42) trans-Pacific "Clipper" the model S-43 was a twin-engined amphibious "parasol" monoplane

Fig. 342. An S-43 operated by Inter-Island Airways of Hawaii.

of the flying boat type. Seating was normally arranged for 16 passengers and a crew of 3, but a coach-style arrangement was able to squeeze in 25 people. Most airlines operated the S-43 as an "amphibian", as did the government services, but on some routes Pan Am operated the ship as a pure flying boat; removal of the big landing gear assembly added at least a half-ton to the payload. Twenty of the S-43 were delivered during 1936 of which several were shipped abroad. Totally suited for an air service that originated on land and terminated in the water, the S-43 inaugurated new airlines in North Africa, Norway, and in Chile. Our own government services (Navy and Air Corps) were using the S-43 for utility service and patrol duties; the U. S. Army Air Corps had 5 as the OA-8 and one as the OA-11. The U. S. Navy air arm had 11 for

patrol duty as the JRS-1. As powered with two 9 cyl. Pratt & Whitney "Hornet" S1EG (geared) engines rated 750 h.p. each at 2250 r.p.m. at 7000 ft. the S-43 was exceptionally fast for an "amphibian" and its all-round performance was outstanding for this type of airplane. Its water characteristics were superb and it was equally deft on land or water; pilots were lavish in their praise for it, whether asked or not. The later model S-43-B was a twin-tailed version that was usually delivered as a flying boat and operated strictly in the water; on some routes this was more practical. The type certificate number for the model S-43 was issued 12-24-35 and later amended to include the S-43-B. No accurate listing was available for the number of examples of this model that were manufactured by the Sikorsky Aircraft Div. at Bridgeport, Conn.

Fig. 343. An S-43 destined for Norway; others were exported to France, Russia, China, and Chile.

Fig. 344. The S-43-B was a twin-tailed version; several were operated by Pan Am.

Listed below are specifications and performance data for the Sikorsky model S-43 as powered with 2 "Hornet" S1EG engines rated 750 h.p. each; length overall 51'2"; height overall (on wheels) 17'8"; wing span 86'0"; max. wing chord 11'6"; total wing area 781 sq. ft.; airfoil at root NACA-2218; airfoil at tip NACA-2212; wt. empty 12,570 (12,750) lbs.; useful load 6430 (6750) lbs.; payload with 400 gal. fuel & 3 crew 3300 (3600) lbs.; gross wt. 19,000 (19,500) lbs.; figures in parentheses as later amended; max. speed 186 at sea level; max. speed 194 at 7000 ft.; max. speed (one engine) 125 at 7000 ft.; cruising speed (.75 power) 167 at sea level; cruising speed (.70 power) 165 at 1000 ft.; cruising speed (.75 power) 181 at 8000 ft.; landing (stall) speed (with flaps) 65; climb 1100 ft. first min. at sea level; ser. ceiling 20,000 ft.; gas cap. 400 gal.; oil cap. 28 gal.; baggage 450 lbs.; cruising range (.75 power) at 84 gal. per hour 775 miles; price not announced. Useful load raised to 7530-7850 lbs. as flying boat.

Specifications and data for model S-43-B same as above except as follows; length overall 52'3"; height overall (on wheels) 17'7"; airfoil at root NACA-2218; airfoil at tip NACA-2209; wt. empty 12,900 (13,482) lbs.; useful load 6600 (6518) lbs.; payload with 400 gal. fuel & 3 crew 3650 (3568) lbs.; gross wt. 19,500 (20,000) lbs.; wts. in parentheses as later amended; max. speed 190 at 7000 ft.; cruising speed (.70 power) 166 at 7000 ft.; cruising speed (.75 power) 173 at 12,800 ft.; landing (stall) speed (with flaps) 65-67; climb 1100-1010 ft. first min. at sea level; ser. ceiling

19,000 ft.; gas cap. normal 400 gal.; gas cap. max. 594 gal.; oil cap. max. 44 gal; cruising range (.70 power) at 80 gal. per hour 800 miles; price not announced.

The two-step hull was a 24-ST alloy semi-monocoque framework laid on a girder-type keel and covered with smooth "stressed-skin" Alclad metal sheet; all framework members were anodized and the "skin" was fastened with flush-type rivets. The 4 main bulkheads provided 5 water-tight compartments of which any 3 could keep the airplane afloat. The spacious interior was normally arranged for 16 passengers, but a coach-style arrangement could seat up to 25. Entry to the main cabin was in the aft section and entry to the cockpit was up forward. Anchor and mooring gear was in the bow, baggage was stowed just behind the pilot compartment, with a steward's pantry and a lavatory in this same area. Passengers were divided into 2 compartments and each passenger was allowed up to 47 lbs. baggage. The huge all-metal cantilever wing was of box-type monospar construction with girder-type ribs cantilevered from the rear face and a detachable leading edge fastened to the front face. The tapered wing, in 3 sections, was mounted above the hull in "parasol" fashion on 2 heavy N-type struts; a streamlined tower in the center, carrying no loads, housed engine and plane controls. Engines were mounted into the center-section, and the C/S also housed four 100 gal. fuel tanks. Ailerons and wing flaps were all-metal (24-ST) structures covered with fabric, and all parts of the wing behind the spar beam

Fig. 345. An S-43-B unloads at Port of Spain, Trinidad.

were also covered in fabric. The all-metal wing tip floats were fastened at a point to prevent wing from heeling into the water. The landing gear of 11'2" tread was of separate units that retracted snugly up into wheel wells in the hull; the 45x17 wheels were fitted with hydraulic brakes and 10-ply tires. The full swivel 18x6 tail wheel was fitted with 6-ply tire. When used as a true "flying boat" the landing gear and tail wheel assemblies were removed for a 1100 lb. gain in payload or fuel for extra range. The "balanced" tail group was an all-metal (24-ST) structure covered with fabric; the horizontal stabilizer was adjustable in flight. The model S-43-B version had a twin-tailed arrangement. Hamilton-Standard controllable propellers, Eclipse electric engine starters, Eclipse generator, Willard battery, fuel pumps, fuel gauges, dual control wheels, navigation lights, landing lights, parachute flares, mooring gear & anchor, Pyrene & Lux fire extinguishers, life jackets, a Very pistol, bilge pump, canvas bailing bucket, first-aid kit, tool kit, and fire-axe were standard equipment. "Constant-speed" propellers, inflatable life raft, radio equipment, "Hornet" S2EG engines, and extra fuel capacity were optional. The next Sikorsky development was the Cyclone-powered S-43-W as described

in the chapter for ATC # 623.

Listed below is partial listing of S-43 entries as gleaned from registration records:

NC-15061;	S-43	(# 4301)	2 Hornet 750.
-15062;	"	(# 4302)	"
-15063;	"	(# 4303)	"
-15064;	"	(# 4304)	"
-15065;	"	(# 4305)	"
-15066;	"	(# 4306)	"
-15067;	"	(# 4307)	"
PP-PAU;	"	(# 4308)	"
PP-PAW;	"	(#)	"
-16925;	"	(# 4316)	"
-16926;	"	(# 4317)	"
-16927;	"	(# 4318)	"
-16928;	"	(# 4319)	"
-16931;	"	(# 4322)	"
-16932;	"	(# 4323)	"
-16933;	"	(# 4324)	"

This approval for ser. #4301 and up; ser. # 4301-02 del. to Inter-Island Airways; reg. no. for ser. # 4307 not verified; ser. no. unknown for PP-PAW; no listing for ser. # 4308 thru 4315 - some of these were del. to Pan Am; reg. no. for ser. # 4315-17-18-19 not verified; ser. # 4320-21 were model S-43-W; S-43 for Army Air Corps and U. S. Navy mfgd. 1937; no listing available beyond ser. #4324.

ATC # 594
(2-13-36)
STINSON " RELIANT", SR-7

Fig. 346. A Stinson "Reliant" SR-7B with 245 h.p. Lycoming engine.

Some of the excitement in the Stinson plant was the hustle of day and night shifts working to complete orders for the tri-motored "Model A", but some of the behind-the-scene excitement was the shaping of a brand-new "Reliant", a revolutionary mating of the familiar fuselage with an adaptation of the unique sesqui-spar wing. The double-tapered wing design had worked beautifully on Stinson's low-winged tri-motor, and it was calculated that the wing would do wonders for the "Reliant" also. C. R. Irvine and Robert Hall designed this wing to mate with a standard SR-6 fuselage and the result as it was rolled out onto the apron was the beautiful SR-7. Because of its double taper and the way it joined the fuselage the airplane soon became popularly known as the "Gull Wing". Those that had a peek at it before national announcement were naturally impressed and came to regard it highly, but those that had no idea what the "new Reliant" would look like were simply amazed. Amazed first at its staunch pose that was tempered with grace, and then amazed with the way the SR-7 conducted itself. Perhaps many people expected some compromise, but there was none; the new SR-7 was every inch a typical "Reliant" and the best-looking of the

bunch, so far. To offer variety with models suitable for any purse or purpose the SR-7 was available with 3 different Lycoming engines. Many options were also available and the airplane was approved to operate on wheels, skis, or floats. The roster of owners was very impressive and production of the first batch of 12 airplanes had customers waiting in the doorway for delivery. Because of necessary price raises the SR-7 was competing with better-built airplanes, so Stinson craftsmen were building the new "Reliant" with extra patience, backed by skill and years of experience; each SR-7 that was rolled out from final assembly was a veritable show-piece. Stinson Aircraft was celebrating its tenth year in the business during Dec. of 1935 and a feature of the celebration was the christening of the prototype SR-7 for 1936 by Mrs. E. A. Stinson, widow of the late "Eddie" Stinson. The inner circle gathered around the airplane was a group of ten-year employees that had helped "Eddie" Stinson build his first airplane that was introduced in 1926. Since that time, Stinson Aircraft had produced more than 1000 airplanes.

The Stinson "Reliant" model SR-7 was a high-winged cabin monoplane with seating arranged for 4 or 5. Because of higher

Fig. 347. The "Reliant" SR-7 was available with 3 different Lycoming engines.

horsepower and greater allowance in gross weight the SR-7B and SR-7C were eligible to carry 5 people. Extra fuel was also allowed for greater range. The SR-7A powered with a 225 h.p. engine was limited to 4 people and 50 gal. of fuel. In general, the SR-7 series was a normal "Reliant", but it is surprising what the new wing had done for its character. With its double taper and max. thickness at the strut station the wing looked rather massive and made the whole airplane appear practically indestructible, but the slender wing tips kept it from looking unwieldy. The wing taper at the roots presented less cross-section in this area, so in effect, visibility was much better. Span-wise distribution of the air-flow split the intensity of all loads to the air-frame and this had a tendency to soften the ride and divert the jolts. Pilots claimed the SR-7 had the stability of a bridge, and rode the rough air like an ocean-liner. As powered with the 9 cyl. Lycoming R-680-6 engine rated 245 h.p. the model SR-7B (the most popular of the SR-7 series) had plenty of hustle and impressed everyone in the way it conducted itself throughout the whole range of flight. As powered with the Lycoming R-680-4 engine rated 225 h.p. it was noticeable that the SR-7A had a little less power, and as powered with the Lycoming R-680-5 engine rated 260 h.p. it was also noticeable that the SR-7C had a little more power. This was the fastest "Reliant" up to now, and owners were quick to brag on it. To operate off water an SR-7B was equipped with Edo pontoons and the performance characteristics were fairly remarkable; a statement by someone "it gets off the water like a scared Teal" is descrip-

tive in part of its capabilities as a seaplane. The SR-7C was also eligible as a seaplane on Edo twin-float gear. The type certificate number for the model SR-7B was issued 2-13-36 and amended to include the SR-7A and SR-7C; some 50 examples were mfgd. in the SR-7 series by the Stinson Aircraft Corp. at Wayne, Mich.

Listed below are specifications and performance data for the "Reliant" model SR-7A as powered with Lycoming R-680-4 engine rated 225 h.p. at 2100 r.p.m. with fixed-pitch metal propeller; length overall 27'0"; height overall 8'6"; wing span 41'7"; max. wing chord 96"; wing chord at tip 38"; total wing area 256.5 sq. ft.; airfoil Clark Y; wt. empty 2260 lbs.; useful load 1090 (1115) lbs.; payload with 50 gal. fuel 587 (615) lbs. (3 pass. & 50 lbs. baggage); gross wt. 3350 (3375) lbs.; wts. in parentheses as later amended; max. speed 144; cruising speed 136 at 3000 ft.; landing speed (with flaps) 53; climb 725 ft. first min. at sea level; ser. ceiling 12,300 ft.; gas cap. 50 gal.; oil cap. 4.5 gal.; cruising range at 14 gal. per hour 475 miles; price $6485. at factory.

Specifications and data for the model SR-7B as powered with Lycoming R-680-6 engine rated 245 h.p. at 2300 r.p.m. with Lycoming-Smith controllable propeller were same as above except as follows; length overall 27'2"; wt. empty 2310 lbs.; useful load 1290 lbs.; payload with 70 gal. fuel 663 lbs. (3 pass. & 100 lbs. baggage); payload with 50 gal. fuel 783 lbs. (4 pass. & 100 lbs. baggage); gross wt. 3600 lbs.; max. speed 146; cruising speed 138.5 at 3000 ft.; landing speed (with flaps) 55; climb 850 ft. first min. at

Fig. 348. An SR-7C with 260 h.p. Lycoming engine used in promotion by Pure Oil Co.

sea level; ser. ceiling 14,000 ft.; gas cap. 70 gal.; oil cap. 5 gal.; cruising range at 14.5 gal. per hour 470-645 miles; price not announced. The SR-7B as seaplane on Edo 39-4000 floats same as above except as follows: wt. empty 2650 lbs; useful load 1200 lbs.; payload with 65 gal. fuel 603 lbs. (3 pass. & 93 lb. baggage); gross wt. 3850 lbs.; max. speed 131; cruising speed 123; landing speed (with flaps) 60; climb 700 ft. first min. at sea level; ser. ceiling 10,000 ft.; gas cap. 70 gal.; oil cap. 5 gal.; cruising range 530 miles; price not announced.

Specifications and data for the model SR-7C as powered with Lycoming R-680-5 engine rated 260 h.p. at 2300 r.p.m. with Lycoming-Smith controllable prop same as above except as follows: wt. empty 2335 lbs.; useful load 1265 lbs.; payload with 70 gal. fuel 638 lbs. (3 pass. & 75 lbs. baggage); payload with 50 gal. fuel 758 lbs. (4 pass. & 75 lbs. baggage); gross wt. 3600 lbs.; max. speed 148; cruising speed 140 at 3000 ft.; landing speed (with flaps) 55; climb 950 ft. first min. at sea level; ser. ceiling 14,500 ft.; gas cap. 50-70 gal.; oil cap. 5 gal.; cruising range at

Fig. 349. The gull-winged SR-7 was one of the most handsome airplanes of this period.

15 gal. per hour 450-640 miles; price not announced. The SR-7C was also eligible as seaplane on Edo 39-4000 twin-float gear at 3850 lbs. gross weight.

The fuselage framework was built up of welded C/M steel tubing, faired to shape with wooden formers and fairing strips, then fabric covered. Entire fuselage was covered in dural metal panels forward of the doors. A luggage compartment was located under the rear seat with allowance for 25 lbs.; the main baggage compartment behind the rear seat was allowed 50-75-100 lbs., according to fuel load carried. The double-tapered sesqui-spar wing was built up with a girder-type spar beam of welded chrome-moly steel tubing with wing ribs of square dural tubing that were riveted together and reinforced with dural gussets; the leading edges were covered with dural sheet and the completed framework was covered in fabric. Slotted wing flaps were vacuum-operated. A 25 gal. fuel tank was mounted in each wing root for 50 gal. cap., and 35 gal. tanks were mounted for a 70 gal. cap., 41 gal. fuel tanks were optional. The semi-cantilever wing was braced by a single heavy-gauge dural strut on each side. The cantilever landing gear of 113 in. tread was wider than on previous "Reliant" models; 8.50x10 low-pressure tires were mounted on 7.50x10 wheels with hydraulic disc brakes. Fittings were furnished on the fuselage for Edo 39-4000 twin-float gear; an aux. fin was required on seaplane. The fabric covered tail group was built up of welded C/M steel tubing; all movable control surfaces were aerodynamically balanced and horizontal stabilizer was adjustable in flight. A fixed-pitch metal propeller (Lycoming-Smith controllable for SR-7B and SR-7C), electric engine starter, 12-volt battery, dual controls, cabin heater, shatterproof glass, navigation lights, parking brake, 10.5 in. tail wheel, ash trays, cabin lights, assist ropes, and first-aid kit were standard equipment. Wheel streamlines, aux. door on right side, metal-lined cabin for cargo, ambulance litter, landing lights, generator, parachute flares, radio equipment, fire extinguisher, and 82 gal. fuel cap. were optional. The next "Reliant" development was the model SR-8 as described in the chapter for ATC # 608.

Listed below are SR-7A, SR-7B, SR-7C entries as gleaned from registration records:

NC-16139;	SR-7B	(# 9650)	Lycoming 245.
-16100;	"	(# 9651)	"
-15173;	"	(# 9653)	"
NC-3040;	"	(# 9654)	"
-15174;	"	(# 9655)	"
-15166;	"	(# 9656)	"
-16101;	"	(# 9657)	"
-16102;	"	(# 9658)	"
NC-2250;	"	(# 9659)	"
-16103;	"	(# 9660)	"
-16105;	SR-7A	(# 9661)	Lycoming 225.
-16108;	SR-7B	(# 9662)	Lycoming 245.
-16104;	"	(# 9663)	"
-16106;	SR-7A	(# 9664)	Lycoming 225.
-16113;	SR-7C	(# 9666)	Lycoming 260.
-16107;	SR-7B	(# 9667)	Lycoming 245.
-16111;	"	(# 9670)	"
-16112;	"	(# 9671)	"
NC-2203;	SR-7A	(# 9672)	Lycoming 225.
-16114;	SR-7B	(# 9673)	Lycoming 245.
-16115;	"	(# 9675)	"
-16109;	"	(# 9676)	"
-16116;	"	(# 9678)	"
-16117;	"	(# 9679)	"
-16118;	"	(# 9680)	"
-16119;	"	(# 9681)	"
-16122;	SR-7A	(# 9684)	Lycoming 225.
-16123;	SR-7B	(# 9685)	Lycoming 245.
-16124;	"	(# 9686)	"
-16125;	"	(# 9687)	"
NS-2205;	SR-7C	(# 9688)	Lycoming 260.
-16127;	SR-7B	(# 9689)	Lycoming 245.
-16128;	SR-7A	(# 9690)	Lycoming 225.
-16131;	SR-7B	(# 9696)	Lycoming 245.
-16126;	"	(# 9698)	"
-16135;	"	(# 9700)	"

This approval for ser. # 9650 and up; ser. # 9652, 9665, 9668, 9669, 9674, 9677, 9682, 9683, 9691, 9692, 9693, 9694, 9695, 9697, 9699 were not listed - some of these may have been exported to foreign countries; ser. # 9672 later modified to SR-7B; ser. # 9680 del. to Alaska; ser. #9688 del. to Penna. State Dept. of Revenue; this approval expired 9-30-39.

ATC # 595
(2-14-36)
TAYLOR "CUB", J-2

Fig. 350. A Taylor "Cub" J-2 with Continental A-40 engine high over Texas.

Several hundred Taylor "Cub" were already flying around the country by late 1935 and some of the annoying little things the owners and operators didn't like about the E-2 had filtered back to the factory. As much as possible, most of these complaints were corrected in the extensively-redesigned Model J-2. So, as rolled out for preview, the new J-2 stood firmly on a wider landing gear, was more graceful in appearance with promise of better performance, was more likely to please, and surely the best value available on the lightplane market. The squared-off look of previous models was eliminated by a nicely rounded fin and rudder, the rounded wing tips tended to shorten the span, and the turtle-back was raised up to meet the wing, thus eliminating that "parasol" look and fashioning the "Cub" into a true cabin airplane. The cabin sides could still be removed for those that preferred to frolic about in the open air. It didn't take long for news about the improved "Cub" to get around and the factory was literally swamped with orders, some sight unseen; 23 of the J-2 were rolled out in March (1936) and 50 were scheduled for April. Before the year was out some 550 of the "Cub" J-2 were assembled and rolled out for delivery. Extremely optimistic of the future, the factory people laid plans to build 2500 airplanes in 1937! Altho'

only 658 of the J-2 were built in that year, because of tragedy at the plant, this was still a phenomenal amount of airplanes to be built and delivered by one company during this post-depression period. The projected plan to build 2500 "Cub" finally came to pass, but it took many years to do it. The "Cub" plant on Emery Airport in Bradford suffered a damaging fire the middle of March in 1937; most jigs and dies were saved and moved to a large hangar on the airport previously used for storage. Here assembly was performed and various other production was conducted in shops scattered nearby to allow assembly of at least one airplane per day. Some fuselage jigs were shipped to Air Associates in Long Beach, Calif., the western assembly plant where production and assembly would continue until Taylor Aircraft could find a new plant site. These were the "Western Cub" and distributed to dealers in the vast western region. Finally deciding on a plant site in Lock Haven, Pa. (June 1937) the new "Cub" plant started production in the middle of July and "Silver Cub" began rolling out as fast as possible to catch up on orders. Shortly after, name of the plant was changed to Piper Aircraft Corp. and plans were laid for a new custom model called the "Cub Sport". Twenty-three of the J-2 were built going into 1938 and by then the famous J-3

Fig. 351. A J-2 floats lazily over the mountain tops.

was already being groomed in the sidelines to take the country by storm.

By 1936 the "Cub" was firmly entrenched as the poor-man's-airplane and used almost universally for pilot-training. Little "flying schools", some just a one-man operation, were sprouting up all over the country. It was just a matter of scraping together $490. for a down payment on a "Cub" and a good pilot was in business. Low operating costs allowed low-cost flight training and this attracted thousands. Some of these enterprising young men were so busy instructing they carried their lunch aloft in a paper bag and ate sandwiches while directing the manipulations of a student. Nearly every airport had a "Cub" or two on hand, and some fields literally swarmed with "Cub" to the extent they were called "Cubville", "Cub Haven", "Cub Country", etc. Many of the J-2 were exported to Europe and other countries; one was shipped to Nicaragua to train Army cadet pilots. Not all the "Cub" were bought by people of modest means; several were used in pursuit of business, and some were owned by sport-fliers on the "Social Register". One such was a custom "Cub" owned by a lady-pilot that had it done up in a hand-rubbed cream finish with plush blue upholstery and called it "Hayseed"; "Hayseed" was her favorite in spite of the fact she could own an airplane costing 10 times as much! The "Cub" J-2, bless her heart, was fun to fly, but she wouldn't hurry nowhere. On a breakfast flight from Los Angeles to Death Valley, the "Cub" pilots were faced with strong winds and arrived to cold bacon and eggs, and coffee about gone. The "Cub" had her limitations, but she made up for this in ways that

a pilot could feel, but were hard to explain. The formula for the success of the Taylor "Cub" model J-2 defies any rational analysis because much of it was based on values other than facts and figures.

The Taylor "Cub" model J-2 was a light cabin monoplane with seating arranged for two in tandem. The improved J-2 was built around an airframe that was basically the same as the'E-2, but so much had been done to alter its shape that you couldn't help but notice that it was an entirely new airplane. The "Cub" now looked like an honest-to-goodness cabin airplane. Each change made was tied to a common complaint, so for practical purposes the J-2 was literally without complaint. Better airflow across the fuselage added 4 or 5 m.p.h. to the speed, it improved the climb-out, lengthened the glide path, and eliminated turbulent airflow over the tail group. The wider landing gear kept things steadier in a cross-wind and allowed taxiing in a breeze without fear of tipping over. Also, the J-2 was rather handsome and people admired it. As introduced early in 1936 the "Cub" was selling for $1470., or for $1035. less engine and prop; most were sold for $490. down and a year to pay. For another $28.00 you could get the cabin enclosure. The "Silver Cub", all done up in "silver dope", was introduced later in 1936 and because it was cheaper to build, and volume sales justified it, the price was reduced to $1270. ($425. down and a year to pay). The 1000th "Cub" was built Dec. 1936 and flown off to the Miami Air Races to celebrate the occasion; the "Cub" had been approved with the twin-ignition Continental A-40-4 engine in November, and

Fig. 352. Amongst all its various uses, the J-2 was most popular for pilot training.

this too was an occasion. The J-2 held its price of $1270. going into 1938 and a free flying course was now included. A seaplane was also available since mid-1936 and it only cost $1895. on Edo twin-float gear ($635. down and a year to pay). As powered with the 4 cyl. Continental A-40 series engines rated 37 to 40 h.p. the model J-2 was a deft little airplane that was fun to fly; comments like "it's the sweetest little airplane I have ever flown" were quite common and unsolicited. The J-2 was an introduction to flying that was pure and simple; every hop was a picnic. It was quite at home in the boon-docks and expanded the joy of cow-pasture flying. Terribly forgiving, the J-2 was ideal for pilot-training and it took a real dumbo to get himself in trouble. The J-2 gave ample warning when it wanted to quit flying and a "full stall" was like falling into cotton candy. The "Cub" was never tricky, but she did enjoy a practical joke now and then, just so she wouldn't be taken entirely for granted. The type certificate number for the "Cub" model J-2 was issued 2-14-36 and more than 1200 examples of this model were manufactured by the Taylor Aircraft Co. at Bradford, Penn.; from July 1937, balance of the J-2 were built at Lock Haven, Penn. Because of differences in opinion and lack of harmony, C. G. Taylor (designer of the "Cub") sold his interests in 1935 and left to develop another airplane; the company was reorganized, but kept the same name. T. V. Weld became pres. & sales mgr.; Walter C. Jamouneau was V.P. & chf. engr.; Wm. T. Piper became sec-treas. & gen. mgr. Johnnie Livingston, famous "Waco" pilot, was with the

"Cub" organization for a time, but left by Aug. of 1937 to become a fixed-base operator back in his home town.

Listed below are specifications and performance data for the Taylor "Cub" model J-2 as powered with Continental A-40-3 engine rated 37 h.p. at 2550 r.p.m., or Continental A-40-4 engine rated 40 h.p. at 2575 r.p.m.; length overall 22'5"; height overall 6'8"; wing span 35'3"; wing chord 63"; total wing area 178.5 sq. ft.; airfoil USA-35B; wt. empty 563 lbs.; useful load 407 lbs; payload with 9 gal. fuel 175 lbs.; gross wt. 970 lbs. (1000 lbs. for ser. # 600 and up); bag. 5 lbs.; max. speed 87; cruising speed (2300 r.p.m.) 70; landing speed 30; climb 450 ft. first min. at sea level; ser. ceiling 12,000 ft.; gas cap. 9 gal.; oil cap. 4 qts.; cruising range (2300 r.p.m.) at 2.75 gal. per hour 210 miles; price $1470. at factory early 1936, lowered to $1270. Seaplane on Edo-D-1070 floats same as above except as follows; height on water 7'7"; wt. empty 657 lbs.; useful load 410 lbs.; payload with 9 gal. fuel 178 lbs.; gross wt. 1058 lbs; max. speed 75; cruising speed 65; landing speed 35; climb 360 ft. first min. at sea level; ser. ceiling 10,000 ft.; cruising range 200 miles; price $1970. at factory, later reduced to $1895.

The fuselage framework was built up of welded chrome-moly and 1025 steel tubing, lightly faired to shape, then fabric covered. Seats were mounted in tandem and a large let-down door provided entry from the right side. The interior covered in Fabricoid was rather bare, but adequate, and all gadgetry was simple and quite functional. The J-2 was a true cabin airplane,

Fig. 353. A "Cub" J-2 on Edo floats.

but enclosure sides could be removed for summer flying; the large Pyralin windshield now had more slant offering full protection and better visibility. A small baggage shelf with allowance for up to 20 lbs. was behind the rear seat. A 9 gal. fuel tank was mounted high in the fuselage ahead of the windshield; a bobber-type fuel level gauge projected thru the cowling. The engine cowling was redesigned with emphasis on better cooling. The wing framework, in 2 halves, was build up of solid spruce spar beams with aluminum alloy (Nicral) wing ribs riveted into truss form; the leading edges were covered with dural sheet and the completed framework was covered in fabric. The wing was braced to the fuselage with vee-type struts on each side of streamlined C/M steel tubing. The split-type landing gear of 72 in. tread was now 16 in. wider and fitted with Rusco shock-cord rings; wheels were 7.00x4 and no brakes were provided. The roly-poly 18x8-3 Goodyear airwheels were optional. The spring-leaf tail skid was fitted with a hardened shoe; a steerable tail wheel attachment was available. The "Cub" J-2 was also eligible on skis and as a seaplane on Edo D-1070 twin-float gear. The fabric covered tail group was built up of welded 1025 steel tubing; the horizontal stabilizer was adjustable in flight. All

Fig. 354. The J-2 worked in fair weather or foul and most often was kept outside.

movable controls were operated by cable. A Sensenich wooden propeller, dual stick-type controls, and a first-aid kit were standard equipment. Navigation lights, battery, carbureter heater, cabin heater, and wheel streamlines (pants) were optional. The next "Cub" development was a version called the "Western Cub" as described in the chapter for ATC # 620.

Below is a partial listing of Taylor "Cub" model J-2 entries as gleaned from registration records:

X-15951; J-2 (# 500) Continental A-40.

Reg. No.		Ser. No.	
NC-15956;	"	(# 501)	"
-15957;	"	(# 502)	"
-15958;	"	(# 503)	"
-15959;	"	(# 504)	"
-15960;	"	(# 505)	"
-15962;	"	(# 506)	"
-15963;	"	(# 507)	"
-15964;	"	(# 508)	"
-15965;	"	(# 509)	"
-15966;	"	(# 510)	"
-15967;	"	(# 511)	"
-15968;	"	(# 512)	"
-15969;	"	(# 513)	"
-15970;	"	(# 514)	"
-15971;	"	(# 515)	"
-15972;	"	(# 516)	"
-15973;	"	(# 517)	"
-15974;	"	(# 518)	"
-15975;	"	(# 519)	"
-15976;	"	(# 520)	"
-15977;	"	(# 521)	"
-15978;	"	(# 522)	"
-15979;	"	(# 523)	"
-15980;	"	(# 524)	"
-15981;	"	(# 525)	"
-15982;	"	(# 526)	"
-15983;	"	(# 527)	"
-15984;	"	(# 528)	"
-15985;	"	(# 529)	"
-15986;	"	(# 530)	"
-16300;	"	(# 533)	"
-16301;	"	(# 534)	"
-16302;	"	(# 535)	"
-16303;	"	(# 536)	"
-16304;	"	(# 537)	"
-16305;	"	(# 538)	"
-16306;	"	(# 539)	"
-16307;	"	(# 540)	"
-16308;	"	(# 541)	"
-16309;	"	(# 542)	"
-16310	"	(# 543)	"
-16311;	"	(# 544)	"
-16312;	"	(# 545)	"
-16313;	"	(# 546)	"
-16314;	"	(# 547)	"
-16315;	"	(# 548)	"
-16316;	"	(# 549)	"
-16317;	"	(# 550)	"
-16318;	"	(# 551)	"
-16319;	"	(# 552)	"
-16320;	"	(# 553)	"
-16321;	"	(# 554)	"
-16322;	"	(# 555)	"

This approval for ser. # 500 and up; ser. #500 thru 599 eligible at 970 lbs. gross wt.; ser. # 600 and up eligible at 1000 lbs. gross wt.; reg. no. for ser. # 512, 514, 526, 528, 536, 541 not verified; no listing for ser. # 531-532; ser. # 658 and up eligible as seaplane — earlier ser. nos. also eligible if modified to conform; because more than 1200 of the J-2 were built, it is impractical to present a complete listing; this approval expired 9-30-39.

ATC # 596
(2-24-36)
AERONCA, MODEL LA, LB.

Fig. 355. The Aeronca LA with 70 h.p. LeBlond engine.

It seemed rather unusual for a dainty, low-winged cabin airplane such as the "Aeronca L" to come out of a plant that had been building comical-looking flivver planes for the past 6 years, but all aircraft engineers do have dreams on occasion that spawn vehicles ahead of contemporary times. Giles E. Barton had such a dream and it was fashioned into reality in 1934. Powered originally with the 2 cyl. Aeronca E-113-C engine of 40 h.p. the prototype was painfully underpowered and the performance that Barton had in mind lay dormant because of lack of power. They say it just barely got off the ground and flew many miles out before it was high enough to turn around! The installation of a 5 cyl. "LeBlond 60" engine unleashed some of the potential and the new airplane took on the stature of a very promising design. Modifying the structure and configuration a little for the bigger engine, the 5 cyl. LeBlond 5DE of 70 h.p. became standard in the model C-70 (Model LA) and the LeBlond 5DF of 85 h.p. was offered in the model C-85 (Model LB). There was no need now to make excuses for these 2 airplanes, they were both terrific. Joe Plosser, the "Aeronca" distributor for So. Calif., ferried the first Model

LA (C-70) from the factory on Lunken Airport to his base at Glendale. The 2475 mile cross-country trip was covered in 27 hours of flying time; total cost of making the trip, including all expenses, was $43.00. The leisurely trip was uneventful and quite enjoyable; pilots showed great interest in the new airplane along the way. A 2 cyl. Aeronca C-3 embarked on the same trip, but it had to take 2 days longer! Orders for the new "Aeronca" were coming in nicely, with the higher-powered (85 h.p.) Model LB the favorite. The roster showed that owners were strung out all over the country. About 40 of the "Aeronca" LA-LB were delivered in 1936 but production was cut for 1937 because interest seemed to be falling off. There was no fault in the airplane, it just seemed to be in an inconvenient price bracket. The popular Aeronca C-3 was still selling well, but already the "Aeronca K" was being groomed to take its place, and it swung into production during May of 1937.

The "Aeronca L" was a low-winged cabin monoplane with side-by-side seating for two. The coupe-type airplane was rather normal except for its sharply tapered cantilever wing and its rakish cantilever landing gear that was fully

Fig. 356. First LA off production line went to Calif.

encased in large metal "boots". As a sport-type airplane the series was offered with 3 different engines; the models LA and LB discussed here were powered with LeBlond engines of 70 h.p. and 85 h.p. respectively. The rugged airframe was dimensioned in good aerodynamic proportion, the airplane had a good amount of charm about it, and it attracted attention wherever it went. Probably not all owners felt the same way, but one exclaimed that it was the most beautiful thing with wings; for him it was love at first sight. Quite likely he still carries a faded photo in his billfold and hallowed are the memories of it. As powered with the 5 cyl. LeBlond 5DE engine rated 70 h.p. at 1950 r.p.m. the model LA was a spritely machine with an engaging personality. Performance was a little above the average and flight characteristics were delightful. Many have said that this "Aeronca" was gentle as a lamb if you steered it straight and easy, but give her a challenge and she became quick as a pussy-cat. As powered with the 5 cyl. LeBlond 5DF engine rated 85 h.p. at 2125 r.p.m. the model LB was, of course, that much better and became the most popular ship of the series. Fifteen horsepower doesn't seem like much, but the "Aeronca L" was sensitive to horsepower and responded with a satisfying increase in performance. Capable of cruising for up to 500 miles on a tank of gas, and quite able to get in and out of all the interesting pasture-airports,

the low-winged "Aeronca" put hours of fun in cross-country flying. It has been many years since the dainty "Aeronca" L graced the skies regularly, but a few are still flying. The type certificate number for the models LA and LB was issued 2-24-36 and some 12 examples of the LA and some 25 examples of the LB were manufactured by the Aeronautical Corp. of America on Lunken Airport in Cincinnati, Ohio. Taylor Stanley was pres.; H. V. Fetick was V.P.; C. S. McKenzie was gen. mgr.; J. C. Welsch was sales mgr.; and Roger E. Schlemmer was chf. engr. Giles E. Barton was factory superintendent. In 1937 Walter J. Friedlander was appointed president.

Listed below are specifications and performance data for the Aeronca model LA as powered with 70 h.p. LeBlond 5DE engine; length overall 22'6"; height overall 7'0"; wing span 36'0"; wing chord at root 72"; aerodynamic mean chord 58.8"; total wing area 150 sq. ft.; airfoil NACA-2218 at root and NACA-2209 at tip; wt. empty 1021 (1036) lbs.; useful load 659 (644) lbs.; payload with 28 gal. fuel 306 (291) lbs.; gross wt. 1680 lbs.; figures in parentheses as later amended; max. speed 115 at sea level; cruising speed (1800 r.p.m.) 100; landing speed 48; climb 500 ft. first min. at sea level; ser. ceiling 12,000 ft.; gas cap. 28 gal.; oil cap. 2 gal.; cruising range (1800 r.p.m.) at 5 gal. per hour 500 miles; price not announced.

Fig. 357. Aeronca LA shows off its graceful form.

Specifications and data for model LB as powered with 85 h.p. LeBlond 5DF engine same as above except as follows; wt. empty 1011 lbs.; useful load 669 lbs.; payload with 28 gal. fuel 316 lbs.; gross wt. 1680 lbs.; max. speed 120 at sea level; cruising speed (1900 r.p.m.) 105; landing speed 48; climb 600 ft. first min. at sea level; service ceiling 14,000 ft.; cruising range (1900 r.p.m.) at 5.4 gal. per hour 500 miles; price was approx. $3000.

The fuselage framework was built up of welded 4130 steel tubing, faired to shape with wooden formers and fairing strips, then fabric covered. The enclosure was more of a Pyralin "greenhouse" affair than a regular cabin, with a side-panel that opened out for step-over entry. Side-panel on left (pilot) side opened out for ventilation. Seating was side-by-side on deep, comfortable cushions, with a large luggage compartment (with allowance for up to 115 lbs.) in back. The engine was mounted in rubber and cowled neatly with a "Townend" ring. The tapered cantilever wing was in 3 sections. The thick center portion of 18 ft. width was built up of spruce and plywood box-type spar beams with spruce and plywood truss-type wing ribs; the 9 ft. tip sections were built up of solid spruce spar beams and truss-type wing ribs. The leading edges were covered with dural metal sheet and the completed framework was covered in fabric. The wing was faired with metal fillets where it joined the fuselage. Ailerons were fitted with mass balance. An air-brake, popping out 90 deg. to the windstream was fitted to lower fuselage between the landing gear legs. Fuel tanks were in the wing and connected to a header-tank for flow

Fig. 358. Prototype Aeronca L on factory field.

Fig. 359. Aeronca LB with 85 h.p. LeBlond engine; shown here in Navy colors.

to the engine. The rather novel landing gear of 77 in. tread was of 2 cantilever assemblies employing double "Aeronca" oil-spring shock struts; 18x8-3 Goodyear airwheels were fitted with disc brakes. Each landing gear assembly was encased in a large, streamlined metal boot. The fabric covered tail group was built up of welded steel tubing; the left elevator was fitted with a "trim tab". A wooden Sensenich propeller, engine and flight instruments, compass, navigation lights, full-swivel tail wheel, fuel gauge, and first-aid kit were standard equipment. Electric engine starter, battery, wind-driven generator, cabin heater, landing lights, parachute flares, dual controls, Pyrene fire extinguisher, 7.00x5 wheels with brakes, radio, bonding & shield, air-brake, and extra instruments were optional. The next "Aeronca" development was the Warner-powered model LC as described in the chapter for ATC #614. Listed below are model LA and LB entries as gleaned from registration records:

X-14558: LW (# 1000) LeBlond 60.
NC-15292: LB (# 2000) LeBlond 85.
  -15282: LA (# 2001) LeBlond 70.
  -15294; " (# 2002) "
  -15727; " (# 2003) "
  -15728; " (# 2004) "
  -15730; LB (# 2005) LeBlond 85.
  -15735; " (# 2006) "
  -15738; LA (# 2007) LeBlond 70.
  -15741; LB (# 2008) LeBlond 85.
  -15743; LA (# 2009) LeBlond 70.

  -15744; " (# 2010) "
  -15747; " (# 2011) "
  -16251; LB (# 2012) LeBlond 85.
  -16253; LA (# 2013) LeBlond 70.
  -16254; LB (# 2014) LeBlond 85.
  -16258; LA (# 2015) LeBlond 70.
  -16266; LB (# 2017) LeBlond 85.
  -16269; " (# 2018) "
  -16271; " (# 2019) "
  -16272; " (# 2020) "
  -16275; " (# 2022) "
  -16278; " (# 2023) "
  -16279; LA (# 2024) LeBlond 70.
  -16280; LB (# 2025) LeBlond 85.
  -16281; " (# 2026) "
  -16284; " (# 2027) "
  -16293; " (# 2031) "
  -16294; " (# 2032) "
  -16297; " (# 2033) "
  -16527; LA (# 2034) LeBlond 70.
  -16526; LB (# 2035) LeBlond 85.
  -16528; " (# 2036) "
PP-TBO;" (# 2038) "
  -16534; " (# 2039) "
  -16537; " (# 2040) "
  -16538; " (# 2042) "
  -16541; " (# 2043) "
  -16561; " (# 2048) "

This approval for ser. # 2000 and up; ser. #1000 (LW) was prototype of L series; no listing for ser. # 2016 and 2041 — may have been exported; ser. # 2002 later as LB, had LeBlond 90 engine late in 1936; ser. # 2038 del. to Brazil; other ser. nos. not listed to #2048 were model LC.

ATC # 597
(3-2-36)
WACO, MODEL DQC-6.

Fig. 360. The DQC-6 with 285 h.p. Wright engine.

The magic formula that Clayton Brukner kept laid away in a drawer at Troy, Ohio was allowing the "Custom Cabin" by Waco Aircraft to get bigger, fatter, and heavier while performance remained just as good in most cases and even better in some. The slight changes in the basic shape were barely noticeable, but the change of a curve, an angle, or a dimension was apparently the secret that overcame some of the drag and eased the burden of progressively bigger loads. On the inside the new "Custom" was no less than elegant, and on the outside the airframe was a nice balance of form and bulk that was distinctive and very pleasant. The "Custom Cabin" went over rather big in the first year (1935) it was introduced, and now promised to be a big part of Waco production for 1936. Among the various "Custom" offerings for the 1936 season, Waco introduced 2 new cabin models that were powered with the famous "Wright" engine; these were the DQC-6 and the EQC-6. The DQC-6 was powered with the 7 cyl. Wright R-760-E1 engine rated 285 h.p. and the EQC-6 was powered with the supercharged 7 cyl. Wright R-760-E2 engine rated 320 h.p. In proper circumstance the "Custom Cabin" was a rather snooty airplane, especially in comparison

with the cheaper "Standard Cabin" that Waco was building also, and fitted more like a limousine for the carriage trade. With the nation-wide depression slowly waning and business improving in general, it is not surprising that the more expensive (320 h.p.) EQC-6 was outselling the (285 h.p.) DQC-6. Victor Fleming, Howard Hawks, Leland Hayward, and Henry King of Hollywood, who were ardent "Waco" fans, each had an EQC-6 as did Henry B. DuPont and Jesse Vincent who were also ardent "Waco" fans. The roster of owners also listed several oil companies, Stokely Bros. Foods, an Aerial Taxi outfit in the Philippines, 2 large newspapers, 2 were shipped to Argentina, and 3 were in use at scattered stations of the U. S. Coast Guard. The new C-6 was attracting impressive clientele and every airplane was a showcase of tribute to Waco tradition.

The Waco "Custom Cabin" for 1936, generally known among pilots as the C-6, was a sedan-type cabin biplane with seating arranged for 4 or 5. To offer choices for varied tastes and purposes the C-6 line was available with a number of different engines. Both the DQC-6 and the EQC-6 were powered with 7 cyl. Wright engines; the DQC-6 was powered with the R-

Fig. 361. The EQC-6 with 320 h.p. Wright engine.

760-E1 of 285 h.p. and the EQC-6 was powered with the R-760-E2 of 320 h.p. Both airplanes were more or less identical and the (320 h.p.) EQC-6 was the top of the "Custom" line for 1936. The "Custom Cabin" were plush airplanes with enough room and comfort for just about everybody, and enough convenience to please even the most critical. Normally, as it left the factory, the C-6 was well equipped, but many extras were still available as options. A fully equipped C-6 bedecked in custom colors was a joy to behold and it turned heads wherever it went. The performance available from either of these 2 airplanes (DQC-EQC) was just short of remarkable and in a subtle manner that was quite deceiving; the airplane was doing better than it seemed. The C-6 was a well-mannered airplane with the stability of a river barge, but it responded well to varying degrees of enthusiasm at the wheel. On the whole, the big "Custom" had no vices, but she did have personality and pilots enjoyed learning her ways. As time went by the "Custom" C-6 made staunch friends and was welcome anywhere. Both the DQC and the

Fig. 362. EQC-6 passes overhead on way to landing.

Fig. 363. The handsome EQC-6 was popular for business or sport.

EQC grew old gracefully confident in the fact that there were more than 100 authorized agents in 35 states and 16 foreign countries to service her needs. The C-6 was a lot of good airplane for the money and most of them graced the skies for many years afterward. The type certificate number for the model DQC-6 was issued 3-2-36 and amended later to include the EQC-6. Eleven of the DQC-6 and 20 of the EQC-6 were manufactured by the Waco Aircraft Co. at Troy, Ohio.

Listed below are specifications and performance data for the Waco model DQC-6 as powered with 285 h.p. Wright R-760-E1 engine; length overall 26'2"; height overall 8'8"; wing span upper 35'0"; wing span lower 24'6"; wing chord upper 72"; wing chord lower 48"; wing area upper 168 sq. ft.; wing area lower 76 sq. ft.; total wing area 244 sq. ft.; airfoil Clark Y; wt. empty 2075 lbs.; useful load 1425 lbs.; payload with 70 gal. fuel 798 lbs.; gross wt. 3500 lbs.; max. speed (105% power) 170; cruising speed (.75 power) 151; cruising speed (2000 r.p.m.) 151 at 6000 ft.; landing speed (with flaps) 55; climb 850 ft. first min. at sea level; ser. ceiling 17,800 ft.; gas cap. normal 70 gal.; gas cap. max. 95 gal.; oil cap. 5-6 gal.; cruising range (.75 power) at 17 gal. per hour 580 miles; price $8975. at factory field. Model DQC-6 also eligible as seaplane on Edo 38-3430 twin-float gear at 3610 lbs. gross wt.; performance with floats was slightly inferior. The empty wt. (landplane or seaplane) went up as extra equipment was added; factory records indicate that most DQC-6 left the assembly line with empty wts. ranging from 2120 to 2249 lbs. Useful loads and payloads were readjusted accordingly.

Specifications and data for the model EQC-6 as powered with 320 h.p. Wright R-760-E2 engine (350 h.p. for take-off) was same as above except as follows: wt. empty 2094 lbs.; useful load 1406 lbs.; payload with 70 gal. fuel 779 lbs.; gross wt. 3500 lbs.; max. speed (105% power) 176 at sea level with controllable propeller; cruising speed (.70 power) 157; cruising speed (2000 r.p.m.) 171 at 9000 ft.; landing speed (with flaps) 55; climb 1000 ft. first min. at sea level; ser. ceiling 19,000 ft.; gas cap. 70-95 gal.; oil cap. 5-6 gal.; cruising range (.70 power) at 19 gal. per hour 550 miles; price $9650. at factory field. Model EQC-6 also eligible as seaplane on Edo 38-3430 twin-float gear at 3610 lbs. gross wt.; performance with floats was slightly inferior. The empty wt. went up as extra equipment was added; factory records indicate that most EQC-6 left the assembly line with empty wts. ranging from 2216 to 2239 lbs. Useful loads and payloads were readjusted accordingly.

The fuselage framework was built up of welded 4130 steel tubing, faired to shape with wooden formers and fairing strips, then fabric covered. The spacious cabin seated 2 in front and the bench-type seat in back was wide enough to seat 3 across; the front seats were adjustable. The cabin interior was sound-proofed and upholstered in fine fabrics; a large baggage compartment, with allowance for up to 125 lbs., was accessible from behind the rear seat or a large outside door on the left side. The large entry door was on the left side, but a door was available on the right side also. Ample window area of shatter-proof glass, and Pyralin, both to the rear and overhead, provided good visibility, and a swing-over wheel provided dual controls; front side windows could be rolled down. The robust wing framework, in 4 panels, was built up of solid spruce spar beams with spruce and plywood truss-type wing ribs; the leading edges were covered with dural metal sheet and the completed framework was covered in fabric.

Fig. 364. An EQC-6 on Edo floats; DQC-6 also eligible as seaplane.

Split-type drag flaps on underside of upper wing were vacuum-operated; there was no intermediate position — only up and down. Interplane bracing was of heavy-gauge streamlined tubing and ailerons were on the upper wing only. One aileron was fitted with a trimming tab. A 35 gal. fuel tank was mounted in root end of each upper wing half; 47.5 gal. fuel tanks were optional. The landing gear of 87 in. tread was a simple tripod arrangement of patented "oleo" legs; 8.50x10 tires were mounted on 6.50x10 wheels with Autofan mechanical brakes. The wheels were encased in streamlined metal wheel pants. The DQC and EQC were both eligible as seaplanes on Edo 38-3430 twin-float gear. The fabric covered tail group was a composite structure of spruce spar beams and dural metal ribs for the fixed surfaces, and steel tube spars and steel formers for the movable surfaces; an elevator "tab" was adjustable for trim. A Curtiss-Reed metal prop, Exide battery, electric engine starter, generator, cabin heater, navigation lights, landing lights, NACA engine cowl, throw-over control column, swiveling tail wheel, drag flaps, parking brake, fire extinguisher, fuel gauges, first-aid kit, tool kit, tie-down ropes, and log books were standard equipment. A Y-type control column, controllable propeller, parachute-type seats, parachute flares, radio, custom upholstery, custom colors, extra door and wing-walk on right side, 95 gal. fuel cap., and seaplane gear were optional. The next C-6 development were the models YQC-ZQC-AQC as described in the chapter for ATC # 598 of this volume.

Listed below are DQC-6 and EQC-6 entries as verified by factory records:

NC-15706: DQC-6 (# 4386) Wright 285.

-15714:	"	(# 4389)	"
-15716:	EQC-6	(# 4391)	Wright 320.
-15715:	"	(# 4394)	"
:	"	(# 4395)	"
-15722:	DQC-6	(# 4396)	Wright 285.
-16500:	EQC-6	(# 4401)	Wright 320.
:	"	(# 4423)	"
-16214:	DQC-6	(# 4425)	Wright 285.
-16218:	"	(# 4427)	"
-16223:	EQC-6	(# 4434)	Wright 320.
-16228:	"	(# 4435)	"
-16233:	"	(# 4440)	"
NC-2213:	"	(# 4441)	"
NC-2277:	DQC-6	(# 4446)	Wright 285.
-16248:	EQC-6	(# 4471)	Wright 320.
-16506:	"	(# 4473)	"
-16502:	"	(# 4475)	"
-16515:	DQC-6	(# 4478)	Wright 285.
-16520:	"	(# 4479)	"
-16525:	"	(# 4480)	"
-16524:	EQC-6	(# 4483)	Wright 320.
-16587:	"	(# 4485)	"
-16591:	DQC-6	(# 4490)	Wright 285.
-16595:	"	(# 4492)	"
NC-500:	EQC-6	(# 4495)	Wright 320.
:	"	(# 4498)	"
-17469:	"	(# 4544)	"
V-157:	"	(# 4545)	"
V-158:	"	(# 4546)	"
V-159:	"	(# 4547)	"

This approval for ser. # 4386 and up; ser. # 4395, 4423 delivered to Buenos Aires, Argentina; ser. # 4434 on Edo floats; ser. # 4498 del. to Philippine Air Taxi of Manila, P.I.; ser. # 4544 del. to Western Air Express; ser. # 4545-4546-4547 del. to U. S. Coast Guard stations at El Paso, Tex., Cape May, N.J., and Wash. D.C. respectively; this approval expired 9-30-39.

ATC # 598
(3-2-36)
WACO, MODEL YQC-6,

Fig. 365. The YQC-6 with 225 h.p. Jacobs engine; ship later modified into ZQC-6 with 285 h.p. Jacobs engine.

The 'Custom Cabin" biplane by Waco for 1936, more often known as the C-6, was a versatile basic airplane that was available with 7 different engines. Because the engine was actually the heart of the airplane, the C-6 in turn became practically 7 different airplanes. In discussion here are the models YQC-6, ZQC-6, and the AQC-6 which were all powered with 7 cyl. Jacobs engines. The YQC-6 was powered with the 225 h.p. Jacobs L-4 engine, the ZQC-6 was powered with the 285 h.p. Jacobs L-5, and the AQC-6 was powered with the 330 h.p. Jacobs L-6; some customers favored the "Jake" engine and this lineup gave them a nice selection to choose from. Each one of these models was like a different airplane because of varying degrees of performance, and to some extent varying characteristics, but each had one thing in common — they were plush, comfortable airplanes with ability to go anywhere and pride enough to mix with any company. The "Custom Cabin" biplanes for 1936 had a subtle tailored look that reflected simplicity with elegance; a nice combination of fashion and function. Altho' leveled at the sportsman and men of business as a personal conveyance the C-6 could put on an apron over her finery and work alongside the best of

them. By design and the builder's promise the C-6 was not basically a working airplane, but a ten-year heritage of pioneer spirit would come quickly to the surface. At $7295. the 225 h.p. YQC-6 (Jacobs L-4) was more than a fair bargain, but the 285 h.p. ZQC-6 (Jacobs L-5) at $7835. was actually the most popular; it had the most talent for the money. When the improved Jacobs L-6 engine became available many of the ZQC-6 were converted into the AQC-6 and found an added measure of spirit. Many of these airplanes were already in Canada where they had been operating year-round on wheels, skis, and floats. The last of the C-6 type (a 330 h.p. AQC-6) was delivered to Alaska in June of 1939.

All models in the Waco C-6 series were custom-built cabin biplanes with seating arranged for 4 or 5. Four passengers and the pilot were a normal load in the YQC-ZQC and the AQC except when in an overloaded condition with radio equipment, parachutes, and extra fuel. As used normally in the U.S.A. the YQC-ZQC-AQC were plush personal transports for the sportsman and men of business; most were gaily finished and lavishly equipped. Because of high performance and large load capacity the 285 h.p. model ZQC-6 projected an aptitude for work "in

Fig. 366. The ZQC-6 in Canada; most were later modified into AQC-6 with 300-330 h.p. Jacobs engine.

the bush", so a freighter version had to be offered with a lined cargo compartment and extra doors. The first of these were delivered to Canada in mid-1936 and at least 30 more followed in succession; the cabin Waco was popular in Canada, the C-6 especially. Occasionally a YQC-6 or a ZQC-6 were boxed up for export and shipped off to places like Argentina, India, or Australia. The point of interest is the fact the roster shows that for many owners this was their second or third "Waco"; it takes a good airplane to impress one to that extent.

As powered with the 225 h.p. Jacobs L-4 engine the YQC-6 could do remarkable things with this amount of power, and it usually took a demonstration to prove it. As powered with the 285 h.p. Jacobs L-5 engine the ZQC-6 was naturally a little better in everything, and even better than people expected; this was the most popular version. When the Jacobs L-6 engine became available it was installed in several of the YQC-ZQC already in service; the modified version was called the AQC-6. With the extra horsepower and the improved engine, swinging a

Fig. 367. The handsome ZQC-6 was popular for sport or business.

Fig. 368. ZQC-6 "Freighter" had extra doors; this version was popular in Canada.

controllable-pitch propeller, the AQC-6 was a much better airplane in hard service. The (225 h.p.) YQC-6 was a little reluctant to do much of anything beyond straight-and-level when loaded to maximum gross weight, but the ZQC and AQC had more "horses" to play with and did get downright frisky at times. Inherently stable, with the self-control of good manners, the C-6 were a pleasure to own and to fly. An AQC-6 served with the USAAF in 1942 as the UC-72G and 5 of the ZQC-6 served as the UC-72H; all were returned to post-war service. The type certificate number for the YQC-6 was issued 3-2-36 and amended to include the ZQC-6 and AQC-6. Some 88 of the Jacobs-powered C-6 were manufactured by the Waco Aircraft Co. at Troy, Ohio. .

Listed below are specifications and performance data for the Waco model YQC-6 as powered with 225 h.p. Jacobs L-4, L-4M, or L-4MB engine; length overall 26'8"; height overall 8'8"; wing span upper 35'0"; wing span lower 24'6"; wing chord upper 72"; wing chord lower 48"; wing area upper 168 sq. ft.; wing area lower 76 sq. ft.; total wing area 244 sq. ft.; airfoil Clark Y; wt. empty 2004 (2050) lbs.; useful load 1346 (1450) lbs.; payload with 70 gal. fuel 719 (823) lbs.; gross wt. 3350 (3500) lbs.; wts. in parentheses as later amended; max. baggage 125 lbs.; max. speed 159; cruising speed (1900 r.p.m.) 140; cruising speed (2000 r.p.m.) 149 at 6000 ft.; landing speed (with flaps) 52-55; climb 760-740 ft. first min. at sea level; ser. ceiling 16,000 ft.; gas cap. normal 70 gal.; gas cap. max. 95 gal.; oil cap. 5-6 gal.; cruising range (1900 r.p.m.) at 13.5 gal. per hour 650 miles; price $7295. at factory field. The YQC-6 was also

eligible as seaplane; limited to 4 place with 95 gal. fuel.

Specifications and data for the ZQC-6 as powered with 285 h.p. Jacobs L-5, L-5M, or L-5MB engine same as above except as follows: wt. empty 2023 lbs.; useful load 1477 lbs.; payload with 70 gal. fuel 850 lbs.; gross wt. 3500 lbs.; max. speed (105% power) 166; cruising speed (1900 r.p.m.) 150; cruising speed (2000 r.p.m.) 158 at 6000 ft.; landing speed (with flaps) 55; climb 850 ft. first min. at sea level; ser. ceiling 17,000 ft.; gas cap. 70-95 gal.; oil cap. 5-6 gal.; cruising range (1900 r.p.m.) at 16.5 gal. per hour 600 miles; price $7835. at factory field. Following data is for ZQC-6 as seaplane on Edo 38-3430 or 39-4000 twin-float gear; wt. empty 2368 lbs.; useful load 1242 lbs.; payload with 50 gal. fuel 735 lbs.; payload with 70 gal. fuel 615 lbs.; gross · wt. 3610 (3800) lbs.; figures in parentheses for ser. # 4700 and up with Edo 39-4000 floats; max. speed 147; cruising speed (1900 r.p.m.) 135; landing speed (with flaps) 60; climb 750 ft. first min. at sea level; take-off fully loaded in 20 secs.; ser. ceiling 15,000 ft.; gas cap. 70 gal.; oil cap. 5 gal.; cruising range 400-540 miles; price with floats not announced.

Specifications and data for the AQC-6 as powered with 300 h.p. (330 h.p. for take off) Jacobs L-6, L-6M, or L-6MB engine same as above except as follows: wt. empty 2050 lbs.; useful load 1450 lbs.; payload with 70 gal. fuel 823 lbs.; gross wt. 3500 (3650) lbs.; 3650 lbs. was allowable gross wt. for ser. # 4700 and up; max. speed (105% power) 170; cruising speed (.75 power) 155; landing speed (with flaps) 55-57; climb 950 ft. first min. at sea level; ser. ceiling 18,500 ft.; gas cap. 70-95 gal.; oil cap. 5-6 gal.;

Fig. 369. The ZQC-6 on Edo floats; YQC-6 and AQC-6 were also eligible as seaplanes.

cruising range (.75 power) at 19 gal. per hour 550 miles; price $8975. at factory field. Following data is for AQC-6 as seaplane on Edo 39-4000 twin-float gear; wt. empty 2370 lbs.; useful load 1240 lbs.; payload with 50 gal. fuel 733 lbs.; gross wt. 3610 (3800) lbs.; gross wt. of 3800 lbs. eligible with Edo 39-4000 floats only; max. speed 151; cruising speed (.75 power) 139; landing speed (with flaps) 60; climb 800 ft. first min. at sea level; ser. ceiling 16,000 ft.; gas cap. 70-95 gal.; oil cap. 5-6 gal.; cruising range at 19 gal. per hour 350-490 miles; price with floats not announced. The empty wt. (landplane) went up as extra equipment was added; factory records indicate that most AQC-6 left the assembly line with empty wts. ranging from 2288 to 2313 lbs. Useful loads and payloads were adjusted accordingly.

The construction details and general arrangement of the models YQC-6, ZQC-6, AQC-6 were practically identical to the DQC-6 and EQC-6 (ATC # 597) except for the engine installation and whatever modifications were necessary to a particular combination. Unless otherwise noted the following pertains to any model in the C-6 series. The standard entry arrangement was one door on the left side, but an extra door and wing-walk were also available for the right side. The interior was normally upholstered in blue and gray "Velmo" mohair, a restful and sound-absorbing fabric. The "freighter" interior, with seats removed and a lined cabin, had an extra large baggage door on the left side; the cargo compartment was allowed up to 800 lbs. The ambulance conversion carried pilot, one-man litter, and one occupant.

Parachute-type seats for the front or rear occupants were available as option in any model. Fuel tanks of either 35 gal. or 47.5 gal. cap. were mounted in the upper wing roots; with an added 25 gal. fuel tank mounted under rear seat the airplane was limited to 4 place. Oil cap. was either 5, 6, or 7.5 gal. depending on fuel cap. normally used. Drag flaps on underside of upper wing not to be lowered above 108 m.p.h. For hard service · "in the bush" or frequent cross-country trips the C-6 was often equipped with oil-cooler, larger battery, an oversize engine starter, oversize generator, emergency exit in the roof, and a sleeping bag compartment. All models were eligible on wheels, skis, or floats. The versions used for sport or business were usually fitted with custom upholstery, night-flying equipment, radio equipment, extra instruments & pilot aids, extra fuel cap., and custom color schemes. A fixed-pitch Curtiss-Reed metal propeller was normally used, but a Hamilton-Standard two-position controllable prop was available and all-round performance was generally improved. The next "Waco" development was the "Standard Cabin" model YKS-7 as described in the chapter for ATC # 626.

Listed below are YQC-6, ZQC-6, and AQC-6 entries as verified by factory records:

NC-15705: YQC-6 (# 4385) Jacobs 225.
  -15709: ZQC-6 (# 4387) Jacobs 285.
  -15712:   "   (# 4388)   "
  -15717:   "   (# 4390)   "
  -15718:   "   (# 4392)   "
  -15719:   "   (# 4393)   "
  -15721:   "   (# 4397)   "

-16201: " (#4398) "
-15724: " (#4399) "
-16202: " (#4400) "
NS-16212: YQC-6 (#4402) Jacobs 225.
VH-UVM: " (#4403) "
NC-16204: ZQC-6 (#4404) Jacobs 285.
-16205: YQC-6 (#4405) Jacobs 225.
-16206: ZQC-6 (#4406) Jacobs 285.
-16207: YQC-6 (#4407) Jacobs 225.
-16209: ZQC-6 (#4420) Jacobs 285.
-16208: " (#4421) "
-16203: " (#4422) "
-16213: " (#4424) "
-16222: " (#4426) "
-16217: " (#4428) "
-16219: " (#4429) "
-16224: " (#4430) "
-16220: " (#4431) "
-16229: " (#4432) "
-16231: " (#4433) "
-16227: " (#4436) "
-16232: " (#4437) "
-16234: " (#4438) "
-16240: " (#4439) "
-16239: " (#4442) "
-16235: " (#4443) "
-16238: " (#4444) "
: " (#4445) "
-16244: " (#4448) "
CF-AZM: " (#4449) "
CF-BBN: " (#4470) "
CF-AZO: " (#4472) "
-16511: " (#4474) "
VT-AIB: YQC-6 (#4476) Jacobs 225.
-16501: ZQC-6 (#4477) Jacobs 285.
CF-AZP: " (#4481) "
-16518: " (#4482) "
VT-AHZ: YQC-6 (#4484) Jacobs 225.
-16584: ZQC-6 (#4487) Jacobs 285.
CF-AZR: " (#4489) "
-16586: " (#4488) "
VT-AII: YQC-6 (#4491) Jacobs 225.
-16594: ZQC-6 (#4493) Jacobs 285.
-16590: " (#4494) "
: " (#4496) "
CF-BBO: " (#4497) "
CF-BBP: " (#4499) "

: " (#4540) "
CF-BBR: " (#4541) "
VT-AIN: YQC-6 (#4542) Jacobs 225.
CF-BDJ: ZQC-6 (#4543) Jacobs 285.
CF-CCV: " (#4590) "
CF-CCU: " (#4591) "
CF-BDO: " (#4592) "
CF-BDL: " (#4593) "
CF-BDM: " (#4594) "
CF-BDQ: " (#4595) "
CF-BDR: " (#4596) "
CF-BDP: " (#4597) "
CF-BDS: " (#4598) "
CF-BDT: " (#4599) "
CF-BDU: " (#4640) "
CF-BDV: " (#4641) "
VT-AJJ: " (#4642) "
CF-BDW: " (#4643) "
VT-AIX: YQC-6 (#4644) Jacobs 225.
VT-AIY: " (#4645) "
CF-CCW: ZQC-6 (#4646) Jacobs 285.
VT-AJI: " (#4647) "
VT-AJL: YQC-6 (#4648) Jacobs 285.
VT-AJK: " (#4649) Jacobs 225.
CF-BDZ: ZQC-6 (#5000) Jacobs 285.
CF-BJP: " (#5031) "
CF-BJR: AQC-6 (#5032) Jacobs 300.
CF-DTA: ZQC-6 (#5033) Jacobs 285.
CF-BJS: AQC-6 (#5034) Jacobs 300.
CF-DTB: " (#5035) "
CF-DTC: " (#5036) "
CF-DTD: " (#5037) "
CF-BJV: " (#5039) "
NC-20906: " (#5040) "

This approval for ser. #4385 and up; ser. #4390 later operated in Mexico as XA-DIC; ser. #4403 del. to Australia; ser. #4445, 4540 del. to Argentina; ser. #4449 was first C-6 del. to Canada, followed by ser. #4470, 4472, 4481, 4489, 4497, 4499, 4541, 4543, 4590, 4591, 4592, 4593, 4594, 4595, 4596, 4597, 4598, 4599, 4640, 4641, 4643, 4646, 5000, 5031, 5032, 5033, 5034, 5035, 5036, 5037, 5039; ser. #4476, 4484, 4491, 4542, 4642, 4644, 4645, 4647, 4648, 4649 del. to India; ser. #4407, 4540, 4543, 4594, 4598, 4640, 5031, 5033 later as AQC-6; ser. #5040 del. to Alaska.

Fig. 370. Stearman-Hammond Y-125 in its early configuration; lay-out featured "pusher" engine and "tricycle" landing gear.

When parked on the apron among regular airplanes the unusual "Hammond Y" stuck out like a sore thumb; everything about it seemed to be wrong. The passengers sat way out in front, the engine was buried in the back, the fuselage extremity which normally carried the tail group was traded off for a couple of tail booms, and the whole thing was perched on a double-tapered wing from which hung a squashy tricycle landing gear. Dean B. Hammond and Carl Haddon (designer & chief engineer respectively) reached way back for most of these features, features that were common even before World War 1, to provide utmost safety and flight characteristics that would coddle the amateur flier. The "Model Y" was designed in 1934 in competition for a U. S. Government program (AB-205) that was calculated to bring the pleasures of flying within reach of the ordinary man in the street; the aim was to develop a low-cost "foolproof" airplane capable of cheap mass production. The target price was $700. per airplane, which seemed impossible even at depression prices, and the only ones of 14 other manufacturers who came close at all to that price had to use converted automobile engines. Because of the way it was built, Hammond couldn't have been striving for the $700. figure in the "Model Y", so consequently, his asking

price came to over $3000. This then was an improbable candidate for "everyman's airplane". The prototype airplane was powered with a 4 cyl. inverted inline Menasco B-4 engine of 95 h.p., and in tests it fell short of speed requirements, so it was ordered into further development.

By this time Lloyd C. Stearman became interested in the project to assist Hammond and Haddon in the redesigning. After another year of further development the new "Stearman-Hammond Y-125", considerably different from the original "Model Y", became acceptable and received its certificate of approval. Ordinary people not familiar with normal airplanes accepted the Y-125 without question and had no trouble flying it, even after only a few minutes of briefing, but seasoned pilots who had spent years learning the ways of the average airplane were befuddled by it and had a heck of a time flying it! For use by their inspectors in the field BAC (Bureau of Air Commerce) finally ordered 15 of these airplanes with an option on 5 more; a portion of the fund originally set aside for 25 aircraft was distributed to other manufacturers who also had entered the competition. A dealer organization was appointed by Stearman-Hammond, mostly in the western states, and roving demonstrators were astounding the

Fig. 371. Prototype Hammond Y was revolutionary concept to provide a "fool-proof" airplane.

viewers at many airports, but despite the airplane's desirable features the price was more than prospects were prepared to pay. Eugene L. Vidal, Director of Aeronautics, launched a campaign for a "poor man's airplane" late in 1933 and had literally startled the aircraft industry with his improbable plan; he believed there was a market for upwards of 10,000 airplanes if they could be sold for $700. For months he was ridiculed by engineers and blessed by the rank and file of the flying public. City fathers and others concerned feared it unwise and a menace to civilization to have literally thousands of cheap airplanes flying around under the

guidance of amateur pilots, and so on. In all, perhaps it was a good idea, but the program never accomplished what it set out to do; perhaps it is just as well. The airplane that practically anybody could fly, and almost anybody could afford to own, is still a dream.

The Stearman-Hammond Y-125 was a low-winged "pusher type" monoplane with side by side seating for two. The unusual arrangement was calculated to provide easy entry from the ground, a broad range of visibility, a comfortable position away from noise and fumes, the whirling propeller was fenced-off by the twin tail booms, and the tricycle landing gear eliminated

Fig. 372. The Y-125 looked odd among regular airplanes.

many of the operating pitfalls experienced by amateur pilots. With the three-wheeled gear it was possible to taxi at 45 m.p.h. and higher, cross-wind landings were hardly a problem, and the plane could actually be dropped in from as much as 20 feet without damage. The Y-125 was so simple to fly that the average person could fly it alone after 2 or 3 hours of instruction. To seasoned pilots "it just doesn't seem real"! It became the most talked-about airplane in America; to California residents who saw it frequently it became known as "The Bug". As powered with the 4 cyl. inverted inline aircooled Menasco C-4 engine rated 125 h.p. at 2175 r.p.m. the model Y-125 was perhaps a little bit sluggish as compared to a regular airplane, but that seemed to be an acceptable trade-off in view of its other outstanding abilities. Many pilots had a grudge against it, muttering that it sure was a wierd contraption, but there were also many that took to it with an open mind and learned to enjoy it. A highly advanced design, perhaps too many years ahead of its time, the Stearman-Hammond Y was trying to make it in a hostile environment and finally fell by the wayside to become only an interesting memory. The type certificate number for the Model Y-125 was issued 4-9-36 and no reliable records were available as to the amount actually built. John Geisse, chief of the development section of the BAC, flew the first Y-125 to Washington, D.C. and Eugene Vidal was one of the first to try it out. There were no civilian deliveries until the BAC contract was filled. The Hammond Aircraft Corp. was founded at Ypsilanti, Mich. in 1932. Dean B. Hammond was president and gen. mgr.; M. C. "Carl" Haddon was chf. engr. In a reorganization as the Stearman-Hammond Aircraft Corp. at So. San Francisco, Calif., Lloyd C. Stearman was pres. & gen. mgr.; Dean B. Hammond was V.P.; Samuel Metzger was sales mgr.; & Carl Haddon was chf. engr.

Listed below are specifications and performance data for the Stearman-Hammond Y-125 as powered with the 125 h.p. Menasco C-4 engine; length overall 26'11"; height overall 7'11'; wing span 40'0"; wing chord at root 83"; wing chord at tip 29"; total wing area 210 sq. ft.; airfoil Clark Y; wt. empty 1400 lbs.; useful load 750 lbs.; payload with 40 gal. fuel 310 lbs.; gross wt. 2150 lbs.; max. speed 118 at sea level; cruising speed (1920 r.p.m.) 108; landing speed (with flaps) 40; climb 600 ft. first min. at sea level; ser. ceiling 15,000 ft.; gas cap. 40 gal.; oil cap. 4 gal.; cruising range (1920 r.p.m.) at 7.8 gal. per hour 520 miles; price approx. $5000. at the factory. Max. baggage allowance was 100 lbs.

The cabin pod was an all-metal, semi-monocoque structure of riveted 24-ST dural members covered with smooth "Alclad" metal sheet. A large door on each side provided step-up entry right from the ground. The wide, padded seat sat 2 across and a 11 cu. ft. baggage compartment in behind was allowed 100 lbs. There was considerable window area and visibility was excellent over the short nose. The "pusher" (backwards) engine was mounted on a steel tube frame and completely cowled in; an air scoop run across the top bringing cool air under ram pressure from the front. The thrust line was high enough so that the propeller was above and ahead of the wing's trailing edge to provide protection against kicked-up gravel and flying debris. The all-metal (24-ST) cantilever wing framework, in 3 sections, was built up around a single main box-type spar beam with truss-type wing ribs of riveted square dural tubing; the leading edges were covered with dural sheet and the completed framework was covered in fabric. Fuel tanks were mounted in leading edge of the center-section panel. Split-type trailing edge wing flaps covered more than half the span. The three-wheeled landing gear of 109 in. tread consisted of cast aluminum wheel forks attached to long-stroke oleo shock struts; two wheels were under the wing and one in the nose, a pattern for better ground stability. Goodyear 18x8-3 airwheels were fitted with hydraulic disc brakes. Each wheel was encased in a metal fairing. The horizontal stabilizer was fastened between the 2 all-metal (24-ST) monocoque tail booms; tail booms were each fitted with a fin and rudder. The elevator was fitted with an adjustable trim tab. A wooden propeller, electric engine starter, battery, generator, fuel pump, fuel gauge, compass, dual controls, bonding & shielding, navigation lights, and first-aid kit were standard equipment. Fire extinguisher, and 21 in. streamlined wheels were optional. The next Stearman-Hammond development was the model Y-1-S (Y-150) as described in the chapter for ATC # 644.

No accurate listing was available for model Y-125 production.

ATC # 600
(4-14-36)
FAIRCHILD, MODEL 24-C8E.

Fig. 373. The Fairchild 24-C8E with 145 h.p. Warner "Super Scarab" engine.

Fairchild engineers, company pilots, and their factory craftsmen, were bent on continually improving the "Twenty Four", never losing sight of the fact that quality and ease of flying combined to make the best possible airplane for the private owner. Enlarged slightly to carry 3 in 1934, the "Twenty Four" for 1936 was still basically similar, but developments in the industry and owner comment fostered a few changes for convenience and a bow to overall styling. More and more the private airplane was compared to the automobile, probably to create sales appeal among a larger cross-section of potential buyers. Airplane interiors were now compared to the fine auto, ease of servicing and the elimination of frequent maintenance was also compared to the auto, and more and more, the airplane was being suggested as a week-end replacement of the automobile. Then too, people were becoming more affluent as economic conditions improved, more families now had automobiles, and a big spurt in aircraft sales was being predicted. Fashioned in the new trend, the Warner-powered Fairchild 24-C8E for 1936 offered more operating convenience, some added comfort, and a rather pleasant styling. Over 4 years of continuous development had made this new "Twenty Four" a sturdier airplane, involving less upkeep, providing almost effortless handling, and within the contours of this new design

were all the talked-about features that appealed to private ownership. For years now the improving of airplane designs had largely revolved around the increase in horsepower; Fairchild was proving that airplanes can be better without continually resorting to power increases.

The Fairchild model 24-C8E for 1936 was a compact high-winged cabin monoplane with seating arranged for 2 or 3. The so-called "rumble seat" in back, which would normally be occupied by a third person, could be folded back out of the way to make room for piles of luggage, golf bags, hunting and fishing gear, or just about enough of anything for a nice, long vacation. On occasion the 24-C8E could even fill-in as a freighter with up to 500 lbs. strapped down in the cabin, or a 20 gal. fuel tank could be mounted in place of the rear seat for 2 hours extra range. Even with 3 husky people aboard there was still allowance for 165 lbs. of baggage or paraphernalia whether it be boxes, bags, or special gear. Standing there quite tall, there was no need to crouch when walking up to this airplane, and getting in was just an easy step-up. The modish, auto-like interior was serviceable enough for everyday use, but it did promote a desire to fly more often in one's finer dress. The reasonably quiet interior instigated light conversation along the way and visibility was quite adequate from any seat. As powered with the 7

Fig. 374. 24-C8E also available on sport-type landing gear.

cyl. Warner "Super Scarab" engine rated 145 h.p. at 2050 r.p.m. the 24-C8E had a satisfying performance that brought out smiles of surprise. A friendly airplane with pleasant manner, the model C8E was quite easy to fly well and it instilled early confidence in even the most timid; however, the proficient amateur and the expert pilot enjoyed it also because of its proper response to professional handling. The "Twenty Four" owners had a way of saying "I am amazed at the excuses I can find to justify my flying somewhere"! The rugged innards of the 24-C8E were also designed to withstand all sorts of abuses, and every assembly was designed to require the minimum in maintenance. As a bonus, all this was wrapped up in a pleasant appearance that promoted pride and proper care. The 24-C8E was naturally an improvement over earlier "24" and it was also eligible as a seaplane. The type certificate number for the model 24-C8E was issued 4-14-36 and some 50 examples of this model were manufactured by the Fairchild Aircraft Corp. at Hagerstown, Md.

Listed below are specifications and performance data for the Fairchild model 24-C8E as powered with the 145 h.p. Warner "Super Scarab" (Series 50) engine; length overall 23'9"; height overall 7'4"; wing span 36'4"; wing chord 66"; total wing area 173 sq. ft.; airfoil N-22; wt. empty 1463 lbs.; useful load 937 lbs.; payload with 40 gal. fuel 505 lbs. (2 pass. & 165 lbs. baggage); gross wt. 2400 lbs.; max. speed 135 at sea level; cruising speed (1900 r.p.m.) 120 at sea level; landing speed (with flaps) 46; landing speed (no flaps) 55; climb 715 ft. first min. at sea

level; ser. ceiling 17,000 ft.; gas cap. 40 gal.; oil cap. 3 gal.; cruising range (1900 r.p.m.) at 9 gal. per hour 480 miles; price $5390. at factory. Take off (flaps up) 534 ft., take off (flaps down) 402 ft.; cruising speed 124 at 8000 ft.

Specifications and data for 24-C8ES as seaplane on Edo 44-2425 twin-float gear same as above except as follows: length overall 28'6"; height overall 12'0"; wt. empty 1685 lbs.; useful load 865 lbs.; payload with 40 gal. fuel 432 lbs. (2 pass. & 92 lbs. bag.); gross wt. 2550 lbs.; max. speed 120 at sea level; cruising speed 107 at sea level; landing speed (with flaps) 50; landing speed (no flaps) 58; climb 620 ft. first min. at sea level; ser. ceiling 12,100 ft.; cruising range (1900 r.p.m.) at 9 gal. per hour 430 miles; price for seaplane not announced.

The fuselage framework was built up of welded 4130 steel tubing, heavily faired to a slightly different contour with wooden formers and fairing strips, then fabric covered. The modish auto-like interior was arranged to seat 2 or 3; the 2 front seats were side by side and a folding "rumble seat" was extended for a third person in back. Baggage was placed on either side of the rear seat, or the seat could be folded up and the whole area used for luggage; various amounts of baggage were allowed according to payload available. The cabin walls were lined with Kapok, and upholstered in Bedford cord or leather. The large dash-board had ample room for radio and extra instruments, and was fitted with a handy glove compartment. The windshield of shatter-proof glass was slanted at more of an angle and all other windows were of

Fig. 375. Prototype 24-C8E flies over Maryland countryside.

heavy Pyralin. A large door and assist straps on each side provided easy step-up into the cabin; the pilot's seat was adjustable and visibility was adequate from any seat. The interior was reasonably quiet, and all plane-engine controls operated on ball bearings; adjustable sun-shades and dual controls (stick-type) were also provided. Cabin ventilators and a cabin heater were available as an optional extra. The sturdy wing framework, in two halves, was built up of solid spruce spars routed to an I-beam section with spruce and plywood truss-type wing ribs; the leading edges were covered with mahogany plywood sheet and the completed framework was covered in fabric. Freise-type "slotted" ailerons were very effective; trailing edge wing flaps steepened the approach and lowered the landing speeds. A 20 gal. fuel tank was mounted in root end of each wing-half; a 20 gal. fuel tank could be mounted in place of the rear seat. The streamlined wing-bracing struts were combined effectively into a rigid truss with the outrigger landing gear. The new semi-cantilever landing gear of 112 in. tread was designed to create less drag, but it was a little spindly as compared to the earlier sport-type gear; if desired, the sport-type gear was available as replacement. Low-pressure (6.50x10) tires on Warner wheels were equipped with brakes; Fairchild oleo-spring shock struts had 8 in. travel. Fittings were provided in the fuselage for Edo 44-2425 pontoon gear; skis were also eligible. The tail group was a composite structure of cantilever design; the horizontal stabilizer and vertical fin were of spruce spars and ribs covered with mahogany

plywood. Rudder and elevators were of welded steel covered with fabric; right elevator was fitted with a trim tab. A Hartzell wooden propeller, electric engine starter, 12-volt battery, wheel brakes, parking brake, tail wheel, wiring for navigation lights, fire extinguisher, compass, safety belts, assist ropes, ash trays, first-aid kit, and tool kit were standard equipment. A metal propeller, engine or wind driven generator, navigation lights, landing lights, parachute flares, radio set, bonding & shielding, oil-cooling radiator, clock, sport-type landing gear with wheel pants, seaplane gear, skis, and aux. fuel tank were optional. The next development in the Fairchild 24 was the model 24-C-8F as described

Fig. 376. 24-C8E shows off its wide stance and large "air brakes".

in the chapter for ATC # 610.

Listed below are 24-C8E entries as gleaned from registration records:

NC-15954:	24-C8E	(# 2800)	Warner 145.
:	"	(# 2801)	"
:	"	(# 2802)	"
NC-15990:	"	(# 2803)	"
-15991:	"	(# 2804)	"
-15992:	"	(# 2805)	"
-15993:	"	(# 2806)	"
-15994:	"	(# 2807)	"
-15995:	"	(# 2808)	"
-15996:	"	(# 2809)	"
-16349:	"	(# 2810)	"
-16350:	"	(# 2811)	"
-16351:	"	(# 2812)	"
-16352:	"	(# 2813)	"
-16353:	"	(# 2814)	"
:	"	(# 2815)	"
:	"	(# 2816)	"
:	"	(# 2817)	"
-16357:	"	(# 2818)	"
-16358:	"	(# 2819)	"
-16800:	"	(# 2820)	"
-16801:	"	(# 2821)	"
-16802:	"	(# 2822)	"
NS-2813:	"	(# 2823)	"
-16804:	"	(# 2824)	"
:	"	(# 2825)	"
-16806:	"	(# 2826)	"
-16807:	"	(# 2827)	"
:	"	(# 2828)	"
-16809:	"	(# 2829)	"
-16820:	"	(# 2830)	"
-16821:	"	(# 2831)	"
-16822:	"	(# 2832)	"
-16823:	"	(# 2833)	"
-16824:	"	(# 2834)	"
-16825:	"	(# 2835)	"
-16840:	"	(# 2836)	"
-16839:	"	(# 2837)	"
:	"	(# 2838)	"
-16837:	"	(# 2839)	"
-16841:	"	(# 2840)	"
-16842:	"	(# 2841)	"
-16843:	"	(# 2842)	"
-16844:	"	(# 2843)	"
-16845:	"	(# 2844)	"
-16846:	"	(# 2845)	"
-16847:	"	(# 2846)	"
-16848:	"	(# 2847)	"
-16849:	"	(# 2848)	"
--16850:	"	(# 2849)	"

This approval for ser. # 2800 and up; no listing for ser. # 2801, 2802, 2815, 2816, 2817, 2825, 2828, 2838; ser. # 2820 and up had sport-type landing gear with wheel pants; ser. # 2805, 2814 on Edo floats as 24-C8ES; ser. # 2823 del. to N.Y. State Dept. of Conservation; this approval expired 9-30-39.

APPENDICES

BIBLIOGRAPHY

BOOKS:

Boeing Aircraft Since 1916; Peter M. Bowers
The Stinsons; John W. Underwood
Legacy of Leadership; Trans-World Airlines
Revolution In The Sky; Richard Sanders Allen
Yesterday, Today, Tomorrow; Fairchild-Hiller Corp.
Winged-S; Igor I. Sikorsky
Of Monocoupes and Men; John W. Underwood
Staggerwing!; Robert T. Smith
Ryan, The Aviator; William Wagner
Aircraft Year Book (1934-37); Aero. Chamber of Commerce of America, Inc.
Days Of Trial and Triumph; Lockheed Aircraft Corp.
Jane's All The World's Aircraft (1935-36); Sampson Low
The Vintage and Veteran Aircraft Guide; John W. Underwood

PERIODICALS:

Flying
Aviation
The Antiquer
Aero Digest
AOPA Pilot
Sport Aviation
Western Flying
American Airman
The Pilot
Antique Airplane News
Journal of AAHS
Waco Pilot

SPECIAL MATERIAL FROM INDIVIDUALS:

Ray Brandly
John W. Underwood
Roger Besecker
John Sommerfeld
Don Hartsig
Mitch Mayborn
Walter M. Jefferies
Earl Reed
C. G. Taylor
Theron K. Rinehart
Richard S. Allen
Boardman C. Reed
Henri D'Estout
Peter M. Bowers
George Townson
Lloyd Child
Bob Von Willer
E. L. "Jack" Wright
Wm. T. Larkins
James Borden
Harry Gann
William Wagner
Ken M. Molson
J. R. Nielander
David D. Hatfield
Doug Rounds

PHOTO CREDITS

Gregory C. Krohn: Fig. 29-36-42-55

Billy Lee: Fig. 243 (B. Ralph Hall)

Chas. Mandrake: Fig. 177

Mitch Mayborn: Fig. 17-150-151-152-153-213 (Pan American World Airways); Fig. 245 (Aviation Hist. Soc. of N. Z.); Fig. 301-302-307-308-309-337-338-339-340-344-345 (Pan American World Airways)

McLaughlin Photo Ser.: Fig. 352

F. C. McVickar: Fig. 46-102

Morris A. Mills: Fig. 64

Ken M. Molson: Fig. 86-92-121-130-158-182-186-227-238-281-330-331-366-372

Ralph Nortell: Fig. 156

Edward O'Brien Coll.: Fig. 287

Will D. "Billy" Parker: Fig. 203-204-205

Everette J. Payette: Fig. 289

Edward Peck: Fig. 28-30

Pratt & Whitney Div.: Fig. 76-77-78-178-180-181-207-208-211-212-224-225-234-251-252-253-254-304-305-306-328-329-341-342-343

Earl C. Reed: Fig. 286

Ryan Aero. Corp.: Fig. 139-255-256-257-259

Sikorsky Aircraft Div.: Fig. 223

Robt. T. Smith: Fig. 239 (Beech)

Smithsonian - Nat. Air Museum: Fig. 226

Emil Strasser: Fig. 34-38-40-63-65-83-98-99-104-108-185-191-210-237-261-270-285-295-311-348-349

Geo. Townson: Fig. 23-24-25-26 (Driscoll A. Nina)

Frank Turgeon, Jr.: Fig. 351

John W. Underwood: Fig. 70; Fig. 132 (O. R. Phillips); Fig. 183-184-190-197-198-201-202-327 333-334-335-370-371

Truman C. Weaver: Fig. 73 (Van Rossem)

Dick Whittington: Fig. 135

Gordon S. Williams: Fig. 5-9-12-35-37-43-51-52-53-59-60-62-66-67-72-90-93-95-96-97-100-101 105-106-107-110-111-120-122-124-126-140-141-144-148-157-162-165-176-193-194-203- 206-209-229-262-263-266-267-268-276-277-288-354-357-358-359-361-362-363-369

E. L. "Jack" Wright: Fig. 186-187

Wm. F. Yeager: Fig. 6-7-129-149-195-250-269-300-323-367

INDEX